WELFARE AND WORK IN THE OPEN
VOLUME I
FROM VULNERABILITY TO COMPETITIVENESS

——— 'The Political Economy of Europe in an Era of Interdependence', in Herbert Kitschelt, Peter Lange, Gary Marks, and John D. Stephens (eds.), Continuity and Change in Contemporary Capitalism. Cambridge, UK: Cambridge University Press, 135–63.

——— and TAYLOR, ROSEMARY C. R. (1996). 'Political Science and the Three New Institutionalisms', in Karol Soltan, Eric M. Uslaner, and Virginia Haufler (eds.), Institutions and Social Order. Ann Arbor: University of Michigan Press, 15–44.

HAMPSON, IAN, and MORGAN, DAVID E. (1999). 'Post-Fordism, Union Strategy, and the Rhetoric of Restructuring: The Case of Australia, 1980–1996', Theory and Society, 28: 747–96.

HARRIS, RALPH, and SELDON, ARTHUR (1987). Welfare without the State. London: Institute of Economic Affairs.

HAY, COLIN, and WATSON, MATTHEW (1998). 'Rendering the Contingent Necessary: New Labour's Neo-Liberal Conversion and the Discourse of

Welfare and Work in the Open Economy

Volume I. From Vulnerability to Competitiveness

Edited by

FRITZ W. SCHARPF

AND

VIVIEN A. SCHMIDT

UNIVERSITY PRESS

OXFORD

UNIVERSITY PRESS

Great Clarendon Street, Oxford ox2 6DP

Oxford University Press is a department of the University of Oxford.
It furthers the University's objective of excellence in research, scholarship,
and education by publishing worldwide in

Oxford New York

Athens Auckland Bangkok Bogotá Buenos Aires Cape Town
Chennai Dar es Salaam Delhi Florence Hong Kong Istanbul Karachi
Kolkata Kuala Lumpur Madrid Melbourne Mexico City Mumbai Nairobi
Paris São Paulo Shanghai Singapore Taipei Tokyo Toronto Warsaw
with associated companies in Berlin Ibadan

Oxford is a registered trade mark of Oxford University Press
in the UK and in certain other countries

Published in the United States
by Oxford University Press Inc., New York

British Library Cataloguing in Publication Data
Data available

Library of Congress Cataloging in Publication Data
Data available
ISBN 0–19–924088–4

3 5 7 9 10 8 6 4 2

Typeset by Hope Services (Abingdon) Ltd.
Printed in Great Britain
on acid-free paper by
Biddles Ltd.,
Guildford and King's Lynn

PREFACE

Since the demise of the cold war with its fear of a nuclear doomsday, 'globalization' has become the current specter of public debates in western Europe, threatening to wipe out the achievements of advanced welfare states in providing full employment, social security and greater social equality for their citizens. At the same time, these debates have seen an ever more rapid succession of 'model' countries that seemed to have found some miracle solution, and that were displaced by the next one when, on closer inspection, the miracle turned out to be less than perfect. Thus Japan, celebrated as the world leader in industrial productivity, was succeeded by the 'Rhineland model' of social consensus and stability, which in turn was forgotten when admiration shifted first to New Zealand's radical liberalization, and then to the 'great American job machine', which subsequently was overshadowed by the Dutch 'polder model', by growing attention to the Danish achievements in defending high levels of employment and social protection, and now by peak-level discussions about 'multiple Third Ways'.

When we first began to talk about the possibility of a joint project that would clarify these issues in early 1997, the academic literature was split between theoretical contributions: some warning of inexorably tightening economic constraints that were reversing postwar advances in the democratic civilization of capitalism, and others celebrating the ultimate liberation of economic dynamics from the fetters of state control. The available empirical research provided either statistical tests of hypotheses focused narrowly on a few quantifiable indicators or case studies dealing in depth with selected issues in one or a few countries. Thus, what was needed in our view was empirical and comparative research that would utilize much more information about specific problems and policy responses of advanced welfare states than was possible in statistical studies, and that would also be more comprehensive with regard to issues as well as the number of countries than had been possible in the available case studies. In a series of discussions among ourselves and with knowledgeable colleagues, we concluded that such a project would have to include at least Sweden and Denmark among the Scandinavian welfare states; Austria, Germany, the Netherlands, Belgium, France, Switzerland, and Italy in Continental Europe; and the United Kingdom, Australia and New Zealand among the Anglo-Saxon countries. We also decided to focus on employment as well as social policy systems and to cover the period from the early 1970s to the present.

Even though our substantive research interests as well as the geographical reach of our first-hand knowledge were complementary rather than overlapping, we never thought we could carry out a comparative study of this scope by ourselves. At the same time, the manpower requirements and costs of a project based on original empirical research covering the policy experience of a dozen countries over three decades would have been prohibitive. Instead, we decided to organize a highly structured conference project that would rely on the cooperation of colleagues who are experts on the countries to be covered, and who could draw on their background knowledge as well as a limited amount of additional research for the preparation of comparable country reports that could then provide the foundation for comparative analyses. Even so, the financial needs of the project would by far exceed the resources that could be provided by the Cologne Max Planck Institute for the Study of Societies, where the project was to be located.

We count ourselves extremely lucky in obtaining the early, and in many cases enthusiastic, commitment of so many competent colleagues to what turned out to be an extremely demanding common project. At the same time, our needs for financial support were eased by a pump-priming allocation of the President of the Max Planck Society, and then met by a major grant from the Volkswagen Stiftung, a grant from the Fritz-Thyssen Stiftung for a smaller coordinated project, and by the support of the Robert Schuman Center of the European University Institute for one of the project workshops. We are deeply grateful to all these sponsors. Their support allowed us to bring Anton C. Hemerijck and Vivien A. Schmidt for half a year to Cologne, where the project was supported by a competent team including Steffen Ganghof, Martin Schludi, Eric Seils, and Torben Vad. Vad and later Ganghof acted as overall project coordinators.

In order to ensure a common focus among all participants, we began the project by formulating a 50-page 'background paper' that reviewed the available literature and explicated a comprehensive set of working hypotheses on the possible first- and second-order impacts of changes in the external economic environment on the employment and social policy systems of advanced welfare states, on the likely effectiveness of possible policy responses, and on the institutional conditions favoring effective policy responses (Scharpf, Schmidt, and Vad 1998). In order to allow contributors to locate their country studies in a quantitative context, the Cologne team also compiled a common data base consisting mainly of OECD time series on the economic performance, employment, public finance, capital markets, social policy, wages, and distributive outcomes for all countries, starting in the 1970s, wherever possible (Schludi, Seils, and Ganghof 1998).

Both documents were made available to the participants of an opening conference in Cologne early in 1998, in which the overall design of the project, the questions to be addressed, and their goodness of fit for the countries to be covered were discussed by the future authors and several expert commentators. At the same time, it was agreed that a number of important issues needed to be addressed in special studies. First drafts, which were expected and delivered in the early Fall of 1998, were subsequently discussed in great detail in a series of smaller workshops in Cologne and Florence. Second drafts as well as first drafts of the comparative chapters were then prepared for discussion among all participants and again a number of knowledgeable commentators in a concluding conference, convened in February of 1999 in the snowbound isolation of the Max Planck Society's Ringberg Castle in the Bavarian Alps.

By that time, Oxford University Press had agreed in principle to publish the outcome of the project in two volumes—one containing the country chapters and special studies, the other comparative chapters—provided we would be able to meet its page limitations and its timetable. This implied that all authors received not only detailed comments from the editors, on themes to be elaborated and additional information to be supplied on the basis of the Ringberg discussions, but also precise instructions about how much of the text had to be cut in producing the final draft that was due at the beginning of the Summer. By the end of the Summer, a second round of comments from the editors and revisions by the authors led to 'final-final drafts' of the country chapters and special studies, which then went to Jeremiah Riemer, our most demanding language editor, whom we cannot thank enough for his skill and diligence in translating texts from German-English, Italian-English or Danish-English into lucid and elegant American-English.

We have described the process in some detail to show that unlike many conference projects, where participants produce loosely connected papers based on ongoing work, ours did demand a great deal more of contributors, not only because of the range of issues we asked them to address but also because of the very specific guidelines we suggested they follow in writing their papers, the common hypotheses which we expected them to address, the comparative data by which we expected them to contextualize their analyses, and the numerous rounds of editing and requests for revisions under increasingly tight deadlines with which we badgered them. We are extremely grateful for their willingness and ability to produce first-rate contributions under these very demanding conditions. Similarly, we are grateful to the expert commentators in our series of conferences and workshops who were willing to read many and very long drafts and to offer extremely helpful critiques and suggestions, both theoretical and empirical. Their input proved invaluable to the authors and to the project as a whole. Since they will not appear among the authors, we name them here in alphabetical order: Jens Alber, University of Konstanz; Peter Hall, Harvard University; Franz-Xaver Kaufmann, University of Bielefeld; Stephan Leibfried, University of Bremen; and John D. Stephens, University of North Carolina.

However, after we had—almost—succeeded in meeting Oxford's December 1999 deadline for the country chapters and special studies destined for Volume II, we discovered to our dismay that the completion of the comparative chapters in Volume I took considerably more time than we had allowed. Since each of our drafts had interpreted its allotted page limits liberally, and none had allowed for tables, figures, and bibliographies, the drastic cuts that were required amounted to a rewriting of what had essentially been finished chapters. Worse yet, in the process of fine-tuning the coordination between these chapters, we had to become each others' best editors and worst critics, and it is remarkable that all four authors still seem to be on friendly terms with each other. We are grateful to Amanda Watkins, our editor at Oxford University Press, for bearing with us and for remaining supportive and encouraging throughout this difficult phase.

As in the preface to Volume II, we again thank the staff of the Cologne Max Planck Institute, including Christina Glasmacher, Jürgen Lautwein, Thomas Pott, and Christel Schommertz, who helped to make the project and this publication possible. But at this time our very special thanks must go to Sonja Jerak, who took full responsibility for managing the completion process and who cheerfully and competently resumed her editorial functions every time a chapter that was thought to be completed was revised not just once or twice, but just once more again. Whether the result was worth her efforts, the reader must judge.

Fritz W. Scharpf
Vivien A. Schmidt

Cologne and Boston
23 March 2000

CONTENTS

LIST OF FIGURES

LIST OF TABLES

LIST OF APPENDIX TABLES

ABBREVIATIONS

The following abbreviations are used to indicate various countries in some of the tables and figures:

A	Austria
AUS	Australia
B	Belgium
CAN	Canada
CH	Switzerland
D	Germany
DK	Denmark
F	France
FL	Finland
I	Italy
IRL	Ireland
JAP	Japan
N	Norway
NL	Netherlands
NZ	New Zealand
S	Sweden
UK	United Kingdom
USA	United States of America

Other abbreviations used:

EC	European Community
EMS	European Monetary System
EMU	European Monetary Union
EU	European Union
GATT	General Agreement on Tariffs and Trade
GDP	Gross Domestic Product
ILO	International Labour Office
IMF	International Monetary Fund
ISIC	International Standard Industrial Classification of All Economic Activities
OECD	Organization for Economic Cooperation and Development
PPP	Purchasing Power Parity
WTO	World Trade Organization

NOTES ON CONTRIBUTORS

ANTON HEMERIJCK is Senior Lecturer in the Department of Public Administration, Leiden University, the Netherlands, and visiting researcher at the Max Planck Institute for the Study of Societies in Cologne. He studied economics at Tilburg University, and political science at Oxford University (Balliol College), where he wrote his dissertation, and MIT, Cambridge, MA. He has published widely on issues of comparative social and economic policy and welfare reform. Together with Jelle Visser, he wrote *'A Dutch Miracle': Job Growth, Welfare Reform and Corporatism in the Netherlands*, which is now available in English, German, Italian, and Dutch. A Japanese edition is currently in preparation.

FRITZ W. SCHARPF, Professor of Political Science, is director at the Max Planck Institute for the Study of Societies, Cologne, Germany. Recent publications in English include: *Crisis and Choice in European Social Democracy* (Ithaca, NY: Cornell University Press, 1991); *Games Real Actors Play: Actor-Centered Institutionalism in Policy Research* (Boulder, Colo.: Westview, 1997); *Governing in Europe: Effective and Democratic?* (Oxford: Oxford University Press, 1999).

MARTIN SCHLUDI is a doctoral fellow at the Max Planck Institute for the Study of Societies in Cologne. He studied public policy at Konstanz University and Gothenburg University. His research interests include comparative political economy, especially welfare state retrenchment and pension reform.

VIVIEN A. SCHMIDT, Professor of International Relations at Boston University, has written extensively on European political economy and public policy, including *From State to Market?* (Cambridge: Cambridge University Press, 1996), *Democratizing France* (Cambridge: Cambridge University Press, 1990) and articles in journals such as *Publius*, *Daedalus*, *Comparative Politics*, *Current Politics and Economics in Europe*, *Government and Policy*, *Governance*, *Journal of Common Market Studies*, the *Journal of European Public Policy*, and *West European Politics*. Currently, Professor Schmidt is working on a two-volume project on the impact of European integration on national economies, institutions, and discourse in France, Britain, and Germany.

1

Introduction

FRITZ W. SCHARPF AND VIVIEN A. SCHMIDT

The emergence of advanced welfare states was a product of the 'Great Transformation' of capitalist economies that Karl Polanyi (1957) had analyzed. It had become possible in the postwar period, when the integration of the capitalist world economy had reached a low point following the rampant protectionism of the 1930s and World War II while domestic economies were expanding rapidly. At that time, the international regime of 'embedded liberalism' (Ruggie 1982), with effective capital exchange controls, fixed but adjustable exchange rates, and optional barriers to trade, had imposed few constraints on domestic policy choices. Since exit options for investors, producers, and consumers could be controlled, national policymakers had considerable freedom to regulate the conditions of investment, production, employment and distribution without endangering the international viability of the national economy. At the same time, Keynesian economics offered a set of tools that promised to—and for a time did—dampen the cyclical crises associated with capitalist accumulation.

In advanced welfare states, these new capabilities were used to create institutions through which market interactions became re-embedded in a framework of politically shaped rules that defined boundaries for the 'commodification' of labor and modified the distributional effects of the market. In the postwar decades, the state and organized labor expanded their roles in advanced capitalist economies to assure not only civic and political rights but also social rights of citizenship (Marshall 1950). At minimum, these included a political commitment to high levels of employment in 'good jobs' for all those who were expected to work for a living, universal access to health care and education, social insurance for sickness, disability, unemployment, and old age, and social assistance to prevent poverty in the absence of other sources of support (Esping-Andersen 1990). And in spite of widely differing levels and types of market-correcting state intervention and collective agreements between unions and employers, all countries covered by our project continued to maintain dynamic capitalist economies whose viability was barely constrained by the international economic environment in the early postwar decades.

In the meantime, all that has changed. The control of the nation state over its economic boundaries has eroded again: most completely for the member states of the European Union that are also members of the European Monetary Union, but to a considerable degree for all other countries as well. Capital exchange controls have been removed or lost their effectiveness, exchange rates are determined by transnational capital movements, and trade barriers have been abolished or drastically reduced. In other words, national economies are no longer shielded against their international environment, and at least in that sense it must be true that 'Polanyi's Great Transformation is over' (Cerny 1994: 339). The question is whether that also implies that the social embeddedness of markets has come to an end, and that the decommodification achieved by advanced welfare states has ceased to be economically viable.

In the rapidly growing literature on the consequences of 'globalization', some authors predict a downward convergence resulting from regulatory and tax competition among national governments in internationalized capital and product markets (for example, McKenzie and Lee 1991; S. Sinn 1993; Tanzi 1995; Strange 1996; Rodrik 1997), whereas others assert the continuing viability of divergent policy choices at the national level (for example, Rhodes 1996; Garrett 1998; Swank 1998; Soskice 1999). At the theoretical level, however, the arguments presented on both sides in these controversies often seem to be either very general or very narrowly focused, and hence not mutually incompatible, while the empirical evidence appears to be inconclusive. What was lacking when we started our project in 1997 were systematically comparative and sufficiently detailed reports on changes in the structure and performance of a wide variety of advanced welfare states that could be attributed to their increasing exposure to the international economic environment.[1] We chose to address this deficiency by commissioning expert studies of the processes and outcomes of adjustment in employment and social policies after the early 1970s in a set of twelve countries that included examples from all three 'families' of welfare states that Esping-Andersen (1990) had identified; with Sweden and Denmark representing the 'Scandinavian' or 'social democratic' model, Austria, Belgium, France, Germany, Italy, and the Netherlands as members of the 'Continental' or 'Christian democratic' family, and Australia, New Zealand, and the United Kingdom as examples of the 'Anglo-Saxon' or 'liberal' type, important characteristics of which are also shared by Switzerland. These country reports are presented in Volume II together with cross-cutting studies on the develop-

---

[1] Relying on a combination of multivariate statistical analyses and historical and empirical research on selected countries, Huber and Stephens (2001) will change this assessment of the literature.

ment of female labor participation and early retirement, on tax competition, and on the consequences of public-service liberalization.

The basic empirical message of our project is expressed in the subtitle of Volume II: 'Common Challenges and Diverse Responses'. The policy experiences described do not suggest convergence, not even among countries originally as similar as Sweden and Denmark, Australia and New Zealand, or Belgium and the Netherlands. In this volume, we present second-order interpretations of these experiences from three comparative perspectives: economic vulnerabilities and institutional capabilities (Chapter 2), sequences of policy failures and effective responses (Chapter 3), and the role of values and discourse in the politics of adjustment (Chapter 4). Again, the overall message is expressed in the subtitle— 'From Vulnerability to Competitiveness'—suggesting that even advanced welfare states could remain competitive in the open economy. Unlike the subtitle of Volume II, however, this one is descriptive of only some countries included in our project. For others it reflects at best possibilities, rather than achievements.

1.1 Common Challenges

Our project focuses on the adjustment of advanced welfare states to challenges to their employment and social-policy performance that have arisen from the international economic environment. The selectivity of this perspective is justified, first, by the primacy of work and welfare for the life chances of ordinary citizens and, by implication, for the political legitimacy of democratic polities, and, second, by the far-reaching changes in the relationship between national economies and their international environment during the last three decades.[2]

The focus on challenges and responses also distinguishes our approach from that of most current research on the political economy and comparative politics of the welfare state. There, the primary interest is in identifying the effects of various independent variables—different constellations of socioeconomic interests, class-specific power resources, party-political power balances, institutional arrangements, and so forth—on policy outputs and outcomes. For us, the primary question is whether the actual policy choices can or cannot be considered effective responses to the policy

---

[2] This is not meant to deny the importance of endogenous challenges to the postwar welfare state arising from changes in demography, family structures, or social values, nor is it derived from a dogmatic belief that 'globalization' should explain all that has gone wrong in the management of national economies over the last three decades. Nevertheless, given the state of academic and public debates, a selective focus on the effects of increasing international exposure on employment and the welfare state appears to us highly worthwhile.

challenges we identified. It is only when we are then trying to explain why given countries did or did not adopt effective responses that we will of course refer to the interests, strategies, and institutional capabilities of unions, interest groups, political parties, and government actors—along with all other factors that seem to have explanatory power. In committing ourselves to the primacy of a problem-solving perspective, we are fully aware of the risks involved in taking our own definitions of either problems or solutions for granted. Both are normatively charged concepts whose meanings in the specific case are outcomes of political processes and may be currently controversial. In the context of the present project, however, we accept this risk in the belief that rampant inflation, mass unemployment, rising poverty, and increasing inequality were in fact considered as problematic in all the countries whose policy responses we are comparing.

When deciding to focus on challenges arising from the early 1970s onward, we had assumed that the expansion of state responsibility for employment, social security, and redistribution had culminated at the end of the 'golden age' in the late 1960s, and that international economic constraints became a major concern only thereafter. As will be seen in the country chapters and in Chapter 2 in this volume, this stylized background assumption does not apply in all cases. In some countries— Britain, Australia, and New Zealand, in particular—welfare states were exposed to severe international economic challenges before the 1970s; and in other countries—Sweden, Denmark, Italy, and Switzerland, for instance—the expansion of the welfare state continued in the 1970s and even the 1980s. Nevertheless, the focus on the period beginning in the early 1970s is justified by the fact that from then on all advanced welfare states were affected by common challenges.

The sequence of these challenges will be fully discussed in Chapter 2. They began with the breakdown of the Bretton-Woods system of fixed but adjustable exchange rates and with the first OPEC oil-price crisis of 1973–75. The first created an environment of floating exchange rates and accelerated the growth of 'offshore' capital markets that were not under the control of any of the major central banks. The second confronted oil-dependent industrial economies with the macroeconomic challenges of 'stagflation', that is, the simultaneous impact of cost-push inflation and demand-gap unemployment. Under these conditions, Keynesian strategies of fiscal and monetary demand management were no longer able to ensure acceptable outcomes on inflation and employment at the same time unless they were assisted by sustained union wage restraint—which depended greatly on the prevailing industrial-relations institutions.

Since in fact only few countries were able to achieve an effective coordination between macroeconomic and wage policies following the first oil shock, most governments were confronted with the shock of the second oil-price crisis at the turn of the 1980s at a time when unemployment, inflation, and budget deficits were considerably higher than they had been at the onset of the first crisis. In addition, real interest rates in the international capital markets in which most countries had become heavily indebted increased steeply from rates at or below zero in the late 1970s to 8 percent plus in 1984. Hence monetary reflation was no longer available to prevent the rise of unemployment, and massive wage restraint was required to raise the expected profitability of productive investments above the level that could be earned with risk-free government bonds.

By the end of the 1980s finally, when the international macroeconomic environment of capitalist economies seemed once more relatively benign, the protective barriers that had shielded their internal structures in the postwar decades were rapidly disappearing. The internationalization of markets for goods, services and capital was again reaching levels that equaled, and then exceeded, the degree of international economic integration that had existed in the decades before World War I. Capital exchange controls, which still protected the domestic financial markets of most countries in the early 1970s, had practically disappeared.[3] The European Community, moreover, had liberalized financial services, and most countries had deregulated their domestic financial markets as well. As a consequence, financial capital was now again internationally mobile, and the minimal rate of return that investors could expect was no longer defined by reference to interest rates set by the national bank but rather by the attractiveness of competing worldwide opportunities for speculative, portfolio, or direct investments.

At the same time, successive rounds of GATT and WTO negotiations had progressively lowered the tariffs and quantitative restrictions protecting national markets for goods, services and investments. Going beyond that, Australia and New Zealand, which had extensively relied on trade protection in the past, opted for radical liberalization in the mid-1980s; and among the member states of the European Community, the Single-Market program had also eliminated the non-tariff barriers that still impeded the full integration of product markets. For most EU countries, moreover, the completion of the internal market was followed by the

[3] According to an indicator of capital-exchange liberalization constructed by Dennis Quinn on the basis of IMF data, where a score of 14 marks total liberalization, in 1970 eleven of 20 OECD countries had scores below 10, and only one country—Germany—had a score of 14 By 1993, only one country—Greece—still scored below 10, and nine countries now had a score of 14 (Table A.31).

commitment to create a monetary union which would not only remove monetary and exchange rate policy from the control of national governments and impose severe constraints on the conduct of national fiscal policy but which also would remove the last important barrier to real-capital mobility. By the same token, it had become much easier to move mobile tax bases—in particular business profits and other forms of capital incomes—to locations offering the least burdensome tax regimes.

Since governments and unions are no longer dealing with captive capital owners and captive consumers, national systems of taxation, regulation, and industrial relations have now become vulnerable to the extent that they reduce the attractiveness of the national economy to mobile capital and the competitiveness of nationally produced goods and services in international product markets. This has major impacts on employment in the internationally exposed sectors of the economy and on the financial viability of the welfare state.

1.2 Differences Matter

In this project, our concern is with the ability of advanced welfare states to adjust to the challenges arising from the external economic environment. We define successful adjustment by the dual criteria of economic viability and political legitimacy (Penz 1999). The relevance of economic viability is obvious, and it can be measured and compared by reference to generally accepted indicators of economic success, whereas the connection with legitimacy is more elusive and contingent. Given the fact that we are dealing with democratic polities, however, it is clear that legitimacy must ultimately relate to the interests and normative preferences—values—of democratic constituencies.[4] That suggests that it may be undermined by manifest failures of economic viability—as was true of the German Weimar Republic in the early 1930s—as well as by failures to maintain the promises of the welfare state. Since these promises have shaped the life plans of citizens, the political salience of the interests affected could hardly be overestimated. Moreover, since the welfare state involves redistribution, it has come to be supported by norms of appropriateness whose violation may mobilize the opposition even of groups whose self-interest is not affected. Hence, the legitimacy, and the discursive legitimization, of

---

[4] This is not the place to elaborate a theory of democratic legitimacy, except to note that it comprises both an input-oriented dimension of political responsiveness—'government by the people'—and an output-oriented dimension of political effectiveness—'government for the people' (Scharpf 1999: ch. 1).

adjustment strategies designed to maintain or restore economic viability may be a critical precondition of their success (Chapter 4).

But that only adds to the difficulties of comparative analyses and explanations of more or less successful adjustment. These arise from the fact that the countries included in our project differ so much in their vulnerability to external challenges and in their capacity to respond to them as a consequence of institutional differences in their welfare states, industrial relations systems, corporate governance systems, and political systems. The variety of factors and their variance defies comprehensive generalizations, and so we have adopted selective perspectives in the comparative chapters that follow in order to specify the conditions that seem to make a difference. Nevertheless, it seems useful at this place to provide a summary overview of the most salient institutional features of the twelve countries in our project.

1.2.1 Welfare States

All welfare states included in our project are providing more security and a more equal distribution of life chances than could be expected from the unfettered operation of capitalist economies. They differ greatly, however, not only in the extent but also in the type of market-correcting intervention and in the normative aspirations of the 'good society' that these interventions are meant to achieve. As a first cut, these differences are usefully summarized by Esping-Andersen's (1990) distinction between 'liberal', 'christian-democratic' and 'social democratic' families of welfare states; but, as the country studies in Volume II demonstrate, even within these groups differences may be highly significant. Thus, all countries in our project provide free primary and secondary education, and all provide social assistance to avoid extreme poverty. Beyond that, however, the 'golden-age' models differ fundamentally from one another along two dimensions: the extent to which welfare goals are pursued through the regulation of labor markets and employment relations or through the 'formal welfare state' of publicly financed transfers and services, and the extent to which 'caring' services are expected to be provided informally in the family or through professional services. The first of these differences divides the Continental and Scandinavian groups from the Anglo-Saxon welfare states, while the second one sets the Continental welfare states off against the Scandinavian model, and to some extent also against the Anglo-Saxon countries.

1.2.1.1 The Formal Welfare State and the Regulation of Employment In the first dimension, the Anglo-Saxon welfare states placed their trust primarily on the regulation of employment. The egalitarian Beveridge model limited the formal welfare state to providing universal and flat-rate social security benefits that were high enough to prevent poverty, but would not maintain the living standards of workers with medium or higher wages. At the same time, however, the lean welfare state was complemented by a political commitment to full employment that would allow better-paid workers to use private savings to maintain their living standards during short spells of unemployment and in retirement. The regulation of employment relations for social-policy purposes went farthest in Australia and New Zealand, where full employment was maintained through highly protected import-substituting industrialization while the state arbitration courts assured the male breadwinner a 'living wage' sufficient to support a family of five, whereas in Britain full employment was maintained through Keynesian demand management in the 1950s and 1960s.

The Scandinavian countries, by contrast, where social-security benefits had originally been universal, tax-financed and flat-rate as well, responded to rising worker incomes in the postwar decades by introducing earnings-related unemployment insurance and an additional level of occupational pensions that prevented the development of private-sector alternatives and maintained the political support of skilled workers for the welfare state. At the same time, however, the employment system was instrumentalized for welfare-state purposes by strategies reducing the inequality of primary incomes through a 'solidaristic wage policy' that was designed to minimize wage differentials between regions, sectors, and skill groups. Moreover, Sweden also implemented measures of regional and sectoral industrial policy and of active labor market policy that were designed to eliminate the incidence of open unemployment.

In Continental welfare states conforming to the Bismarck model, social security systems were traditionally segmented by occupational categories, and earnings-related benefits were generally financed by wage-based contributions from employers and workers. Since benefits became more generous in the postwar decades while the coverage of public insurance systems was extended, there was again no reason for more affluent workers to resort to private arrangements. Given the existence of relatively generous social insurance, there was less of a political commitment to full-employment policies than was true in the Anglo-Saxon countries and in Sweden, but Keynesian demand management was in fact practiced successfully in some countries in the 1960s, and countries like France, Italy, or Austria had large sectors of state-owned industries that could be required to avoid layoffs in a recession. In contrast to the Scandinavian welfare states, reducing the inequality of primary incomes was not a widely shared goal of wage policy, but in some countries state minimum-wage legislation did in fact compress wage scales, and in others the same effect was achieved by coordinated collective bargaining.

In spite of these fundamental structural differences, all three models could be considered functionally equivalent solutions for the problems of income security at the end of the golden-age period. Under conditions of assured full employment, private top-ups on flat-rate benefits could be as satisfactory as earnings-related public benefits; as segmented Continental insurance systems expanded their coverage, they could approximate the universalism of Anglo-Saxon and Scandinavian systems; and within the boundaries of national economies, general taxation and wage-based social-security contributions did not differ in their economic viability. With the onset of the new international challenges, however, the functional equivalence was lost. As unemployment increased, Anglo-Saxon welfare states lost their capacity to assure income maintenance whereas Continental and Scandinavian welfare states had to bear the fiscal burdens of their institutionalized promises. With the international integration of product and capital markets, finally, the differences between tax-financed and contribution-financed welfare states also increased in importance. But these are matters to be discussed in the following chapters.

1.2.1.2 Caring Services by the Family, the State and the Market The second dimension, regarding the nature and level of service provision, separates the Continental systems primarily from the social-democratic Scandinavian welfare states and to a lesser extent from the liberal Anglo-Saxon model. Initially, it is true, the Bismarck model of work-based social insurance for the male breadwinner and his family had been shaped by conservative and statist efforts to defuse the revolutionary potential of the labor movement. But its reconstruction and expansion in the postwar decades occurred under the influence of christian-democratic parties and Catholic social philosophy, which emphasized the importance of the family and the principles of subsidiarity and corporatist self-organization. As a consequence, the original Bismarck system, which had of course reflected the gender roles of the time, was reinforced and extended rather than transcended, and it was supplemented by child benefits and significant tax privileges favoring single-earner families. By the same logic, it was taken for granted that caring services for the young, the sick, and the old would normally be provided by women within the family, while supplementary social services for the needy by publicly subsidized churches and charities were of limited importance.

In the Scandinavian countries, by contrast, where the welfare state had come later than in Germany, its development was shaped by egalitarian ideals promoted in the labor movement and social-democratic parties.

Under their influence, social insurance became universal and tax-financed, rather than work-based and contribution-financed. Moreover, even though actual labor markets of the time were as male-dominated and gender roles as traditional as in other countries, the further development of the welfare state took its directions from a feminist interpretation of egalitarianism which, in the words of Alva Myrdal, was no longer just claiming the 'married woman's right to work', but insisted on the 'working woman's right to marry and have children' (Myrdal 1945: 121, as cited in Holmwood 2000: 39). The implication was that caring services for the young, the sick, the handicapped, and the old should be professionally provided and collectively financed. The political realization of these demands from the 1960s onward has resulted in an expansion of public-service employment and female labor participation that was not equaled anywhere else.

In Britain, it is true, the trajectory of public-service employment, primarily within the National Health Service, had not lagged far behind until the end of the 1960s. The difference, however, is that the basic structures of the universalist Anglo-Saxon welfare state were gender-neutral rather than expressly devoted to gender equality, as in the Scandinavian countries. But in contrast to the christian-democratic model, the liberal model at least had not institutionalized specific disincentives that made it unattractive for married women to seek paid employment.[5] Thus, when public-sector expansion was stopped by the economic crises of the 1970s and then by Thatcherism, the Beveridgean welfare state did not stand in the way of an expansion of female employment in the private-sector services in the United Kingdom, or in Australia and New Zealand, for that matter.

These and other differences between the Anglo-Saxon, Scandinavian, and Continental ideal types of the welfare state are summarized in Table 1.1 (see also Bonoli and Palier 1998). However, the success or failure of countries was affected not only by differences in their welfare-state configurations, but also by differences in their systems of industrial or employment relations and of corporate governance.

---

[5] In the ideal-typical Continental country, a married housewife is protected by her husband's health insurance and pension insurance, and her husband's income tax is significantly reduced by tax 'splitting'. If she works, she has to pay insurance contributions from which she will gain no additional benefit, and her wages will be taxed at the marginal rate defined by the joint income.

Table 1.1 *Constellations of welfare states*

Characteristics and properties	Anglo-Saxon	Scandinavian	Continental
Rights	Individual	Individual	Family
Responsibility	Individual	Collective	Collective
Claiming principles	Need	Citizenship	Work/family needs
Beneficiaries	Poor	All citizens	Male breadwinner
Goal	Poverty alleviation	Equality/income maintenance	Income maintenance
Social security transfers	Flat-rate	Flat-rate/ contribution related	Contribution related
Caring services	Family/market	State	Family/ intermediary groups
Type of financing	Taxation	Taxation/ contribution	Contribution
Source of financing	State/market	State	State/earner
Gender and status effects	Neutral	Pro-equality	Differentiated

1.2.2 Industrial Relations Systems

Employment relations, we suggested above, may be instrumentalized to serve welfare-state purposes through the regulation of wage differentials and of the conditions of employment. To the extent that they are, they are now implicated in the problems of national adjustment to the internationalization of capital and product markets in much the same way as is true of other types of welfare-state regulation. In the 1970s and 1980s, however, economic adjustment had depended on the capacity of industrial relations systems to avoid wage inflation in the face of international macroeconomic shocks. In both regards, what mattered were institutional differences that are generally described in the literature by the shorthand distinction between 'corporatist', 'statist', and 'fragmented' systems. The analytical usefulness of these descriptors is increased, however, by an understanding of two underlying dimensions—the degree of coordination among collective-bargaining units, and the degree of state involvement— which then suggests the existence of four, rather than three, different constellations (Fig. 1.1) at the end of the 'golden age' period.

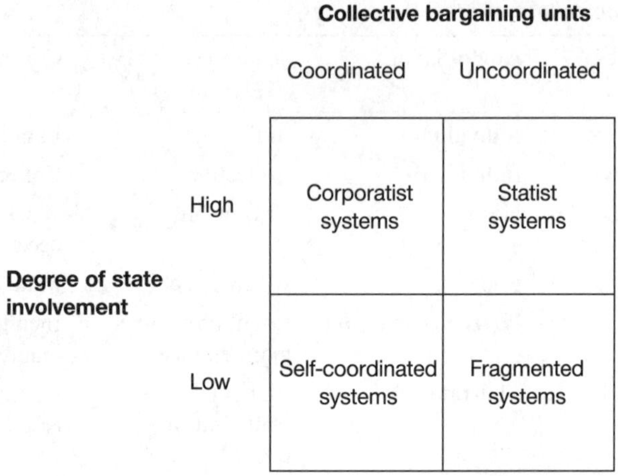

Collective bargaining units

Coordinated   Uncoordinated

	Coordinated	Uncoordinated
High	Corporatist systems	Statist systems
Low	Self-coordinated systems	Fragmented systems

Degree of state involvement

Figure 1.1 Types of industrial relations systems

1.2.2.1 Coordinated Collective Bargaining From the perspective of ideal markets, all collective bargaining systems must seem problematic since they have the capacity to set wages and employment conditions at levels that differ from the hypothetical market equilibrium. In the absence of market coordination, coordinated collective bargaining implies the capacity and willingness of negotiators in individual bargaining units to reflect the joint impact of bargaining outcomes in all units on the state of the national economy. Such coordination may be achieved through institutional centralization, as when the peak federations of Swedish unions and employers' associations were able to negotiate nation-wide settlements which they were able to enforce against deviant tendencies among their sectoral, regional, and local subunits. In principle, it may also be achieved through horizontal self-coordination among subunits.

While the state is never totally removed from the industrial-relations arena, its role may vary between the determination of general rules of the game through labor law and industrial relations legislation and the direct involvement of governments in collective bargaining rounds. It is the latter constellation for which we reserve the term 'corporatist'. This usage corresponds to the 'classical' literature on neo-corporatism and its emphasis on tripartite negotiations between the state and the monopolistic peak associations of capital and labor (Schmitter and Lehmbruch 1979). In the countries classified as neo-corporatist—generally including Sweden, Denmark, Austria and, in certain periods, Belgium and the Netherlands—the pattern is always associated with the involvement of the peak associations of capital and labor—the 'social partners'—in policy choices *of the state*. In the reverse direction, however, the direct and open involvement of the state in collective bargaining between employers and unions is less common. While the social partners in corporatist countries usually have wide channels of informal communication with the government, they also find it necessary to emphasize their formal autonomy. In fact, examples of explicit 'political exchange' (Pizzorno 1978) in the form of 'accords', 'social pacts' or 'alliances for employment', where the government tries to obtain the explicit acceptance of wage guidelines (Ebbinghaus and Hassel 2000), are more characteristic of formerly 'fragmented' industrial relations systems—Australia, Italy and perhaps Belgium in our project— rather than of corporatism. In any case, it is always the role of the state to represent, explicate, and create acceptance for the requirements of an 'incomes policy' reflecting macroeconomic criteria.

In Germany and Switzerland, however, the state does not play a significant role in collective bargaining, nor are industrial-relations institutions sufficiently centralized to allow a degree of hierarchical coordination, as it still exists in Austria, Denmark and the Netherlands. If wage setting in both countries can nevertheless be classified as being coordinated, that is a result of voluntary '*self-coordination*' which must achieve both horizontal coordination among separate bargaining units and vertical coordination between wage policy and monetary policy. The necessary precondition of both is a union organization that avoids inter-union competition for members and hence incentives for escalating wage competition. If that is assured by the existence of jurisdictional monopolies, coordination could be achieved either by cross-jurisdictional negotiations or, less demandingly, by practices of 'pattern bargaining' where the wage leadership of one large industry is informally accepted by all other bargaining units. In Germany, this wage leadership is usually exercised by the large metal workers' union with a view to economy-wide productivity increases and, as will be shown in later chapters, vertical coordination is also achieved by asymmetric adjustment in the sense that unions have learned to adjust to the monetary parameters defined by the Bundesbank (Soskice and Iversen 1998). Similar patterns exist in Switzerland.

1.2.2.2 Uncoordinated Collective Bargaining Regardless of the greater or lesser role of the state, coordinated industrial relations system are generally characterized by more or less cooperative interactions among the social partners. Since both sides share a concern for the macroeconomic effects of their bargaining outcomes, the relative salience of common interests as opposed to competing distributive interests is strengthened at the level of industries, regions, and firms as well. This is not so in countries where coordinative institutional mechanisms are lacking, especially if there are structural conditions creating incentives for inter-union competition. Such incentives exist in the United Kingdom, Australia, and New Zealand, where the industrial-relations structure is *fragmented* into a large number of independent unions, many of them quite small, with overlapping jurisdictions and with highly decentralized bargaining units. They also exist, under very different conditions, in France, Italy, and Belgium—and to a lesser degree in the Netherlands as well—where competing national union federations are divided by party-political or ideological cleavages, and where industrial conflict often—especially in the late 1960s and early 1970s—is an expression of political competition.

In the absence of state intervention, both the Anglo-Saxon and the Latin types of fragmented industrial-relations systems tend to generate high levels of industrial conflict as well as inflationary wage dynamics. By the same token, however, state intervention in these countries is generally more pervasive and intense than is true in countries with a capacity for coordinated collective bargaining. In Britain and Italy, and during the 1970s in Belgium and the Netherlands as well, governments resorted to intermittent bouts of statutory wage freezes and attempts at negotiated 'incomes policy' to dampen inflationary dynamics, but generally without lasting success. But similar difficulties were encountered by countries which, in the absence of coordinated collective bargaining, had developed much stronger instruments and practices of state intervention.

In our project, the group of countries with *statist* industrial relations systems includes France, Australia, and New Zealand. Here, wages and work conditions are seen as matters of state responsibility as much as of collective management-labor responsibilities. In France, the state is involved not only in setting the rules governing the wage-bargaining process but also in organizing the process and, if and when it fails—which it often does—even determining the outcome. Centralized wage-bargaining generally follows from such interventionism, with agreements proceeding from state controlled, sector-wide collective negotiation between management and unions. Moreover, state-owned enterprises take the leadership in establishing workers' social rights on vacations and workplace conditions as well as in promoting modernization of the workplace and the reform of industrial training. In Australia and New Zealand, by contrast, state control was exercised through arbitration courts that set wages and work conditions when voluntary agreements failed—which was much of the time. By making decisions on the basis of 'comparative wage justice', these courts sought to maintain long-standing wage differentials between skill groups and sectors at the same time as they were trying to hold the line against the rising pressures of worker militancy and inter-union wage competition at the end of the 1960s.

In the context of our project, the different types of industrial-relations systems were exposed to their greatest challenges in the macroeconomic crises that marked the end of the golden-age period in the early 1970s and thereafter. As will be seen in the following chapters, none of the countries was able to weather these crises unscathed, but by and large countries with coordinated wage-bargaining systems, and in particular countries with corporatist institutions, were able to adjust more successfully than the others. In fact, by the 1990s, none of the countries with industrial relations system classified here as being either fragmented or statist still maintained the institutional configurations that existed in the early 1970s, whereas countries with corporatist or self-coordinated industrial-relations institutions had changed very little.

The changes in fragmented or statist industrial relations systems suggest that the fourfold classification we introduced at the beginning of this section sits on top of the more fundamental distinction between conditions in which wages and employment conditions are determined by agreements between individual workers and employers and hence regulated by the market, and industrial-relations systems in which individual employment contracts and wages are subject to higher-level regulation, by collective-bargaining agreements and/or by the state. Toward the end of the golden-age period, this more basic distinction had been of purely theoretical interest since in all OECD countries wages and the conditions of employment were in fact subject to collective agreements and varying degrees of state regulation. But by the 1990s, as will be shown in the following chapter, there were a few countries—the United Kingdom, New Zealand, and France—where the regulation of employment relations has been decentralized to a degree that approximates the market model.

1.2.3 Governance Institutions

The industrial-relations systems discussed above can be considered as being part of the problem constellations with which countries had to cope, but, as we will show in the following chapters, in some countries they also needed to be considered as part of the governance institutions within which effective policy responses could be adopted and implemented. The same could be said of economic governance systems. Here, the literature on 'varieties of capitalism' suggests again a threefold distinction between 'market capitalism' 'managed capitalism', and 'state capitalism' (V. A. Schmidt 2000a), whereas in our view the variance among our countries might be better captured by the consideration of two underlying dimensions: the degree of coordination among firms and the degree of state involvement. The resulting possibilities could then again be represented by a fourfold table.

The combination of high degrees of business coordination with high state involvement could be described as 'corporatism on the capital side', with Japan as the paradigmatic case. Among the countries in our project, Sweden and Austria might also be described in these terms during certain periods. Switzerland and Germany, the usual examples of 'managed capitalism', are characterized by relatively low degrees of state direction[6] combined with high degrees of coordination through inter-firm networks achieved through cross-ownership, shareholding banks, strong industrial associations, and the functions of chambers with compulsory membership. The statist model of capitalism would then describe countries— France, but also postwar New Zealand and Australia—combining an intense and pervasive involvement of the state in the conduct of economic affairs with a low degree of self-coordination among economic actors. The model of market capitalism, finally, would fit those countries—present-day Britain and New Zealand, for instance—in which neither the state nor business networks will complement, let alone displace, the coordinative mechanisms of the market. To the extent that these differences have affected the employment performance of countries by facilitating or excluding certain types of industrial-policy responses, they are discussed in the country chapters in Volume II and in Chapter 3 below. The reader should be warned, however, that, given our primary focus on the welfare state and the constraints of an already over-complex project, we have not systematically explored the causal effects of different models of capitalism and corporate governance systems.

Contrary to our original intentions, the same can also be said of our treatment of the effect of different types of political institutions on national adjustment strategies. Here, however, we cannot say that we didn't really try. The authors of our country studies had been asked to pay attention to the politics of adjustment and the institutional factors shaping them, and their reports represent a rich source of empirical information and knowledgeable interpretation and explanation. Moreover, all three of our comparative chapters attempt to account for the effects of institutional differences, and Chapters 2 and 4 specifically focus on these issues. Why is it, then, that we still feel that the potential for institutional and political explanations remains seriously under-exploited in our project?

The primary reason is not a lack of standardized comparative information, even though our case studies necessarily had to focus selectively on those events that were causally significant and politically salient in a given country. Where we thought that non-reported events or even 'non-

---

[6] This does not preclude an 'enabling' role of the state in providing infrastructure and a legal framework that facilitates cooperation.

decisions' might be important from a comparative perspective, we could and did request additional information or rely on other sources. Instead, the main reason is that we found ourselves overwhelmed by the complexity and contingency of the wider factor constellations within which the effects of political institutions and political discourses need to be identified.

We had always been skeptical of the use of simple 'structuralist' hypotheses in comparative political-economy research, at least for the period covered in our project. While the rise of the welfare state in the 'golden-age' period, and the level and shape it had achieved by the end of that period, may have been plausibly explained by the political domination of social-democratic, christian-democratic or liberal parties, or by the 'power resources' of the labor movement, and while the distinction between 'corporatist' and 'pluralist' political systems still had some explanatory power in studies focusing on inflation and unemployment during the 1970s, these factors seem to lose most of their explanatory power in the period of retrenchment and reform in the 1980s and 1990s (Pierson 1996; Huber and Stephens 2001).

But our argument should be made at a more general level. By the design of our project, we had chosen to confront the irreducible contingency of the problem-institutions-actors-politics-policy nexus, and our interest in finding explanations for the greater or lesser effectiveness of national policy responses did not allow us the opt-out of relying on single-factor *ceteris-paribus* hypotheses. Thus, even though we accept the explanatory logic of George Tsebelis' (1995) elegant veto-player theory, which predicts that multi-actor political systems will, under otherwise equal conditions, have a harder time achieving effective political action than single-actor polities, and even though we are impressed by the fact that appropriately specified hypotheses derived from this theory are able to explain 0.1 percent of the empirical variance in multivariate regressions (Bawn 1999), we are still confronted with the fact that multi-actor Germany was better able to respond to the crises of the 1970s than were single-actor Britain, France, or New Zealand. In fact, our country studies and the chapters below abound with instances where the same set of institutions that facilitated effective responses to one type of policy challenge failed dismally when confronted with another type of challenge. In other words, the research questions which we are trying to answer require us to face up to the complexities and contingencies that are otherwise covered by large *ceteris-paribus* clauses in hypothesis-testing empirical studies (Scharpf 1997b: ch. 1).

In the context of our project, the effectiveness of policy responses is conditioned by the simultaneous influence of at least three distinct sets of complex factors: relevant policy challenges resulting from the interaction of changes in the international economic environment with conditions of the domestic economy and national policy legacies, institutional rules defining actor constellations and their modes of interaction, and the orientations—perceptions and preferences—of the policy actors involved. Sometimes, causal inferences may be facilitated by appropriate case selection. Thus, in a study of inflation and unemployment in four European countries in the 1970s (Scharpf 1987) it was possible, by holding challenges (stagflation) and actor orientations (Keynesian) constant, to identify the effects of different institutional structures. Conversely, as will be seen in Chapters 2 and 3 below, in the transition from 1979 to 1980 in Britain, or from 1983 to 1984 in New Zealand, both policy challenges and political institutions remained constant, so that the neo-liberal policy change in both countries may plausibly be explained by a change in actor orientations—which in these cases was facilitated by change of governing parties—from left to right in Britain, but from right to left in New Zealand—while the similar change of orientations in France in 1983 did not even depend on this quasi-institutional factor. Moreover, as will be seen in Chapter 4, even though in the case of Britain and New Zealand there was a similarity of challenges, actor-orientations—neo-liberal—and political institutions—single-actor Westminster model—the longer-term policy outcomes may still differ as a consequence of differences in the quality of policy discourses.

In the chapters below, we have struggled with these contingencies as best as we could, striving for internally and mutually consistent and parsimonious explanations, but always aware of the fact that at this stage of our collective enterprise the search for consistency and parsimoniousness must not yet be allowed to obstruct the efforts to understand and compare the conditions that have affected specific outcomes. We expect that it will be possible to go forward from here toward 'bounded generalizations' by identifying subsets of cases in which the variance of outcomes can be explained by variations in the same set of factor constellations (Scharpf forthcoming). But the chapters in this volume represent the state we have reached as of now.

1.3 The Comparative Chapters

The overall goal of the following chapters is to compare and contrast the impact of the changes in the international economic environment on the postwar social welfare and employment structures, as they had matured by about the early 1970s, of the twelve countries in our project. Although they show that there is no convergence in the welfare state, and that there is no single solution or formula for successful adaptation, these chapters do show that there are indeed several paths toward a successful adjustment of advanced welfare states to international economic pressures.

Chapter 2, by Fritz Scharpf, examines the common pressures on employment and the welfare state that originated from changes in the international economic environment after the early 1970s, and it relates these to national economic conditions and policy legacies in order to identify differences of vulnerability and varying demands on the institutional capacity for policy adjustment. In the earlier period until the mid-1980s, these challenges were of a macroeconomic nature, and the effectiveness of national policy responses depended primarily on the institutional capacity for effective coordination between wage policy and monetary policy. After the mid-1980s, the dominant challenges arose from the global integration of capital markets and the increasing intensity of international competition in product markets. Now the greater or lesser vulnerability of countries was primarily determined by the structure of their welfare states, in particular by the dependence on particular sources of finance and by their effects on service employment in the sheltered sectors. What mattered now was the institutional and political capacity to adopt and implement unpopular changes in the policy legacies of the welfare state.

Chapter 3, by Anton Hemerijck and Martin Schludi, examines the dynamics of policy responses and their ultimate effectiveness. It identifies typical sequences of policy failures, caused by the misfit between new problems and existing policy legacies, which may generate processes of policy learning that ultimately produce effective solutions; but it also points to instances where policy learning is blocked by conflicts of interest or by divergent cognitive orientations in multi-actor institutional settings. Of equal importance are sequences of lateral spillovers where the solutions to problems in one policy area generate new problems that subsequently must be dealt with in adjacent policy areas. In the 1970s and 1980s, these spillovers were most important in countries where major job losses could not be prevented through macroeconomic policy responses, and where the rise of open unemployment was avoided or mitigated by resort to early-retirement and disability pensions. The resulting fiscal burdens became a major problem when the internationalization of capital markets and the commitment to a European Monetary Union came to limit opportunities for deficit financing and for tax increases at the same time. Similar patterns are observed in the policy responses to the new challenges countries faced in the 1990s. In analyzing these sequences of policy failure, learning, and problem displacement, the chapter also is able to compare and assess the greater or lesser effectiveness of the policy responses actually adopted. It is thus able to identify effective responses and successful countries that have been able to adjust to the challenges of the open economy without abandoning their welfare-state goals.

Chapter 4, by Vivien Schmidt, focuses on the role of values and discourse in the politics of successful adjustment. It starts from the assumption that the achievements and aspirations of postwar welfare states have gained a normative salience that is closely associated with the legitimacy of political systems. Thus, policy changes which might otherwise be considered effective responses may not merely violate the interests of groups directly affected, but provoke more widespread protest and discontent that may undermine the political viability of democratic governments. Yet that is not inevitable. Even policies challenging established normative expectations may be justified by persuasive public discourses which either explain and affirm their legitimacy in terms of the prevailing value system or which are able to gain public acceptance for a redefinition of normative aspirations. The chapter examines the institutional and political preconditions of successful discourses on welfare-state reform. More specifically, it demonstrates that in multi-actor polities the 'coordinative discourse' that is necessary to achieve compromises among multiple policy elites may impede the effectiveness of the 'communicative discourse' in which policy makers must gain the attention of, and persuade, the wider public. However, as comparative analyses of Britain and New Zealand or of France and the Netherlands demonstrate, single-actor institutions do not guarantee, and multi-actor constellations do not rule out, successful communicative discourses that gain public acceptance of painful but effective welfare-state reforms.

In the conclusion, we emphasize a number of more general patterns that we have been able to identify in our comparative analyses. Even though we see no need to revise the interpretation we have expressed in the subtitle of Volume II—'common challenges and diverse responses'—we have learned that the variation among the responses of individual countries is far from random. Throughout the periods covered by our project, there have been distinct groups of countries facing similar challenges that would have called for similar responses. And even though the increasing internationalization of the economic environment has narrowed the range of economically viable national policy choices, we are able to show that in each of these groups one or more countries were in fact able to move 'from vulnerability to competitiveness' without abandoning their normative aspirations or jeopardizing the democratic legitimacy of their governments.

2

Economic Changes, Vulnerabilities, and Institutional Capabilities

FRITZ W. SCHARPF

2.1 Introduction

In the decades after 1970, all advanced welfare states were exposed to broadly similar changes in their international economic environment which made it more difficult to maintain the aspiration levels of the postwar 'golden age' with regard to the normatively salient goals of full employment, social security, and social equality. The primary focus of our project, in the country chapters in Volume II as well as in Chapter 3 here, is on national policy responses and their relative effectiveness in adjusting to these changes without abandoning the aspirations of the postwar welfare state. The present chapter is meant to provide an explanatory frame for the discussion of these policy responses by focusing, on the one hand, on the specific nature of the challenges that different countries were facing and, on the other hand, on the specific institutional conditions that either facilitated or impeded the adoption and implementation of effective policy responses.

This combination of perspectives, focusing on seemingly unrelated sets of factors, requires a brief justification. They are treated together in a single chapter because they strongly interact with each other if we consider both of them as 'independent variables' influencing the effective policy responses in which we are interested. The proximate causes of these responses are of course interactions among actors—individual, collective, and corporate—that have a role in the adoption and implementation of policy choices. These actors—prime ministers, government departments, central banks, political parties, labor unions, and so forth—are generally acting in representative roles: that is, under incentives that favor policy choices responding to the interests of the collectivities they represent. But since these roles are institutionalized, institutional 'rules of the game' will define competencies, veto positions, and modes of interaction that circumscribe the repertoire of permissible 'moves' as well as the outcomes associated with particular constellations of moves, and they may also define institution-specific norms of appropriateness that may modify or even supersede preferences rooted in organizational self-interest (Scharpf 1997b). In other words, institutional rules channel and constrain potential moves, they shape incentives, and they may also influence actor perceptions and preferences. There is no question, therefore, that the outcome of policy interactions may be strongly influenced by the institutional setting within which they occur; and thus it should also be possible to show that certain types of institutional settings are more or less conducive to effective policy responses to a given challenge.

The last phrase, however, points to the inherently contingent character of the causal relationship between institutional conditions and policy effectiveness. Institutions create selective capabilities that may be good for some purposes and not for others. For instance, the adoption of major policy changes is generally more difficult in the German political system with its multi-actor and multiple-veto characteristics than is true in the single-actor 'Westminster model' that was approximated in the United Kingdom or in New Zealand until very recently (Tsebelis 1995; Scharpf 1988; Lijphart 1984). Under the economic conditions of the 1960s and 1970s, however, the stop-go policies facilitated by British institutions were clearly less effective than the more steady German pattern; it is only when confronted with the challenges of the 1990s that German institutions have come to be generally considered as a cause of policy failures. In other words, even though institutional differences may provide very powerful explanations for the success or failure of national policy responses, these explanations can be formulated only with regard to specific types of challenges. Hence if they are to be discussed at all, they need to be discussed in the chapter that explicates the challenges with which countries had to cope.

That term also requires elaboration. In the context of our project, the 'challenges' we consider arise from changes in the international economic environment that are likely to have negative effects on the postwar aspirations of advanced welfare states. But while the external changes may be identical for all countries, challenges will differ for three conceptually distinct reasons: First, and perhaps most importantly, challenges may differ because *aspirations* are not the same among countries. Take 'full employment' which, in the early 1970s still meant employment for all 'male breadwinners' in the Continental welfare states as well as in Australia and New Zealand (Schwartz, Volume II), whereas Sweden and Denmark had begun to raise their aspirations to include equal employment opportunities for women. Thus, after the first oil-price crisis, the decline of female participation rates was not considered a challenge to full employment in

Switzerland, Austria or Germany, but it would have been so considered in Sweden. Similarly, 'social security' was associated with universal flat-rate benefits in the 'Beveridge model' of the Anglo-Saxon welfare states whereas it had come to mean status-maintaining income replacements in the Continental welfare states evolving from the 'Bismarck model'. And while 'social equality' in the Beveridge model had required equal access to education and health care, but no more than poverty-preventing income redistribution, in the Scandinavian and some—but not all—Continental welfare states it came to imply equalization of primary incomes through 'solidaristic' wage policy. Thus, even if the real impacts of external changes were the same in all countries, some of these impacts would be considered a severe problem in some countries but not in others.

But neither are impacts the same in all countries. They are mediated through economically relevant structural conditions and policy legacies that may differ considerably between countries. Thus, Britain was hit as hard as most other countries by the first oil-price crisis of 1973–75. But when the OPEC cartel struck again in 1979, North-Sea oil had come on stream, and Margaret Thatcher no longer had to cope with the balance of payments crises that had haunted the Heath, Wilson, and Callaghan governments. By the same token Denmark, with an economic structure dominated by small, family-owned firms is less affected by increasing international capital mobility than is Sweden, which depends much more on the investment decisions of big multinational enterprises. Similarly, under the policy legacies of Continental countries, where unemployment benefits and public pensions are earnings-related, the economic crisis of the early 1970s created greater financial burdens for the welfare state than was true in Anglo-Saxon countries with relatively low and flat-rate benefits.

In the following sections, I will therefore begin by describing first the changes in the international economic environment in a certain period that generally gave rise to pressures for policy adjustment in advanced welfare states. I will then identify subgroups of countries that shared similar vulnerabilities and thus had to face broadly similar policy challenges, and I will finally discuss to what extent differences in the institutional conditions of these countries could plausibly account for differences in the effectiveness of policy responses. For the reader, this form of presentation creates an obvious problem, since our comparative chapters are not only based on the country-specific information presented in Volume II, but also presuppose each other in the sense that my discussion of institutional explanations depends on comparative information about policy responses and about political processes that is fully elaborated only in the following chapters, and *vice versa*. Unfortunately, like airline pilots caught in a landing queue, we can only 'ask for your understanding'.

2.2 The Economic Environment of Advanced Welfare States from the 1950s to the 1980s

The advanced welfare states included in our project have their institutional roots in the last decades of the nineteenth century and the first decade of the twentieth century, when the international integration of capitalist economies had reached a high plateau. But they only achieved their full development in the benign economic environment of the early postwar decades, when demand for industrial products was increasing world-wide, first as a consequence of reconstruction and then pushed onward by the 'Fordist' cycle of rapid productivity increases in the manufacturing of standardized consumer goods, falling relative prices, rising mass incomes, and expanding mass consumption. Economic growth, however, was only one of the conditions facilitating the development of the welfare state. As is pointed out in the Introduction, it was of equal importance that national economic boundaries were still effectively controlled under the international economic regime of 'embedded liberalism' (Ruggie 1982).

2.2.1 The 'Golden Age' of Embedded Liberalism

Behind semi-permeable economic boundaries, national governments and unions could more or less ignore the exit options of capital owners, tax payers and consumers. Thus, the level and the type of taxes that could be imposed on captive tax payers—and hence the level of public services and transfers—were primarily limited by political rather than economic constraints; and since increases of wage and non-wage labor costs, and uniform regulations of the conditions of production and employment, had to be borne by all competing firms, their costs could generally be passed on to captive consumers without endangering the profitability of capitalist production. Moreover, since national interest rate policy was able to determine, and vary, the minimal rate of return that captive capital owners could expect in the market for longer-term investment opportunities, and since government deficit spending could be accommodated by an expansion of the domestic money supply, most governments learned to dampen macroeconomic fluctuations through Keynesian demand management, and to achieve and maintain full employment and relatively high rates of economic growth.

Hence, at the beginning of the 1970s, rates of unemployment in most of the countries covered by our project were low or even close to zero (Table A.4); economic growth was quite vigorous (Table A.2); and low public sector deficits—and, in many countries, surpluses—indicated that welfare state expenditures were not exceeding available revenues (Table A.22). If there was reason for concern, it was mainly over price stability (Table A.3). But these problems did not yet affect citizens in a massive way.

Nevertheless, not all countries were in equally good shape at the onset of the 1970s. *Italy*, which had experienced high economic growth rates in the 1950s and 1960s, was still catching up with countries where modernization had begun earlier (Ferrera and Gualmini, Volume II). It still had the lowest employment rate (Table A.4), and also the highest rate of registered unemployment of all countries in our study. Whereas in the normal postwar development of European economies the rapid decline of agricultural employment was overcompensated by the even more rapid increase of industrial employment (Esping-Andersen 1999: 24–27), this transformation was delayed in Italy. The country thus entered the 1970s with a relatively large agricultural sector which, however, was shrinking rapidly under the modernization pressures of the European Community's common agricultural policy.[1] The consequences were particularly hard on the predominantly rural *Mezzogiorno*, where government-induced industrialization never succeeded in creating sufficient numbers of jobs, whereas the modern and highly competitive manufacturing industries in northern Italy were not large enough to absorb the labor surplus from the south. For similar reasons, slow employment increases in the private and public services were not able to eliminate unemployment even in the 1960s. Together with Austria, which was also late in the transformation from an agricultural to an industrial and service economy, Italy thus entered the 1970s as the least wealthy country in our sample (Table A.1).

In terms of wealth, the *United Kingdom* was not much better off than Italy and Austria, but for very different reasons (Rhodes, Volume II)— which is also suggested by the fact that British employment rates in the early 1970s were among the highest in our group of countries. The British problem was not delayed industrialization but early decline. Throughout the 1950s and 1960s, the United Kingdom had been trying to maintain the British pound as an international reserve currency next to the US Dollar, and it also sought to maintain stable—and preferential—trade relationships with the 'Sterling block' of Commonwealth countries that had tied their exchange rates to the pound. At the same time, British industrial relations had become more decentralized and more conflictual during the 1950s and 1960s. Moreover, the British welfare state was not designed to deal with substantial unemployment. It had been reorganized according to the Beveridge model immediately after World War II, with flat rate

---

[1] Austria had an even larger share of agricultural employment that was falling even more rapidly than was true in Italy. But in Austria, both industry and services were already more developed and could take up more of the workforce that was displaced on the farms.

benefits that were far from income-maintaining except for the lowest wage brackets. But unlike the Scandinavian countries, that had started from similar origins, Britain had never raised replacement rates to a level that would maintain incomes in case of unemployment. Governments were thus under strong normative and political pressure to avoid unemployment in order to protect workers from poverty.

Taken together, these special circumstances created unfavorable conditions for economic development. First, preferential access to Commonwealth markets had limited the pressures to increase the efficiency of British industry. Second, the decentralization of wage bargaining within a fragmented union structure created strong wage pressures in the upswing phase of the business cycles. However, since wage-push inflation had negative effects on the balance of payments and on international confidence in the pound, governments were, third, forced to shift early to restrictive monetary and fiscal measures. But as rising unemployment was considered socially and politically unacceptable, governments also could not afford to pursue a consistent policy of monetary stability, but had to reflate the economy as soon as the downswing resulted in job losses. The stop-go pattern of short-lived macroeconomic interventions, finally, discouraged productive investments (Table A.30) which, in turn, contributed to the slower rise of industrial productivity in Britain compared to other industrial countries.

Australia and *New Zealand* were also exceptional, but again for different reasons. In most of the countries in our sample, it was the industrial sector that was exposed to competition in the international economy, and hence very efficient, whereas agriculture was sheltered against the world market either by national or by European barriers to trade and subsidies. By contrast, Australia, and even more so New Zealand, had traditionally relied on their highly competitive agricultural and raw materials exports[2] to Europe and in particular to Britain in order to pay for industrial imports, mainly from Britain. In the postwar period, however, the worldwide demand for agricultural products did grow more slowly than demand for industrial products, and difficulties increased when access to the European market was restricted by the protectionism of the Common Agricultural Policy. In response to these changes, Australia and New

---

[2] Two other countries found themselves in seemingly similar situations. In the early postwar decades, Denmark had depended on agricultural exports while small and middle-sized industrial firms had mainly served the protected domestic market. From the 1960s onward, however, Danish industrial policy helped small firms to upgrade skills and technologies so as to increase their international competitiveness. In the Swedish economy, iron ore and timber played a similar role in the export portfolio, but they were complemented by highly competitive industrial exports throughout the postwar period.

Zealand chose to reduce their own dependence on industrial imports by fostering import-substituting industrial production through a combination of subsidies, tariffs, and quantitative import restrictions.

The choice was largely motivated by the fact that Australia and New Zealand had also developed Beveridge-type welfare states in the postwar period which, as in Britain, provided flat-rate unemployment and social security benefits which, certainly for skilled and higher-paid workers, were politically acceptable only if the state was committed to maintaining full employment. In that sense, it is indeed meaningful to consider the support of a sheltered industrial sector as an important 'informal' part of these Beveridge-type welfare states (Schwartz, Volume II). But it is also clear that, given the small scale of the Australian and even more so of the New Zealand economy, and the lack of competition, the efficiency of these sheltered industries was quite low, and that they would be extremely vulnerable if they became exposed to international competition.

As a consequence, some of the countries included in our project did in fact enter the 1970s with different sets of economic structures and vulnerabilities than was true in the general case of highly industrialized and internationally competitive welfare states. These differences must be kept in mind when we now turn to the first set of new international challenges in the early 1970s. Moreover, as is pointed out in the Introduction, they also differed greatly in the policy legacies of their welfare states (Esping-Andersen 1990) and in the institutional structures of their industrial relations systems (Crouch 1993; Golden, Wallerstein, and Lange 1999), and their political systems (Lijphart 1984). But since these differences will be the main focus of the subsequent discussion, there is no reason for preliminary descriptions here.

2.2.2 The 1970s: Floating Currencies and Stagflation

The economic environment changed in the early 1970s with the coincident breakdown of the Bretton-Woods system of fixed exchange rates and the first oil-price crisis. They confronted macroeconomic policymakers in advanced industrial countries with the novel challenge of having to cope with 'stagflation'—the simultaneous increase of cost-push inflation and demand-deficient unemployment under conditions of floating exchange rates—challenges for which none of the experiences of the postwar decades provided any guidance.

The first important change was the erosion and ultimately the destruction of the Bretton-Woods regime of fixed but adjustable exchange rates in the early 1970s, and the official shift to *floating currencies* on 9 March 1973. Under the old regime, most countries had been reluctant to devalue, and even more so to revalue, their currencies in response to changing rates of inflation, productivity, and other factors affecting international trade. Hence floating exchange rates caused considerable adjustments in the years after 1972 (Table A.32). The effect was reinforced by the growth of *Euro-dollar* markets that had been under way for some time, but increased in importance in the early 1970s. Because of restrictive American banking rules and the reluctance of the Soviet Union to have its dollar holdings controlled by US authorities, the City of London had come to attract dollar deposits, and so did more exotic banking places which were not under the control of any of the major national banks and in which the conditions for dollar lending and borrowing were highly flexible. During the declining years of the Bretton-Woods regime, the volume of currency trading in these offshore markets had increased sharply. Hence, when finance ministers finally decided to let their currencies float, the expectation that exchange rates would correspond closely to the 'real' value of currencies, as defined by trade flows and inflation rates, was disappointed by the increasing importance of speculative currency transactions. From then on, domestic policy choices could have immediate repercussions on the exchange rates of national currencies, and hence on the competitiveness of exports and the level of inflation.

However, countries could hardly explore the implications of this new international environment before they were confronted with even more difficult challenges to their macroeconomic policy routines in the Fall of 1973, when Arab oil exporting countries reacted to Israel's victory in the Yom Kippur War by cutting oil production within the OPEC cartel— which led to a fourfold increase of crude oil prices in the winter of 1973–74. For oil-dependent industrial countries, the first effect was a massive cost push which greatly accelerated the rise of inflation. Even more ominous, however, was a second consequence. Since industrial economies could not continue to function without oil as an essential fuel and raw material, the price increases resulted in a massive diversion of purchasing power, reflected in an increase of the current-account surplus of OPEC countries from $8 billion in 1973 to $60 billion in 1974 (OECD 1980: 125). Since the OPEC countries could not immediately 'recycle' their new wealth into additional industrial imports,[3] their surpluses corresponded to an equivalent fall of aggregate demand in the oil-importing countries. If nothing was done, the result would be a steep rise of demand-deficient

---

[3] Subsequently, OPEC surpluses were shifted into the offshore dollar markets where they swelled the volume of assets available for speculative transactions as well as for loans. As a consequence, industrial and developing countries were also confronted with the tempting option of using international credit at very low real interest rates (Table A.7) to compensate for the fall in aggregate domestic demand.

unemployment, especially in countries that had just set out on a course of fiscal and monetary retrenchment to fight inflation. For governments committed to practicing Keynesian demand management by switching between fiscal and monetary reflation or deflation, these were entirely new conditions, which confronted them with a veritable dilemma. If they chose to fight unemployment through demand reflation, they would generate escalating rates of inflation; and if they chose to fight inflation through restrictive fiscal and monetary policies, the result would be mass unemployment.

Theoretically, it is true, the dilemma could have been avoided if, in addition to fiscal and monetary policy, wages could also be employed as a tool of macroeconomic policy in a form of 'Keynesian concertation' where the government and the central bank would prevent job losses through demand reflation while the unions would reduce inflationary cost pressures through wage restraint (Scharpf 1991, chs 2 and 6). But, as we will see below, this effective policy response could be achieved only under unusual and very demanding institutional conditions.

2.2.3 *The Early 1980s: Stagflation and the Rise of Capital Interests*

The major challenges of the early 1980s resembled those of the preceding decade because their initial stimulus was another oil-price crisis in 1979–80, which, again, introduced strong impulses of cost-push inflation and demand-gap unemployment. However, the second crisis was not merely a re-run of the first. When it began, most countries were still struggling with much higher levels of inflation and unemployment than had existed in the early 1970s, and also with much higher levels of indebtedness. Since Keynesian policies seemed unable to deal with the challenges of stagflation, monetarist interpretations of the situation gained ground in economics and in the media and finally among political decision makers as well (Hall 1993).

What mattered more than the election of Margaret Thatcher, however, was the fact that the US Federal Reserve, which had responded to the first oil crisis with Keynesian reflation, finally followed the German Bundesbank's earlier switch to monetarism. Its strictly non-accommodating policy combined with the escalating budget deficits of the early Reagan years to produce an unprecedented rise of real long-term interest rates: from minus 0.2 percent in 1979 to more than 8.1 percent in 1984. Since US interest rates also applied in the offshore dollar markets in which most governments had become indebted, and since in any case the effectiveness of national exchange controls was eroding even in countries that had not liberalized their capital markets, the effect was immediately felt throughout

the OECD world. Regardless of the theoretical beliefs and policy preferences of their governments, real interest rates were rising steeply in all
countries—except for safe haven Switzerland—with the consequences that
the burden of serving existing and new debts became very high, and that
fiscal reflation could no longer be considered an effective response to the
steeply rising unemployment rates caused by the second oil crisis. Instead,
fiscal consolidation became a high-priority goal in most countries included
in our project.

At the same time, the minimal expected rate of return that was required
to justify of real investments did increase greatly. As long as the real interest rate associated with financial investments had been zero or negative, all
projects that promised positive profits had been attractive. But when
returns that capital owners could expect from risk-free government bonds
rose to high positive levels, only projects with expected profits significantly
above that level would still have a chance to be financed. In contrast to the
1970s, it was thus no longer sufficient that governments maintained the
level of aggregate demand. Even where that was still possible, business
employment would fall unless there was also a significant increase of business profits—which could be achieved only through a redistribution from
labor to capital incomes.

In short, the challenges of the early 1980s were more severe than those of
the mid-1970s, and policy options had narrowed because monetary reflation was no longer feasible, because the cost of public sector deficits had
greatly increased, and because a rise of business profits had now become a
necessary precondition for maintaining or regaining private sector employment. Nevertheless, countries still had a choice between meeting these constraints in the context of either devaluation or hard currency strategies.

To structure the following discussion, I will group countries by their
expansionary or restrictive monetary and currency regimes. This is justified by the fact that, as a consequence of this basic choice, the external
changes creating the stagflation threat would be transformed into very different types of domestic challenges. Given flexible exchange rates, expansion would entail devaluation, improved international competitiveness,
rising or stable employment, and very high rates of inflation, whereas a
tight-money position would leave national policy actors to cope with the
challenge of mass unemployment.

2.3 Challenges in the 1970s: Stagflation

The economically optimal response to the stagflation challenges of the
1970s was a form of 'Keynesian concertation' that required the coordi-

nated deployment of fiscal and monetary reflation on the one hand, and wage moderation on the other. Both of these requirements depended on institutional preconditions, but the first was generally more easily met than the second.

2.3.1 Fiscal and Monetary Reflation or Deflation?

For most governments, fiscal reflation was a quasi-automatic response as soon as the demand-reducing effects of the oil-price crisis were perceived. Keynesianism was still the dominant economic paradigm; and, starting from low levels of indebtedness in the early 1970s, and even from budget surpluses in Austria, Australia, Denmark, France, and Sweden, and with low or even negative real interest rates, an increase in deficit spending did not seem to imply excessive budgetary risks. Moreover, as voters had come to take near-full employment practically for granted, preventing the rise of unemployment appeared politically imperative for bourgeois and labor governments alike (Scharpf 1987). By 1975, therefore, the budgets of prac-tically all countries included in our project had gone into deficit (Table A.22).

The one exception was *Switzerland*, which had never converted to Keynesian counter-cyclical demand management (M. G. Schmidt 1985), and where in any case the relative size of the central-government budget was not large enough to generate fiscal impulses at acceptable cost.[4] Moreover, even if the independent and stability minded Swiss National Bank would have considered monetary reflation, it could not have achieved it in the turbulent period of the early 1970s. Being considered a safe haven for capital owners throughout the world, Switzerland's problem was to fend off capital inflows that drove up the exchange rate at a speed that greatly exceeded the revaluation of the German mark. Thus, the country was operating under extreme hard currency conditions even though Swiss nominal interest rates were extremely low by international standards, and real long-term interest rates turned negative in some years.

In any case, however, fiscal reflation alone could not stabilize employ-ment unless it was accompanied by an accommodating monetary policy— which, in the face of escalating inflation, would run counter to the habitual preferences of central bankers and their banking constituencies. In most countries, however, central banks were not institutionally independent, and in a conflict their policies could be determined by the government. In

---

[4] Assuming that countercyclical demand management must primarily rely on the national budget, a fiscal stimulus of 1% of GDP would have required a budget deficit of 9.9% in Switzerland, but only of 2.8% in Sweden and of 3.0% in the United Kingdom (Scharpf 1991: 213–14).

the United States, where that was not the case, the Federal Reserve itself was still committed to the Keynesian paradigm, so that the all-important dollar capital markets were also operating under an accommodating monetary regime in the mid-1970s (Johnson 1998). As a consequence, real long-term interest rates had become negative—sometimes strongly—after 1974 in the majority of countries (Table A.29). Here, however, the exception was not limited to Switzerland, but included Germany and a number of neighboring countries which had linked their currencies to the German mark.

In Germany, the government had persuaded its European trading partners to respond to the breakdown of Bretton-Woods in the spring of 1973 by the European Exchange Rate Agreement—the 'Snake'—which implied that their currencies should float jointly against the US dollar. The purpose was to avoid fluctuations between the participating currencies and to dampen upward pressures on the mark that would hurt German exports (Moravcsik 1998, ch. 4). At the same time the Bundesbank, freed from the obligation to support the dollar exchange rate, had adopted a deflationary stabilization program which was also supported by the government's fiscal policy, and generally hailed as the centerpiece of a European 'stabilization pact'. However, when the oil-price crisis struck in the fall of 1973, the German government, like most others, switched to fiscal reflation in an attempt to prevent job losses, whereas the Bundesbank responded to the renewed rise of inflation rates by continuing and even tightening its restrictive course. Since, under flexible exchange rates, fiscal impulses will be neutralized by a monetary constraint, the overall effect was deflationary. Real long-term interest rates, which were strongly negative in the reflation countries, rose to 3.1 percent in 1974 and 4 percent in 1976 (Table A.29); economic growth became negative in 1975; the employment rate declined from 68.5 percent in 1973 to 65.2 percent in 1977 (Table A.5), but the rate of inflation also came down rapidly from a peak of 7.0 percent in 1974 to 2.7 percent in 1978 (Table A.3).

This early switch to a monetarist strategy was facilitated by the statutory independence of the Bundesbank and by the broad public support of its authority (Cukierman 1992; Johnson 1998). In effect, by declaring that henceforth the expansion of the money supply would be limited by the inflation-free growth potential of the economy, the bank imposed an exact reversal of the assignment of functions presumed by Keynesian concertation. Now, monetary policy would determine the level of inflation through its control of the nominal money supply, and it was for the government and the unions to defend employment by adjusting their own claims on the nominal GDP accordingly. If the limit was respected, the growth potential could be fully realized; if it was exceeded by nominal wage increases and public sector borrowing, interest rates would rise and private sector jobs would be lost. Once that strategy had been promulgated, the bank saw no reason to treat the oil-price push as a special case: it would increase unemployment unless unions reduced their wage claims to such a degree that lower production costs and prices would restore real aggregate demand to pre-crisis levels (Scharpf 1991: ch. 7).

The expected result was a steep revaluation of the German mark against the dollar—by 37 percent between 1972 and 1978—which also pulled up the exchange rates of other 'Snake' countries (Table A.32). However, when the negative employment effects of revaluation compounded by the oil crisis made themselves felt, Italy, the United Kingdom, and France quit the Snake forthwith, and Sweden did so a bit later. But Austria—which was not formally a member of the Snake—the Netherlands, Belgium, and Denmark decided to stick to their exchange-rate commitments. This had two important consequences: first, and regardless of whether the national bank was institutionally independent or not, monetary policy now had to be employed to defend the exchange rate with the German mark and thus had to follow the deflationary course of the Bundesbank; and, second, to the extent that it succeeded, the national currency would also rise in relation to economies outside this Deutschmark-zone. In other words, the countries that had linked their currencies to the German mark were thereby forced to practice varieties of 'imported monetarism'.

In the 1970s, we therefore can distinguish two groups of countries, characterized by soft-currency and hard currency strategies respectively. In spite of this basic difference in macroeconomic positions, however, the economic success or failure in both groups of countries depended on the institutional capacity for wage moderation. But the function that wage moderation would have to perform was quite different: In soft-currency countries, it would have been needed to contain the rise of inflation, whereas in hard currency countries wage restraint could have limited the job losses that otherwise were the result of monetary deflation.

2.3.2 Soft-Currency Countries

Given the availability of dollar credits at low or negative interest rates in the international markets, demand reflation was generally successful in employment terms. Thus, the United Kingdom, Italy, New Zealand, and Sweden were actually able to increase employment rates during the period of the first oil crisis, while France, Australia, and Belgium managed to scrape through with relatively small job losses (Table A.5). In Sweden, it is true, very big increases in employment can be explained mainly by the expansion of publicly financed social services, but the other countries in this group did indeed owe their superior employment performance to the fact that, in the face of the stagflation crisis, they initially allowed inflation to run its course and the exchange rate to fall accordingly (Tables A.3, A.32).

If nothing else were done, however, the successful fight against unemployment would come at a high price. Large public deficits combined with a falling exchange rate would greatly add to the inflationary pressures caused by the rise of oil prices. And if unions then tried to increase real incomes through settlements that anticipated the further rise of inflation, the resulting wage-price spiral would continue even though oil prices had stabilized by 1975. But in the absence of unemployment, voters were then likely to consider runaway price increases the most salient policy failure. Hence governments that were not yet willing to control inflation by letting unemployment rise depended for their political survival on wage moderation to combat inflation (Scharpf 1987). For unions, however, whose *raison d'être* is to achieve better outcomes for their members than these could achieve for themselves in the market, that was a tall order.

As long as the government continued to assure full employment, market-determined wages would continue to rise at least in step with anticipated inflation. What Keynesian concertation called for, then, was an institutional capacity to keep wage increases *below* the level of market outcomes. More precisely, what was required were wage settlements resulting in a sustained decline of real unit labor costs (Table A.17) which, in countries with high rates of inflation, would also imply falling real wages (Table A.16). Within a short-term perspective, that surely made no sense for rational, self-interested workers and unions. Worse yet, they found themselves in a prisoner's dilemma where unions practicing unilateral wage moderation would see the real wages of their members decline even more rapidly than they had bargained for if other unions continued with aggressive wage strategies.

Yet in a longer-term perspective, the defense of real incomes could degenerate into a vicious wage-price spiral in which even Keynesian governments might be forced to switch to deflation or, more likely, would be replaced by a 'monetarist' government with preferences that ranked price stability above the defense of full employment. Anticipating these dismal consequences, the labor movement as a whole surely ought to have had second thoughts about the wisdom of free-riding on governments committed to Keynesian full-employment policies. But the extent to which this collective and longer-term self-interest was, or could have been, reflected in the actual decisions of wage-setting actors depended greatly on institutional structures of industrial-relations systems that would favor an inclusive and longer-term perspective.

In the face of upward market pressures under conditions of full employment, this capacity would be limited, even under favorable institutional conditions. Nevertheless, it would differ, and the differences should be related to the institutional distinctions introduced in the Introduction. The capacity for wage settlements below the market level should be weak in 'fragmented' collective-bargaining systems where multiple unions may be powerful within their own segments of the labor market, but have no institutional mechanisms for coordinating their bargaining strategies. In collective bargaining systems 'coordinated' through centralized negotiations or through horizontal self-coordination, this capacity may exist within the union organization (Calmfors and Driffil 1988),[5] and in 'statist' systems it may be supplied by *ad hoc* state intervention or by a more permanent role that state actors play in wage-setting decisions.

2.3.2.1 Wage Setting by Coordinated Collective Bargaining In our project, *Sweden* was the only country with a clear soft-currency policy that also had an institutional capability for coordinated wage setting. The active role of the peak organizations of capital and labor in the preparation of government economic and social policy initiatives (Korpi 1983; Immergut 1992) and the practice of centralized wage negotiations between the peak employers' association (SAF) and the dominant blue-collar union federation (LO) had in the 1950s and 1960s made possible an extremely successful form of consensual macroeconomic management. In spite of the growing resentment of white-collar and public sector unions of LO's hegemonic role, that capacity was still available in the 1970s and even in the 1980s (Scharpf 1991, ch. 6).

Since Sweden initially benefited from the raw materials boom of the early 1970s, the negative employment effects of the oil-price crisis were relatively late in coming, whereas inflation reached almost 10 percent already in 1974. Thus the government's first response was to tighten its fiscal policy, raising the public sector surplus to 4.5 percent in 1976 (Table A.22). But when the fall of international demand finally hit Sweden, the defense of full employment was automatic even though the social democrats had been replaced by a bourgeois coalition in 1976. In fact, the new government nationalized the hard-hit shipbuilding and steel firms in order to avoid layoffs, and subsequently to organize the restructuring of these industries. Moreover, Sweden left the European currency Snake when the rise of the German mark became a problem, and it tried to improve

---

[5] While it generally makes sense to focus on the union side exclusively in analyzing wage-setting systems, for the wage restraint required in soft-currency countries in the 1970s, the capacity of employers' associations to police wage concessions by individual firms was also important.

competitiveness through three devaluations in 1977–78. As a consequence, industrial employment declined very little, while overall employment continued to rise because of the rapid expansion of tax-financed social services. The rate of inflation rose to 11.4 percent in 1977.

All the while, wages had risen faster than the rate of inflation, and unit labor costs in national currency almost doubled between 1973 and 1978 (Table A.18). Clearly, unions were not doing their share in the Keynesian-concertation scenario. The reason, however, was a lack of incentives, rather than a lack of institutional capacity. When the crisis began to reach Sweden, the bourgeois coalition government, coming into office after more than forty years of social-democratic rule, was committed to defend full employment at all costs. Since there was no danger of a 'monetarist' switch, Swedish unions saw no reason to accept real-wage sacrifices in order to ease the inflation-unemployment dilemma of an unloved government. However, when manufacturing employment actually began to decline in 1977–78, LO was willing to support the devaluation strategy of the government, and the rise of unit labor cost in national currency came to a halt in 1978 (Table A.18); relative to the OECD average, unit labor costs even declined by 16 percent between 1976 and 1980 (Table A.19). In other words, the institutional capability for wage restraint was still intact, but unions had no incentive to make use of it as long as their members were not directly affected by a threat of unemployment.

2.3.2.2 Statist Wage Setting Systems   In theory, countries with a potentially strong involvement of the state in the wage-setting process might also have had the capacity to practice Keynesian concertation. Among the soft-currency countries of the 1970s, this group included France, Italy, Australia, and New Zealand. As it turned out, however, none of them succeeded in controlling the rise inflation through a dampening of wage increases. The reasons for failure are interesting.

In *France*, unions were highly politicized and divided along party-political lines. In terms of membership and organizational capacity, they were comparatively weak, but their capacity to mobilize workers for strikes and protest actions in the name of political as well as economic goals had remained very strong. Given the organizational weakness of unions, and of employers' associations as well, the government's role in the wage-setting process was a very large one: it participated in, or even organized, wage-bargaining rounds, and if agreement was not forthcoming, it could determine the outcome unilaterally. In doing so, its only effective constraint, apart from the economic conditions of the industry, was the capacity and willingness of unions to organize strikes against the imposed settlement. Given the very unfavorable strike record of French industry, and the near-revolutionary mass mobilization during *les évènements de mai* in 1968, however, Gaullist governments were extremely wary of provoking union protests. Hence, though French wages after 1974 were mainly determined by the government, a policy of effective wage restraint to support the strategy of fiscal and monetary reflation was not seriously attempted. Instead, the Barre Government decided to abandon Keynesian full-employment policies and switched to a more restrictive fiscal and monetary position after 1976—which brought down inflation from 13.7 percent in 1974 to 9.1 percent in 1978, but also allowed the unemployment rate to rise from 2.8 percent in 1974 to 5.2 percent in 1978. At the same time, the government used nationalized firms as an employment buffer and tried to prevail on private sector firms to avoid mass layoffs (V. A. Schmidt 1996b). Moreover France, like other Continental countries, used early retirement to limit the rise of registered unemployment—which reduced the participation rate of men over the age of 55 from 75.4 percent in 1970 to 66.4 percent in 1978 (Table A.13).

In *Italy*, the state was also organizing wage bargaining rounds and also had the constitutional powers to impose wage settlements. Political divisions among unions also resembled the French pattern, but their organizational strength and their potential for strategic action were much greater. However, after the radicalization of the rank and file in the *autunno caldo* of 1968, industrial relations in the 1970s were characterized by high levels of militancy. As in Sweden, the political risks associated with aggressive wage policies were minimal. There was no danger that a Keynesian government might be replaced by a monetarist opposition, and the series of short-lived coalition governments were politically too weak to switch from loose-money and deficit-spending patterns to fiscal and monetary deflation, or to impose restrictive wage settlements. Instead, the dramatic rise of unit labor costs in national currency was even overcompensated by the rapid devaluation of the Lira, which lost half its value between 1970 and 1980. As a consequence, economic growth was strong in all years except 1975, total employment rates remained fairly stable throughout the 1970s, but the rate of inflation never came down to single digits between 1973 and 1984 (Table A.3).

Institutional conditions in *Australia* and *New Zealand* differed fundamentally from these European variants of statist industrial relations (Schwartz, Volume II). In both countries, wage setting had traditionally been performed by state arbitration courts whose 'awards' were legally binding on unions and employers. In Australia, the minimum wage set by the federal court was explicitly defined by reference to a decent standard of living for a family of five, whereas specific awards for branches and skill groups were to ensure equal wages for all workers doing the same kind of work. In New Zealand, general criteria were less explicitly formulated, but the arbitration awards also assured high minimum wages and considerable wage equality. Since all recognized unions and employers' associations had standing in arbitration proceedings while awards were binding on non-members within their domain as well, the legal system created strong incentives to form specialized associations rather than incentives for organizational concentration and centralization. The result was an extremely fragmented and decentralized union organization—which did not much matter as long as wages were effectively determined by the arbitration awards.

While these courts enjoyed judicial independence from the government, their mandate included references to the health of the economy, and the government had standing in the proceedings and did argue its view of macroeconomic requirements in important cases. But when the courts did in fact attempt to dampen wage increases under conditions of labor scarcity in the late 1960s, they were no longer able to enforce their awards against employers succumbing to market pressures and local strikes. In the raw-materials boom of the early 1970s, therefore industrial relations in *New Zealand* degenerated into a highly fragmented and decentralized pattern of British-style 'free collective bargaining'. Since both the Labour and the National—that is, conservative—parties were fully committed to maintaining full employment through demand reflation, this did not change with the onset of the oil-price crisis. In the absence of organizations that would be competent to strike binding agreements at the national or sectoral levels, moreover, attempts by consecutive governments to promote a negotiated incomes policy never had a chance. Unit labor costs in national currency doubled between 1973 and 1979, but, as in Sweden and Italy, their rise was overcompensated by devaluation (Table A.19). As a consequence, unemployment in New Zealand remained below 1 percent until 1977, and never rose above 2 percent until the end of the decade; but inflation reached 16.9 percent in 1976 and did not decline much thereafter.

In *Australia*, by contrast, the political risks were more real. The Labor government that had won elections in 1972 on a platform of welfare-state expansion and full employment was defeated in 1975 and its conservative successors were in fact willing to use more restrictive monetary policies to fight inflation, which had risen to 15 percent by 1974 but came down to 7.9 percent in 1978. At the same time, the government also began to reduce the level of trade protection. In the process, it accepted the rise of unemployment from 2.3 percent in 1974 to 6.1 percent in 1978. Since the award system continued to protect real incomes, the rise of unemployment did not have much effect on wages: as in New Zealand, unit labor costs in national currency doubled between 1973 and 1979 (Table A.18), and again the rise was overcompensated by a falling exchange rate (Table A.19). Institutionally, however, developments in Australia differed in two respects from New Zealand. First, under the pressure of rising unemployment and their declining economic bargaining power, unions had to resort to the arbitration courts to defend real wage levels. Second, since only the Australian Confederation of Trade Unions (ACTU) had standing before the federal court to initiate increases of the minimum wage, which greatly gained in importance as local bargaining power was reduced by unemployment, the 1970s saw successful efforts at organization building, concentration, and centralization. In the process, the ACTU extended its domain beyond its traditional membership of industrial unions to include also white-collar and public sector unions, thus creating the institutional preconditions for corporatist peak-level negotiations over the 'Accords' of the 1980s (Schwartz, Volume II).

2.3.2.3 Concertation in a Fragmented Industrial Relations System   In the *United Kingdom*, Conservative and Labour Governments had at various times in the postwar decades tried to contain the inflationary wage pressures of a fragmented industrial relations system through statutory wage freezes, but never with lasting success. In the early 1970s, Edward Heath had simultaneously tried to strengthen the role of the central union federation, the Trades Union Congress (TUC), through his industrial-relations legislation and to negotiate an agreed incomes policy. Under pressure from its member unions, however, the TUC leadership rejected both initiatives. Within the traditional Keynesian framework, Heath then tried to fight inflation through fiscal and monetary restraint but switched back to reflation plus wage-freeze legislation at the onset of the oil-price crisis in the winter of 1973–74. At the same time, Harold Wilson's opposition Labour party had succeeded in negotiating a 'social compact' with the TUC, in which it had foresworn the use of statutory wage controls and promised repeal of Heath's industrial-relations act plus significant improvements in social benefits in exchange for the unions' political support in the upcoming elections and promises of voluntary wage restraint.

After the narrow Labour victory in February 1974, the government had kept its promises, whereas the TUC leadership was unable to deliver on its side of the compact under the unchanged conditions of British industrial-relations institutions. Given the existence of more than 100 unions within the TUC—some of them 'general', some organized by industry, others by skills, and many of them quite small—and given the increasing decentralization of wage bargaining that had occurred in the preceding decade, there was no effective way of preventing the thousands of individual bargaining units from exploiting the ability to pay of firms that were facing high levels of demand thanks to the government's policy of fiscal and monetary expansion. As a result, the rate of inflation shot up to 24 percent in 1975, there was another run on the pound and desperate negotiations for international credit, and the government was losing one by-election after another while still keeping its promise to avoid statutory wage freezes. In this predicament, the TUC leadership decided to resort to a strategy that ran counter to all institutional incentives of its member units. It offered the government a new 'social contract' that would limit all wage increases to a flat sum of seven pounds a week—which gave the lowest-paid workers a small gain in real terms, while all others had to accept massive real-wage losses (Table A.16).

The dramatic nature of the problem and of the proposed solution allowed TUC leaders to gain the support of member unions and to launch, together with the government, a highly moralistic and emotional campaign, with appeals to the 'spirit of Dunkirk', asking union members and shop stewards 'to give a year to Britain'. In its first year, the campaign was a total success (Table A.17), mainly because moral pressures combined with the simplicity and high visibility of the flat-rate rule had made evasion difficult. As inflation began to come down in 1976, the TUC majority agreed to extend the social contract for another year, but now skilled workers and craft unions became increasingly resentful of the growing distortion of wage relativities, and firms began to circumvent the flat-rate rule through promotions and job reclassifications in order to attract or keep skilled workers. Thus, when the government proposed to extend the social contract for a third year on even tighter terms in order to finally break inflationary expectations, negotiations broke down; and when the government then tried to impose its rule in the public sector, an explosion of strikes brought the country to a standstill in the 'winter of discontent' of 1978–79—which then opened the way to Margaret Thatcher's landslide victory in May 1979 (Scharpf 1991, ch. 5).

The case shows that it is indeed possible to override even a very unfavorable institutional structure of incentives through discourses communicating convincing appeals to solidaristic values. But it also shows that such appeals depend on great moral pressure and effective monitoring, and that their effectiveness erodes rapidly if the fairness of requirements can be challenged and/or if universal compliance cannot be assured. It also shows that the simplicity and rigidity of a flat-wage rule, which may be an important precondition of its suitability for a short-term moral campaign, may be totally unsuited in the longer term for a wage-setting system in which 'comparability' has a high normative salience, and which must also be sufficiently flexible to respond to changes in productivity, profitability, and relative scarcity.

2.3.3 Hard Currency Countries

The group of countries which responded to the stagflation crisis of the 1970s with a non-accommodating monetary policy that resulted in a rise of the exchange rate included Switzerland, Germany and the members of the 'Deutschmark-zone'—Austria, Belgium, Denmark, and the Netherlands—that had tied their currencies to the mark. As expected, this policy was effective in moderating the rise of inflation, which by 1976 was only half a high—6.75 percent—on average among these six countries than it was among the six soft-currency countries—13.93 percent. But the fall in demand also caused an average fall of total employment rates between 1973 and 1977 in the order of 2.23 percentage points in the hard currency group, as compared with employment gains of 0.33 points in the soft-currency countries (Table A.5).[6] The one exception was Austria, where the total employment rate actually increased during the first oil-price crisis.

2.3.3.1 Austro-Keynesianism: Hard Currency, but Not Tight Money   The Austrian success in avoiding job losses while maintaining an effective hard currency position was owed to exceptional institutional capabilities. Austria's policymakers and public had shared the German aversion to inflation, and Austrian unions were among the strongest supporters of a hard currency policy which made it easier for them to practice wage moderation. As elsewhere, however, the initial response to the oil-price crisis was expansionary, and on the basis of Keynesian analyses produced by the one and only Austrian Institute of Economic Research, unions, employers, the government and the central bank misjudged the credibility or the effectiveness of the switch to a monetarist strategy announced by the German Bundesbank's in the Spring of 1973. As a consequence, wage increases negotiated in 1973 and 1974 were far too high in light of the fact that the Austrian exchange rate was rising along with the appreciation of the German mark.

Once the problem was correctly diagnosed, however, the institutional capacity of Austrian corporatism came into its own. Rather than punishing unions for their excessive wage settlements, which the Bundesbank did in Germany, the Austrian National Bank found ways to soften the domestic impact of its external hard currency position by keeping nominal interest rates below the German level—which was possible since capital-transfer controls were still effective at the time (Hemerijck, Unger, and Visser, Volume II). In addition, the government further reduced monetary

---

[6] In both groups, the average is improved by the fact that in Sweden and Denmark the rapid expansion of public-sector employed continued during the 1970s.

constraints by subsidizing the interest rates of investment loans, and it pre-
vailed on the large sector of nationalized industries to avoid layoffs. In
effect, therefore, Austria was part of an international hard currency regime
without paying the price of domestic tight-money policies. The unions, for
their part, responded by reducing their wage demands in the following
years. In the second half of the 1970s, therefore, Austrian inflation rates
were only bettered by hard currency Switzerland and Germany—both of
which suffered massive job losses—and the Austrian employment performance was about as good as that of the soft-currency countries, which had
much higher rates of inflation.

The institutional conditions that facilitated this remarkable concerted
action have often been described (Lehmbruch 1967; Marin 1982;
Katzenstein 1984; Scharpf 1991, ch. 4). They were developed in the early
postwar years to prevent the return of the class war of the early 1930s, and
to provide substitutes for state action that was crippled by a four-power
occupation regime, through institutionalized cooperation between the
'black' and 'red' *Lager*. Each of these two 'camps' could rely on an infrastructure of 'chambers' with compulsory membership, each of them
was closely associated with one the two major parties—the christian-
democratic ÖVP and the social-democratic SPÖ—and both of them
depended on the allocation of career opportunities in the state and in the
large nationalized industries by strict parity ('*Proporz*'). Other essential
elements were a highly concentrated and centralized union organization,
strong influence of peak-level coordination on sectoral wage negotiations,
an institution for the joint discussion of economic and social policy issues
between the 'social partners' and the government, and a central bank
jointly owned by the social partners and the government.[7] Under these
conditions, once a realistic cognitive map of the new situation was available, there was no question that all parties involved—the government, the
central bank, employers and unions—would do their part in a complex
hybrid strategy—the celebrated 'Austro-Keynesianism'—that worked well
for Austria in the 1970s.

2.3.3.2 Should Institutions Matter?   Apart from Austria, all hard currency
countries suffered major job losses in the 1970s. According to the
Bundesbank's version of monetarism, however, which also finds support
in a 'modern' version of Keynesian macroeconomic theory (Carlin and
Soskice 1990), these losses could be mitigated or perhaps avoided if constraints on nominal aggregate demand were compensated by falling unit
labor costs and prices, so that real aggregate demand could be maintained.

---

[7] Cukierman (1992) ascribes relatively high independence to the Austrian national bank,
which may reflect its policies but not its institutional position.

In other words, in a non-accommodating monetary environment, the assignment of macroeconomic policy functions is a mirror image of the one discussed above in the context of the Keynesian concertation strategy. Now monetary authorities assume exclusive responsibility for price stability, while employment is controlled by wage-setting institutions (Soskice and Iversen 1998; Iversen 1999).

Above, in the discussion of soft-currency countries, I argued that union wage restraint, which was a necessary precondition for the success of Keynesian concertation strategies, depended greatly on the institutions of wage setting: feasible in coordinated collective-bargaining systems, and theoretically possible in statist systems as well, but highly unlikely in fragmented wage-setting institutions. In that classification, one would describe the industrial relations systems in Switzerland, Germany, Denmark, and the Netherlands as variants of the 'coordinated' model, whereas Belgium was more similar to the French 'statist' system. Theoretically, however, institutional differences should not matter in a non-accommodating monetary environment, when wage restraint is required to control the rise of unemployment, rather than the rise of inflation.[8] Analytically, price stability is a collective good, and the fight against inflation appears as a prisoner's dilemma where, in the absence of coordination, individual bargaining units will 'free ride' on the efforts of others. By contrast, unemployment and the threat of further job losses are 'private evils' that each bargaining unit, regardless of its size, should wish to avoid. In other words, institutional differences should not matter, and we should expect to see the government-union game in all countries converging on a hard-money/wage-restraint equilibrium outcome (Scharpf 1987).

In reality, however, convergence was incomplete. If we look at the period from the monetarist switch in Germany (1973) to the end of the decade (1980), and if we consider only employment rates in the private sector,[9] losses in Germany amounted to 3.5 percentage points, the Netherlands lost 4.1 points, Switzerland 4.8, Belgium 5.1, and Denmark lost as much as 5.9 percentage points of the business-employment rate (Table A.7).

[8] Soskice and Iversen (2000) and Iversen (1999) argue that under a non-accommodating monetary regime sectoral bargaining is most likely to produce job-protecting wage restraint, whereas in centralized collective-bargaining institutions the influence of public-sector unions and low-wage groups might prevent economically rational outcomes. For the 1970s, we do not have enough institutional variance in our group of hard currency countries to assess the empirical plausibility of this proposition for highly centralized systems. Practically all countries considered here would be classified as having sectoral bargaining institutions; and they did vary greatly in their wage-setting performance.

[9] In the same period, business-sector employment losses were partly compensated by increases of government employment, which amounted to 0.3 percentage points in the Netherlands, 0.8 points in Germany, 1.0 in Belgium, 1.2 in Switzerland, and as much as 2.7 percentage points in Denmark (Table A.6).

Clearly, then, none of the industrial relations systems in these countries was fully able to perform the employment-stabilizing function assigned to wage-setting in the monetarist scenario. Still, the differences are significant, and it is also worth noting that in Switzerland and Germany, after a steep initial fall, business employment was stabilized by 1976–77 and increased slightly thereafter, whereas in the other three countries the decline continued to the end of the decade and beyond.

These differences are not explained by differences in the development of exchange rates. On the contrary, between 1973 and 1977, the effective trade-weighted exchange rate of the Swiss frank appreciated by 42.5 percent and the German mark rose by 39.4 percent. By contrast, the effective exchange rate of the Dutch guilder increased only by 15.4 percent, the Belgian franc by 10.7 percent, and with an increase of only 4.3 percent the Danish krone remained practically stable (Table A.32). Obviously, the commitment to a hard currency position was not equally strict in all countries—presumably because central banks confronted with higher wage pressures would find it more difficult to maintain the target exchange rate. This much is suggested by the fact that, with regard to the increase of unit labor costs in national currencies during the same period, the rank order of countries is exactly reversed: the highest in Denmark at 48.5 percent, followed by Belgium at 47.1 percent, the Netherlands at 34.5 percent, Germany at 23.6 percent, and the lowest in Switzerland at only 17.2 percent (Table A.18). In short, while exposed-sector employment in Switzerland and Germany suffered most from rising exchange rates, business employment in Denmark and Belgium, and to a somewhat lesser degree in the Netherlands, was even more negatively affected by increases of unit labor costs—whose impact was not limited to the exposed sector but would destroy jobs in the sheltered branches as well.

So what needs to be explained are differences in the wage-setting performance of these hard currency countries. But, as will be seen, these differences are not primarily institutional. What seems to have mattered more are cognitive differences in the appreciation of the economic and employment implications of a hard currency environment. Here, conditions in Switzerland and Germany seem to have been more favorable than in countries practicing versions of 'imported monetarism'.

2.3.3.3 Switzerland and Germany The steep rise of the Swiss exchange rate severely hurt exports and domestic activity. In fact, Switzerland suffered the deepest recession of all OECD countries, with a growth rate of minus 6.7 percent in 1975 (Table A.2) and a fall of the employment rate from 77.4 percent in 1973 to 73.0 percent in 1976 (Table A.5). Despite these heavy job losses, however, the appearance of open unemployment (Table A.4) was prevented by the cumulative effect of repatriating foreign workers (Table A.15) and of persuading married women to reduce their participation in the labor force (M. G. Schmidt 1985; Bonoli and Mach, Volume II). At the same time, however, the institutional conditions for a downward adjustment of wage claims in the face of threatening job losses were best in Switzerland. Here, the organizational strength of the labor movement was moderate to low; industrial relations had been 'cooperative' since the late 1930s; wage levels were high in international comparison; and wage negotiations were decentralized to industrial sectors or individual firms and highly sensitive to sectoral and regional differences in profitability. In fact, unit labor costs in national currency were actually *reduced* by 10 percent between 1975 and 1977 (Table A.18). As a consequence, the loss of jobs was stopped early, and employment rates increased again after 1977.

In Germany, the employment turnaround came a year later. It was also achieved through wage moderation. Unit labor costs in manufacturing did not rise in 1976 and increased by less than the rate of inflation in the following years. But this response came only after a head-on collision between monetary policy and wage policy had pushed up open unemployment from 1.0 percent to 4 percent (Table A.4).[10] The conflict arose even though German unions, while not as centralized as their Austrian and Swedish counterparts, were practicing a form of coordination through wage leadership that also had a considerable institutional capacity for macroeconomic rationality (Thelen 1991). Organized by large industrial sectors, some of these unions had highly competent central staffs, and while the peak union federation (DGB) was not directly involved in collective bargaining, it did provide a forum for strategic discussions among all union leaders, and its research institute (WSI) did provide economic analyses in preparation for the annual bargaining rounds. Moreover, as a consequence of their participation in the supervisory boards of stock companies and the more general participation rights of workers under German co-determination rules, unions were on the whole well informed about the economic well-being of firms within the branches for which they negotiated wage settlements.

But the conflict of 1974–75 was not between sectoral unions and their employers: it was between monetary policy and wage policy and it was, at bottom, cognitive. Unlike in Austria, where the social partners owned the

[10] Here, the rise of unemployment corresponded more closely with the magnitude job losses. Increasing female participation in the labor force was counterbalanced by the increasing resort to early retirement and disability pensions, reducing the participation rates of men over the age of 55 (Tables A.12, A.13). To a lesser extent than in Switzerland, the number of foreign workers was also reduced (Table A.15).

central bank and staffed its top positions, German unions and the Bundesbank traditionally observed each other from a distance, anticipating or responding to each other's moves in the mode of 'mutual adjustment' (Scharpf 1997b, ch. 5).[11] Thus, when the Bundesbank announced and explained its monetarist strategy in 1973, union economists were puzzled, rather than persuaded. From their Keynesian perspective, what mattered for employment was fiscal policy rather than monetary policy;[12] and since the government budget was expansionary, they expected rising inflation rather than rising unemployment for 1975. In hindsight, therefore, wage increases in 1974–75 were too high, just as they were in Austria. In contrast to Austria, however, there was no common effort to contain the damage caused by this 'mistake'. Seeing the credibility of its new strategy at stake, the Bundesbank used the occasion to demonstrate the real effectiveness of sharply restrictive monetary measures by single handedly reversing the rise of inflation—from 7 percent in 1974 to 6 percent in 1975—in the face of fiscal expansion and excessive wage increases. That unemployment would shoot up as a consequence was regrettable, but useful for proving the point. As it turned out, both the government and the unions did learn this lesson, and during the second half of the 1970s Germany could be considered a model of coordinated monetary, fiscal, and wage policies, with low inflation, above-average economic growth, and increasing employment. But it was a highly asymmetric form of coordination, in which the bank had established, and gained acceptance for, its first-mover privileges (Scharpf 1991, ch. 7; Johnson 1998).

2.3.3.4 Coping with Imported Monetarism In countries practicing forms of 'imported monetarism' as a consequence of their membership in the Snake, governments and unions were less directly exposed to the ex-cathedra teachings of the Bundesbank and thus had greater difficulty in learning the same lesson.

In *Denmark*, the onset of the crisis was even more dramatic than in Germany. Between 1973 and 1975, business employment had fallen by 3.9 percentage points, and open unemployment had shot up from 0.9 percent

---

[11] In the heyday of 'concerted action' between 1967 and 1970, it is true, there had been attempts at more intense communication and explicit coordination. But when agreed-upon wage restraint had resulted in wildcat strikes and excessive wage drift in the overheated economy of 1969, the unions found it necessary to pacify their rank and file militants by insisting on large and inflationary wage increases in 1970–71. This, in turn, persuaded the bankers that there was no sense in further attempts at concertation, and relations became arms-length again.

[12] The Keynesian literature, discounting the importance of monetary policy, had focused on the effects of an *expansion* of the money supply, expressed in Karl Schiller's memorable quip that 'you can lead the horses to water, but you cannot make them drink'.

to 4.9 percent and continued to rise to 8.3 percent by 1978. Nevertheless, there was no wage moderation. Unit labor costs in national currency increased by 80 percent between 1973 and 1980—as compared with 46 percent in Germany—and consumer price inflation continued at 10 percent in 1978—when it had fallen to 2.7 percent in Germany. All the while, the efforts of the national bank to defend the exchange rate in the European currency Snake resulted in real long-term interest rates considerably above the German level, reaching 6.6 percent in 1976 and 8.6 percent in 1979 (Table A.29). However, as we have seen above, these efforts were not enough to stabilize the krone in relation to the German mark. In other words, Denmark in the 1970s had the worst of both worlds: a hard currency policy whose unsuccessful defense failed to contain the rise of inflation but succeeded in producing the highest rates of unemployment among the countries in our project.

The blame for this dismal outcome must be shared about equally by the actors responsible for monetary policy and wage policy. The Danish national bank enjoys a relatively high degree of institutional autonomy, but its authority is not reinforced by the same public aversion to inflation that exists in Germany and Austria. Moreover, while the government's—initially wavering—decision to join the European Snake[13] accorded with the preferences of the bank, the implications of a serious commitment to a hard currency position were never generally communicated and understood, and certainly not accepted by unions in the way that was true in Austria. Thus, the Danish hard currency position was not treated as being fully credible by financial markets, and the bank had to raise interest rates significantly above the German level to support the currency alignment (Iversen 1999, ch. 5).

However, when unemployment began to increase steeply as a consequence, neither the government nor the unions interpreted this as a compelling reason to reverse existing policies. Instead, unions saw the rise of unemployment as a betrayal of government commitments to full employment which in their view relieved them of any obligation to practice wage restraint as a *quid pro quo* (Iversen 1999: 138).[14] Legislated wage

---

[13] As Iversen (1999: 137) points out, the hard currency policy was mainly supported by the Radical Party—on which the government depended—whose farmer clientele would have suffered from a divergence between the official exchange rate and the 'Green krone' defining support prices for agricultural products in the European Community.

[14] There is a literature on 'political exchange' which, following Alessandro Pizzorno's (1978) seminal article, assumes that union wage restraint needs to be rewarded by the government in one way or another: tax benefits, social wages, and so forth (Lange and Garrett 1985; Marin 1990; see also the discussion of Australian 'Accords' in the 1980s by Herman Schwartz in Volume II). In the strict sense, however, this exchange logic applies only in the context of 'Keynesian concertation', when the government assures full employment and depends on union wage restraint to contain inflation. In a non-accommodating monetary

settlements were imposed in 1975, 1977, and 1979 without achieving much of a dampening effect. Beyond that, the rapid expansion of publicly-financed social services continued throughout the decade, increasing the employment rate of the government sector from 13.9 percent in 1970 to 21.7 percent in 1980 (Table A.6). This did wonders for the participation of women in the labor market, but little or nothing to reduce industrial unemployment.

In effect, therefore, imported monetarism in Denmark produced none of the beneficial effects for inflation and, ultimately, employment which it had in Germany. But even though it was unable to stabilize the exchange rate, the Danish central bank was unwilling to moderate its high interest rate policy in response to rising unemployment. At the same time, the multi-party coalition governments under social-democratic leadership were too weak either to explicitly abandon the ineffective hard currency commitment and switch to Swedish-style devaluation strategies, or to actively support the anti-inflation efforts of the national bank through fiscal consolidation, the abolition of wage-indexing, and the imposition of effective wage controls. The greater puzzle, however, is why industrial unions did not resort to wage moderation in response either to the hard currency stance of monetary policy or to the rise of unemployment.

The answer is only in part institutional. In the literature, the Danish industrial relations system is often treated as being similar to the Swedish. That is true for the high degree of unionization, which in both countries benefits from the unions' role in managing the unemployment insurance systems. In both countries, moreover, the federation of blue-collar unions (LO) had the leading role in peak-level negotiations with employers' federations that are meant to define the frame within which actual wages are then determined by sectoral and local bargaining. On the other hand, the number of LO's affiliate unions is considerably larger than in Austria, Germany, or Sweden, and they are primarily organized as either general or craft unions rather than by industrial sectors. As a consequence, interorganizational competition and local wage drift are a much greater problem for negotiated wage restraint than is true in Sweden, let alone in Austria and Germany (Visser 1998; Golden, Wallerstein, and Lange 1999). However, as I said above, organizational fragmentation and decentralization should not have mattered much after unemployment had begun to rise in the mid-1970s. From then on, even small unions and decentralized bargaining units should have found it in their self-interest to practice wage moderation in order to save the jobs of their own members. It seems likely,

environment, however, when unemployment is allowed to rise, union wage restraint to avoid further job losses should need no external reward. What matters, instead, is whether unions do in fact share the belief that wage restraint would save jobs.

therefore, that cognitive misperceptions of the role of wages in a non-accommodating monetary environment played a critical role. In any case, it is clear that the monetarist assignment of macroeconomic functions was ignored, and with dismal results, by Danish unions in the 1970s.

In *Belgium*, monetary policy was more effective than in Denmark in suppressing inflation after a peak of 12.8 percent in 1975, and the Belgian franc lost only 12.5 percent of its value in relation to the German mark between 1973 and 1980—as compared with 37 percent for the Danish krone. Nevertheless, the rise of unit labor costs in national currency was almost as steep as in Denmark, amounting to 75 percent between 1973 and 1980 (Table A.18). As a consequence, Belgian products were priced out of international markets; business employment fell continuously, from a rate of 51.4 percent in 1974 to 46.4 percent in 1980 (Table A.7); and open unemployment increased equally continuously from 2.4 percent in 1973 to 8.0 percent in 1980 (Table A.4).

Here, the institutional conditions favoring policy failure are spelled out clearly in the country chapter (Hemerijck, Unger, and Visser, Volume II). On the one hand, membership of the European currency Snake and a strict hard currency policy was credible because the national bank had the full support not only of all political parties, but also of the unions. At the same time, however, the economic implications of a hard currency position were not understood. Short-lived coalition governments were preoccupied with the search for federalizing solutions that would keep the country together under the growing tensions of the linguistic conflict. They had no mind to develop an integrated strategy that would combine a hard currency position with a viable set of 'Austro-Keynesian' full-employment policies. Instead, the almost absent-minded response of Belgian governments to manifestations of the economic crisis was to throw money at problems when and where they arose. Thus, rapidly rising early retirement and an excessive proliferation of subsidies to declining industries generated escalating public sector deficits that rapidly pre-empted all room for fiscal maneuver. As in Denmark, moreover, wage-indexing was left intact even though in the environment of the 1970s it was contributing to, rather than dampening, inflation.

Given this pattern of public policy, it would have been difficult for unions to practice voluntary wage restraint even under favorable institutional conditions. In fact, however, conditions were definitely less than favorable. While Belgian unions are powerful, they are divided along party-political lines and increasingly afflicted by internal linguistic cleavages. Thus, given the pressures of inter-union competition and the radicalization of their members after the late 1960s, moderation would have been difficult even if union leaders had believed in its necessity. The fact is, however, that they didn't. As was true of their German colleagues in 1974, Belgian trade union leaders did not appreciate the economic effectiveness of a firm monetary constraint. But while German union strategists, regardless of their Keynesian theories, came to respect the *de facto* power of the Bundesbank after their defeat in the 1974–75 confrontation, Belgian unionists 'continued to believe that wage restraint would not help but only depress demand and aggravate the crisis' (Hemerijck, Unger, and Visser, Volume II). Since tripartite negotiations about subsidized reductions of working time also failed to produce results, above-average real-wage increases continued until the early 1980s alongside the rapid increase of unemployment.

In the *Netherlands*, finally, hard currency policy was even more effective than it was in Belgium. Between 1973 and 1980, the Dutch guilder lost only 5 percent of its value *vis-à-vis* the German mark. And even though the rate of inflation was always higher than in Germany—partly as a consequence of the comprehensive inflation-indexing of private and public sector wages and welfare benefits—the Dutch commitment to a hard currency position was sufficiently credible to allow real long-term interest rates to remain at or even below German levels (Table A.29). Nevertheless, the rate of business employment fell by 4.1 percentage points between 1973 and 1980, as compared with 3.5 percentage points in Germany.

A closer look reveals that in Germany business employment fell steeply between 1973 and 1976—by 3.8 percentage points—but bottomed out in 1977 and rose again toward the end of the decade, whereas business employment in the Netherlands fell more steadily throughout the decade. The difference may in part be due to a relatively high share of declining industries: coal mining, textiles and clothing, and shipbuilding. But the comparison with Germany also suggests an institutional explanation. In Germany, coordination between monetary policy, fiscal policy and wage policy was traditionally based on nothing more demanding than the mechanisms of 'mutual adjustment'. These had failed for a year, when the unions misinterpreted the Bundesbank's switch to monetarism. But once the effectiveness of this switch was understood and grudgingly accepted, mutual adjustment was again effective, expectations were stabilized and business confidence was restored.

By comparison, the Netherlands, like Austria, had developed more ambitious and potentially more capable 'corporatist' institutions for policy coordination between government and the social partners. But whereas Austrian corporatism achieved its greatest triumphs in the 1970s, its Dutch counterpart simply ceased to function. As the country chapter explains, overheated labor markets had in the 1960s destroyed the effectiveness of postwar statutory wage controls. In their place, the Wage Act of

1970 had re-installed wage-setting through collective bargaining. When the crisis hit, it was still unclear which role central corporatist institutions—the Foundation of Labor (STAR) and the Social Economic Council (SER)—and the government should play in the wage-setting process. At the same time, unions came under rank and file pressure to demand a radical democratization of industrial relations, while a neo-liberal opposition to corporatist cooperation gained ground among employers. In short, not only was there no chance for Austro-Keynesian consensus strategies, but Dutch policy actors also lost the assurance that they could correctly anticipate each others' preferences and strategic options, which is the precondition for German-type coordination through mutual adjustment. Thus, if the success of Austro-Keynesianism was owed to the stabilization of expectations in a turbulent economic environment (Seidel 1982), the 'Dutch disease' of the 1970s was a consequence of desta-bilized expectations which seem to have depressed business confidence even more than was warranted by objective conditions.

2.4 Challenges in the 1980s: Stagflation and the Rise of Capital Interests

For two reasons, the second oil-price crisis was more than a replay of the stagflation challenges of the mid-1970s. First, all countries had come out of the 1970s with much higher levels of public debt, and most of them also had higher levels of inflation and higher levels of unemployment—all of which helped to discredit the Keynesian paradigm that had guided government responses in the mid-1970s. Second, and more important, the international monetary environment was rapidly changing from low or negative real interest rates to very high positive rates, with the consequence that interest rates in all countries had to follow suit if massive capital out-flows were to be avoided, and that deficit spending changed its character from a viable policy option to a perhaps unavoidable policy failure. Nevertheless, countries still had a macroeconomic choice between expansionary and restrictive strategies. But now, however, expansion could be achieved only by devaluation of the currency rather than by fiscal and monetary reflation.

2.4.1 Devaluation Countries

Of course, not all countries could have devalued at the same time to increase international competitiveness and thus aggregate demand, and a cycle of competitive devaluations might have had disastrous consequences for the world economy. But since the US dollar continued to rise in the early 1980s while the member countries of the European Monetary System (EMS)—created in 1979 to replace the increasingly ineffective Snake—struggled to maintain a hard currency position, that danger was remote. In contrast to the expansion of domestic demand in the 1970s, however, the devaluation strategy could not defend employment unless the competitive advantage and higher profits were maintained by wage restraint—which could be achieved either through coordinated collective bargaining or through the market.

2.4.1.1 Coordinated Wage Setting The coordination of devaluation and wage restraint depended on the same institutional capabilities that successful Keynesian concertation had required in the 1970s. During the last years of the bourgeois coalition governments in *Sweden*, inflation had risen to 13.7 percent in 1980 (Table A.3), public deficits had reached the record level of 7 percent of GDP in 1982 (Table A.22), business employment rates had fallen steadily from 57.5 percent in 1975 to 53.6 percent in 1982 (Table A.7), and, in spite of the massive use of active labor market policy, open unemployment had risen to 3.1 percent in 1982 (Table A.4). Thus, when the Social Democrats returned to power in 1982, the sense of crisis was acute enough to support an austerity package that combined fiscal consolidation with a 16 percent devaluation of the krona and a massive appeal to union wage restraint. The institutional conditions for that had deteriorated in the late 1970s as a consequence of conflicts between LO and SAF over the creation of 'wage earner funds', conflicts between LO and white-collar and public sector unions over wage leadership, and conflicts within LO and SAF over the continuation of centralized, and extremely egalitarian, wage negotiations. Nevertheless, the sense of crisis and the renewed *entente* between Social Democrats in government and organized labor was sufficient to ensure wage settlements that allowed Sweden to maintain the competitive advantage gained through devaluation well into the second half of the 1980s.[15] As a consequence, the superior employment performance of Sweden in the 1980s was not primarily due, as is often assumed, to the increase of public sector employment—which was quite modest, rising from an employment rate of 25.0 percent in 1982 to 25.7 percent in 1990—but to an increase in the rate of business employment from 53.6 percent in 1982 to 55.7 percent in 1990 (Table A.7). In the process, the share of labor in national income had fallen from 73.7

[15] Torben Iversen's (1999: 144 and 190, n. 28) claim that there was a 'rapid deterioration of Swedish competitiveness' is not supported by the data. Between 1981 and 1987, relative unit labor costs in manufacturing in Sweden fell by 16%, whereas they increased by 24% in Germany and by 27% in Denmark. The advantage of the 1982 devaluation was only fully eroded in 1990 (Table A.19).

percent in 1982 to 69.9 percent in 1987 (Table A.20). Beyond that point, however, the economic preconditions for coordinated wage restraint were destroyed by a real-estate and construction 'bubble' which, by hindsight, appears as a major failure of policy coordination.

Traditionally, Swedish credit markets had been highly regulated, and housing credit had been tightly rationed, while home owners and consumers could deduct interest payments from their taxable income. When credit markets were deregulated in 1985–86, these tax exemptions were initially left unchanged. The result was a credit-financed explosion of consumer spending and housing construction with rapidly rising inflation that peaked at 10.4 percent in 1990, when the OECD average was at 5 percent. There was no chance that these market forces could be contained by voluntary wage restraint. In order to suppress inflation, the government then switched to extreme fiscal retrenchment. Moreover, since exchange controls had also been removed in the late 1980s, monetary policy was required to defend the exchange rate that had been defined by the devaluation of 1982. To increase the credibility of this new commitment to a hard currency policy, the government decided in late 1990 to peg the krona to the ECU—which then pulled Sweden into the EMS crisis of 1992, in which its expensive defense of the exchange rate was finally overwhelmed by currency speculation. In combination, these events threw the Swedish economy into its deepest postwar recession.

But these challenges will concern us in the next section. What matters here is whether there are institutional explanations for the policy failures that caused the bubble and the crash at the end of the 1980s. In the literature, much attention is paid to the protracted and inconsistent maneuvers of SAF, LO, and the government which, in effect, destroyed the old institutions of centralized wage setting and corporatist cooperation. But given the policy failures of the late 1980s and their inflationary effects, no system of collective bargaining could have ensured effective wage restraint after 1988. As for the policy failures, they are usually ascribed to cognitive misperceptions and the accidental coincidence of home-made and international crises. In the country chapter, there is also a suggestion that the effectiveness of policy coordination within the government may have suffered in the 1980s since policies of capital-market deregulation were defined more or less in isolation by economists in the national bank and in the finance ministry[16] rather than being integrated into a comprehensive strategy whose implications were well understood by other government departments and the social partners (Benner and Vad, Volume II).

---

[16] This fact is interpreted as evidence of a neo-liberal conspiracy involving finance minister Kjell-Olof Feldt and his advisers, in Canova (1994).

Devaluation was also part of the strategy adopted by *Australia* after the Labor party returned to power in 1983,[17] and as in Sweden the competitive advantage could be maintained for a number of years. This success was due to the ability and willingness of union leaders to negotiate a series of peak-level 'Accords' with the government that combined commitments to welfare-state reform with agreements on wage settlements that allowed real wages to fall in order to allow profits to rise. Under the earlier conditions of organizational fragmentation and decentralization, the adoption and implementation of these Accords would have been difficult. What made them possible was, first, the process of organizational concentration mentioned above which had increased the membership of the central union federation (the ACTU), and second, the fact that, in contrast to New Zealand, the authority of arbitration courts had survived the challenges of the 1970s. Since only the ACTU had standing to apply for increases of the basic wage in the Federal Court, the federation had become a potential partner for a strategy that would reflate aggregate demand through massive devaluation, and that depended on wage restraint to preserve the competitive advantage and the rise of profits.[18] Faced with the prospect of a monetarist alternative, the ACTU was willing to cooperate with the government, and local wage drift was held in check by a Federal Court ruling under which local wage increases above the minimum would be allowed only if there were above-average productivity increases. This last feature was of particular importance since the Labor government also embarked on a gradual but persistent course of liberalizing, deregulating, and privatizing an economy in which industrial production had been sheltered from foreign competition, and in which services and infrastructure had been nationalized or highly regulated. Given the relative inefficiency of production, and managers newly confronted with a more competitive environment, adjustment was helped by the fact that local unions had strong incentives to search for productivity-increasing solutions, and to collaborate in their implementation, rather than to oppose them.

While it lasted, the combination of devaluation and wage restraint was even more successful than in Sweden. Relative unit labor costs fell by 33 percent between 1982 and 1987 (Table A.19); the share of labor fell from 62.3 percent of national income in 1984 to 59.5 percent in 1988 (Table A.20); the rate of business employment increased from 52.4 percent in

---

[17] The devaluation was achieved by downward floating rather than by a single decision, but it was no less effective than in Sweden. Between 1982 and 1987, the effective exchange rate of the Australian dollar declined by 37.8% (Table A.32).

[18] For a critical review of this strategy, from a left-union perspective, see Hampson and Morgan (1999).

1984 to 58.0 percent in 1989 (Table A.7); and unemployment fell from 9.9 percent in 1983 to 6.1 percent in 1989 (Table A.4). But, as in Sweden, the success story came to an end in the late 1980s when the sudden liberalization and deregulation of capital markets produced an overheated domestic real-estate and consumption boom that destroyed the economic preconditions of continuing wage restraint, and that ended in a deep recession in which the rate of business employment fell from 58.0 percent in 1989 to 54.7 percent in 1993, while unemployment rose again to 10.9 percent.

In both countries, it is interesting to note, the coordination between exchange-rate policy and wage policy was remarkably successful for a while, and then failed for the same reasons when the deregulation of capital and credit markets generated domestic demand inflation. Even under the most favorable institutional conditions, unions are unable to hold the line against local wage pressures and wildcat strikes in an overheating economy. Thus, coordination between exchange-rate policy and wage policy was not enough to ensure lasting success; it would also have been necessary to consider the impact on industrial relations of policy choices in such fields as banking regulation and tax policy. It may be true, therefore, that coordinated or 'tightly coupled' policy solutions are potentially more effective than simpler strategies (Freeman 1995). But it is also true that they depend crucially on effective communication and a mutual understanding of the pressures and constraints facing actors in separate policy arenas. Given the ubiquitous bias of 'selective perception' associated with the division of labor in organizations (Dearborn and Simon 1958), these conditions are difficult to achieve even under stable conditions. In a turbulent economic environment, when policy initiatives must chart new courses, attempts to pursue complex coordinated strategies are likely to have a high rate of failure.

2.4.1.2 Fragmented Wage Setting In *New Zealand*, devaluation was also a major element shaping the challenges and options of the 1980s, with the effective exchange rate falling by 40 percent between 1980 and 1990. Since the government was maintaining full employment, strong but organizationally fragmented unions did fully exploit their opportunities for wage maximization, and the awards of arbitration courts could easily be overturned by local strikes. Nevertheless, the conservative government of the early 1980s continued with demand reflation, protectionism, and even intensified the commitment to import-substituting industrialization in its 'Think-Big' investment program. The change came in 1984, with the surprise election of a Labour government that had a mandate to break with past policy legacies. After an initial attempt to achieve an Australian-type agreement on wage restraint had failed, the free-market wing of the governing party gained the chance to implement a program of liberalizing reforms that was much more radical than the parallel reforms in Australia. Compared with Britain, however, the neo-liberal program of the New Zealand Labour Party was incomplete in its exclusive focus on product and capital markets.

Beginning with the reduction of external tariffs and quantitative restrictions in product markets, and the liberalization and deregulation of financial markets, the government also proceeded to privatize public sector services and to reduce top marginal tax rates in accord with textbook neo-liberal policy prescriptions. In contrast to Britain, however, social policy was more generous, combining institutional decentralization with a steep increase in total social spending, from 17 percent of GDP in 1984 to 22.6 percent in 1991 (Tables A.27, A.27a), and high public sector deficits (Table A.22). Even more important, the New Zealand Labour Party did nothing to either reform or destroy the dysfunctional industrial-relations system with its fragmented and decentralized institutional structure and its all but impotent arbitration courts, even though it was less dependent on union support than the British and Australian labor parties.

Overall, the economic record of the neo-liberal Labour government in office between 1984 and 1991 was dismal. After an excessive boom in 1984, economic growth was far below the OECD average, and per-capita GDP, measured in purchasing-power parities (PPP), fell from 69 percent of the US level in 1983 to 60 percent in 1991. New Zealand was the only OECD country to experience such decline (Table A.1). While nominal effective exchange rates fell by more than 20 percent between 1984 and 1991 (Table A.32), unit labor costs in national currency increased by 66 percent during the same period (Table A.18). Since inflation also shot up again to two-digit levels between 1985 and 1987, at a time when it was at the lowest point since the early 1970s in the OECD average (Table A.3), the Labour government now found it necessary to switch to a strictly non-accommodating monetary regime. Real long-term interest rates shot up from zero in 1987 to 7.1 percent in 1989 (Table A.29), bringing the rate of inflation down from 15.7 percent in 1987 to 1.0 percent in 1992 (Table A.3), while the rate of business employment fell by 5.5 percentage points between 1987 and 1991 (Table A.7)—by which time unemployment had also risen from 4.1 percent in 1987 to 10.3 percent.

At this point, however, the Labour party had fallen apart, and the neo-liberal program was completed by the new conservative government. It adopted a course of rigid fiscal consolidation, replacing a budget deficit amounting to 4.7 percent of GDP in 1990 with a budget surplus of 3 percent in 1994 (Table A.22) and reducing total social expenditure from 22.6

percent of GDP in 1991 to 18.8 percent by 1995 (Tables A.27, A.27a). Like Margaret Thatcher, moreover, the new government was finally politically free to tackle the industrial-relations problems underlying the economic malaise, and in contrast to Australia its strategy was radically destructive rather than constructive. The Employment Contracts Act of 1991 emasculated unions by allowing employment contracts to be freely negotiated between individual workers and their employers. At the same time, arbitration courts lost the competence to adjust wages by reference to criteria of comparability across firms, branches or skill groups. The result was a radically decentralized, market-determined system of wage determination, whose effects, however, could be observed only in the next decade.

To conclude: countries that resorted to devaluation in order to cope with the second oil-price crisis depended even more on sustained wage restraint than had been true of soft-currency countries in the 1970s. It could be achieved for a while in Sweden, where the corporatist capacity for coordinated collective bargaining still existed, and in Australia, where it was newly created. Wage restraint could not be achieved under institutional conditions of fragmented collective bargaining in New Zealand.

2.4.2 Hard Currency Countries

The majority of countries did not devalue, but followed the American lead by adopting a non-accommodating monetary policy in response to the second oil crisis. For countries that had done so already in the 1970s, therefore, the 1980s brought more of the same problems and solutions, whereas others had to go through a dramatic turnaround of macroeconomic policy that created new challenges for wage-setting as well. If employment was to be maintained in hard currency countries in spite of the very high real interest rates in the early 1980s, wage restraint had to be even more effective than in the previous decade; and in theory this might have been achieved in coordinated as well as in fragmented collective bargaining systems, or through statist intervention.

2.4.2.1 Coordinated Wage Setting   The fewest difficulties in adjusting to the conditions of the 1980s were encountered in *Switzerland*, even though the Swiss franc continued to appreciate against other currencies. While the employment rate in industry declined somewhat through the 1980s (Table A.9), services expanded so vigorously that the rate of business employment increased by 9.1 percentage points between 1979 and 1991, reaching by far the highest level among all OECD countries (Table A.7). That suggests that the existing institutional structure of highly decentralized wage setting and highly decentralized government was well positioned to cope

with the second oil price shock, and then to take advantage of the generally favorable business climate of the second half of the 1980s.

Other countries that did not choose devaluation and that nevertheless
had some success in maintaining employment in the private sector of the
economy included Germany, Denmark, Austria and, in a spectacular
turnaround, the Netherlands. Of these, *Germany* was similar to
Switzerland in the constant upward pressure on its currency which, however, was a consequence of the restrictive monetary policy of the Bundesbank rather than the result of security-oriented capital inflows happening
in spite of a policy of low nominal interest rates in Switzerland. Coming at
the end of a brief recovery at the end of the 1970s, this tight-money
response to the second oil shock again caused another deep recession in
which the rate of business employment fell almost as much as it did in
Margaret Thatcher's Britain: from 56.5 percent in 1980 to 52.1 percent in
1984 (Table A.7). Unlike in Britain, however, the German system of industrial relations and collective bargaining was not destroyed or even seriously damaged either by the recession or by the change from Helmut
Schmidt's social-liberal to Helmut Kohl's christian-liberal government in
the fall of 1982. Unions had learned to respect the effectiveness of monetary restraint, real unit labor costs in national currency were falling
between 1981 and 1985 (Table A.17), and the share of labor in national
income continued to decline from 66.7 percent in 1982 to 61.3 percent in
1990 (Table A.20), even though the rate of business employment rose
again from 52.1 percent in 1984 to 55.0 percent in 1990—the last year
before German unification. In other words, German unions seemed to be
aware of the importance of wage costs and profits for private sector
employment, and the institutional conditions of sectoral wage bargaining—which provided little opportunity for local wage drift[19]—allowed
them to pursue effective strategies reflecting this insight.

Austria, which had long pursued a hard currency strategy, had fixed its
exchange rate even more firmly to the Deutschmark after a brief vacilla-
tion in 1979. As in the early 1970s, its interest rate policy was a bit less
restrictive than was true in Germany, but in contrast to the first oil-price
crisis, its level of business employment declined even more than in
Germany this time around: from 55.9 percent in 1980 to 50.8 percent in
1984. Even more significantly, the decline was not reversed after the end of
the second oil crises but continued more slowly until 1987. The reason,
however, was not aggressive wage settlements. Relative unit labor costs
actually decreased through the 1980s (Table A.19). Instead, the main rea-

---

[19] In contrast to Sweden, Denmark, and Austria, there are no local bargaining rounds
in Germany. Within firms, workers' interests are not represented by unions but by works
councils which are not empowered to negotiate about wages (Rogers and Streeck 1995).

son for the decline of business employment was the need for restructuring the large sector of nationalized basic industries that had been used as an 'employment buffer' in the crisis of the 1970s. In the meantime, it had become so much of a burden on the economy and on the state budget that rationalization and then privatization were considered inevitable. In agreement with the social partners, however, the restructuring was implemented gradually to avoid mass layoffs and a dramatic rise of unemployment (Table A.4).

In *Denmark*, the ineffective policies of the 1970s had continued until 1982 when the social-democratic government was replaced by a conservative-led coalition with a mandate for change. The new government was committed to fiscal consolidation and a serious hard currency position, and the central bank now had its full political support in defending the exchange rate of the krone in the European Monetary System. At the same time, automatic wage indexation was abolished to allow private sector wages to adjust more quickly to labor market conditions. In its own terms, this austerity program was quite effective; inflation came down from 10.1 percent in 1982 to 3.7 percent in 1986 (Table A.3). At the same time, real unit labor costs (Table A.17), real wages (Table A.16) and the labor share in national income (Table A.20) were falling, with the consequence that the rate of business employment—which had fallen continuously from 1970 to 1983—increased steeply from 50.1 percent in 1983 to 55.2 percent in 1987 (Table A.7). But in comparison with Switzerland and Germany, the change was short lived. After the failed attempts at centrally negotiated wage restraint in the 1970s, industrial relations had reverted to highly fragmented bargaining patterns in the 1980s, which facilitated wage restraint under the pressures of high unemployment but could not sustain it when employment conditions improved again. The government's attempts to impose statutory wage controls proved ineffective; real wages, real unit labor costs and the labor share rose once more, and the decline of business employment turned into a deep fall in the recession of the early 1990s. In response to this experience, Danish wage-setting procedures were reformed in the late 1980s, but the new pattern of 'centralized decentralization' could take effect only in the following decade (Due *et al.* 1995).

The *Netherlands* had entered the crisis period of the 1980s in an even more desperate condition, with total employment having fallen continuously from an already comparatively low rate of 61.6 in 1970 to 50.8 percent in 1984—the lowest level among all OECD-18 countries (Table A.5)—and with unemployment rising continuously from the early 1970s to a peak of 11.0 percent in 1983 (Table A.4), even though the labor force participation of men over the age of 55 had been drastically reduced from 80.6 percent in 1970 to 50.3 percent in 1984 through the use of early retirement and disability pensions (Table A.13). As a consequence, the total burden of taxes and social security contributions had risen from 37.1 percent of GDP in 1970 to 46 percent in 1983 (Table A.23), while public deficits had nevertheless continued to climb to 6.6 percent of GDP in 1982 (Table A.22).

It is remarkable, in light of the present admiration for the 'Dutch Miracle', that the eventual turnaround was achieved within the same institutional settings that had brought about the 'Dutch Disease': a multiparty political system, coalition governments, an independent central bank and institutions for corporatist consultation between a plurality of unions and employers' associations and the government. Until the early 1980s, these institutions had produced a macroeconomic disaster. Militant unions were pushing up wages while the hard currency policy of the independent central bank reduced international competitiveness and domestic demand; at the same time, politically weak coalition governments under social-democratic prime ministers were unwilling to act without the agreement of the social partners—which, however, were unable to agree on anything. But after the general elections of 1981 had produced another patchwork coalition government that achieved nothing and simply gave up after nine months, new elections brought a majority for a christian-liberal coalition led by Rud Lubbers, who was committed to a 'no-nonsense' austerity program—which implied a shift from Keynesian to monetarist preferences in the sense that a further rise of unemployment was now considered more acceptable than a further decline of business profits and of state finances.

The policy agenda of the new government included many of the standard elements of neo-liberal reforms in Britain: deregulation, privatization, tax cuts for business, and the elimination of automatic linkages from private sector wage increases to public sector pay and social benefits. From an institutional perspective, however, it mattered even more that these policy reversals were chosen autonomously by the government without asking for the agreement of the social partners (Hemerijck 1995). In comparison with Austria, this dramatic break with past practice was legitimized by the deep public discontent with the non-functioning of corporatist institutions during the preceding decade; in comparison with Germany, it was facilitated by the institutions of a unitary state that did not allow the opposition to influence national decisions through the veto position of a second federal chamber (Lehmbruch 1986, 1989).

However, as was shown for New Zealand, and Denmark, a neo-liberal and monetarist program of the state could not achieve positive employment effects under the conditions of the 1980s unless it was accompanied by sustained wage restraint. Thus, the most important element among the factors explaining the Dutch turnaround was the strong comeback of corporatist institutions after the government had asserted its capacity for unilateral action, and its willingness to stick to a course of fiscal and monetary retrenchment, even as unemployment rates were shooting up from 5.8 percent in 1981 to 11.0 percent in 1983. Since the Lubbers government was no longer willing to accept political responsibility for the consequences of conflictual industrial relations and wage competition, unions and employers only had to look across the English Channel to see the fate that awaited them unless they did get their act together: a collapse of organizational capacity and bargaining power for the unions, and an even deeper decline of international competitiveness for the employers.

The essence of the Dutch miracle thus lies in the fact that, after a decade of conflict and mutual recriminations, unions and employers were in fact able to respond to these dismal prospects by shifting from competitive to cooperative 'interaction orientations' (Scharpf 1997b: 84–89) that allowed them to conclude the bipartite 'Accord of Wassenaar' in November of 1982. Since the focus now was on the common interest in defending the viability of the Dutch economy, agreements among the social partners on a great variety of employment-increasing measures, including the expansion of part-time work, proliferated in following years (Visser and Hemerijck 1997). Of greatest immediate importance among these was agreement in principle on a policy of wage restraint which from then on kept real-wage increases in Dutch industry consistently below those in Germany (Table A.16). And given the fact that the social partners now assumed bipartite responsibility for the adjustment of wages and employment relationships to the macroeconomic conditions, the conservative government, unlike Margaret Thatcher, did not hesitate to return to the corporatist fora for discussing government initiatives in the fields of tax policy, budget consolidation, and welfare-state reforms. But it remained clear that the government was able to, and would, act on its own even if all-round agreement could not be achieved.

This turnaround of industrial relations and wage-setting practices did help to reverse the decline of employment. Even though the effective exchange rate increased by 29.5 percent between 1982 and 1991 (Table A.32), relative unit labor costs actually decreased by 13.9 percent in the same period (Table A.19). The share of labor fell from 66.1 percent of national income in 1980 to 58.5 percent in 1985, and it remained at about that level thereafter (Table A.20), even as the rate of business employment increased from 42.7 percent in 1984 to 48.0 percent in 1991, and continued to rise thereafter (Table A.7).

2.4.2.2 Statist Wage Setting   In employment terms, *Belgium* was in the same bad shape as the Netherlands in the early 1980s, with a steady decline of the business-employment rate from 51.6 percent in 1970 to 42.6 percent in 1984 (Table A.7). The main institutional cause of that decline was the combination of a central bank that was able and willing to pursue an ambitious hard currency policy with an industrial-relations system in which politically and linguistically divided unions were structurally incapable of practicing the wage restraint that would have mitigated job losses. As in the Netherlands, the crisis produced a political turnaround in the early 1980s which, however, followed a 'statist' institutional trajectory that was as different from the Dutch restoration of corporatist concerta-tion as it was from the market-oriented transformation in Britain and France.

The center-right coalition that came to power in 1981, having failed ini-tially in its appeals for union wage restraint, set out to reverse the decline of the economy on the basis of 'enabling laws' that allowed it to govern by decree, and hence without further dependence on a parliament that was preoccupied with the complications of negotiating and managing consti-tutional solutions to the linguistic conflict. Beginning with a modest devaluation of the currency, the government sought to protect the com-petitive advantage by an initial freeze of wages and prices, a temporary suspension of wage indexation, and a subsequent four-year suspension of collective bargaining. At the end of that period, unions and employers were again allowed to engage in wage negotiations, but the government had obtained special powers to impose a settlement if negotiations should fail—which they promptly did. After the socialists had re-entered govern-ment in 1987, which mitigated the blocking strategy of the socialist union, wage increases were again the object of peak-level negotiations among the social partners; but these negotiations were conducted 'in the shadow' of state intervention and under very tight government guidelines.

The direct economic impact of this extreme form of statist intervention in the wage-setting process was in fact as favorable as the effect of corpor-atist wage moderation had been in the Netherlands: real wages declined from 1982 to 1987 (Table A.17) while relative unit labor costs decreased by 26 percent between 1981 and 1983, and increased again only by 8.4 per-cent until 1990 (Table A.19). The labor share of national income, which had reached its high point at 65.4 percent in 1981, fell continuously to 56.3 percent in 1989, and then continued at about that level (Table A.20). Nevertheless, employment in the business sector, which had reached its low point at 42.6 percent in 1984, increased only slowly to 45.5 percent by 1991—which was a good deal less than the increase from 42.7 percent to 48 percent during the same period in the Netherlands (Table A.7)—partly because Belgium did not achieve anything like the Dutch increase of part-time employment (Table A.14).

The institutional explanation for the less successful Belgian perform-ance can perhaps be described as the 'weakness of the isolated state'. Belgian governments, politically weak in other respects, still had the power to set and enforce wage rates by decree, which allowed them to shore up the price competitiveness of Belgian industry. But they had little else. Government by decree could neither motivate the social partners to search for new forms of work organization that would increase opportunities for part-time employment, nor bring about the rapid expansion of domestic service jobs which would have required parliamentary majorities that were willing to deregulate certain aspects of the labor market and to modify social security legislation in ways that were unpopular with the voters. Moreover, in order to gain the passive acceptance of unions for wage restraint by decree, the government had to maintain extremely attractive early-exit options that reduced the labor force participation of older work-ers to the lowest level among OECD-18 countries (Table A.13) and that continued to require very high public sector deficits (Table A.22). At the same time, imposed wage settlements were made more acceptable by allowing above-average wage increases for the lowest-paid workers, with the consequence that Belgium is among the very few countries where D5:D1 wage differentials narrowed rather than widened during the 1980s (Table A.21).

In short, the rise of average wages could be contained in Belgium and in the Netherlands. But whereas the restoration of corporatist capabilities required Dutch unions to face economic necessities directly, the govern-ment assumed responsibility for imposing these necessities in Belgium, and statist wage-setting remained bound to a logic of political exchanges in which acceptance had to be bought by political concessions.

Finally, *Italy* can also be included among the countries that switched from a soft-currency to a hard currency position in the 1980s. Since it had become a member of the new EMS, albeit with wider margins for adjust-ment, the central bank had been granted greater autonomy from the gov-ernment in order to defend the lira. Thus the effective exchange rate, which still had declined by 20 percent between 1980 and 1984, was practically stable from then on until 1991 (Table A.32). As in Belgium, the state was heavily involved in the wage-setting process, but short-lived coalition gov-ernments did not have the power to impose Belgian-style settlements. However, even though tripartite negotiations over an anti-inflation social pact in 1983 did not establish a longer-term pattern, the politically divided but organizationally strong unions did respond to the macroeconomic shift. In comparison with the 1970s and early 1980s, the increase of unit labor cost in national currency slowed down considerably after 1983, and relative unit labor cost was actually stable between 1983 and 1989 (Table A.19). As a consequence, the business employment rate, which had declined by 2 percentage points between 1980 and 1984, was stabilized and even increased slightly thereafter.

However, since the hard-money constraint was not externally imposed but politically chosen by weak governments, the wage restraint also had to be bought by 'political exchanges' in which union cooperation was rewarded by more generous pensions and other social-policy concessions. Even though total taxation was also rising (Table A.23), these concessions were largely financed by very high public sector deficits (Table A.22), which then added to the fiscal challenges that had to be faced in the 1990s (Regini and Regalia 1997).

2.4.2.3 Fragmented and Market-Oriented Wage Setting   After the election of Margaret Thatcher's monetarist government in 1979, the initial British response to the second oil crisis was an extreme form of hard currency policy. Thus, the early Thatcher years had seen a 20 percent rise of the effective exchange rate of the pound between 1978 and 1981, that was caused by a very restrictive monetary policy and high interest rates combined with the fact that North-Sea oil was finally coming on stream. As a result, British industry lost its international competitiveness and was in large part destroyed. However, the power of militant and fragmented unions, which had brought down the last Labour government in the 'winter of discontent' of 1978–79, was not yet broken. Thus, unit labor costs in national currency continued to increase by 40 percent between 1979 and 1982 (Table A.18), and inflation again reached a peak of 18 percent in 1980 (Table A.3). As a consequence, the business-employment rate fell from 55.8 percent in 1979 to 50.2 percent in 1983 (Table A.7), and open unemployment rose from 4.5 percent in 1979 to 11.8 percent in 1986 (Table A.4).

Since one of the early Thatcher 'reforms' had eliminated earnings-related unemployment compensation—leaving only the low flat-rate basic benefit—the steep rise of unemployment undermined the capacity of unions to bargain for wage increases and to mobilize strikes. The effect was made permanent by Thatcher's industrial-relations legislation. Unlike the reforms introduced by Heath, and repealed by Wilson against his better judgment, the new version was not intended to reduce the fragmentation and decentralization of collective bargaining which, from the perspective of corporatist capabilities, was the root problem of the British wage-setting system (Streeck 1978). Instead it aimed directly at the base of British-style union power, by denying legal force to closed-shop agreements, by requiring strike ballots, by disallowing sympathy strikes, and by making unions legally liable for the damage caused by illegal strikes. While outside observers might consider these rules perfectly fair, and while none of them would have interfered with union activity in the highly regulated industrial relations systems of, say, Germany, they all but destroyed the power of British unions which, under the ground rules of legally uncon- strained 'voluntarism', had mainly depended on mobilization and peer pressures at the shop floor, on 'spontaneous' action, and on the ideolog- ical solidarity of other unions in the case of strikes and lockouts (Crouch 1993). Thus, through policies introduced during her first term in office, and through the pressure of mass unemployment, Thatcher had in fact destroyed what institutional support there had been for collective action in wage bargaining, and may even have brought about 'the end of institu- tional industrial relations' (Purcell 1995).

The resulting pattern of extremely decentralized wage setting was highly responsive to local market conditions. Unit labor costs in national cur- rency actually declined from 1982 to 1983, and increased much more slowly than before during the rest of the decade. This then allowed the government to let the effective exchange rate of the pound slide by more than 20 percent between 1981 and 1988 (Table A.32), which also reduced relative unit labor costs by the same magnitude (Table A.19). The share of labor incomes in GDP fell from 67.8 percent in 1980 to 61.8 percent in 1987 (Table A.20); and the rate of business employment, after reaching its low point in 1983, increased by more than 7 percentage points until the end of the decade (Table A.7). Unemployment rates, however, remained above 10 percent until 1987, but then fell to 5.9 percent in 1990.

Institutionally, the dramatic turnaround in the early 1980s has a straightforward explanation in the awesome power which the Westminster model bestows upon governments with a secure electoral majority and a prime minister who is unchallenged in her own party. But why couldn't the same concentrated power have been used by the last Labour Government under Jim Callaghan, or by the last Conservative government under Edward Heath, for that matter, to avert the crises of the British economy that caused their political demise? The answer is that Heath, Wilson, and Callaghan had been committed to Keynesian full employment policies, and given the expectations of their voters they could not have risked a dra- matic rise of unemployment. But in order to make good their commitment without an unacceptable escalation of inflation, they had become hostage to the unions and their ability and willingness to practice wage restraint. Margaret Thatcher's monetarist credo, by contrast, gave priority to break- ing inflationary expectations through monetary restraint even if that would entail a temporary rise of unemployment. To the extent that voters could be persuaded by this discourse, the success of her macroeconomic program was not dependent on the capacity and willingness of unions to practice voluntary wage restraint (Scharpf 1987). After the 'winter of discontent', moreover, confronting the unions had become a politically profitable strategy for the Conservative government rather than the liability which it had been for Edward Heath in 1973–74 (King and Wood 1999). In other words, unlike her predecessors, Margaret Thatcher was not constrained either politically or economically from making full use of the capabilities for decisive action that are provided by the single-actor Westminster model of government.

In *France*, the cautious turn to monetarism of the Barre Government in the late 1970s was reversed in 1981, when the new socialist government initially opted for massive increases of public expenditure and extensive nationalization in order to create jobs and to improve social benefits. By now, however, the central bank was obliged by France's membership in the European Monetary System to raise real interest rates to very high levels in order to stem the capital flight that was caused by the government's untimely reversion to fiscal Keynesianism. As a consequence, inflation remained at two-digit levels and the small increase in public sector employment (Table A.6) was not nearly enough to compensate for the fall in business employment from a rate of 51.2 percent in 1980 to 46.8 in 1984.

The socialist government's sudden conversion to hard currency and free-market policies in 1983 was as dramatic as the policy turnarounds adopted by incoming conservative governments in Denmark, the Netherlands, and Belgium in the early 1980s. The new strategy combined the macroeconomic policy of the *franc fort* with a commitment to the liberalization program of the Single European Act, and while the nationalization program of 1981 was not reversed, the priorities of *dirigiste* industrial policy now shifted from protecting existing jobs to increasing the international competitiveness of public and private firms alike through mergers and through the introduction of productivity increasing reforms of management practices and work organization (V. A. Schmidt 1996b).[20]

But while it succeeded in stabilizing the currency and reducing the rate of inflation dramatically, the new strategy did not improve the employment situation (Lordon 1998). In contrast to the 1970s, however, the power of fragmented but militant unions was no longer to blame. In fact, French industrial relations were—unintendedly, perhaps—transformed in almost the same way as in Britain by the industrial-relations legislation of the socialists. In the interest of work-place democracy, the *Auroux* laws of 1982 required the establishment of worker-management dialogues in public- and private sector firms. Private sector managers, who had opposed

---

[20] The process was greatly accelerated when the conservative Chirac government of 1986–88 proceeded to privatize a large part of these public firms.

the legislation, soon found it more attractive to deal directly with representatives of their own workforce rather than with the functionaries of organizationally weak, but ideologically radical and competing unions—with the consequence that wage-setting by fragmented collective bargaining with heavy state involvement came to be replaced by plant-level agreements from which the state could safely withdraw.

Nevertheless, the rate of business employment continued to decline. As in Austria, one of the reasons was the restructuring of state-owned enterprises that had served as employment buffers in the 1970s, and that were now required to become competitive in the Single European Market—which also required the liberalization and deregulation of telecommunications, air and road transport, and financial services. In combination with the monetary constraints imposed by the *franc fort*, these were conditions in which wage moderation alone was not sufficient to stop the decline of business employment. Since public sector employment also stagnated, unemployment remained at about 10 percent until the end of decade (Table A.4); but it would have been even higher if early retirement had not been used so extensively to reduce the labor force participation of older workers from 68.6 percent in 1980 to 45.8 percent 1990 (Table A.13).

As in Britain and New Zealand, the highly centralized French political system imposed no institutional constraints that could have prevented the government from carrying out any economically feasible policy that served its political preferences. In contrast to Margaret Thatcher's Britain, however, French governments of both political camps were constrained in the electoral arena by the need to respect the values of social solidarity and civic equality that are deeply held by the constituencies of right-of-center governments as much as by the left (V. A. Schmidt, this volume), and by a stronger contestational tradition that allowed worker protests to count on public support. This prevented a course of more radical liberalization, privatization and labor-market deregulation than was in fact pursued after 1983. It also explains the massive use of welfare-state exit options to reduce the labor supply (Levy, Volume II). But it does not explain the generally poor labor market performance which France shares with other Continental welfare states, and which is the subject of the next section.

To conclude: in countries that maintained or adopted a hard currency policy in response to the more intense macroeconomic challenges of the 1980s, sustained wage restraint was a necessary, but not always a sufficient, condition for limiting job losses in the early 1980s, and for achieving employment increases in the second half of the decade. Such wage restraint could generally be produced in countries with coordinated collective bargaining systems, where unions were now sufficiently aware of the causal connection between wage increases and job losses. In countries with fragmented collective-bargaining structures, governments could not, or did not dare to, rely on the collective intelligence of the 'social partners'. Instead, Belgium and, to a lesser extent, Italy resorted to statist wage-setting practices whose acceptability had to be bought by political concessions to union demands on related issues. By contrast, Britain, France and, in the 1990s, New Zealand destroyed the institutional bases of union power and collective bargaining, with the consequence that wages came to be determined by market forces and ceased to be a policy variable that could be coordinated with government strategies in other policy areas.

2.5 The 1990s: Employment and the Welfare State in the Open Economy

The challenges discussed so far came as external macroeconomic shocks that could, in principle, be met by a standard set of macroeconomic policy responses, which in some countries could be adopted within existing institutional structures and in others required institutional changes in the industrial relations system. By contrast, the international challenges that came to the foreground in the 1990s had been building up slowly over the preceding decades, and some countries had begun to respond to them even in the 1970s. Even more important, while the external macroeconomic shocks of the 1970s and 1980s had affected all industrialized economies in more or less the same way, the changes of the international economic environment that came to a head in the 1990s manifested themselves as very different challenges in different countries, depending on the structural characteristics of their economies and even more so on the policy legacies that had shaped national employment systems and welfare states. For the same reason, it is now no longer possible to identify a standard set of optimal policy responses, and then to discuss the factors that did or did not allow individual countries to adopt these. Instead, it will be necessary to identify potentially effective responses for groups of countries facing similar challenges. But what were these challenges?

By the second half of the 1980s, oil prices had returned almost to pre-crisis levels, inflation was under control, real dollar interest rates had receded from their 1984 peak to more moderate—but still comparatively high—levels, and most industrial economies were recovering from the decade of external macroeconomic shocks. Nevertheless, by the early 1990s these same economies were again in a deep recession, with low or negative real growth (Table A.2), and a new peak of unemployment that was significantly higher than in the early 1980s (Table A.4). On the face of it, this was a stabilization recession, exacerbated by the fact that it occurred in many countries more or less simultaneously. The general economic upturn in the second half of the 1980s had let inflation rates creep up again (Table A.3), and monetarist central banks lost no time to respond with rising interest rates (Table A.29). In addition, there had been credit-financed real estate and consumption bubbles in Japan, the United Kingdom, Australia, New Zealand, and Sweden, which provoked particularly radical monetary responses in these countries. And then there was the fall of the Berlin Wall, and the German government's initial decision to finance unification through deficit spending rather than through tax increases—which initially boosted the west German and other west European economies, but deepened the recession in EMS-Europe when the Bundesbank responded by raising interest rates and tightening the money supply. In Europe, moreover, recovery was delayed by the Maastricht Treaty and its obligation to reduce public sector deficits in order to meet the criteria for membership in the European Monetary Union.

In short, there are good macroeconomic explanations for the general economic slowdown in the early 1990s, and for the particularly severe problems of particular countries. At the same time, however, the international economic environment in which countries were dealing with these seemingly conventional problems had been in a process of transformation that reached its culmination in the 1990s as well. By now, the international integration of product and capital markets, which had been increasing throughout the postwar decades, again surpassed the level that capitalist economies had once achieved before World War I (Dicken 1992; Hirst and Thompson 1995; Bairoch 1997; McKeown 1999; Simmons 1999). The result has been greatly increased competition in product markets and much higher capital mobility. Moreover, by the mid-1980s the fiscal constraints arising from capital-market integration combined with rising levels of social spending to create serious challenges to the financial viability of existing welfare-state programs. It is the ability of countries to adjust to these changes which has come to determine the economic viability of advanced welfare states.

2.5.1 Increasing Economic Integration

The process of economic integration was accelerated through a series of political decisions and political events, such as the fall of the Berlin Wall and the return of central and eastern Europe to the capitalist world, the increasing scope and effectiveness of the world-wide free-trade regime represented by the transition from the GATT to the WTO, the successful implementation of the 1992 Single-Market program in the European

Community, the rapid diffusion of policies deregulating and privatizing telecommunications, air, road and rail transport and other infrastructure functions and, perhaps most important, the wholesale liberalization and deregulation of financial markets even in those countries that had heavily relied on exchange controls and the *dirigiste* allocation of credit until the early 1980s.[21] In Europe, moreover, membership in the EMS and the subsequent commitment to create a European Monetary Union had created a common monetary environment that imposed increasingly tight constraints on autonomous national fiscal-policy choices as well. The cumulative result of these politically induced changes of the international economic environment were greatly intensified competition in product markets and greatly increased capital mobility.

On the whole, however, the countries included in our project were quite successful in defending their overall shares in the international markets for goods and services (Table A.33). What mattered more was that the removal of tariff and non-tariff barriers, and in Europe the prospect of monetary union, greatly increased the international mobility of real capital, and that the liberalization of financial markets also increased opportunities for avoiding and evading taxes on capital incomes (Ganghof, Volume II). In parallel to the greater spatial mobility of real and financial capital, there was also an increase in the 'functional mobility' (Watson 1999) between different types of capital assets: from the ownership of real estate, industrial property and physical objects through secured credit, portfolio investments in tradable government and industrial bonds and company stock, all the way to hedging and purely speculative investments in currencies, raw materials, bonds and stocks futures and index contracts, and in an increasing variety of financial 'derivatives' that are even further removed from transactions in the 'real' economy (Scitowski 1998).

These 'secondary' money markets are absorbing an increasing volume of capital that is driven by expectations of speculative gains, and that may never 'touch down' in the sense of ultimately being used to finance productive investments. The result, it is claimed, is a capital shortage in the real economy that upsets the balance between demand and supply in the labor market (Watson 1999: 65). In any case, the level of profitability that is required to justify business investments seems to rise even in periods when real interest rates are relatively low.

---

[21] According to an indicator of capital-exchange liberalization constructed by Dennis Quinn on the basis of IMF data, the maximum score of 14 was reached by only one country—Germany—in 1970, whereas eleven of 20 OECD countries had scores below ten. By 1993, only one country—Greece—still scored below ten, and nine countries now had scores of 14 (Table A.31).

One reason is that patterns that are characteristic of the Anglo-American model of capitalism are also appearing in Continental and Scandinavian countries. Business investment is less easily financed by long-term credit from 'house banks' or by 'patient' equity capital; instead, large projects must meet the profitability benchmarks of highly mobile institutional investors and their professional analysts for whom the whole world is a potential site for real, portfolio, or speculative investments. For corporations, moreover, the pressure to increase profits—and, even more, the expectation of future profits—is also related to the fact that a high market capitalization provides some protection against hostile takeovers. Conversely, there is reason to think that the present surge of mergers, acquisitions and divestments, in manufacturing as well as in financial services, in communications as well as in the media or in retail marketing, is driven not only by the gains in technical efficiency and market power that are generally associated with bigness and specialization, but also by the incentives for managers and investment bankers that are associated with successful takeover bids. In short, internationally integrated and competitive capital markets are adding their own impulses to the pressures of competition in product markets.

As a consequence of these cumulative changes in the international economic and legal environment, national governments and national labor unions are no longer able to rely on the protective barriers that facilitated the achievement of their policy goals in the postwar decades. That is not to say that they have lost all capacity to pursue the welfare goals they had chosen in the postwar decades, but it does imply that these goals must again be pursued within the constraints of international capitalism; and it suggests that, in contrast to the 1970s and early 1980s, a capacity for macroeconomic coordination and union wage restraint is no longer sufficient for coping with the new challenges. What matters more is now the shape of the welfare state itself. But before it is possible to discuss the greater or lesser vulnerability of different countries, it is necessary to specify more precisely the mechanisms through which the pursuit of employment, social security and social equality goals is constrained by economic internationalization. In the following subsections, I will focus on the two areas that are most directly affected: private sector employment and the financial viability of the welfare state.

2.5.2 Implications for Private Sector Employment

In the course of the last two decades, the international product markets served by advanced industrial economies have changed in two respects. On the one hand, lower-cost competition from newly-industrializing and central and eastern European countries is forcing producers in high-cost countries to automate production or to specialize in 'upmarket' industrial products of high technical or esthetic quality, and in highly productive services. Assuming that wages and non-wage labor costs are downward inflexible, skill requirements will rise, and demand for unskilled workers will shrink as a consequence.[22] At the same time, and of greater practical importance, competition among advanced industrial countries has also become more intense, contributing to the greater volatility of increasingly specialized markets for 'diversified quality production' (Streeck 1997). Hence employment in internationally exposed sectors of the economy can be maintained only through continuous product and process innovations that reduce the costs of production and/or improve the quality of products and their flexible adaptation to the volatile demand in specialized market niches (Streeck 1999). In other words, international competition will necessarily drive up productivity in those firms that are able to survive—which in the aggregate will limit employment opportunities even in those countries that are doing well in the international markets. In fact, employment rates in those sectors of the economy that are exposed to international competition[23] have declined practically everywhere in the advanced industrial countries since the early 1970s (Table A.8). Employment gains were achieved only in the sheltered branches of ISIC 6 and 9: that is, in 'wholesale and retail trade, restaurants and hotels' and in 'community, social, and personal services' (Table A.10).

In the exposed sectors, firms have become price takers, and among the member states of the European Monetary Union governments have also lost the option of correcting a loss of international competitiveness through adjustments of the exchange rate. As a consequence, above-average cost increases can no longer be passed on to consumers. At the same time, firms are now facing investors who are no longer limited to national investment opportunities but will compare—post tax!—rates of return achieved by real or portfolio investments with benchmarks defined by the most profitable investment opportunities available internationally. Moreover, the resulting pressures are felt not only in the exposed sectors of the economy, but also in sheltered branches supplying local goods and services to internationally exposed firms, as well as in capital-intensive branches providing services that are locally produced and consumed.

[22] Given these conditions, the dispute about the major cause of the deteriorating position of low-skilled workers—technical change or competition from low-wage countries—seems quite pointless. If low-wage competition does not displace production in high-wage countries, it will speed up productivity-increasing technical change.

[23] Since competition works at the margin, we have chosen to define employment in production and in production-related services—ISIC 1–5, 7, and 8—as being 'exposed', regardless of the degree of 'openness' of the economy in question.

As a consequence, private sector firms are now much less able and willing to cross-subsidize less profitable lines of production, or less productive jobs. Instead, and most obviously within the European Monetary Union, each product—and in the extreme, each job—must now earn its full costs of production plus an adequate rate of return on capital at internationally uniform prices. For governments and unions that implies that the employment risks associated with strategies aiming at the 'de-commodification of labor' (Esping-Andersen 1990) have greatly increased. Solidaristic union wages, government minimum-wage legislation, social policies raising the reservation wage of unemployed job seekers, and taxes and regulations imposing non-wage labor costs—all of these are now more likely than before to entail job losses. Obviously, these risks will most affect service jobs whose productivity cannot easily be increased, and hence the employment opportunities of less skilled workers. In short, it is now generally more difficult than before to instrumentalize private sector employment relations for the achievement of egalitarian welfare goals. If such purposes were in the past pursued through collective bargaining and government regulations of employment conditions—for example, arbitration awards in Australia that were meant to provide a 'living wage' for a family of five—their continuing realization has come to depend to a larger degree on the formal welfare state and the tax system. These options, however, are also constrained by the impact of economic internationalization on welfare state revenue.

2.5.3 Implications for the Financial Viability of Welfare States

In the average OECD country, the share of taxes and social security contributions in GDP has risen steeply until the mid-1980s, but stagnated thereafter (Table A.23). In Italy, Switzerland, and Denmark, it is true, total tax revenue continued to increase, and in the United Kingdom it declined somewhat, but otherwise, annual figures seem to fluctuate at about the level reached in the mid-1980s. Remarkably, moreover, differences between countries have remained about as high as before, with Australia collecting about 30 percent of GDP, Switzerland, the United Kingdom, New Zealand, and Germany clustering around or above 35 percent, the Netherlands, Italy, Austria, France, and Belgium around or above 45 percent, and Denmark and Sweden above 50 percent. In other words, there seems to be no convergence over time. Instead, the stagnation of tax revenues seems to have had more or less the same constraining effect on Scandinavian high-tax countries, Anglo-Saxon low-tax countries and the Continental welfare states with their intermediate levels of taxation.

In order to understand this pattern, we must consider the upward as well as the downward pressures on public sector revenue. The upward pressures that had increased tax burdens everywhere in the 1970s and early 1980s have not, of course, abated thereafter. Unemployment, early retirement, pensions and health care for an aging population, poverty, and rising demands on education and on business-oriented infrastructure—all would under earlier circumstances have required, and justified, further increases of taxation. As for the downward pressures, the usual suspects are governments competing for revenue from internationally mobile tax bases—in particular from corporate profits and capital interest—and for internationally mobile investments and production. As a result, most countries have significantly cut nominal tax rates on capital incomes since the mid-1980s (Ganghof, Volume II). However, as is frequently pointed out in the literature, one nevertheless cannot observe a general 'race to the bottom' of *effective* rates of capital taxation (Garrett 1998; Quinn 1997; Swank 1998).[24] Instead, countries that cut their top rates have generally tried to defend their revenue position by simultaneously broadening the tax base. Even though the generally assumed superiority of that solution is open to challenge,[25] countries seem to have been pushed toward it by the disadvantages associated with the alternative courses of action among which they would have had to choose if revenue from mobile sources were significantly reduced. These alternatives include increasing public sector deficits, reductions of public expenditures, and a shift from mobile to less mobile bases of taxation. Closer inspection reveals, however, that each of these options is confronted with obstacles or associated with negative side effects that reduce their feasibility or attractiveness (Ganghof, Volume II).

Deficit spending had increased in most countries during the 1970s, and even though it was continued in the 1980s, its budgetary costs increased dramatically with the rise of real interest rates. In the 1990s, the Maastricht criteria for membership in the European Monetary Union had the effect of foreclosing the deficit option for most European welfare states, and under conditions of high capital mobility other countries also tried to demonstrate their fiscal conservatism in order to avoid paying high risk premia on their public debt and speculative runs on their currencies. In short, sustained deficit spending was no longer considered viable in the 1990s (Table A.22). At the same time, however, significant cuts in public expenditures were difficult to adopt in multi-party and corporatist political systems with multiple veto actors, and they were also difficult in Westminster-type two-party systems where the governing party had to

[24] On the difficulties of empirical confirmation or falsification, see Ganghof (Volume II).
[25] The elimination of tax exemptions could reduce the *relative* attractiveness of real as compared to portfolio investments (Sinn 1989).

fear negative electoral reactions to significant and visible cuts in welfare benefits (Pierson 1994, 1996). In most cases, therefore, massive expenditure cuts were not, and are not, a solution that governments could pursue without incurring heavy political costs.[26] That leaves the option of shifting the burden to less mobile tax bases. Among these, the ones with the largest revenue potential are taxes on consumption, social security contributions, and taxes on income from labor, all of which are relatively immune to international tax competition;[27] but, unfortunately, they may have negative impacts on employment. It seems worthwhile to consider these in some detail.

2.5.3.1 The Employment Effects of Taxation As one should expect, neoliberal rhetoric notwithstanding, the statistical association between the *total* burden of taxes and social security contributions, measured as a share of GDP, and *total* employment, measured as a share of the working-age population, is very weak ($R^2 = 0.10$). In fact, Denmark, the country with the highest tax burden, does as well as or better in employment terms than the lowest-tax economies of the United States and Japan (Fig. 2.1). Among the twelve countries covered by our project, the highest employment rates are achieved by low-tax Switzerland together with high-tax Denmark and Sweden, while the low-tax Anglo-Saxon countries have intermediate and the remaining moderate-tax Continental countries have the lowest employment scores (Table A.5).

Even though *total* taxation does not seem to have an influence on *total* employment, it seems plausible to search for causal effects by examining differences in the structure of employment as well as differences in the structure of taxation. On the employment side, the first distinction is between public and private sector employment. As is to be expected, there is a positive association between the total tax burden and government employment rates (Fig. 2.2). The relationship is not very strong, however ($R^2 = 0.38$) and a closer inspection of the scattergram suggests that it would disappear altogether if Sweden, Denmark, and Norway[28] were left out of the picture. Apparently, it is only these highly developed Scandinavian welfare states that have systematically translated high tax

---

[26] But, obviously, political constellations do matter: Margaret Thatcher in the 1980s and the conservatives in New Zealand in the 1990s faced a divided opposition that could not win under plurality election rules; and in the Netherlands, welfare cuts were adopted by inclusive coalition governments (Green-Pedersen 1999a).

[27] For the value-added tax, that is true as long as it is raised according to the 'country of destination' principle, by which exports are exempted and imports taxed at the domestic rate.

[28] The Norwegian position is influenced by the availability of oil revenues which do not count as taxes.

Total employment as % of pop. 15–64

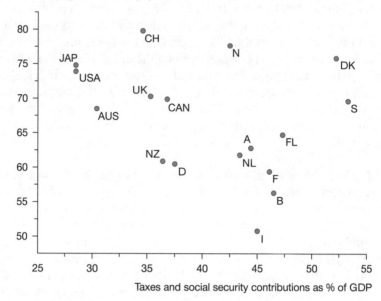

Figure 2.1 Total tax burden and total employment, 1997

Sources: OECD, *Revenue Statistics* (Paris: OECD, 1997); OECD, *Economic Outlook* (Paris, 1997).

revenues into high levels of publicly financed social services, whereas Continental countries tend to cluster below the regression line. By contrast, the expected negative association between total taxation and business employment (Fig. 2.3) appears to be much stronger ($R^2 = 0.62$) but again Denmark and Sweden are doing better, and Continental countries are generally doing less well, than would be expected on the basis of relative tax burdens.

Private sector employment, however, includes diverse branches whose sensitivity to tax burdens may differ considerably. One theoretically meaningful distinction is between employment in those branches that are or are not actually or potentially exposed to international competition i.e. primary and secondary production-related services, such as transport, communications, financial and business services (ISIC 1–5) and (7+8). Contrary to widespread assumptions about international competitiveness, there is practically no statistical association ($R^2 = 0.12$) between the overall tax burden and employment in the exposed sectors (Fig. 2.4). It is also remarkable that both high-tax countries like Denmark and Sweden and medium-tax countries like Austria and Germany have more jobs in the

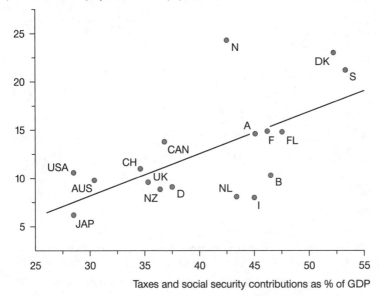

Figure 2.2 Total tax burden and public sector employment, 1997

Sources: OECD, *Revenue Statistics* (Paris: OECD, 1997); OECD, *Economic Outlook* (Paris: OECD, 1997).

exposed sectors of the private economy than is true of the United States, one of the two countries with the lowest tax burden (Table A.8). The conclusion seems to be that employment in those branches which are facing international competition is relatively insensitive to the overall tax burden.

By implication, that suggests that the strongly negative impact of tax burdens on business employment represented by Fig. 2.3 must primarily affect employment in the consumption-oriented private services that are domestically produced and consumed. In the OECD statistics, these services are included in ISIC 6 (wholesale and retail trade, restaurants, and hotels) and ISIC 9 (community, social and personal services). But since the latter category includes both public and private sector jobs, and jobs with high labor productivity (in health care, education, and the media, for instance) as well as jobs with low labor productivity, data on employment in ISIC 6 should provide a clearer test for the causal effect of taxation on employment in domestic service branches with low average labor productivity (Fig. 2.5). It is in fact strongly negative ($R^2 = 0.62$). Yet, again, there are interesting differences, with Denmark and Austria as positive, and Belgium, France, Italy, and Germany as negative outliers.

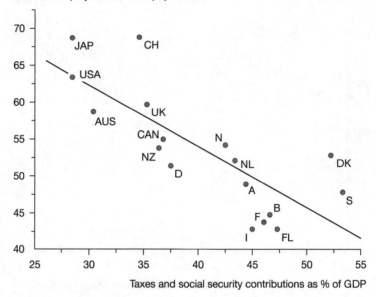

Figure 2.3 Total tax burden and private sector employment, 1997

Sources: OECD, *Revenue Statistics* (Paris: OECD, 1997); OECD, *Economic Outlook* (Paris: OECD, 1997).

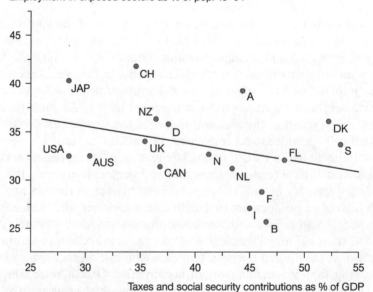

Figure 2.4 Total tax burden and employment in sectors ISIC 1–5, 7, and 8, 1997

Sources: OECD, *Revenue Statistics* (Paris: OECD, 1997); OECD, *Labour Force Statistics* (Paris: OECD, 1997).

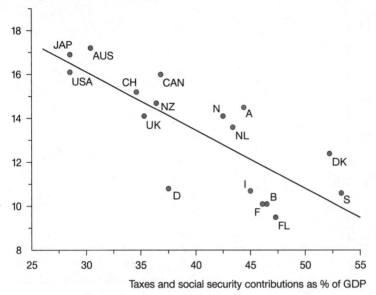

Figure 2.5 Total tax burden and private sector employment, 1997

Sources: OECD, *Revenue Statistics* (Paris: OECD, 1997); OECD, *Labour Force Statistics* (Paris: OECD, 1997).

Thus, the next question is whether differences in tax structures may explain some of the observed variance in negative employment effects. If we distinguish between three major blocks of revenue—personal and corporate income taxes (Table A.24), consumption taxes (Table A.25) and social security contributions (Table A.26)—it appears that the high-tax Scandinavian welfare states as well as the low-tax Anglo-Saxon countries are primarily relying on personal and corporate income taxes for their revenue, whereas in most of the Continental welfare states social security contributions provide the lion's share of revenue. There is less of a clear pattern for consumption taxes.

Considering private sector employment as a whole, one might conclude from current policy debates that taxes on corporate and personal incomes, which are thought to depress private demand and discourage business investments, should have the strongest negative effect. Remarkably, however, this expectation is again not supported by the data (Fig. 2.6). There is no statistical association ($R^2 = 0.07$) between business employment and the GDP share of personal and corporate income taxes. That leaves social security contributions and consumption taxes which, because they are relatively immune to international tax competition, are generally considered

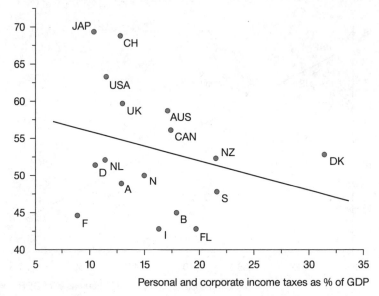

Figure 2.6 Income taxes and business employment, 1997

Sources: OECD, *Revenue Statistics* (Paris: OECD, 1997); OECD, *Economic Outlook* (Paris: OECD, 1997).

the most promising targets of burden-shifting policies. Taken separately, each of these has a moderately negative effect on overall business employment as well as on employment in ISIC 6. In combination, they have strong negative effects on business employment in general (Fig. 2.7) as well as on ISIC-6 employment (Fig. 2.8), with R-squares of 0.49 and 0.58, respectively.

The interpretation of these patterns is straightforward. Employment in those sectors that are exposed to international competition—manufacturing, but also to transport, communications or financial services—is little affected by the overall tax load, since high productivity allows the burden to be shifted to workers whose relatively high take-home pay is reduced accordingly. By contrast, market-clearing wages in the less productive services might be at or near the level of social assistance benefits that define the lowest reservation wage in advanced welfare states. Hence the cost of taxes and social security contributions levied on such jobs cannot be shifted to employees but would have to be borne entirely by the employer, with the consequence that such services may be priced out of price-elastic markets.

The same argument explains the variation in the impact of different types of taxation. Consumption taxes reduce demand for all products, but they fall most heavily on services whose low productivity makes them vulnerable to automation on the one hand, and to self-service (Gershuny 1978) or tax evasion on the other hand.[29] Similarly, social security contributions are usually, but with a growing number of exceptions,[30] raised as a proportional tax on total wages, with a cap at medium wage levels. Hence they fall heavily on low-wage jobs, while the burden on highly

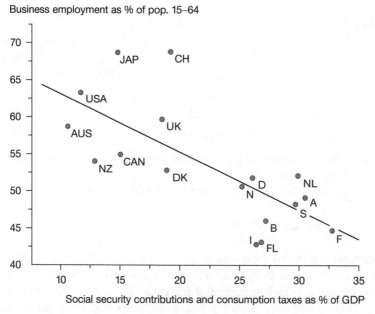

Figure 2.7 Social security plus consumption taxes and business employment, 1997

Sources: OECD, *Revenue Statistics* (Paris: OECD, 1997); OECD, *Economic Outlook* (Paris: OECD, 1997).

[29] As a consequence, the European Commission is recommending a reduction of VAT rates on a range of less productive services, and several EU member states have begun to do so (Directive 1999/85/EC).

[30] In the Netherlands, the major part of social security contributions was integrated into the income-tax schedule after 1990. Thus employee contributions are collected only on incomes above the basic exemption of 8,700 guilder per year and at the lowest rate of the income tax schedule. In addition, since 1994 the remaining employers' contributions have been practically eliminated for workers earning up to 115% of the full-time adult minimum wage. France, Austria, and Belgium have also reduced payroll taxes on low-paid workers, and in the United Kingdom employers' social security contributions are progressive above a basic exemption (OECD 1999e; OECD 1999d: 121).

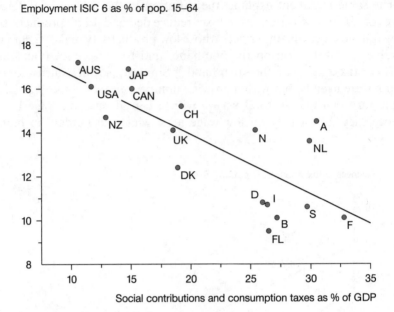

Figure 2.8 Social contributions plus consumption taxes and private service employment, 1997

Sources: OECD, *Revenue Statistics* (Paris: OECD, 1997); OECD, *Labour Force Statistics* (Paris: OECD, 1997).

productive and highly paid jobs is relatively smaller. By contrast, personal income taxes are not collected on wages below a basic-income exemption, and since their rates are generally progressive, taxes on the income elements that exceed the exemption begin at lower rates. Thus, the burden of income taxes on the cost of low-wage jobs and part-time jobs tends to be minimal, and while they may have some effect on the ability of firms to attract high-wage professionals from low-tax countries, their negative impact on business employment is much weaker than is true of consumption taxes and social contributions.

2.5.3.2 Wage Differentiation and Employment Protection Tax levels and tax structures are surely not the only factors having a negative impact on employment in the private services. Government minimum wage legislation and solidaristic union wage policies may also have the effect of raising the labor costs of less productive services above the market-clearing level (Iversen and Wren 1998). The best available indicator is the D5:D1 ratio of earnings in the median decile to earnings in the lowest-decile of the

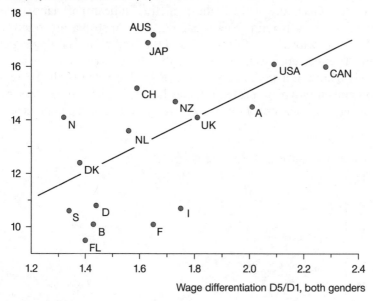

Figure 2.9 D5/D1 wage differentiation (1994/1995) and private service employment, 1997

Sources: OECD, *Labour Force Statistics* (Paris: OECD: June 1996); OECD, *Labour Force Statistics* (Paris: OECD, 1997).

wage distribution for both genders (Table A.21). While the association between this indicator of wage differentiation and private-service employment is positive (Fig. 2.9), it is not very strong ($R^2 = 0.29$). Nevertheless, it may help to explain some of the outlier positions in Fig. 2.8. Thus, the fact that Austria has more ISIC-6 jobs than is explained by the tax factors may indeed be related to the fact that, for both genders,[31] the D5:D1 ratio is higher in Austria than in any other country included in our project.

A second factor which is often assumed to have a negative impact on service employment is the difficulties, and the costs, associated with hiring and firing, which are thought to prevent employers from responding flexibly to uncertain increases of demand (OECD 1994). The OECD attempted to capture these differences in a synthetic index integrating various dimensions of 'employment protection legislation' (EPL) in a single

---

[31] For men, the D5/D1 wage differentiation in Austria was 1.67 in 1994: still higher than in the Scandinavian and other Continental countries, but somewhat below the UK and New Zealand, and far below the United States. In other words, the employment effect seems to be mainly due to lower wages for typical 'women jobs' in retail trade, hotels, and restaurants.

rank ordering (Table A.34). Of the countries included in our project, Italy, France, and Germany score highest on this indicator of labor market rigidities, whereas Britain, New Zealand, and Australia are rated most flexible, with Switzerland, Denmark, and the Netherlands following close behind. As expected, the association with ISIC-6 employment is negative (Fig. 2.10), but it is also not very strong ($R^2 = 0.39$). Thus, while wage dispersion and employment protection may help to explain some of the residuals in Fig. 2.8, their impact is not as strong as that of the tax factor.[32]

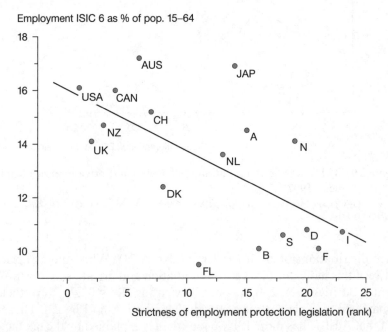

Figure 2.10 Strictness of employment protection and private service employment, 1997

Sources: OECD, *Employment Outlook* (Paris: OECD, June 1999); OECD, *Labour Force Statistics* (Paris: OECD, 1997).

We can thus conclude that economic integration creates strong but partly contradictory pressures on welfare states that are committed to the values of full employment, social security, and equality. Employment in the exposed sectors of the economy is eroding and becoming less stable as a consequence of more intense competition in product markets and of the

---

[32] In a multivariate analysis including all three factors, only the effects of social security plus consumption taxes on ISIC-6 employment turned out to be statistically significant. But the signs of the other two factors were in the expected direction.

rising profit requirements of mobile capital. These same factors also constrain the ability of governments to tax profits and factors of production; they have practically destroyed the power of unions to change the functional distribution of incomes in favor of labor; and they have greatly reduced the capacity of governments and unions to equalize primary incomes through minimum-wage legislation and solidaristic wage settlements. At the same time, however, efforts to raise welfare-state revenue through higher taxes on those bases that are not internationally mobile, in particular consumption taxes and social-security contributions, are particularly damaging to those segments of private sector employment which, in general, have shown the greatest potential for expansion in recent decades.

But while fiscal constraints are tightening, high unemployment and the greater inequality of primary incomes are increasing the demands on the social-security and equalizing functions of the welfare state. Moreover, most countries also face rising expenditures for pensions and health care that had nothing to do with economic internationalization and competition, resulting instead from falling birth rates, increasing longevity and the rising health costs of an older population. Confronted with these rising demands on the welfare state, even countries like the United Kingdom and New Zealand, that have converted to radical versions of the neo-liberal creed, have not yet been very successful in reducing the total tax burden (Table A.23). Instead, countervailing pressures seem to have immobilized levels of taxation in all countries since the mid-1980s, and there is no reason to think that low-tax countries should be less constrained than high-tax countries.

But these simultaneous pressures on employment and on welfare-state finance are affecting countries that have very different patterns of employment and of welfare-state finance and benefits. Hence countries differ greatly in the extent to which the continuing achievement of their welfare-state goals—which also differ—is vulnerable to the pressures and constraints of an internationalizing economy, and they also differ greatly in their institutional capacity to adopt and implement effective policy responses to the specific challenges which each of them is facing.

2.6 Differing Vulnerabilities, Agendas, and Institutional Capabilities

If all countries were unique, however, comparison would serve no useful purpose. For the 1970s and the 1980s, it was possible to identify groups of countries facing roughly the same challenges because their primary responses to the external macroeconomic shocks—reflation or deflation;

devaluation or hard currency—were similar. For the 1990s, there is no such challenge-defining basic choice among master strategies, just as there are no theoretically first-best solutions comparable to 'Keynesian concertation' in the 1970s. However, since it is the structure of national employment systems and welfare states through which the impact of increasing competition in product markets and capital mobility is mediated, we find it useful to refer to Esping-Andersen's (1990) distinction of three different 'families' of welfare for grouping countries that had to face similar challenges in the 1990s.[33] These have been variously labeled as 'Scandinavian' or 'social-democratic', 'Anglo-Saxon' or 'Beveridgean' or 'liberal', and 'Continental' or 'Bismarckian' or 'christian-democratic'. As the country chapters in Volume II have shown, not all of these labels fit all of the countries in each group. In particular, Switzerland is more 'liberal' than other Continental countries, and I will discuss it in the context of the Anglo-Saxon group, even though it also does not fit perfectly there.

In the following sections, I will begin by describing the common characteristics of employment and welfare-state structures in each group and the specific challenges to which these have become exposed in the 1990s, and I will conclude by a discussion of the institutional characteristics that have facilitated or impeded effective policy responses to these challenges. For EU member states, one might think that the multi-level characteristics of European policymaking should also be discussed here. However, while Europe has played a major role in promoting the internationalization of product markets and investment choices, it has not yet assumed a major role in coping with the problems created thereby (Scharpf 1999).

2.6.1 Scandinavian Welfare States

Sweden and Denmark are generally considered exemplary manifestations of the Scandinavian or 'social-democratic' welfare state. Yet their trajectory through the last three decades has been quite different. For one thing, Sweden became relatively poorer, starting in 1970 from 78 percent of the US level in purchasing-power-parities (PPP) per capita, and falling to 69 percent by 1997, whereas Denmark became richer, starting at 72 percent and reaching 83 percent by 1997 (Table A.1). Also, Denmark has been

---

[33] To check the continuing plausibility of these groups, I did a series of cluster analyses on the twelve countries in this project. Based on the latest available data for total employment rates, government employment rates, female participation rates, GDP shares of total taxation, total social expenditure, social security contributions, and D5/D1 wage differentials, different clustering algorithms consistently generated the following three clusters: (1) Sweden and Denmark; (2) Australia and New Zealand, the United Kingdom and, at somewhat greater distance, Switzerland; and (3) Austria and France, Germany and the Netherlands with Belgium, and Italy at some greater distance to both subgroups.

struggling with relatively high unemployment ever since the mid-1970s, whereas Sweden was able to defend full employment until the early 1990s. Structurally, however, the similarities are indeed very striking.

2.6.1.1 Employment Structures and Policy Legacies Both countries have very high total employment rates (Table A.5) and very high female employment (Table A.12). Since business employment is about at the OECD average (Table A.7), these characteristics are produced by public sector employment rates that are almost twice as high as the OECD average (Tables A.6). They, in turn, are due to exceptionally high employment in publicly provided services for the aged, for the sick, for the handicapped and for families with small children, which in other welfare states are either performed outside of the formal labor market by women in the family or provided by commercial services and private charities (Table A.28). This Scandinavian departure from common employment patterns had begun in the high-growth period of the 1960s. Thus it was not resource-constrained initially, and then was driven by a positive-feedback mechanism where the expansion of social services allowed housewives to enter the labor market, and at the same time created new jobs which women could fill. Politically, therefore, families benefiting as consumers as well as providers of social services became the constituency supporting the high levels of taxation that were necessary to finance further expansion. The fact that expansion slowed down and came to a halt in 1980s could be explained as a 'growth to limits' effect (Flora 1986) since female participation in the labor force had by then risen to more than 80 percent in Sweden and was almost as high in Denmark.

In the exposed sectors of the economy, employment rates in the early 1970s were significantly above the OECD average in Sweden, and about average in Denmark (Table A.8). In the meantime, Swedish rates have declined to the OECD average, whereas Denmark has risen above that level. In the sheltered sectors, employment rates in Sweden and Denmark have been and are considerably above the OECD average (Table A.10) as a consequence of their high public sector employment. To assess their position in the sheltered-sector *private* services, data on ISIC-6 employment—wholesale and resale trade, restaurants, hotels—must serve as a proxy (Table A.11). In this segment, both Sweden and Denmark have traditionally been below the OECD average—which is usually explained by the sensitivity of less productive services to the high Scandinavian tax wedge and to the effects of very low wage dispersion (Table A.21) and high minimum wages (Iversen and Wren 1998). However, whereas Swedish employment rates decreased by 11 percent between 1989 and 1997, the Danish rate increased by 15.9 percent during the same period—much faster than the OECD average. Part of that difference is surely explained by the greater depth of the Swedish recession in the early 1990s. But, as discussed above, the fact that Denmark relies to a much lesser degree than Sweden on social-security contributions for the financing of its welfare state (Table A.26) must also be part of this explanation.

The regulation of employment conditions is largely left to collective-bargaining agreements in Sweden and Denmark. Since union density is very high—74 percent in Denmark and 83 percent in Sweden in 1989—the coverage of these agreements is also high (Golden, Wallerstein, and Lange 1999: table 7.1); and since Swedish and Danish unions have been committed to very strong norms of equality, regulations of employment relationships tend to be uniform, and wage differentials are the lowest among OECD countries. Even though in Sweden the Rehn-Meidner model of solidaristic wage setting and active labor-market policy had been explicitly designed to speed the transition of workers from less productive firms and industries into more productive ones (Moene and Wallerstein 1999), employment protection legislation is very strict. In the OECD's synthetic EPL-indices, Sweden ranked twenty-second among 27 in protection against individual dismissals, whereas in Denmark labor market flexibility is almost as high as in the Anglo-Saxon countries, ranking sixth for individual dismissals and eighth for overall strictness (Table A.34). In the absence of active labor-market policies, Denmark was unable to prevent unemployment as effectively as Sweden had done, but it provides very generous—at least for low-paid workers—and long-term unemployment benefits which made it possible for unions to accept the lack of employment protection.

Total social spending is the highest among OECD countries, reaching a peak of 36.9 percent of GDP in Sweden in 1993 and of 32.4 percent in Denmark in 1994 (Tables A.27, A.27a). But if expenditures for social services for elderly and disabled persons and for families are counted separately—above 5 percent of GDP in Sweden and in Denmark, as compared with 1.36 percent in Germany, 1.14 percent in France, or 0.28 percent in Belgium (Table A.28)—it is clear that, even at its peak, the Scandinavian welfare state could not be considered excessively generous in providing social insurance benefits. Public or publicly mandated expenditures on health care and sickness benefits, for instance, are at or below the OECD average, and the same is true of pensions, where Sweden and Denmark spend less than Italy, Austria, France, Belgium, Switzerland, or Germany. In fact, the only area where Scandinavian social insurance could be called 'generous' is in expenditures on unemployment benefits and active labor market policies (OECD 1999f).

On the revenue side, it is clear that the overall burden of taxes and social security contributions is highest in the Scandinavian welfare states, amounting to 52.2 percent of GDP in Denmark in 1996 and to 53.3 percent in Sweden in 1997, as compared with 30.4 percent in Australia, 35.3 percent in the United Kingdom, 37.5 percent in Germany, and 46.1 percent in France (Table A.23). But since high Scandinavian taxes are in fact buying a high volume of social services and paying for a large number of jobs, they cannot, by themselves, be considered a problem in terms of either general welfare or employment. In fact, it cannot even be said that high Scandinavian taxes are crowding out a large volume of potentially more valuable private sector employment. As was shown above, employment in the exposed sectors was at or above the OECD average, and until the deep recession in the early 1990s, the Swedish rate of business employment was consistently above the OECD average, and Denmark is even now doing better than France, Austria, and Germany (Table A.7)—all of which have lower levels of taxation.

As shown above, one explanation of this favorable pattern seems to be a relatively employment-friendly tax structure which relies heavily on personal and corporate income taxes that generally have little negative effect on business employment (Fig. 2.6). In 1996–97, these amounted to 31.4. percent of GDP in Denmark, and 21.6 percent in Sweden, as compared with 10.5 percent in Germany and 8.9 percent in France (Table A.24).[34] Social-security contributions, by contrast, which have a strongly negative effect on private-service employment, play a minimal role in Denmark (1.8 percent of GDP in 1994), but have increased to a level of 17.7 percent in Sweden—almost as high as in France (Table A.26)—which may help to explain the recent decline of private-service employment in Sweden. Denmark, it is true, imposes relatively high taxes on goods and services, which in general have also a strongly negative impact on private-service employment: 17.1 percent of GDP in 1996, as compared with 12 percent in Sweden and 10.4 percent in Germany (Table A.25). But since a considerable part of this revenue comes from very high 'luxury taxes' on imported goods, the impact on the price of low-paid services is mitigated.

2.6.1.2 Challenges The basic structures and policy legacies of Scandinavian welfare states appear to be relatively robust against the pressures of economic internationalization. Since the tax structure is business friendly, the very high level of public sector employment does not exert strong downward pressures on private sector employment. As small open economies, both countries had been well adapted to competing in contested international product markets. The liberalization of capital

---

[34] Moreover, the Swedish 'dual income tax' system greatly reduces the tax burden on business profits, and Denmark has differentiated tax schedules favoring mobile capital assets (Ganghof, Volume II).

exchanges came late, however (Table A.31), and at least Sweden found it initially very difficult to deal with deregulated financial markets. Moreover, Sweden, with its large share of multinational companies, is more vulnerable to the relocation of industrial investments than the Danish economy, which is dominated by less mobile small and medium-sized enterprises. Thus, after a brief decline in the early 1990s, the rate of gross fixed capital formation returned to its pre-crisis level of about 20 percent in Denmark, whereas it fell from 22 percent of GDP in 1989 to 13.7 percent in 1997 in Sweden (Table A.30). By the same token, business employment in Denmark has returned to the pre-recession levels of about 53 percent, whereas in Sweden the decline continued, from 55.67 percent in 1990 to 47.8 percent in 1997 (Table A.7). The same difference between both countries can be observed in the employment rates of the exposed sectors (Table A.8).

While the much steeper initial decline in Sweden is explained by the policy failures discussed above, the reasons for the much slower recovery of private sector employment after the recession are not so obvious. In the exposed sectors, Swedish relative unit labor costs fell by almost 30 percent between 1990 and 1998, whereas in Denmark they actually increased by 11 percent in the same period (Table A.19). However, as the country chapter argues (Benner and Vad, Volume II), Denmark was lucky in the timing of expansionary fiscal impulses in the early 1990s, whereas Swedish governments were raising taxes and cutting expenditures in a successful effort to achieve fiscal consolidation at the bottom of the recession. Moreover, it seems plausible that recovery in Denmark benefited from having less rigid employment-protection rules than Sweden.[35] Since firms were able to reduce employment at less cost in the downswing, they would also be more ready to hire additional workers earlier in the upswing, even when they could not yet be sure of the durability of increasing demand. Arguably, employment dynamics in Denmark also benefited from the move toward a 'centralized decentralization' of wage negotiations at the end of the 1980s which, while asserting greater central control over average wage increases, was meant to allow a greater wage differentiation between skill groups and branches (Due *et al.* 1995; Iversen 1999).[36]

[35] Given the multiplicity of other factors influencing the labor markets of countries at widely differing stages of economic development, the OECD (1999c) study of employment protection legislation in 27 countries expectedly did not find very strong causal effects in cross-country regressions. However, the differences between Denmark and Sweden in dynamic performance indicators all point in the expected direction. From the late 1980s to the mid-1990s, Denmark had higher job turnover, more short-term employment spells, and higher unemployment inflows and outflows (OECD 1999c: chart 2.3).

[36] These effects do not show up in the OECD data on D5/D1 wage dispersion (Table A.21) as either changes over time or a difference between Denmark and Sweden. It is

In the sheltered sectors, the obvious challenge facing the Scandinavian welfare states is to maintain the exceptionally high levels of employment in the public services, and at the same time to improve the conditions for an expansion of private services. As for the first, the question is whether they are able to maintain high levels of taxation to finance both the provision of public services and expensive social transfers. However, the problem is not, or no longer, international tax competition and increasing capital mobility. These have been accommodated by the dual income tax in Sweden and by differentiated tax schedules in Denmark, which are precisely targeted to reduce the tax burden on the most mobile tax payers and tax bases (Ganghof, Volume II). The more salient question was, therefore, whether the very high level of taxes on non-mobile tax payers and bases could be politically sustained. As of now, the answer for Denmark seems positive. Total tax revenues fell only briefly, from 51.7 percent of GDP in 1988 to 48.7 percent in 1990, and then increased again to the all-time high of 52.2 percent by 1996 (Table A.23). Quite obviously, the generous Danish welfare state, providing not only universal social-security benefits but also high-quality social services for families with children and for the aged together with the concomitant public sector jobs, has succeeded in creating a large middle-class constituency supporting its continuation—which is reflected in the fact that in a 1999 poll 70 percent of Danish respondents said that they approved of paying high taxes (V. A. Schmidt, this Volume).

In Sweden, the recession-related fall in total revenue was much steeper—from 55.6 percent of GDP in 1990 to 49.6 percent in 1995—but so was the recovery to 53.3. percent by 1997. It was possible only because the social democrats, after their return to power in 1994, decided to fight the escalating public sector deficit—12.3 percent of GDP in 1993—by raising, rather than reducing, taxes at the bottom of the recession, mainly by increasing the share of social-security contributions from 14.4 percent of GDP in 1993 to 17.7 percent in 1997 (Table A.26). Whatever damage that policy may have done to private sector employment, it shows that political tax resistance was also not considered a binding constraint in Sweden. But tax increases alone would not have been sufficient to achieve the breathtaking consolidation of the budget, which moved from a deficit of 12.3 percent of GDP in 1993 to a surplus of 2.1 percent in 1998 (Table A.22). Also needed were changes in the level and structure of expenditures that would allow the Swedish welfare state, which was designed for conditions of full employment, to operate within its means under conditions of

possible, however, that greater differentiation among firms within the same branches and among workers in the same skill groups will not affect the overall distribution among wage deciles.

relatively high unemployment. By a wide variety of measures, described in the country chapter (Benner and Vad, Volume II), the replacement rates of social-security benefits have been reduced, waiting days introduced, and eligibility conditions tightened, without, however, altering the basic structure and philosophy of the Swedish model. In the process, total social expenditure was in fact reduced dramatically, from a peak of 36.9 percent of GDP in 1993 to 33.0 percent by 1995 (Tables A.27, A.27a), even though unemployment was at an all-time high during that period.

The one area where the aspirations of the pre-crisis model seem to have been more than marginally reduced is public sector employment. The rate of government employment has fallen continuously from 25.7 percent in 1990 to 21.2 percent in 1998 (Table A.6), mainly as a consequence of reduced central-government subsidies for regional and local social services. Even more significantly, the extreme fall of the total employment rate by 11.7 percentage points between 1990 and 1998 was only in part reflected in the rise of open unemployment, corresponding to a reduction of the employment rate by 4.6 percentage points. The larger part was absorbed by a fall of the labor-force participation rate by 6.5 percentage points, which was shared almost equally by men and women. In contrast to other countries, moreover, this was not due to a large increase of early retirement. In fact, participation rates of men and women between 55 and 64 have held up quite well during the 1990s (OECD 1999b: Statistical Annex B and C). Instead, large numbers of persons in their prime working age seem to have dropped out of the labor market, perhaps staying in educational institutions to avoid youth unemployment, perhaps choosing parental leave, or finding other alternative roles and sources of income.[37]

If that pattern should persist, Sweden may have to relax its exalted moral commitment to the values of the 'work society' (V. A. Schmidt, this volume). However, if the higher levels of unemployment and inactivity should be considered unacceptable, Sweden would either have to restore earlier levels of public sector employment or accept greater wage dispersion and more variable employment conditions in order to facilitate an expansion of less productive and lower paid private sector services (Iversen and Wren 1998; Iversen 1998a). Assuming that fiscal constraints will rule out the first option, the second does seem to strain the limits of the remarkably high institutional capacity for effective policy responses from which Sweden has benefited so far.

In Denmark, as we have seen, the fall in tax revenues was brief and has been made up again; total social spending increased with the rise of unem-

---

[37] The number of recipients of social assistance did increase steeply in the early 1990s; and they have practically no incentive to seek low-paid employment (Eardley *et al.* 1996; Buhr 1999).

ployment from 28.2 percent of GDP in 1989 to a peak of 32.6 percent in 1994, but began to fall thereafter; public sector deficits remained below 3 percent of GDP throughout the 1990s, and by 1997 the budget was in surplus. As in Sweden, fiscal consolidation was accompanied by reductions in replacement rates and tighter eligibility criteria for some welfare-state benefits which did not change the character of the system.[38] In contrast to Sweden, however, the public sector employment rate was barely reduced at all in the recession of the early 1990s; and it has risen to an all-time high of 23 percent in 1998 (Table A.6). While the total employment rate fell by 5.1 percentage points between 1989 and 1994, as compared with 11.1 percentage points in Sweden, almost all of that loss had been recovered by 1998. Nevertheless, labor force participation was 3.1 percentage points lower in 1998 than it was in 1990, even though unemployment rates declined from a peak of 12.1 percent in 1993 to 6.5 percent in 1998 (Table A.4). Conceivably, this is less a symptom of value changes than a consequence of 'activating' rules introduced in the early 1990s which reduced the maximum period of unemployment benefits from seven to five years and, more importantly, did require participation in labor market programs after the second year.

2.6.1.3 Capabilities   Having avoided the Swedish policy failures of the late 1980s and early 1990s, and given a policy legacy that was generally more favorable to employment in the private sector and in private services in particular, Denmark was not confronted with challenges that overtaxed the institutional capabilities of the public-policy and industrial-relations systems. After a brief episode of anti-tax politics in the early 1970s, public support, including the support of middle-class voters, for the welfare state became so manifest that expansion continued even under the bourgeois governments between 1982 and 1993 (Green-Pedersen 1999a). While that would not assure consensus on specific policy initiatives, it helped to dampen the ideological confrontation between social-democratic defenders and neo-liberal attackers of the welfare state that occurred elsewhere. What may have been more important, as the country chapter points out, is the fact that traditionally weak Danish governments were significantly strengthened by a change in institutional practices (Benner and Vad, Volume II). In the past, Denmark, like other multi-party systems, was governed either by a majority coalition that could easily be blocked by

---

[38] The replacement rate of unemployment benefits, for instance, remains extremely generous at 90% of previous earnings; but since the ceiling of maximum weekly payments has been reduced to about £350 per week, only workers with below-average wages remain fully protected. As a consequence, for most workers the pressures to seek new jobs have increased.

internal disagreement, or by minority governments that had to resign when they lost a vote in Parliament. Under the current rules, however, the government's defeat on a substantive issue is not treated as a vote of no confidence: it is free to try again with a new bill. Hence a politically skilled minority government can use its power as an agenda setter to gain majority support from ad hoc coalitions for a much wider variety of policy proposals than would be accessible to a firm coalition government (McKelvey 1976; Shepsle and Weingast 1987). The Danish industrial-relations system, in turn, was still not capable of practicing voluntary wage restraint under conditions of tight labor markets. But the new structures of 'centralized decentralization' seemed well suited to avoiding excessive wage pressure when confronted with the threat of unemployment under conditions of a non-accommodating monetary policy (Iversen 1998a, 1999). Moreover, the effective decentralization of collective bargaining facilitates adjustment to diverse and volatile conditions in international niche markets, and it also favors the expansion of private services in the sheltered sector.

In Sweden, governing capabilities have traditionally been much greater than in Denmark because of the hegemonic positions of the social democrats in the party system, and of LO in the industrial relations system (Korpi 1983; Esping-Andersen 1985) which had allowed a close coordination between government policy guided by a long-term strategic vision of social-democratic welfare capitalism, and union strategies guided by a 'solidaristic wage policy' committed to full employment and wage equality. While the ideological hegemony of social democracy and centralized industrial relations were eroding in the 1980s (Rothstein 1998b; Pestoff 1995), and could not prevent the coordination failures that caused the deep crisis of the early 1990s, they were still sufficient to facilitate consensual policy responses to this crisis. In comparison with some other countries, it appears particularly remarkable that the Swedish social democrats during their period in opposition between 1992 and 1994 still considered themselves so much the natural governing party that they were ready to work out the harsh cutbacks in welfare-state programs in cooperation with the conservative Bildt government (Hinnfors and Pierre 1998). It is also a credit to the continuing 'corporatist' orientations of unions that they were generally willing to accept these cutbacks as necessary and legitimate.

What was not acceptable to the union federations were recommendations by an expert commission which included proposals to extend the maximum period of temporary contracts and to allow local unions to negotiate agreements on hiring and firing criteria and working time that differed from centrally agreed rules. These proposals would have increased the differentiation and flexibility of employment conditions in ways which in Denmark had contributed to the greater resilience of employment in the recession, and to the rising number of private-service jobs. The social democrats, again in office after 1994, did enact a few of these recommendations, but then backed down in the face of fierce union opposition and mass demonstrations (Mahon 1998). In other words, the strong role of unions in Swedish corporatism, and the tight coupling between the social-democratic party and the central union federation, LO, which had been one of the most important 'power resources' of the Swedish labor movement (Korpi 1983), continued to give unions a veto over social-democratic policy choices.

Swedish unions had been willing to accept financial cutbacks that reduced the level, while maintaining the structure, of social-security transfers and social services on which their members had come to rely,[39] but they have so far been unwilling to accept policies that seem to violate deeply held norms of universalism and egalitarianism (Rothstein 1998b; V. A. Schmidt, this Volume). But while egalitarian wage policies were fully compatible with employment success when the macroeconomic challenges of the 1970s and 1980s could be met by *general* wage restraint (Swenson 1989), they constrain employment growth in the less productive private services (Iversen and Wren 1998). Apparently, Swedish unions are not interested in these less secure and less well paid jobs. They are committed to the norm of 'good jobs for everybody', in industry and in public services, and if there are not enough of these to match the supply of labor, active labor-market policies and welfare transfers with high replacement rates must fill the gap. For the same reasons, they are as opposed to Danish-type 'activation' measures, that would require recipients of unemployment benefits to accept lower-paid jobs, as they are to any liberalization of the very restrictive employment protection and temporary employment rules, even though replacement rates for unemployed workers with average wages are even more generous than in Denmark (Table A.34). Given the fact that Sweden still has very high levels of employment, and that open unemployment has been falling again in the second half of the 1990s, one surely cannot say that, with regard to the interests of their members, this is an irrational position. In any case, however, compared with the relative freedom of Danish governments to seek political support in various quarters for pragmatically plausible policy initiatives, the institutional capacity of the Swedish political system is constrained by a *de facto* veto of unions over a range of policy initiatives that were gaining in importance under the challenges of the 1990s (Vartiainen 1998; Iversen 1999).

---

[39] The loss of public sector jobs did not affect the core workforce of local and regional governments, and it was associated with a decline of part-time employment (Table A.14).

2.6.2 Anglo-Saxon Welfare States and Switzerland

The four countries which are discussed together here must appear as a heterogeneous group. For one thing, they include the two poorest countries and the richest country in our twelve-country project. Measured in PPP, New Zealand was down to 61 percent of the US GDP per capita in 1997, the United Kingdom did somewhat better at 69 percent, and Australia at 73 percent was still below the OECD average, whereas Switzerland at 88 percent was by far the richest country in our project (Table A.1). Nevertheless, while their actual welfare-state policies are quite different, both the Anglo-Saxon countries and Switzerland are appropriately described as being 'liberal' if the relatively small size of the 'state' is taken as the dominant criterion, and they also have similar employment structures.

2.6.2.1 Employment Structures and Policy Legacies Historically, Switzerland, Australia, and New Zealand were among the countries with the lowest tax burdens and the lowest GDP-shares of public expenditures on social transfers and social services, whereas in the United Kingdom, with its National Health Service, taxes and social expenditures were closer to the OECD average. In all four countries, social security transfers were at a low level, designed to provide a safety net protecting against poverty, rather than status-maintaining income replacement in cases of unemployment, sickness, disability and in old age. More complete insurance against these risks was considered an individual responsibility. If all four countries could nevertheless be considered advanced welfare states, it was because the state assumed responsibility for full employment which, given the bargaining power of organized labor, allow the male breadwinner to support a family and to make private provisions for the risks that were elsewhere covered by public insurance.

During the postwar decades, the way in which the state attempted to assure full employment differed greatly from country to country. In the United Kingdom, Keynesian macroeconomic management, constrained by recurrent balance of payments crises, was the main instrument of employment policy. Employment was also stabilized by the existence of an extensive range of nationalized industries and service branches. In Australia and New Zealand, full employment was maintained by extensive trade protection and state subsidies for import-substituting industrialization, and wages and employment conditions were regulated by the arbitration courts. In Switzerland, finally, trade protection was assured for agriculture and local services, while the size of the foreign workforce was regulated through the extension and restriction of temporary work permits. By the 1990s, however, these protective structures had disappeared.

In Britain, Keynesian full employment policies had been abandoned, and the nationalized industries had been closed down or privatized along with a wide range of public services and infrastructure facilities. In Australia and New Zealand, trade protection for inefficient industries had been removed; and deregulation and privatization had intensified competition in services as well. While agriculture was still protected in Switzerland, services had been liberalized and foreign workers could no longer serve as employment buffers.

As a consequence, none of these four countries was able to maintain full employment throughout, and Australia and New Zealand reached two-digit unemployment in at least two years, the United Kingdom did so in eight years, whereas for Switzerland even the rise of unemployment to much lower levels in the early 1990s came as a severe shock (Table A.4). New Zealand was in a particularly unfavorable position since the combination of aggressive unionism with the radical neo-liberal competition policy and the strictly non-accommodating monetary policy of the Labour government at the end of the 1980s had caused a deep fall of employment rates. While business employment picked up after 1992, when the new conservative government had passed legislation allowing individual wage contracting in place of wage setting by collective bargaining, the improvement was short-lived (Table A.7).

Nevertheless, by the mid-1990s, after the full-employment promise had been disappointed, the four countries still had the lowest GDP shares of social expenditure in our project, ranging from 15.7 percent in Australia to 22.5 percent in the United Kingdom, as compared with an OECD-18 average of 24 percent and a top rate of 33 percent in Sweden (Tables A.27, A.27a); and they also shared significant characteristics of their employment structures. Except for New Zealand, total employment rates in 1998 are above the OECD average of 66.5 percent, ranging from 68.2 percent in Australia and 70.3 percent in the UK to the OECD record of 79.8 percent in Switzerland. Moreover, and again with the exception of New Zealand, these rates are higher than in 1980 and as high as or higher than in 1970—which is also true for Denmark, but not for any other country in our project (Table A.5). At the same time, all four countries have rates of female participation which are higher than those in all Continental countries, and in the case of Switzerland even higher than in Denmark (Table A.12). But whereas the high Scandinavian rates are primarily due to extremely high employment in the public social services, the rates of government employment are below the OECD average in all four countries and have recently declined further except in Switzerland (Table A.6). Instead, and once more with the exception of New Zealand, business employment rates have, against the OECD trend, increased during the last two decades and were in 1998 significantly above the OECD average, ranging from 58.7 percent in Australia to the OECD record of 68.8 percent in Switzerland (Table A.7). However, this success was not achieved in the exposed sectors of the economy, where employment rates in all four countries are now lower than they were in 1980 and, with the exception of Switzerland, not significantly above the OECD average (Table A.8). Obviously, the large losses in industrial employment (Table A.9) were not fully compensated by the rise in internationally exposed service branches—transport, communications, financial, and business services. While these trends are also true for Switzerland, the level of exposed-sector employment remains the highest among OECD countries, which is explained not only by the attractiveness of Swiss banks as a safe haven for footloose capital assets but also by the continuing competitiveness, in spite of high wages and a rising exchange rate, of Swiss high-quality manufacturing exports produced by a highly trained workforce in the context of cooperative industrial relations.

Even in Switzerland it is true, however, that the above-average performance in business employment was realized by the expansion of private services in the sheltered sectors—which, however, are difficult to identify in the available OECD employment statistics. It is clear that they must be located in the branches ISIC 6—'wholesale and retail trade, restaurants and hotels'—and ISIC 9—'community, social, and personal services'. For the reasons discussed above, data on ISIC-9 employment are hard to interpret, so I will again focus on ISIC-6 branches, where services are in general provided in the private sector and where employment rates in all four countries have increased since 1980, and are now above the OECD average, ranging from 14.1 percent in the UK to 17.2 percent in Australia in 1997 (Table A.11). It is here, therefore, that the rise of business employment in liberal countries must find part of its explanation.

In general, the productivity of service jobs in wholesale and retail trade, hotels and restaurants is relatively low, which means that economically viable market wages must also be low. In the literature, employment in less productive private services is therefore associated with relatively high wage dispersion in the lower half of the earnings scale (Iversen and Wren 1998; Esping-Andersen 1999, ch. 6). In fact, in 1994–5 and for both genders, the rate of median earnings (D5) to earnings in the lowest decile (D1) of the wage distribution was moderate to relatively high in all four countries: 1.59 in Switzerland, 1.65 in Australia, 1.73 in New Zealand and 1.81 in the UK, as compared with 1.34 in Sweden and 2.1 in the United States (Table A.21 and Fig. 2.9). However, only in the UK has there been a steep increase of the D5:D1 ratio—from 1.67 in 1980 to 1.81 in 1995—whereas wage dispersion in the other countries seems to have been remarkably stable over time. Contrary to theoretical expectations, however, the increase of ISIC-6 employment rates since 1980 is considerably higher in Australia and New Zealand than in the UK.

The high level of business employment in all four countries is also associated with a relatively low total tax burden, ranging from 30.4 percent of GDP in Australia in 1997 to 36.4 percent in Zealand (Table A.23 and Fig. 2.3). Even more important for private-service employment is the generally employment-friendly tax structure. Relying relatively heavily on personal and corporate income taxes, ranging from 12.8 percent of GDP in Switzerland to a 'Scandinavian' rate of 21.5 percent in New Zealand—as compared with 10.5 percent in Germany and 8.9 percent in France (Table A.24)—all four countries go easy on social-security contributions and consumption taxes, both of which add directly to the cost of less productive private services. The combined GDP-share of both amounts to only 10.6 percent in Australia, 12.9 percent in New Zealand, 18.5 percent in the UK, and 19.2 percent in Switzerland, as compared with 26 percent in Germany and 32.8 percent in France (Tables A.25 and A.26, and Fig. 2.8).

Flexible employment conditions are also supposed to facilitate employment in the private services. In fact, in the OECD's overall assessment of employment protection legislation, the United Kingdom ranked second in flexibility, New Zealand third, Australia sixth, and Switzerland seventh among 27 countries (Table A.34 and Fig. 2.10). For the UK, flexibility is the result of the traditionally low salience of state law in the regulation of employment relations under the maxims of 'free collective bargaining' (Crouch 1993), combined after 1979 with the determined weakening of union bargaining power by the Thatcher Government. In New Zealand, the erosion of the regulatory competencies of the arbitration courts in the 1970s has also taken the state out of industrial relations even before collective bargaining was dismantled by the Employment Contracts Act of 1991. In Australia, as we have seen, the role of arbitration courts continued longer than in New Zealand. Nevertheless, the judicial form of regulation through case-by-case awards did allow for a degree of flexibility and responsiveness to special circumstances that could not be achieved through legislation or centralized collective agreements aspiring to uniform standards. In Switzerland, the state also imposes few constraints on the employment relationship, and flexibility is maintained by highly decentralized patterns of collective bargaining, as well as by the fact that unions are traditionally weak in the sheltered-sector private services.

In short, what is distinctive about the employment structures of these four countries are relatively high levels of total employment and female participation which, in contrast to the Scandinavian countries, are associated with above-average employment rates in sheltered-sector private services rather than with public sector employment. The expansion of private services is facilitated by relatively low tax burdens with an employment-friendly tax structure, by relatively high wage dispersion, and by flexible and differentiated regulations of employment relations. At the same time, however, levels of social spending, both public and mandated private, are still lower than in all other countries covered in our project except for Italy, and range in 1995 from 15.5 percent of GDP in Australia to 25.5 percent in Switzerland (Tables A.27, A.27a). In that sense, it is still true that the full-employment goal must play a critical role in the normative legitimization of these political economies. But what if full employment could not be assured any longer?

2.6.2.2 Challenges   Switzerland had experienced massive job losses as a consequence of the macroeconomic shocks of the mid-1970s. Even though these did not result in manifest unemployment, the result was a major change of the original welfare-state configuration. Compulsory unemployment insurance with comparatively generous replacement rates was introduced in 1977; in 1985, the compulsory basic pension insurance of 1948 was supplemented by the 'second pillar' of a mandatory but private occupational pension (Brombacher-Steiner 1999); and in the 1990s the voluntary but publicly subsidized health insurance system, which had resisted reform efforts for most of the century (Immergut 1992), was finally made mandatory. Together with further reforms of the basic pension insurance, the result was that, of all countries covered in our project, Switzerland has experienced the steepest rise of total social expenditures, from 16.1 percent of GDP in 1980 to 25.5 percent in 1995 (Tables A.27, A.27a). With some exaggeration, one might thus say that Switzerland was being transformed from an 'Anglo-Saxon' to a 'Continental' welfare state with high social insurance transfers and high social-security contributions. But if that is the case, it still is the Continental country with by far the most flexible labor market regulations and by far the lowest overall tax burden. In this new configuration, in other words, the Swiss welfare state seems to have achieved a much higher level of social protection without undermining its superior economic viability in an internationalized economy.

In contrast to Switzerland, and also to the Scandinavian countries, the major economic challenge for Britain, Australia, and New Zealand had been an endemic lack of international competitiveness which was finally addressed in the late 1970s or early 1980s by governments that were committed to neo-liberal economic policies. Predictably, the initial consequences for employment were disastrous. Nevertheless, the Anglo-Saxon countries did not increase public social expenditures to nearly the same degree as was true in Switzerland. Instead, they maintained—or, in the case of Britain, returned to—the lean Beveridgean character of their formal welfare states. A case in point are flat-rate public pensions, with expenditures ranging from 3.4 percent of GDP in Australia to 7.6 percent in the United Kingdom, as compared with 11 percent in Switzerland, 12.2 percent in France, and 13.4 percent in Austria (OECD 1999f). In other words, for most citizens, retirement income depends primarily on private savings and insurance. In contrast to the United Kingdom, however, where the Thatcher Government did its best to erode the mandatory occupational pension insurance by creating attractive opt-outs, Australia moved in the opposite direction in 1986 by making participation in private occupational pension funds obligatory (Gern 1998).[40]

Even more important, flat rate unemployment benefits mean that losing one's job is associated with a drastic loss of income for single workers with average wages. In Australia and New Zealand, moreover, benefits have the character of means-tested social assistance payments, reaching only 37 percent of the average production-worker (APW) wage. At the same time however, social-assistance benefits for families with children are more generous, reaching replacement rates that are comparable to those in Continental or even Scandinavian welfare states (Table A.34). For single workers, therefore, unemployment means poverty, and 'welfare without work' is not an option that someone might prefer to a regular job. Given 'flexible' labor markets, decentralized wage setting, and low unemployment benefits, the neo-liberal assumption is that the creation of jobs could and should be left to the markets; and, by and large, the policy responses in all three countries are presently based on this assumption. For 'breadwinners' and their families, however, these constellations create two types of problems.

On the one hand, in many of the service jobs created in flexible labor markets, productivity-related wages are not high enough to support a family with children. On the other hand, the fact that the relatively generous social-assistance benefits for families are means tested—implying prohibitive withdrawal rates—may create unemployment traps that prevent any member of an assisted family from accepting a low-paid job. In New Zealand, the conservative government coming into office in 1991 opted for a straightforward neo-liberal solution by cutting benefits drastically in order to create more work incentives—with a concomitant steep increase of inequality (Easton 1996).

Beyond that, the problems of the 'working poor' are addressed by family-related 'in-work benefit' programs in all three countries. In Australia, the dominant approach has been to allow families with low income from

---

[40] Apparently, the benefits paid by these funds are not included in the OECD data cited.

work to receive a range of benefits available to recipients of social assist-ance, and since 1995 the withdrawal rate of unemployment benefits has been reduced from 100 percent to 75 percent. In New Zealand, a relatively low 'Family Tax Credit' is supposed to increase the attractiveness of low-paid work. In the United Kingdom, the more extensive Family Credit available for households with dependent children and a parent working at least 16 hours a week in a low-paid job has been transformed into the Working Families Tax Credit administered through the tax system (Kalisch, Aman, and Libbie 1998: tables 5.3, 5.8). At the same time, the refusal of recipients of unemployment benefits and social assistance to accept available low-wage jobs is being more strongly sanctioned by the withdrawal of benefits. In order to reduce the fiscal burdens on the welfare state, moreover, means tested student fees have come to play a significant role in the financing of higher education in Australia and Britain.

In short, in contrast to Switzerland, the other three countries are clearly not moving toward the traditional Continental model. Instead, they have been restructuring their welfare-state policies so as to maximize the incen-tives to seek paid work at whatever wages are obtainable rather than to rely on social incomes. The resulting problems of the 'working poor' are not ignored, but they are dealt with in the form of in-work benefits that increase rather than counteract the incentives to work. In addition, the intention is to increase the redistributive effect of the welfare state, and reduce total social spending at the same time, through a more precise tar-geting of expenditures to the needy and more effective sanctions against 'welfare chiseling'.

2.6.2.3 Capabilities In their political institutions, the four countries dis-cussed here could not be more different from each other. Switzerland represents the extreme case of a multi-actor system with a federal struc-ture in which competencies are more decentralized than in any of the other eleven countries, and with a national decision structure with insti-tutionalized veto positions among the four parties included in the semi-permanent governing coalition and between both houses of the federal parliament. In addition, relative small groups in the electorate have the right to challenge legislation passed by parliament in a popular referen-dum. Australia also is a federal state, with decentralized competencies, sometimes coalition governments, and a bicameral parliament with pro-portional representation in the second chamber. Britain and New Zealand, by contrast, were unitary states with first-past-the-post election systems that normally would guarantee single-party governments. The fact that New Zealand changed to a proportional election system and that in Britain some competencies have been delegated to the Scottish parliament in 1999 has not yet affected the policy choices discussed in the country chapters.

Britain and New Zealand did enact the most far-reaching changes of existing policy legacies in the 1980s and 1990s, which they were able to do in the absence of effective veto positions under the institutional conditions of their Westminster political systems. The question is why they chose to move in the direction they did. One obvious reason is the 'goodness of fit' between a monetarist-neo-liberal interpretation and the economic crises with which these countries were confronted in the late 1970s and early 1980s, and the fact that neo-liberal beliefs included not merely a theory about the functioning of economies but also strong normative propositions about the role of the state and of individuals in society (V. A. Schmidt, this Volume). But at least in Sweden, Germany, Switzerland, and the Netherlands, these beliefs also had broad support among economists, in the business press, in business associations and in business-oriented political parties. But, by and large, their influence on public policy was limited to the liberalization, deregulation, and privatization of economic activities, whereas welfare-state cutbacks, where they occurred, were accepted grudgingly, under the pressures of economic and fiscal necessity, but never pursued as a normatively desirable policy goal, as was true in Britain and New Zealand.

The explanation is in part institutional. In Westminster-type unitary states with two-party systems, the proponents of the neo-liberal world view had to capture at least one of the large parties in order to gain any influence at all on public policy; but if they succeeded in this, the concentration of political power allowed them to implement not only the economic policies but also the social policies of the neo-liberal program. In multi-party systems with multiple-veto institutions, by contrast, it is easier to capture or create a pro-business party, but its influence on public policy will be constrained by multiple veto positions representing non-business interests. Thus, even the weak constraints of the Australian constitution had the effect of limiting the thrust of neo-liberal welfare-state reforms, and in Sweden and Germany, neo-liberal coalition parties were never able to effectuate their program beyond the economic sphere. In Switzerland, moreover, the institution of the referendum led to the paradoxical outcome that precisely those policy initiatives which responded to neo-liberal demands contributed to the expansion of social insurance programs in order to overcome popular opposition that would otherwise have assured their defeat (Bonoli and Mach, Volume II).

But then, even in Westminster-type political systems governments face electoral constraints and should be sensitive to popular opposition (Pierson 1994). This suggests that differences in electoral feasibility should provide another partial explanation. In the Scandinavian countries, as we have seen, the social democratic welfare state created its own political constituency by providing services and jobs for middle class families as well as generous insurance against social risks for average-income workers. In other words, there is no chance that an explicit anti-welfare-state program could find the electoral support of a majority of self-interested voters. In Continental countries, the Bismarckian welfare state does not directly provide employment opportunities, but it provides generous social insurance to a sufficiently large majority of the electorate to make even marginal cutbacks appear as a high-risk operation. The Swiss example shows, moreover, that in times of increasing uncertainty voters may in fact favor the expansion of compulsory insurance programs over voluntary arrangements. In Beveridgean Australia and New Zealand, however, and also in the United Kingdom after the Thatcher reforms had eliminated earnings-related unemployment benefits and reduced the attractiveness of earnings-related public pensions, middle-class voters have little or no stake in the residual welfare state, except for the provision of health care. By necessity, they had learned to fend for themselves, and their ability to do so was best served by low levels of taxation. Thus, the redistributive social-assistance programs for the 'truly needy' are not defended by self-interested majorities, and if neo-liberal arguments succeed in allaying the scruples of an altruistic morality, it may in fact be politically profitable to propose welfare cutbacks along with a tightening of eligibility criteria and 'workfare' requirements—which may explain why the Blair Government is almost concealing, rather than advertising, its considerable expansion of redistributive programs.

2.6.3 Continental Welfare States

The Continental welfare states in our project—Austria, Belgium, Germany, France, Italy, and the Netherlands—differ in levels of employment and unemployment, in their industrial relations systems and in their political institutions. But they have two important conditions in common: all of them are now part of the European Monetary Union (EMU), which also means that they were operating under tight-money conditions and fiscal constraints through most of the decade, and all of them have welfare-state structures that are still influenced by the original Bismarck model, which emphasized social insurance for the male breadwinner and his family, whereas the care of children, of sick persons and of the aged was supposed to be provided by mothers, wives, and daughters in the family (Esping-Andersen 1990).

2.6.3.1 Employment Structures and Policy Legacies As in the other groups of countries, the structure of employment was strongly shaped by the characteristics of the welfare state. Given their Bismarckian roots, Continental welfare states responded to economic growth in the postwar decades by increasing the coverage and the generosity of health, unemployment, disability, and pension insurance rather than by expanding social services—with certain exceptions for childcare in France. As a consequence, at the end of the 'golden age', public sector employment rates (Table A.6) and female labor force participation (Table A.12) were much lower than in the Scandinavian welfare states, and no higher than in Anglo-Saxon countries, while the participation rates of men were at comparably high levels in all countries (Daly, Volume II). At the same time, financing and spending patterns were also shaped by the path-dependent evolution from Bismarckian origins. Whereas Scandinavian and Anglo-Saxon welfare states were mainly financed from progressive income taxes, and were at least initially committed to providing equal flat-rate social-security benefits to all citizens, Continental welfare states developed according the logic of compulsory insurance against the loss of wage incomes. Hence they continued to rely primarily on wage-based and proportional social-security contributions of workers and employers (Table A.26), and their benefits, except for the provision of health care, were generally contribution- and earnings-related—with the consequence that part-time work and the typically incomplete work biographies of married women would not provide minimally adequate pensions.[41] The one exception is the Netherlands, where the inadequate pension insurance was in 1956 replaced by a flat-rate basic pension for all citizens. Everywhere else, however, social security continued to depend on the life long and full-time employment of the male breadwinner, which created additional disincentives for female participation.[42]

The fact that the welfare state was primarily financed by payroll taxes adding to non-wage labor costs also had an influence on the level and structure of employment in the private sector. At the end of the 'golden age', only Austria and Germany had business employment somewhat above the OECD average, and in the 1990s all six of our Continental

---

[41] The existence of a large number of 'mini-pensions' explains the fact that in spite of very high pension expenditures, the 'implicit replacement rates'—calculated as the ratio of *average* pensions to average wages—of Continental pension systems are quite low when compared to the much less expensive flat-rate pension systems of Scandinavian and Anglo-Saxon welfare states (Gern 1998: table 1).

[42] The fact that female participation in the Netherlands was nevertheless extremely low at the end of the 'golden age' must thus be explained in terms of conservative or 'christian-democratic' value orientations (V. A. Schmidt, this Volume). But once these changed, the Dutch welfare state was no obstacle to the amazing increase of participation rates.

106   *Fritz W. Scharpf*

welfare states were below the average (Table A.7). But since the higher non-wage labor costs could be more easily passed on to consumers or absorbed by workers in highly productive jobs, the relative employment position of Continental countries was better in the industrial sector (Table A.9) than in the less productive private services (Table A.11).

Beyond these basic similarities, the six countries shared patterns of agricultural protection, monopolistic or cartelized transport, communications, and energy infrastructures, and highly regulated financial services. With the exception of Germany and the Netherlands, they also had relatively large sectors of state-owned industries. Where they differed most, however, was in the institutional structures and practices of industrial relations: corporatist and generally cooperative in Austria and, to a lesser extent, in Germany and the Netherlands, conflictual and statist in Belgium and France, and conflictual and highly politicized in Italy. These were discussed more fully in the preceding sections. Continental countries also differed greatly in the degree of wage differentiation (Table A.21), but were very similar in the high degree of legal protection for existing jobs (Table A.34).

2.6.3.2 Challenges Given these conditions, Continental welfare states were particularly vulnerable to two types of international challenges: the job losses caused by the two oil-price crises and later recessions, and intensified international competition in the industrial sector.

In the 1970s, only Italy and Austria had been able to avoid heavy job losses, and in the early 1980s these two countries were hit even harder than the other four (Table A.5). Compared with Beveridgean and Scandinavian systems, however, Continental welfare states are more threatened by declining employment. Earnings-related benefits make unemployment more tolerable for average-income workers, and they also increase the attractiveness of reducing the labor supply through disability and early-retirement pensions for all parties involved: governments are able to avoid the rise of politically salient unemployment statistics, employers can avoid conflict-ridden and expensive mass layoffs, unions are less constrained in their wage demands, and for older workers the prospect of early retirement with a full pension may appear very tempting (Ebbinghaus, Volume II; Manow and Seils, Volume II). By 1997, therefore, the six Continental countries had the lowest participation rates of men over the age of 55 among all countries included in our project—falling from about 80 percent at the beginning of the 1970s to 33.9 percent in Belgium, 40.7 percent in Austria, 42 percent in France, 44.2 percent in the Netherlands, 54.6 percent in Germany, and 55.9 percent in Italy—as compared with 63.6 percent in the UK, 71.3 percent in Sweden and 81.9 percent in Switzerland (Table A.13).

At the same time as expenditures on welfare-state benefits are driven up, declining employment also reduces revenues from social-security contributions. As a consequence, Continental welfare states were confronted with the unattractive choice of either cutting benefits just when they are needed most by people who always paid their contributions, or increasing state subsidies to the insurance funds just when the state budget is also in a fiscal squeeze, or raising contributions just when an increase of non-wage labor costs appears economically most counterproductive. For a while, Italy, Belgium and to a lesser extent the Netherlands attempted to evade these dismal choices by going deeper into deficit (Table A.22). But the high real interest rates of the 1980s increased the fiscal costs of this solution, and in the 1990s, given their political commitment to the European Monetary Union, all six countries were forced to pursue a restrictive fiscal policy in order to meet the Maastricht public-deficit criterion of 3 percent of GDP and the somewhat less compelling public-debt criterion of 60 percent of GDP. The challenge was greatest in Italy, where the public deficit was still at 9.5 percent in 1993; but Belgium with a deficit of 7.1 percent was also deeply in trouble. As it turned out, all six countries had difficulty in meeting the deficit criteria, but with the help of combinations of tax increases, expenditure cutbacks, privatization, and creative book-keeping, in the end all of them did squeeze in. By contrast, the equally ambitious Maastricht criteria on inflation were easily met by all countries; even Italy was able to match the German inflation rate at 1.8 percent by 1997 (Table A.3).

The tightening fiscal constraints meant that all Continental welfare states were eventually forced to follow the pattern already set by Germany in the 1970s of combining retrenchment with increases of social security contributions. But whereas Germany was able to stabilize both expenditures and contributions by the early 1980s, total social spending continued to increase until the mid-1980s in Austria, Belgium, France, and the Netherlands, and until the early 1990s in Italy (Tables A.27, A.27a). So did the GDP-shares of social-security contributions (Table A.26). However, even those countries which had been able to consolidate their welfare budgets in the late 1980s saw expenditures rise again in the recession of the early 1990s, with increases amounting to 4.8 percent of GDP between 1990 and 1995 in unified Germany, 3.4 percent in France, 2 percent in Austria, and 1.5 percent in Belgium. Remarkably, however, Italy was now able to push expenditures down again by 1995, and in the Netherlands the GDP-share of social spending in 1996 was actually 3 percentage points below the 1990 level.

In contrast to previous periods, however, when social expenditures and social-security contributions had moved more or less in parallel everywhere, countries differed in their fiscal responses in the 1990s. In its determined effort to meet the Maastricht deficit criteria, Italy continued to increase social contributions even as it stopped the rise of social expenditures, and to a lesser extent the same was true in the Netherlands. At the other extreme, the steep further increase of expenditures in France, where contributions had already reached an extremely high plateau of 20 percent of GDP in the mid-1980s, was entirely financed by rising income and consumption taxes. In Austria, spending and contributions continued to rise in parallel, whereas in Germany the dramatic rise of social expenditures after unification was financed in part by temporarily higher deficits and in part by higher social security contributions. In spite of these differences, however, social security contributions in the mid-1990s were higher in all Continental welfare states than in any other OECD country except for Sweden, ranging from 14.8 percent of GDP in Belgium to 20.2 percent in France (Table A.26). From the analyses presented above, one should expect that this high level of non-wage labor costs had a constraining effect on employment in the private services.

If we turn to employment challenges more generally, it is clear that employment in the investment-intensive industrial sector in all advanced countries was most vulnerable to the double effects of economic internationalization: more intense international competition in product markets and higher profit requirements imposed by internationally mobile capital. In the OECD average, therefore, employment rates in industry (ISIC 2–5) have continuously declined, altogether by 29.6 percent, from 1970 to 1997. The decline was smallest in Japan and the United States, where exports and imports are relatively insignificant compared with large internal markets. Among the countries in our project, the losses of the Continental welfare states are not exceptionally high. Belgium and France, at 42.6 percent and 41.6 percent respectively, lost the most, but they were closely followed by the United Kingdom at 40.3 percent, Switzerland at 40 percent, Australia at 39 percent, and Sweden at 36.2 percent. Losses in the Netherlands and Germany, at 32.7 percent and 30.1 percent, were close to the OECD average; and Austria and Italy at 26.9 percent and 26.8 percent were not much worse than the least affected country, Denmark, where the rate of industrial employment declined by only 24.8 percent (Table A.9). But even where this decline was not exceptionally steep, Continental welfare states suffered relatively more from it because, given their low employment rates in the public sector and in private services, the industrial sector generally played a larger role in their employment structures.

The industrial decline continued in the 1990s, with the largest losses between 1990 and 1997 suffered by Austria, France, and Germany—3.8, 2.8., and 2.2 percentage points, respectively—whereas in the Netherlands,

Belgium, and Italy de-industrialization seems to have bottomed out at a low level. During the 1990s, however, international competition was no longer limited to agriculture and industry. All six countries in our Continental group were greatly affected by EU and national policies exposing the formerly protected transport and communications services (ISIC 7) to intense international and national competition, with the consequence that overall employment rates in ISIC 7 stagnated at best but more often declined during the 1990s (OECD, *Labour Force Statistics*, various years). There are, however, great and interesting variations in the employment performance of different service branches and in different countries (Héritier and S. K. Schmidt, Volume II). In all Continental countries, financial and business services (ISIC 8) also became more exposed to international competition from the late 1980s onward, whereas the speed and intensity of deregulation and market-oriented re-regulation differed considerably among countries. As a consequence, while employment rates in ISIC 8 increased in all six countries during the 1990s, the rise was particularly steep in Austria and in the Netherlands (OECD, *Labour Force Statistics*, various years).[43] The Netherlands is also the only country in the Continental group where employment in the 'exposed sectors' as a whole, including production (ISIC 1–5) and production-related services (ISIC 7 and 8) did increase during the 1990s (Table A.8).

The general challenges in these exposed sectors have been discussed sufficiently in the preceding section. What is specific for the six Continental countries is the fact that these challenges must now be met under the conditions of the European Monetary Union, where there is no more hope or fear of exchange-rate adjustments to compensate for a loss of competitiveness, and where wages and prices will be expressed in the same currency. Since the political and industrial-relations decisions that are affecting wages, prices, and the conditions of production continue to be nationally confined, this creates an entirely new situation, especially for countries which in the past had difficulty in controlling cost-push inflation. In contrast to the other challenges discussed so far, however, it was difficult to say in the abstract in which direction national actors would, in the absence of international policy coordination, be pushed by competitive pressures in the Euro zone (Eichengreen, Frieden, and Hagen 1995; Dyson and Featherstone 1999). The theoretical discussion is structured by two competing prisoner's-dilemma scenarios. The first assumes that national unions and governments treating the impact of their decisions on price stability as an externality will produce spiraling inflation. The second

---

[43] A more detailed statistic for 1997 shows that the Netherlands, along with the United Kingdom and Sweden, is exceptionally strong in business services, whereas Austria has relatively more employment in banking and insurance (European Commission 1998: table 5).

assumes that national governments and unions trying to defend production and jobs at home will be forced into beggar my neighbor wage concessions, tax cuts, and deregulation that will leave all of them worse off. These issues have not been explicitly addressed in the present project, and they cannot be treated here. Nevertheless, the national policy experiences of the 1990s described and analyzed in Volume II do in fact throw some empirical light on the likely responses to this challenge.

For now, however, it is useful to repeat that the Netherlands is in fact the only one among all advanced industrial countries in which employment rates in the exposed sectors increased measurably—by 2.4 percentage points—between 1990 and 1997 (Table A.8). In general, however, employment gains in the 1990s, if any, could be achieved only in the consumption-oriented services (ISIC 6 and 9) where the OECD-18 average increased by 1.2 points between 1990 and 1997 (Table A.10).[44] With the exception of Belgium and Italy, such gains were also achieved in all Continental countries, but they were by far the largest in Austria—plus 4.2 percentage points—and in the Netherlands—plus 3.4 percentage points. As mentioned before, the ISIC-9 category includes an extremely heterogeneous mix of services, of which health, education, and social services constitute the largest block whose expansion, because they are financed by the state or by social security contributions, has been severely constrained by the fiscal crises of Continental welfare states discussed above.

Thus, if there were significant employment gains in the sheltered sector in the 1990s, they had to be achieved in the private services. If we again take ISIC-6 data as a proxy, the picture is quite clear. Employment rates increased much more than the OECD average in the Netherlands—plus 2.9 percent points—and in Austria—plus 2.3 percentage points—and their level was also above the OECD average in both countries (Table A.11). In all other Continental countries, ISIC-6 employment was stagnant or falling between 1990 and 1997, and employment rates in 1997 were considerably below the average.

---

[44] The reader may notice that data for exposed- and sheltered-sector employment rates do not add up to total employment rates for all countries. The reason is that we must draw on different OECD data sources. Employment data by ISIC branches are only available in the *Labour Force Statistics* which, however, are afflicted with gaps in time series and with wholly implausible jumps from one year to the next. In some cases these seem to be due to a change of definitions or a switch to another data source that may or may not include marginal forms of employment. To make matters worse, these changes are often applied retroactively, so that a new edition of the *Labour Force Statistics* may change the employment history of a country even for the 1970s. Hence we have chosen to rely on *Economic Outlook* data where these are available—total employment, government employment and business employment—because definitions appear to be consistent over time and the available series are more complete.

To conclude: the challenge of the 1990s for the employment policies of Continental welfare states was to stabilize employment in the exposed sectors and to increase employment in private services in the sheltered sector. Among the Continental countries, the Netherlands was the only one that was able to improve its position in both the exposed and the sheltered sectors. Austria was unable to prevent a decline of its very high level of exposed-sector employment—the highest after Switzerland and Japan—during the 1990s, but its gains in sheltered sector services between 1990 and 1997 were higher than in any other country in our project. In terms of total employment, however, the Netherlands was the clear winner, increasing its employment rate by altogether 7 percentage points between 1990 and 1997, more than any other OECD-18 country. At the opposite extreme, Germany lost 4.3 percentage points, a loss which was exceeded only by Sweden and Finland.

2.6.3.3 Path Dependent Success Stories and Failures Beginning with the *Netherlands*, the clear winner in the Continental group, it needs to be understood that the story of the 'Dutch Miracle' (Visser and Hemerijck 1997) is not about very high *levels* of employment, but about a successful *turnaround* which, after a deep fall from 61.6 percent in 1970 to 50.8 percent in 1984, brought total employment rates back to 61.8 percent in 1998, a level that is still below the OECD average and about par with Austria, Germany, and France (Table A.5). But since employment in all other Continental welfare states is far below the levels of the early 1970s, a successful turnaround is indeed a remarkable achievement. The employment turnaround was also associated with a dramatic rise of female labor participation, but at least up to now this has also been a story about *catching up* with the moderate rates in neighboring Continental countries rather than about a rise to Scandinavian or Swiss levels (Table A.12). Moreover, the Dutch employment success was not associated with a proportional increase in the volume of work, but was in part[45] due to a dramatic expansion of part-time employment, rising from 10 percent of the working-age population in the early 1980s to 21.4 percent in 1996 (Table A.14)—a rate which is equaled only in Switzerland and Norway, but far higher than in other Continental countries.

---

[45] Between the beginning of the turnaround in 1983 and 1997, the annual hours worked per person in dependent employment fell by 10.7% to a record low of 1,365 hours (OECD 1999b: Annex, table F). During the same period, however, the number of persons in dependent employment, corrected for a break in the series, increased by 32.7% (OECD *Labour Force Statistics 1977– 97*). It is not true, therefore, that shorter working hours explain all or most of the Dutch Miracle. Nevertheless, part-time work accounted for 70.6% of total employment growth between 1993 and 1997 (OECD 1999d: table 4.4).

Remarkably, moreover, the rise of part-time employment was, at least initially, less a result of well-designed policy choices than a development facilitated by policy legacies that existed for other reasons. The basic pension introduced in 1956 had removed a disincentive that impedes the rise of part-time employment in other Bismarckian insurance systems. The same is true of income-tax rules providing for the separate taxation of married couples (Daly, Volume II). A further incentive was added by the tax reform of 1990 which integrated a large part of the social-security contributions of employees into the proportional income-tax schedule, with the effect that contributions are not raised on wages below the basic tax exemption of 8,700 guilder annually. But even here it is not clear that the tax reform had been designed as an incentive to part-time work (Hemerijck, Unger, and Visser, Volume II). It was only after the erosion of traditional gender roles, when women—and, to an unusual degree, men as well (OECD 1999c: Statistical Annex, table E)—began to avail themselves of these opportunities, that Dutch unions found themselves forced to treat the remaining disadvantages of part-time work as an issue that required attention in collective bargaining and government policy (Visser 1999a).

With regard to the sectoral distribution of employment gains, policy legacies rather than explicitly designed employment strategies also seem to account for the unusual increase in production-oriented services—ISIC 8, and to some degree also ISIC 7. The Netherlands has always been a liberal trading nation; together with Britain it has been in the avant-garde pressuring for the liberalization of services in Europe; and it was ready and willing to fully exploit its competitive advantages as an early liberalizer (Héritier 1997) as well as its position as port of entry into Continental Europe. Moreover, its tax policy was and is explicitly designed to attract the headquarter functions of multi-national enterprises (Ganghof, Volume II). In part, the above-average employment rates in ISIC 6 depend on the same factors. A more detailed EU statistic shows that in 1997 the Netherlands was below the European average in 'hotels and restaurants', but above-average in 'distribution', and that in this subcategory the truly exceptional employment rate was in 'wholesale trade' rather than in 'retail trade' (European Commission 1998: table 4)—a profile which fits well with the opportunity structure provided by an internationally competitive trading and service economy.

The other country in our Continental group which has been doing relatively well in employment terms is *Austria* (Auer 1999). While its unemployment rate did rise in the 1990s, it was still the lowest until 1996, when it was bettered by the Netherlands (Table A.4). According to our OECD *Economic Outlook* data, its 1998 rate of total employment was the highest in the Continental group (Table A.5). However, the Austrian rate of total employment declined by 2.7 percentage points between 1992 and 1997, and recovery seems to be slow. In sectoral distribution, Austria still has above-average, though declining, rates of industrial employment (Table A.9). As in the Netherlands, employment gains were achieved in the service branches of ISIC 6 and ISIC 8, with an emphasis on 'hotels and restaurants', 'retail trade' and 'banking' (European Commission 1998: table 5). The rate of government employment is also above average among Continental countries, and it continued to increase until the mid-1990s (Table A.6). Beyond that, the Austrian configuration shares the typical Continental characteristics: a hard currency policy combined with fiscal constraints that rule out deficit spending, a relatively high level of taxation (Table A.23) and social spending (Tables A.27, A.27a), a very high share of social security contributions—18 percent in 1997—and moderate to high levels of employment protection (Table A.34).

So what could explain the relatively good, but not superior, employment performance in the 1990s? The main explanation, surely, is historical: the fact that Austria was able to avoid the big mistakes in macroeconomic policy that other countries had made in the 1970s, the 1980s or the early 1990s. Hence overall employment had suffered less than in other Continental countries. Beyond that, there are two endemic differences that may reduce the vulnerability of Austrian employment under the conditions of the 1990s. The first is a tradition of relatively high wage dispersion. Thus, in the 1993–95-period, the D5:D1 ratio for both genders[46] was 2.01 in Austria, as compared with 1.34 in Sweden, 1.44 in Germany, 1.56 in the Netherlands, 1.65 in France—and 2.1 in the United States (Table A.21). Since the median wage in Austria is not excessively high, this 'American' degree of wage dispersion implies a low minimum wage and the existence of a relatively large low-wage sector facilitating high levels of employment in less productive private services. The second peculiarity is that in Austria wages respond more flexibly than in any other OECD country—except for Japan—to changes in unemployment (Pichelmann and Hofer 1999: 36). This suggests that in a downturn, job losses will be limited by downward wage flexibility, whereas in an upturn existing capacity can be used without delay. Unlike in the Netherlands, however, employment gains have not been amplified by deliberate wage restraint. In short, Austria is well placed to defend existing employment, but less able to create opportunities for dynamic expansion.

If the Netherlands and Austria are the relative successes among the Continental welfare states in the 1990s, united *Germany* is the failure.

---

[46] For men, the Austrian D5/D1-ratio of 1.67 in 1994 is much closer to the Continental average, and significantly below the US level of 2.13. This suggests that the low-wage sector is mainly providing jobs for women.

Compared with the West German rate of total employment in 1990, job losses to 1998 amounted to 4.3 percentage points (Table A.5), and while the decline seems to have bottomed out in 1998, there is as yet no sign of a vigorous turnaround. The dominant factor, surely, is German unification and the way it was dealt with (Manow and Seils, Volume II). In effect, East German industries were destroyed by the adoption of a common currency at an economically unrealistic exchange rate, and by the rapid approximation to West German wage levels. After 1992, moreover, the restrictive response of the Bundesbank to the government's initial resort to deficit-financing instead of tax increases caused a deep recession in western Germany that had wide repercussions in other European countries. Since a considerable part of the costs of unification was then shifted to social insurance, this had the effect of increasing non-wage labor costs, which, under conditions of exchange-rate stability, reduced international competitiveness. But even then, Germany's inability to recover from the unification shock, as it had done from the first and the second oil-price shocks, requires an explanation.

Given its high rate of industrial employment—still the highest among OECD-18 countries except for Japan (Table A.9)—Germany was more affected than other countries by intensified international competition, and German firms were able to defend their position only by a combination of outsourcing—mainly to central and eastern Europe—and massive efforts to increase productivity. While west-German industrial unions were unwilling to make a Dutch-style commitment to long-term wage moderation,[47] cooperative industrial relations at the level of firms did facilitate rapid productivity increases. In terms of international competitiveness, these adjustment strategies succeeded: German trade surpluses were as high or higher in the 1990s than they had been in the late 1980s (OECD 1999b: Annex, table 48), and the decline of the German share of world exports in the early 1990s was stopped by 1994 (Table A.33).

However, the loss of industrial jobs could not be compensated by the weak growth in service employment. Here, the reasons are complementary to the arguments explaining Dutch and Austrian employment successes. The classical Bismarckian pension system and income-tax splitting among married couples creates disincentives for part-time employment. Social-security contributions are high, and they are not mitigated by progressive rates or by a tax exemption favoring low-wage or part-time employment. Employment-protection legislation is stricter than in the Netherlands and Austria in all dimensions considered in the OECD study (Table A.34).

---

[47] Relative unit labor costs increased by 6% between 1991 and 1998, whereas they fell by 5% in the Netherlands, by 11.6% in Austria and, due to the 1992 devaluation, by 25% in Italy (Table A.19).

Wage dispersion, finally, is almost as low as it is in the Scandinavian countries; and, contrary to the general trend, it actually became more compressed in from the mid-1980s to the mid-1990s (Table A.21). In combination, these factors impede the expansion of less productive private services as well as the expansion of part-time employment, and they are also not favorable to the rapid development of innovative business services. Thus, the employment rate in the low-wage branches of 'distribution' plus 'hotels and restaurants' was 4.2 percentage points lower than in Austria, and in 'computing and data processing' plus 'business activities' it was 2.7 percentage points below the Dutch rate (European Commission 1998: table 5).

Belgium, France, and Italy, which had done more poorly in the 1980s, did not suffer the massive job losses experienced by post-unification Germany, but neither have they been able to initiate structural changes that could lead to a dynamic expansion of employment as it is occurring in the Netherlands. For Italy and Belgium, meeting the Maastricht deficit criteria to achieve membership in the EMU was the major challenge, and the major achievement, of the 1990s. In Italy, this did require tax increases as well as a reduction of total social expenditures, from 25.9 percent of GDP in 1993 to 23.7 percent in 1995 (Tables A.27, A.27a), which was mainly achieved through cutbacks in the public financing of health care and in active labor market policy (OECD 1999f), while the substantial reforms of the pension system will have fiscal effects only in later years (Ferrera 1997; Gualmini and Ferrera, Volume II). In Belgium, the rise of total social expenditure seems at least to have been halted in 1993, whereas in France increases continued unabated from 25.7 percent in 1989 to 30.1 percent in 1995, mainly as a consequence of rising outlays for pensions and health care. Even though tax revenues also increased, fiscal consolidation did depend to a large extent on the proceeds of privatization (Maclean 1995; V. A. Schmidt 2000c). While there has been some liberalization of working-time rules in France and in Belgium in the late 1980s (Bastian 1994), all three countries rank high on the OECD scale of employment-protecting legislation (Table A.34). Moreover, there is no evidence in any of the countries, except for the Netherlands, of major efforts to break the mold of the Bismarckian configuration.[48] Instead, we see defensive measures which, on the one hand, aim to reduce the supply of labor through early retirement and, in the French case, the legislated move to the

[48] In France, it is true, some of the burden of welfare-state finance was shifted from social-security contributions to an earmarked proportional income tax (*Contribution Social Généralisée, CSG*) that was introduced in 1990 and has been increased several times since then. Nevertheless, social security contributions, at 20.7% of GDP in 1996, are still the highest in our project.

35-hour week, and which, on the other hand, aim to extend the financial viability of the welfare state through incremental cutbacks of benefits, a tightening of eligibility rules, and marginal increases in contributions. Beyond that, the hope in all four countries was to increase employment through economic growth. In France, it seems that the efforts directed at industrial restructuring are finally paying off in high growth rates at the turn of the decade, and France as well as Belgium have also introduced major programs to reduce employers' contributions at the low end of the wage scale in order to stimulate employment in the private services. In these two countries at least, it seems that the characteristic structural weakness of Continental welfare states is by now being recognized and addressed, whereas similar proposals in Germany (Zukunftskommission der Friedrich-Ebert-Stiftung 1998) have so far not led to policy changes.

In general it remains true, however, that with the exception of the Netherlands, the *de facto* agenda of Continental welfare states in the 1990s responded to the requirements of fiscal consolidation imposed by the Maastricht criteria, but did not generally include structural changes that could have increased employment opportunities to the level achieved in the Anglo-Saxon, let alone the Scandinavian, welfare states. The question is whether there were institutional reasons preventing the choice of effective policy options.

2.6.3.4 Capabilities   The six Continental welfare states differ greatly in their political structures, with France and the Netherlands being unitary states, Italy a unitary state with a greater degree of autonomy of its provinces, Austria and Germany federal states with highly centralized competencies, and Belgium a federal state with decentralized competencies. At the national level, all countries in this group have plural or multi-party systems that usually require coalition governments, but even if bicameral parliaments exist, the second chamber does not usually constitute an effective constraint on governments that are supported by a majority in the first chamber. The one exception is Germany, where a majority of Länder votes in the second chamber is able to block national legislation, and is likely to do so under conditions of 'divided government'. In France, the strong position of the president, and of a prime minister who has the support of the president, generally facilitates a high concentration of powers which, however, may turn into a dualist power structure under conditions of *cohabitation*. In Belgium, the parties in any governing coalition are themselves internally divided by the linguistic conflict, and in Austria, legislation in the fields of economic and social policy has practically depended on consensus among the 'social partners'. In the abstract, however, these institutional differences do not seem to explain the differences of policy responses in the 1990s. It seems more promising therefore to take a look at the relatively more successful Dutch and Austrian solutions, and to ask what institutional obstacles could have stood in the way of adopting and implementing these in the other countries.

The relatively high level of private-service employment in Austria, as we have seen, depends in part on the existence of very high D5:D1 wage differentials, higher than in the United Kingdom, and as high as in the United States. But whereas the widening wage differentials in the United Kingdom and the United States are generally attributed to the weakening of union power (Iversen 1999), Austrian unions are organizationally strong, concentrated, and centralized and, as in Germany, wage-setting is highly coordinated through mechanisms of wage leadership (Traxler 1995b). Thus unions would surely have had the institutional capability to achieve and enforce at least the German degree of wage compression. That they did not do so has an explanation that is technically of an institutional nature. Sectoral wage agreements are oriented to the ability to pay of weaker firms in the industry, and works councils in more profitable firms are able to achieve considerable wage drift in informal 'second rounds' of wage bargaining—which also explains the high flexibility of Austrian wages in response to changes in the demand for labor. But according to theoretical expectations (Iversen and Wren 1998), these institutional practices could surely have been changed by the organizationally strong and highly centralized Austrian unions, and so the more important explanation must lie in the normative and cognitive orientations of Austrian unions according to which the protection of existing jobs always had much higher salience than aspirations for greater wage equality (Guger 1998; Visser 1998; V. A. Schmidt, this volume).

In Germany, by contrast, egalitarian value orientations have strongly influenced union policy, with the effect that wage settlements resulting in real-wage losses in the 1970s and 1980s generally included above-average increases for the lowest-paid groups. This also explains the economically disastrous commitment to the rapid achievement of west-German wages in eastern Germany, and the adamant political resistance of German unions to policy proposals facilitating the development of a subsidized low-wage sector. Similarly, the egalitarian orientation of Italian unions has long prevented wage differentiation between the *Mezzogiorno* and the prosperous regions of northern Italy (Ferrera and Gualmini, Volume II). In Belgium, where the decline of D5:D1 wage differentials in the 1980s was a result of government policy, we have also seen that allowing above-average increases for low-wage groups was the price the government had to pay for the acquiescence of powerful but divided unions to wage-setting by decree. Even more interesting is the Dutch experience, where successive governments had lowered the relative value of the minimum wage (OECD 1998d: table 2.3 and chart 2.2), but where the *de facto* wage dispersion did not change at all (Table A.21). It seems, then, that unions in all Continental welfare states apart from Austria share the 'Scandinavian' commitment to egalitarian values, and that where they have the power to do so, they will defend these values even against strong economic incentives.

In France, finally, where unions were greatly weakened in the 1980s, decentralized wage setting also did not result in greater D5:D1 wage dispersion. Here, however, the explanation must be political, since the legal minimum wage—*SMIC*—is determined by the government. In the 1970s and early 1980s, political pressures ensured a steep rise of the *SMIC* relative to average wages; and this high level was more or less maintained subsequently. By 1997, at 68.5 percent of the basic median wage, the *SMIC* was the highest of all OECD countries with minimum-wage legislation (OECD 1998d: table 2.3 and chart 2.2). What prevented greater wage differentiation in France was thus not union power, but the power of conservative governments fearful of protests in the streets, and of socialist governments with a normative commitment to equality.

In other words, the Austrian option of expanding fully insured employment in the less productive private services through very high wage dispersion could not be realized, for normative and political reasons, in the other Continental countries. That leaves the policy options that seem to explain the Dutch success story. Some of these, I have tried to show, depend on comparative advantages and historical policy legacies that could not have been recreated elsewhere by policy choices in the 1990s. But that is not true of other elements contributing to the 'Dutch Miracle': (1) the sustained commitment of the social partners to competition-oriented wage moderation; (2) the measures facilitating private-service employment; and (3) the efforts to reduce the attractiveness and the fiscal burdens of exit-options provided by the welfare state.

As for the first element, the 'Accord of Wassenaar' has come to define the aspirations of governments and employers' associations in a number of European countries which, when confronted with the prospect of the Monetary Union, saw a need for longer-term and reliable commitments ensuring that national wage increases would not exceed those in competitor countries (Ebbinghaus and Hassel 2000). Among the Continental countries in our project, such efforts have been effective in Belgium and Italy, while similar attempts in Germany have run into major difficulties. In Belgium, the government had tried to negotiate a tripartite 'alliance for jobs' in the early 1990s which would have included an obligation to orient future settlements to wage increases in Belgium's three most important trading partners (Vilrokx 1998). But when negotiations failed once more because of conflicts among unions, the government nevertheless was able to impose the substance of the draft framework agreement by legislation. Apparently, strong but competing unions found it easier to accept a government *diktat* than to bear the blame for agreeing to solutions which their members must find distasteful; but once the statutory framework was in place, annual wage increases were again determined through collective bargaining.

In Italy, by contrast, unions have been able and willing to conclude altogether four tripartite pacts between 1992 and 1998, in which not only the abolition of the *scala mobile* and severely restrictive wage guidelines but also a wide range of painful measures of welfare-state retrenchment and labor-market deregulation were agreed upon. The reason could be that Italian governments even in the 1990s would not have had the political strength to impose unpopular solutions, Thus, if organizationally strong Italian unions were impressed with the urgency of the fiscal crisis of the welfare state and with the need to control inflationary wage pressures in order to remain economically viable under conditions of Monetary Union, they did not have the Belgian option of putting the blame on a scapegoat government. Instead, they had to assume responsibility in order to legitimize government action. In Germany, by contrast, matters are institutionally complicated by the extremely high symbolic value that unions place on the constitutional guarantee of *Tarifautonomie*, which is understood to rule out any government intervention in the regulation of wages and working conditions through collective bargaining. Since actual negotiations are conducted at the sectoral level, even voluntary inter-sectoral agreements are seen as highly problematic, and while sectoral unions have often practiced effective wage restraint, they have never been willing to do so on the basis of an explicit, longer-term commitment.

Among the second set of Dutch policies, measures facilitating low-wage service employment have also found some imitators. Thus, while social-security contributions are high in the Netherlands, the share paid by employers was traditionally among the lowest in Europe (OECD 1999d: table A.4). Nevertheless, employers' contributions were further reduced in the 1990s, and are now close to zero for workers earning up to 115 percent of the statutory minimum wage (OECD 1999e: figure V.b). Similar measures reducing the social-security wedge specifically for wage-jobs have been adopted in France and more recently in Belgium. But, once more, the contrast with Germany is instructive. There, proposals to reduce or eliminate social-security contributions for low-paid jobs were introduced in the context of discussions over the 'alliance for jobs', where they were

blocked by a union veto. What mattered, apparently, was the framing of
the issue in terms of equality: Should one encourage the expansion of a
low-wage and low-skill segment of the labor market with inevitably less
attractive and less secure employment conditions than are enjoyed by the
shrinking core workforce? As was true of Swedish unions in 1995, the
dominant response among German unions was negative; and since the
government, by putting the proposal on the agenda of the alliance, had
granted them a veto, that settled the matter. The same fate would have
awaited proposals emulating the Dutch moves toward 'flexicurity', which
somewhat relaxed employment protection for regular jobs while improving the employment opportunities and employment conditions of outsiders trying to enter the labor market through temporary employment
agencies and other non-standard forms of work (Pennings 1999).

Dutch unions have accepted or even proposed such measures because
the rise of part-time and temporary employment had already changed the
composition of their membership and their strategic orientations. That is
not meant to suggest, however, that Dutch reform policies did not run into
strong opposition. But the big political battles were fought over the third
set of policies aiming at the fiscal consolidation of the welfare state
through a reduction of very high 'inactivity rates', in particular by tightening eligibility criteria and reducing the attractiveness of disability pensions, by reducing the level of social assistance—which was tied to the
minimum wage—and by 'activating' measures that have increased the
pressure on recipients of social assistance and unemployment benefits to
accept available jobs or withdraw from the labor market (Van der Veen
and Trommel 1999). In comparative perspective, these measures were neither very drastic nor very successful in their own terms (Alber 1998). The
share of inactive persons supported by the welfare state is still high, and
participation rates of older workers are still quite low.

Nevertheless, the opposition to some of these measures was so fierce
among the unions and the general public that the political survival of the
government was at stake. It is most remarkable, therefore, that the christ-
ian-democratic-labor coalition under Lubbers nevertheless stuck to the
reform program even though it predictably led to a catastrophic defeat in
the 1994 elections that radically changed the Dutch multi-party system
(Irwin and Holsteyn 1997). It is equally remarkable that the labor party,
whose losses were only marginally smaller than those of the Christian
democrats, continued to pursue the retrenchment program in a new labor-
liberal coalition after 1994. The proximate explanation of this course of
action was an extremely strong cognitive orientation, shared by political
elites in the governing coalition as well as in the liberal opposition, of the
necessity to reduce the unfavorable active/inactive ratio of the Dutch labor

market or, what is the same thing, to increase the employment rate (NEI 1998).

But as under very similar circumstances the conservative Juppé government in France dropped its plans for cutting public sector pensions in the face of strikes and protest demonstrations in the fall of 1995 (Levy 1999a, Volume II), the tenacity of the Lubber coalition needs a further explanation—which is in part institutional. The institutional angle becomes clear if we add Germany and Austria to the comparison. In Germany, the Kohl government's tax reforms of 1997 were adopted by the Christian-liberal majority in parliament but blocked by the social-democratic majority in the Bundesrat. In Austria the relevant comparison is Chancellor Vranitzky's first attempt to put together a fiscal consolidation package without the prior agreement of the social partners in 1994, which he had to withdraw when it became clear that the unions would prevail on a sufficient number of social democratic deputies to vote against the package (Hemerijck, Unger, and Visser, Volume II). In Austria and Germany, in other words, the government was confronted with institutionalized veto positions that it could not overcome by unilateral action, and in both cases the opposition was not primarily driven by disagreement over the substance of the government's policy[49] but by institutional or organizational self-interest: the Austrian social partners defending their corporatist control over the economic and social-policy choices of the government, and the German social democrats, after 15 years in opposition, trying to demonstrate the impotence of the Kohl government in the run-up to the 1998 elections.

In the Dutch unitary state with a unicameral legislature, the parliamentary opposition could criticize the government's unpopular program, but in contrast to Germany it held no veto position and was thus never confronted with incentives to block a program it considered substantively necessary in order to defend its organizational self-interest. Compared with Austria, it mattered that after the deep frustrations of the 1970s, Lubber's conservative-liberal 'no-nonsense government' of 1982 had changed the ground rules of Dutch corporatism. From then on, it was understood that the government and its parliamentary majority had the legitimacy to act unilaterally. Corporatist institutions remain important, and consensus with the social partners is always sought and often achieved, but it is no longer considered a necessary precondition for government action (Mair

---

[49] The Austrian social partners designed an even tougher consolidation package a year later, which was then passed by a wide majority in parliament; and the German social democrats, after their return to power in the fall of 1998, adopted a similar combination of fiscal consolidation and tax reform, which was now opposed by a christian-liberal opposition in the Bundesrat.

1994). Thus, unlike in Austria, the massive opposition of the unions to the social-security reforms of the early 1990s could not stop the government and the parliamentary parties supporting its program (Visser and Hemerijck 1997).

In Belgium, effective policy solutions were made much more difficult by internal cleavages within any governing coalition, and by the negotiations necessary to accommodate the competing claims of institutionally entrenched subunits defined by linguistic identities. It appears that these have generally been able to agree on investing the government with the authority to impose wage settlements by decree, but that reforms with negative electoral repercussions were and are not politically feasible. In Italy, by contrast, corporatist pacts with the unions have allowed politically weak governments to achieve significant cutbacks in overly generous areas of a highly uneven welfare state.

That leaves France, a unitary state where the executive is able to legislate without depending on delegation from the relatively weak parliament, where governments do not lack political legitimacy, and where unions are organizationally weak, with a precarious role in wage negotiations and without any institutionalized voice in the policy choices of the state. So what explains the conservative Juppé government's retreat from the pension reforms it considered necessary for the fiscal consolidation of the welfare state? The answer is electoral politics and the discourses shaping them, which are discussed elsewhere (V. A. Schmidt, this volume). But these politics are also shaped by institutional background conditions that distinguish French politics in the Fifth Republic from other European countries.

In comparison with all other countries in our project except for the UK and New Zealand, France lacks an infrastructure of interest-intermediating associations which could effectively oppose, but also legitimize, moderate, and implement government policy. In particular, it lacks 'social-partnership' institutions that have a potential for public-interest oriented self-organization at the 'meso' level of economic sectors (Levy 1999a). If these institutions are functioning effectively—which, as we have seen, is a big 'if'—they relieve the government of the hard choice between exercising total, and inevitably schematic, state control over wages and working conditions, and leaving these matters entirely to the vagaries of macroeconomically ignorant and indifferent local bargains or confrontations. In France, the government is never relieved of the dilemma of having to choose between ineffective centralization and irresponsible decentralization. Still more important for present purposes, if intermediating organizations exist, they must, for the specific sectors which they organize, share the government's concern for the resolution of economic crises. They may take matters into their own hands, as in the Netherlands, in Austria and perhaps in Italy, or they may deliberately acquiesce in unilateral government action, as in Belgium, but they cannot ignore the crises with which the government is struggling and then oppose measures that would relieve them.

In France, however, the state is too strong and unions and other associations are too weak to allow even for this implicit partnership. The state has adopted a 'heroic' style of policymaking, in which initiatives are developed, with little input from organized interests, by a small and relatively homogenous bureaucratic-political policy elite, and imposed by executive decree or by legislation in a pliant parliament (V. A. Schmidt 1996a). But since the state is not buffered by intermediary institutions against the anger and potential violence of 'the masses', it must generally be ready to retreat if massive opposition becomes manifest subsequent to its decisions (V. A. Schmidt 1996a, 1996b, 2000c; Levy 1999a). The government was, perhaps, extreme in its readiness to 'negotiate with the street', but it was following a pattern that had been established by de Gaulle himself and his successors in the aftermath of *les évènements du mai* in 1968. In the Netherlands, by contrast, the legitimacy of representative government and parliamentary democracy was and is unquestioned, and practices of consultation in the preparation of policy initiatives are so extensive that, once the government has made up its mind on a politically controversial issue, there is no legitimate reason for it to capitulate in the face of public protests.

2.6.4 *Conclusion*

After the drastic policy reversals in Britain and New Zealand, the Anglo-Saxon welfare states have become lean, private-service intensive, and economically viable in the 1990s. The challenges which they face arise from the increase in inequality and poverty. To meet them through investments in education and training on the one hand, and through poverty-alleviating reforms of social assistance on the other hand, appears to be more a question of value orientations, public discourses and political support-building strategies than a problem of economic or institutional constraints. At the other extreme, the economic viability of the generous and public-service intensive Scandinavian welfare states seems also relatively secure, but more so in Denmark than in Sweden. While tax burdens are very high, the tax structure is business- and employment-friendly, and its political viability seems to be assured by broad support for the employment effects and benefits of universal and high-quality social services and for generous social insurance programs. However, a normative challenge may arise from the potential conflict between the continuing commitment to egalitarian values and the necessary flexibility and differentiation of employment conditions in segments of private services which must expand if aspirations for full employment are to be maintained.

More severe challenges are confronting the transfer-generous but service-lean Continental welfare states whose economic viability is constrained by an employment-unfriendly tax structure and by relatively rigid regulations favoring the protection of existing jobs over the creation of new jobs. They are in difficulties because most of the policy changes that would have improved their economic viability in the 1990s were definitely unpopular with the groups affected by welfare state retrenchment and by the liberalization and deregulation of employment relationships. Thus their capacity for effective policy responses is effectively constrained by the existence of institutional veto positions in multi-actor political systems and by the anticipation of negative electoral responses in single-actor political systems.

3

Sequences of Policy Failures and Effective Policy Responses

ANTON HEMERIJCK AND MARTIN SCHLUDI

3.1 Introduction

During the 'golden age' most advanced industrial societies developed their own country-specific brands of welfare capitalism. The various models of welfare capitalism were built upon relatively coherent policy mixes of macroeconomic policy, wage policy, taxation, industrial policy, social policy, and labor market regulation. The comparatively smooth interplay among these interdependent policy domains contributed to the achievement of economic growth, full employment, social protection, national solidarity, and political stability. Moreover, the international economic regime of 'embedded liberalism' (Ruggie 1982; see Scharpf, this volume) gave national policymakers a substantial degree of freedom to pursue relatively independent economic and social policies without undermining domestic and international stability.

The virtuous dialectic between economic growth and social policy development was suddenly brought to an end in the early 1970s. In the wake of the manifold recessions that followed in the mid-1970s, early 1980s, and early 1990s, it became increasingly difficult for advanced welfare states to deliver on their core commitments to full employment, social protection and equality. Already in the late 1960s, problems of labor discipline and accelerating inflation threatened to erode the historical settlement between capital and labor (Crouch and Pizzorno 1978). Since then, three important changes in the international political economy unsettled the relative 'goodness of fit' across important policy areas and between the domestic and international political compromises (see Scharpf, this volume). First, after the *first oil price shock of 1973*, the problem of stagflation—the contemporaneous rise of inflation and unemployment—came to haunt national economies. Second, the emergence of a very restrictive international economic environment, with extremely high real interest rates, in the wake of the *second oil crisis of 1979*, pushed up unemployment to levels not seen since the Great Depression. Low growth, rising social expenditures, and recurrent external disequilibria led to fiscal crises in many of the countries in our project. Third, since the mid-1980s the *liberalization and deregulation of capital and product markets*, most notably the creation of a single European market with a single currency, further constrained national fiscal and monetary policy and extended the need for austerity in social and employment policy. Moreover, manifold policy failures to manage the crises of the 1970s and 1980s brought on a distinct shift in the balance of political power from the left to the right.

Despite mounting economic and political pressures, scholars of comparative social policy have so far found the policies and institutions of the advanced welfare states remarkably resistant to change (Pierson 1994, 1996; Esping-Andersen 1996). By treating the welfare state as a rather static policy structure, narrowly defined in terms of social protection against the exigencies of the market, they have tended to overlook the interaction effects among different areas of social and economic regulation over time that go beyond the welfare state's core 'distributive' social security programs. These include: (1) macroeconomic policy—including fiscal, exchange rate, and monetary policy; (2) incomes policy and industrial relations; (3) industrial and competition policy and regulation; (4) tax policy; (5) labor market policy and regulation; and, finally, (6) social security policy. Although this set is not exhaustive, these six areas of social and economic regulation have been highly relevant for reaching the key objectives of full employment, social security and equity in advanced welfare states. During the 'golden age', Keynesian economic management, explicitly designed to meet the goal of full employment, gained a hegemonic position in a majority of the countries in our project. Systems of industrial relations and collective bargaining have been crucial in terms of employment and income distribution, through systems of wage indexation. In the 1970s incomes policy measures were used to expand the welfare state in exchange for wage moderation. In the area of industrial, trade and competition policy, nationalized industries were important employers while tariff barriers on imports also helped to protect employment in countries with very large home markets. Moreover, public utilities in transport and postal services provided secure jobs for a large part of the workforce (Héritier and S. K. Schmidt, Volume II). Social services in education and health care, provided by the state, served to guarantee universal access, security, continuity, and affordability. Systems of progressive taxation, necessary for the financing of the welfare state, were used to reduce the level of inequalities. Labor market regulation, laying down the ground rules governing working conditions and job protection, served to protect workers from, among other things, unfair dismissals. While the 'right to work' is difficult to uphold in any capitalist economy, in the 1960s and 1970s many countries adopted some elements of 'active labor market' policy whose primary aim was to avoid structural unemployment by assisting the geographic and sectoral mobility of workers and by upgrading their skills. Finally, social security, the core policy area of the welfare state, was designed to protect the aged, the sick, the unemployed, and the poor by providing them with adequate sources of income and decent levels of public assistance.

Over the past three decades, all advanced welfare states have been reconfiguring, under cumulative international constraints, the basic policy mix upon which national welfare states were built after 1945. The consecutive changes in the international political economy have disturbed the once stable postwar 'equilibria' of employment-friendly macroeconomic policy, collective wage setting, active industrial policy, progressive taxation, generous social security policy, and protective labor market regulation. As a consequence, many of these policy areas have become the object of reform. These policy changes, in turn, have put cumulative constraints on the capacity of policy-makers to reconcile the goals of welfare and work in the open economy. The shift to monetarism and restrictive fiscal policy in the 1980s and 1990s undermined the capacity of national policy-makers to use macroeconomic policy instruments to achieve full employment. Open capital and product markets put severe limits on solidaristic wage policies and progressive taxation. Collective bargaining was decentralized and wage indexation eliminated. In the area of industrial policy, the deregulation, liberalization, and privatization of public monopolies undermined labor hoarding strategies, and thus added to already high levels of unemployment in many countries. Downward pressure on tax levels reinforced the predicament of permanent austerity for the welfare state. In the 1990s, finally, the core areas of the welfare state, social security and labor market policy, moved to the frontline of the adjustment effort. In the process, the policy changes triggered by external economic challenges over the past decades have interacted with the ongoing endogenous social changes of demographic aging, family change, increased female participation in the labor market and the shift from manufacturing to services.

The guiding question of this chapter is this: how, and to what extent, have the relatively stable postwar policy profiles been reconfigured by policy changes, prompted by important changes in the international economy? In this chapter, we explore the substantive causal mechanisms between changes in the international political economy and domestic policy adjustment, understood as a *system-wide search* for a new, economically viable, politically feasible, and socially acceptable profile of social and economic regulation.

The chapter first presents our theoretical perspective on the 'sequential' logic of policy adjustment, understood as a *dynamic* political process of *problem-induced* policy learning. We next examine how and why the twelve countries in our project responded the way they did to the successive challenges of the international political economy and assess the relative effectiveness of their policy responses in the 1970s, 1980s and 1990s. We then try to specify the central requirements and identify novel mixes of policy programs for effective adjustment in the first decade of the twenty-first century on the basis of the more successful countries in the 1990s. In conclusion, we turn to the question of whether there is a pattern of policy adjustment that is in any sense typical of the advanced welfare states.

3.2 The Sequential Logic of Policy Adjustment

3.2.1 Policy Learning in the Welfare State

The current predicament of the welfare state is best described as an endeavor to match equity and efficiency. Today, many observers fear that the welfare state is haunted by a tragic tradeoff between economic efficiency and social justice (Esping-Andersen 1996; Iversen and Wren 1998). Policy adjustment in the new era of global competition takes place in a highly charged political context (Pierson 1998; Hall 1999b). Although governments may no longer be able to rely on their protective postwar policy profiles to achieve the objectives of full employment, social protection and equality, the nation state still is the principal site of policy change. Policy changes have to be endorsed by elected governments and parliament and continue to be mediated by national political parties, organized interests, and other relevant institutional structures like bureaucracies and systems of interest intermediation (Hirst and Thompson 1997).

The predicament of policy adjustment under international constraints very much revolves around creating a political consensus over 'what to do' and 'who should pay'. Political actors simultaneously have to solve a production problem—the search for economically effective solutions to the pressures of international competition—and a distribution problem—agreement over the distribution of the cost and benefits—associated with selected policy alternatives. Policy adjustment is an extremely risky political endeavor. Governments that fail to adequately respond to key challenges in the international political economy run the risk of being voted out of office. The 1979 election, which brought Thatcher to government in the United Kingdom, is a telling example of how economic mismanagement under Labour was punished by the voters. Distributive conflict over welfare reform is likely to intensify political controversy over the adjustment process. The extraordinary elections of 1997 in France, which brought the socialists back into office under Jospin, is illustrative of the political risks of welfare retrenchment and the deep-seated popularity of social policy. In short, any government's success in the electoral arena over the past decades has been critically dependent on its ability to steer the process of adjustment between the Scylla of economic mismanagement and the Charybdis of dismantling the welfare state.

Policy adjustment under international constraints is about making deliberate and purposive changes in the instruments and goals of social and economic regulation in response to the cumulative pressures of the international political economy. Policy adjustment has two basic characteristics. It is *reactive* and *not routine*, in the sense that standard lessons from past policy experience no longer seem adequate. In agreement with the canons of organizational theory, we regard policy adjustment as driven by 'problem-induced search', with an eye toward resolving problems and restoring basic policy efficacy (March 1994).The starting point for policy adjustment is the prevalence of pressing policy problems or challenges. We employ a behavioral conceptualization of policymakers as 'problem-solving' actors. We do not ignore institutional self-interest, opportunism, or rent-seeking, and political calculations that influence policy actors' decisions. Strategic considerations matter a great deal. The world of policy and politics operates on a different logic of decision-making and interaction than is true for the market economy. Policy choices are always taken in the context of public debate, argumentation, deliberation and persuasion and with regard to the political community of which actors are members (Majone 1989). Under conditions of crisis, institutional self-interest is often pushed into the background. Moreover, even within the narrow boundaries of institutional self-interest and normative orientations of political actors, there is considerable scope for problem-oriented policy responses. The Dutch experience of welfare reform shows that political actors, especially in a severe economic crisis, may even be willing to risk electoral defeat if they consider their decisions necessary and 'good for the country'.

Policy adjustment is best portrayed as a trial and error process of policy learning, in which pressing problems are considered and various policy alternatives tried in the hope of restoring policy satisfaction. In the social sciences, the literature on 'policy learning', 'policy oriented learning', 'lesson drawing', 'government learning', and 'organizational learning' has become a veritable growth industry (Argyris and Schon 1978; Bennet and Howlett 1992; Feick 1992; Goldstein and Koehane 1993; Huber 1991; Rose 1993; Sabatier and Jenkins-Smith 1993; Cohen and Sproull 1996;

Olsen and Peters 1996; Braun and Busch 1999). The different proponents of the variegated concept of learning are in agreement over a number of dimensions: First of all, learning serves the purpose of better goal attainment. Second, learning is problem- or failure-induced. However, third, policy problems are riddled with ambiguities and, fourth, policy actors are mere boundedly rational satisficers. Fifth, policy learning combines policy analysis and political decision-making.

Peter Hall (1993: 278) has defined policy learning as a 'deliberate attempt to adjust the goals or techniques of policy in the light of the consequences of past policy and new information so as to better attain the ultimate objects of governance'. Although policy learning is *directed* at better goal attainment, learning should not be mistaken for generating positive outcomes *per se*. Policymakers, pressed to make swift decisions, are likely to make mistakes because policy problems are inherently ambiguous. In the 1960s economists believed that no economy could simultaneously suffer both from high inflation and high unemployment: the condition of inflation would stimulate the economy, and unemployment would serve to reduce inflation. After the first oil price shock, it took a long time before economists and then policymakers recognized that the problem of stagflation was both empirically and theoretically possible. This goes to show that political decision-makers are critically constrained in their capacities to diagnose the new problem constellations, to design and implement viable policy proposals. Moreover, policymakers often do not have the time to be optimizers to consider all possible alternatives and choose the 'best solution'; they have to accept *satisficing* rather than optimal solutions. Under conditions of bounded rationality (Simon 1976, 1996) policy actors are likely to pursue strategies of adjustment which they wrongly believe to be feasible at a certain point in time, but serve only to reinforce policy pressures rather than relief. By the same token, policy actors under the same pressure to make a swift decision may fail to be aware of the full range of policy alternatives and therefore do not adopt the most effective policies.

Before policy alternatives are placed on the political agenda, the status quo must be considered unsatisfactory. Politically, current problems must be considered so daunting that the costs of inaction and non-decision outweigh the costs of policy change. Policymakers keen on *satisficing* are, more often than not, biased towards routine policymaking. As long as policy performance matches acceptable targets, political actors will be cautious about proposing drastic reforms. Organizational theorists emphasize the role of organizational 'slack' in processes of organizational change (Cyert and March 1963). Slack accumulated in good times can serve as a buffer in bad times. In the face of organizational decline, managers discover ways to decrease slack by cutting costs and through organizational restructuring. In the world of the policy and politics of the welfare state, however, normative aspirations and prior political commitments do not swiftly adapt to a decline in policy performance. The 'golden age' of rising expectations saw the institutionalization of welfare programs, which in due course came to be seen as inalienable rights. The institutionalization of expectations as rights, to be sure, raises substantial difficulties for the politics of reneging on earlier policy commitments.

When policy performance falls below acceptable targets, as in the case of stagflation becoming structural, search activity is increased to close the 'competency' gap. Crisis and unexpected shocks can trigger the search for effective adjustment. In periods of sustained poor performance, political pressure intensifies, which eventually induces even the most entrenched policymakers to see problems and policies in a new light.

3.2.2 Policy Analysis and Decision-Making

Policy adjustment is as much the outcome of 'puzzling'—diagnosing the nature and magnitude of the problems at hand, setting priorities, and identifying potentially effective policy solutions—as it is a product of 'powering', skillfully rallying political and societal support for the selection of particular solutions (Heclo 1974). Choices about where to search for effective solutions reflect cognitive as well as political factors, ideas as well as interests. Accumulated policy failures can induce a readiness for policy learning, provoking in turn an 'unfreezing' process in which old ideas loose their portent and new insights can be accommodated in the policy process (Hall 1993). Seen as learning, policy adjustment is an open and creative process.

Political decision-makers must want to learn something that they do not already know. Policy learning requires a readiness to subject pre-established policy ideas to critical insights, new information, and experience across time and place. Policy learning is about the mobilization of ideas and expertise to identify problems and propose solutions. In terms of *puzzling*, what matters is the capacity of policy actors to achieve an informed and accurate diagnosis of ongoing changes in the international economic environment, to arrive at an appropriate understanding of the prevailing policy profile's vulnerabilities, based not only on sound evaluation of past policy performance but also on new insights and ideas from academic circles.

Of special importance is the organization of swift dissemination of policy analysis within the policy system; the storage of memory and new information and insights. Policy learning is institutionally nested. Of key relevance are institutions that are able to span the boundaries between experts, policymakers and other interested parties. Such 'boundary spanning' institutions structure the policy discourse by shaping the perceptions of actors over what is desirable and feasible, and thus affect policy outcomes (see V. A. Schmidt, this volume). These institutions can help to recognize fundamental changes in the policy environment at an early stage, to communicate adequately policy-relevant research to policymakers, and to suggest courses of action that might be effective and recognized as legitimate. For a common understanding of problems and policies, the provision of trustworthy information, or 'commonly understood facts', is crucial. Although there is always the danger of 'group think', a high level of coherence in policy analysis is likely to facilitate a shared understanding of problems and solution than an fragmented landscape of many think-tanks and consultancy firms.

Policy development, however much dependent on effective policy analysis, is ultimately about the mobilization of authority: governments are making binding decisions and seeing to it that they are implemented accordingly. In terms of *powering*, what is important is to orchestrate a consensus over 'what to do' among key policy actors and to implement feasible strategies which can be legitimized by relevant interests in terms of prevailing normative orientations through the relevant political institutions.

While policymakers may be overwhelmed by mounting policy problems, they are seriously constrained in their capacity to act by prevailing institutions, policy legacies, past commitments of standing programs, and the numerous actors in different policy areas, pursuing multiple and often contradictory goals. For the countries in our project, we observe considerable variation in policy content, methods of provision, and modes of institutional governance across different policy sectors (Hollingsworth and Boyer 1997). In some countries the sphere of industrial relations is, for instance, fully autonomous from state intervention; in others there is a strong tradition of state intervention in industrial relations. In corporatist political economies political authority over industrial relations is 'shared' by the state and the social partners. A similar variation applies to the area of social security. In Bismarckian Continental regimes, there is a strong tradition of associational self-regulation as a corollary of payroll financing. The upshot is that for areas where policymaking authority is shared between the state and non-state corporate actors, adjustment requires the explicit or tacit agreement of many of the parties involved. And the more participants there are in the adjustment process, each with its conflicting objectives and divergent understandings of the problems at hand, the greater the controversy over the direction of policy adjustment is likely to become.

Policy changes are more often the result of temporary political disequilibria than the outcome of intelligent policy analysis *per se*. At best, the two go together. A shift in the balance of power, to be sure, allows certain political actors to impose their definition and diagnosis of policy failure along with an appropriate solution on the rest of the policy community. Power, however, is often negatively correlated with learning: Karl Deutsch aptly defined power as 'the ability to afford not to learn' (Deutsch 1963: 111). In this respect, the return to strategies of coordinated wage moderation in many countries in our project the 1980s can be interpreted as the result of a learning process, triggered by a shift in the balance of power between labor and capital in favor of the latter, whereby unions recognized at the cognitive level the idea that sustained wage moderation could help to restore profits, which would in turn lead to new investments and ultimately jobs.

Policy adjustment is usually characterized by long periods of stability, with only incremental changes in the policy profile and brief periods of 'episodic' change when both the *means* and *ends* of policy become fundamentally contested. Dramatic policy mistakes, by raising the overall problem load, can prompt a readiness for policy adjustment, triggering swift policy responses with long-term consequences for subsequent policy developments. Undesirable and unexpected economic shocks may widen the scope for path-breaking policy change, especially when policies that were effective in the past come to be identified as the core reason for policy failure. This creates important windows of opportunity for restructuring policies and institutions (Keeler 1993; Cortell and Peterson 1999). In many countries the recession of the late 1970s served as a 'triggering device', discrediting many left of center coalitions and providing the new conservative governments with a major opening for a restrictive policy package of fiscal consolidation, privatization, and welfare retrenchment. Mistakes are not necessarily a waste of time; they can energize the policy process by allowing political decision-makers to overcome institutional rigidities that would persist under normal circumstances.

Policy actors constantly learn from their ongoing assessment of the policies they are engaged with on a daily basis. The lessons they draw from their assessments lead to conclusions about both the instruments and objectives of public policy. Following Hall, lessons over the means or policy instruments are usually advanced by insider experts. A more fundamental type of policy learning, concerning the goals of public policy, which Hall coins 'social learning', usually originates outside the policy inner circle, as a result of the politicization of dramatic policy fiascos. This form of learning is accompanied by a change in prevailing policy paradigm, which he defines as the overarching set of ideas specifying 'how the problems facing [policymakers] are to be perceived, which goals must be attained through policy and what sort of techniques can be used to reach those goals' (Hall 1992: 91). We would like to add a third dimension. In the context of a severe performance crisis, often not only do objectives and instruments become the object of adjustment but also institutional rules, responsibilities and the once stable boundaries between policy areas get redrawn. In short, the rules of the game become political variables, objects of reform and obstacles to overcome. Policy failures not only energize the policy process in a search for new instruments and goals; they also unleash a search for new rules. As a consequence, institutional parameters lose some of their primacy as explanatory variables.

3.2.3 Profiles, Problems, Performance, and Adjustment

As a consequence of cumulative changes in the international political economy and ongoing interaction effects among interdependent policy areas, policy adjustment essentially follows a 'sequential' pattern in which political attention and policy action shift from one area to another. In the wake of each of the recessions of the mid-1970s, early 1980s, and early 1990s, policy actors entertained different options for changing or maintaining the existent policy profiles. Their options depend, among other things, on the available room of maneuver across policy areas at the different stages in the process of economic internationalization. For instance, compensation for a dramatic fall in aggregate demand in the mid-1970s was addressed by very different responses. One response was to use industrial policy in support of ailing firms so as to maintain employment. Another would be to increase public sector employment or to stimulate effective demand by welfare expansion.

It is very important to emphasize that the range of policy alternative choices and the relative importance of single policy areas in the process of adjustment changes over time, in correspondence with the rise of new problem constellations in the international economic environment. In the 1970s, macroeconomic policy was still considered a vital tool for maintaining full employment. In the 1990s macroeconomic policy changed its character to become a necessary, but not sufficient, background condition for economic stability.

Policy adjustment follows essentially a sequential logic for three reasons. The first has to do with exogenous shocks in the policy environment, like the first and second oil crises. If such shocks no longer allow government to achieve their preferred employment and social policy goals through policies that were successful and feasible in the past, they are forced to consider non-routine adjustment. The swift liberalization of capital markets in the 1980s precluded the kind of reflationary fiscal and monetary policy strategies that were pursued in the 1970s. By the same token, EMU restrictions on monetary and fiscal policy led policymakers in Italy and France to bring social policy and labor market regulation to the center of the adjustment process in the 1990s.

The second reason for sequential adjustment stems from endogenous second-order *spillover* effects in the policy profile environment. Policy-makers have short attention spans and usually focus on politically salient, area-specific problem constellations, ranging from rising unemployment to industrial decline, accelerating inflation, escalating budget deficits and the fall in the demand for low-skilled labor in the context of globalization. In the event of an external shock, policymakers usually work out a resolution to one set of problems, prevailing at a certain point in time, within the specific policy area that seems to be immediately affected. However, if this fails, the burden of adjustment is endogenously shifted to other policy areas. This is especially true in the case of policy failures. In Britain, the Netherlands, and Belgium, mismanagement of the crisis of stagflation through fiscal relation triggered a shift to a tight fiscal and a hard currency policy in the early 1980s under the conservative governments. As a consequence, the burden of adjustment was shifted on to the labor market and different systems of industrial relations in these countries. By the same token, successful policy responses early in the adjustment process make it easy to delay subsequent adjustments to new problem constellations at a later stage. In Fig. 3.1 we display the general character of the sequence of policy adjustment prompted by the shifting problems constellations in the 1970s, 1980s, 1990s. What is of great importance in the diachronic pattern of adjustment are: (1) the starting constellation of the national policy profile; (2) the basic policy response to any challenge; and (3) the relative success or failure in meeting the challenge, which determines to a large degree the future room for maneuver and the need for more path-breaking policy reforms at later stages in the process of policy adjustment.

Changes in the international political economy engender a multitude of diachronic spill-over effects across interdependent areas of social and economic regulation. The degree of interdependencies across the policy areas of macroeconomic policy, wage setting, industrial and competition policy, taxation, social security, and labor market regulation, however, differs. In some welfare states such interdependencies are the product of policy design. For instance, elaborate systems of wage indexation affect public financing. By the same token, the revenue basis of payroll-financed welfare states is critically dependent on levels of employment.

The crucial issue in the case of strong interdependencies between different policy areas is how policy interdependencies are *politically* managed.

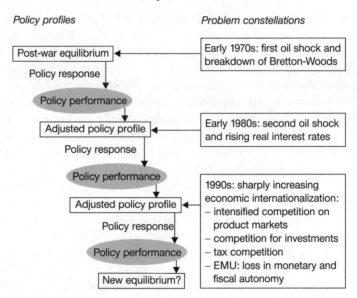

Figure 3.1 Sequence of policy adjustment

In an elementary fashion, we can distinguish between 'loosely' and 'tightly' coupled welfare states (Weick 1976; Freeman 1995; Ebbinghaus and Manow 1998; Hemerijck and Kersbergen 1999). Loosely coupled welfare states are characterized by a high degree of mutual indifference at the level of decision-making. Tightly coupled welfare states, by contrast, are characterized by decision-making institutions that enable policymakers to coordinate policy interdependencies. Historically, the Swedish model of the 1960s and 1970s is a perfect example of a 'tightly coupled', highly interdependent welfare state. The Swedish policy profile revolved around four tightly connected policies: a loose fiscal and monetary policy, supported by centralized wage moderation, an active labor market policy pushing workers to new job opportunities and out of unemployment, and a solidaristic wage policy, in line with egalitarian normative principles, to speed up structural change by not allowing inefficient firms to stay in the market. To be sure, the manifold interdependencies among the different policy areas of the Swedish welfare state required positive coordination among the key players in the Swedish model. It should be emphasized, however, that there is not necessarily a direct link between the degree of interdependency at the level of policy problems and the degree of coordination at the level of decision-making structures.

In an ideal-typical fashion, policy adjustment in loosely coupled welfare states follows a pattern of spontaneously crosscutting spillover. It typically takes place without design. Even though policy adjustment is not a product of explicit coordination, policy change is not necessarily chaotic. Although policy change in one policy area often involves unintended and unanticipated consequences for other areas, adjustment takes place through local adaptation: policymakers in the affected policy areas are likely to behave in a systematic way by adapting their behavior to changes made in neighboring policy areas. The advantage of loose coupling lies in the swift mobilization of knowledge and resources to address local problems effectively through decentralized elaboration, innovation, and implementation of policy goals. In terms of coordination, policy actors in these systems, at best, follow a strategy of 'negative coordination' in trying to avoid negative externalities and spillovers (Mayntz and Scharpf 1975).

Effective policy adjustment in tightly coupled welfare states requires 'positive coordination', on the basis of a common agreement on overarching policy goals. In an ideal-typical fashion, policy actors in different areas coordinate their behavior in such a way that each can cope adequately with sector-specific constraints while at the same time contributing to joint problem-solving at the macro-level of the economy and the polity. Thus, effective policy adjustment in tightly coupled welfare is the product of coordinated change and issue-linkage across different policy areas. *If* positive coordination can be reached, tightly coupled welfare states are able to pursue effective adjustment by widening the space for effective policy mixes going beyond the narrow scope of merely 'negative coordination'. Although strong policy interdependencies require overarching institutions of policy coordination, this does not guarantee that positive coordination does in fact take place. Tightly coupled welfare states always run the risk of institutional self-blockage, thereby foreclosing any possibility of effective policy responses being elaborated, adopted, and implemented (Scharpf 1997b).

3.3 The Effectiveness of National Adjustment Patterns in a Changing International Political Economy

As the empirical evidence provided in this projects suggests, the effectiveness of policy adjustment differs across countries, periods and policy areas. Since policy adjustment is inherently related to both the prevailing domestic and international problem constellation at different points in time, there is not likely to be a superior policy mix for all countries at all times. This section thus tries to shed light on the effectiveness of certain policies under specific and changing conditions in the policy environment. We focus in particular on the capacity of actors to deal with the manifold *interdependencies* and *spillover* effects between the various areas of social and economic regulation. We also highlight the importance of the *timing* of reforms. In adopting, finally, a more dynamic perspective of *policy learning*, we go beyond the argument of path-dependency and regime-specific pathologies to show how experiences of policy learning, often triggered by severe economic crises, can push the adjustment process in directions which substantially deviate from traditional trajectories.

3.3.1 Changing Problem Constellations in the International Political Economy and the Process of Adjustment [1]

For the 1970s the economically advanced welfare states were confronted with the problem of stagflation—the simultaneous rise in both inflation and unemployment—mainly triggered by the combined effect of the breakup of the Bretton-Woods system of fixed exchange rates in 1971 and the sharp increase of raw oil prices in 1973–74 (see also the previous chapter). The degree to which countries were able to avoid stagflationary crises is best grasped by juxtaposing the development of inflation and employment levels. [2] There is a remarkable variation across countries in the extent to which they have been able to get to grips with the problem of stagflation in the 1970s. As shown in Fig. 3.2, which juxtaposes changes in employment rates and average levels of inflation for the 1970s, we observe that only Sweden managed to expand employment considerably, while keeping inflation at medium levels. Austria displayed a slight increase in employment levels and low levels of inflation. While employment was relatively stable in Italy, New Zealand, and the United Kingdom, this came at the price of escalating inflation. At the opposite end of the spectrum Germany and Switzerland were most successful in fighting inflation, but they experienced a significant decline in employment. The same is true for Belgium, though at a significantly higher level of inflation. The Netherlands, facing similar inflationary pressures as Belgium, suffered the most dramatic drop in employment. At slightly higher levels of inflation, on a par with Sweden, Denmark stabilized its level of employment, while Australia and France faced both a modest fall in employment.

Success or failure in containing stagflation was critically dependent on the ability of political actors to organize a coordinated interplay among monetary, fiscal, and income policy. As sketched out in Fig. 3.3, our coun-

[1] The quantitative information is based on the data appendix at the end of this volume. Where we use other sources, this is indicated in the text.
[2] While the rate of open unemployment does not adequately reflect a country's real employment performance, we look primarily on the employment/population ratio—share of total employment as % of persons aged 15–64—as a more valid indicator for the success of national employment policies.

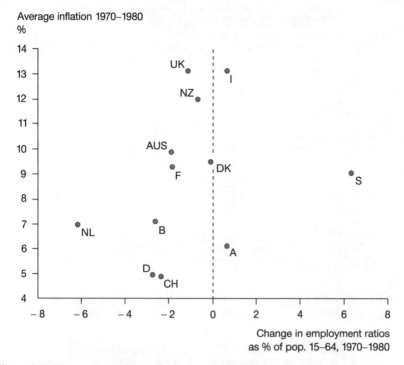

Average inflation 1970–1980

Figure 3.2 Macroeconomic performance in the 1970s

Sources: OECD, *Statistical Compendium: Economic Outlook* (Paris: OECD, 1999); own calculations.

try samples' relative successes or failures during the 1970s were the result of very different national trajectories of macroeconomic policy adjustment. While there has not been a single superior strategy of success, it seems clear in retrospect that wage restraint has been a necessary, though not sufficient, precondition of any successful strategy against stagflation.

In the wake of the second oil crisis of 1979, the international economic environment changed again significantly. While the problem of stagflation lost some of its salience in the 1980s,[3] increasing levels of economic internationalization and the sharp rise of real interest rates became the key challenges for advanced welfare states in this decade. As a consequence, the question of international competitiveness and profitability gained the upper hand in the policy debate. As a starting point for the evaluation of the effectiveness of national adjustment patterns in the 1980s we rely on

---

[3] This is, among others, indicated by time-series data on inflation: between 1980 and 1986 rates of inflation within the OECD–18 cluster subsided from 11.5% to 3.7%, thus displaying a mirror image to the development in the first half of the 1970s.

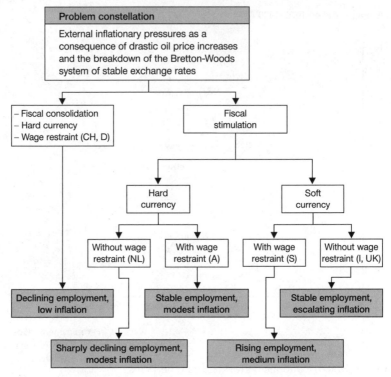

Figure 3.3 Patterns of macroeconomic adjustment in the 1970s: the problem of stagflation

two empirical indicators: change in employment levels and public deficits. In terms of policy effectiveness, the improvement of public finances became more important as liberalized capital markets and high real interest rates drove up the costs of public deficits.[4] While the persistent reliance on massive deficit spending in some countries throughout the 1980s might have been effective in terms of preserving the level of employment for some time, this strategy clearly came at the price of rapidly growing state debt. As Fig. 3.4 illustrates, in the 1980s there is again a considerable cross-country variation in policy performance. While a number of countries, such as Sweden, the United Kingdom, Australia and in particular Switzerland, successfully improved employment throughout the decade, others, such as Italy, Austria, France and especially New Zealand, experienced a significant deterioration of their employment performance in the

---

[4] For the average of the 18 richest OECD countries, outlays to serve the public debt have increased from 1.5% to 3.4% of GDP between 1979 and 1986 (OECD, *Economic Outlook*, various years).

1980s. The remaining countries, by and large, maintained their employment record. With respect to the degree of fiscal consolidation, the differences within our country sample are striking, too. The majority of the countries were able to keep public deficits on average below 3 percent of GDP in the 1980s. Switzerland, again, stands out, displaying practically a balanced budget throughout the decade. The Netherlands and New Zealand show a medium performance with public deficits between 4 percent and 5 percent. Belgium and Italy, clearly, score lowest in that respect, displaying average deficits of about 9 percent and 11 percent, respectively.

Until the late 1980s the macroeconomic environment was, by and large, relatively favorable. In most countries inflation and public deficits could be brought under control, while economic growth picked up. However, the reunification of Germany prevented a soft landing of European economies. As the Bundesbank feared that monetary unification and

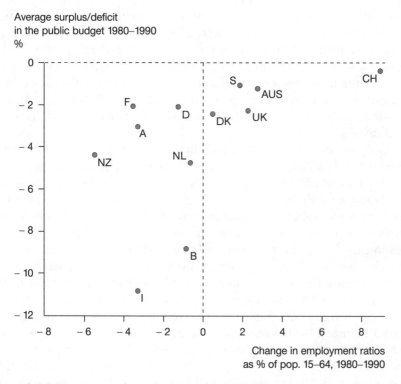

Figure 3.4 Macroeconomic performance in the 1980s

Sources: OECD, *Statistical Compendium: Economic Outlook* (Paris: OECD, 1999); own calculations.

sharply rising budget deficits might endanger price stability, it switched to a very restrictive monetary policy in 1991–92. Pegged to the Deutschmark, in part through the EMS, the other European economies had to follow suit. However, some countries were not able to credibly abide by the constraints on monetary policy imposed by the EMS. As a consequence Italy, Sweden and the United Kingdom had to devalue their currencies substantially. Partly as a result of the currency crisis, most European countries went into recession in the early 1990s, marking another rise in unemployment. As a result of high interest payments on the public debt and rising unemployment, public debt rose considerably in the majority of countries in our sample. If countries were to reduce their debt and the corresponding debt service in line with the EMU convergence criteria, some of the countries, especially Belgium and Italy, would have to run a primary budget surplus of over 5 percent for several years.

Against the background of these developments, policy attention and policy reform efforts increasingly gravitated to the core areas of the welfare state, that is, social policy and labor market regulation. This holds especially true for those countries which so far had been able to shield their systems of social security and employment protection from the pressures of adjustment. In particular, the reform of public pensions, which absorb a very large part of the public budget, was placed on the political agenda (for an overview on pension schemes and recent reforms, see Table 3.2), often triggering intense political conflict. Clearly, the difficulties of pension reform are inherently related to the status of pensions as an acquired right.

Policy performance in the international economic environment of the 1990s refers fundamentally to the effectiveness in increasing, or maintaining high levels of, employment in the private sector. In contrast to the 1970s and early 1980s, the expansion of the public sector can no longer be seen as a viable solution to the employment problem as this would require either an increase in taxes or higher deficit spending, strategies which have become unrealistic for both political and economic reasons. If we look at the changes in private employment during the 1990s, the performance record among the countries in our sample is again mixed. Most of the Continental welfare states suffered more or less strong losses in employment or, like Belgium, improved their very low employment record only slightly. Among the Continental welfare states, only the Netherlands display a dramatic increase in employment levels. The Anglo-Saxon countries, by contrast, all display an improvement of their employment performance. While Denmark proved able to maintain the level of employment in the private sector throughout the 1990s, Sweden at the same time faced a dramatic decline.

Table 3.1 *Changes in business employment levels and income distribution in the 1990s*

	Business employment ratio			Income inequality	
	1990	1998[a]	Change 1990–98	Ranking of countries in the mid-1980s[b]	Change from mid-1980s to mid-1990s[c]
Australia	57.9	58.7	0.8	11	+
Austria	51.0	48.9	−2.1	3[d]	++
Belgium	45.2	46.0	0.8	2	+
Denmark	53.0	52.8	−0.2	3[d]	++
France	46.9	44.6	−2.3	9	+
Germany	55.0	51.4	−3.6	5	+
Italy	45.2	42.8	−2.4	8	+
Netherlands	46.9	52.1	5.2	6	++
New Zealand	49.2	52.3	3.1	7	+++
Sweden	55.7	47.8	−7.9	1	+++
Switzerland	72.5	68.8	−3.7	12	+
United Kingdom	57.7	59.7	3.2	9	+++
Average	53.0	52.2	−0.8		

[a] 1997 for the Netherlands and Sweden.
[b] 1 refers to the country with the least unequal, 12 to the country with the most unequal income distribution.
[c] 1980s for Australia.
[d] Estimate.
Notes: + refers to a rise in income inequality between 2% and 7%; ++ refers to a rise in income inequality between 7% and 15%; +++ refers to a rise in income inequality of more than 15%.
Sources: Employment: OECD (1999g); own calculations. Income distribution: OECD (1996b, 1998c); Easton (1996).

As policy reforms increasingly touch upon the areas of social policy and labor market regulation, it also has become a major challenge for political actors to preserve the central functions of the welfare state: providing a certain level of income—and job—security, avoiding poverty and reducing inequality. As time-series data on poverty and income security are not available for all countries, we look at the change in income inequality in recent years as a proxy for the change in the redistributive capacity of the welfare state (Table 3.1). As the empirical evidence shows, there has been a general rise in income inequality since the mid-1980s. However, both the degree of changes and the level of income inequality differ considerably across countries. Among the countries in our project, income inequality rose most sharply in New Zealand, the United Kingdom, and Sweden. By contrast, Australia, Belgium, France, Germany, Italy, and Switzerland faced only a slight increase of income inequalities. Finally, a number of countries display medium increases, such as Austria, Denmark, and the

Table 3.2 *Synoptic overview of old-age pension systems and recent reforms*

	Public pension system 1995					Occupational pensions 1993			Recent significant reforms
	Type of benefit	Financing	Expenditures (% GDP)	Assets (% GDP)	Eligibility requirement for full basic pension	Type	Coverage (% employees)	Assets (% GDP)	
A	CR	Contributions (state subsidized)	8.8	—	No basic pension	Voluntary	10	—	Change of indexation from gross to net wages (1993); reduction of preferential treatment of public sector employees (1997)
AUS	MT	Taxes	2.6	—	10 years of residence (income/asset tests)	Compulsory	92	45	Introduction of a pattern of mandatory fully funded occupational pensions (since 1986)
B	CR	Contributions (state subsidized)	10.4	—	No basic pension	Voluntary	31	10	
CH	Mix of UF/CR/MT	Contributions (state subsidized)	6.7	6.0	Contribution during all years from age 21	Compulsory	90	70	Funded occupational pensions made mandatory (1985); only minor changes to public system
D	CR	Contributions (state subsidized)	11.1	1.1	No basic pension	Quasi-compulsory for public sector employees	42	6	Change of indexation from gross to net wages; reduction of benefits for early retirees, gradual increase in the normal retirement age for women (1992)

DK	UF/MT[a] CR[b]	Taxes[a] Contributions (fully funded)[b]	6.8	—	40 years of residence	Quasi-compulsory	80	21	Extension of coverage of occupational pension schemes through collective bargaining; pensioners taxed in the same way as other taxpayers (1994)
F	CR	Contributions (state subsidized)	10.6	−0.5	No basic pension	Compulsory	Universal	3	Change of indexation from gross to net wages (1984) and to inflation (1988); only private sector scheme: increase in the period of reference earnings (1994), transfer of non-contributory rights to a tax financed 'solidarity fund' (1993)
I	CR	Contributions (state subsidized)	13.3	0	No basic pension	Voluntary	5	4	Suspension of indexation to gross wages (1992); shift towards a more uniform contribution-based system with improved actuarial fairness and an effective reduction in average benefits (1995); introduction of tax incentives for individual retirement savings

Table 3.2 *cont.*

	Public pension system 1995					Occupational pensions 1993			Recent significant reforms
	Type of benefit	Financing	Expenditures (% GDP)	Assets (% GDP)	Eligibility requirement for full basic pension	Type	Coverage (% employees)	Assets (% GDP)	
NL	UF	Contributions	6.0	—	50 years of residence	Quasi-compulsory	83	85	Contributions to public pensions included in the personal income tax system (1990); introduction of the old-age pension savings fund (1996); calculation of benefits in occupational pension schemes on the basis of lifetime rather than last earnings (in progress)
NZ	UF	Taxes	5.9	—	10 years of residence	Voluntary	22	—	Link to 80% average wage (for couple) was abolished, relative value now below 70%; gradual increase of the statutory retirement age from 60 to 65 (1992–2001)

S	UF[a] CR[b]	Taxes[a] Contributions[b]	11.8 25.8	40 years of residence	Partly compulsory 90	16	Improved actuarial fairness, increased means-testing of basic pension, shift towards a defined- contributions scheme, increased prefunding through individual accounts (1998)
UK	CR	Contributions	4.5 −0.2	No basic pension	Voluntary 75[c]	82	Introduction of personal pensions as an option to contract out of the public scheme (1987); measures to increase the attractiveness of opting out (1986, 1995); replacement rate of public earnings-related scheme reduced from 25% to 20%, calculation basis extended from 20 years to all working years

[a] General basic pension.
[b] Supplementary pension.
[c] Including personal pensions.

Notes: MT: means-tested. CR: contributions-related benefit. UF: universal flat benefit.
Sources: Compiled on the basis of Gern (1998); Kalisch, Aman, and Buchele (1998).

Netherlands. On the whole, there is no systematic relationship between the change in income inequality and the change in levels of private employment in recent years. Thus, there is little evidence of an unavoidable trade-off between employment and equality. High levels of social security and employment are neither mutually exclusive nor mutually reinforcing. However, institutions are needed to bring these goals in line with one another.[5]

3.3.2 National Adjustment Patterns

The order in which we treat the country experiences loosely follows a regime-specific categorization. This allows to compare countries with 'similar' policy repertoires. We begin with Germany, which, as the biggest economy among the countries in our project, also marked out the room for manoeuver for other European countries in monetary policies. This holds especially true for Austria, the Netherlands and Belgium, which had pegged their currencies to the Deutschmark ever since the foundation of the European currency snake. Subsequently, we treat the other continental welfare states which have pegged their currencies at least temporarily to the Deutschmark: France and Italy. These countries are followed by Switzerland, which displays the lowest degree of economic integration with the EU among the Continental welfare states. We continue with the countries of the Scandinavian cluster. Within this cluster we first look at Denmark, which has been economically and politically more integrated into the EU than is the case for Sweden. We end with the Anglo-Saxon countries, of which we treat the United Kingdom first, since its inherited policy profile has more similarities to the other European welfare states than those of Australia and New Zealand.

3.3.2.1 Germany   In line with the prevailing macroeconomic policy paradigm, the majority of the countries in our sample initially responded to the first oil crisis with a strategy of fiscal reflation (Manow and Seils, Volume II). The exceptions were Germany and Switzerland. In Germany, the breakdown of Bretton-Woods allowed the Bundesbank to regain control over the supply of money. Faced with a massive inflow of capital and provoked by high wage agreements in 1974, eased by the commitment of the

---

[5] Taking the changes in private employment and income distribution as the primary performance indicators for the 1990s is not to play down the importance of price stability and consolidated public finances as necessary preconditions for effective adjustment. However, in recent years all countries in our project have effectively moved towards a policy of macroeconomic stability. Thus, cross-country differences in rates of inflation and budget deficits have declined tremendously.

Social Democratic government to full employment, the central bank decided to fight inflation, which had reached about 7 percent in 1973–74, by turning to a restrictive monetary policy. As a consequence, the effective exchange rate appreciated by almost 40 percent between 1972 and 1979. With respect to fiscal policy, the decentralized federal structure of the state made it difficult to organize an effective strategy of countercyclical demand management. In combination with the first oil-price shock, these factors triggered a deep recession in 1975, resulting in a sharp decline in the employment rate from 68.5 percent in 1973 to 65.7 percent in 1975 (Hennings 1982). The drop occurred almost exclusively within the industrial sectors, which were especially vulnerable to currency revaluations. In the second half of the 1970s Germany performed much better in terms of employment and inflation. This was mainly the result of a smoother interplay among fiscal, monetary, and wage policy. Since trade unions had switched to a moderate wage policy, anticipating the non-accommodating policy of the Bundesbank, the latter was able to loosen the reins of monetary policy. Moreover, fiscal policymakers adopted a more expansionary stance in 1978. As a result, employment levels rose slightly in the late 1970s, while inflation, though rising, could still be kept at a comparatively low level. The generally tighter stance in fiscal policy brought about some incremental cuts in social benefits. As a consequence, welfare spending, which had been growing considerably up to this point, more or less leveled off. Quite remarkably, Germany is the only country in our sample that spent a smaller share of its national income on social security in 1980 than it did in 1975. In contrast, most countries in our sample continued to expand their welfare state spending throughout the 1970s (see Table 3.3).

Germany's performance during the 1980s reveals a mixed picture. Clearly, Germany entered the decade with comparatively favorable conditions: inflation was modest and public deficits were within tolerable limits while unemployment was still at a comparatively low level of 3.2 percent in 1980. In the wake of the second oil crisis, however, the central bank, faced with a still expansionary fiscal policy, stepped on the brake by sharply raising interest rates. Moreover, when the economy started to recover in 1983, policymakers decided not to support the recovery process by way of monetary and fiscal expansion, although wage policies were moderate. As a result, employment levels fell sharply, from about 66 percent in 1980 to 61.6 percent in 1984. In the second half of the 1980s macroeconomic policy and wage policy worked together again much more smoothly. Inflation fell from 6.3 percent in 1981 to minus 0.1 percent in 1986 as a result of moderate wage policies and falling oil prices. Due to some monetary and fiscal stimulation, the economic recovery also paid off in terms of rising employment, reaching a level of almost 65 percent at the

Table 3.3 *Social security transfers and government final consumption as % of GDP in the 1970s*

		A	AUS	B	CH	D	DK	F	I	NL	S	UK	Aver.
1971	Social security transfers	15.6	5.7	14.2	8.3	12.9	11.2	17.1	13.1	18.5	12.1	8.4	12.5
	Government final consumption	14.8	12.5	14.1	10.9	16.9	21.3	13.4	15.5	16.9	22.5	17.8	16.1
	Sum	30.4	18.2	28.3	19.2	29.8	32.5	30.5	28.6	35.4	34.6	26.2	28.6
1975	Social security transfers	16.9	8.8	18.8	12.5	17.5	13.8	20.4	15.6	24.0	14.2	9.9	15.7
	Government final consumption	17.2	15.4	16.4	12.6	20.5	24.6	14.4	15.4	17.4	23.8	21.8	18.1
	Sum	34.1	24.2	35.2	25.1	38.0	38.4	34.8	31.0	41.4	38.0	31.7	33.8
1980	Social security transfers	19.0	8.8	21.0	12.7	16.5	16.6	23.2	15.8	25.8	17.8	11.5	17.2
	Government final consumption	18.0	16.5	18.0	12.7	20.1	26.7	15.2	16.4	17.9	28.8	21.3	19.2
	Sum	37.0	25.3	39.0	25.4	36.6	43.3	38.4	32.2	43.7	46.6	32.8	36.4

Source: OECD (1985).

end of the decade (Franzmeyer, Lindlar, and Trabold 1996). In institutional terms, a kind of implicit coordination between monetary policy and wage policy developed, whereby wage demands came to mirror the publicly announced money supply growth target to which the central bank committed itself.

The German economy's international competitiveness, based on high wage/high quality production, was strong for much of the 1980s. This competitive policy mix, however, required very high levels of productivity, reflected in declining demand for low-skilled labor in the industrial sectors. Manow and Seils (Volume II) show how German labor market problems are related to the failure to create enough jobs in the sheltered service sector for those laid off in the industrial sector. They argue that the design of German social security policy is a root cause of the German labor market predicament: due to its strong reliance on payroll financing, which boosts the costs of labor, the German welfare state tends to price out less productive employment from the market. As a consequence, and in spite of the German model's overall competitive success, the welfare system was increasingly used as an instrument of labor shedding after 1980. Under increased competitive pressure, German firms in high wage sectors could survive only if they were able to increase productivity. This was, in part, achieved through labor-saving investment strategies, raising workers' productivity levels through high-quality vocational training and education, and/or by laying off less productive or 'too expensive', mostly elderly, workers. The sheltered service sectors, on the other hand, were not able to compensate sufficiently for job losses in the industrial sector. This is mainly due to the rising tax wedge at the lower end of the income scale, which tends to price out low-skilled labor from the market.[6] While the employment ratio in the exposed sectors during the 1980s declined by 2.8 percentage points, the increase in the sheltered sector made up for only 1.5 percent of the working age population. As a consequence, the unemployment rate in 1990 was substantially above the level in 1980: 6.2 percent as compared with 3.2 percent.

To be sure, since as early as the mid-1980s there has been a growing concern that Germany was losing its attractiveness as a *Standort*—business location—for international investors owing to high levels of taxation and numerous rigidities in the labor market and welfare state. Against the background of favorable conditions in the world economy, however, pressure for adjustment remained limited until the end of the decade. In 1990 unification changed things dramatically. The East German economy

---

[6] This is also reflected in the degree of earnings dispersion at the lower half of the income scale—D5/D1—which decreased from 1.68 in 1984 to 1.44 in 1993 (see Manow and Seils, Volume II).

collapsed immediately in the face of western competition. Intra-German monetary unification's conversion rate of 1:1 for cash deposits and 2:1 for savings, reflecting a political decision in the run-up to federal elections rather than sound macroeconomic analysis, more or less destroyed the competitiveness of East German companies and led to a collapse of production and employment. Moreover, wage increases during the initial unification boom and rising budget deficits triggered inflationary pressures. While inflation for the OECD–18 fell on average from 5 percent in 1990 to 2.9 percent in 1992, the opposite was true for Germany, where inflation rose from 2.7 to 5.1 percent over the same period. The Bundesbank, strictly committed to maintaining price stability, reacted with a very restrictive policy between 1990 and 1993. As a result, the Deutschmark appreciated massively against other currencies. Tight money and currency appreciation combined to trigger a deep recession in 1993. While the loss of competitiveness was compensated by labor shedding, the resulting increase in social security contributions created additional wage pressure. The price was paid in the form of sharply falling employment. Ill-fated decisions in fiscal and wage policy contributed to the economic mismanagement of the early 1990s.

Fiscal policy, to begin with, suffered from bad timing. While, from an economic point of view, a more restrictive stance in fiscal policy would have been required during the unification boom, the Kohl Government decided to implement a demand-stimulating tax reform in 1990. Moreover, instead of financing the rapidly growing transfers to the east through higher value-added taxes (VAT) and lower public consumption expenditures in the west, the government raised the deficit and increased social security contributions. While the growing deficit reinforced the Bundesbank's restrictive monetary policy, the rise in social contributions added massively to the rising cost of labor. Like fiscal policy, wage policy also adjusted badly to the challenge of unification. During the reunification boom, trade unions pressed for high wage increases, which aggravated inflationary pressures. When the recession forced them to return to a moderate wage policy, however, the Bundesbank was too reluctant to loosen the monetary policy reins. This form of 'negative coordination' between organized labor and the Bundesbank sheds light on a fundamental weakness of the German wage bargaining system. While German trade unions have generally not followed a very aggressive course in their wage demands, typically lowering their aspiration levels swiftly in periods of sluggish growth, so far they have proved unable to commit themselves to long-term wage restraint. Broadly speaking, German unions considered wage restraint as a necessary evil so as to maintain existing jobs for 'insiders' rather than to create new jobs for the unemployed. Thus, German unions so far have not refrained from lifting wages above the market-clearing level. To some extent, this lack of restraint results from the fact that the tax burden on labor increased rapidly throughout the 1990s.[7] In order to expand the leeway for wage moderation it would have been necessary to reduce, rather than increase, the tax burden for wage earners. This, again, proved to be politically difficult. In order to reduce income taxes, the Kohl Government needed the support of the Social Democratic opposition, which had a majority in the Bundesrat, and this was not forthcoming. Moreover, a significant reduction of social contributions would have required a change in the indexation of public pensions. Since pensions are linked to net wages, any reduction in taxes or social contributions for wage earners spills over into higher pensions, which again would require higher contributions—thereby partly offsetting the reduction of the tax burden for the wage earners. However, since pension benefits in Germany are largely perceived as acquired rights, for which workers' own contributions have been paid, any reform in this area is likely to meet stiff political resistance.

As a consequence of the 'stop-go' pattern in wage demands, a smooth interplay between monetary policy and wage policy is difficult to sustain. Moreover, the investment behavior of capital owners is likely to be negatively affected if the commitment to wage restraint is not credible in the long run. A second fundamental mistake in wage policy refers to the fact that East German wages were quickly increased so as to catch up with the West German wage level. As these increases were not matched by corresponding levels of productivity, a sharp rise in unemployment could not be avoided. Moreover, as wage rounds are typically based on the principle that wage differentials within and across sectors should be kept within narrow limits, wage flexibility does not sufficiently reflect differences in productivity.

Another weak point in the German system of social and economic regulation that hampered effective adjustment concerns political actors' limited capacity for adequately linking solutions to problems in industrial relations and social security. In 1996 the Kohl Government called both unions and business associations to the bargaining table to talk about moderating wage settlements in the west, delaying the adjustment of eastern wages to western levels, and stepping up investments in the new *Länder*. The talks about an 'Alliance for Jobs' failed in the face of the government's sick pay reform package in 1996.

The lack of policy coordination is also a fundamental obstacle to pension reform. Basically, there is an agreement among the central political

[7] Between 1990 and 1998 social security contributions rose from 35.6% to 42.1% (see Manow and Seils, Volume II).

actors that a stronger emphasis on private, fully-funded pensions would strengthen the overall viability of the system. So far, however, they lack the strategic capacity for issue-linkage along those lines. Private pension saving and provision for occupational pension schemes are only partly encouraged by tax policy. Moreover, the rising burden of social contributions has crowded out the savings capacity of private households. Finally, the expansion of occupational pensions based on collective agreements is hampered by insufficient wage restraint on the part of the trade unions.

In terms of policy effectiveness, the German record of the 1990s is mixed. While its employment performance declined steadily, it faced only a minor increase in income inequality. After the unification boom employment levels fell continuously, from 66 percent in 1991 to 60.5 percent in 1998. Moreover, the lion's share of this job loss occurred in the private sector, where employment declined from 55.4 percent in 1991 to 51.4 percent in 1997–8. Thus, Germany displays, after Sweden, the largest drop in employment among the countries in our project during the 1990s. At the same time, unemployment almost doubled, reaching a record high of 11.4 percent in 1997. Also, other macroeconomic indicators reveal a below-average performance. Economic growth remained persistently below the international average after 1993. Public finances did not improve until 1996 and recovered only slightly thereafter. While the public deficit amounted to 3.5 percent of GDP in 1993, it was reduced only to 2.5 percent in 1998, as compared with a decline of deficits from 5.1 percent to 0.3 percent for the OECD–18 average. However, Germany proved very successful in fighting inflation, which was reduced to 0.9 percent in 1998. In combination with the compression of wage differentials at the lower end of the earnings scale, this might explain why income inequality has increased only a little bit in recent years. The welfare state suffered only incremental cuts for the 1990s. The lack of structural reform or is very likely to create problems of sustainability of the German welfare state, especially in the area of pensions in the first decade of the twenty-first century.

3.3.2.2 Austria   In contrast to Germany, Austria proved not only able to contain inflation but also to stabilize its level of employment throughout the 1970s (Hemerijck, Unger, and Visser, Volume II). When Austria faced the first oil price shock, the social-democratic government was determined to defend full employment. Austrian policy actors, including employers' organization and the conservative opposition party, adhered to a Keynesian diagnosis of the ensuing recession. A shared understanding of the crisis helped Austrian policymakers pursue a common policy strategy, coined 'Austro-Keynesianism'. Expansionary fiscal and monetary policies were deployed to stabilize effective demand and employment, and a hard currency policy was adopted as the appropriate instrument to curtail inflation, which rose from 4.4 percent in 1970 to 8.4 percent in 1975. Since 1976, the Austrian Schilling has been tied to the Deutschmark, resulting in a fall of inflation to 3.7 percent in 1979. Although the peg to the Deutschmark meant a continuous effective appreciation of the Schilling after 1976, the overall consensus in favor of the strong currency policy was never challenged. The social partners took responsibility for competitiveness by way of adopting a moderate wage policy.

Compared with most other west European countries, Austria seems to have escaped the polarizing impact of the resurgence of class conflict after 1968. In this respect, Austrian unions never pursued ambitious distributive goals. Full employment was regarded as the most effective distributive policy by all the actors involved in Austrian corporatism. Austria also had a unique administrative system of price controls, whose effectiveness was, however, limited. Export subsidies were used to ease the burden of the hard exchange rate on ailing industries. Another element of the successful Austro-Keynesian response to the first oil price shock was a substantial increase in the VAT on luxury goods, for the purpose of balancing a substantial current account deficit. Nationalized industries, finally, were effectively hoarding labor in the 1970s.

Owing to the high degree of coordination between fiscal policy and incomes policy—that is, between the state and the social partners—the Austrian economy's macroeconomic performance compared particularly well with other countries pursuing a hard currency policy during the stagflation period. While the Austrians were successful in maintaining full employment for most of the 1970s, this was partly the result of reducing the supply of foreign workers, as in Switzerland. All in all, Austria did remarkably well in maintaining above-average employment levels, remaining at about 68 percent throughout the 1970s, while simultaneously keeping inflation far below the international average at about 6 percent on average throughout the 1980s.

The second oil crisis in 1979 hit the Austrian economy much harder than the first, but not as hard as many other countries. This surely reflects the advantages of Austria's effective response to the first oil price shock. Nevertheless, Austria failed to 'dive through' the second oil crisis, as Hemerijck, Unger, and Visser (Volume II) argue. An isolated expansionary fiscal policy was no longer tenable. Moreover, the public deficit increased after 1975, reaching a high of 4.4 percent in 1987. Low growth throughout the decade, a growing current account deficit, and rising inflation had to be paid for by higher interest rates, which made debt servicing a mounting problem. Fiscal consolidation thus gained priority over full employment. Tax increases were enacted in 1983 but these produced no lasting relief. The stabilizing elements of the Austrian model—that is, the hard currency and the unions' moderate wage policy—were maintained. In short, the Austrian model lost some of its glory, but its performance kept up. While unemployment increased quite substantially, from 1.6 percent in 1980 to about 5 percent in the late 1980s, this was still low by international standards. However, employment levels fell from 67.5 percent in 1980 to below the OECD–18 average, reaching a low of 62.7 percent in 1987.

In the face of a structural crisis in the international steel industry in the mid-1980s, Austrian policymakers embarked on a program of large-scale restructuring of nationalized industries. In the late 1970s, firms in public ownership had employed about 9 percent of all workers, which amounted to no less than 25 percent of manufacturing employment. The steel crisis drove up unemployment and public deficits. The reorientation of industrial policy from 'government-led growth' to 'industrial adjustment' brought on a large-scale privatization of industry with negative implications for employment. In retrospect, it could be argued that the success of Austro-Keynesianism served to conserve old and outdated industries, hampering structural adjustment and technological change.

The Austrian response to mounting labor market problems in the 1980s followed the continental strategy of easy exit through the expansion of early retirement and disability pensions. In the process, the number of elderly workers fell dramatically. As a consequence, the ratio of beneficiaries of social transfers to active citizens in the working population rose substantially. After the mid-1980s, the government began to follow a policy of incremental retrenchment, introducing reductions in public employment, cuts in transfer payments, and a wage freeze on public employees. Social insurance contributions were also raised. By the late 1980s, the qualifying period for pensions was raised from ten to 15 years.

In 1988 a tax reform was enacted to boost regime competition. Corporation taxes were reduced and in 1989 marginal tax rates and the average level of income taxation was reduced significantly, but progression in income taxes increased. In 1993 asset taxation was abolished altogether. Throughout the decade, there was a moderate rise in earnings inequality, which increased even further wage differentials that were already much larger than in the other Continental and Scandinavian welfare states.

At the beginning of the 1990s, the Austrian economy was in relatively good shape, with lower levels of unemployment than in most other European economies. After the fall of the Berlin wall, Austria suffered from a dramatic supply shock of about 200,000 immigrant workers, amounting to 7 percent of the labor force. The restrictive policy of the

Bundesbank, moreover, engendered a strong appreciation of the Schilling, which dampened domestic demand and economic growth. This led to a rise in unemployment from 4.7 percent in 1990 to 6.4 percent in 1997. Moreover, the EMU required additional measures to reduce the budget deficit, which had increased from 2.4 percent in 1990 to 5.1 percent in 1995. Again, wage moderation helped to soften the combined effects of a hard currency. After 1995 a strict budget consolidation policy package was adopted, with the support of the social partners, to fulfil the Maastricht criteria. The *Sparpaket*—savings package—of 1995 involved cuts in benefits, reductions in social services, the expansion of means testing and qualifying periods, stricter regulation for unemployment benefits and early retirement, and a cap on health care spending, compensated by minor improvements in maternity leave and tax credits for families. The pension reform of 1997 extended once again the qualifying period from 15 to 18 years, while indexation of pension benefits was suspended for one year. In the area of social assistance legislation, the right to a benefit was made more contingent on willingness to work, enforced by tough sanctions.

Recently, active labor market policy measures, now under the joint jurisdiction of the social partners, have gained in importance. So far, only small adjustments have been made to regulations on working time. It should be stressed that Austria suffers from the least flexible labor time regulation in the European Union. In the 1990s the Austrian labor market was unable to absorb labor supply resulting from the swift increase in female participation and the large inflow of foreign workers. Overall employment fell again in the 1990s, from 65.2 percent in 1992 to 62.5 in 1997. The fall in business employment was partially compensated by a small increase in public sector jobs. Due to rising unemployment and significant cuts in social benefits, Austria faced a substantial, though not dramatic, rise in earnings inequality. Although Austria has thus managed to adjust incrementally to external economic pressures, it still has much to do to promote greater flexibility in the labor market and it has only just begun to institute reforms that would ensure the sustainability of the welfare state.

3.3.2.3 Netherlands While Austrian policymakers, operating under a hegemonic cognitive framework of Keynesian economics shared by all interested parties, managed to resolve the crisis of stagflation in the 1970s, their Dutch counterparts lacked a consensus on the nature of the mid-1970s recession (Hemerijck, Unger, and Visser, Volume II). In the early 1970s policymakers in the Netherlands responded to the collapse of the Bretton-Woods monetary system by bringing the guilder in line with the Deutschmark inside the Snake. The labor-led Den Uyl Government, which came to power in 1973, initially pursued an expansionary macro-economic policy. It strengthened purchasing power by increasing public expenditures. The social partners, however, and especially the trade unions, were unable to support fiscal expansion through wage modera-tion. With a fragile consensus on Keynesian reflation, trade unions were unprepared to moderate their wages. As a result, inflation shot up, from 3.6 percent in 1970 to 10.2 percent in 1975. In the face of an inflationary wage-price spiral, exacerbated by an elaborate system of wage indexation, employment levels fell sharply and public expenditure rose steeply because of the rapid increase in the number of social security recipients. Already in the 1970s, the Dutch continental welfare state embarked on a large-scale strategy of shedding older and less productive workers, mainly through disability pensions. The 'Dutch disease' was aggravated by gas exports that drove up the exchange rate—with negative side effects for exports—increased imports, and crowded out domestic products. While both public and private consumption rose, business investment fell considerably. After the mid-1970s, the government abandoned its demand-side policies of job creation. As the government's attempts to bring about centralized wage moderation failed, it imposed a number of wage freezes to contain the wage-price spiral. In the process, inflation came down from 10.2 percent in 1975 to 4.2 percent in 1979. By the end of the 1970s, rising unemployment, increasing public deficits, declining competitiveness and falling growth rates put the Netherlands in an extremely tight corner. In the process employment suffered a sharp decline from 61.6 percent in 1970 to 55.4 per-cent in 1980.

After the onslaught of the second oil price shock, the Dutch economy experienced a more severe recession than any other country in our project. Real demand suffered a serious decline, while unemployment reached double digits, employment fell to an all-time low of 51 percent, and the public deficit jumped up to 5.8 percent in 1983. The depth of the crisis of 1981–82 was a catalyst for policy change. In the face of rising real interest rates, the main policy objective now became fiscal retrenchment. The newly elected center-right coalition government under Lubbers in 1982 immediately threw its support behind a deflationary macroeconomic pol-icy program. In 1983 the guilder was officially pegged to the Deutschmark. Wage indexation was suspended, and a freeze was imposed on the mini-mum wage after it had been reduced by 3 percent. Public sector wages were also cut by 3 percent. Because of the outright failure to save the Dutch shipbuilding industry in the 1970s, industrial policy initiatives were virtu-ally suspended.

The shifts towards fiscal retrenchment and a hard currency meant that changes in the international economy had to be met by voluntary wage restraint and/or productivity increases. With soaring unemployment and declining union membership, after a decade of failed tripartite encounters, the Lubbers coalition's entry into office was crowned by the now famous 'Wassenaar Accord' in November 1982. With the Accord, the unions recognized that for a high level of investment, essential for job creation, an even higher level of profitability was required. They agreed to keep wage increases below productivity growth in exchange for a modest reduction in annual and weekly working hours. Ever since then organized wage moderation became the core element of the Dutch adjustment strategy. In the process, Dutch wage setting underwent a transition from a highly centralized but faltering system in the 1970s to a system dominated by industry-level bargaining under the shadow of central coordination. At the level of the bipartite Labor Foundation and the tripartite Social and Economic Council, central union, employers' organizations and government officials issued non-binding framework agreements. By doing so they tried to influence the bargaining agendas at the sectoral level. This form of two-level social dialogue and coordination proved particularly effective in establishing a 'goodness of fit' between the requirements of macroeconomic stability and microeconomic flexibility at the levels of firms and sectors, while creating a climate of a 'broad ownership' of the interconnected problems facing the Dutch economy. Wage restraint in the Netherlands ultimately paid off in terms of revolutionary job growth. After 1984, when the Netherlands fell to the lowest employment ratio of all the countries in our project—50.8 percent—employment increased steadily to a ratio of 54.8 by 1990, still about 13 percent below the OECD–18 average.

By the late 1980s a new mix of macroeconomic policy and wage policy was achieved, with fiscal policy oriented towards stabilizing the business cycle, monetary policy towards a fixed exchange rate *vis-à-vis* the Deutschmark, and incomes policy towards wage moderation. The record of adjustment in the contentious areas of social policy was mixed, however. In the 1970s, the Dutch welfare state had to absorb large job losses. This policy of subsidizing the exit of elderly, less productive workers and encouraging women to stay at home, mainly through the tax system, proved difficult to reverse in the 1980s. The heavy use of the generous disability scheme and early retirement facilities explains the fact that, in spite of fiscal retrenchment, the public deficit remained at about 5 percent throughout the decade. By the late 1980s, it became obvious that the Dutch welfare state, despite economic recovery through wage restraint, was trapped in a vicious cycle of 'welfare without work'. Cuts in benefit levels by 10 percent in 1987 were not enough to manage the 'crisis of inactivity'.

In the early 1990s, policymakers became aware that the low level of labor market participation was the Achilles' heel of the extensive but passive Dutch welfare state. With the participation of the social democrats in the third Lubbers administration, index-linking among contractual wages, minimum wages, and benefits was restored, but this was made contingent upon the ratio of inactives—welfare recipients—to actives—insurance contributors—in the population. This conditional indexation procedure encouraged the social partners to internalize the employment effects of wage bargaining.

The long period of wage moderation in the 1980s and 1990s had resulted in a strong competitive position by the early 1990s. Exports continued to increase much faster than the European average, while the downturn of 1992–93 was not as disastrous as in other European countries. While German unification first boosted economic growth, high interest rates started to dampen economic activity soon thereafter. As a consequence, the decline in unemployment immediately came to a halt. In the wake of the downturn, the government felt obliged to cut expenditures again and to impose another freeze on social security benefits. Moreover, as a result of the currency turmoil in the summer of 1992 the effective rate of the guilder rose by over 5 percent. This prompted the social partners to conclude a new bipartite agreement, called 'A New Course', in which the partners renewed their commitment to a *responsible wage policy*. Under this compromise, which reinforced the trend towards decentralization of collective bargaining and a greater degree of involvement by sectoral and firm-level negotiators, employers gave up their blanket resistance to shorter working hours, while unions promised to keep up wage restraint. Both pledged to improve the unfavorable employment/population ratio and agreed on more flexible employment.

For governments, the political exchange logic behind wage moderation changed character in the 1990s. Increasingly, wage moderation was matched by lower taxes and social contributions by employers, made possible by improved public finances and a broader tax base. During the 1990s the budget deficit fell from 5 percent to just over 1 percent. The new exchange logic was also supported by the tax reform of 1990, which integrated taxes and social security charges and lowered rates while limiting deductions.

Unemployment fell from a high of 7.6 percent in 1994 to below 4 percent at the end of the decade, and the rate of employment increased from about 56 percent to 62 percent, which brought employment back to the level of 1970. While public employment remained more or less stable, the growth in employment took place in the private sector, especially in the sheltered service sectors. Most remarkably, private employment in the 1990s surged from 47 percent in 1990 to over 52 percent in 1998.

After the first and second Lubbers Governments had exhausted the 'price' policy of bringing expenditures under control through the freezing and lowering of benefits, the emphasis in the 1990s shifted to the 'volume' policy aimed at reducing the number of recipients. Unavoidably, the political crisis of the Dutch welfare state came to revolve around the extended use of disability pensions for reducing labor supply. In spite of massive popular resistance, replacement rates were cut and stricter rules were applied to new medical examinations. In the elections of 1994, the third Lubbers coalition was effectively voted out of office. However, the new 'purple' coalition of Dutch social democrats, conservative liberals, and progressive liberals, the first government since 1917 without a confessional party, did not slow down the reform effort. The Partij van de Arbeid (PvdA) had a bottom-line condition: not to tamper with the level and duration of social benefits. From this position, the government committed itself to the 'jobs, jobs, and more jobs' strategy. This approach made its imprint on all kinds of social security and labor market policy initiatives. There were efficiency improvements in social security, including the introduction of financial incentives through a partial re-privatization of social risks—that is, shifting the financial responsibility for sickness benefits to individual employers—and a managed liberalization of social policy administration, which reduced the involvement of the social partners in social security administration. A second string of measures concentrated on the introduction and intensification of activation obligations for the long-term unemployed. In the area of labor market policy, an underdeveloped area in the Dutch postwar policy profile, many new initiatives were launched. Additional job programs for unemployed youths and the long-term unemployed gained in importance, while the public employment service was liberalized. Finally, the government introduced several kinds of employment subsidy schemes based on a reduction of social security contributions paid by employers.

Labor market flexibility has become an integral part of the new Dutch policy mix. Legislation removing constraints on shop opening hours, business licenses, temporary job agencies, working time, and dismissal law consolidated this development. Since 1993 Dutch unions and employers have increasingly come to exchange shorter working hours, an expansion of leave arrangements, the warranty of income stability throughout the year and lower overtime rates against the annualization of working hours and an expansion of work in the evenings or on Saturdays. The social partners are also in agreement that employers should honor workers' requests to work part-time unless there are compelling firm-related reasons for rejection. In 1995 unions and employers signed the first collective agreement for temporary workers, introducing a right of continued employment and pension insurance after four consecutive contracts or 24 months of service. This agreement subsequently paved the way for a virtual paradigm shift in Dutch labor market regulation with the adoption of the 'flexicurity' law in 1998. The 'flexicurity' law, as Hemerijck, Unger, and Visser (Volume II) argue, is a compromise whereby a slight relaxation of dismissal protection for regular employment is exchanged for improving the rights of temporary workers and introducing the presumption of an employment relation in the case of freelance work. Temporary employment agencies no longer need a license, but the law assumes that the agencies take on the responsibilities of employers.

The incremental individualization of the tax system since 1984 improved opportunities for switching from full-time to part-time jobs, and the removal of all remaining elements of discrimination on the basis of working hours have all contributed to a 'normalization' of part-time employment. With the expansion of the service sector, together with the revolutionary growth in part-time jobs, female participation increased from a very low level of just over 30 percent in the early 1970s to just under 65 percent in the late 1990s. As compared with the vast majority of the countries in our project, participation rates for men aged 55 to 64 increased significantly in recent years, from 41.5 percent in 1993 to almost 47 percent in 1998, which, however, is still comparatively low by international standards (OECD 1999b).

In retrospect, as Hemerijck, Unger, and Visser (Volume II) argue, Dutch unions have consistently placed jobs before income ever since 1982. Employment growth and macroeconomic stability subsequently created economic and political preconditions for the path-dependent transformation of social security and labor market policies. The positive interaction effects among sustained wage moderation, the expansion of part-time work, the shift to services, and the revolutionary increase in female employment have been supported since the early 1990s by social and employment policy reform. In the lengthy and painful learning process between the early 1970s and the late 1990s, the Dutch welfare state has been transformed from one of the least sustainable in the early 1980s to one of the most by the late 1990s.

3.3.2.4 Belgium Nothing akin to the positive learning experience of the Dutch social partners and policymakers occurred in Belgium, where trade unions, employers and the government remained stuck in a condition of corporatist immobilism (Hemerijck, Unger, and Visser, Volume II). Belgian trade unions did not accept that wage restraint and the suspension of wage indexation were necessary for economic recovery and job growth. In part, this reflects the continued strength of the Belgian unions compared with their Dutch counterparts. Belgian governments had to impose wage restraint rather than oil the wheels of negotiated wage moderation through tax reductions. Imposed wage restraint sacrificed micro-flexibility for the purpose of macro-adjustment. This also made any form of issue linkage between different areas of social and economic regulation difficult to achieve.

Between 1968 and 1973, the radicalization of the Belgian trade union movement resulted in a marked increase in strike activity. Under conditions of resurgent class conflict, relations between trade union and employers' associations were at a postwar low. As in the case of the Netherlands, the elaborate system of wage indexation, designed to protect workers from imported inflation, began to feed on itself as wage claims rose. The result was an unparalleled price-wage spiral, with inflation rising from 3.9 percent in 1970 to 12.8 percent in 1975. Any attempt to tamper with indexation in the face of high inflation met with stiff resistance from the trade unions. Moreover, indexation served the unions' egalitarian objective by helping to protect solidarity between the low- and high-paid. The spillover effect of spiraling inflation through the indexation mechanisms gave Belgian macroeconomic policymakers little choice but to squeeze imported inflation through a hard currency policy, resulting in a massive fall in effective demand and employment. Like Dutch governments at the time, Belgian governments thereby sought to gain wage concessions from the unions in the fight against inflation and rising wage costs, without daring to touch the automatic stabilizers, in return for improvements in social security and the extension of early retirement, introduced in 1976, to reduce open unemployment. In 1977, Belgium became probably the first country in which sectoral agreements to lower the working week to 39 hours were reached. The government's policy of fiscal reflation also focused on bailing out crisis sectors and on expanding the public sector. Eventually, this saddled the Belgian economy with a huge public deficit, which increased continuously from 2.2 percent in 1970 up to two-digit levels in the early 1980s. In the course of the 1970s, due to the lack of wage restraint and a hard exchange rate policy, Belgium faced a substantial deterioration in employment levels, which fell from about 60 percent—already low by international standards—to 57.3 percent in 1980. Partly due to massive fiscal reflation, however, overall employment losses in the 1970s were less strong than in the Netherlands.[8]

The Belgian economy, like the Dutch, was in particularly bad shape when it faced the second oil-price shock. Stagnant growth, rising unemployment and sharply increasing deficits were again aggravated by domestic political problems that made it extremely difficult for Belgian

---

[8] It should be noted, however, that the sharper decline of the employment/population ratio in the Netherlands during the 1970s also results from the fact that the working age population—15 to 64 years—grew much faster than in Belgium and other OECD countries.

policymakers to orchestrate and implement an effective package of negotiated change. In contrast to the Netherlands, the depth of the recession
did not generate a consensus on sustained wage moderation. Wage moderation in the 1980s was forced on the social partners by the government
through special enabling laws, suspending free collective bargaining. This
form of nation-wide imposed wage restraint, necessary to achieve nominal
stability after the devaluation of the franc in 1982, implied that wage differentials continued to narrow, leading to very high compression of the
wage structure and, as a consequence, to employment losses at the low end
of the labor market.

After a devaluation of the Belgian franc by 8.5 percent against the
Deutschmark in 1982, the Belgian currency followed the Deutschmark. In
the fight against inflation the hard currency peg was successful, but at the
cost of very high real interest rates. Belgian competitiveness in terms of
unit labor costs improved slightly after 1982, but unemployment soared to
a level of more than 13 percent in 1983–84. The budget deficit remained a
double digit percentage of GDP and fell only after 1983. Employment fell
by almost 4 percentage point in the early 1980s, reaching a low of 53.4 percent in 1984. In the second half of the 1980s, employment rose slightly to
reach 56.4 percent in 1990, still 11 percentage points below the OECD–18
average. When free collective bargaining was again allowed, after 1986,
wage increases again outpaced productivity increases. The combination of
real wage growth, rising non-wage labor costs, and a strong external constraint explains the shift to labor-saving and capital-intensive production
in Belgian industry.

The Belgian state proved unable to reverse the pathological cycle of
'welfare without work'. This cycle resulted from a highly incoherent mix
of policies that were sometimes helpful but entirely counterproductive at
other times. Early retirement schemes were massively extended in 1982,
triggering a sharp decline in participation rates for older workers, from
50.6 percent in 1983 to about 35 percent throughout the 1990s—the lowest value among the countries in our sample. In 1985 the minimum wage
for the young was lowered together with unemployment benefits, while
waiting days were extended. Employer subsidies were introduced to
encourage the exit of older workers in order to refill vacancies with young
unemployed workers. The *Maribel* program to create more jobs was
'flanked' by an agreement on a 5 percent reduction in working hours, combined with a 3 percent wage sacrifice and a 3 percent increase in hiring.
Under the original *Maribel* scheme of 1981, subsidies were intended to
compensate exporting firms in difficulties from the hard currency policy
and to slow down the decline of jobs in industry. Because of its selective
character, in the 1990s the European Commission repeatedly criticized

Maribel as a distortion of competition. In response, subsidies have been extended to the service sector.

With the entry of the Socialists into Martens' seventh cabinet, of 1988–91, free wage bargaining was restored, albeit under the 'shadow of hierarchy'. In the absence of any form of domestic consensus, the government turned to an external benchmark. The 1989 Competitiveness Act authorized the government to intervene, *ex post*, if wages in Belgium had risen faster than the average trend among its six major trading partners. The performance of the period of free collective bargaining was mixed; as wages increased, determined by productivity gains in industry, they outpaced productivity increases in services, which were four times lower. Hence investment and employment in services stagnated at a low level throughout the 1990s.

At the beginning of the 1990s, Belgium was a textbook illustration of *Eurosclerosis*: high structural unemployment, slow productivity and employment growth in private services, monetary instability, a large deficit of about 7 percent of GDP, and a huge public debt of over 125 percent of GDP. The international slow-down in economic growth and the restrictive policies in the run-up to the EMU magnified this problem constellation. In 1990 the monetary authorities, anxious to forestall a speculative attack against the franc, formally pegged the Belgian currency to the Deutschmark. Following the EMU decision in 1991, the Dehaene Government was strongly committed to complying with the Maastricht criteria, particularly with respect to the public deficit. The public deficit was indeed gradually reduced to 1.9 percent in 1997. For most of the 1990s Belgium had to run a primary surplus of around 6 percent of GDP in order to lower the massive debt ratio. In 1996 a special 3 percent EMU tax surcharge was implemented.

After the recession of the early 1990s, the Belgian economy recovered, but its sub-par labor market performance persisted. The rate of employment increased slowly from 54.8 percent in 1994 to 56.3 percent in 1998. Unemployment, which had risen from below 9 percent to above 13 percent between 1990 and 1994, fell only little thereafter. While government employment dropped from 11.2 percent in 1990 to 10.3 percent 1998, business employment remained stable at about 45 percent until 1997 and increased to a still very low level of 46 percent in 1998.

The year 1995 was a turning point in Belgian social and economic policymaking. Once more, the government made an attempt to persuade the social partners to sign a social pact. After another failure, wage increases beyond what the watered-down price indexation formula warranted remained banned until 1996, when the second Dehaene Government, of 1995–99, dictated that wage increases must remain below the *average* wage increases in Germany, France, and the Netherlands. This was a clear tightening of the old law of 1989, as it introduced a wage norm *ex ante* instead of a rationale for intervention *ex post*. The 1998 bargaining round, for 1999–2000, did produce an agreement. The social partners agreed to a maximum wage increase of 5.9 percent for two years. This sign of self-restraint was eased by the government's decision to reduce social security contributions over the next five years.

Belgian welfare reform in 1990s focused largely on pensions. In 1997 the pension system changed from wage indexation to price indexation. Moreover, measures were adopted to raise the retirement age for women— to 65, as was already the case for men—and improve coverage for people working under atypical contracts. Since 1995 the federal government has also phased in an additional 'low earnings' subsidy scheme, applicable to workers at or around the minimum wage, whose social security charges are lowered by between 2 percent and 12 percent of total wage costs. In terms of equity, Belgium has experienced only modestly rising income inequality since the mid-1980s. Thus, as a result of low wage dispersion and high social spending, Belgium still displays a very egalitarian income distribution by international standards.

Hemerijck, Unger, and Visser (Volume II) argue that the linguistic conflict and the cumbersome federalization process negatively interfered with the resolution of pressing problems in social and employment policy. As certain elements of social security have been progressively devolved to the regions and the communities, federalization did undermine the capacity for coordination and issue linkage at the national level. Moreover, the fiscal leeway of Belgian governments has been heavily restricted by massive spending on interest on, and repayments of, the huge public debt. Thus, effective adjustment under the prevailing international constraints of the early twenty-first century relies heavily on the construction of feasible political and societal coalitions able to reduce the plethora of veto powers in the Belgian political economy and level out their cognitive and normative disagreements.

3.3.2.5 France France, like Belgium, faced a more or less continuous decline in employment throughout the period under study (Levy, Volume II). In the 1970s, French governments pursued an inflationary growth strategy based on what was, by and large, a soft monetary policy and on a loose fiscal policy. While demand stimulation allowed for comparatively high rates of economic growth, it also pushed inflation to double-digit levels in the mid-1970s, which offset the effects of currency depreciation on competitiveness. Only in autumn 1976 did France start to deal with inflationary pressures by adopting the so-called *Barre Plan*, inspired by the perceived superiority of the 'German model' of low inflation and a strong currency. Conceptually, the *Barre Plan* indicated a switch to a more supply side-oriented strategy, including a tighter stance in monetary and fiscal policy, a relaxation of price controls, and greater domestic competition. In practice, however, macroeconomic policy responses adopted in the late 1970s revealed a more mixed picture, in which elements of *dirigisme* remained important. Industrial policy continued to play an important role, albeit more targeted towards 'strategic industries'. By and large, French performance in the 1970s may be characterized as mediocre. Employment levels declined modestly from 66 percent to about 64 percent, while inflation still hovered above 10 percent at the end of the decade (Boltho 1996; Sautter 1982).

The socialist government under Mitterrand, which came to power in 1981, decided to adopt an alternative macroeconomic policy strategy, based on a distinctly Keynesian diagnosis of the second oil crisis. Mitterrand's expansionary *program commun* included a rise in the minimum wage by over 10 percent, additional jobs in the public sector, the lowering of the retirement age to 60, one extra week of vacation to five weeks in total, two devaluations of the franc, and the large-scale nationalization of banks and industries. In the midst of low growth and a highly restrictive international economic environment, this policy proved wholly ineffective. To begin with, employment levels could not be stabilized. The slight expansion in public employment did not outweigh the drop of 0.8 percent in private employment between 1981 and 1982. At the same time, unemployment increased from 7.4 to 8.0 percent. While the rise in unemployment was still moderate by international standards, the strategy of 'socialism in one country' was disastrous in terms of macroeconomic stability. Mainly as a result of massive wage increases, inflation remained at double-digit levels, exceeding the German level by about 7 percentage points. Public deficits, which were reduced to zero in 1980, rose much more quickly than in other countries, although still at an acceptable level of 2.8 percent in 1982. At the same time, the current account deficit also increased rapidly from 0.8 to 2.2 percent of GDP. A currency crisis in 1983 forced the French socialists to make a complete U-turn from the Keynesianism *program commun* to the policy strategy of *désinflation compétitive*, a rather orthodox strategy of monetary stability and fiscal retrenchment (Boltho 1996).

Wage policy also became more restrictive. For one, the legal minimum wage was decoupled from inflation in 1983 and 1984. What is more, since the government had direct control over wages in the public sector and nationalized industries, which made up about 38 percent of all employees in the mid-1980s, it was able to regain control over wage increases in these areas. Against the background of sharply rising unemployment, a disciplinary effect on private sector wages also emerged. To some extent, wage restraint was favored by the gradual 'marketization' of the French bargaining system resulting from the *Auroux* laws passed in 1982. These laws, although designed to bring more stability into the fragmented system of French industrial relations by giving the unions a legal status in wage bargaining at the plant level, only reinforced the fragmentation of the wage bargaining system (Boltho 1996; Collignon 1994). As a consequence, from 1983 onwards wage increases were largely brought under control again. However, the effects of wage restraint on total labor costs were partly offset by an increase in payroll costs, mainly as a result of rising unemployment and the growing number of early retirement beneficiaries. In the first half of the 1980s the share of social contributions and payroll taxes rose above 20 percent of GDP and more or less remained at this level thereafter.[9] Nevertheless, as unit labor costs increased only a little since 1984, wage moderation clearly strengthened the international competitiveness of French companies.

Alongside the paradigm shift towards *désinflation compétitive*, interventionist or *dirigiste* principles were gradually abandoned. The heavy subsidization of selected industrial sectors was turned back, nationalized companies were privatized, credit, price, and capital controls were lifted, and restrictions on layoffs and temporary and part-time employment were relaxed. By pegging the franc to the Deutschmark in the second half of the 1980s, monetary policymakers hoped to bring inflation down to the German level and to lower interest rates by reducing the risk premium for foreign investors. Thus, at the end of the 1980s, *désinflation compétitive* was firmly rooted in French macroeconomic policy. In the course of disinflation, macroeconomic key indicators indeed converged towards German levels. Long-term interest and inflation rate differentials *vis-à-vis* Germany shrank steadily from the mid-1980s onward. Moreover, the public deficit was brought down to a low of 1.2 percent in 1989.

While France proved comparatively successful in improving macroeconomic stability, the shift from Keynesian demand management toward competitive disinflation was linked to high transition costs in terms of employment. Mainly as a result of large-scale privatization of nationalized industries, employment in this sector declined continuously through 1988. Among the countries in our project, France displayed by far the sharpest drop in industrial employment, falling from 22.3 percent to 17.3 percent between 1980 and 1988, as compared with 22.5 percent and 20.0 percent, respectively, for the OECD–18 average. Moreover, this decline was only

---

[9] Thus, France displays, together with the Netherlands, the highest share of social contributions as a percentage of GDP in our country sample.

partly compensated by job growth in the domestic service sectors. As a consequence, total employment levels declined during the 1980s from 64.1 percent to 60.6 percent. Since it was only in 1987 that employment growth finally picked up again, the period of upswing was too short to restore pre-crisis employment levels. In particular, while France displayed very high rates of economic growth in the late 1980s, rigid labor markets hampered employment growth.[10] In order to ward off resistance to the strategy of *désinflation compétitive*, the French socialists expanded the welfare state. Consistent with responses in other Continental welfare states, the French response to industrial decline was to establish so-called 'conversion poles', again with heavy state subsidies, which allowed for early retirement on a full pension at age 50 in many cases. Moreover, the general age of retirement was reduced from 65 to 60. As a consequence, during the 1980s France experienced the sharpest decline of any OECD country in the participation rate of males between the ages of 55 and 64, falling from 68.6 percent to 45.8 percent).[11]

The employment crisis was exacerbated during the recession of the early 1990s when macroeconomic policy remained highly restrictive. In contrast to Italy, Sweden, and the United Kingdom, France was able to defend its currency against speculative attacks in the 1990s and thus remained in the EMS. While this had a positive effect on price stability, the appreciating franc brought employment levels down even further. Total employment rates fell from 60.6 percent in 1990 to 58.7 percent in 1994 and stagnated thereafter. The French employment record in the 1990s appears even worse if we look only at private sector employment, which declined even more sharply, from about 47 percent in 1990 to 44.5 percent in 1993, and then more or less leveled off in the ensuing years. The expansion of public sector employment from 13.7 percent in 1990 to 14.8 percent in 1998 compensated partly for the sharp decline in private employment.

The welfare state, which hitherto had been heavily used to absorb the workforce laid off in the industrial sector, moved to the center of the adjustment process in the 1990s. Like other continental countries, France suffered from the problem of generous minimum wages and high

---

[10] Interestingly, while the average rate of economic growth was about the same in France and the United Kingdom between 1986 and 1990—3.2% and 3.3%, respectively—employment outcomes differed tremendously: While the total employment rate increased by only 1 percentage point in France, Britain experienced an increase of 6 percentage points at the same time.

[11] The low participation rates of older workers might also, to some extent, be attributed to the fact that wages for older workers—55 to 64 years—are on average 7 percentage points higher than wages for persons aged 45 to 54. This contrasts sharply with wage profiles in other countries, where earnings for elderly workers are on average 9% *lower* than for middle-aged workers (OECD, 1998e).

non-wage labor costs, which hampered the creation of the kinds of low-skill, low-productivity jobs needed to bring down unemployment. High unemployment, high levels of subsidized non-employment, and low levels of employment led to chronic deficits in the social insurance funds. This was especially true for the pension system, which proved particularly vulnerable to socioeconomic changes. Since the pension system is financed by contributions rather than by taxes, the decline in employment increasingly eroded the revenue basis of the system. This development was reinforced by the decrease in the effective retirement age to 55, which is amongst the lowest in the world (Gern 1998). Moreover, French pensions are almost exclusively financed on a pay-as-you-go basis, which might become highly problematic when demographic aging accelerates after 2005. In 1991, Prime Minister Rocard introduced a new social security tax which, in contrast to social security contributions, was imposed on all earnings, including capital and property—although minimal at this time, it was to prove an important tool for later governments to shift contributions from the payroll tax to more general tax. In 1993 Prime Minister Balladur was able to curtail the generosity of the pension schemes for the private sector by shifting the calculation of reference salary from the average of the best ten years to the average of the best 25 years of a worker's career. In addition, the reform required a minimum of 40 years before retiring, as opposed to 37.5 years previously. Balladur also increased social security taxes. In the next round of reforms, Prime Minister Juppé proposed to extend the changes in the pension introduced by Balladur to the public sector. He was especially bent on eliminating the special measures that allowed public employees to retire at 50. The response to the Juppé plan was a six-week strike that paralyzed the country and incurred substantial losses for the economy. Popular resistance forced Juppé to back down on his pension reform proposal. However, important changes in the institutional design of French social policy were realized through (1) the constitutional amendment that allowed the Parliament to vote on the social security budget and (2) a change in the administration of the social security funds whereby state officials gained influence at the cost of the social partners. As such, argue Bonoli and Palier (1997), the Juppé plan involved a major restructuring of French social security. This change in the governance structure and policy content reflects the effort by the government to gain better information and control over social spending.

Jospin was elected as prime minister on the promise to carve out an efficient and equitable alternative. Following Levy (Volume II), Jospin not only demonstrated the government's commitment to a leftist agenda, but also gave a leftist turn to measures of austerity and liberalization. In public health, insurance coverage was extended and charges for low-income groups abolished. An ambitious youth employment program was launched, expected to create 350,000 jobs by 2002. The working week was to be gradually reduced from 39 hours to 35 coupled with an annualization of working hours so as to meet employers' demands for higher flexibility in working hours. Moreover, the Jospin Government shifted the tax burden in a more progressive direction, away from worker contributions to general social contributions, applying to all incomes, by raising the social security tax originally introduced by Rocard. Jospin also strove for a more equitable and fair approach towards welfare retrenchment, for instance through scaling back tax breaks for children enjoyed primarily by the affluent and through making savings in the health care sector mainly by lowering reimbursements to affluent doctors and pharmaceutical companies. Jospin also supported the creation of private pension funds which were to be managed collectively by employer and union organizations, rather than by private companies, which has been the case up to then. Moreover, there has been a partial shift in the financing of the health care system, away from contributions and towards the use of taxation.

While social policy reform gained in importance during the 1990s, the cuts in benefit levels remained very limited by international standards. As Levy (Volume II) points out, the end of *dirigiste* economic policy has by no means marked the end of state activism. On the contrary, while continuing to play a crucial role in cushioning the transformation from a *dirigiste* to a more liberal economic policy, the French welfare state has actually gained in importance during the 1990s: between 1989 and 1995 social spending increased from 25.7 percent to 30.1 percent of GDP. This might also explain why income inequality grew only a little in recent years. It should be noted that mediocre performance in terms of economic growth, fiscal consolidation and employment, which France displayed through about 1997, has been improving rapidly quite recently. This suggests that the Jospin government might indeed have found the 'middle ground' for reconciling equity and efficiency.

3.3.2.6 Italy   Italy resembles France not only with respect to its comparatively late switch to a tight macroeconomic policy, but also with respect to its relatively passive, insider-biased welfare state and its rigid system of employment protection. It was only in the 1990s, pressed by the impending Maastricht entry exam and the growing pressure from international financial markets, that Italian policymakers were able to turn a vicious cycle of industrial decline, budgetary crises, welfare without work for some and poverty for many, into a virtuous policy cycle of *risanamento*. Crucial in the analysis of Ferrera and Gualmini (Volume II) of the 'quality jump' in Italian social and economic policymaking is that the *risanamento* coincided with a turnover in the Italian political system from the First to the Second Republic, which gave the Amato, Ciampi, and Dini Governments the much-needed autonomy to govern the economy and to support the development of a responsive form of policy concertation with the trade unions and employers' associations.

After the collapse of the regime of Bretton Woods in the early 1970s, strong speculative attacks on the lira forced the Italian currency to devalue. The devaluation exacerbated an already spiraling inflation, which rose from a low level of 4.8 percent in 1971 to a postwar high of 19 percent in 1974. Italian governments in the 1970s sought the support of the trade unions in their attempt to manage the recession by persuading the unions to moderate wage claims. In return, the trade unions were offered more limits on overtime and expanded social protection, especially for disability pensions. When the first oil price shock pushed Italy into a recession, however, with GDP dropping 4 percent, the system automatically indexing wages to the rate of inflation (*scala mobile*) only reinforced the vicious cycle of self-sustaining inflationary expectations. Moreover, the *scala mobile* brought about a considerable reduction of wage differentials, which were partly offset by additional wage increases granted to the higher paid that only added to the inflationary spiral. At the end of 1975 the government lowered interests rates, which led to a new speculative attack on the lira, causing another large and unintended devaluation. This time the devaluation did bring relief: Between 1976 and 1979, an expansionary macroeconomic policy and strong depreciation served to sustain employment, albeit at a low level. But the recovery was fragile and of short duration. The social contract of 1978 proved unable to curtail the vicious cycle of devaluation, inflation, and indexation. By 1980 the rate of inflation reached more than 21 percent. In terms of employment, Italy weathered the economic crises of the 1970s comparatively well, as the employment/population rate in 1980 was even 0.7 percentage points above its 1970 level of 56.1 percent in 1970—still very low by international standards. In terms of social policy developments, the 1970s were marked by a very rapid growth of expenditures on public pensions, mainly as a result of generous reforms. As the reforms' generosity was not even approximately matched by a corresponding increase in revenues, public deficits soared by the mid-1970s, reaching a high of 12.4 percent of GDP in 1975 and not falling below 8 percent until the mid-1990s.

The expansionary macroeconomic policy strategy and strong depreciation of the lira in the late 1970s served to sustain Italian competitiveness. But the recovery, based on a stop-go monetary policy, was again short. Double digit GDP percentage levels of public deficits and escalating inflation made a re-orientation of macroeconomic policy inevitable. In 1979 entry into the EMS enabled the *Banca d'Italia* to pursue a stricter policy of currency stability and disinflation. The so-called 'divorce' between the government and the central bank in 1981 implied that the *Banca d'Italia* was no longer obliged to finance residual government debt. The Bank also dismantled credit controls so as to lend more credibility to its anti-inflation policy. The Bank's restrictive policy pushed the government to adopt a policy of budgetary restraint, which, however, did not suffice to reduce the double-digit budget deficit, since rising real interest rates required higher spending on public debt serving, which grew from 4.4 percent of GDP in 1979 to almost 11 percent in 1993 (OECD, *Economic Outlook*, various years). Nevertheless, the tighter stance in macroeconomic policy had a depressive effect on domestic economic activity. Although tight money brought inflation down from 21.2 percent in 1980 to a low of 4.6 percent in 1987, employment fell from the already low level of 56.8 percent in 1980 to 53.4 percent in 1985. In spite of a growing world economy in the second half of the 1980s, employment remained stagnant, at about 53 percent, for the rest of the decade.

In the area of wage policy the *scala mobile* reinforced inflationary spirals. In 1983 a social pact over incomes policy and fiscal policy was reached, but it failed to tackle the issue of indexation because of the relative weakness of wage bargaining institutions. Unions were unable to control the wage push from below, which provoked employers to demand a shift in the locus of wage bargaining to the plant level (Treu 1994). Although the power of the trade unions was considerably weakened in the 1980s by rising unemployment, this did not provoke a political attack on the Italian trade unions or on the *scala mobile*. Rather, in the face of industrial decline, weak governments continued to seek union approval for their economic policy proposals.

Italian governments' social policy record in the 1980s was mixed. Although policymakers introduced a number of restrictive reforms designed to keep inflation and public expenditures at bay, they left the guiding principles of Italian social policy intact. Italy's social security systems largely followed the continental pattern of a transfer-oriented, pay-roll-financed social insurance system. Social protection in Italy, however, is more skewed in favor of insider groups in the labor market than in Germany and the Netherlands. As Ferrera (1996) argues, Italy's path-breaking advances in welfare expansion during the 1960s and 1970s, in such areas as old age, disability, survivor, and short-term income compensation, disproportionately benefited the older generation of labor market insiders at the expense of unprotected, younger cohorts working under atypical contracts. By the late 1980s, Italy was becoming a pension state rather than a modern welfare state, with pension benefits absorbing about

50 percent of total social expenditures. Given the relatively low level of contributions, public deficits had to finance Italian welfare. In addition, the polarized system of Italian social protection had a territorial component reflecting the split between the rich, industrialized northern regions and the poor, underdeveloped *Mezzogiorno*. For most of the postwar period, clientelism reinforced the high degree of labor market segmentation and dualism in social protection. Finally, the insider-outsider cleavage was reinforced by the fact that, as in many other continental welfare states, the administration of the social security funds was largely in the hands of the social partners, primarily concerned about the interests of their core constituency. While some proposals were put forward to rationalize the pension system and restore its financial balance by raising the age of retirement and changing the benefit formulas, no progress was attained beyond incremental cuts. The insufficiency of these measures to reverse fiscal imbalances set the stage for far more radical reforms in the 1990s.

The rapid growth of the public debt until the early 1990s favored a new round of speculative attacks on the lira in the *annus fatalis* of 1992. Italy had to withdraw from the EMS. The Maastricht entry exam for EMU, however, made fiscal restraint indispensable. A strong devaluation of 30 percent in 1992 formed the stepping stone for a miraculous recovery and a succession of major policy reforms in the areas of industrial relations, social security, and labor market policy and regulation. In the course of the 1990s, at long last, the public deficit came down—from more than 11 percent in 1990 to 2.6 percent in 1998—outlays for public debt serving fell steadily from 1995 onwards, and inflation dropped—from 6.5 percent in 1991 to 1.7 percent in 1998—which allowed Italy to join the EMU in 1999. However, Italy's very restrictive fiscal policy had a depressing effect on domestic demand, which also left its mark on employment. Unemployment jumped again from 8.6 percent in 1991 to 12.3 percent in 1997, the rate of employment fell from 53.5 percent in 1990 to 50.6 percent in 1997, the lowest level among the countries in our project. While public employment remained stable at a rate of 8 percent, private employment fell from a rate of 45.2 percent in 1990 to a record low of 42.3 percent in 1995, after which it slowly increased to a mere 42.8 percent in 1998. Moreover, regional employment disparities widened throughout the 1990s: while the unemployment rate in the center/north was 7.6 percent in 1997, it amounted to 22.2 percent in the *Mezzogiorno*, with even higher rates for women and youth and high levels of long-term unemployment.

Strengthening the central bank's power in the Italian political economy had already changed the nature of the social conflict over inflation and curbed the power of the trade unions. Against the background of the political corruption scandals that marked the political transition from the First to the Second Republic, and in light of the constraints imposed by international financial markets and the EMU's entrance exam, Italian policymakers were forced to find a way to cut the massive public deficit. In this context of domestic and external turmoil, an extraordinary responsive pattern of policy concertation emerged, which led to a number of important tripartite agreements (Ferrera and Gualmini, Volume II) . In 1992 the unions, employers, and the government agreed to suspend the *scala mobile* and hold pay increases below the expected rate of inflation. By giving up on the sacrosanct tool of wage indexation, the Italian unions agreed to share the costs of adjustment so as to attain the long-term benefits of the single currency. A year later the technocratic government led by Ciampi negotiated a tripartite protocol on collective bargaining reform that acknowledged the aim of cutting labor costs. In the wake of the 1993 accord, a new collective bargaining system was established, based on two levels of negotiations: one at the national macroeconomic and one at the firm or territorial microeconomic level. Biannual tripartite meetings at the national level allowed for more coordination between incomes policy and fiscal policy, geared towards flexible adjustment to the expected level of inflation. Plant-level supplements were allowed on the basis of productivity growth. The foundational accords of 1992 and 1993 were followed by a number of other social pacts, some of which went clearly beyond wage policy, such as the pension reform agreements of 1995. In 1998 the social partners agreed to keep wage increases below the expected EU inflation rate, again with plant-level supplements allowed on the basis of productivity growth. The combination of the Maastricht Treaty's stiff fiscal constraints and the changeover to the Second Republic opened a policy window for welfare reform. The Amato pension reform included a rise in retirement age for women and men to be phased in by 2002, a rise in the minimum contribution requirement for old age benefits, and the gradual extension of the reference period for pensions, together with new increases in contributions. In 1993 the government enforced temporary cost savings in state pensions and initiated legislation on supplementary pension funds subject to collective negotiation. After widespread protests and a general strike against Prime Minister Berlusconi's retrenchment plans, which included the abolition of seniority pensions, the Dini caretaker government negotiated a pension reform with the unions. This agreement included a shift from the old, overly generous 'defined benefit' formula to a new, less generous 'defined contribution' formula, to be phased in gradually. Through this agreement unions managed to exempt older workers from most of the phased-in changes. Moreover, seniority pensions, claimable after 35 years of contribution with no age threshold, will be phased out by 2008. The government and the social partners also agreed on the gradual standardization of rules for public and private employees. Finally, strict rules on disability benefits and incomes from work as well as tighter controls on beneficiaries were implemented.

The social pacts since 1993 not only contributed to the fulfillment of EMU entry conditions by effectively taking inflation out of the labor market, but also included agreements on negotiated flexibility and job security. In 1997, the Prime Minister Treu package on labor market reform was adopted, which legalized temporary work agencies as well as fixed-term and part-time work contracts, and simultaneously sought to protect or to improve the rights and entitlements of workers in these kinds of jobs. It seems that Italian unions are moving away from their strong defense of rigid labor market regulation at all costs to a policy of more flexible bargaining practices seemingly better able to resolve the threat of deskilling and growing segmentation. Other path-breaking reforms in labor market policy include the breaking up of the public employment service monopoly. Placement activities were transferred to the regions, and private agencies were allowed to set up temporary work agencies. This type of labor market deregulation and flexibility was designed to stimulate part-time work, benefiting women and the young. Territorial pacts and area contracts for underdeveloped areas, involving not merely social partners but also banks and regional chambers of commerce, came into vogue, following the success in the Italian industrial districts. As in France, introducing a 35-hour working week is back on the policy agenda, but has yet to receive significant support from the Italian trade unions and employers' associations.

While these reforms had positive effects on inflation and public finances, Italy still has the strictest employment legislation among the countries in our project, a factor that might have contributed to Italy's persistent employment failure (OECD 1999b). With respect to the distribution of income within the society, Italy experienced only a modest increase in inequality since the mid-1980s, albeit on a comparatively high level. All in all, although Italy still has some way to go to put its house completely in order, its turnaround since the early 1990s has been impressive.

3.3.2.7 Switzerland Swiss financial markets have always been much less regulated than those in the other continental welfare states we have studied (Bonoli and Mach, Volume II). Switzerland also never experimented with any kind of Keynesian macroeconomic steering. As a result, the Swiss currency appreciated even more strongly than the Deutschmark, which triggered a deep recession in 1975. In the wake of the economic crisis, employment levels dropped from 77.1 percent to 73 percent between

1974 and 1976. As a response, a large share of immigrant workers with insecure and temporary working contracts, and lacking secure residence permits, were forced to repatriate. Women were also forced to retreat from the labor market. Since coverage in unemployment insurance was only some 22 percent in the mid-1970s, benefiting first and foremost the core male workforce, the use of foreigners and women as an employment buffer did not burden the lean Swiss welfare state. Moreover, open unemployment remained clearly below 1 percent throughout the 1970s. Nevertheless, inflation was reduced to very low levels in the second half of the 1970s. While employment rates fell from 76.6 percent in 1970 to 74.3 percent in 1980, this was still very high by international standards. A heavily subsidized agricultural sector and soft anti-cartel legislation shielded large parts of the Swiss economy from competitive pressures and thus constituted an important employment buffer, complementing the underdeveloped *formal* welfare state.

Thus, Switzerland entered the 1980s with a relatively favorable start-up constellation. Due to its stability-oriented macroeconomic policy, Switzerland was very well equipped to counteract the shock of the second oil crisis. At a time when other countries had to abandon their traditional macroeconomic policy measures in the wake of the multiple recessions of the 1970s and early 1980s, Switzerland was more or less unaffected. As a consequence, Switzerland was able to stabilize its position in the international economy and maintain relatively low interest rates—since Switzerland was regarded as a 'safe haven' of international capital markets—which also paid off in relatively stable employment rates during the first half of the 1980s.

When the world economy started to recover, Switzerland experienced impressive growth in employment, from about 74 percent in 1984 to more than 83 percent in 1990—the strongest jump within our country sample. This 'employment miracle' was favored by a range of different factors: low interest rates during the 1980s and generous lending criteria created a veritable boom in the construction industry. More importantly, for much of the 1980s the social partners were able to agree on wage moderation in spite of tight labor markets, which contributed to low levels of inflation throughout the decade. This can be partly explained by the relative weakness of Swiss trade unions and the ability of Swiss employers to coordinate their efforts at restraining wage increases. Wage restraint was also supported by two other factors. Wage bargaining followed a pattern of 'implicit coordination' in which wage demands were dampened by the pronounced non-accommodating stance of the independent central bank. In addition, the strongly federalized political system lacked any capacity to use fiscal policy for demand management. Thus, Swiss trade unions were aware of the fact that neither monetary nor fiscal policy would accommodate excessive wage increases. The decentralized structure of the wage bargaining system also provided for a sufficient degree of flexibility at the micro-level.

Despite the massive appreciation of the Swiss franc, export industries performed well throughout the period under study. This was due to two factors. First, Swiss exports have always been highly specialized, competing in niche markets. Second, reductions in the profit margins for a number of large companies, together with the progressive removal of barriers to trade, seem to have provided the right incentives for effective strategies of industrial restructuring, rationalization, outsourcing, and lean production. The favorable economic record of the 1980s was also reflected in the public budget, which was more or less balanced throughout the decade. The favorable fiscal conditions in effect allowed for an expansion of the lean Swiss welfare state. For instance, coverage in occupational pensions and unemployment insurance was made universal in the 1980s.

During the 1980s, Switzerland more or less gave up on the buffer of foreign workers and women. Many of the insecure work permits in use in the 1970s and early 1980s were gradually converted into permanent residence permits. Second, a change in mentality and attitude towards female employment materialized: female work was increasingly perceived as the rule rather than the exception. The likelihood of a swift and large withdrawal of women and foreigners from the labor force in an economic crisis was accordingly reduced. Moreover, with the introduction of compulsory unemployment insurance, job losses were to a higher degree reflected in the unemployment statistics, as the unemployed had a weaker incentive to withdraw completely from the labor market. With the institutionalization of social and employment rights for women and foreign workers, the more inclusive, but still lean, Swiss welfare state became more vulnerable to the vicissitudes of the international economy.

This increased vulnerability became apparent in the early 1990s when the combined effect of recession, economic internationalization, and European integration put pressure on the Swiss economy. Between 1991 and 1994, rates of economic growth were negative, and the employment ratio dropped from 83.7 percent to 79.8 percent before stagnating for the remainder of the decade. Since government employment remained stable throughout the 1990s, the decline in employment took place first and foremost in the private sector. As the buffer function of unprotected foreign workers and women had largely disappeared, this simultaneously resulted in an increase in open unemployment from practically zero to almost 5 percent. The reasons for the employment crisis were manifold. Clearly the strong appreciation of the Swiss franc had a depressing effect on employment in the exposed sectors. Moreover, the protected sectors of the Swiss economy forfeited their role as employment buffers, when a number of protective mechanisms were removed so as to strengthen price competitiveness abroad by increasing competition on domestic markets. These measures included more restrictive cartel legislation, the gradual introduction of the free movement of persons between Switzerland and the EU, a removal of protectionist barriers in the agricultural sector, and the liberalization of public utilities. While these reforms are likely to have strengthened the international competitiveness of the Swiss economy, they also had a depressing effect on employment in the hitherto protected sectors. This holds especially true for the ISIC 6 sector—wholesale and retail trade, restaurants and hotels—where Switzerland experienced the sharpest drop in employment of the countries in our project. Moreover, the boom in the construction industry collapsed in the early 1990s, when property prices dropped following the international downturn and Swiss banks tightened their lending criteria. As a result, employment levels in the construction sector fell dramatically in the early 1990s.

The awkward economic predicament of the early 1990s also stimulated a series of responses in taxation, industrial relations, labor market regulation, and social policy, which clearly went beyond the incremental reforms of the 1980s. These adjustments have not altered the Swiss model much, but they do reveal that even Switzerland has become more internationally constrained in its policy choices (Bonoli and Mach, Volume II). In the wake of sluggish growth and swiftly rising unemployment, public deficits rose quickly, reaching a high of about 4 percent of GDP in 1993. As a consequence, the consolidation of the public budget gained priority in tax and fiscal policy. In 1995 the existing turnover tax was replaced by a value added tax (VAT)—a policy novelty for the Swiss. With the restructuring of the tax scale in 1997, the tax rates on corporate and capital income have come down slightly, maintaining Switzerland's rates among the lowest in the OECD area.

Major adjustments also took place in the wage-setting system, as employers in export industries pressed for radical decentralization down to the firm level. Their successful campaign led to a more decentralized and flexible collective bargaining system.

Rising unemployment and fiscal deficits also affected social policy. While the 1980s still saw the Swiss welfare state expand, making up for its backwardness compared with other Continental welfare states, this trend was reversed in the 1990s, when the retirement age for women was raised and cuts in unemployment benefits were enacted. These reforms succeeded in the referendum process (where other, more radical reforms were defeated) mainly because they balanced cuts with improvements in gender equality and expanded active labor market programs.

Despite a lengthy period of low economic growth and falling employment in the first half of the 1990s, Switzerland remains the richest country in our project and displays the highest level of employment within the OECD. Unemployment has risen considerably but is still low by international standards. Moreover, as Bonoli and Mach (Volume II) point out, owing to relatively generous unemployment and social assistance benefits, rising unemployment did not trigger a sharp rise in income inequalities. As such, Switzerland, having already started from a position of strength in the 1970s, managed to maintain this, while bringing its welfare state up to the level of other Continental countries. Most recently, Swiss policymakers have pursued incremental reforms in both social and labor market policy.

3.3.2.8 Denmark   Unlike Switzerland and Austria, Denmark proved incapable of stabilizing its macroeconomic approach in the 1970s (Benner and Vad, Volume II). The Danish experience of that decade is characterized by economic mismanagement, that is, by a stop-go macroeconomic policy and a failed incomes policy. For three years after Denmark joined the European monetary Snake in 1973, the Danish krone appreciated by 18 percent, which seriously harmed international competitiveness and exacerbated a chronic current account deficit. While an expansionary fiscal policy ought to stimulate domestic demand, expansion was not accompanied by moderate wage agreements. As a result, inflation soared to double-digit levels in the mid-1970s. Wage inflation was reinforced by automatic indexation mechanisms and growing wage competition between public and private sector unions. As a result, economy-wide wage contracts regularly failed in the second half of the decade. While the government reacted by imposing statutory wage settlements designed to curtail wage inflation, success was limited: since the greatest wage increases were conceded to low-income workers, higher-paid wage earners sought to restore previous wage differentials. As a consequence, wage restraint imposed by way of government decrees was partly eaten up by increasing wage drift. By 1979 Denmark decided to devalue the Krona, but the devaluation was too small to have a strong positive effect on private domestic demand and competitiveness. To make things worse, with Danish inflation higher than Germany's, interest rates were also much higher. In 1979 interest rates were so high that housing construction almost came to a complete halt, while the public debt rose exponentially and the current account balance remained in deep deficit in spite of attempts to restrict domestic demand by higher indirect taxes (Iversen 1998b; Nannestad 2000).

Unemployment rose throughout the decade, from 1.3 percent in 1970 to over 6.9 percent in 1980. The rise in open unemployment would have been even stronger if Denmark had not expanded its public sector massively through the early 1980s, as indicated by an increase in government employment levels from about 14 percent in 1970 to almost 23 percent in 1982. While the expansion of public employment helped stabilize Danish employment levels within a favorable corridor between 73.3 and 75.7 percent throughout the 1970s, inflation could not, by and large, be kept under control. Inflation rose from 5.8 percent in 1970 to 12.3 percent by the end of the decade.

The Danish experience in the 1980s provides striking evidence for the fact that severe crises often trigger a process of policy learning, as a result of which pathological trajectories can be reversed—to this extent, Denmark's story resembles the Dutch case. When the second oil crisis hit Denmark, the macroeconomic situation was, as already noted, very unfavorable. While the Social Democratic-led government initially pursued repeated devaluations combined with tighter incomes and fiscal policies, it was politically too weak to keep up this strategy. Lacking a majority in parliament, it tried to maintain support from the trade unions. As a consequence, fiscal policy was loosened again, and a minimum wage was introduced and then raised as a way of lowering income inequality, thereby offsetting the attempts to contain wage inflation. The result was a largely incoherent and ineffective policy mix incapable of maintaining employment levels or bringing inflation under control. In 1982, when a bourgeois government came into office, the direction of policy adjustment changed significantly: Sound fiscal policy and a reduction of the current account deficit became priorities. By the same token, there was an end to the expansion of public employment and of active labor market policy. By joining the EMS, Denmark committed itself to a hard currency policy. Moreover, in 1982 automatic wage indexation, like the link between public and private sector wage increases, was suspended or abolished, as a result of which wage increases dropped by half. Interestingly, these measures went hand in hand with a change in policy style, as support from the trade unions was no longer an indispensable precondition for political action. While substantial cut-backs in social benefits were enacted,[12] there was no ideological blueprint for dismantling the welfare state. Thus the basic structure of the Danish welfare state remained intact. By the same token, taxes were raised substantially in order to balance the public budget. This policy package contributed to a remarkable economic recovery,

---

[12] Most notably the introduction of a waiting period of one day for sick pay and a freeze in the maximum rate of daily cash benefits through 1987, thereby exempting the low-paid from benefit cuts.

as it allowed for a sharp decline in real interest rates, the expansive effects of which outweighed the contractionary effects of the government's tighter fiscal and wage policies (Iversen 1998b, 1999). The fruits of this policy change became visible not only in higher growth rates, lower inflation, and a massive improvement of the public budget within only a few years, but also in a major rise of employment through 1987. The flip side of the coin, however, was a further worsening of the current account balance, which reached a record deficit in 1986. As a result, the government tightened fiscal policy even more—the so-called 'potato diet'—by raising taxes to dampen domestic demand. Somewhat later the government, confronted with a substantial loss in popularity—partly as a result of the 'potato diet'—in the election year of 1987, loosened its restrictive stance in incomes policy and allowed wages to grow by more than 10 percent, which seriously eroded Denmark's competitive position. Moreover, a tax reform that reduced deductibility for interest payments on real estate mortgages triggered a wave of insolvencies among home-owners. The cumulative effect of these measures was a sharp deterioration in the economic climate, resulting in low economic growth, rising unemployment, and a re-appearance of budget deficits in the late 1980s and early 1990s. Thus, Denmark was practically decoupled from the international economic boom of the late 1980s. Partly as a result of the recession, inflation was brought under control, and the current account balance improved continuously, leading to a stable surplus from 1990 onwards. This was supported by innovations in the wage bargaining system: the social partners had signed a 'declaration of intent' in 1987 to keep wage increases below the level of Denmark's main trading partners. Moreover, they had turned to a system of coordinated sectoral bargaining, in which the social partners at the central level bargained only over a minimum wage, which, on average, makes up only 60 percent of total wages, thereby allowing for an appropriate adjustment of wages to local conditions (Schröder and Suntum 1998). By and large, the macroeconomic situation was clearly more favorable at the end of the decade than it was at its beginning (Nannestad 2000). Thus, it was in the 1980s that the macroeconomic foundation was laid for the Danish employment 'miracle' of the 1990s.

Low inflation, comparatively sound public finances, and a considerable current account surplus in the early 1990s provided successive Danish governments with considerable leeway not only to pursue an anti-cyclical fiscal and tax policy, but also to experiment with innovative labor market policies. In 1992, when unemployment had again reached double-digit levels, a job rotation scheme was introduced in the final days of the Conservative-led government. After that government resigned in January 1993, successive center-left governments returned to a cautious Keynesian economic policy based on an—at least temporarily—expansionary income tax reform and stronger reliance on active labor market policy. The 'activation' content of labor market policy was increased by extending job and education offers for the long-term and youth unemployed and making participation obligatory after a certain period of unemployment (Benner and Vad, Volume II). While the level of unemployment benefits remained unchanged, the maximum period for unemployment benefits was restricted and eligibility criteria tightened so as to strengthen work incentives. Thus, while the Danish welfare state became more employment-friendly in the 1990s, it did not become subject to major retrenchment. The element of private mandatory insurance, however, was strengthened in the early 1990s by making occupational pension schemes quasi-compulsory through collective wage bargaining. As these are fully-funded defined contribution plans, the reform increased the Danish pension system's robustness in the face of demographic change. Moreover, these schemes' positive impact on national saving contributed to the remarkable improvement in the Danish current account balance, which had been in chronic deficit until the late 1980s. In macroeconomic policy, the Social Democratic government did not abandon its fixed exchange rate policy and orientation towards price stability (Nannestad 2000). This policy mix proved very successful: from 1994 onwards, Denmark not only saw a sharp decline in open unemployment, falling from 12.0 percent to 6.5 percent in 1998, which was partly the result of massively extended paid-leave arrangements in the mid-1990s, but also an above-average increase of 4 percentage points in employment levels—already very high by international standards, and part of which must be attributed to an expansion of the public sector. Moreover, the deficit in the public budget turned into a surplus in 1997, while both inflation and the current account balance remained within tolerable limits. Like the Netherlands, Denmark faced a substantial increase in income inequality since the mid-1980s, though less pronounced than in New Zealand and the United Kingdom. But Denmark still displays a very egalitarian income distribution by international standards. And its turnaround since the 1980s has been truly remarkable, as its incremental reforms appear to have created a sustainable Scandinavian welfare state.

3.3.2.9 Sweden Unlike Denmark, Sweden proved very successful at orchestrating a smooth interplay among monetary, fiscal, and wage policy in the 1970s (Benner and Vad, Volume II). The initial Swedish response to the first oil shock centered on fiscal stimulation to boost demand and maintain full employment. As a result, growth rates were comparatively high in 1974 and 1975. The expansive macroeconomic policy package included large state subsidies to ailing industries and extensive labor market training programs. The government also reduced income taxes in 1974 in an attempt to lower the pressure on wage increases. But as these reductions were financed out of increases in payroll taxes, the costs of production increased and exacerbated inflationary pressures. In combination with the initial commitment to a 'hard currency' policy, this led to an effective appreciation that eroded Sweden's international competitiveness. Swedish policymakers reacted with a tightening of fiscal policy, as a result of which the Swedish economy went into a recession in 1977. However, Sweden was remarkably successful both in restoring competitiveness and maintaining employment levels. First, the Krona was devalued in 1976 and 1977 in order to restore international competitiveness. A reduction in social contributions also contributed to lowering labor costs. Most importantly, the Swedish system of highly centralized wage bargaining was able to revive a strategy in which the gains of strategic devaluations for improved international competitiveness were not eaten up by higher wage demands (Schelde, Andersen, and Åkerholm 1982). As a result, inflation could be dampened significantly between 1977 and 1979. Moreover, the modest fall in employment within the exposed sectors—from about 42 percent of the working-age population in 1976 to 40.5 percent in 1978— was more than balanced by a swift expansion of the public social services and active labor market policy. In short, Swedish macroeconomic policy, industrial relations, and labor market policies were fairly effective for most of the 1970s in creating jobs and the right incentives for industrial restructuring. As a consequence, and with high and increasing levels of employment, rising from about 73 percent in 1970 to almost 80 percent in 1980, the Swedish social security system was relatively unaffected by the recession-prone 1970s. Still, inflation was not exceptionally high by international standards: on average about 9 percent throughout the decade, far below the inflation figures for New Zealand, the United Kingdom, and Italy.

During the 1980s, Sweden continued to do comparatively well in terms of employment. In spite of the recession in the early 1980s open unemployment increased only slightly up to 3.5 percent in 1983. Moreover, unemployment declined steadily thereafter, reaching a low of 1.5 percent in 1989. Employment levels, already very high by international standards, were stabilized at about 79 percent in the first half of the 1980s, and they even shot up to 81.3 percent in 1990. Moreover, the public deficit, which had gone up to 7 percent by 1982, was turned into a surplus of 5.4 percent in 1989, with the assistance of higher indirect taxes. Initially, Sweden also proved successful in containing inflation: starting from a level of 13.7 percent in 1980, inflation was steadily reduced to 4.2 percent in 1986. Thus, during most of the 1980s Sweden managed the tradeoff between full employment and inflation quite effectively.

In 1982 Sweden devalued the Krona by 16 percent, following a 10 percent devaluation from the previous year. The devaluation was highly successful in helping to restore high levels of growth and to maintain full employment. The resulting improvement in public finances also allowed Sweden to preserve its very generous social security system throughout the 1980s. In spite of the strong devaluations, wage increases were held within tolerable limits in the following years, bringing inflation down from 13.7 percent in 1980 to 4.2 percent in 1987. However, from 1988 onwards inflationary pressures grew rapidly again, reaching double-digit levels in 1990. A range of different factors contributed to this outcome. The deregulation of the domestic capital market in the mid-1980s led to a speculative housing boom, massively stimulating domestic demand. In combination with a more expansionary fiscal policy, such as improved pensions and sickness benefits, and increasingly tight labor markets, the upsurge made it extremely difficult to maintain wage restraint. As a consequence, international competitiveness deteriorated quickly, which also became manifest in a sharply rising current account deficit. Moreover, rising tensions within the trade union camp had contributed to a gradual erosion of the centralized wage bargaining system and aggravated wage competition between the public and the private sectors, thereby undermining their capacity to bring about coordinated wage restraint under conditions of tight labor markets (Jochem 1998). Confronted by an overheated economy in 1989, Sweden was faced with the choice between cooling down the economy in an attempt to regain control over inflation or to restore competitiveness by another round of devaluation. Political actors responded by a major shift in macroeconomic policy priorities, whereby full employment was replaced by price stability as the primary macroeconomic target. While the Swedish strategy of competitive devaluation was relatively successful under conditions of closed capital markets, this option was ruled out by financial markets that were now more open. The same was true for any expansion of public employment, which had reached its financial limits in the 1980s. The Swedish government applied the brakes and embraced a hard currency policy, pegging the Krona to the ECU in 1991. This resulted in a sharp drop in domestic demand. Moreover, the 1990 tax reform cooled down the economy at a time when it was already moving into recession.

Between 1991 and 1993 GDP dropped by almost 5 percent, and the rate of unemployment increased from 1.6 percent in 1990 to 8.2 percent in 1993. Employment levels dropped sharply, from 81.3 percent in 1990 to 70.2 percent in 1994, without picking up again in the following years. This trend reflected a decline in both public and private employment. While the rate of government employment fell from 25.7 percent to 21.2 percent in the 1990s, business employment levels shrank from 55.7 percent to 47.8 percent. Moreover, public finances deteriorated rapidly, moving from a surplus of 4.2 percent in 1990 to a deficit of 12.3 percent in 1993.

In order to defend the Swedish Krona, the bourgeois government in office from 1991 to 1994 reached an agreement with the Social Democrats on two 'crisis packages' (Benner and Vad, Volume II). These included cuts in replacement rates, the introduction of a one-day waiting period for sickness benefits, lower pensions, changes in eligibility criteria, and an expansion of active labor market policy. Moreover, the tax burden for business was lowered. Since these measures proved unable to defend the Swedish Krona, however, the government was forced to let the currency float in 1992. While the bourgeois government was first and foremost concerned about Sweden's attractiveness to international investors, it was the reduction of taxes for capital and employers' social contributions rather than the consolidation of the public budget that had priority. This changed when the Social Democrats re-entered office in 1994. While welfare cutbacks were even greater than under the bourgeois government, the Social Democrats also increased taxes in order to balance the public budget. Quite remarkably, the top marginal rate on income taxes, having been reduced from 72 percent to 51 percent in 1991, was pushed back up to 60 percent. Thus, while total taxation dropped from 55.6 percent of GDP in 1990 to 49.6 percent in 1995, the subsequent tightening of fiscal policy contributed to a rise in levels of taxation to 53.3 percent by 1997. Due to the system of the dual income tax—distinguishing between income from labor and income from capital—the increases in taxes on income did not directly affect income on internationally mobile capital (see Ganghof, Volume II). Moreover, political resistance against tax increases was restrained by two factors. First, in a country that had remarkable surpluses in the public budget for most of the 1970s and 1980s, the massive and unprecedented disruption of public finances allowed the Social Democratic government to appeal credibly to the Swedes' readiness to make sacrifices. Second, as the middle classes have a strong interest in a highly developed welfare state, both in their role as welfare beneficiaries and in their role as providers of social services, their willingness to pay high taxes is likely to be higher than in the residual Anglo-Saxon welfare states and the comparatively service-lean Continental welfare states. In terms of budget consolidation, the policy of simultaneous cuts in benefit levels and increases in employees' social insurance contributions as well as taxes on personal income proved remarkably successful. The benefit cuts and tax increases brought the budget back into surplus within only a few years. The tax increases, however, did add massively to the costs of labor: while unit labor costs fell by 13 percent between 1991 and 1994, they rose again by more than 10 percent until 1997, as compared with about 2 percent for the OECD–18 average. This might partly explain why employment rates shrank again from 70.8 percent in 1995 to 68.9 percent in 1997.

Both the sharp rise in unemployment and the substantial cutbacks in welfare programs have made Swedish income distribution more unequal. Next to New Zealand and the United Kingdom, Sweden displays the sharpest rise in income inequality since the mid-1980s among the countries in our project. However, by international standards Sweden still has a very egalitarian income distribution.

While the numerous cutbacks did not alter the basic structures of the Swedish welfare state, the same cannot be said about the recent pension reform, which involved important structural changes from the previous system. First, the old universal basic pension is going to be replaced by a guaranteed minimum pension. As the latter is basically means-tested, the reform deviates from the principle of universality in social benefits, and thus runs the risk of eroding middle class support. The second tier of the new pension system is based on a defined contribution of 16 percent. The level of future benefits is thereby made dependent on demographic changes and the growth rate of real wages. Elements of redistribution are much weaker than in the old system, so as to strengthen the 'actuarial fairness' of the scheme. Moreover, the system will be funded by equal payroll contributions from employers and workers and have autonomy from the state budget. The new system, though mainly working on a pay-as-you-go basis, also contains a moderate individual pre-funded component, saved in a fund chosen by each individual (Ministry of Health and Social Affairs 1998).

It was only quite recently that Sweden's employment performance improved again. Since 1998 there has been a clear upwards trend in employment. Open unemployment, still stagnating at about 8 percent in 1997, will fall to 5.3 percent in 2000, according to OECD projections (OECD, *Economic Outlook*, various years). Moreover, since 1997 public finances have recovered sufficiently to allow for another cautious expansion of social benefits. At the same time, inflation was brought down to 0.4 percent by 1998. Thus, while Sweden is unlikely to reduce unemployment to the extremely low levels it used to have in the 1980s, the country seems to have found a new equilibrium combining macroeconomic stability and high levels of employment with a still very generous welfare state.

3.3.2.10 United Kingdom   While Sweden pursued an effective Keynesian adjustment strategy in the 1970s, this strategy failed miserably in Great Britain (Rhodes, Volume II). Unemployment rose from 2.4 percent in 1970 to more than 6 percent in 1980, while inflationary pressures escalated dramatically throughout the decade. Moreover, rates of economic growth in the 1970s remained very low by international standards. Thus, Britain in the 1970s could indeed be described as the sickest of the sick men of Europe. This can be attributed to a range of partly interrelated factors.

First, while most of the countries in our sample experienced the postwar period as a 'golden age' characterized by rapidly rising productivity and continuously high levels of economic growth, this does not hold true for Great Britain, which was plagued by macroeconomic imbalances and slow productivity growth in the industrial sector. The reasons for the misery are manifold (see Scharpf, this Volume). As a result of this unfavorable start-up constellation, Britain entered the 1970s in a state of sluggish growth, low profitability, accelerating inflation, and sharply rising unemployment.

Moreover, British political actors adopted an incoherent and inconsistent policy mix. They failed to break the typical stop-go pattern in macroeconomic policy already prevalent in the 1950s and 1960s. Successive British governments were trapped in an institutional and ideological setting that did not allow them to overcome the problem of stagflation. Britain had presided over an underdeveloped *formal* welfare state, and the expansion of social services and transfers was severely constrained by the relative weakness of the British economy in the postwar era. The more important aspect of the British welfare state, shared by Australia and New Zealand, lay in its *informal* dimension, that is, the commitment to full employment. However, the British system of voluntarist and adversarial industrial relations with strong but highly decentralized unions[13] and weakly organized employers counteracted the policy of full employment by triggering a disastrous wage-price spiral. Successive British governments tried to gain a trade union commitment to wage moderation without giving up the goal of full employment. When inflation skyrocketed to more than 24 percent in 1975, the union peak organization (TUC) was able to persuade its member organizations that wage restraint was indispensable. However, due to British unions' scattered structure, wage inflation was brought under control only in the short run. It was the severe economic crisis of the late 1970s and, related to this, the massive ideological shift brought about by the newly elected Thatcher government that allowed for a decisive reversal of the British pathology: by the late 1970s disorientation and a sense of complete and utter failure pervaded the political debate over Britain's perennial malaise.

---

[13] It should be added that British unions are craft- rather than industry-based. As a consequence, several unions are often simultaneously represented within a single firm, exercising a monopoly over their craft-based constituencies and being interested above all in advantageous wage deals for their clientele with little concern for macroeconomic consequences.

The election of Thatcher marked the turning point in the British pattern of policy adjustment. Monetary policy change stood at the top of her list of priorities. After the recurrent failures of incomes policy, tight monetary and fiscal policy was considered the only alternative for controlling wage inflation. Under tight control of the money supply and a restrictive fiscal policy, the unions were soon to learn that irresponsible wage setting would sharply drive up unemployment. The new macroeconomic paradigm was particularly effective in bringing down inflation, which went from 18 percent in 1980 to 4.6 percent in 1983. At first the policy of disinflation aggravated the recession of 1980–81. Employment fell sharply, from 70.8 percent in 1979 to 64.6 percent in 1983. This was partly due to the large-scale privatization of nationalized industries. After 1982, an extended period of high economic growth set in. In the process employment rose again to 72 percent by the end of the decade. The recovery also paid off in terms of fiscal policy: The budget deficit, which had risen up to 4 percent in 1984, decreased quickly thereafter and gave way to a surplus in 1988.

Supported by an absolute majority in parliament, facilitated by the Westminster model of democracy and legitimized by the ideology of neo-liberalism, Thatcher's supply-side policies included substantial tax cuts for middle- and higher-income brackets, the privatization of nationalized industries, and the deregulation of product and labor markets. Corporate tax rates were also substantially reduced. To make up for losses in the budget, indirect taxes were raised, a shift that clearly favored the better-off.

Trade unions were especially hard hit by the new legislation, which massively reduced their scope for collective action, especially their capacity to strike. Labor market deregulation in all its forms facilitated the expansion of temporary jobs for young people and stimulated the growth of non-standard, mostly part-time, employment. Most restrictions on hiring and firing of temporary workers were simply abolished. Special policies were introduced to encourage employers to hire workers at low wages. A subsidy scheme supporting the creation of small enterprises proved fairly successful. Public housing was privatized on a large scale. Institutional reforms were enacted in the area of social service delivery that introduced elements of market competition and decentralization into education, benefit delivery and the National Health Service (NHS). In pensions substantial cuts were enacted. Moreover, a 'contracting-out' clause was set in place that allowed the switch from public to private schemes if the latter offered at least the same benefit level as the state scheme. Since private pension schemes were also encouraged by tax concessions, they increasingly crowded out public pensions, thereby gradually undermining the support for public welfare provision. Unemployment benefits also became subject to retrenchment: earnings-related supplements to the basic income allowance were abolished in 1982, while unemployment benefits became liable to taxation.

These cuts also had a disciplinary effect on unions' wage bargaining position. First, the cuts effectively lowered the reservation wage, constituting a floor for the entire wage scale, and thus allowed wages to fall. Second, the higher the loss in income due to unemployment, the more likely it is that wage earners will accept wage restraint. The reduction of benefit levels went along with a stronger reliance on means-tested benefits, such as housing allowances, whose proportion in total benefits almost doubled during the Thatcher years. As a consequence, in-work benefits were expanded in the late 1980s and throughout the 1990s so as to provide more incentives to make work pay and remove poverty traps.[14] In combination with the shift to a more regressive tax system and a rise in earnings dispersion resulting from massive labor market deregulation, welfare state retrenchment led to a rapid increase in poverty and inequality.

In spite of Thatcher's comparatively successful micro supply-side strategy, the Conservatives, partly as a result of economic mismanagement, proved unable to break the typical 'stop-go' cycle of the British economy. In the late 1980s inflationary pressures flared up again for a number of reasons. Unemployment had fallen from 11.8 percent in 1986 to about 6 percent at the end of the decade. Moreover, the liberalization of credit markets and easy mortgage finance fed a frenzied consumption boom. The situation was aggravated by the 1988 tax reform, which entailed massive reductions in income taxes. As a consequence, inflation rose rapidly from 3.4 percent in 1986 to 9.5 percent in 1990. Moreover, the current account balance deteriorated, turning from a surplus of 0.6 percent of GDP in 1985 into a deficit of 4.3 percent in 1989. At the same time, actors in monetary policy tried to keep the British pound within the EMS. As a consequence, interest rates were raised sharply to control the money supply. By the same token, Britain was affected by the steep rise of German interest rates induced by unification, with higher interest rates having a depressing effect on domestic demand. The outcome was a deep recession at the beginning of the 1990s. Employment levels fell from 72 percent in 1990 to 67.8 percent in 1993, and open unemployment increased from 5.9 percent to 10.3 percent at the same time. But inflation also fell to a low of 1.6 percent in 1993.

---

[14] The expansion of means-tested and in-work benefits may partly explain why total social spending as a share of GDP did not decline altogether during the Thatcher era. In social security the number qualifying for supplementary benefit income support rose in line with poverty. Moreover, the relative stability of social expenditure ratios must also be attributed to higher spending in numerous areas in response to popular demand, such as in health care.

Britain recovered remarkably quickly from the recession, however. The recovery process was supported by an expansive monetary and fiscal policy. British membership in the EMS was cancelled in 1992, which led to a substantial lowering of the exchange rate and a sharp fall in short-term interest rates. Fiscal policy was quickly loosened, allowing the budget deficit to rise to 8 percent in 1993. This had a stimulating effect on the economy, which also paid off in terms of employment. Between 1993 and 1997 the employment ratio increased from 67.8 percent to 70.2 percent. This is all the more remarkable in light of how government employment was shrinking at the same time. The overall improvement in employment performance thus underestimates the employment success story in the business sector, where we observe an even steeper increase, from 55 percent in 1992 to 60.7 percent in 1997. Unemployment rates dropped from 10.3 percent in 1993 to 6.5 percent in 1998. Britain's impressive employment record in recent years suggests that the employment intensity of economic growth is quite high. There is reason to believe that the flexibility of British labor markets has contributed to this favorable development.

The policy profile in the key areas of social and economic regulation that had emerged under the Conservative governments did not change dramatically after Labor re-entered office in 1997. The legacy of 'Thatcherism' clearly constrains the policy options for New Labour. As Rhodes (Volume II) argues, Labour's 'Third Way' is a mix of modest and incremental innovations which is aimed to build and improve on that legacy. The fact that the Bank of England obtained full political independence underscores the fact of strong continuity in macroeconomic policy. While there has been some minor re-regulation on the labor market, such as the introduction of legal minimum wages and new trade union recognition rights, the United Kingdom still has the most liberalized labor market within the European Union. However, there has been a modest improvement in a number of social transfers, such as family allowances, as well as a shift from 'welfare to work' through new resources for childcare, education, training and subsidized employment, in particular for young people and single mothers, based on a 'sticks and carrot' strategy so as to strengthen work incentives. Moreover, health spending was expanded significantly. By and large, however, there is a relative continuity of policy responses under the Blair government, suggesting that the Conservatives were able to alter the political economy of the British welfare state. Not only did the Conservatives fundamentally change the policy profile around which the British welfare state was organized. They also transformed the political support basis of the welfare state by destroying the power resources of the trade unions and undermining middle class support for the welfare state by making public programs residual while expanding options for exit into private schemes. The exceptions to the rule are the NHS and education, which remained very popular with the middle classes. The result is a welfare state that remains lean in its provisions, continues to have problems with poverty, but seems to have largely solved the problems of high unemployment and low employment that continue to affect many of the Continental welfare states.

3.3.2.11 The Antipodes   Australia and New Zealand display striking similarities in their inherited policy profiles, deviating strongly from the modes of social and economic regulation in the European welfare states (Schwartz, Volume II). Like Britain, they share a tradition of stop-go macroeconomic policy cycles with balance of payments and exchange rate problems, together with the overriding importance of the *informal* welfare state—that is, the commitment to full employment and reliance on socially defined rather than market-based wages—in contrast to a formal system of social transfers and services. Most importantly, and in stark contrast to the British experience, the postwar models of the Antipodes operated on the basis of a strong interdependence between trade policy and domestic industrial policy through the strategy of 'import substitution industrialization'. Both countries extracted rents from their highly efficient and competitive primary sectors[15] so as to protect local manufacturing through high tariffs and thereby generate sheltered full employment. In wage policy, state-run arbitration courts in both countries created highly regulated labor markets and set working conditions and wages at *socially defined*, relatively high levels, with only limited influence from both union and employer representatives.

From this highly interventionist pattern of wage setting, a tendency emerged favoring wage and input cost increases in sheltered sectors, which squeezed rents out of the export sectors. This dynamic became particularly problematic when export prices fell in the late 1960s and 1970s, especially when Britain joined the EU in 1973. In the end, the sheltered sectors got too big for the exposed sectors to support. Under conditions of full employment, policymakers were tempted to deploy the arbitration courts as an instrument of incomes policy to contain inflation and keep exports profitable. Tight labor markets in the late 1960s and union militancy in New Zealand and Australia, however, made it difficult for governments to impose wage restraint through the courts. In the wake of the breakdown of Bretton Woods and the first oil shock, inflation and current account deficits became the overriding policy problems. In order to persuade the unions to pursue wage restraint, Labor governments in both New Zealand

---

[15] Dairy, meat, wool, and timber in New Zealand; coal, mineral wool, meat, wheat, and dairy in Australia.

and Australia expanded the formal welfare state. By the mid-1970s conservative governments realized that effective adjustment required a more fundamental change in the operation of wage arbitration within the confines of the import-substitution industrialization policy. In the 1980s Australia was gradually able to orchestrate and negotiate a viable incomes policy. The failure to do so in New Zealand eventually set the stage for a path-breaking neo-liberal paradigm shift in the first half of the 1980s.

New Zealand. In the early 1970s policymakers responded to accelerating inflation and current account deficits with contractionary policies. When unemployment rose they immediately shifted back to an expansionary stance. They also borrowed heavily overseas so as to sustain the old employment model. In so doing they generated international financial obligations that the existing economic structure could not sustain. Moreover, the arbitration system proved unable to enforce wage restraint. The Labour government's efforts to expand the formal welfare state, by introducing a flat-rate pension and various forms of disability pensions, restored the real value of several means-tested benefits that had been eroded by inflation. However, these were not enough to integrate the unions into a European-style social pact for wage restraint. Strikes, under conditions of full employment, made employers give in, while policymakers again responded with a loose fiscal policy and accommodating monetary policy. As in the British case, the lack of a credible threat to punish aggressive unions with a restrictive monetary policy drove up inflation. Having failed to orchestrate an incomes policy, Prime Minister Muldoon resorted to price controls and credit allocation. In 1978 he adopted a final exaggerated version of the old model, coined the 'Think Big' program, designed to expand steel production, increase refinery capacity, and create a synthetic fuel plant. Heavy borrowing and monetary financing by the Think Big project drove inflation above 17 percent in 1980, while the current account deficit moved up to 4.4 percent of GDP.

The severe recession after 1981, rising unemployment, and a growing current account deficit caused a widespread sense of disillusion with the previous policy record. After the disastrous last round of import substitution industrialization, the center-right coalition was effectively voted out of power in 1984. Labour set out to transform the old model in a market-oriented direction during the 1980s . The new profile included financial deregulation, tax cuts for the middle classes, decentralization of wage bargaining, large-scale privatization and, albeit only in the 1990s, welfare retrenchment.

Amidst a foreign-exchange crisis, the incoming Lange Government, forced by a run on the New Zealand dollar, adopted a large devaluation of

20 percent in 1984. An independent central bank was subsequently set up. This macroeconomic policy shift was accompanied by massive financial liberalization. This helped boost foreign investments. Central bank autonomy and radical trade liberalization profoundly changed the economy by placing high profitability requirements on enterprises. This forced inefficient firms in labor-intensive manufacturing firms to shed excess labor. With high real interest rates, falling trade protection drove up the rate of open unemployment—which had still been below 2 percent throughout the 1970s—to more than 10 percent in the early 1990s. At the same time, employment levels fell from about 65 percent to around 57 percent.

In the second half of the 1980s numerous state-owned enterprises were privatized. Labour also restructured the tax system by broadening the tax base and lowering the top marginal income tax rate from 48 percent to 33 percent. The additional revenue from a new goods and service tax was insufficient to fund income tax cuts on a sustainable basis. Moreover, spending on social welfare and the high servicing costs of New Zealand's large foreign currency-denominated public debt, in the context of high interest rates, also caused by the 1984 devaluation, resulted in a growing budget deficit, amounting to 6.5 percent in 1986. The net impact of the tax policy changes was highly regressive.

The Labour government, however, did not fully attack the old, informal welfare state. It pursued a mix of carrots—increases in the social wage—and sticks—tight fiscal and monetary policy—to enforce wage discipline. With the 1987 Labor Relations Act, the room for enterprise bargaining was extended, which broke up the automatic transmission of wage gains from the sheltered to the exposed sectors. Public sector bargaining was brought in line with private sector practices. There was some compensatory expansion of the formal welfare state. At the same time, social transfer spending rose along with unemployment. Labour implemented the Guaranteed Minimum Family Income in 1986, a kind of negative income tax, guaranteeing working families roughly 80 percent of the average post-tax wage. However, the government also pursued some retrenchment by, among other things, changing the basis for indexation in public pensions and by increasing the eligibility age from age 60 to 65. Finally, in health care a more market-based governance structure was established. In education vouchers and tuition fees were introduced and expanded. It is important to emphasize that most of these far-reaching policy reforms were adopted and implemented by stealth. They were not suggested in any kind of white paper.

The 1990 election led to the inauguration of the more pronounced neoliberal National governments under Bolger. The rise in unemployment in the late 1980s and early 1990s put severe pressure on public finances. The crisis unleashed a whole range of additional policy changes, ranging from the individualization of wage setting and the privatization of social policy to further liberalization of trade policy. The Bolger Government followed a radical strategy of decentralization and deunionization on the premise that flexible and decentralized wage setting would lead to higher levels of productivity and economic growth. In the process, union density plummeted and wage dispersion widened dramatically. While the wage share declined, unemployment fell from 10.3 percent in 1990 to 6.7 percent by 1997. Employment levels, which had fallen from 63.4 percent in 1986 to 57.1 percent in 1992, were made up in the mid-1990s, when employment rose again to 63.3 percent by 1996. After a significant drop from 53.3 percent in 1986 to a record low of 48 percent in 1990, business employment went up to 54.4 percent in 1996, followed by a decline to 52.3 percent in 1998.

Bolger's primary goal of budget consolidation affected the government's policy towards cutting the *formal* welfare state, which did expand during the 1980s. Most importantly, the National administration curtailed social assistance, with a cut in benefits averaging 10 percent. Far sharper cuts in social assistance were adopted for able-bodied males and childless females, with the objective of pushing them back into the labor market. Eligibility requirements were also considerably tightened. In order to reduce public involvement in spending on the formal welfare state, the National government introduced market principles in social security, especially in housing and education. The government failed, however, to introduce markets in health care and old age pensions. Still, it did increase the effective tax rate on old age pensions and suspended indexation for two years. In the process the public deficit was transformed into a sizeable surplus of about 3 percent in the mid-1990s.

The radical reforms of the 1980s and 1990s under Lange and Bolger created a climate of serious discontent, which eventually led to a referendum in 1993. In 1994 this led to the introduction of multi-member proportional representation into the electoral system. As a result, the National Party needed to forge a coalition with the more centrist New Zealand First Party after the 1996 elections. The 1999 election produced a Labour-Alliance coalition government. Both coalitions served to slow down the pace of reform in New Zealand. But until the 1999 election, there was no reversal of the radical reforms in social policy and the labor market which had taken New Zealand from one of the most generous of the Anglo-Saxon welfare states to the leanest.

Australia. The more incremental and negotiated character of Australian adjustment can partly be explained by the existence of a more effective, less politicized arbitration system. Still, the system was not able to keep inflation at bay. As in New Zealand, tight labor markets at the beginning of the 1970s and flaring union militancy had led to high wage claims. As a consequence, inflation increased from about 4 percent in 1970 to a record of 15.1 percent in 1975 and 1976, and it remained above 8 percent for the rest of the decade. Profitability declined while the labor share increased. Firms shed labor, pushing up unemployment from 2.3 percent in 1973 to about 6 percent by the end of the decade. At the same time, employment levels fell from 68.4 percent to 66.3 percent. Deteriorating terms of trade drove the current account deficit up to 3.8 percent of GDP by 1978. In 1974 the government lowered tariffs by 25 percent, in the hope that this would moderate wage militancy. Talks about an explicit social contract failed, however, although the encounter between the government and the unions at least signaled that Australian trade unions were willing to discuss wage restraint. Whitlam supported the arbitration court's introduction of centralized wage indexation and expanded the formal welfare state with new public health and social assistance programs. Subsequently, the Fraser Liberal-National coalitions (1975–83) introduced a mild form of monetarism, targeting public sector wages and cutting public investment. Fraser's policy response restrained but did not change the old model. In 1979 rising commodity prices provoked a doubling of foreign direct investment into Australia, including a 35 percent increase in investment for mineral production. Tight labor markets made the unions press for higher wages. In the face of significant strike activity, Fraser made a pre-election wage concession well above the arbitration court's guidelines for 1980. As a consequence, inflation again reached double digits in 1980.

While the reforms of the 1980s in New Zealand were radical and comprehensive, Australian policymakers pursued a more cautious strategy of 'negotiated change'. As in New Zealand, the perceived mishandling of the economy by the Liberal-National coalition put Labor in power. In the wake of the recession of 1981, unemployment had nearly doubled, to 10 percent, by 1983. Before the 1983 election, the Australian Labour Party (ALP) negotiated a 'foundational' Accord with the trade unions, so as to signal to voters that the ALP could be trusted to run the economy without inflation. As in New Zealand, speculative pressures on the Australian dollar persuaded the newly elected Labor government to let the currency float and to abolish exchange controls in December 1983. In 1984 the government committed itself to a package of fiscal restraint to fight the budget deficit, which had grown from 0.5 percent in 1982 to almost 4 percent in 1983.

The 16 percent depreciation of the Australian dollar in 1985 created the need for a new kind of wage bargain. The government made it clear to the employers and the trade unions that it would no longer guarantee full employment in the absence of responsive wage setting. Under the shadow of financial deregulation and a floating dollar, a second Accord was concluded between the government and trade unions. Under the Accord, renegotiated on several occasions between 1983 and 1989, unions accepted a sustained reduction in labor's share of national income in exchange for public policies designed to expand employment and social benefits.

The Accord procedures gave the Labor government a number of distinct advantages in handling the predicament of Australia's adjustment to an open and competitive economy. Most importantly, it created a stable environment and gave the government time to introduce market reforms in highly sensitive policy areas. The Accord was the appropriate instrument for breaking down the old horizontal pattern of wage parities between the exposed and the protected sectors, which had been responsible for pricing exports out of world markets. It allowed for the decentralization of collective bargaining while still preserving basic social protection through a centrally set minimum wage. The agreements encouraged part-time and female employment as lower trade barriers were destroying full-time jobs. Finally, the Accord gave Labor a foundation of broad public support for its reform strategy.

Australian trade unions realized that declining manufacturing employment was a secular trend and thus had a strong preference for reaching an agreement on wage restraint rather than enduring a government-imposed wage freeze. Their experience with arbitration in the 1970s in preserving real wages and containing inter-union rivalries also convinced unions to exchange wage restraint for a managed expansion of the formal welfare state in the 1980s.

Social policy reforms were enacted to cushion the newly unemployed and to facilitate the entry of women into the workforce. The emergence of dual or one-and-a-half income families and the topping up of single or no-income families through social assistance served to preserve disposable incomes for families caught up in the transition to a more robust export economy. The establishment of a system of national health insurance was a major policy innovation. Targeted subsidies helped cushion the transition from covert to overt unemployment, and from full-time to part-time employment. Social assistance programs were redesigned to top up the wages of those now working for lower pay. The universal child benefit was changed into a means-tested family benefit—now Basic Family benefit—following the logic of a negative income tax and boosting benefits for the worst-off groups. This supplement also reduced the problem of poverty traps.

Under conditions of very high growth after 1992, policy reform in Australia continued at a gradual pace. This incremental approach also helped consolidate the public budget, which had tumbled into a precipitous deficit after the economy went into recession in 1991. The downturn was induced by an overheated asset market and then reinforced by a restrictive monetary policy. The rate of unemployment rose from about 6 percent in 1989 to almost 11 percent in 1993, then declined gradually to about 8 percent in 1998. At the same time, the rate of employment fell from a healthy 69 percent to a low of 65.5 percent in 1993, after which it gradually recovered to reach 68.5 percent by 1998. Business employment, however, developed more favorably than total employment in the 1990s. While the business employment rate fell sharply, from almost 58 percent in 1990 to 54.7 percent in 1993, it soon bounced back. In 1998 business employment was at 58.7 percent, surpassing the pre-crisis level by about 0.8 percentage points. Thus, Australia's mediocre performance in terms of total employment during the 1990s was only due to the decline in government employment, which fell from 11.2 percent in 1990 to 9.8 percent in 1998. It should be added that, in both countries, the employment record was improved substantially by the expansion of part-time employment.

On the basis of quantitative data, the negotiated trajectory of Australia seems to have been more effective than New Zealand's 'shock therapy'. The period from 1984 to 1990 in New Zealand was one of stagnation, although policymakers were able to bring inflation down from an all time high of 17.1 percent in 1980 to 6.1 percent in 1990. Australia enjoyed steady economic growth until 1989, during which inflation was brought down from 10.2 percent in 1980 to 7.3 percent in 1990. From 1984 to 1989, labor market outcomes were also better than those in New Zealand. Australian unemployment oscillated between 6 percent and 8 percent throughout the decade, while the rate of unemployment in New Zealand rose steadily from 2.5 percent in 1980 to 10.3 percent in 1990. Employment levels in Australia first fell from 66.3 percent in 1980 to 62.9 percent in 1983, but then recovered remarkably and skyrocketed to 69.2 percent in 1989. By contrast, employment in New Zealand declined continuously, from 64.3 percent in 1980 to 58.8 percent in 1990. Moreover, New Zealand's poor performance was accompanied by growing inequality, whereas in Australia the effects of growing inequality in market incomes were in part offset by progressive changes to welfare policies (Quiggin 1998).

As Schwartz (Volume II) shows, over the past three decades both New Zealand and Australia have fundamentally transformed their social and economic policymaking profiles in a market-based direction. The core element of the old model, import substitution industrialization, has completely vanished. With unemployment on the rise in Australia during the late 1970s and in New Zealand during the 1980s, informal welfare was replaced by an expansion of formal welfare provision. However, welfare retrenchment was clearly more pronounced in New Zealand than in Australia. While Australia opted for a stronger targeting of benefits and improvements in transfers to the worst-off groups, New Zealand followed a more radical course of retrenchment. Welfare benefits were cut on a broad scale, some by more than 20 percent. As Easton (1996) shows, the lowest income quintile suffered most heavily from the welfare cuts of the early 1990s, leading to a decrease in this quintile's spending power by 21.3 percent—as opposed to a slump of just between 0.6 percent and 7.8 percent for the upper four quintiles. It should thus not come as a surprise that income inequality increased by far less in Australia than in New Zealand. Moreover, poverty increased sharply in New Zealand during the early 1990s.[16] Australia, in short, managed to transform both the structure and content of employment and social policy through a more negotiated, moderate reform process than New Zealand, and with better results.

3.4 Effective Policies at the End of the Twentieth Century

In the preceding sections we have primarily analyzed the dynamic character of the adjustment process. As we have seen, the content of policy reforms and their relative effectiveness is shaped by changing conditions in the international political economy as well as by the relative success of policy reforms and learning from mistakes at previous stages of the adjustment process. The following section provides a more static account of policy effectiveness under the contemporary conditions of an open economy. On the basis of the more successful countries in our project, we want to identify those policies which seem to have contributed to bringing employment and social policy goals closer in line with one another in the 1990s.

3.4.1 Comparative Performance

The challenge of economic internationalization for the welfare state raises the question of how to reach a balance between the competing values of social and employment policy and the changing requirements of international competition. To be sure, policy effectiveness defies easy categorization. We try to assess policy performance along three dimensions: macroeconomic performance (see Table 3.4), employment performance

---

[16] On the basis of the poverty line set by the Royal Commission on Social Security, Easton (1996) reports a rise in poverty by 35% between 1989–90 and 1991–92.

Table 3.4 *Macroeconomic performance*

	Annual GDP growth (%)[a]	Annual inflation (%)[b]	Structural balance (% GDP, 1998)[c]	Current account balance (% GDP)[a]	GDP per capita (1997)[d]
Australia	4.4	1.3	0.1	-4.5	72
Denmark	3.6	2.0	0.6	0.8	83
Netherlands	3.2	2.1	-2.0	5.8	75
United Kingdom	3.1	2.6	-0.4	0.0	69
New Zealand	2.8	1.6	1.8	-4.5	61
Sweden	2.6	0.7	3.2	2.0	69
France	2.4	1.3	-2.4	1.6	72
Belgium	2.4	1.6	-0.7	4.5	77
Austria	2.4	1.2	-2.0	-2.1	79
Germany	2.0	1.4	-1.4	-0.6	76
Italy	1.8	2.4	-1.4	2.4	73
Switzerland	1.0	0.4	-1.5[e]	7.6	88
Average	2.6	1.6	-0.4	1.1	75

[a] Average 1994–98.
[b] Average 1996–98.
[c] General government.
[d] USA=100; in purchasing power parities.
[e] Estimate for 1997.
Sources: OECD (1999g, 1999h); own calculations.

(see Table 3.5), the level of social protection (see Table 3.6), and the distributive outcomes in terms of wage dispersion, income equality, and poverty (see Table 3.7).

The various performance indicators reveal considerable cross-country differences in each of these dimensions. With respect to macroeconomic performance (see Table 3.4) the picture is very mixed. If we look at GDP growth as main indicator for macroeconomic performance, Australia, Denmark, the Netherlands, the United Kingdom, and New Zealand displayed clearly an above average record in recent years, while Germany, Italy, and Switzerland experienced only meager rates of economic growth. However, it needs to be emphasized that Switzerland is still the by far richest country in our project.

In terms of employment performance, we also observe substantive variation (see Table 3.5). National employment records display a span in employment/population ratios from 79.8 percent for Switzerland to 50.8 percent for Italy. For unemployment the span reaches from 3.7 percent in Switzerland to 11.7 percent in France. Cross-national differences are even more pronounced with respect to the level of long-term unemployment. Interestingly, those countries which display an employment performance significantly below average—Germany, Belgium, France, and Italy—are welfare states of the Continental regime type. The Netherlands is the exception to the rule, since it has been able to reverse the vicious cycle of 'welfare without work'.

With respect to levels of social protection (see Table 3.6), we again continue to observe tremendous cross-national variation. By and large our figures corroborate the picture of welfare state variation along the lines developed by Esping-Andersen (1990). Denmark and Sweden continue to be the most generous welfare states with very high levels of spending, especially on social services. The Continental welfare states remain at intermediate levels of generosity and clearly spend less on social services than their Scandinavian counterparts. At the lower end of the scale of social protection we find the liberal Anglo-Saxon welfare states, lean in terms of both transfers and public services.

Welfare state generosity is also reflected in the distributive performance of the welfare state (see Table 3.7). The Anglo-Saxon countries display not only high levels of wage dispersion but also comparatively high poverty rates and a comparatively inegalitarian distribution of disposable household income. The outlier here is Australia, which displays medium levels in distributive outcomes. The Continental welfare states are by and large located in the middle range, displaying a medium performance in terms of distribution. However, within the sample of Continental welfare states, the spectrum is wide. Italy, with average levels of wage dispersion, reveals

Table 3.5 *Employment performance 1998*

	Employment ratio[a]	Unemployment ratio[b]	Long-term unemployment[c]	Female employment ratio	Youth unemployment[d]	Inactivity/activity ratio[e]
Switzerland	79.8	3.7	1.4	71.0	4.9	—
Denmark	75.8	5.1	1.3	70.2	10.6	0.402
United Kingdom	70.3	6.3	2.4	64.2	14.7	0.422
Sweden	69.6	8.3	3.0	69.4	15.7	0.401
Australia	68.5	8.0	2.9	59.2	14.8	—
Austria	62.8	4.7	1.3	59.0	6.9	0.593
Netherlands	61.8	4.0	2.1	59.4	12.1	0.394
New Zealand	60.9	7.5	1.7	62.1	11.7	—
Germany	60.5	9.4	4.9	55.6	8.0	0.425
France	59.4	11.7	5.1	52.3	26.3	0.502
Belgium	56.3	9.5	5.7	47.5	20.5	0.665
Italy	50.8	11.9	7.9	36.7	32.0	—
Average	64.7	7.6	3.2	58.9	14.9	0.476

[a] Total employment as % of pop. 15–64 years.
[b] Standardized ratio.
[c] Long-term unemployed (12 months and over) as % of labor force.
[d] 15–24 years; 1996 or last year available.
[e] Proportion of persons relying on income replacement benefits relative to the proportion of active persons within the pop. 15–64 years; 1996.

Sources: OECD (1998b, 1999b, 1999g); Ministerie van Sociale Zaken (n.d.); own calculations.

Table 3.6 *Level of social security*

	Social expenditure ratio 1995[a]	Social transfers		Social services 1995		
		Public pensions: replacement rate[b] (%)	Net replacement rate of unemployment benefits[c] (%)	Level of social assistance in PPPs[d]	Elderly and disabled services as % of GDP	Family services as % of GDP
Sweden	33.4	74	81	124	3.37	1.72
Denmark	32.6	56	83	129	3.04	2.10
France	30.1	65	82	96	0.78	0.37
Germany	29.6	55	75	95	0.58	0.78
Belgium	28.8	68	71	88	0.15	0.13
Netherlands	28.0[e]	46	83	133	0.67	0.36
Austria	27.1	80	66	98	0.36	0.49
Switzerland	25.5	49	78	141	0.47	—
Italy	23.7	80	42	128	0.20	0.10
United Kingdom	22.8	50	68	111	0.68	0.48
New Zealand	18.8	61	59	82	0.05	0.09
Australia	15.7[e]	41	59	128	0.35	0.21
Average	26.3	60	71	113	0.89	0.62

[a] Total social expenditures as % of GDP.

[b] Average of four cases, 1995.

[c] 1995; net replacement rates after tax; average for different family types (single, married couple, couple with 2 children, one parent with 2 children) and two earnings levels (APW level and 66.7% of APW level); including unemployment benefits, family, and housing benefits in the first month of benefit receipt; it is assumed that waiting periods are met; APW = average production wages.

[d] 1992; OECD mean =100, average for different family types, after housing costs; PPPs = purchasing power parities.

[e] Total social spending is considerably underestimated as private (quasi-)mandatory pensions are not included in the figures.

Sources: OECD (1998a, 1999f); Blöndal and Scarpetta (1998); Eardly *et al.* (1996); own calculations.

Table 3.7 *Distributive performance*

	Poverty rate[a]	Gini coefficient[b]	Wage dispersion D9/D1[c,f]
Sweden	7.3[f]	22.9[f]	2.1
Denmark	6.9[f]	24.0[f]	2.2[e]
Belgium	5.5[f]	23.0[f]	2.3
Western Germany	11.4[f]	25.6[d]	2.4
Netherlands	6.2[e]	27.2[e]	2.6
Switzerland	—	—	2.7
Australia	9.2[e]	31.7[f]	2.9
United Kingdom	10.6[f]	34.6[f]	3.3
Italy	12.8[f]	34.6[f]	2.8
New Zealand	—	—	3.1
France	15.9[e]	32.4[e]	3.3
Austria	—	—	3.6
Average	9.5	28.4	2.8

[a] % below 50% of median income.
[b] Lower figures indicate a more egalitarian structure of distribution of disposable income.
[c] D1 refers to the lowest income decile, D9 refers to the highest income decile.
[d] 1983–87.
[e] 1988–91.
[f] 1992–95.
Sources: OECD (1996a); Huber, Ragin, and Stephens (1998); own calculations.

strong disparities in terms of post-tax and transfer income distribution and poverty. This should perhaps be interpreted as a consequence of its pension-heavy and clientelistic, insider-biased welfare state and the lack of an adequate safety net for youth, single mothers, and the long-term unemployed. On the other hand, Belgium, Germany, and the Netherlands, although belonging to the Continental cluster, reveal a comparatively favorable performance along all three dimensions, coming close to the Scandinavian welfare states in this respect.

The performance figures suggest that relatively successful employment and social policies are possible under very different welfare state arrangements. Australia, Denmark, the Netherlands, and Switzerland, respectively originating from the Liberal, Social Democratic and Conservative worlds of welfare capitalism—with Switzerland located between the Liberal and the Conservative cluster—are cases in point (Esping-Andersen 1990). As the empirical evidence suggests, these countries perform relatively well both in terms of efficiency and in terms of equity. This finding leaves us with the intriguing puzzle that employment and welfare state goals can be achieved simultaneously in different regime types, suggesting that there is no inherently pathological model. To be sure, different welfare states are affected differently by the various dimensions of economic internationalization. As a result, they face different problems of policy adjustment. Effective policy adjustment, however, is not only about tackling the challenge of *international competition*. Effective policy responses have also to address *regime-specific problems*, which often go beyond competitiveness *per se*.

The main problems confronting the *Scandinavian* countries are, first of all, difficulties in financing their costly welfare states under conditions of high capital mobility. Second, there is a need to expand private sector employment to compensate for the stagnation or decline of job opportunities in the public sector. The *Anglo-Saxon* welfare states, by contrast, while displaying a reasonable employment performance, provide only meager levels of social protection, which are often not sufficient to avoid poverty and social exclusion. Finally, the *Continental regimes*, though presiding over a reasonable standard of social protection, display on average only low levels of employment, in both the private and the public sectors, and a problematic gap between labor market insiders with extensive coverage and under-protected labor market outsiders.

There are, however, clear examples of countries that seem to be moving away from the purportedly 'pure' real types of welfare capitalism. More importantly, it is precisely those countries that are deviating from their original clusters in selected policy areas that have proven particularly effective in addressing the most typical problems to emerge from regime-specific structures. The empirical performance comparison reported above showed that Australia, Denmark, the Netherlands, and Switzerland in particular today do comparatively well along the performance dimensions sketched above. We argue that the favorable record of these four countries can be attributed to a policy mix that combines specific comparative advantages from different regime-types.

Our argument is that the basic requirements for a successful policy adjustment can be met by different strategies as long as an appropriate measure of 'goodness of fit' is built into the policy responses, a fitness capable of addressing both the general problem of international competitiveness and regime-specific challenges. The following section identifies the essential requirements for successful adjustment in the relevant policy areas of social and economic regulation and highlights the strategies which proved particularly effective in meeting these requirements. However, we do not only focus on the 'quartet' of the high-performing countries identified above, but also illuminate effective policy responses, which can be observed in the other countries of our project.

3.4.2 Requirements and Strategies for Successful Adjustment

In an era of economic internationalization all advanced welfare states need to be competitive. As welfare states have become increasingly constrained on the fiscal side, they have to increase the efficiency of their welfare programs if they were unwilling to renege on the core commitments of the postwar welfare state. Below we will catalogue the general requirements of a competitive, employment-friendly, and equitable welfare state as well as the various policies that proved effective in fulfilling these requirements. This is not to say, however, that the same policies work under each welfare regime. Rather, we argue, that each country basically has a set of regime-specific instruments at its disposal to pursue effective adjustment under conditions of economic internationalization. Thus, while the available solutions typically differ from one country to another, they are often functionally equivalent and might well be comparable in terms of policy effectiveness. The general requirements may be summarized as robust macroeconomic policy, wage moderation and flexibility, employment-friendly and efficient social policy, and labor market flexibility.

3.4.2.1 Robust Macroeconomic Policy   Macroeconomic policy under conditions of liberalized capital markets faces a tradeoff among three broad policy aims: capital mobility, monetary autonomy, and a fixed exchange rate cannot be achieved at the same time. Where financial capital is mobile, national autonomy in interest rate policy can be reached only at the price of an unstable currency, while a fixed exchange rate does not allow national control over interest rates (Mundell 1962). Since the countries in our sample are highly dependent on access to international capital markets, most of them have opted for open capital markets and stable exchange rates at the price of an independent monetary policy (Simmons 1999). By the same token, strategic devaluations, which Sweden still implemented in the early 1980s, run the risk of massive capital flight. As a consequence, price stability and budgetary discipline have become key elements of any sustainable macroeconomic policy. Moreover, high budget deficits increase the debt burden of the state. Italy and Belgium, which had to pay about 10 percent of their GDP to service their public debts in the early 1990s, are cases in point (OECD, *Economic Outlook*, various years). Furthermore, if fiscal imbalances drive up interest rates, this may crowd out investment in the business sector. Conversely, a strict fiscal policy helps to bring down interest rates, which, over time, may stimulate the economy, reduce the public debt burden, and strengthen the confidence of consumers and potential investors in the economy. Finally, if the structural budget deficit is low on average, there will be some leeway with which to activate the stabilizing function of fiscal policy in periods of low economic growth. The Danish tax reform of 1994 is a case in point, insofar as Denmark's comparatively low structural budget deficit allowed the tax reform to be temporarily underfinanced and a low-growth economy to be stimulated. By and large, the perceived role of macroeconomic policy has drastically changed, from nearly omnipotent instrument of full-employment policy to necessary, but not sufficient, background condition for limited damage control. Employment creation, however, must be pursued by other policy instruments.

As empirical evidence suggests (see also Table 3.4), the 'quartet' of countries we identified as comparatively successful in reconciling the goals of employment and social security—Australia, Denmark, the Netherlands, and Switzerland—has pursued a policy pattern of budgetary discipline in recent years. The policy actors in these countries, including the trade unions, also arrived at the insight that monetary policy has to be geared primarily towards price stability rather than to full employment.[17] As Australia, Denmark and Switzerland—which are not members of the EMU, although Denmark remains a member of the EMS—also followed a course of macroeconomic stability, there is reason to believe that this recognition basically gained acceptance irrespective of the Maastricht criteria.

3.4.2.2 Wage Moderation and Wage Flexibility The general shift from full employment towards price stability as a primary policy goal in the 1980s meant that macroeconomic policy could no longer serve as a buffer shielding other areas of social and economic regulation from the burden of external adjustment. In the more restrictive international economic environment since the early 1980s, wage restraint remained an important requirement for successful adjustment . In the context of high levels of unemployment, wage increases which remain below the rate of productivity growth help to boost profitability, which in turn allows for higher investments and job growth. The beggar-thy-neighbor argument, which suggests that modest wage increases—given a fixed exchange rate—lower unemployment merely at the expense of trading partner countries is misguided. As the Dutch experience suggests, the employment effects of wage restraint are most pronounced in the domestic service sector. Moreover, if wage restraint leads to higher employment and a concomitant growth in domestic demand, the overall effects of wage restraint on the current account are unclear.

---

[17] Australia's high current account deficits and somewhat higher rates of inflation should be viewed as a phenomenon accompanying a booming economy and concomitantly extensive investments rather than as indicators of an inflationary macroeconomic policy.

To the degree to which wage developments in the private and the public sectors are coupled, modest wage increases also lower the public sector wage bill (Ebbinghaus and Hassel 2000). As a second-order effect, rising employment may contribute to lowering the costs of social security. Hereby the revenue basis of the welfare state can be broadened. Moreover, there is some empirical evidence that wage restraint allows for a smoother interplay among incomes, monetary, and fiscal policies, thus stimulating economic growth while keeping inflation low. Those countries we identi-fied as displaying an above-average employment performance have pur-sued a responsible incomes policy along these lines.

Although there was a strong tendency towards the decentralization of collective wage bargaining in the 1980s, more recently we observe a remarkable resurgence of corporatist forms of social pacts and policy coordination in a number of countries, notably Australia, the Netherlands, Denmark, and Italy, but also in countries like Finland, Ireland, Spain, and Portugal, countries not covered in our study (Schmitter and Grote 1997). It seems that the shift to a hard currency regime in Denmark and the Netherlands during the early 1980s brought the social partners closer together. Similarly, the completion of the single market and the EMU entrance exam provided the key impetus for the social pacts in Ireland, Italy, Portugal, and Spain in the 1990s. In short, the effects of economic internationalization seem to have rekindled the need to find cooperative, positive-sum solutions to the predicament of adjust-ment.

Interestingly, many of the countries that have successfully pursued a coordinated strategy of wage restraint do not rely on the traditional pre-requisites, such as the strong, centralized, hierarchically ordered interest associations, of 1970s neo-corporatism. Organized wage moderation in the 1980s and 1990s can be delivered under far less demanding institu-tional preconditions than in the 1970s (see Table 3.8). The state remains an important sponsor of these new accords, offering reductions in taxes and social contributions or promising to maintain social benefits in case wage moderation proves effective (Traxler 2000; Cameron 2000). In Australia, Denmark, Italy, and the Netherlands, governments entered into package deals with the social partners, rewarding the willingness of unions to pursue wage restraint by delivering various kinds of side payments ranging across working time reduction, tax cuts, increased spending for active labor market policy and vocational training. Mandatory contribu-tions to occupational pensions paid by the employers also gained in importance as a module of bipartite or tripartite package deals. Especially in the Continental welfare states, wage bargaining increasingly revolved around the 'social wage' in a broader sense rather than around nominal

Table 3.8 *Differences between neo-corporatist bargaining and modern forms of policy concertation*

	Neo-corporatism (1970s)	Policy concertation (1980s–90s)
International context	Breakup of embedded liberalism	Internationalization of capital markets
Problem constellation	Stagflation	Declining competitiveness High real interest rates High unemployment Rising inactivity
Labor market conditions	Full employment	Rising unemployment High levels of non-employment
Response	Demand side incomes policy, mostly under conditions of an accommodating macroeconomic policy	Supply side incomes policy, typically under the shadow of a non-accommodating macroeconomic policy, targeted at comparative labor costs and inflation
Issue linkage	Narrow: wage restraint in return for fiscal reflation, expansion of welfare state and solidaristic income policy	Broad: wage moderation in exchange for labor time reduction, tax reduction, flexicurity, higher spending for active labor market policy and education
Strategy	Political exchange	Intense concertation
Structure	Centralization	Organized decentralization
Initiating party	Government/employers	Government/trade unions
Dominating party	Trade unions	Employers

Sources: Adapted from Traxler, Blaschke, and Kittel (2000), and Negrelli (1997)

gross wages (Ebbinghaus and Hassel 2000). Moreover, governments may also offer to preserve social benefits and standards in employment protection. In the Netherlands during the 1980s, organized wage restraint was exchanged for working time reduction first and tax concessions later. In Denmark a basic agreement over paid leave schemes, highly subsidized by the state, helped to dampen the wage demands of the country's relatively well-organized unions. Although no 'foundational' social pact has been signed in Switzerland, the consensual character of decentralized wage negotiations and the relative weakness of trade unions have allowed for a sufficient degree of both wage moderation and wage flexibility, even under the conditions of tight labor markets.

In the 1970s consensual wage restraint was part and parcel of the success of Austro-Keynesianism and the Swedish model. Corporatist bargains in these two countries were struck under conditions of full employment and accommodating fiscal and monetary policies. In order to contain stagflation pressures, incomes policy agreements were pursued, geared towards securing social peace, price stability, and full employment. This was achieved by way of exchanging wage moderation for welfare state expansion and a more egalitarian wage structure. In the context of full employment, employers were the weaker party, more dependent on wage restraint to contain inflationary pressures. The trade unions, by contrast, were the dominant party, only willing to deliver wage moderation if policy adjustment corresponded to their solidaristic preferences (Traxler and Kittel 2000). The effectiveness of corporatism in Sweden and Austria was contingent on a range of elementary preconditions: high levels of centralization, concertation mechanisms in wage bargaining processes, and tight disciplinary control over rank and file union membership.

By contrast, the revitalized corporatist bargains in the 1980s and 1990s, first of all, take place in the context of high unemployment, internationalized capital markets, and non-accommodating fiscal and monetary macroeconomic policies. Under these conditions, wage policy not only has to be in line with price stability but also has to allow for profitability and competitiveness (Iversen 1999). Under high levels of unemployment and increased exit options for employers, the unions have become the weaker partner in this constellation. Employers agree to the new deals only if they support competitiveness and allow for greater flexibility of working conditions. For their responsible behavior, unions receive working time reduction and the promise of jobs and apprenticeship places. However, the unions have to shelve their earlier concerns for a more egalitarian income distribution. Due to the institutional anchoring of price stability and fiscal consolidation by independent central banks and the EMU convergence criteria, unions can no longer expect that excessive wage increases will be accommodated by expansionary macroeconomic policies. As a consequence, expansionary wage policy is likely to backfire and trigger rising unemployment. Under the shadow of this imminent threat, the institutional preconditions of the new social accords are less demanding than in the case of Keynesian corporatism. Still, the new social pacts continue to rely on the presence of fairly well-organized interest associations, capable of both developing a longer-term perspective on problems of adjustment and of convincing their members to abide by a coordinated strategy.

The Danish and Dutch systems of industrial relations are marked by a low intensity of industrial conflict and a high degree of consensual concertation between the state and the social partners at various levels. Their bargaining systems are organized around two processes of intermediation: from the micro-level up and from the macro-level down. The format of 'organised decentralization' (Crouch and Traxler 1995), to be sure, requires relatively strong interest associations, though not necessarily encompassing hierarchies, and nationwide institutional structures of social partnership. While matters of wage bargaining and work organization are largely autonomous in Denmark and the Netherlands, the social partners are involved in macroeconomic policy, where trilateral consultation with government actors and experts in various formal and informal policy arenas takes place. Strong associations and stable institutions of social partnership institutions are an asset, but perhaps more important are high levels of trust not only between the social partners at the national level but even more so between sectoral negotiators and central leadership. Wage coordination thus relies less on organizational strength *per se* and more on the capacities of policy actors who operate the system at different levels of interaction and the way they are supported by the institutional infrastructure. Embedded in such an institutional environment, unions find it much easier to adopt a more macroeconomic and long-term perspective as they negotiate wages.

What has become increasingly important over the past decades is the manner and extent to which the social partners managed to combine decentralized bargaining autonomy with macroeconomic considerations in setting wages. The Australian, Danish, and Dutch—as well as the Austrian—experiences suggest that two-level wage bargaining systems, placing sectoral or decentralized negotiations within the confines of a broader national framework accord, are comparatively successful in combining macroeconomic objectives with micro-level adjustment, that is, wage flexibility. Agreements in two-level systems allow sectoral bargainers to strike decentralized deals over productivity, training, and job opportunities for less productive workers within the framework of a more long-term commitment to macroeconomic stability, still essential for containing inflationary pressures (Rhodes 2000). Also, the expansion of the service sector has made wage flexibility at the meso- and micro-levels more important in the 1980s and 1990s than in it had been in the 1970s, when the primary concern was about *average* wage increases in the face of stagflation. There is reason to believe that two-level bargaining arrangements are even superior to largely market-driven wage bargaining systems that now prevail in France, the United Kingdom, and New Zealand. Clearly, market-driven systems are more effective than both statist wage determination—as in Belgium or in France until the 1980s—and fragmented collective bargaining—as was most clearly the case in Britain during the 1970s—in producing market-clearing wage levels. However, while market-driven systems are only able to have a retroactive effect, coordinated systems may act in an anticipatory manner, so as to avoid wage inflation. Coordinated bargaining systems in these countries often produce a strong 'institutional memory' which keeps actors from repeating earlier mistakes. By the same token, coordinated systems may even be able to set wages, at least temporarily, *below* the market clearing level when there is a danger of an overheated economy. This is unlikely to occur in market-driven wage bargaining systems, where employees and trade unions tend to exploit their bargaining power fully.

The state's capacity to intervene in self-governed policy fields in order to overcome reform blockages remains of crucial importance. However, in the 1970s and 1980s wage intervention often led to wage compression, which can undermine micro-flexibility—as the Belgian experience illustrates. In the Netherlands there has been no political intervention in wage setting since 1982. This is not to say that the Dutch state has lost the political power to help set wages. As in Denmark, there is no unlimited *Tarifautonomie*. In the Netherlands, prewar laws authorize the labor minister to declare collective bargaining agreements legally binding for all workers and employers in a certain branch of industry. This provision was routinely applied until the early 1990s, but since then it has been used as a bargaining chip to obtain certain 'public-regarding' objectives from wage negotiations. The government's more independent position has actually strengthened its influence in wage bargaining, and fear of government intervention has, in turn, driven unions and employers closer together (Visser and Hemerijck 1997).

It is important to emphasize that the resurgence of an effective wage policy in Denmark, the Netherlands and Italy came after the trade unions were forced to give up on their long cherished indexation systems, which increased real-wage stickiness and made inflation tolerable to labor. As higher prices ended up in uncontrollable wage increases, indexation undermined competitiveness and led in turn to continuous layoffs, which then resulted in higher social security costs.

3.4.2.3 Employment-Friendly and Efficient Tax and Social Policy   Since, as we argue, redistribution through egalitarian wage policy leads to non-market-conforming wages and thus has negative consequences for employment, the goal of redistribution is best pursued by social and tax policy. Capacities for expanding welfare spending, however, are severely restricted. To begin with, as tax systems are increasingly challenged by international competition, increases in taxes and social contributions have negative side effects. Moreover, in the face of slow economic growth they are likely to trigger resistance from taxpayers. This also applies to those countries in which overall tax levels are comparatively moderate by international standards, a finding indicated by the relative stability of taxation levels since the mid-1980s across virtually all countries in our sample. Moreover, in the context of liberalized capital markets, expanding social expenditures through increased deficit spending is no longer an option. For these reasons, the only way to achieve a higher degree of redistribution without harming employment is to increase welfare efficiency, that is, to redistribute available public revenues in a more targeted manner while reducing organizational slack. Moreover, and partly related to the efficiency aspect of the welfare state, taxation and social protection systems also affect in different ways and to different degrees the growth of employment in national economies.

We start by evaluating the effects of different welfare state arrangements on employment. Empirical evidence suggests that social spending levels *per se* are a not a good predictor of employment performance. In contrast to the United Kingdom and New Zealand, our 'quartet' of successful countries has performed comparatively well in employment terms without a radical dismantling of the welfare state. We argue that social spending is not just to be regarded as a cost factor hampering business in international competition. Social security arrangements may well play a supportive role for the economy as a whole. It is the structure of financing and spending, rather than the expenditure level alone, that affects the welfare state's impact on economic and employment performance. For example, the Danish mix of intensive spending on social services and active labor market policies is arguably more productive in terms of employment than mere income maintenance programs concentrating on the aged—such as one finds, above all, in Italy. This is especially true of activation programs for the most vulnerable groups on the labor market.

Similarly, the continental strategy of labor supply reduction, mainly through early retirement and disability pensions, comes at a high price. First, these strategies proved rather ineffective in creating new job opportunities for the young. France and Italy, though relying heavily on early exit options from the labor market, display very high levels of youth unemployment. Moreover, since these supply-reduction measures are geared toward fighting open unemployment rather than toward increasing employment, they tend to aggravate the financial burden imposed on the active part of the population and further boost labor costs. By the same token, as strategies to expand labor force participation help to broaden the revenue basis of the welfare state, this is also likely to reduce the financial pressure to cut benefits. Denmark, Switzerland, and Australia have traditionally had high levels of workforce participation and did not, by and large, fall into the Continental pattern of workforce shedding. The Netherlands has recently been able to reverse this vicious cycle of 'welfare without work' by restricting access to, and curtailing heavy misuse of, their disability schemes. As Ebbinghaus (Volume II) argues, the extent to which early exit options from the labor market are used is contingent upon a variety of 'push' and 'pull' factors setting different incentive structures for both employers and employees in different regime types. Strategies of gradual retirement through partial pension schemes may help to reduce the total costs of early retirement, avoid dismissals, and preserve the health status of older workers. Swedish experience seems to confirm the viability of this option (see Delsen 1996). To be sure, temporary reductions in labor supply might be necessary during economic crises. However, as empirical evidence suggests, such solutions have a tendency to become permanent. In a period of low economic growth, Denmark's schemes for sabbatical, educational, and parental leave are more appropriate measures for temporary labor supply reduction than is the Continental strategy of permanent labor shedding. Moreover, paid leave schemes, as well as active labor market policies, may be regarded as a 'transitional labor market state' serving partly as 'buffer zones' around the regular labor market while containing hysteresis effects, which typically contribute to the persistence of long-term unemployment (Auer 1999, 2000; Schmid 1996).

Generally, policies aimed at expanding employment are likely to be more successful if they are supported by the social partners. The Netherlands, which has strengthened the incentives for the social partners to raise the degree of activation by making the level of minimum wages and social benefits dependent on the ratio of inactives—welfare recipients—to actives—insurance contributors—in the population, is a case in point.

Employment performance is also affected by the financing structure of the welfare state. This holds especially true for employment at the lower end of the earnings scale, which is likely to be crowded out by high payroll taxes particularly if high legal minimum wages or high levels of social assistance set a high reservation wage below which net wages cannot fall. As a consequence, in welfare states mainly financed by payroll taxes, the tax wedge at the lower end of the labor market is typically higher than in welfare states primarily financed out of general taxation, such as Australia and Denmark. To some extent, this also applies to the Swiss welfare state, where the health insurance system and the large second tier of old-age provisions are organized as a private, but still mandatory, insurance scheme and, as such, do not show up in the tax wedge. The Netherlands, whose welfare state is primarily financed out of payroll taxes, has reduced the tax wedge for low-paid workers by integrating general social insurance contributions into the tax system. This means that the general basic income tax exemption is extended to some branches of the social insurance system. Moreover, a special cut in employer contributions for low-paid workers has been implemented.

There is also clear empirical evidence that the specific arrangements of income and payroll taxes have an impact on employment patterns—that is, the combination of full- and part-time work—within households. As a recent study comparing these systems and their effects in ten countries shows (Dingeldey 1999), it is not primarily the formal regulation of tax systems—individualized versus a splitting system—that matters; more important for explaining cross-country variation in the distribution of working-time within families is the formal system's interaction with tax-free allowances and progressivity. Sweden is exemplary in that respect: the Swedish social insurance and tax system is completely individualized and does not even provide an additional tax-free allowance for families with a single earner—as is the case in other countries with individualized systems. As a result, egalitarian employment patterns between men and women are highly favored, which again contributes to Sweden's very high female participation rate (see also Daly, Volume II).

The design of systems of social security and taxation also matters in terms of cost efficiency: the welfare state has different redistributive functions, such as reducing poverty, limiting income inequality and providing a certain level of income protection against social risks. While the fulfillment of these goals is severely limited by fiscal constraints, there is a range of policies which effectively moderate this dilemma. Here again, an analytic distinction between the revenue and the benefit sides of the welfare system is helpful. On the revenue side, there are a number of instruments to finance social security which do not increase the overall tax burden on the various factors of production. An option widely used in the Anglo-Saxon welfare states and Switzerland is the strong reliance on user charges and copayments for the financing of public social services—health, elderly and child care, as well as education. This does not necessarily impinge on social equity, as economically vulnerable groups might be partly exempted from the payment of these fees.

Another financing option, particularly with regard to pensions, which has comparatively little detrimental effect on employment is private mandatory contributions. Australia, Denmark, the Netherlands, and Switzerland have made occupational pensions mandatory in recent years, either by the state or through collective agreements (Gern 1998). Those countries have thus adopted a combination of a pay-as-you-go financed basic pension—or a means-tested minimum pension in Australia—and a fully funded and income-related pension on an occupational basis. This mix is superior in two respects. First, this combination allows for a higher degree of risk diversification. Due to their high degree of prefunding, such pension systems are likely to be comparatively robust against demographic changes. Moreover, the advantage of both individual private and occupational pensions—often paid for by employers—versus public pensions lies in the fact that contributions are perceived as part of private consumption rather than as part of the tax wedge and thus are likely to generate fewer work disincentives than contributions to public social insurance schemes. By the same token, pension systems which display an institutional separation between a pay-as-you-go financed basic pension and a fully funded private mandatory insurance also allow for a more targeted assignment of the various redistributive and insurance functions of the welfare state and are thus less likely to generate distributive conflicts than is the case with pension systems which combine these functions within one tier. In addition, funded schemes tend to have a higher rate of return than pay-as-you-go schemes, since real interest rates are clearly higher than growth rates for real wages. Finally, the problem stemming from the fact that low-wage earners are typically less able to accumulate sufficient contributions through private or occupational pension schemes has been successfully addressed in Australia, where contributions from low-wage earners are subsidized by the state.

The revenue base for national pension schemes also varies in terms of coverage, most notably with respect to the inclusion and exclusion of civil servants and the self-employed. Arguably, universal pension schemes are less vulnerable to changes in employment patterns than categorically fragmented schemes of the Continental type. In that respect, too, Denmark, the Netherlands, and Switzerland display a more robust policy profile.

What is more, the robustness of public revenues in general is clearly higher in tax systems which combine modest nominal tax rates, which are also more advantageous in psychological terms, with a broad tax base. Moreover, those tax systems are more transparent and equitable. Finally, tax regimes which rely strongly on consumption taxes are likely to be more robust in the face of rapidly aging populations than levies on a shrinking work force. By the same token, indirect taxes are less vulnerable to cyclical fluctuations in the level of employment.

There is also considerable variation in the degree to which policies have proven to be effective in reducing welfare expenditures without compromising the central functions of the welfare state. The Anglo-Saxon countries have tried to increase welfare efficiency through a stronger reliance on means-tested benefits so as to concentrate welfare spending on the truly needy. However, the disadvantages of this strategy must not be underestimated. First, means-testing benefits require careful and administratively costly procedures in order to prove need, which may also have stigmatizing effects. Second, they often create strong work disincentives, or 'poverty traps', if they are provided only up to a certain income level—although, to some extent, high effective marginal tax rates for low-income earners resulting from means-testing can be alleviated through various forms of in-work benefits. By the same token, in the case of pensions, means-testing is likely to hamper incentives to make advanced contribution payments for individual pension claims. In Australia, the incentive problem caused by the means-tested character of the public pension scheme was addressed by making occupational pensions compulsory. Third, means-tested benefits exclusively geared towards lower income strata are not in the interest of the middle class and may thus, from a political perspective, be more vulnerable to retrenchment. This was, for instance, the case in the United Kingdom and New Zealand, where the eroding or absent middle-class support for a higher level of means-tested benefits might, at least partly, explain why these countries display for the time being much higher poverty rates than other welfare regimes.

Other countries have found strategies to keep the growth of social expenditures under control while avoiding the drawbacks of means-testing. The taxation of social benefits is a case in point. As recent empirical studies from the OECD have shown (Adema 1998) cross-country variation is considerably higher in gross social expenditure ratios—before taxation—than it is in net social expenditure ratios—after taxation. The reason for the difference is that taxation of social benefits differs widely from country to country. In countries with little taxation of social benefits this may induce perverse distributive results. For example, since public pensions are barely taxed in Germany, net replacement ratios for high-wage retirees are higher than those for low-wage retirees. Denmark, the Netherlands, and Switzerland, which tax pensions at a higher rate, thus achieve a more equitable intra-generational income distribution without higher total costs (see also Kohl 1994).

Denmark and the Netherlands have enforced a further cost-cutting strategy in social policy which did not undermine the redistributive effectiveness of the welfare state. The criteria for paying social assistance and unemployment benefits were applied more strictly, making them dependent on recipients' willingness to accept suitable work or participate in activation measures. As such, this strategy proved also superior in terms of employment.

3.4.2.4 Labor Market Flexibility Growing international competition, technological progress, and changed family patterns have tremendously altered the conditions under which national employment systems operate. Generally, these developments require more flexibility in labor markets with respect to working patterns, wages, and working time. While there is a broad range of possible strategies for increasing labor market flexibility, many of these alternatives are counterproductive in terms of equity and social security. The basic challenge for effective employment policy lies in reconciling labor market flexibility with measures to avoid social exclusion. As the empirical evidence provided by our country studies suggests, there is no inherent contradiction between the objectives of flexibility and equity. To the contrary, the general acceptance of flexible arrangements in the labor market is likely to be increased if flexibility is matched by a decent standard of social protection. Denmark and the Netherlands offer telling examples of how both excluding large parts of the workforce from the labor market—a pressing problem in many Continental and especially Mediterranean welfare states—and marginalizing vulnerable groups within the labor market—typical for Anglo-Saxon welfare regimes—can be avoided. Innovative employment policy and important changes in labor market regulation in these countries concentrate on bridging the gap between employers' preferences for flexibility and workers' interest in stability and security, thereby making labor market flexibility more socially acceptable. The successful policy mixes adopted in Denmark and the Netherlands can be subsumed under the label of 'flexicurity' a concept developed in the Netherlands. Flexicurity is based on a number of different, though mutually reinforcing, strategies. In the following sections, we highlight five central dimensions.

Increasing the demand for low-skill work. Mainly as a result of technological change, all advanced welfare states have to cope with the problem of declining demand for low-skill work in the industrial sectors. The countries covered in our study differ, however, in the degree to which they have been able to compensate for this development by promoting demand for low-skill jobs in the service sector. Generally, the demand for low-skill work is related to the level of female labor force participation. Higher employment of women typically raises the demand for regular jobs in the areas of care for children and other dependants as well as for consumer-oriented services in general. Thus, demand and supply in service employment are mutually reinforcing (European Commission 1998). By the same token, it should not come as a surprise that the rapid increase of employment in these service areas in the Netherlands since the mid-1980s occurred simultaneously with the quick expansion of female labor force participation.

Our 'quartet' of successful countries has managed to lift the demand and supply for jobs in the sheltered services on to a high equilibrium level. This was, among others, brought about through different techniques effectively reducing the tax wedge at the lower end of the labor market. Australia, following the logic of a negative income tax, offers subsidies in the form of tax credits to workers in low-paid jobs. The aim is to avoid the strong work disincentives associated with the poverty traps typical of Anglo-Saxon welfare states with their strong reliance on means-tested benefits. By contrast, employers in the Netherlands hiring low-skilled workers are exempted from social contributions which typically constitute a major obstacle to more low-skill hiring in the Continental welfare states. These strategies are of minor importance in mainly tax-financed welfare states such as Denmark, where the tax wedge at the lower end of the income scale is already rather low.[18] The same holds true for Switzerland, where health insurance and the second tier of the pension system are organized as private mandatory insurance and thus do not have the effect of a tax on labor.

Expanding part-time work and flexibilization of working hours. The changing socioeconomic environment also requires more flexibility in working hours. This allows not only for a better use of resources at the level of the firm, but also for a better fit between the firm and employees' needs, which are increasingly deviating from the traditional pattern of lifelong full-time employment. By and large, a voluntary reduction of individual working hours is likely to have fewer negative side-effects than a general reduction in working time. Uniform, across the board reductions of the working week can lead to evasion strategies by employees and firms, which in turn could lead to an expansion of the black economy. Moreover, if such reductions are linked to compensatory hourly wage increases, the resulting jump in unit labor costs might even be counterproductive in terms of employment. In contrast, the expansion of part-time work seems to be a more advantageous strategy. As empirical evidence shows, high levels of employment are usually connected with above-average part-time ratios.

[18] Moreover, in Denmark, as well as in Sweden, the state is an important employer as a provider of social services.

The tremendous job growth in the Netherlands in recent years is partly the product of a rising share of part-time employees. For young people in particular, part-time contracts may serve as a bridge leading to regular employment (Auer 1999, 2000). While the socioeconomic changes sketched above suggest that the potential for expanding part-time employment is considerable, the countries in our sample vary greatly in the degree to which they have exhausted this potential. This again suggests that an appropriate country-specific policy mix is critically important for setting the right incentive structure for employers and employees to expand the demand and supply, respectively, of part-time work. This policy mix can be based on a broad range of instruments. Cutting individual working hours is more attractive in those countries that have a basic-pension system and partial individualization of social security entitlements. By contrast, in countries, such as Germany, that combine a system of complete tax splitting between spouses with a strictly earnings-related pension system, part-time employment is punished not only by unfavorable tax treatment but also by more or less proportional cuts in pension entitlements. The propensity for individual reduction in working hours can be enhanced by lowering the tax burden at the lower end of the labor market to compensate partly for any loss in gross wages. Finally, the standard of social and job protection for part-time workers should not substantially deviate from the level of protection provided for full-time workers (see Walwei 1998). This points to the central importance of labor market 'desegmentation',[19] another essential cornerstone of flexicurity.

Labor market desegmentation. Labour market desegmentation is geared towards negotiating a relaxation of employment protection for the stable, full-time, core workforce and linking these new standards to increased protection for the peripheral, unstable, part-time, and temporarily employed in the rest of the economy. This helps to contain the growth of precarious jobs, which we have seen in France among other places. The Danish welfare state is illustrative in this respect: very high levels of unemployment benefits make employees and trade unions more willing to accept weak protection against dismissals. Evidence from Italy suggests that social protection and dismissal protection are *functional equivalents*. Weak social protection goes together with restrictive dismissal protection and *vice versa*. While a lower standard of protection against dismissal might affect overall employment levels only a little—since a more rapid rise in employment during an economic upswing is likely to be outweighed by a faster cutback in jobs during a downturn—long-term unemployment

---

[19] The concept of labor market desegmentation has been suggested to us by Jonathan Zeitlin, for which we are grateful.

with its highly undesirable hysteresis effects might well be kept at a more modest level than in countries with high and rigid standards of employment protection. This assumption is also empirically supported by a recent study from the OECD (1999b). As a consequence, systems combining restrictive dismissal protection with meager unemployment benefits essentially cater to the interests of insiders, whereas systems based on minimal job protection but offering decent standards of social protection for the unemployed bridge the gap between insiders and outsiders more easily. In this respect the Danish strategy is clearly superior to its functional equivalent in the Mediterranean countries. The Netherlands has followed a different strategy of labor market desegmentation. As already pointed out above, the legal status of part-time workers has been raised. The same is true for employees in temporary job agencies, which experienced massive growth in past decades. This also meets the interests of employers, whose demand for labor is subject to fluctuations. As such, the increased use of temporary work agencies in the Netherlands is functionally equivalent to low levels of employment protection in Denmark, Switzerland and the Anglo-Saxon countries.

Reconciling work and family life. This is another policy line to increase labor market flexibility. As quantitative data show, there is considerable cross-country variation in the level of female labor force participation reaching from about 44 percent in Italy to about 75 percent in Denmark, Sweden, and Switzerland (see Daly, Volume II). In the Netherlands, female labor force participation has increased the most rapidly of the countries in our sample, displaying a doubling of participation rates since the early 1970s. Clearly, this went in hand with rising part-time opportunities allowing women to combine child rearing and participation in the labor market. As a consequence, in many Dutch households the low wage increases that result from long-term wage restraint are compensated for by an additional family income that comes from women's growing job opportunities. Reconciling work and family life is also the driving force behind the Danish—and Swedish—strategy to expand childcare facilities and parental leave arrangements. As Daly argues, public support of caring, and to a lesser degree, tax provisions have a strong influence on the decisions of women to participate in the labor market. On the demand side, the structure of the labor market, in particular the size of part-time and service sector employment, is an important explanatory factor for the degree of female labor force participation.

Increasing the activation content of labor market policy and tightening eligibility criteria for unemployment benefits. Australia, Denmark, the

Netherlands, and Switzerland have substantially increased spending on active labor market policy in recent years, thereby emphasizing the activation content of labor market policy instead of just relying on passive transfers to the unemployed. Moreover, strategies of labor shedding through early retirement, disability pensions, and the like, which were widely used especially in the Netherlands, have also been revised. Finally, as already mentioned, the impact of activation programs has been strengthened by stronger pressure on the unemployed to accept suitable job offers or participate in education programs.

High levels of employment and social security, to sum up, can no longer be pursued by the limited arsenal of macroeconomic policy alone. Given the high degree of economic internationalization reached at the end of the twentieth century, the effective delivery of employment and social policy objectives is critically dependent on a consistent mix of policies across various areas of social and economic regulation. Above all, labor market and social policies have to be (re)designed so as to foster employment growth rather than to subsidize non-employment. As the empirical evidence provided above suggests, there is a broad range of viable policy options to reconstruct a new equilibrium of the welfare state.

3.5 Conclusion

Policy adjustment under international constraints is difficult, but it happens. Over the past three decades a number of sudden shocks and more incremental changes in the international political economy have disturbed the once stable postwar 'equilibria' of macroeconomic policy, wage setting, industrial policy, taxation, social policy, and labor market regulation. In this we have examined how different welfare states responded to the process of economic internationalization. By adopting a policy learning perspective, we have been able to trace the diachronic, sequential self-transformation of twelve economically advanced welfare states across six policy areas. Having highlighted the composite effects of policy changes on the overall effectiveness of policy adjustment in countries that appear in good shape at the onset of twenty-first century, we would turn to the question of whether there is particular pattern of policy adjustment that is in any sense typical of the economically advanced welfare states.

While all countries have faced similar challenges, the timing, politics, content, and outcomes of policy change have been quite different. Some of the countries in our project have implemented policy change across the entire gamut of policy areas, one after the other, for the past several decades. This goes to show that the welfare state, broadly understood, is a dynamic policy structure. Other countries have bundled more radical changes in several policy areas into a single shock therapy package, usually triggered by severe failures in economic management and large shifts in the political balance of power. In yet other countries the process of adjustment seems to have come to a—possibly temporary—standstill as the result of strong popular opposition and institutional self-blockage across policy areas.

In this chapter we have identified some of the general causal mechanisms behind different experiences of policy adjustment. First and foremost, national trajectories of policy adjustment were conditioned to a considerable degree by the overall starting constellation of their respective policy profiles before the onset of the external shocks of the 1970s. Second, the relative success or failure to respond adequately to the successive changes in the international political economy by and large determined the available room for maneuver when new international constraints made themselves felt. Third, policy fiascos often triggered fundamental learning processes that led to significant modifications in the country-specific policy profiles and rules of the game governing various policy areas. Fourth, to the degree that policy responses required some issue linkage between different policy areas, successful adjustment depended on various forms of coordination available to policymakers.

Our approach of sequential and 'problem-induced' policy learning has enabled us to analyze and sketch diachronic trajectories of policy adjustment without forcing ourselves to choose between the dichotomous academic categories of *convergence* and *divergence* (Berger and Dore 1996). Although the capacity for policy adjustment has become more circumscribed, a fair number of advanced welfare states have proved highly responsive to the challenge of economic internationalization, in terms of both efficiency and equity. Over the past three decades, countries have had to give up strategies that previously enabled them to protect the core policy areas of the welfare state, which once allowed them to legitimize broad social and employment policy objectives. In the process, the terms of the policy debate has revealed a shift from macroeconomic adjustment to social security reform. In the wake of the recessions of the mid-1970s, the early 1980s and early 1990s, the key issues of the policy debate about the joint pursuit of economic and social objectives changed considerably. In the 1970s, against the background of the emerging problem of stagflation, the debate revolved around macroeconomic management to contain inflation and unemployment. In the context of rising real interest rates and of accelerating public debt, the policy debate in the early 1980s moved towards issues of competitiveness and fiscal austerity. While the fight against unemployment continued, more emphasis was placed on supply-side measures. In the 1990s the policy debate again changed. As the international integration of capital and product markets intensified, the core areas of the welfare state, social security, and labor market policy moved to the forefront of the adjustment effort. In the area of macroeconomic policy, particularly monetary policy, we do observe almost full convergence involving a sharp reduction in national autonomy. Today, monetary policy in the European Union falls within the jurisdiction of the independent European Central Bank. While fiscal policy and tax policy continue to remain within the orbit of the nation state, international constraints, most notably the EMU convergence criteria, place important limits on the scope for domestic fiscal policy. In the context of an emerging post-industrialization in employment patterns and of the predicaments caused by demographic aging, the focus in the 1990s gravitated towards pension reform on the one hand, and the search for a novel balance between flexibility and security on the other.

It is extremely difficult, beyond these fairly general observations, to draw definitive conclusions from the adjustment trajectories and their effectiveness. This is largely because the end is not yet in sight for policy adjustment under international constraints. Pension reform is clearly unfinished business. At this stage we wish to confine ourselves to a more tentative theoretical conclusion based on a number of noteworthy empirical observations. We have seen many reversals of social and employment fortunes over the final quarter of the twentieth century. No single welfare state did equally well in responding to the three waves of economic internationalization. Having praised the Dutch model of the 1990s in the preceding section, we think it is important to remember the high social costs of Dutch corporatism's policy mistakes in the 1970s, that country's drastic monetary and fiscal corrections, its sustained wage moderation induced by high unemployment during the 1980s, and its painful welfare reform in the 1990s. Correcting for past policy mistakes took the Netherlands 15 to 20 years and a combination of intelligent policy choices, all in order to reach the modest level of employment it experienced in the early 1970s. The Swedish model's historical success lay in pursuing a fully-fledged Keynesian full employment policy when the advanced welfare states were still in a position to do so. As a result, Sweden experienced a unique and large increase in employment during the crisis-prone 1970s. Although the Swedes mainly expanded the public sector, this has had the lasting positive side-effect of strengthening middle-class support for the service-intensive Scandinavian welfare state. Strong societal support for the Swedish welfare state also survived when the model crashed in the early 1990s.

A particularly striking finding is that policy reforms in the welfare state's core 'distributive' areas arrived so late in the adjustment process.

This is less true for the United Kingdom and New Zealan
institutions and principles of the welfare state were effectivel
conservatives. The resolution of this puzzle is related to the ⟨
ical risks of policy adjustment: the more reform efforts reach
'distributive' areas of the welfare state, the more political conflict is likely
to flare up. Conceptually, in a thought experiment, we can place the six
policy areas that make up the welfare state on a spectrum displaying the
extent to which they are, on the one hand, directly affected by changes in
world markets and, on the other hand, politically protected from market
pressures (see Fig. 3.5). While no policy area is totally shielded from the
international economic environment, policy responses in macroeconomic
policy, incomes policy, and industrial policy, because they operate under
the shadow of open markets, are basically oriented towards strategies of
external adjustment. As we move closer to the core areas of the welfare
state, like social policy and labor market regulation, we encounter provisions, like social security benefits, minimum wages, and dismissal protection, that are deliberately designed to protect workers and citizens from
market exigencies. These policy areas are based on established industrial
and social rights granted to citizens irrespective of their market power.
Most of these policy programs, as we have seen above, have become implicated in the process of adjustment mainly through endogenous spillover
effects from policy areas where the corridors of adjustment have narrowed
significantly due to external changes and endogenous policy failures.

Although the obvious political risks of welfare state retrenchment make
it impossible to separate the objective of competitiveness from the goal of

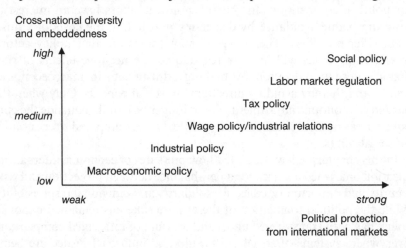

Figure 3.5 Domestic political protection and cross-national diversity of policy
areas

social justice during the process of adjustment, we believe that electorally accountable political decision-makers have an interest in broadly dispersing, and thereby hiding, the costs of economic adjustment. Different policy issues induce different forms of political mobilization. Changes in macroeconomic policy, which are of major importance to ordinary citizens' material life chances, are often subjectively perceived as mere technical interventions in the eyes of the electorate. As such, they remain shielded from mass political mobilization. A significant rise in interest rates by an independent central bank does not lend itself easily to political dramatization. A more explosive political climate is ignited when cuts in benefit levels are discussed or when large national firms go bankrupt. When the process of policy adjustment starts to impinge on social security and labor market policy, often because the room for policy adjustment in the more 'exposed' policy areas has been exhausted or has become severely constrained, distributive conflict looms large. As social and employment policies are based on deeply held normative understandings of equality, social justice, and national solidarity, reforms made there are likely to endanger the legitimacy, and thereby the efficacy, of policy adjustment. Moreover, as industrial and social rights are usually attached to relatively strong interest groups, like trade unions, which typically resist curtailments of acquired rights, reform is likely to make the adjustment process rather unpredictable. If internationally exposed wages are sticky, as economists argue, then generous pensions, wage indexation, job protection regulation, and the like, all enshrined in law, are probably even stickier. After all, the politics of 'dismantling the welfare state' is not an attractive ticket for political competition. In general, political actors have an interest in fostering blame avoidance by dispersing and hiding the costs of adjustment (Pierson 1994). Therefore, we may conjecture that policy actors, whenever possible, will initially respond to the negative effects of economic internationalization by making adjustments in macroeconomic policy, and thereby avoiding direct cuts in social benefits. Only when the burden of economic adjustment can no longer be handled outside the core policy areas of the welfare state are political actors prepared to economize on social rights.

In this chapter we have observed how pressures of economic internationalization unleashed a search for a new balance between protection and risk, security and opportunity, collective solidarity and individual responsibility. While the political foundation of the welfare state has remained national, policy has been transformed under the pressure of intensified competition. Everywhere systems of social citizenship and industrial justice are being scrutinized in terms of their implications for productivity and competitiveness. Effective responses are aimed at accommodating economic internationalization rather than opposing it. Interestingly, the more successful countries we have encountered deviate considerably from the 'purer' ideal-typical welfare regimes of the 1970s. Over the past two decades, countries like Denmark, the Netherlands, Switzerland, and Australia have developed appropriate policy mixes for reconciling equity and efficiency under the constraints of economic internationalization. These effective policy mixes did not emerge overnight; rather, they were the outcome of a lengthy and often painful adjustment process. By the same token, successful patterns of policy adjustment were decidedly not predicated on comprehensive reform blueprints covering all policy areas at once and supported by strong political leadership. To the contrary, they are typically the products of failure-induced learning processes. All the successful countries have followed a trajectory of negotiated change. In the two most tightly coordinated economies, Denmark and the Netherlands, the 1990s reforms and strategies crossing different policy areas were mutually reinforcing through issue linkage. Together the impact of concerted adjustment was powerful. Perhaps the reforms would have been less successful and more difficult to implement in isolation. They surely benefited from a 'shared ownership' of policy problems, triggered by the memory of deep crises and policy failures. We would like to stress that negotiated reforms based on shared ownership of policy problems are less likely than radical change to endanger the overall stability of the economic and political system. Radical 'big bang' reforms packages generate massive uncertainty and instability in the period of transition, and can undermine economic performance—at least in the short run—reduce the propensity to take economic risk, and possibly even lead to greater social conflict. An erosion of social cohesion, furthermore, is likely to undermine trust in the economic and political system, foster an unstable environment for long-term investment, and have a negative impact on consumer behavior and policy development. The purported success of the New Zealand model compared with Australia's recovery in the 1980s is a case in point. Throughout the 1980s economic performance, based on almost all relevant indicators, has been much poorer in New Zealand, not only compared with the OECD average but also, interestingly, with Australia, which followed a more incremental pattern of negotiated change based on a social pact among the state, trade unions, and employer organizations (Quiggin 1998). We observe a similar downturn in the United Kingdom, reflected in sharply rising unemployment immediately after the Conservatives came to power in 1979.

If welfare states wish to adjust to ongoing changes in the foreign and domestic policy environments, they not only need to change their policy structures; perhaps more importantly, they must also raise their general capacity to adapt, that is, their institutional learning capabilities. The more successful countries stand out because they have been able to inaugurate innovative policy mixes attempting somehow to synchronize horizontal coordination across policy areas with vertical coordination among macro-, meso-, and micro-levels of decision-making in a positive-sum game. This form of flexible coordination requires an elaborated software for issue linkage, information sharing, communication, and trust-building among different actors, something possibly even more important than the institutional hardware itself. It is not by chance that the Netherlands and Denmark stand out within the European Union as the countries whose citizens display by far the highest degree of trust in the problem-solving capacity of their countries' political institutions (Becker 1999).

4

Values and Discourse in the Politics of Adjustment

VIVIEN A. SCHMIDT

4.1 Introduction

Since the 1970s, the achievements of the advanced welfare state have been challenged by a wide variety of external economic pressures often summarized under the rubric of globalization, which are related in particular to the increasing competition in capital markets, in product markets, and in tax regimes. As we have seen in previous chapters, the changes in welfare states in response to such economic adjustment pressures vary widely depending upon such things as countries' relative economic vulnerability to those pressures, the relative capacity of their institutional structures to promote successful strategies for reform, and the relative success of the repertoire of policies they mustered in response. Success, however, is not only a matter of economics, institutions, or policies. It also depends on politics.

In the classic policy science foursome of problem, policy, polity and politics, this means that my focus in this chapter would be on the last dimension: on the dynamic processes of political interaction which, within a given institutional structure—polity—and confronted with specific vulnerabilities—problem—would generate specific responses—policy. In effect, this would require me to recount and systematize the contemporary history of the politics of adjustment in our twelve countries. But the recounting has largely been done in the country chapters (in Volume II). And it is not certain that the systematization of these country-specific stories could produce much generalizable knowledge that is not already contained in the earlier chapter discussing institutional capabilities. What could be added here are analyses of class alliances and interest group politics, of party-political and electoral constellations, of the disincentives confronting single-party governments and the members of coalition governments when policy reform would go against the interests of important

In addition to members of the conference project, I would like to thank Paulette Kurzer, Peter Hall, and Jonas Pontusson for their comments.

groups in the electorate and/or their own constituencies, and of the incentives for opposition parties and affected interests to mobilize protests against such reforms. Most of these incentive- and interest-based interpretations are pretty straightforward and not very edifying. Thatcher could carry out her program because the opposition was divided and had no chance of winning under British electoral rules, and the German social democrats won an election by mobilizing voters against the retrenchment policies of the Kohl government, which after a few months in power they must carry even further—but now against the vociferous opposition of the former government parties.

In other words, such an approach would get me little farther than providing an account of politics as usual, according to which one assumes that in the politics of retrenchment, those who lose will be opposed (see Pierson 1996, 1998) and that, more generally speaking, under the normal rules of democratic politics, policies that go against the interests of large groups, let alone a majority of the electorate, are bound to fail—and this whether one expects defeat to come from disagreement among the veto-players in multi-actor—federal and/or multi-party—polities or from anticipated voter reactions in unitary and single-party governments. But this does not square with what goes on in the real world, where policy initiatives that go against the narrow self-interest of electoral majorities succeed more often than one would expect—in Britain in the Thatcher years after 1979, in the Netherlands and Denmark after 1982, in France after 1983, in New Zealand after 1984, in Italy and Sweden after 1992, and potentially in Germany after 1999. In some of these cases, institutional conditions gave governments a free hand, but in others that was clearly not the case. The most interesting question to explain, then, is how governments actually managed to overcome narrow self-interest enough to persuade electoral majorities and even the most affected interests of the merits of a new policy program.

My focus in this chapter is on those aspects of democratic politics that facilitate successful adjustment in the face of interest-based opposition. These involve forms of political communication which, in the continuum between 'bargaining' and 'arguing', are located closer to the arguing pole. To describe them, I will use the term of 'policy discourse'. While this discourse must necessarily provide the cognitive definitions of the problem and the cause-and-effect relationships defining effective solutions, the emphasis here is on the normative content of arguments proposed to justify unpopular policy initiatives. The reason is worth spelling out.

The welfare state itself is a socio-political construct which, since it involves insurance and redistribution, could not exist without the support of strong normative arguments and moral convictions. As a consequence, its existing structures of obligations and benefits are supported by a sense of appropriateness that generates moral support for the status quo also among those who are unaffected or would even benefit by its reform. It is such moral convictions that explain the wide public support for protests organized in December 1995 by French public-sector unions against proposed cuts in civil service pensions, which were much more generous than the pensions expected by ordinary citizens. In order to succeed with unpopular reforms, therefore, governments must be able to dissociate the self-serving protest of disadvantaged interest groups from the support of the moral majority. This, I suggest, can be achieved only through discourses that seek to demonstrate that reform is not only necessary, by giving good reasons for new policy initiatives, but also appropriate, through the appeal to values (V. A. Schmidt 2000b). Such normative legitimization, moreover, may involve appeal to the very values of solidarity that the traditional welfare state was built upon—as when the norm of intergenerational solidarity is now invoked to justify less generous pensions in order to relieve the burdens on the younger generation—to competing values that also have broad moral support—self-reliance versus solidarity—or, finally, to higher values of the collective good, as when a government calls for sacrifices to save the nation from economic disaster. There is, of course, no assurance that such appeals will help the government survive an impending election. But I will try to show that no major and initially unpopular welfare-state reform could succeed in the medium term if it did not also succeed in changing the underlying definition of moral appropriateness.

Thus, this chapter will explore the democratic legitimization of reform of the welfare state by considering how governments actively sought to justify policy change through normative discourse. By focusing on moments of crisis or transition when values are generally made explicit in public debates as opposed to continuing as unquestioned background assumptions embedded in institutional practice, this chapter seeks to offer comparative insights not only into the values that remain central to different polities' notions of social justice but also into the discourses that appeal to values in their efforts to legitimize policy change. Moreover, it considers not only the substantive content of those discourses but also how the national institutional context affects the locus of discourse as well as the course of reform. Finally, it raises questions about whether there is a new emerging value consensus about the appropriate kinds of policies for a new, less vulnerable, more competitive welfare state in the open economy.

The chapter begins with a short theoretical discussion related to the use of values and discourse as primary explanatory variables. It then considers in turn each of three different families of welfare states, Anglo-Saxon, Scandinavian, and Continental, first by briefly discussing the postwar constellation of values as they had crystallized by the 1970s and, second, by then examining the role of normative discourse in the dynamics of policy reform in the 1980s and 1990s. In this latter part, the emphasis is on those reform initiatives in any given country that represented a major challenge to deep-seated national values and conceptions of social justice, and which therefore were the object of significant public deliberation and debate. In the conclusion, the chapter turns to more theoretical questions about normative discourse in policy reform in an effort to generalize about the conditions for its success or failure in promoting policy change in different institutional contexts.

4.2 The Role of Values and Legitimizing Discourse in Policy Change

The appeal to values in legitimizing discourses is a complex process. All societies have a plurality of values, many of them conflicting or applying only under certain conditions or to special choice situations—or 'spheres of justice'—and most changing over time, with some emphasized or de-emphasized at any one time or another. Therefore, when governments construct a legitimizing discourse, the appeal to values always has the character of 'selective activation', by focusing on a particular value within a limited repertoire of other values that could also be invoked in the situation—and which may be invoked by the opposition. Societies differ from one another, however, not only in their normative orientations, that is, in the weight they accord to particular values, but also in their degree of normative integration. Some societies tend to have greater agreement about the norms and values appropriate to any given policy area than others, which may have several rival normative orientations, one or another of which may predominate at any given time. And therefore, the more complete the normative integration, the fewer are the strategic choices open to governments in the appeal to specific values.

Discourses differ across countries not only in the range of values to which they may appeal but also in how they are constructed and where they are focused. This is because different institutional contexts tend to frame the discursive process, determining who is involved in the initial elaboration of the policy program and discourse and toward whom the discourse is directed (see V. A. Schmidt 2000b, 2000d). In some countries, the elaboration of the program is by a restricted, government-centered policy elite, and the discourse directed toward the general public to communicate the government's policy decisions. This 'communicative discourse', as we shall see, is more prevalent in single-actor systems where power is concentrated in the executive, such as Britain, New Zealand, and

France. In other countries, the elaboration of the policy program is the product of a much wider cross-section of policy-related elites, while the discourse tends to be directed towards those very policy elites involved in the original elaboration, as a way of coordinating the policy construction. This 'coordinative discourse' is much more prevalent in multi-actor systems where governmental power and/or societal representation are more dispersed, such as Germany, Austria, and the Netherlands. While most countries privilege one or the other form of discourse, there are certain countries in which under certain circumstances both forms of discourse tend to have equal weight, as has been the case for Switzerland.

These differences in discursive practices are important not only because of what they tell us about differences in countries' democratic legitimation processes but also because of how they affect the course of welfare reform itself. For even countries that resemble one another in postwar welfare state values may nevertheless end up with very different policy outcomes because of differences in discursive contexts, as we shall see in the cases of multi-actor Australia by contrast with single-actor Britain and New Zealand, or of multi-actor Italy by contrast with single-actor France.

By focusing on discourse, then, this chapter suggests that we can gain insights into the reasons for success or failure of policy reform which go beyond explanations in terms of interests and/or institutions alone. Although the chapter makes no claims to being able to predict which particular discourses will prove influential, or to which particular values an influential discourse will appeal, it does have hypotheses about the conditions under which governments' discourses are more or less likely to act as a significant influence on policy reform, given certain kinds of institutional contexts and constellations of interests, and given a particular range of values to confront in their efforts to reform the welfare state. It also suggests that a government's discourse can best be shown to exert a separable, causal influence—enabling change as opposed to simply accompanying it—when it is used to justify policies that go against the immediate or perceived interests of its own constituency. In fact, one of the few tools a government has to gain or retain public and/or policy elite support when potentially faced with an opposition mobilized in protest and appealing to majority interest is to appeal to values, whether to values of national solidarity or the public good, or more specifically to alternative societal values not being furthered by the current policies. Cases where discourse can be shown to have mattered to the success or failure of welfare reform, as we shall see, are Britain, which had a successful discourse, by contrast with New Zealand, Denmark by contrast with Sweden, the Netherlands by contrast with Belgium, and Italy beginning in the early 1990s by contrast with France until the late 1990s and Germany still today.

4.3 The Challenges to the Values of the Postwar Welfare State

For most of the advanced welfare states under consideration, the early 1970s represented the apotheosis of the 'golden age' model. Many were still in the process of construction as the first oil shock hit, and some even expanded subsequently, with only one or two—Germany and Austria—beginning the belt-tightening that would take place in earnest for a number of countries in the 1980s, and for others only in the 1990s. Major welfare reform initiatives were not seen until the 1980s in the Anglo-Saxon welfare states, and for most Scandinavian and Continental welfare states not until the 1990s, if then. For all countries, however, the pressures had been building ever since the end of the 'golden age', as the welfare state absorbed the fallout from countries' economic restructuring in response to challenges related to increasing competition in product markets and worldwide capital mobility (Scharpf, this volume). Faced with rising unemployment, growing welfare costs, and decreasing ability to fund their programs, countries' traditional welfare state commitments to full employment, a given level of social security, and/or equality came increasingly under threat.

Economic problems, however, were not the only threat to the traditional welfare state. Endogenous social changes, reflected in the new 'post-industrial' values related to changing lifestyles, attitudes toward work, and the role of women in particular, also had a significant impact on the welfare state, especially with regard to questions of equality of opportunity in employment and gender income parity. Moreover, the neo-liberal ideas that had served as an impetus to the transformation of the structure of the economy were now also increasingly being applied to the structure of welfare and work, promoting individual responsibility for social security above a certain basic minimum, preferring market solutions over state or other provision in social services and pensions, pushing flexibility in wages and work conditions in place of equal pay and job protections, and approving greater differentiation in income to reflect the individual's contribution to society. Such ideas, though, gained currency to varying degrees and in different ways in different countries. Much depended upon the actual structures of the welfare state, and the interests and values to which governments could appeal in seeking reform.

It should come as no surprise that Anglo-Saxon welfare states have been the most receptive to neo-liberal ideas. Such ideas found fertile ground not only because of the historical liberalism of Anglo-Saxon countries but also because of the very structure of the welfare state. The low level of benefits and services, which entailed that the many had to pay for the few while themselves having to rely on the market with regard to employment and social security above the minimum level, made welfare retrenchment harder to resist in those areas where it was in the self-interest of the majority (see Scharpf, this volume). By contrast, neo-liberal ideas have seemingly penetrated the least in the 'social-democratic' Scandinavian welfare states, not only because of the long-standing value placed on equality in Scandinavian countries—which also ensured the greatest receptivity to post-industrial values related to women—but also because the universalistic nature of the welfare state, with its high level of services as well as of employment and social security for all, ensured that the maintenance of a generous welfare state was in the interests of all (Rothstein 1998c). Interestingly enough, neo-liberal ideas have also not made much headway so far in most 'Christian-democratic' Continental welfare states, mainly because of the high level of social insurance for all, despite lower levels of services, somewhat greater differentiation in benefits, and less certain employment. Here, post-industrial values have instead been the major force for change in the welfare state, by challenging the family-based, male-breadwinner model.

Such differences among welfare states help explain the fact that, confronted with the economic challenges of the 1970s, 1980s, and 1990s, countries with different kinds of welfare states faced different questions. The major question for Anglo-Saxon countries was how far to go in a liberal direction with regard to the promotion of individual responsibility and market-reliance. The question for Scandinavian countries was how to protect social-democratic ideals of collective responsibility and equality in the face of retrenchment needs. And the question for Continental countries was in whether and/or how much to alter their Christian-democratic family-based, gender and status differentiated model to promote either liberal or social-democratic ideals.

4.4 The Anglo-Saxon Welfare State

For the three Anglo-Saxon countries in our project, Britain, New Zealand, and Australia, major external economic pressures appeared earlier than for most of the other countries in our sample, and only intensified in the 1970s. The policy responses to those pressures also began earlier, in the 1980s rather than the 1990s, and basically challenged the normative orientations of the already 'liberal' postwar welfare state in the name of liberalism. The policy changes, however, went a lot farther for New Zealand than Britain, and for both much farther than Australia. But whereas such changes were largely accepted by the general public in Britain and

Australia, they were not in New Zealand. While the differences in the extent of reform can be explained by institutional structures that made single-actor Britain and New Zealand better able to impose radical reform than multi-actor Australia, the differences in public responses owed a great deal to the persuasiveness of the communicative discourse in Britain and of the coordinative discourse in Australia by contrast with the lack of communicative discourse in New Zealand.

4.4.1 Postwar Anglo-Saxon Welfare State Values

The Anglo-Saxon countries are often labeled 'liberal welfare states' because of their emphasis on individual responsibility in a residual welfare state. In such welfare states, social assistance is understood as a right differentiable according to need, with the beneficiaries, the poor, and the goal, poverty alleviation. Only in publicly provided or subsidized services such as education and health care are rights seen as universalistic and non-differentiable. This is totally in keeping with the Beveridge model, which assumed that anything more than a minimum of state provision with regard to income replacement would be a disincentive to work, but that one must ensure equal access to health and education, since if you are sick you can't work, and if you are uneducated, you cannot work to your fullest potential. But if work was therefore a necessity as much as a moral obligation for the individual who, without work, would lose self-respect as well as an acceptable standard of living, full employment became something of a moral obligation for the state, as well as a major source of political legitimacy (see Scharpf, this Volume).

For the United Kingdom, New Zealand, and Australia, this general description of liberal values institutionalized by way of a modest welfare state serving as a safety net for a system based on full employment held throughout the postwar period until the 1970s or later. But there were none the less significant differences among the countries; and in all countries such liberal values were contested by strong social-democratic aspirations.

For Britain in particular, it could be argued that the minimalism of the welfare state was less a product of clear moral conviction than of both the economic vulnerabilities that from very early on were an impediment to the expansion of the Beveridge model and of the lack of any agreement among political elites on the desirability of state intervention or welfare expansion. Britain throughout the postwar period was in fact a normatively fragmented society in which the values and discourse of the two major parties differed greatly in emphasis and imagery, given the paternalism of the Tory rhetoric, with its strong liberal impulses, by contrast with the class-based, egalitarian language of Labour, with its strong social-democratic and egalitarian impulses. Despite this, the two political parties ended up quite close in consensual style as well as in economic policymaking from the 1950s to the 1970s, in which policy decisions appeared to be matters of tweedledum or tweedledee. Thus, although the Conservatives were ideologically opposed to state interventionism, holding as early as the 1950s that full employment was the ultimate substitute for universal social provision—although many nevertheless also held to the 'One Nation' tradition that the alleviation of poverty was critical to the maintenance of British institutions (Greenleaf 1983, ch. 7)—when in power they instituted policies that were much more interventionist and expansionary with regard to social welfare measures, however inadequate, than their ideological commitments would seemingly have allowed. And similarly, whereas Labour was in principle committed to equality and income redistribution, insisting that equality of opportunity and social mobility were not enough and needed to be combined with measures 'to equalize the distribution of rewards and privileges so as to diminish the degree of class stratification, the injustice of large inequalities, and the collective discontents which come from too great a dispersion of rewards' (Crosland 1956: 237), they did little practically to foster either equality or redistribution when in power and only intermittently engaged in the greater interventionism to which they were ideologically committed (see Rhodes, Volume II).

In Britain, in short, although the parties disagreed on the need for interventionism in the economy and the expansion of social welfare, these had little effect on the policies, which were quite similar throughout the postwar period until the 1970s. The right wanted to do less but could not avoid doing more, while the left wanted to do more but was unable to avoid doing less.

In New Zealand and Australia, by contrast, throughout the postwar period parties of the left and the right were agreed on the need for a more interventionist role of the state in the industrial sector. And they had a moral commitment to offsetting their even more modest welfare state through the 'informal welfare state'. In Australia, this had a long history going back to the Harvester decision of 1907, which established the basic principle by which the arbitration court would make its judgements, to wit, that the minimum wage for an unskilled worker should be determined by 'the normal needs of the average employee regarded as a human being living in a civilized community' (Castles 1988: 99) and expected to support a wife and three children. Moreover, in both countries, the arbitration courts made decisions on the basis of 'comparative wage justice', with awards that sought to maintain wage relativities among occupations on the basis of long-standing wage differentials—and that led to wage compression, especially in New Zealand (Schwartz, Volume II). This resulted in a greater society-wide commitment to equality and security in Australia and New Zealand than in Britain,[1] even though both antipodal countries also shared Britain's underlying liberal emphasis on individual responsibility and the work ethic along with full employment.

4.4.2 Values and Discourse in Anglo-Saxon Welfare State Reform

Some might argue that much of the turn to greater liberalism by all three Anglo-Saxon welfare states in response to the major economic crises beginning in the 1970s could have been anticipated, given the traditional liberal ideology that had kept social assistance at a minimum in order to ensure that it did not take the place of work, and the long-standing economic problems that kept more egalitarian impulses in check. But what could not have been anticipated are the differences among countries in the ultimate acceptance or rejection of reform. And this had much to do with the legitimizing discourses that served Britain and Australia in their different ways better than New Zealand.

4.4.2.1 The United Kingdom Britain, which had struggled economically through much of the postwar period, overburdened by war debts that the other countries in our project did not have, was hit particularly hard by the economic crises of the 1970s. And the initial governmental responses, which sought to revive the old solutions, failed especially dramatically. The Labour party, which by this time had moved much farther to the left than in the earlier postwar period as it propounded a more clearly socialist ideology—with a high degree of interventionism, nationalization of industry, and so forth—along with continued support for corporatist business-labor-government relationships, at first at least seemed to have found the answer. Its coordinative discourse had successfully persuaded the unions to engage in wage restraint through appeal to the self-sacrificing 'spirit of Dunkirk' and 'to give a year to Britain'. The resulting 'corporatist' incomes policy lasted only a short time, however, and was followed

---

[1] It is important to note, however, that the values of equality and security were focused on the core wage earner. In Australia, for example, while there has consistently been a relatively equal pay distribution among 'core' workers, overall inequality has been relatively high. This can be explained by the presence of part-time workers, Asian immigrants—especially given the early 'White Australia' policy—and women who were generally not afforded the same work protections or guarantees as the white male core workforce. Other factors are the limited redistributive effects of Australia's small welfare state and the effects of capital incomes on overall inequality (see discussions in Svallfors 1993; Saunders 1994; Mitchell 1991).

by the wide-scale strikes of the 'winter of discontent' of 1978–79 (see Scharpf, this volume), worsening economic problems, and the inevitable victory of the Tories, who by this time had moved farther to the right under the leadership of Margaret Thatcher, advocating greater *laissez faire* capitalism to solve the problems of economic decline and industrial unrest. And once in power, Thatcher used all the resources of the Westminster system as well as her control over party and policies to impose her ideological commitments.

There can be no doubt that Thatcher's success in instituting neo-liberal reform owes a great deal to institutional capacities afforded her by the British single actor system, to economic policies that eliminated government dependence on union cooperation, and to fortuitous political circumstances, including a divided opposition and the Falklands war, that insulated her electorally (see Scharpf, this volume). However, the fact that such reform took hold, lasting despite subsequent changes in governments, owes much to the highly effective accompanying communicative discourse through which Thatcher sought to persuade the general public not only of the superior logic of market capitalism, which she contrasted both with the Labour Party's 'socialism' and 'corporatism' and the Tory 'paternalism' of her own party, but also of its appropriateness in terms of the country's long-standing adherence to a limited state and liberal economic principles, with their basis in deep-seated British values (Marquand 1988).

The neo-liberal ideology propounded by Thatcher and the Conservative government defended the people's right 'to be unequal' with claims that the pursuit of equality weakened incentives and penalized success (Evans and Taylor 1996; Leydier 1998); that inequalities were necessary to stimulate individual talents and raise British economic performance; that government attempts to reduce inequalities were not only costly and ineffective but also dangerous because of their detrimental effects on the economy and on the population, creating a dependency culture with a nanny state; and that inequalities were morally justifiable in any social order to provide rewards and incentives that would encourage the 'spirit of entrepreneurship' as well as provide a warning by the example of the less well-off (Wilding 1994; Leydier 1998). Thus, Thatcher talked of 'rolling back the frontiers of the Welfare State', and promoting an 'enterprise culture' in order 'to change Britain from a dependent to a self-reliant society. From a give-it-to-me to a do-it-yourself nation; to a get-up-and-go instead of a sit-back-and-wait-for-it Britain' (*Times*, 9 February 1984, cited in Hedetoft and Niss 1991). She appealed to Victorian values as she insisted on distinguishing between the 'deserving' and the 'undeserving' poor when providing assistance, that is, between 'those who had genuinely fallen into difficulties and needed some support till they could get out of them' and 'those who had simply lost the will or habit for work and self-improvement' (Thatcher 1993). And instead of government being responsible for solving Britain's problems, she sought to shift the onus to the people (Riddell 1989: 1).

Interestingly enough, while Thatcher's discourse was largely successful in helping to gain acceptance for radical changes in the structure of the economy and work through anti-inflation austerity budgets, deregulating and privatizing industry, and shattering the unions, it did less to help her overcome public resistance to changes the structure of welfare. In the end, despite her vow to 'end the dependency culture', Thatcher actually did not cut overall social welfare expenditures or the National Health Service (NHS), where public opposition to retrenchment was greatest, given that it was an area where the notion of rights was universalistic and the middle classes benefited. But while Thatcher found herself repeatedly defending her record on the NHS, and pointing to greater spending on the NHS as proof that she valued it, she had much less difficulty legitimizing cuts in social assistance programs and housing allowances, where she could distinguish between the 'worthy poor' and the feckless and the idle, for example, the unemployed, single mothers, and youth. Moreover, although Thatcher did not threaten the universalism of the basic pension, she limited its redistributive effect, by de-linking pensions from earnings, at the same time as she reinforced individual responsibility and exposure to market risks by promoting individual recourse to private pensions beyond the basic pension. Finally, although Thatcher did not interfere in principle with the universalism of health or education, the institution of competition in the NHS and in tertiary education was a way of encouraging 'capitalist' values of entrepreneurialism in place of—in Thatcher's view—'socialism'.

The question, then, is to what extent Thatcher succeeded in promoting neo-liberal values as she changed policies. Public opinion surveys suggest that Thatcher did manage to move the British toward more capitalist values when it came to acceptance of inequalities, individual responsibility, materialism, and entrepreneurialism, all of which followed from her reforms of the structure of the economy and work,[2] but that she did not by any means eradicate 'socialist' values, especially with regard to health and welfare (see Crewe 1991), where resistance to reform was more successful. This is evidenced in a 1988 MORI poll on peoples' views of the ideal society, which shows that whereas on the two out of five questions

---

[2] To be more precise here, we should probably say that Thatcher was engendering a return to long-standing 'capitalist' values which had been overshadowed by the so-called 'socialist' ones (see Hetzner 1999).

focused on work issues, majorities came out in favor of a capitalist society which emphasized increasing efficiency rather than keeping people in work—50 percent versus 42 percent—and allowing people to make and keep as much money as they can—53 percent, versus 43 percent for emphasizing similar incomes and rewards for everyone—on the remaining three focused on welfare, majorities came out in favor of a socialist society—49 percent, versus 43 percent for a capitalist society—which emphasized social and collective provision of welfare—55 percent, versus 40 percent for encouraging the individual to look after himself—and rewarded caring for others—79 percent, versus 16 percent for wealth creation (Hetzner 1999: 124).

The polls also suggest that even though the British continued to espouse socialist values with regard to health and welfare, when it came right down to it they were unwilling to pay for them. For example, when asked a general question about whether they supported increasing expenditures on the National Health Service, education, or social benefits, the British appeared to be more and more in favor—with a British Social Attitudes survey finding a dramatic rise between 1983 and 1991, from 32.2 percent to 64.9 percent in 1991 (Jowell *et al.* 1992: 217). However, when asked direct questions about how much they were willing to see their own taxes raised in order to pay for the increase in social services and benefits, polls found that the answer was for the most part very little—an IEA survey noted that of the 82 per cent polled who claimed to be willing to pay more for social services and benefits of various kinds, only slightly more than 10 per cent of the sample would be 'prepared to pay the equivalent of an additional 3p in the £ on the standard rate of income tax' (Harris and Seldon 1987: 27, cited in Hetzner 1999: 181). Moreover, many considered their own taxes already high enough—a 1985 British Social Attitudes survey found that 55.1 percent felt their taxes were too high and only 25.1 per cent just right, versus 0.7 per cent too low (Brook *et al.* 1991: F-16, cited in Hetzner 1999: 178). It is also significant that at the same time as pollsters found general support for tax increases to pay for health and welfare, the voters were re-electing Thatcher at least in part because of the tax cuts she had instituted.

If nothing else, then, we could say that despite continued collectivist values with regard to welfare, Thatcher's promotion of the capitalist values of the 'enterprise culture' had had great effect. Further confirmation for this can be found in the election results, and in the rhetoric of the politicians whose political lives and livelihoods depended on guessing right and thereby winning elections. It is telling that over a period of 18 years the British re-elected first Thatcher and then Major, who continued the Thatcherite policy program and discourse, albeit with a somewhat less confrontational style, and that the only way the Labour party was able to

return to power was in adopting much of the Thatcherite neo-liberal policy program and discourse.

One should not forget that, during Thatcher's first mandate, the Labour
party had espoused the exact opposite set of values from those of
Thatcher, with its 1983 election campaign promising socialism in one
country—and opposing further European integration because of this—
pledging more nationalization, and a more generous and egalitarian welfare state. Labour's repeated election defeats convinced it that it could not
win with such policies, and the mid-1980s to the mid-1990s represented
the long march back to the center. The gradual acceptance of capitalism
and neo-liberal economic policies beginning in the mid-1980s culminated
with the 1992 election manifesto claiming 'not to replace the market but
to ensure the market works properly' (Hay and Watson 1998) and the 1995
renouncing of one of the last vestiges of 'socialism', with the elimination
of Clause IV of the Labour Party Constitution which justified nationalization. But whereas Labour slowly but surely seemed to have undergone
a complete neo-liberal conversion with regard to the structure of work and
the economy, the conversion was more nuanced with regard to welfare.

Throughout the Thatcher and Major years, in fact, Labour leaders continued to express concerns about poverty, inequalities, and the attacks on
welfare and education. By the late 1980s, Labour had completely reversed
its earlier opposition to European integration because it saw this as a way
to defend social policy in Britain, in particular with the Social Chapter of
the Maastricht Treaty—for which Major had gained an opt-out. At the
same time as Labour was seemingly continuing to defend traditional
social policy, however, it was increasingly espousing neo-liberal social values of opportunity, responsibility, individual merit, and the 'challenge of
the Market' as the best mechanism to allocate most goods and services
(Shaw 1994; Leydier 1998).

Labour's mixed approach to social issues—appealing to public concerns about growing inequalities and declining services while claiming to
offer solutions in keeping with the new neo-liberal ethos—clearly resonated with the public. This was evidenced by the fact that in the 1987 and
1992 campaigns, the electorate seemed to favor Labour on the issues,
although they nevertheless brought back the Conservative Party because
they thought they were more capable of governing, and more in favor of
its leadership. By the 1997 election, however, and the first one with Tony
Blair as a candidate, the Labour party had both issues and leadership in
its favor (Denver 1998).

In the run-up to the election of May 1997 and subsequently, Blair with
his 'New Labour' Party constructed a communicative discourse that represented very much a renewal of the Thatcherite discourse. It sought to

convince the public that 'New Labour' had taken a 'third way' between the left and the right, between 'the failed world of Old Labour', with its appeal to values of equality, community, and socialism, and Thatcherite neo-liberalism, with its appeal to the values of individualism and *laissez faire* capitalism, by embracing the 'risk society' resulting from globalization and providing a new politics of the radical center, with an active, inclusive civil society, in which one must reconstruct the state, rather than shrink or expand it (Featherstone 1999). Subsequently, moreover, the third way became something which, rather than setting a new course 'between conservatism and progressivism', takes a progressive course which distinguishes itself 'from all conservatisms, whether of the left or the right', and ensures that 'after a century of antagonism, economic efficiency and social justice finally work together' (Speech to the Labour Party Congress, Bournemouth, 28 September 1999).

In this discourse, moreover, globalization has a special place, since it serves as the rationale for New Labour's neo-liberal turn (see Hay and Watson 1998; V. A. Schmidt 2000d). Unlike Thatcher's discourse, where support for globalization followed from the ideology of neo-liberalism, in Blair's discourse, support for neo-liberal policy follows from the reality of globalization. And this was used as justification for government policies that sought to promote greater flexibility in the labor markets, to 'attack the real wage'—by keeping public sector wages down and urging the private sector to exercise restraint—and the social wage—by downgrading benefit entitlements and redefining welfare as workfare (Chancellor's budget speeches, July and November 1997, cited in Hay and Watson 1998).

Given Labour's longstanding defense of social welfare, it could seem all the more ironic that Blair has essentially done what neither Thatcher nor Major dared in terms of welfare reform, by introducing workfare for social assistance recipients and tuition fees for students in tertiary education at the same time that it has continued means-testing in social assistance and gone further with the introduction of the market into pension systems. But for New Labour, all of this is perfectly consistent with a discourse that emphasizes reversing 'social exclusion' and fostering social mobility, and which has put its money where its mouth was, so to speak, by providing greater funding for education, training, and welfare-to-work programs (Teles 1998). Thus, Blair could claim that he had taken positive action to 'promote opportunity instead of dependence' through education and workfare as opposed to the Conservatives' mainly negative action with regard to the 'dependency culture' focused on limiting benefits and services. Moreover, in higher education, the breach in the principle of universality of access through fees, remedied partially by scholarships for the poorest, did not have to be seen as an attack on redistributive principles, since university fees are essentially a tax on the middle classes and the rich. What is more, 'New Labour' has also been somewhat more redistributive in its social policies with regard to the very poor, by raising the level of social assistance and by instituting a minimum wage for the first time ever, even if these redistributive aspects of Blair's welfare policies have seemingly been 'by stealth', since they have had much less attention in the discourse (see Rhodes, Volume II).

Thatcher may have succeeded in creating a neo-liberal revolution in the economic arena, then, but it took Blair to complete that revolution with regard to the social arena. At the same time that Blair has reinforced neo-liberal values of individual responsibility and the virtues of the market, however, his discourse of the 'third way', along with his less emphasized redistributive policies, have also tapped into the deep-seated 'socialist' values of compassion, equality—at least of opportunity—and social justice which have consistently been reported in the public opinion polls. Many Britons in fact remained uncomfortable with the Conservative government's moralizing about the very poor as feckless and idle and its seeming lack of concern about rising poverty. They seem much more comfortable with putting the poor to work, to force their inclusion in society, and with being a little more compassionate about the lot of those who cannot for whatever reason become part of the 'active society'.

Thus, in Britain, Thatcher's communicative discourse was an important element in gaining British acceptance of neo-liberal change in the structure of the economy and work, so much so that Blair remained true to the basic policy goals and discourse, and even furthered those goals with regard to the structure of welfare. In New Zealand, something very different happened, in part because of the lack of a sufficiently legitimizing communicative discourse. The public showed its ultimate displeasure with even more radical neo-liberal changes than in Britain through a referendum that dismantled the very institutional arrangements that made radical welfare changes possible in the first place.

4.4.2.2 New Zealand In the contrast between Britain and New Zealand, both Westminster models of single-actor systems, it is important to remember that where Britain maintained a rather meager formal welfare state that was minimally interventionist and had already experienced growing unemployment in the 1970s, New Zealand had had a more generous informal welfare state which became significantly more formally generous in the 1970s, had continued low unemployment in the 1970s, and had increased its state interventionism and protectionism as well in that period. Equally significant is the fact that while Britain was struggling economically through much of the postwar period, New Zealand had ranked among the world's top ten countries in per capita income, with its inhabitants seeing themselves as enjoying the world's best quality of life in 'God's Own Country' (Nagel 1998). Thus, the fall from grace, as major economic crises hit beginning in the 1970s, was comparatively much farther. Moreover, the reforms in response to those economic crises were much more radical and far-reaching than in Britain, and also took New Zealand a much greater distance from its initial starting point.

Beginning in the mid-1980s with the introduction of market principles, the dismantling of state interventionism and protectionism, and the rise in unemployment, followed in the 1990s by the drastic reduction in the generosity of the welfare state and the deregulation of the labor market with even greater market liberalization, New Zealanders experienced a comparatively greater challenge to their postwar value system than the British. And they also had much less of a choice. Whereas the British could have chosen to reject Thatcherite neo-liberal policy in favor of traditional left-wing Labor policy in election after election, but did not, the New Zealanders had two parties, both of which had majorities from the mid-1980s on that propounded neo-liberal policies. Moreover, whereas in Britain the changes were facilitated by an elaborate communicative discourse which consistently sought to persuade the public of the benefits of the neo-liberal policies as well as to convert them to its underlying values, this was not the case in New Zealand. Here, the political parties never made clear what their plans were going to be in their election campaigns, instituted radical reforms when in power without much consultation or communication, and did this mostly against the wishes of large parts of the population. The result was tremendous public discontent, which culminated in the referendum, voted in 1993, replacing the majoritarian electoral system—as of 1996—that had made it possible for governments to impose such radical reform in the first place.

Much of the explanation for the way in which change came about can be attributed to the progressive dealignment of the major parties' electorates and the rise of ideologically-driven minority wings of those parties that were able to exploit the institutional framework to capture power and impose their policies with impunity. Even more so than with Thatcher in Britain, these committed minorities broke not just with the policies of the past but also with the consensual style of policymaking.

Through much of the postwar period, there had been relatively little difference in the policies of the two major New Zealand parties, Labour and National, both of which had agreed on the liberal social-democratic policy framework settled on in the 1950s (James 1986; Nagel 1998: 232–33) and for which political conflict consisted in 'jostling' one another for the 'safe middle ground' (Mitchell 1969: 140). This changed, however by the late 1960s, with the rise of divisions over foreign policy—especially with regard to French nuclear testing—environmentalism, group rights—in particular the Maori—and social norms—with changing sex roles and patterns of family life. These in turn fueled changing party alignments, as the Labour Party began to gain more and more votes—and leadership—from the young and rising professionals concerned with non-economic issues while its traditional working class constituency was eroding, the result of the changing class composition of the workforce and the growing appeal of the increasingly populist National Party under the leadership of Robert Muldoon in power beginning in the mid-1970s (Gustafson 1976, 1986; Nagel 1998). National's policies, however, which shifted from a moderate economic liberalism during the mid-1970s to an emphasis on economic security and greater state interventionism—the 'Think-Big' import-substitution projects—by the late 1970s in turn led to a growing split in the party, which culminated in an out and out revolt by the free-marketeers in the run-up to the 1984 election with the creation of the break-away New Zealand Party (Nagel 1998), and ultimately ushered in a new Labour government.

When the Labour Party came to power in 1984 after almost a decade of rule by the National Party, the economy was in crisis and in danger of defaulting on its international obligations. In its election campaign, Labour had left its plans with regard to economic policy rather vague, although there was general acceptance that something had to be done. But there was certainly little suggestion that it would engage in such radical neo-liberal economic reform. Much the contrary, given campaign refer-ences to ensuring an 'active role for government', instituting 'prices and incomes policy' and an 'investment strategy', which gave the impression that a new Labour government would be as interventionist as its prede-cessor (Mulgan 1990; Nagel 1998).

Labour's shift to neo-liberal economic policies can in large measure be explained by the discrediting of the old economic solutions. But it also had to do with electoral considerations, primarily its efforts to attract upper middle class voters in marginal districts supportive of economic liberal-ism, and thereby to overcome a systemic disadvantage that had given it a plurality of votes but not of seats in Parliament in the previous two elec-tions (Nagel 1998). Moreover, Labour calculated that even with neo-lib-eral economic policies, it could still expect to retain the loyalty of its traditional constituency of the poor and the working classes as long as it continued to support the industrial relations and welfare systems, and of its more left-wing followers by its support of certain non-economic causes, in particular by being anti-nuclear but also pro-women, environmentalist, sensitive to Maori claims, and so forth (Vowles 1990; Nagel 1998).

The radicalness of Labour's turn to neo-liberalism, however, can explained only by the seizure of control over the Labour policy agenda by a small coterie in the Labour Party led by Roger Douglas, the Finance Minister, seconded by the Treasury, and supported by big business and the financial community (Nagel 1998). This 'elite conspiracy' was possible not only because of the near-monopoly role of the Treasury with regard to economic advice (Boston 1989) but also because the Labour Party's particular rules of cabinet solidarity and of party discipline in parliamentary voting allowed a very small, well-organized minority of the Labour government to impose its views (Boston 1990; Nagel 1998; Schwartz 1994). The reforms were carried out in the name of a revival of the values of classical liberalism and *laissez faire* in order to disembed the economy from the society through an autonomous, self-regulating system of markets. They were implemented single-mindedly and as fast as possible—in 'blitzkrieg' fashion—in order to keep the initiative in the hands of the government, to leave no room for modification or re-evaluation, and to avoid allowing vested interests to coalesce in opposition to the reforms (Easton 1997: 80–81).

Thus, with the Labour government in New Zealand beginning in 1984, the construction of the policy program by a very restricted group ensured that there was a minimum of coordinative discourse among policy elites—much as in Britain beginning in 1979 with the Conservative government. The difference is that there was almost no communicative discourse either. Whereas Prime Minister Thatcher sought to convince the electorate through public discourse about the normative merits of her policies, and wanted everyone to believe what she believed as she imposed reform, Finance Minister Douglas, as the prime architect of Labour economic policy from 1984 to 1990, did not feel the same compulsion, and seemed to assume that everyone would come to believe what he believed once he had imposed reform (Quiggin 1998: 82). Only occasionally did Prime Minister David Lange step in to talk about the necessary sacrifices given the economic crisis when Douglas was under attack. But mostly, public attention was deflected from the economic issues by a focus on the non-economic in the government's communicative discourse, especially with regard to the issue of nuclear testing by the French in Muroroa and the blowing-up of the Greenpeace boat—which, one could say, was Lange's Falklands War.

Thus, the Labour Party was re-elected in 1987, this time with an even less clear set of electoral promises—a full manifesto was published only two weeks after the election. And it then proceeded with even more radically neo-liberal policies that again were either not forecast in the pre-election campaign or violated campaign promises, such as tax reforms benefiting the rich, privatization, and fees for university students (Mulgan 1990;

Nagel 1998). But now, the Labour Party's electoral appeal began to erode during the second term as a result of increasingly bitter internal divisions in the party over economic policy and the slide into economic recession.

Labour's appeal for most of its two terms in office was based on the fact that it managed to balance its unpopular, radically liberal economic policy with much more popular social policies. Despite its introduction of competition in both the production system and the welfare system, and the emphasis on market principles and user charges, Labour retained a certain amount of 'collectivism' with regard to both welfare and work, by maintaining and even reinforcing the industrial relations system while expanding the welfare state (see Schwartz, Volume II). With regard to the welfare state in particular, there was an effective communicative discourse in which Labour claimed to introduce competition into the formal welfare system in order to save it, by making it more sustainable even as it increased spending on social assistance. Similarly in health and education, Labour increased spending even as it introduced greater competition in the provision of education—for example, through a voucher-like system for primary education—and charged tuition fees for tertiary education—providing low income students with targeted allowances, however, making the reform redistributive. As such, Labour's social reforms managed to appeal to long-standing values of equality even as it sought to promote individualism and self-reliance and challenged long-standing values of security with economic reforms that radically altered the structure of the economy.

The National Party came to power in 1990, largely because of a split in the Labour Party over neo-liberal economic reform. The electorate, moreover, was voting for a change—but not necessarily in the direction of more neo-liberalism. Whereas in the 1987 election opinion polls suggested that voters were satisfied with the direction and speed of Labour's economic policy reform (Vowles 1990), by 1990 a large majority considered it to have gone too fast or headed the wrong way (Vowles and Aimer 1993). National, however, in the words of David Lange, gave them 'more of the same, or worse' (*New Statesman & Society*, 10 May 1996). Having won in part as a result of the misleading, at least to the average citizen, campaign promise of 'Creating a Decent Society', National instituted an even more radically neo-liberal program by targeting the welfare state and industrial relations system in addition to engaging in further privatization and deregulation of the economy. Thus, the National Party, led by Jim Bolger, rejected the 'collectivism' of Labour in favor of a radical shift of the management of risk from society to the individual. It sought to destroy rather than save or expand the welfare state by introducing even greater competition and by drastically reducing a wide range of social programs and services, restricting eligibility, and attacking even such seemingly accepted universalistic rights as health care through the introduction of rationing. Moreover, it radically decentralized wage bargaining, with the resulting collapse of unions. And it did all of this with even less attention to public opinion than Labour (Schwartz, Volume II). Here too, reform was the product of a narrow coordinative discourse among a restricted group in the National Party, together again with the Treasury, which found the National Party more receptive to its radical ideas about reform in welfare and industrial relations system than Labour (Nagel 1998). And again there was almost no communicative discourse about the economic reforms.

Public discontent was increasingly apparent. Opinion polls showed a precipitous drop in confidence in politicians—from 33 percent in 1975 to 4 percent in 1992 (Jackson 1993: 17)—while voter turnout had also decreased significantly—from 86 percent in 1984 to 76 per cent in 1990 (Vowles and Aimer 1993: 43). The best evidence of public dissatisfaction with the National and earlier Labour government policies, however, was the referendum initiative, supported by dissatisfied members of both major parties, which proposed to eliminate the majoritarian, first-past-the-post system in favor of a German-style, mixed member proportional representation system—voted in 1993 and instituted in 1996 (McRobie 1993). In this way, it would alter the very institutions that had allowed successive governments to reform without regard to public opinion. The public, in fact, spoke loudly through its favorable vote on the referendum about its dissatisfaction not just with the policies but with a system that so concentrated power that the government felt such little need to try to legitimize its policies, or to listen to the public debates in response, let alone to enter into public deliberation with those opposed. That public communication in single-actor systems is adversarial goes without saying, but it need not be, should not be, unilateral, which is what it seemed to have been in New Zealand.

The fact that the new institutional set-up made it much more difficult for any government to go back on the reforms that were the real object of protest is one of the great ironies of the changes. But the focus of change is not as strange as all that, once we realize that it brought in an electoral system that would produce a government that required the kind of negotiation and deliberation that characterized the more multi-actor Australian system, which had also reformed in a liberal direction, but had not gone nearly as far as in New Zealand. And the electoral reform did usher in something of a new era, making it difficult for any coalition government to continue with radical reform and ensuring, in the words of Ruth Richardson, Finance Minister in the National government from 1990 to 1993, that 'the wimps have won' (*Economist*, 19 October 1996: 19).

A National-led coalition government was elected in 1996 not because National was more popular but rather because the opposition was divided, with the Labor party in particular still torn by tensions between the free-marketeers and the others, while a new party, New Zealand First, drew on anti-immigrant and right-wing populism. Moreover, the National campaign led by Jim Bolger promised to go more slowly on reform; and the National-led coalition government did indeed reverse some of the most unpopular aspects of the reforms, by shifting from an emphasis on profitability in health care to public service.

The 1999 elections proved to be the first since the early 1980s which presented a clear choice between continuing with radical reform or halting at least some of its least popular aspects. While the losing National Party candidate, Jenny Shipley, party leader since late 1997, had pledged to continue with free-market policies and offered tax cuts for business and individuals, her successful Labour party opponent, Helen Clark, echoed Blair's 'third way', pledged to increase taxes in order to pay for better social and health services and a higher level of social assistance, and promised 'a fair society, good education, good health system, dignity in retirement and an absolute commitment to a growing economy which shares opportunity and work' (*New York Times*, 28 November 1999). What this suggests is that while Clark's new Labour Party, just as Blair's 'New Labour', could not turn back the clock on 15 years of neo-liberal reform, accepting the greater insecurity and individual responsibility associated with open economies and deregulated markets, it would not give up on collectivism entirely. Given the lessons of recent history and the constraints of the new electoral institutions, moreover, its reform efforts are most likely to follow the example of Australia since the 1980s, by relying on negotiation among a wider group of policy elites and paying greater attention to public response.

4.4.2.3 Australia The contrast in the history of liberalizing reform between Britain and New Zealand on the one hand and Australia on the other is striking, and points out the importance of institutional differences and how they play themselves out in the discursive process. Although in Australia in the mid-1980s, much as in New Zealand, a newly elected Labor government pledged to economic interventionism in its campaign turned instead to radical neo-liberalism, equally influenced by the 'economic rationalists'—including the Treasury, big business and the financial community—who had a monopoly on economic advice (Quiggin 1998: 80–81), it could never impose reform in the way that the New Zealand government did. Nor did it want to. Australia got adjustment with a human face not only because change required consensus, given a more multi-actor system that demanded much more consultation and negotiation, but also because the politicians themselves, such as Prime Minister Hawke, valued this, in sharp contrast to Douglas in New Zealand. In Australia, the reforms themselves were implemented over a much longer period of time, with care taken to moderate their socioeconomic impact and to debate their merits with the relevant actors in order to assure consensus. In multi-actor Australia, this meant negotiating with a wide set of actors at the federal and State level; with the House of Representatives, elected on the basis of constituencies—like New Zealand—and the Senate, elected by proportional representation; and with the trade union movement, which most importantly for Australia and unlike New Zealand were willing and able to be cooperative (Evans *et al.* 1996; Quiggin 1998: 82).

Moreover, in Australia there was nothing like the party dealignment experienced by New Zealand beginning in the late 1960s, and there was no earlier trading back and forth of power as in Britain in the 1950s and 1960s. Rather, the Labor Party remained out of power in the 1950s and 1960s, pushing for more generous social policies from the sidelines for its traditional working class constituency, with little impact on the Liberal-Country governments until the late 1960s, when Labor began to pose a serious electoral threat. In the election campaigns of 1969—which it lost—and 1972—which it won—Labor promised ambitious social programs which were to transform Australia's residual welfare state into a full-blown, Scandinavian-style welfare state. These it largely delivered once in power, increasing social spending, instituting universal health insurance (Medibank), and equal pay for equal work. (Schwartz, Volume II). Its loss of power in 1975, due to a deteriorating economic situation and rising unemployment, brought in a Liberal-National Party coalition headed by Malcolm Fraser. The new government, as in New Zealand, began with neo-liberal reform but, unlike New Zealand, stuck to it, and also went much farther in cutting the welfare state by reversing many of Labor's reforms—in particular Medibank. By the early 1980s, however, rising unemployment and a newly deteriorating economic situation led to its defeat in the December 1983 election, bringing the return of Labor, which also then engaged in much greater neo-liberal reform. But, unlike in New Zealand, Labor engaged in reform in conjunction with other policy actors, thus ensuring greater moderation and acceptance of the policies instituted.

The balance between liberalizing the economy and maintaining or expanding social policy was assured from the mid-1980s through much of the 1990s mainly because of a cooperative relationship in the employment relations sphere that traded wage restraint for a social wage, that is, for a continued high level of social assistance, albeit means-tested, and universal social services in health and education. In fact, part of the Australian success in instituting more moderate and better accepted reform has to do with the development of a quasi-corporatist set of relations between employers, labor, and government. This began in the early 1980s with the first of the Accords that produced wage restraint through incomes policies, and which Labor saw as the only way to save the welfare state while dividing or neutralizing potential business opposition (Schwartz, Volume II). This was what made for Australia's economic success and New Zealand's failure in the second half of the 1980s. The unions' willingness to compromise was facilitated by the fact that they were persuaded by the arguments of 'post-Fordism', which represented flexibility in work conditions and restraint in wages as the means for Australian manufacturing to become internationally competitive (Hampson and Morgan 1999).

Finally, the policy discourse, which performed as much of a coordinating function with regard to the multiple actors as a communicative function for the larger public, was one with much debate and deliberation, where reforms that were opposed by substantial numbers of actors were withdrawn, not imposed.[3] This is illustrated by the fate of a goods and services tax (a value-added tax) proposed by governments in both Australia and New Zealand in the 1980s, which was abandoned in the former country because of lack of support by unions, welfare groups, and business and imposed in the latter country despite lack of popular support (Quiggin 1998: 84). (It was only after the Liberals won the 1996 elections that the tax, which had been proposed three times since the mid-1980s, passed, with many exemptions, however.) Moreover, whereas the New Zealand parties in power did comparatively little to explain their economic programs to the public, the Australian parties consistently provided a legitimizing discourse. Australia's Labor Party was intent on articulating the rationale behind its pragmatic and cautious approach as one of following a middle way between adhering to traditional Labor's irrelevant shibboleths and to the contemporary conservatives' free market dogmatism (Quiggin 1998: 85). This helps explain the party's success in election after election, even though its discourse and policies ultimately did not save it from the consequences of increasing disaffection among its traditional working class constituency. Labor's electoral support kept dropping, from a high of 49.5 percent in the first preference vote in 1983, to 45.8 percent

---

[3] This kind of simultaneous public/private discourse may very well be characteristic of Australia because of a combination of country size and the difficulty of carrying on such discussions behind closed doors, given a tradition of open public debate on all issues.

in 1987, to 39.4 percent in 1990, and to a historic low of 38.8 percent in 1996, when it lost the election to the Liberals (Quiggin 1998: 92). And the Liberals benefited from this erosion of support for Labor, and then proceeded to go farther in a neo-liberal direction.

Australia, in brief, had a much more moderate history of liberalization in the economic and social policy arenas than either Britain or New Zealand, mainly because of differences in its institutional structures which affected the manner and pace of neo-liberal reform as well as the character and locus of discourse. The population also seemed more satisfied with government action in the welfare arena, as evidenced by attitude surveys in which fewer Australians than Britons in 1985 saw the need for more spending on health—62 percent versus 88 percent; old age pensions—55 percent versus 75 percent; education—64 percent versus 75 percent; and unemployment benefits—13 percent versus 41 percent (Jowell, Witherspoon, and Brook 1989: 41). This may, however, also have had to do with the fact that Australians had experienced an increase in social spending in the mid-1980s by contrast with British perceptions that the welfare state was under threat. Or it may reflect the fact that Australians expected less from a formal welfare state by comparison with Britain, as evidenced by their more modest views of government responsibility to provide health care for the sick—60 percent versus 86 percent; to provide a decent standard of living for old people—62 percent versus 79 percent; to provide a decent standard of living for the unemployed—15 percent versus 45 percent; and to reduce income differences between rich and poor people—24 percent versus 48 percent (Jowell, Whitherspoon, and Brook 1989: 41). On this last redistributive dimension, in 1990 Australia was again lower than Britain, although both had significantly increased their support for government responsibility to reduce income differences—42.2 percent versus 56.9 percent; but in 1992 Australia remained steady while Britain shot up even higher—42.6 percent versus 65.2 percent—probably reflecting increasing discomfort in Britain with growing poverty (see Table 4.1, Questions 3, 6, 14). New Zealand, included for the first time in the 1992 surveys, fell between the two—53.1 percent—as it has on all other questions regarding redistribution and equality, possibly also reflecting concerns about the impact on the poor of cuts in the welfare state (see Table 4.1, 1992 Survey).

But whatever the differences among Anglo-Saxon countries' liberal welfare state structures, experiences of adjustment, or values and attitudes, the differences from other country clusters are what sets them apart. On issues of inequality and redistribution, attitude surveys suggest that the populations of the liberal Anglo-Saxon countries accept greater levels of inequality and are more divided between the 'haves' and the 'have-nots' on

Table 4.1 *International social attitudes surveys (in percentages)*

	A	AUS	D	GB	I	NZ	S	NL
1992 Survey								
1) Large differences in income necessary for prosperity	17.2	24.7	21.0	19.1	28.2	17.2	30.4	
2) Good business profit improves everyone's standard of living	41.8	50.5	41.1	45.5	63.2	46.6	44.6	
3) Government to reduce differences in income between high and low	69.5	42.6	65.5	65.2	80.0	53.1	53.0	
4) Government to provide job for everyone who wants one	72.1	39.4	66.3	56.1	86.2	49.1	77.4	
5) Government to provide everyone who guaranteed basic income	51.2	50.9	58.1	66.1	68.7	60.5	43.3	
1990 Survey								
6) Government to reduce differences in income between high and low		42.2	56.4	56.9	69.7			
7) Government to provide job for everyone who wants one		41.5	74.2	63.3	84.9			
8) Government to provide decent standard of living for unemployed		55.8	78.3	80.0	77.8			
1987 Survey								
9) Large differences in income necessary for prosperity		28.0	24.0	26.0	18.0			16.0
10) Good business profit improves everyone's standard of living		53.0	40.0	53.0	57.0			31.0
11) Financial incentives necessary to work hard		72.0	69.0	61.0	54.0			36.0
12) Financial incentives necessary to take extra responsibility		82.0	64.0	82.0	77.0			64.0
1985 Survey								
13) Government to provide job for everyone who wants one	47.0	2.0		35.0	38.0	52.0		
14) Government to reduce differences in income between high and low	41.0	24.0	28.0	48.0	48.0			
15) Government to provide decent standard of living for unemployed	16.0	15.0	24.0	45.0	40.0			

Sources: 1992 Survey: ISSP 92/ZA–No. 2310, V23, V24, V 57, V59, V62 (Social Inequality II); 1990 Survey: ISSP 90/ZA–No. 1950, V24, V49, V54 (Role of Government II)—submission from Rolf Uher, Zentralarchiv, Köln; 1987, 1985 Surveys: Jowell, Witherspoon, and Brook (1989: 38, 41, 62, 69, 70).

the issue of redistribution than other countries in our sample.[4] A 1987 international survey of social attitudes, for example, shows more consistent societal acceptance of inequalities, with Australia and Britain more agreed that large differences in income are necessary for national prosperity—at an average of 27 percent versus an average of 19 percent for Germany, Italy, and the Netherlands; more agreed that allowing businesses to make good profits is the best way to improve everyone's standard of living—53 percent versus an average of 43 percent for the other countries; and more agreed that financial incentives, meaning pay inequalities, are needed if people are to work hard—an average of 67 percent versus an average of 53 percent for the others—and if they are to take extra responsibility—82 percent versus an average of 68 percent for the others (see Table 4.1, Questions 9, 10, 11, 12). Moreover, in a 1985 survey, responses to a question about whether it is government's responsibility to reduce income differences between those with high and low incomes showed much more significant divides between richer and poorer respondents in the Anglo-Saxon countries, with the spread between poorest quartile and wealthiest quartile in Britain and Australia both at 21 points by contrast with a spread of 11 points in West Germany, 8 in Austria, and 15 in Italy (Jowell, Whitherspoon, and Brook 1989: 50).

4.5 The Scandinavian Welfare State

For the two Scandinavian countries in our project, Sweden and Denmark, external economic pressures had different effects at different times, leading to different kinds of policy responses: incremental for Denmark beginning relatively early on, later and more drastic for Sweden. Despite these differences, both countries have largely maintained their basic commitment to equality, even as they have had to diminish the generosity of the welfare state. But within this context, it is now Denmark that appears to have taken the place of Sweden as the ideal social-democratic model, having gradually moved over time from a position of somewhat lesser welfare state equality, generosity, and normative integration than Sweden to one of somewhat greater equality, generosity, and integration. This is in part the result of the fact that while Denmark was able to maintain successful coordinative discourses in both work and welfare arenas among a wide array of key policy actors, Sweden has had difficulties sustaining its

---

[4] I focus here only on the comparative surveys dealing with inequality. This is because surveys which measure attitudes about government responsibility for welfare provision and levels of support are much too contingent on differences in welfare state structures and perceptions of government action at the time to prove useful for my purposes.

coordinative discourse in the work arena, while its communicative discourse on welfare has not served as a spur to the necessary changes.

4.5.1 Postwar Scandinavian Welfare State Values

The Scandinavian countries are generally termed 'social-democratic' welfare states because of their emphasis on equality, and their collective notions of responsibility for the provision of generous benefits and extensive public services to all. Here, welfare is universalistic and non-differentiable. The principle upon which claims are based is citizenship and the beneficiaries, all citizens. The goal is equality of income, albeit graduated according to accustomed earnings, and equality of access to social services to the highest of standards—that is, to the level of the new middle classes—as opposed to equality of minimal needs, as in Anglo-Saxon welfare states (Esping-Andersen 1990). For Scandinavian welfare states, moreover, as for Anglo-Saxon welfare states, work comes before welfare. But whereas this is the result of necessity in Anglo-Saxon welfare states, in Scandinavian welfare states it is a matter of individual fulfillment, with work itself enshrined as a basic right, almost coequal with the right to an income in this system (Esping-Andersen 1990).

In work, just as in welfare, equality has been a central value, whether with regard to wages or to gender. The Scandinavian welfare state fostered a solidaristic wage policy that entailed not only equal pay for equal work but also a compression of wage scales—for Sweden in particular in the 1970s, where the notion of the 'same pay for similar work' was transformed by the increasingly radicalized labor movement into the 'same pay for all work' (Vartiainen 1998: 26). Such wage compression was significantly greater than in Continental welfare states—discussed below—let alone in Anglo-Saxon ones. Although we have data on wage differentials only from 1979 on, a glance at the numbers shows that Sweden and Denmark have much lower earnings dispersion by far, and that these persist over time (for more detail, see Iversen 1998a and Table A.21), by comparison with Anglo-Saxon welfare states which in the cases of New Zealand and the United Kingdom (but not Australia) only increased over time (see Fig. 4.1).

The Scandinavian welfare state's commitment to wage equality was joined by commitment to gender equality. By the early 1970s, the newly emerging 'post-industrial' feminist values were in the process of institutionalization, with women able to move into the workplace in increasing numbers as a result of changes in the workplace, such as wage parity laws and openness to part-time employment, and of welfare reforms that vastly expanded state-provided family and day care services, and also created large numbers of public sector jobs (see Daly, Volume II).

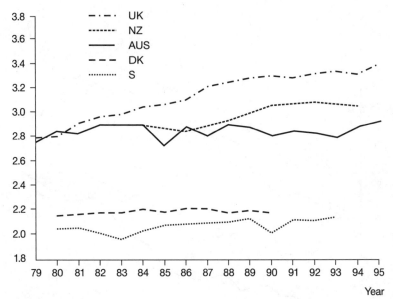

Figure 4.1 Earnings dispersion (D9/D1) in Scandinavian and Anglo-Saxon countries

Notes: D1 and D9 refer to the upper limits of, respectively, the first and the ninth deciles of employees ranked in order of their earnings from lowest to highest, i.e. 10% of employees earn less than D1 earnings limit and 90% less than the D9 earnings limit. D5 thus corresponds to median earnings. For Belgium there is a break in series after the year 1988.

Source: OECD, *Statistical Compendium: Labour Force Statistics* (Paris: OECD, 1998).

The result is female labor participation rates that are far above other countries. Again, although the data are at times spotty, the figures show that, over the course of the 1970s and into the 1980s and 1990s, the Scandinavian countries stayed a good 10 to 20 percentage points above all other countries in female participation, moving from around 60 percent female participation in the early 1970s to 75 percent in the mid-1990s (see Fig. 4.2 and Table A.12). By comparison, Anglo-Saxon welfare states, including Britain, New Zealand, and Australia, which differed greatly in female participation rates in the 1970s, had all increased significantly by the 1990s, up to around 60 percent (see Fig. 4.2)—a testimony, perhaps, to the liberalized economy's ability to generate jobs and the liberal welfare state's neutrality with regard to gender issues, given the need for two incomes—but they still remained around 15 percentage points below the Scandinavian welfare state (for a more detailed analysis, see Daly, Volume II).

Both Sweden and Denmark, in short, have consistently demonstrated much greater levels of equality in both income and gender than other

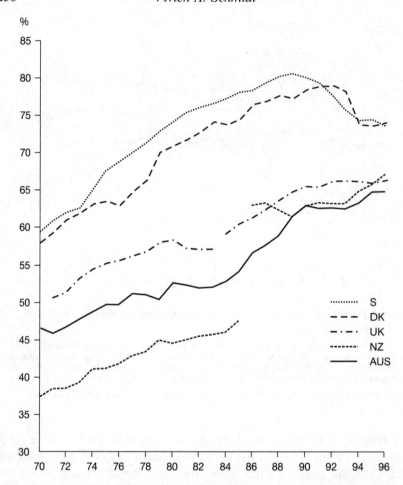

Figure 4.2 Female labor force participation rates in Scandinavian and Anglo-Saxon countries

Source: OECD, *Statistical Compendium: Labour Force Statistics* (Paris: OECD, 1998); own calculations.

countries. Of the two, however, Sweden shows slightly higher levels. The fact that Sweden was more normatively integrated, with its 'work society' values reinforced by a strong Social Democratic party that held power either alone or in coalitions from the 1930s on, meant that it was easier for it to implement social-democratic reforms than in Denmark, where the power and control of the weaker Social Democratic party was often contested, including by a tax revolt in the early 1970s (Benner and Vad, Volume II).

4.5.2 Values and Discourse in Social-Democratic Welfare State Reform

In response to economic crisis in the 1980s in Denmark and the 1990s in Sweden, little changed in the basic welfare state commitments. Where tradeoffs had to be made, core values of equality and work were defended more vigorously than the generosity of transfers, with cutbacks acceptable as long as sacrifices were shared equally. Support in Scandinavian countries for the traditional welfare state continued not only because of the value consensus, however. It was also because of the universalist structure of the welfare state which guaranteed support from a large middle class constituency and most women (see Rothstein 1998c), thereby avoiding the split between the haves and have-nots in liberal welfare states that made it easier to retrench in non-universalist social policy areas; and because of the structure of the electoral system, based on proportional rather than majoritarian representation, which made it much harder for neo-liberals to break the consensus by capturing a large party and imposing reform, as in Britain and New Zealand. On this latter dimension, however, there were nonetheless differences between the two countries. For whereas in Sweden the predominance of the Social Democratic party meant that neo-liberal forces remained outside the parliamentary majority and had little impact other than when they were in power in the early 1990s, in Denmark since the 1980s the recourse to *ad hoc* majorities gave neo-liberals greater influence (see Scharpf, this volume).

The main puzzle with regard to Sweden and Denmark, in fact, has less to do with a retreat from basic values, which did not occur, than with how the two changed places: Denmark managed to liberalize work and reform welfare through incremental adjustments that left it, by the late 1990s, with a still generous universalist welfare state that appeared fully sustainable and with a more flexible set of work relations that enabled its industries to remain internationally competitive. Sweden, which did not have to adjust until the economic crisis of the early 1990s, reformed its welfare state through more radical adjustments, but may still face problems of sustainability in the future and has yet to promote significant flexibility in work relations. The explanation lies not only with differences in economic vulnerability and institutional contexts but also with the differing discourses in the two countries beginning in the 1980s, with Swedish discourse less effective in convincing the public of the legitimacy of the move toward a somewhat more 'liberal' social-democracy than Denmark.

4.5.2.1 Sweden

For Sweden, change has in many ways been harder than for Denmark, mainly because it avoided the need for reform until the 1990s, when it came all of a sudden, in response to economic crisis in the early 1990s. In the 1980s, Sweden continued its highly redistributive system, maintained employment at high levels, and still expanded the public services sector. The crisis, however, did not lead to any major re-evaluation of the egalitarian basis of welfare state policies, only attempts to contain costs across the board. There has been no 'system shift' in a liberal direction, despite market-leaning reform of the public services or a move from tax-financed toward individual social insurance. Moreover, although business, in particular the Swedish Employers' Association (SAF), has become increasingly active in advocating neo-liberal reform (see Pestoff 1995), it has not succeeded in bringing about a hoped-for sea change in public attitudes toward the welfare state. With the exception of the Conservative coalition of 1991 to 1994, when major reforms were instituted, the neo-liberals have not gained much of a hearing in Parliament. The Social Democrats, moreover, would be certain not to espouse neo-liberal values, although they too supported reform when the Conservatives were in power and instituted their own when back in power, but not with the same justifications. This can be explained in large measure by their basis of support among the unions, which have remained strong in their belief in the traditional social-democratic ideals for the structure of welfare as well as work. Such union support, in fact, also helps shed light on why the Social Democrats cut transfers only to a limited extent between 1994 and 1998, while services were the main target (Benner and Vad, Volume II). What this meant, however, is that values of security for the worker—reflected in the unions' much stronger defense of maintaining the safety net for the core worker than of the service jobs of workers who often had a more marginal attachment to the workforce—took priority over the right to work for all.

All in all, the reforms have ensured that while the welfare state is 'leaner', it remains comparatively generous in its treatment of the unemployed and loyal to the 'work society' ethic that seeks to treat all citizens as productive individuals able to live up to their full potential. Moreover, although the commitment to wage equality, defined in 1970s terms as the same pay for all work, ended in the early 1980s with the breakdown of centralized wage bargaining, commitment to wage parity largely continued, as wage differentials still did not grow significantly, moving slowly upward to reach or only slightly exceed the level of Denmark (see Fig. 4.1). The main challenge to the society's egalitarian values has primarily been the rise in unemployment, which reduces the effectiveness of the ideological commitment to the work society.

Sweden's continued support for traditional welfare state values is also reflected in attitudinal surveys. In a comparison of social-democratic Sweden—in a 1992 survey—with one of the most egalitarian of liberal welfare states, 'Labourist' Australia—in a 1987 International Social Survey Project (ISSP) survey—the Swedes saw less need for financial incentives, meaning pay inequalities, to get people to take extra responsibility than the Australians—75.5 per cent of Swedes versus 84.5 per cent of Australians; were more in favor of government providing a decent standard of living for the unemployed—61.2 per cent of Swedes versus 36 per cent of Australians; and fewer agreed that allowing business to make good profits is the best way to improve everyone's standard of living—44.4 per cent of Swedes versus 54.4 per cent of Australians (see Svallfors 1993: 22, 24). Moreover, in an ISSP survey in 1992 that asked whether the government should provide a job for everyone who wants one, Sweden came out dramatically higher than any of the Anglo-Saxon welfare states as well as of two of three Continental welfare states, Germany and Austria, but not Italy (see Table 4.1, Question 4).

On the question as to whether it is the responsibility of the government to reduce the differences in income between people with high incomes and those with low incomes, by contrast, the Swedes appeared as less redistributive than the British, by 12.2 points, as well as the Continental Austrians by 16.5 points, Germans by 13.5 points, and Italians by 23 points (see Table 4.1, Question 3). Rather than suggesting a values clash between the system people have and the one they think they deserve, however, it may very well be that people simply felt that the changes had gone far enough—in Sweden, too far in the direction of wage equality, since it has one of the lowest rates (see Fig. 4.1), and of redistribution, given its extremely high tax rate; in Britain, too far in the direction of wage dispersion—it has one of the highest rates (see Fig. 4.1)—and cutbacks in the redistributive functions of the welfare state, given rising poverty and inequality following Thatcherite reform. This is further supported by the Swedes' surprisingly high agreement with the statement that large differences in income are necessary for a country's prosperity; at 30.4 percent, it was way above the Australians, New Zealanders, British, Germans, and Austrians, with only the Italians coming close (Table 4.1, Question 1). Moreover, such a response was probably to be expected in 1992, when Sweden was feeling the full effects of the economic crisis, and was agreed on the need to cut back the welfare state.

In the face of economic crisis, the Swedish discourse of the 1990s focused almost entirely on the need for social solidarity and the acceptance of moderate cutbacks in the generosity of transfers, even if the Conservative-led government of 1991 to 1994 added an element of neo-liberal ideology to its arguments while the Social Democratic government after 1994 used only economic arguments (Rothstein 1998c). Legitimization has therefore not been much of an issue because governments presented themselves as defending basic values even as they cut benefits. In support of this, by 1996, once the economy had recovered somewhat, the Social Democrats restored benefit levels in a couple of the major income-related insurance programs, demonstrating the government's political will to defend core sectors of the welfare state (Hinnsfors and Pierre 1998). The electoral campaign of fall 1998, moreover, was almost entirely focused on how to maintain the welfare state, with the main topic that of redistribution, not growth. And after another victory of the Social Democrats, albeit with their smallest share of the vote in 78 years, forcing them to seek alliances with the Greens and former communists, they were all the more determined to defend the welfare state, as evidenced by Prime Minister Goran Persson's budget speech in October 1998 promising lots more welfare, although with few details on how to pay for it, even as they continued to try to rein in social spending (*Economist*, 23 January 1999).

The legitimizing discourse itself has been primarily of the communicative variety with the larger public, rather than coordinative with the social partners and private providers, as it often is in corporatist countries, mainly because in Sweden, the state has increasingly taken primary responsibility for the welfare state. A fully coordinative discourse has also been lacking with regard to work ever since the main employers' association, on the impetus of large-scale, internationalized business, rejected centralized collective bargaining in the early 1980s. They had lost trust in such bargaining because of the 1970s radical labor support for a more equal distribution of wages which had made it harder for them to compete with international competitors on wages or to attract and keep needed high-skilled workers (see Pontusson and Swenson 1996; Iversen 1996). The now endemic distrust between the two parties, moreover, has meant that Swedish labor has lacked not only the inclination but also the means to negotiate greater flexibility in wages and work conditions centrally. In consequence, it will be less able to moderate the effects of increasing flexibilization, as other Scandinavian corporatist countries such as Denmark or even Finland have managed through central negotiations (Vartiainen 1998: 31–32). In fact, in the face of the failure of the social partners to reach any common understanding, let alone agreement, on adapting labor laws to meet demands for greater flexibility in the organization of production, the Swedish government enacted changes in 1996 which were protested by the unions and rejected as insufficient by employers (Rothstein 1998c).

In short, the reform of welfare and work is left to the government in Sweden, which finds it hard to reconcile its continuing commitment to equality and full employment with the retrenchment policies it has had to institute in the interests of fiscal responsibility. In fact, the Social Democratic government has yet to decide whether to follow a more liberal course, by promoting deregulation and a more flexible, meaning inegalitarian, wage structure in order to return to full employment, or a more Christian-democratic course, sacrificing employment to continued wage equality, which, however, allows for greater inequality through the marginalization of those excluded from full participation in the economy (Iversen 1998a; Iversen and Wren 1998). The problem is that the government hesitates in the face of the fact that either policy course violates the country's continuing basic egalitarian and cooperative values, and that the government has yet to come up with a coherent discourse to legitimize either course of action, let alone a coherent policy for a discourse to legitimize. This is especially problematic given the dramatic drop in public confidence in Sweden's central political institutions, where between 1986 and 1996 trust in Parliament and government went from plus 30 percent to minus 20 percent (Holmberg and Weibull 1997, cited in Rothstein 1998c). Moreover, the large middle-class constituency supportive of the welfare state at its current high level of generosity makes major retrenchment, as opposed to emergency adjustment measures, politically unfeasible for any of the major parties in government. What is more, given the breakdown of national level corporatist concertation since the 1980s, the government has been less able than in the past to negotiate policy change with the social partners through a more coordinative discourse. Instead, the state is more alone in having to make choices which it will then have to communicate to a less trusting public.

4.5.2.2 Denmark   For Denmark, the current challenge to the welfare state has been even less marked than in Sweden, mainly because the problems came earlier, and were dealt with incrementally. Generally speaking, while these changes diminished the generosity of the welfare state, they also did not impinge much on the country's basic commitment to equality: much the contrary, in fact, in the cases of expanded benefits for the elderly, women, and students. Some reforms, however, did seem taken out of the neo-liberal book, such as user charges and private copayments in education and health. In the context of Denmark's still highly generous welfare state, however, this served to guarantee universality of access at the same time as it helped to contain costs since the charges and fees remained low enough not to deter anyone from using the services.

   In areas related to work, Denmark also sought to limit the expense without jeopardizing its principles of equality, for example, by reducing replacements rates and tightening eligibility in unemployment compensation. Because the extremely generous unemployment system was increasingly seen as a disincentive to work, such measures were assumed to be compatible with Denmark's own values with regard to work. The 1990s saw even more such cost-cutting, plus workfare. By comparison, other areas of potential reform which clashed more with long-standing egalitarian commitments were not changed nearly as much as originally proposed by the conservative government in the 1980s—for example, the reduction in the progressiveness of the tax system—given resistance by the Social Democratic opposition (Benner and Vad, Volume II).

Generally speaking, such incremental change in the Danish welfare state was made easier by the ongoing economic crisis in the 1980s and 1990s, in which necessity was the justification for political parties and the social partners to agree to active reform measures. This was apparent not only in the communicative discourse of government, which constantly reminded citizens of the crisis as they presented their reform programs, but also in the coordinative discourses of political elites within the legislative context and of the social partners in wage bargaining. Economic crisis, in other words, helped promote normative integration, as political parties in government became more willing to engage in 'policy and party shopping' in their efforts to solve major problems by brokering *ad hoc* coalitions for reform, while the social partners became more willing to compromise in the wage bargaining process (Benner and Vad, Volume II). One could even argue, therefore, that the 'threat from without' helped consolidate the normative consensus around the need for reform, and thereby served to overcome the fragmentation of a political system characterized by weaker governments and many more veto points than the Swedish system.

For all the consensus around the need for reform in the face of economic crisis, however, there were significant limits placed on conservative, bourgeois governing coalitions by the opposition in the 1980s. Although the government's discourse on the need to take the economy away 'from the brink of the abyss' had convinced the electorate in the early 1980s of the need for the abolition of the automatic indexation of wages and the freezing of a range of social security benefits, despite union and Social Democrat opposition, by the mid-1980s the opposition had begun to sway public opinion in their direction. The Social Democrats' protests against government retrenchment policies on the grounds of social fairness, with advertising campaigns showing the image of the people sliding into mass social graves as a result of the proposed shortening of the duration of unemployment benefits, caused the government to moderate its legislative program significantly (Green-Pedersen 1999b). From 1987, moreover, the government's loss of electoral strength meant that it consistently compromised with the Social Democrats, engaging in a larger coordinative discourse which resulted in the expansion of many aspects of the welfare state, as noted above. It is only once the Social Democrats took office as of 1993 that significant welfare retrenchment programs again began, with support from the conservative opposition and despite dissatisfaction from rank-and-file members of the Social Democratic party. There was now a clear consensus among policy elites on the need for reform, and a government of the left in a better position to pass policies of the right (Green-Pedersen 1999b). Here, it is clear that the Social Democratic government's ability to form *ad hoc* majorities with support from the right made significant welfare reforms much more feasible in Denmark than in Sweden, where the government could not turn to the right for support given not only that it was locked into a coalition with other left-wing parties but also that the stronger Swedish unions could exercise a veto over any such policies.

Since the mid-1990s, moreover, the political debate has been dominated by the question of how to make the welfare state work most efficiently and equitably, as distinct from the Swedish discourse on the defense of the welfare state, and there have been no promises to cut taxes, despite the fact that Denmark is second only to Sweden in its high taxation rate. But in Denmark, support for high taxes has remained high, with 70 percent of respondents in an opinion poll in September 1999 saying that they liked paying high taxes (*Financial Times*, 17 December 1999)—and a far cry from the tax revolt of the early 1970s.

The result is a welfare state that seems to have replaced Sweden as the ideal social-democratic welfare state in a more competitive world. Denmark has already faced the choices that Sweden has not on whether to follow a more liberal or a more Christian-democratic course. And it has chosen to go some way in both directions—by allowing for somewhat higher unemployment on the one hand and for somewhat greater flexibility and inequality in wages on the other—without, however, destroying its overall commitments to equality. On the one hand, the recognition that something less than full employment would have to be tolerated came already in the 1970s, by contrast with Sweden's rude awakening in the 1990s. And it was not seen as undermining social democracy because of the generous unemployment compensation system that cushioned its effects. On the other hand, even at the height of the 'golden age' of corporatism, as we have already seen, Denmark has always been somewhat more 'liberal' in its approach to employment than Sweden, with greater employment flexibility built into the system. Moreover, because militant unions in the 1970s, in the face of greater crisis as well as less centralized labor control, could never impose the radical wage equality demands of Swedish labor, it did not thereby destroy management trust in wage-bargaining with labor. This ensured that Denmark's somewhat less centralized corporatist concertation system survived the 1970s, enabling it to promote wage restraint centrally—through the setting of a maximum wage level—by the mid- to late 1980s, without undermining the flexibility of the increasingly decentralized bargaining process and the growing number of individual-ized and local contracts. Perhaps most revealing on this differing evolution of Denmark and Sweden on wage equality are the results of a European Values Survey in 1981 and a World Values Survey in 1990 asking respond-ents whether they agreed that a faster secretary should be paid more: Denmark showed an increase of 16 points—from 60 per cent to 76 per cent—and Sweden only three points—from 59 per cent to 62 per cent—leaving the latter the most egalitarian in our sample on views of pay equal-ity (Klingemann and Fuchs 1995: 404).[5]

In short, Denmark has in many ways already managed the transition to a more 'liberal' social-democratic welfare state while remaining largely true to its original egalitarian and universalistic principles. By contrast, Sweden finds itself as yet unable to make or legitimize the move to a more 'liberal' social-democratic welfare state, which in turn may ultimately undermine its ability to uphold its original even more egalitarian and uni-versalistic principles. As an ideal, therefore, Denmark may very well have taken the place of Sweden.

4.6 The Continental Welfare States

For the seven Continental countries in our project, Germany, Switzerland, Austria, the Netherlands, Belgium, France, and Italy, economic pressures hit at different times with different degrees of intensity, with the first three countries little affected until the 1990s and the last three confronting major economic crisis much earlier. The challenges to the welfare state, however, were not only economic, with pressure for reductions in the level of social spending and increases in labor market flexibility. They also included the newly emerging post-industrial values, in particular with regard to the role of women, which challenged the normative orientations of the postwar Continental welfare state, and in particular its emphasis on the family. The policy responses and public reactions varied, however. Germany and Austria have reformed the least; but whereas in Germany the prospects of reform remain uncertain as a result of the breakdown of the coordinative discourse among social partners and government and the failures of the communicative, Austria has continued to have a coordinative discourse

[5] This left Sweden at least eleven points below all other countries in the surveys except social-democratic Norway, which showed 0% increase from 54%. By contrast, Britain showed an eleven-point increase, from 68% to 79%; W. Germany a 14 point-increase, from 71% to 85%; the Netherlands an eleven-point increase, from 61% to 72%; France a 16-point increase, from 63% to 79%; and Italy a 30-point increase, from 49% to 79%.

which has proven effective in slowly facilitating change, although it is now in trouble. The Netherlands has reformed the most, having increased flexibility in the structure of work following the return to a coordinative discourse after the break-down of corporatist concertation in the 1970s, and revamped the structure of welfare following the turn to a more communicative discourse. In Belgium, by contrast, where the state has imposed reform without much coordination or communication, reform has not been as extensive or effective as in the Netherlands, leaving the country with continued problems with regard to job flexibility and welfare state sustainability. Switzerland has also liberalized moderately, mainly because reforms following an exclusively coordinative discourse have been held in check by the periodic turn to a more communicative discourse through referendum, which acts as a brake on policies that do not gain a wide consensus. Finally, France has had trouble instituting much welfare reform until recently, despite its strong state, mainly because of the failures of its communicative discourse, while Italy since 1992 has managed to overcome long-standing state paralysis and institute necessary reforms as a result of effective coordinative discourse among social partners and government and persuasive communicative discourse with the general public.

4.6.1 Postwar Continental Welfare State Values

The Continental countries are often called 'Bismarckian' or 'Christian-democratic' because of their emphasis on the family in a reasonably generous welfare state, with collective responsibility focused on maintaining the family unit. Here, the principle upon which claims are based is work, with the beneficiaries, the core workforce of male bread-winners, and the goal, income maintenance. Welfare is understood as a right differentiable according to gender and social strata, with welfare services more limited, leaving much to the family, and to some extent provided by non-state charities, even though typically financed or subsidized by the state or by state-mandated health insurance. The Christian-democratic state's patterns of welfare provision according to the principle of subsidiarity and financing through wage earners, moreover, tend to favor the status quo in terms of income and status, with few of the market-expansion pressures found in liberal states and few of the redistributive and gender-equality effects seen in social-democratic states.

Clearly, full employment of the entire population is not a consideration here, as it is in Scandinavia, given the gender division that often keeps women at home. Unemployment of the male breadwinner, by contrast, is a much greater catastrophe, given that it jeopardizes the entire family's future, and not just that of the individual earner. Job security for the core male breadwinner, therefore, is a welfare value that also spills over into the work realm. Women's work, by comparison, may be less valued, and the woman therefore more likely to leave work first in the event of a crisis and ensuing high unemployment, whether out of choice or because dismissed. For this reason among others, 'work before welfare' is neither a necessity nor a value for all those other than the core male breadwinner upon whom the entire family depends, given that 'welfare before work' can be not only attractive, given the relatively high level of benefits, but also morally acceptable when there are fewer jobs and non-objectionable exit options through disability and early retirement (see Ebbinghaus, Volume II).

Despite similarities in the structural characteristics of the Continental welfare states, there are nevertheless significant differences among Continental countries. Germany and Austria have probably been the most conservative and normatively integrated of the societies considered herein, with both highly influenced by the values of Catholic social democracy or its Protestant equivalent in the case of parts of Germany. Their welfare state structures, moreover, seemed to do the most to reinforce gender differences, as the core male labor force benefited from comparatively high levels of social protection while women experienced great inequalities, in particular married women for whom the pension systems and tax laws, especially in Germany, set disincentives for labor force participation, as did the low level of public childcare services and the lack of availability of part-time work (Manow and Seils, Volume II).

Although the Netherlands and Belgium resembled the two conservative Christian-democratic welfare states in their earnings-related, reasonably generous, gender and status-differentiated systems, they also differed in substantial ways. The Netherlands was notable for the even greater generosity and extensiveness of its welfare system, for its more universalist understanding of welfare as a non-differentiable right, and for its even greater gender differentiation, with strong tax incentives for married women to stay out of the workforce and few job protections from dismissal for women in the workforce; only in 1973 was a law forbidding dismissal for reasons of marriage or pregnancy passed. Moreover, the Netherlands was highly normatively integrated, despite, or perhaps because of, its 'pillarization' into distinct political, social, and religious camps, although it was not as integrated as 'segmented' Austria, which was divided mainly along political lines. In Belgium, by contrast, the pillarization along linguistic and cultural lines on top of political, social, and religious divisions made for greater normative fragmentation, and was also a factor contributing to the widespread clientelism and patronage in service provision.

Switzerland was in many ways an outlier compared with the other Continental countries not only because its low level of welfare provision resembles that of the Anglo-Saxon welfare states but also because it reflected little of the influence of Christian social democracy which had shaped the systems of the other countries. However, it was as normatively integrated as Austria or the Netherlands, despite a system which was in many ways more segmented or pillarized than even Belgium, given more linguistic and cultural differences on top of political, social, and religious ones. And it has traditionally been as conservative as the others with regard to family relations and gender roles, with the man as *pater familias*. Thus, although more willing to allow women into the workforce, as evidenced by its higher female participation rates than the others in the early 1970s, it was also readier to send women home in the event of crisis in order to protect the core male workforce, which it did, along with immigrant workers, in the mid-1970s in response to the first oil crisis (Bonoli and Mach, Volume II): something which both the Germans and the Austrians did less of with regard to women, although Austria also sent home immigrant workers, but still fewer than the Swiss (see Hemerijck, Visser, and Unger, Volume II).

Although France and Italy consolidated their welfare states later than the other Continental countries, they also ultimately fit the model of the Bismarckian, Christian-democratic welfare state in terms of their reasonably generous, gender and status-differentiated systems. Italy, however, had much less state capacity than most of the other Continental countries, tended to be most traditional in terms of its emphasis on the family and women's place in the home, and was also much more normatively fragmented and clientelistic in service provision than all the other countries in our sample except possibly for Belgium. This was the result of the ideological division between the moderate Catholic subculture and the more radical communist subculture; the regional dualism between the rapidly industrializing north and the backward south; and the work-related dualism between the fully protected core workers and more peripheral ones, itself only further complicated by the veritable 'labyrinth' of status-differentiated, categorical privileges when it came to welfare benefits (Ferrera 1996; Ferrera and Gualmini, Volume II).

In France, by contrast, welfare provision was much more centralized and state-led than in any of the other Continental countries. Moreover, although its welfare state was certainly more normatively integrated than that of Italy or Belgium, France's institutions represented the sedimentation of successive and sometimes competing welfare agendas and values. These began with the early postwar universalistic Beveridgean aspirations, which were quickly submerged by the more Bismarckian Christian-democratic values of the Fourth Republic, supportive of differentiated rights and providing fragmented, clientelistically-based services—also typical of the prewar years—along with strong family policies intended to keep mothers at home. These values were then replaced by the more 'Republican' aspirations of de Gaulle, who emphasized universal rights and saw welfare provision as a matter of state obligation. This added a layer of centralized, universal state services not only with regard to health services and education but also in terms of family services and day care, which in turn had the effect of giving women the option of choosing home or work, and thereby increasing the female participation rate. But the Gaullist reforms did not do away with other elements of the earlier system that continued to support gender and status differentiation: for example, family 'allocations', or special subsidies to families, and state cofinancing of service provision by some charitable groups (see Levy, Volume II).

The Continental countries discussed herein, in short, shared a range of basic features with regard to the structure of welfare, although they nevertheless differed in levels of generosity, degrees of normative integration, and treatment of women. They also differed on work with regard to whether they were more or less reinforcing of wage and gender equality.

In some corporatist countries, wage equality was almost as important a value as in the Scandinavian welfare states, with solidaristic wage policies often resulting in wage compression. This was the case in the Netherlands, where the high minimum wage in particular had an egalitarian effect for the lower-waged workers. In Germany, wage dispersion was also low, due in part to solidaristic wage policies that in times of low wage increases would include provisions in contracts for a flat amount that would give disproportionate benefit to the low-wage groups. By contrast, other Continental countries with corporatist relations tolerated a much greater and rising level of inequality, in the case of Austria as a tradeoff for higher rates of employment (see Fig. 4.3).

In countries with statist rather than corporatist relations, there were also significant differences among countries on wage differentiation, but for different reasons (see Fig. 4.3). Whereas in France wage inequalities were high to begin with and remained high, given the state bowing to management preferences for differentiation as a way of buying worker cooperation, in Italy they decreased over time as union power and solidaristic policies increased, and became comparable to Germany for much of the 1980s (see Fig. 4.3). In Belgium, where the unions were also very strong, state intervention led to relatively small wage differentials, mainly because the state allowed above-average wage increases for the lowest-paid workers (see Scharpf, this volume).

The record on female participation in Continental countries was also mixed, and of course lower than in any of the Scandinavian countries, given the male-breadwinner model. The differences in female particip-

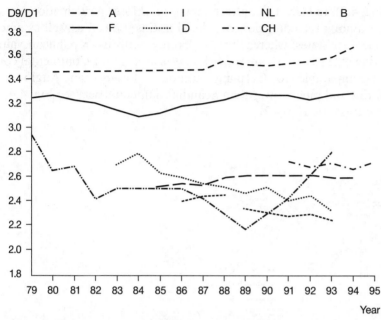

Figure 4.3 Earnings dispersion (D9/D1) in Continental countries

Notes: D1 and D9 refer to the upper limits of, respectively, the first and the ninth deciles of employees ranked in order of their earnings from lowest to highest, i.e. 10% of employees earn less than D1 earnings limit and 90% less than the D9 earnings limit. D5 thus corresponds to median earnings. For Belgium there is a break in series after the year 1988.

Source: OECD, *Statistical Compendium: Labour Force Statistics* (Paris: OECD, 1998).

ation rates among Continental welfare states can be explained by a wide range of factors, that include the availability of public or private day care and other family services, the availability of part-time and service sector jobs, the tax system, the wage differentials between men and women, and so forth (see Daly, Volume II). Continental welfare states generally moved from the upper 40 percent range in the early 1970s to the upper 50 to low 60 percent range in the mid 1990s, with Belgium remaining at lower levels throughout while the Netherlands, which had equally low levels in the 1970s, moved up to the Continental average by the 1990s, due in large measure to the expansion of part-time jobs (see Fig. 4.4). Among Continental welfare states, only Switzerland had high levels of female employment in the early 1970s, higher than in all other countries in our sample other than the Scandinavian, but this dropped in the mid-1970s—when women went home—slowly to move up again, to on a par with and then slightly above those of the Anglo-Saxon welfare states by the 1990s. This suggests that more liberalized economies, even within more corporatist contexts, may be more open to female employment (for the comparisons, see Fig. 4.2). In Italy, by contrast, female workforce participation was the lowest among the countries considered in this project, as well as among EU member-states, whereas that of France, with its 'republican values' ensuring extensive day care provision, was average for Continental countries—comparable to Germany—although lower than Anglo-Saxon countries and much lower than Scandinavian countries (see Fig. 4.4; for the contrast, see Fig. 4.2).

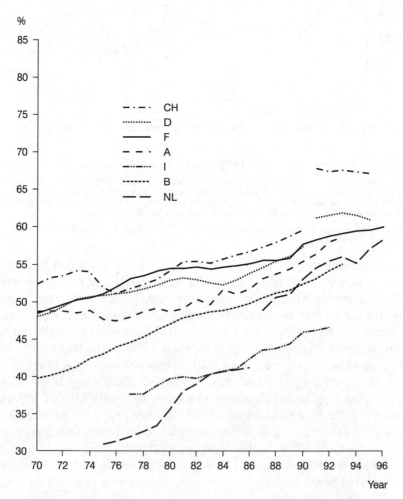

Figure 4.4 Female labor force participation rates in Continental countries

Source: OECD, *Statistical Compendium: Labour Force Statistics* (Paris: OECD, 1998); own calculations.

4.6.2 Values and Discourse in Continental Welfare State Reform

Unlike the Anglo-Saxon or Scandinavian welfare states, the Continental welfare states could not justify new welfare policies in response to growing economic problems through appeal to traditional welfare state values, given the unsustainability of a welfare system based on the traditional family as supported by employment and social protection of the core workforce. One of the main reasons for such unsustainability naturally comes from the rise in unemployment, which brings with it growing welfare costs as well as an increasing divide between the 'haves' in the core workforce and the 'have-nots' left outside. But it is also related to the movement toward greater gender equality and the rise of 'post-industrial' values, with a greater number of women in the workforce and the rise of two-income households that demand fairer treatment. And this also challenges the Continental welfare state's bias in favor of income maintenance for the long-term, full-time employed, and therefore generally male breadwinner (see Esping-Andersen 1999).

The challenges to the welfare state are also embedded in the very economics of the system, given that the earnings-related benefits are treated as near-property rights (see Introduction, this volume). Cutting costs, in other words, is difficult, to say the least. But the alternative is to retreat generally from the high level of benefits and services in all areas, something very hard to legitimize in societies where people have come not just to expect them but to place great value on them. How then to afford the current system? One answer would be to move toward full employment of the Scandinavian variety in order to take advantage of the full human resource potential of the society. But this would not just mean abandoning the traditional postwar values of the family and the core male breadwinner model by increasing part-time work and welcoming great numbers of women into the workforce; it would also require most Continental welfare states to generate a much higher level of day-care and family services, whether provided by the state as in Scandinavian countries and France, by the market as in Anglo-Saxon countries to a lesser extent, or by the nonstate and intermediary groups through state cofinancing, as could be done in Continental countries. But if provided either by the state or through state cofinancing, it would require much higher levels of taxation—just when taxes need to be cut.

What is most interesting about the Continental welfare states is how varied their responses to challenges to their values have been, especially by contrast with the Anglo-Saxon and Scandinavian welfare states. For example, while Switzerland, as one of the most traditionally liberal of Continental welfare states, and which expanded its welfare provision only beginning in the 1980s, liberalized further, Germany and Austria, as two of the most traditionally conservative of Continental welfare states, remained relatively unchanged. Moreover, whereas the equally traditionally conservative Netherlands experienced something of a revolution in both the structures of welfare and work that have made it the most 'liberal' of Christian-democratic welfare states, Belgium has not managed to reform either as extensively or effectively. Finally, whereas France liberalized the structure of work beginning in 1980s but has only begun to tackle seriously the reform of welfare, Italy since 1992 has incrementally reformed its inequitable system of welfare and work. For all these countries, the reasons for the differential course of events has to do not only with economics and institutions but also with the differing success of legitimizing discourses.

4.6.2.1 Germany   In Germany by the mid-1990s, it was already clear that major reforms to the structures of welfare and work were needed to sustain international competitiveness as well as the welfare state. Once unification had hit and the pressures of global competition had intensified, sending unemployment and social spending costs skyrocketing, something had to be done to reform a social security system which relied on high payroll taxes that discouraged internal investment and in which the relatively high wages of the lowest paid and the high social assistance levels encouraged 'welfare without work' and discouraged the move toward service sector jobs (Manow and Seils, Volume II). And yet, as of the late 1990s, meaningful reform had yet to be undertaken.

The lack of reform cannot be understood without reference to the German multi-actor system, with its federal institutional structure, its corporatist policymaking processes, and its patterns of public conflict followed by compromise and discursive consensus-building behind closed doors among a wide cross-section of policy elites. In Germany, the coordinative discourse is most elaborate, given that this is where compromises tend to be worked out. By contrast, the communicative discourse in Germany is necessarily very thin. This is because once the agreements have been worked out, the discourse is essentially over, with the government communicating the outcome in general terms to the larger public, and the other parties to the discourse communicating to their own constituents. The communicative discourse is more elaborate primarily during election periods—which are actually quite frequent, since these involve not just federal elections but also the sixteen Land elections over four years, which affect the composition of the upper house and are fought over federal issues. But here the communicative discourse may work at cross-purposes with the coordinative, as the adversarial rhetoric in the campaign for election may obviate cooperation. Governments may also turn to the communicative discourse when the coordinative discourse breaks down, in an effort to convince the general public and key policy actors of a better course of action and to provide a frame for a new coordinative discourse.

In Germany, then, coming to agreement is not necessarily easy, given the decentralization of the institutions and the normative fragmentation of the different parties to any compromise. But the possibilities of agreement have over the course of the postwar period been none the less good, mainly because the various parties to the discursive process also shared a set of understandings about the values and goals of the welfare state embedded in the 'social market economy', and a commitment to cooperation reinforced by institutional rules that promote such cooperation and enforce negotiated agreements. The postwar consensus on the social market economy and the liberal social-democratic discourse which served to legitimize it were essentially set by the late 1950s, once the Social Democrats signaled their conversion to both program and discourse with the Bad Godesberg program; and it lasted largely unquestioned up until the 1990s. For the major parties throughout this period, Christian Democrats as much as Social Democrats, the social market economy meant essentially the same thing: a market system which, although competitive, was accepted as politically instituted and socially regulated; firms which were seen as social institutions; a state which was expected to act in an 'enabling' manner; an economic governance system which was to be managed primarily by publicly enabled associations engaging in widespread, organized cooperation and bargaining; and a welfare system which was to provide a protective net against the pitfalls of the market (Streeck 1997). Moreover, although the party discourses differed somewhat over time, the core of the liberal social-democratic discourse differed little: the liberal side of the discourse emphasized the market-oriented nature of the economy and the federal state's limited powers with regard to the economy, while the social side focused on the cooperation of business and labor in the setting of wages and work conditions in their own separate sphere of activity, and on the generous welfare state.

There were few challenges to the program or the discourse until the 1990s. Although in the mid- to late 1960s, neo-Keynesianism took hold for a time, as the 'Grand Coalition' government engaged in greater market interventionism than the program was originally assumed to allow, by the mid-1970s any pretence to neo-Keynesianism was gone, with the monetarist conversion of the Bundesbank and the switch by the government to more conservative fiscal policy, followed by the unions' acquiescence to wage restraint under Bundesbank leadership. Moreover, although Kohl came to power in the early 1980s echoing the neo-liberal themes of Thatcher while the CDU's junior coalition partner, the Free Democrats, called for a return to individual responsibility and independence through cuts in social programs, the rhetoric was not followed by real reform. What cuts there were resulted from the need to balance the budget, not from ideology, and these were in any case partly offset by increases in other areas of the welfare state (see Lehmbruch 1994).

The lack of neo-liberal reform in the 1980s can be attributed in part to the fact that there was no economic crisis equivalent to the ones that helped justify major reform initiatives in the liberal welfare states and Denmark and the Netherlands, given the strength of the German economy. But it was also because Kohl lacked not only the will or the ideology of a Thatcher in Britain or a Douglas in New Zealand but also their capacity to impose more radically neo-liberal policies, given the institutional context. The high level of autonomy of government ministries, together with the strength of organized interests as well as the Länder in the policy process, meant that the lack of consensus on the need for reform ensured that there was little way to institute any.

There was also relatively little electoral support for change. The small Free Democratic Party was the only party propounding serious neo-liberal reform, and its voting score never rose above single digits in the 1980s. The public itself appeared happy with the structure of welfare and work as it was. They remained highly focused on 'family values' and did not seem to favor the kinds of policies that are normally associated with neo-liberal reform. The continuing focus on the family emerges in responses to an International Social Justice Project Survey (ISJP) conducted in 1991 and 1992, where Germany was by far and away more sympathetic to basing decisions on family characteristics than Britain and the Netherlands, with family size the basis for priority in getting an apartment—48 percent versus 28 percent and 12 percent—and being treated by a hospital—15 percent versus 5 percent and minus 15 percent—or for receiving higher pay—47 percent versus minus 33 percent and minus 60 percent (Marshall *et al.* 1999).

Germany's lack of support of neo-liberalism also comes out on a wide range of questions in a number of ISSP surveys. In 1992, Germany, at 41.1 percent, was the most opposed of the seven countries sampled to the liberal notion that allowing business good profits is the way to improve everyone's standard of living, coming in on an average of 8 points below the other countries. In 1987, Germany was equally opposed at the same level—40 percent—and below the other countries by between 13 and 17 points, with only the Netherlands, not present in the later sample, scoring lower, by 9 points (see Table 4.1, Questions 2 and 10). Moreover, in 1992, Germany was also not convinced that large differences in income were necessary for a country's prosperity, given an absolute score that was low at 21 percent, and which came in slightly below the average of the seven countries in the sample and slightly above that of the five countries sampled in 1987 (see Table 4.1, Questions 1 and 9). And finally, Germany in 1987 was also much less convinced than most other countries that financial incentives—that is, pay inequalities—were necessary for people to take extra responsibility—on a par with the Netherlands at 64 percent but otherwise way below other countries by between 13 and 18 points (see Table 4.1, Question 11). But although the Germans were clearly not neo-liberals if we judge from their answers to these survey questions, they were also not necessarily egalitarians when it came to questions of pay. In the ISJP survey of 1991–92, large percentages agreed that people who work hard deserve to earn more than those who do not—90 percent versus 93 percent for Britain and 84 percent for the Netherlands—and people are entitled to keep what they have earned, even if it means that some people will be wealthier than others—83 percent versus 72 percent for Britain and 77 percent for the Netherlands (Marshall *et al.* 1999).

By the 1990s, moreover, when economic crisis hit, it did little to challenge the public's values with regard to the welfare state. Much to the contrary, it seemed to reinforce them. In 1985, on the question of whether the government has a responsibility to reduce differences in income between high and low incomes, Germany, at 28 percent, scored far lower than all countries in the sample—between 13 and 20 points below—other than Australia, which is in keeping with the typical Christian-democratic pattern of maintaining income differentials—which in Germany were in any case not very great (see Fig. 4.1). By 1992, however, it had reversed itself, and Germany, at 65.5 percent, was much more redistributive than Sweden, New Zealand, and Australia, on a par with Britain, and only slightly below Austria, although way behind Italy. The same question asked in 1990 shows a somewhat similar spread (see Table 4.1, Questions 3, 6, 14). This suggests that maintaining existing income differentials, although acceptable in 1985 when they were not very large, was no longer acceptable in 1992, when unification produced potentially huge income inequalities with the incorporation of East Germany into the Federal Republic. A similar shift in responses occurred with the question as to whether government should provide a job for everyone who wants one. In 1985, Germany, at 35 percent, came out more opposed than all other countries except for Australia. By 1990, Germany had reversed itself, coming out on the high end, at 74.2 percent, much more in favor of government responsibility for job provision than Australia—32.7 points above—and

Britain—10.9 points above—and behind only Italy—10.7 points below.[6] What is more, although by 1992 Germany's support had slipped a bit, by 7.9 points, perhaps recognizing the impossibility of providing a job to all those out of work in Eastern or Western Germany, it still remained high at 66.3 percent (Table 4.1, Questions 4, 7, and 13). In a similar pattern, finally, whereas in 1985, Germany, at 24 percent, scored low on government's responsibility to provide a decent standard of living for the unemployed, above Austria and Australia but much below Britain and Italy—both of which had been experiencing unemployment problems— by 1990 it was very high, at 78.3 percent, much higher than Australia, on a par with Italy, and only slightly lower than Britain (see Table 4.1, Questions 8, 15). This shift is also confirmed by responses on the ISJP survey of 1991–92 where Germans were more in favor of government guaranteeing everyone a minimum income—at 76 percent—than Britain—at 70 percent—and the Netherlands—at 62 percent) (Marshall *et al.* 1999).[7]

At the same time that the economic crisis which began with unification seemed to reinforce redistributive values in the public, it also served to reinvigorate, as least for a time, the postwar paradigm of the social market economy and the liberal social-democratic discourse that served to legitimize it. Unification extended the West German social market economy to the East, legitimizing this through a communicative discourse in which the government sought not only to re-emphasize the liberal rhetoric of the early 1980s but also to evoke the traditional values of social solidarity and economic liberalism contained in the initial, postwar concept of the social market economy. This communicative discourse, which was the construction of a restricted governmental elite, actually replaced the usual coordinative discourse. This was not only because the crisis situation demanded quicker decision-making than normal but also because there was little chance of consensus among the usual policy actors and little possibility of agreement between the opposition and the government, given the intense electoral competition for new voters in the run-up to the 1990 elections (Lehmbruch 1994: 222–25).

Subsequently, as unemployment continued to rise and privatization proved problematic, the government returned to more corporatist concertation and cooperation with the opposition. By the mid-1990s, however, the renewed consensus was threatened by business leaders who began to

---

[6] I do not make much of the major increase in % of support, because all countries jumped significantly between 1985 and 1990. One could note, however, that the jump in support in Germany, by 39.2 points between 1985 and 1990, was greater than all the other countries by an average of 12.6 points.

[7] Although unemployment was higher in 1985 than in 1990 in West Germany—8% in 1985 versus 6.2% in 1990—it was extremely high in East Germany, and had become a major political issue as well.

propound a neo-liberal discourse focused on the challenges to German competitiveness from globalization and the problems from the lack of flexibility and high wages that were undermining productivity. But while they became increasingly confrontational in their public exhortations to do something about excessively high wage-bargains and rigid employment conditions, labor became increasingly resistant to cutting back wages or benefits. The conflict came to a head with the massive strikes related to the sick pay controversy that began in late 1996, which also led the unions to abandon the 'Alliance for Jobs' talks. Once it was resolved to the basic satisfaction of both management and labor, however, it was followed by a return to more cooperative, coordinative discussions among the social partners. In those areas where they were largely autonomous from government, they went ahead with liberalizing compromises related to wages and conditions of work that served to balance somewhat management's desires for greater flexibility and lower wage rises with labor's concerns about job security. But while the social partners moved forward, government became increasingly paralyzed in the run-up to the September 1998 elections, unable to reach compromise with the opposition on its tax and welfare reform initiatives.

Here, politics was the main obstacle to change. The political rivalry between government and opposition—in control of the upper house—in the run-up to the 1998 election blocked any compromises on welfare state cuts and tax reform. The campaign for election, in which the conflicting communicative discourses of government and opposition were of necessity more elaborate, worked at cross-purposes with the coordinative discussions behind closed doors, which were particularly non-cooperative, as each side accused the other in its election campaign of responsibility for the lack of reform. And while Kohl ran on his record, Social Democrat Schröder sought to appeal to business with promises to liberalize and modernize the economy and to labor by pledging to preserve Germany's generous welfare state through the rollback of the Christian Democrat government's modest cuts in pensions and sick pay.

From the time of its election to the end of 1999, however, the Schröder Government had yet to institute major reform either in tax or welfare policy, although Schröder kept some of his electoral promises to the unions with regard to reversing certain Christian Democrat reforms. In the early months after the elections, Schröder deliberately stayed in the background, expecting that the coordinative discussions behind closed doors organized in conjunction with the social partners in the *Bündnis für Arbeit* (Alliance for Jobs) would lead to a wide range of liberalizing reforms on welfare and work. But these dragged on without producing substantial movement. Tax as well as welfare reforms were also stymied in consequence of the successive elections in the Länder, which quickly reversed the Social Democrats' majority in the Bundesrat. The constant electioneering ensured that a communicative discourse focused on the voters worked at cross-purposes with any compromise on tax or welfare reform between government and opposition. In fact, even minor reform proposals generated protest from the Christian Democrats in opposition, who accused the Social Democrat-led government of seeking to destroy the security of the pension system—with reform initiatives similar to those they themselves had proposed while in office—in much the same way as the Social Democrats in opposition had accused the Christian Democrat-led government of dismantling the welfare state.

Finally, the government also confronted difficulties finding its own voice. First, in the spring of 1999, it seemed that the government was speaking with two different voices, that of Chancellor Schröder, who appealed to business with his espousal of market liberalization, and that of Minister of Finance and party leader Oskar LaFontaine, who appealed to the left of the party and the unions and appeared to reject market liberalization with his espousal of neo-Keynesianism. Only once LaFontaine resigned did Schröder become the sole voice of government, but this did not ensure his effectiveness. Over the summer, the Chancellor briefly adopted Blair's 'third way' in an ill-conceived and ill-received coauthored policy paper on the need to promote 'a go-ahead mentality and a new entrepreneurial spirit at all levels of society'. By September, however, Schröder had turned for legitimization of his proposed austerity package and limits on state pensions—with rises kept to the rate of inflation for the next two years—to an appeal to intergenerational solidarity, on the grounds that Germany could no longer 'devour the resources that should nourish our children' (*New York Times*, 17 September 1999). However, in the face of continued electoral defeat and massive protests by members of his own party and trade unionists against his proposed budget cuts, Schröder moved on to a discourse which had much more in common with that of the French socialists, with an appeal to the values of social justice. Only in December, once Schröder made clear that he was intent on protecting the traditional social market economy even as he sought to liberalize it, by speaking out against a foreign hostile takeover attempt of one firm—of Mannesmann by Vodafone—and intervening to avoid bankruptcy for another, Holzmann, did he regain credibility. Ironically enough, however, the late December 1999 tax reform proposals to eliminate the 50 percent rate of capital gains tax on firms selling shares in other firms would probably do more to undermine the network-based interfirm relations that underpin the traditional German social market economy than any other of Schröder's reform initiatives. But this clearly neo-liberal reform had not been part of the discourse, which has focused instead on the benefits to business of tax cuts.

Schröder's problems suggest that in a country such as Germany, where the complexity of the institutions and rules of interaction lead to a 'joint-decision trap' when the coordinative consensus breaks down (Scharpf 1988), there is still a place for a forceful communicative discourse. And given Germany's current problems, where what is required is nothing less than a recasting of the traditional postwar liberal social-democratic discourse to legitimize a more liberal turn in the social market economy, only a coherent communicative discourse will do. But for this, Schröder would have needed to construct a discourse that convinced the public not only of the necessity of reform but also of its appropriateness in terms that resonated better than the Blairite 'third way'. Even this would not have been enough, however, since, unlike in more single-actor systems, where a persuasive communicative discourse accompanying the imposition of reform may be sufficient—since a public that is persuaded of the necessity and appropriateness of reform is most likely to vote the reform party back into office—in multi-actor Germany such a discourse can be only the first step in the process of reform. For in a system of joint decision-making where the government does not have the capacity to impose, a communicative discourse is not sufficient. Here, reform also depends upon the further ability of the communicative discourse to frame the coordinative discourse among the social partners, the opposition, the Länder governments, and the federal government. Schröder, in other words, would have to construct a discourse capable of appealing to the general public while at the same time providing key policy elites with the language and set of concepts that would enable them to reconstruct their coordinative discourse and, with it, to create a new basis for consensus. It remains to be seen whether Schröder will find his way.

4.6.2.2 Austria In Austria, as in Germany, welfare state adjustment has been incremental, and major reforms have yet to take place (see Hemerijck, Visser, and Unger, Volume II). Here, too, the challenge to the postwar welfare state structure resulting from the need to reform has only recently begun. Austria, moreover, has consistently shown even greater support for welfare state values of equality and redistribution than Germany. Thus, it has been even more in favor of reducing differences in income than Germany, in 1985—41 percent versus Germany's 28 percent—and 1992—69.5 percent versus 65.5 percent—despite, or perhaps because of, much higher wage inequalities that, as noted above, were accepted as a tradeoff for ensuring high rates of employment (Table 4.1, Questions 3 and 14). And it has been even more in favor of government providing a job for everyone who wants one, both in 1985—47 percent to Germany's 35 percent—and in 1992—72.1 percent versus 66.3 percent

(Table 4.1, Questions 4 and 13). Moreover, Austria has been as opposed as Germany to the liberal notion that allowing business good profits is the way to improve everyone's standard of living—41.8 percent versus Germany's 41.1 percent in the 1992 survey; and it has been even less convinced that reducing differences in income increase the country's prosperity—17.2 percent versus Germany's 21 percent in 1992 (Table 4.1, Questions 2 and 1).

Austria, then, much as Germany, has had a solid consensus on the importance of maintaining a reasonably generous welfare state centered on the core male breadwinner model. But, unlike Germany, Austria has not had the same kind of public conflict related to maintaining or reforming the welfare state. This is not only because of grand coalition governments which avoided the German split between government and opposition but also because of a highly consensual policy concertation process between business, labor, and government that has been wider and deeper than in any other European country and regarded as highly politically legitimate not only by the social partners themselves but also by the general public (Compston 1999). In this context, conflict is limited by coordinative deliberations which tend to be relatively informal, involving gentlemen's agreements; highly confidential, if not entirely secret—so if conflict occurs, it is not publicly known; very flexible—which helps avoid conflict in the first place; and wide-ranging (Heinisch 1999).

Rarely does any conflict spill out into the public sphere, as it did in the mid-1990s. And in this case, it occurred because the social partners were for the first time since the 1950s cut out of the negotiation process by the coalition government with regard to a budget consolidation package. The trade unions' vocal, negative response, which criticized the package as 'socially disequilibrated' because of the kinds of cuts it proposed in such areas as maternity leave, early retirement, fees for health care, and the like, ensured that the initiative itself failed; and a much less extensive reform was finally put into place. Ironically, the subsequent budget package, with government defining the issues in the agenda while the social partners worked them out behind closed doors, recommended cuts that went far deeper than any the government would have dared propose on its own (see Hemerijck, Visser, and Unger, Volume II). What is more, they were more readily accepted by the general public because the social partners themselves, and not just the government, engaged in a communicative discourse to legitimize the changes.

This new role of the social partners, as indispensable 'modernization brokers', has also been evident with respect to Austria's hard currency policies and EU membership. In the run-up to the referendum on accession to the EU, employers' associations and unions were instrumental in overcoming the resistance of small business and organized labor, mounting a large publicity campaign together with government (Hemerijck, Visser, and Unger, Volume II; Heinisch 1999). The communicative discourse about membership, moreover, which began in the late 1980s and peaked in intensity in 1994 just prior to the referendum—which passed by 66 percent—appealed to national pride, to wit, that Hungary might one day surpass Austria if it became a member of the EU while Austria remained outside, and to the need for modernization. Moreover, the opposition by the extreme right helped consolidate mainstream party support and to ensure a taboo against criticism, such that the public communication was something of a monologue by government coalition partners and social partners, while no mention was made of the budget cuts that would necessarily follow membership in order to fulfill the Maastricht criteria.

In fact, it would appear that the role of the social partners has been changing in the late 1990s because they now follow government more than lead it with respect to the vast range of policy decisions, working out the details and implementing what government proposes (Hemerijck, Visser, and Unger, Volume II). But while the government may set the agenda, the social partners set the pace of reform, and make it palatable to a public which has increasingly shown greater faith in the institutions of corporatism than those of government. Thus, in a 1995 SWS opinion poll, corporatist institutions ranked second, fifth, and eighth in trustworthiness, whereas government came in ninth and political parties tenth, with the Catholic Church eleventh (Heinisch 1999). As such, it is the social partners in Austria who seem to have smoothed the transition from demand-side to supply-side corporatism (Traxler 1995b).

The problem for Austria today is that the kind of coordinative discourse of transition to supply-side corporatism may not be sufficient to allay public fears of change, especially when a communicative discourse has emerged from the extreme right in a country which, unlike Germany, has not dealt with its past, and thus may remain much more vulnerable to populists and demagogues who make thinly-disguised allusions to Nazism. The large showing of Jörg Haider's Freedom Party in the 1999 elections to Parliament, which put his party, at 27 percent of the vote, slightly ahead of the conservatives, brought down the grand coalition government, and has led to a new coalition between the conservatives and the extreme right. Moreover, it showed that in Austria too, a communicative discourse can appeal—even when it comes from outside the normal channels, or perhaps because it does—if it appears to engage in a provocative and open discussion of the country's problems, by contrast with the coordinative discussions behind closed doors among policy elites, about which the general public is most often kept in the dark. Opinion polls reported at the time suggested that Haider's popularity owed as much to the electorate's concerns about a lack of sufficient oversight over the government—evident from recent corruption scandals unearthed by Haider—and desires for a 'breath of fresh air' as it does to their view of Haider as representative of their interests or favoring stricter control over immigration. The 1999 election very much showed public weariness with the grand coalition governments which have ruled almost without a break throughout the postwar period, and with the *Proporz* system underpinning it. It remains to be seen whether the new right wing coalition will be able to move forward with welfare reform, and whether the public will accept it.

4.6.2.3 The Netherlands By comparison with Austria and Germany, as well as with all of the other Continental welfare states, the Netherlands has experienced a near revolution in the structures of both welfare and work (see Hemerijck, Visser, and Unger, Volume II). From one of the most traditional of 'Christian-democratic' welfare states, where the woman's role was clearly defined as being in the home and the man's at work, and with some of the lowest female labor participation rates in the 1970s (see Fig. 4.2), it has become much less traditional through rapid growth in women's participation in the workforce through part-time employment, with significant change in gender roles—female participation is now average, on a par with Germany—comparatively high rates of male part-time work, and greater flexibility in work conditions. The turning away from traditional Christian-democratic 'family values' is borne out in the ISJP 1991–92 survey, where the Netherlands' high degree of opposition to basing decisions about housing, health care, and pay on family size contrast markedly with those of Germany—see above. Moreover, from one of the most 'social-democratic' of welfare states, whether because of its view of welfare as a universal, non-differentiable right or its more egalitarian approach to wages, it has become one of the most 'liberal', having privatized and marketized social service provision and having accepted higher levels of profit for business, although it remains reasonably egalitarian with regard to wages (Visser and Hemerijck 1997).

  The Netherlands' success in liberalizing is all the more surprising if one were to consider the country's answers on an attitude survey in 1987, which found the Dutch more consistently and significantly opposed than other countries to liberal propositions that large differences in income were necessary to prosperity—at 16 percent, the country was an average of 8 points below the other countries; that good business profits improved everyone's standard of living—at 31 percent, an average of 20 points below the others; and that financial incentives were necessary to work hard—at 36 percent, an average of 28 points below the others—or to take extra responsibility—at 64 percent, an average of 12 points below the others (Table 4.1, Questions 9, 10, 11, and 12). Moreover, this opposition to neo-liberalism continued over time, with the ISJP survey of 1991–92 finding that the Dutch were much less convinced than the Germans or British that large differences in income were an incentive for greater individual effort—34 percent versus 51 percent and 46 percent—remained unconvinced that financial incentives were necessary to take extra responsibility—55 percent versus 72 percent and 72 percent—or that good business profits benefited everyone in the end—at 7 percent, more convinced than Britain, at minus 5 percent, but still less than Germany, at 11 percent. The country also remained highly egalitarian, with the ISJP 1991–92 survey showing the Netherlands significantly less supportive of pay differentials than Germany or Britain even where employees have greater responsibility—73 percent versus 96 percent and 93 percent—show greater individual effort—61 percent versus 98 percent and 91 percent—have more unpleasant working conditions—57 percent versus 91 percent and 83 percent—have higher levels of education—26 percent versus 83 percent and 56 percent—work harder—84 percent versus 90 percent and 93 percent—or have longer lengths of service—34 percent versus 63 percent and 68 percent. So how do we explain the dramatic changes in the structures of welfare and work?

The severity of the economic crisis beginning in the early 1980s was clearly a central part of the explanation. At this time, the Netherlands was in much deeper trouble than Germany or Austria, a result of the breakdown in the 1970s of the social concertation system and wage restraint as well as of the failure of all the traditional remedies to pull the country out of economic crisis. The country that had once been touted as the ideal-typical 'corporatist' country because of its highly cooperative labor-management relations and centralized concerted bargaining, that had been seen as one of the more successful of consociational democracies because of its consensual political relations by large coalition governments in a highly 'pillarized' society, seemed to be careening toward economic disaster and incapable of doing anything about it because of political deadlock. By the early 1980s, however, the process of recovery began, the result of a social learning process in which the social partners became more willing on their own to negotiate the necessary adjustments in wages and work conditions and the government to institute welfare reforms, even in the face of major opposition (Visser and Hemerijck 1997).

The arrival of the 'no-nonsense' Ruud Lubbers coalition government of Christian-Democrats and conservative Liberals in 1982 signaled the start of the process of change. First and foremost, the government's declaration that 'it is there to govern', with or without the social partners' consent, helped precipitate the Wassenaar agreement. This agreement put an end to the 'corporatist immobility' of the previous decade (see Hemerijck 1995) and ushered in a new era of 'responsive corporatism' with social concertation and wage restraint based on union acceptance of 'organized decentralization' in wage bargaining and of the principle that a higher level of business profits was necessary for the higher level of investment required for job growth (Hemerijck, Visser, and Unger, Volume II; see also Hemerijck and van Kersbergen 1997; Visser and Hemerijck 1997). With this responsive corporatism, moreover, came a coordinative discourse that continued through the 1990s, serving as the primary manner in which wage restraint was maintained, wage negotiations decentralized, and work conditions made more flexible. By contrast, in the welfare domain, the government engineered a 'corporatist disengagement', by progressively diminishing social partners' powers and responsibilities over the administration of social programs on the grounds that the coordinative negotiation process had contributed to immobilism (Visser and Hemerijck 1997).

Thus, the Lubbers Government took upon itself the responsibility for welfare reforms for which neither business nor labor was willing or able to gain agreement among its own membership, instituting alternative remedies drawn from the example of the liberal welfare state. In the 1980s, the Netherlands saw cutbacks in welfare state funding of pensions, unemployment compensation, and other benefit programs, although the government also took care to cultivate its social image through policies such as special benefits for the 'real social minimas', families with only one income at subsistence level (Green-Pedersen 1999b). These reforms did not go far enough to solve the problems of the welfare state, however, as employers' associations and right-wing parties were already complaining by 1986, even as trade unions and left-wing parties were protesting their inequitable impact (Aarts and Jong 1996: 51; Ebbinghaus, Volume II). The 1980s reforms were followed in the 1990s, under governments that now included the Social Democrats, by the large-scale reorganization of the welfare system through the tightening of eligibility requirements for disability benefits, the minimalization of the role of the social partners in the administration of welfare, and the marketization of a significant portion of the pension system (see Hemerijck, Visser, and Unger, Volume II).

The radically liberalizing 1990s reforms were not popular. The 'tough medicine' which, in the televised speech of Prime Minister Lubbers in 1989, was necessary for such a 'sick country', where one million of its seven million workers were out on disability insurance, did not go down well either with the unions, which organized the largest protest in the postwar period, or the general public, which saw the reforms as an attack on established rights. But the government coalition went ahead anyway, seeing the problem as not simply financial but as a crisis of governability that could not be allowed to continue (Visser and Hemerijck 1997). The public was not convinced, however, and voted its dissatisfaction in the 1994 elections. The result was a 'political earthquake' when the ruling coalition of Christian Democrats and Social Democrats went down to a resounding defeat, with the Social Democrats having emerged extremely weakened but still the largest party and thus in a position to form the next government, by contrast with the Christian Democrats who, for the first time in a very, very long time, found themselves in opposition. But this did not stop the subsequent left-Liberal government under Prime Minister Wim Kok from continuing with its unpopular reforms (see Hemerijck, Visser, and Unger, Volume II). Since the mid-1980s, in fact, there had been few differences among the major parties on the need for retrenchment, with the last time the Social Democrats challenged the government on 'the fairness issue' having been in the election campaign of 1986 (Green-Pedersen 1999b). In 1994, the only difference in policy from that of the previous government was that the new government promised not to tamper with the level and duration of benefits, and turned instead to revising eligibility requirements and to instituting market-oriented reforms (see Hemerijck, Visser, and Unger, Volume II). And this meant that the public really had no alternative, given the conviction of party elites across the political spectrum of the need for austerity measures and liberalizing reform.

Government willingness to persist with reform, even in the face of public opposition, clearly has much to do with normative commitments to act for the 'general good' or 'collective interest', despite the fact that this clearly went against narrow party self-interest. Government capacity to reform, moreover, has much to do with the strength of the Dutch unitary state, which is able to take action even in the face of opposition by the general public or the social partners—in this case labor—as long as it manages to coordinate agreement among government coalition members. Such agreement was facilitated by the fact that this more restricted coordinative discourse, which included not just the political parties but also experts on advisory committees while excluding the social partners—and thus was a much wider discourse among multiple actors than the truly restrictive ones of Britain and New Zealand—achieved a high degree of consensus on the need for welfare reform beginning in the 1980s. And therefore, even if the communicative discourse of government failed to convince the public in 1994, the coordinative discourse among government parties and experts succeeded in consolidating a coalition for reform.[8] The strength of the Dutch state, in short, is not dissimilar to that

[8] See Rochon (1999) on the long tradition of elites, experts, and relevant actors making decisions while ignoring the voter.

of the New Zealand state, despite the former's multi-actor system and many veto points by contrast with the latter's single-actor system and few veto points until 1996, since both have had tremendous ability to institute reform in the face of popular opposition. And in both cases, it was the normative conviction that liberalizing reform was necessary and appropriate, regardless of the electoral consequences for party self-interest, along with the absence of an electoral alternative, that were the bases for successful welfare state reform.

There are two main differences from New Zealand, however, having to do with institutional context as well as communicative discourse. First, the presence of multiple parties in Dutch coalition governments meant that the liberalizing reforms were moderated by the necessary compromises between right-leaning and left-leaning parties, by contrast with New Zealand, where a small extremist wing was able to impose its views without compromise. Second, in the Netherlands, unlike New Zealand, the public has come to accept the new welfare state arrangements. This is because of a variety of factors including the discrediting of the old system through official inquiries into its abuses and the clear success of the new system in getting people back into gainful employment through jobs programs, through the closing of exit routes, as well as through measures increasing labor market flexibility. The general vibrancy of the economy in which the syndrome of 'welfare without work' seems to have been reversed by Prime Minister Kok's focus on 'jobs, jobs, and even more jobs' also helped. And, of course, the Dutch social welfare system remains reasonably generous, despite all the cutbacks (Hemerijck, Visser, and Unger, Volume II).

But most importantly, the Dutch government was able to follow a 'left-progressive' strategy in which it turned 'vice into virtue' by attacking inefficient inequities in the system, such as paying generous disability pensions to vast numbers of able-bodied people, and by ensuring that equity would not be sacrificed to efficiency. This it did, for instance, by balancing the possible negative effects of wage restraint through compensatory, targeted tax breaks for low wage workers, and thereby ensuring continued, comparatively low wage differentials; by avoiding an unregulated race to the bottom through the upgrading of hourly wages and benefits of part-time and temporary workers; and by reducing gender inequalities—although it in no way eliminated them—by enabling women to get out of the house through the availability of part-time work (Levy 1999b). The government's communicative discourse about its policies emphasizing the fact that it had not forgotten about the concerns of social equity even as it pursued liberalizing efficiency, although clearly nothing as elaborate as the communicative discourse in Britain under Blair, clearly resonated with the public subsequent to the 1994 election, as evidenced by the resounding electoral success of the left-Liberal coalition in 1998.

4.6.2.4 Belgium Belgium offers a striking contrast to the Netherlands with regard to its response to economic crisis and the process of reform. The lesson here is that economic crisis alone is not enough to get the key policy actors in a multi-actor system to act cooperatively. It may have worked in Denmark and the Netherlands but, over and over again, as Belgium went from crisis to crisis, it was never enough to convince the strong unions in particular to compromise. The coordinative discourse among social partners and coalition governments never managed to ensure the necessary cooperation or to achieve sufficient consensus on what was to be done, despite countless initiatives, pacts, and plans seeking to get unions to agree to wage restraint and employers to agree to create jobs, let alone to agree on welfare reform. And in the absence of agreement, coalition governments more often than not simply imposed decisions, while buying off coalition members' clienteles through concessions on this or that in the process.

The differences from the Netherlands are best illustrated by events in the early 1980s, when the social partners missed the opportunity to reach their own Wassenaar accord, given low trust on the part of the negotiating parties and no stable government at the time to enforce any resulting compromise. Subsequently, despite an unprecedented public appeal by the King to 'put our differences aside' as if 'we were at war . . . for the preservation of our economy', the necessary steps to solve the problems of the economy were not taken (Hemerick, Visser, and Unger, Volume II)—there was no 'spirit of Dunkirk' here. After the general elections of 1981, however, the new conservative-liberal government did take action. In the face of the difficulties of gaining agreement through a coordinative discourse with the social partners, the government ended up ruling more or less by decree on wages and social security reform. It was empowered to do so by Parliament in an annual vote of confidence that effectively silenced not only the opposition but even dissenting members of the Prime Minister's own party. In other words, as if taking a page out of the New Zealand book, in Belgium, too, there was no significant coordinative discourse— not with the social partners, not with Parliament or the parties—only the very restricted one of the Prime Minister, close advisers, and political allies in the government. 'Less democracy for a better economy', defended by Prime Minister Martens as 'an unavoidable step', put Parliament and social partners 'in preventive custody' until 1986 (Hemerick, Visser, and Unger, Volume II). After this, wage bargaining was again left to the social partners, albeit limited by a law allowing government to intervene after the fact when it deemed necessary, which was often. By the mid-1990s, however, the return to limited freedom in wage bargaining was over, first with new government-imposed decisions around the 'Global Plan' to trim the welfare state and then, by 1996, with the passage of a framework law setting the allowable limits of wage rises. With this law, the government managed to avoid not only the need for much coordinative discourse with the social partners but also for any intervention on its own part after the fact, and thus coordinative discourse with coalition partners, members of Parliament, and so forth. Although wage-setting by statute is not the best instrument for an economy, it made sense for a polity riven by divisions among social partners and government parties.

The problem for Belgium was not only the impossibility of an effective coordinative discourse, but also the lack of a communicative one capable of gaining public support for change in the absence of cooperation from the social partners. Undoubtedly, communicative discourse is more difficult in multi-actor systems, although the Netherlands ultimately made it work in the case of welfare reform. But the Netherlands is a unitary state, and Belgium is federal, with problems even greater than those of Germany in terms of the government's ability to speak in one voice, let alone to make itself heard. And in Belgium, given the increasingly significant linguistic divides on top of the political, social, and religious differences, a veritable cacophony of voices in two—or three—different languages was increasingly raised on any and all issues. Most importantly, moreover, those voices were primarily focused on the linguistic divides themselves, and on the federalization of Belgium, rather than on the pressing economic issues. The country was, in the words of Michel Albert, attending to 'linguistic squabbles' while the ship was sinking (Hemerijck, Visser, and Unger, Volume II). In other words, where there was a communicative discourse from government, it focused on issues other than the economic, thus missing a chance to appeal to the public around the social partners in the way that the Netherlands did with regard to welfare reform, even if that discourse did fail initially.

It is important, however, to give Belgium its due. What is amazing about the country is the fact that it was able to reform at all, given the increasingly federalized and fragmented political system and problems that were of much greater magnitude than in the Netherlands: not only a much worse economic situation, with a budget deficit that was rivaled only by Italy and much higher unemployment, but also much greater normative fragmentation of the society. What is more, the economic troubles widened the regional disparities and deepened governmental paralysis. And the government had to address the regional issues before anything could be done about the economic. When considering this, one would have to conclude that Belgium has actually muddled through reasonably well, even without successful coordinative or communicative discourse, although this has meant that it has still lagged in the extent of reform not only in welfare but also in work, especially in terms of job flexibility and active labor market measures.

4.6.2.5 Switzerland Switzerland provides a fascinating comparison with Austria, the Netherlands, and Belgium, in particular with regard to institutional capacity for change. Switzerland, originally the most conservative as well as leanest of Continental welfare states, really only caught up with the other countries in terms of welfare benefit levels in the 1980s—but catch up it did with high social insurance transfers and high social security contributions—and in terms of gender-equality in the 1990s. Moreover, much of its welfare state modernization, which occurred primarily in the 1990s, also brought with it retrenchment and the attempt to contain costs (Bonoli and Mach, Volume II). And all of this came about within institutional structures that had, if anything, even more veto points than Belgium, given a highly decentralized federal system with significant independent powers for the multiple levels of local government and separation of powers between executive and legislature; over-sized coalition governments reflecting myriad political and religious divisions that required wide policy agreement; and a referendum system that allowed a small portion of the public—50,000 signatures—to challenge any law. Like Austria, however, the country benefits from strong consensus and a high level of normative integration. And therefore, although Switzerland has linguistic and cultural differences as great as those of Belgium, it still manages to achieve a high level of agreement in its coordinative discourse. But unlike all three other consociational/corporatist democracies with Continental welfare states, where agreement among the policy elites through a successful coordinative discourse is all that is necessary for reform to be instituted, in Switzerland the referendum system means that those reforms that are contested are subject to further public debate and deliberation. This adds another stage to the policymaking process, where communicative discourse becomes paramount as policymakers must justify publicly compromises made in private. And although this referendum system, along with the federal institutional structure, may have proved an impediment in the past to the rapid expansion of the welfare state (Obinger 1998), it has also proved an impediment in the present to any equally rapid retrenchment of the welfare state.

In Switzerland, the perception of the need for reform came only in the early 1990s, in response to economic difficulties which were, however, nowhere near those of most of the other countries in this study. This is when the largest internationalized employers, outside of the context of traditional business associations, began demanding radical change in economic and social policy in order to preserve the competitiveness of Swiss industry in the face of global pressures, and advocated a 'more liberal order' through privatization and deregulation while the employers' association called for a 'social moratorium' on any further expansion of the welfare state (Bonoli and Mach, Volume II). For the most part, the discourse created a sense of urgency which coalitions in favor of reform were able to exploit, as already liberal Switzerland liberalized even more, and at a more rapid pace than ever before, through privatization, deregulation, tax reductions, decentralization of the wage bargaining system, and cutbacks in social spending. In those areas dominated by labor-management agreements in particular, employers were generally able to gain great concessions, although not without resistance from labor, including the decentralization of wage bargaining from the sectoral to the firm level where it had not already been the case, the negotiation of wage indexation every year, and greater flexibility of working time. In areas dependent upon legislation, by contrast, reform was not nearly as extensive as the employers had hoped, whether in laws governing welfare or work. This is mainly because where an issue affected the electorate generally, as in the case of social policies and work rules, as opposed to narrow segments of the population such as farmers and domestic producers, the referendum system ensured that agreement among policy elites was not enough to secure change.

Policy reform 'in the shadow of the referendum system' means that policymakers generally make laws with an eye to immediate public response. Whereas policymakers in the Netherlands can institute reforms largely without regard to public opinion, except for elections every four years, policymakers in Switzerland cannot do so, since any reform could be subject to immediate public review and referendary defeat. This means that reforms that withstand the test of the referendum tend to be more moderate and mixed in the challenges to values, in the case of welfare reform by combining expansion with retrenchment measures. For example, the 1995 reform bill was not defeated in referendum because it mixed an appeal to values of gender-equality, through pension reform beneficial to women, with an attack on established rights as women's retirement age went from 62 to 64. By contrast, the 1997 bill reducing unemployment benefit levels, which had no balancing benefit, was defeated. A similar fate befell the labor reform bill of 1993, mainly because it went against the consensus established in coordinative discussions by the tripartite federal labor commission on the original bill, when a small right-wing majority in Parliament, supported by the employers' association, made the law much more liberal by allowing night work for women while eliminating the provision for compensation in terms of free time and adding other deregulatory measures. In the ensuing public debate prior to the referendum, union and Social Democrats communicated their dissatisfaction on the grounds that the law departed from the original consensus, and won the referendum with a large majority (see Bonoli and Mach, Volume II).

The moderating effect of institutions in Switzerland by comparison with the Netherlands brings to mind the contrast between Australia and New Zealand, where the Australian institutional structures—equally federal and increasingly corporatist, although less 'pillarized' or linguistically and culturally diverse than the Swiss—also insured against radical changes. But in Switzerland, most importantly, the moderating effect has been enhanced by the referendum system, which has ensured that in addition to the coordinative discourse among governing coalitions and social partners, there has been significant communicative discourse among the wider public in the debate leading up to the referendary vote.

4.6.2.6 France In France, there was never much of a welfare state discourse during the postwar period. French governments' focus was primarily on industrial policy: not on macroeconomic policy, on industrial relations, or on welfare policy, all of which were seen as secondary to the industrial policy which they were designed to support. And the discourse of *dirigisme*, or the glories of state interventionism to promote economic growth and modernization, initiated by the founder of the Fifth Republic, Charles de Gaulle, reflected this.

The communicative nature of the discourse followed naturally from the institutional arrangements of the single-actor system of the Fifth Republic set up by de Gaulle, where power was concentrated in an executive which formulated 'heroic' policies largely without interest group or societal input—and therefore provided at best a thin coordinative discourse, if that—but which allowed for accommodation in the implementation, or risked confrontation (V. A. Schmidt 1996a). Given this institutional structure, the importance of a powerful communicative discourse cannot be overemphasized. This is because, in the dynamics of French policymaking, where as often as not the most affected interests protest against the policies for which they had no input, the persuasiveness of the discourse may very well determine the policy outcome.

The Gaullist discourse of *dirigisme* was largely successful until the mid- to late 1960s, but was displaced more and more in the 1970s and replaced in the early 1980s by a socialist discourse advocating even greater *dirigisme* through nationalization, industrial restructuring, and generous socioeconomic policies. While the Socialists' economic policy program was more a reinvigoration of Gaullist ideas than a rejection of them, the policy program's normative legitimization was completely different from the Gaullist. Although the appeal to traditional political values and national pride remained with regard to the role of the state in restoring French economic prowess, there was also a postwar Marxian ideology which infused the discourse, reflected in talk of equality and social justice, of a 'break with capitalism' through nationalization of the means of production, of the capitalist 'wall of money', and of the CEOs of major firms as exploiters. Once in power beginning in 1981, however, the Socialists slowly moderated their discourse, increasingly justifying nationalization in nationalistic terms—that is, to save firms from foreign takeover—as opposed to Marxian terms, rehabilitating business by calling CEOs no longer 'exploiters' but 'creators of riches', and by treating profit no longer as a dirty word (V. A. Schmidt 1996a, ch. 4).

By 1983, however, with the 'great U-turn' in economic policies in response to economic crisis brought on in part by those very policies, which forced an emphatic end to traditional *dirigisme* and state interventionism as we knew it, the Socialist discourse was itself abandoned. The communicative discourse which followed offered justification for the shift to a moderate neo-liberal economic policy program in terms of the '*contrainte extérieure*' or the external constraints imposed by globalization and the need to remain in the European Monetary System, which would act as a shield against globalization. But while the Socialists made clear how necessary the new economic program was to relaunch growth and fight unemployment, they did little to demonstrate its appropriateness in terms of the socialist values they had espoused throughout the postwar period—nor could they. Instead, they fell back on the appeal to French national pride, and spoke of the economic combat for national survival, of national revival and modernization.

When the Socialists lost power in 1986, it was to a right wing coalition that had seemingly abandoned the Gaullist discourse in favor of a somewhat Thatcherite, neo-liberal discourse espousing the 'retreat of the state'. This discourse was in turn abandoned for the most part by the right with its electoral defeat in 1988. And thereafter, in place of an overall legitimizing discourse of the left or the right, successive governments continued to use the rhetoric about the need to rise to the challenge of Europeanization as a guard against the threat of globalization to justify continued industrial reform (V. A. Schmidt 1997a). This rhetoric worked reasonably well with the general public only until the recession of the early 1990s, at which point Europe itself seemed to generate economic problems, with the commitment to monetary union seemingly demanding cutbacks in a welfare state. This is when the lack of an overall legitimizing discourse became particularly problematic, and the need for a discourse capable of reconciling neo-liberal economic policies with the underlying welfare state values of 'social solidarity' and avoidance of 'exclusion' became paramount.

In France, although there was much talk about the crisis of the welfare state before the mid-1990s, little or nothing was done while the welfare state continued to expand as it absorbed the costs of restructuring industry through generous early retirement benefits and unemployment compensation. During the 1980s, as industrial restructuring proceeded, the right as much as the left took pains to reassure the electorate that the welfare state would not be negatively affected. President Mitterrand, after the 'great U-turn' in economic policy in 1983, set himself up as the 'guarantor of national unity and social justice' (cited in Labbé 1990: 157–58) while Prime Minister Chirac in 1986 to 1988 repeatedly made clear that his policies would not challenge the 'republican consensus'. Beginning in 1989, moreover, under Prime Minister Rocard, the Socialists sought to demonstrate their continued concern with issues of social justice through new reforms targeted specifically at the problems of 'exclusion'. For the Socialists, however, the definition of social justice had changed, and now instead of being linked to the concept of equality it was associated with the notion of solidarity, which represented the unarticulated acceptance of the inequalities of income necessitated by a more neo-liberal approach to economic management (Jobert and Théret 1994: 72–78).

By the mid-1990s, all agreed that reforms were necessary if the country was to meet the Maastricht criteria as well as its future obligations with regard to the near-bankrupt social security system. This turned out not to be easy, since the experience of macroeconomic and microeconomic reform since the early 1980s had left the public distrustful of further reform in the socioeconomic arena (Levy, Volume II). Moreover, whatever the public's acceptance of neo-liberal macroeconomic and microeconomic reforms, the large majority remained squarely behind the social security system, and certainly unwilling to see it dismantled. While in a 1983 SOFRES poll 89.5 percent responded that 'it would be very serious to eliminate social security'—ahead even of the right to vote, at 81 percent—in a 1993 Espace Social Européen survey, 85 percent had confidence in the ability of the social security system to solve the problems it confronted, by contrast with 39 percent with confidence in the administration. Moreover, 69 percent were unwilling to take out private insurance, 74 percent were unwilling to pay more social security tax, and 75 percent unwilling to pay more income tax (cited in Jobert and Théret 1994). What is more, the public remained fully behind a continued state role in the provision of public interest services. Not only was the public against privatization, with 49

percent against any at all in 1989, and opposed in particular to the privatization of the schools—59 percent—hospitals—53 percent—and social
security—52 percent (SOFRES, 20–24 January 1989), but large majorities
of the public also retained great confidence in national infrastructural services as well as social services, considering that they worked well or had
even improved over time, with only the social security administration reg-
istering a loss of confidence—52 percent in 1989 down to 49 percent in
1995 (SOFRES, 8–9 September 1995).

Successive conservative governments in the mid-1990s which sought to
institute spending cuts along with regressive tax policies were unable to
reform as they had hoped, mainly because of negative public reaction
which came as much in response to the process as to the substance of
reform. Prime Minister Balladur's tactic of floating reforms like trial bal-
loons, to be withdrawn in the face of protest, involved little attempt to
communicate with the public about the legitimacy of the reforms or to
coordinate with the social partners on the substance of reform. None the
less, he successfully implemented a major reform of private sector pensions, mainly because the measure involved some prior consultation and a
quid pro quo with the unions, in marked contrast to Prime Minister
Juppé's failure to institute a similar reform of public sector pensions
(Bonoli 1997). Juppé's approach, which was a throwback to the old 'statist' approach of imposing 'heroic' reform without prior consultation (see
V. A. Schmidt 1996a), seemingly rejected even the notion of communication or coordination. That Juppé proudly announced that he had put the
reforms together nearly single-handedly is illustrative of the problems. The
result was the withdrawal of reform in the face of the biggest set of strikes
in years. The protests themselves gained widespread public support not so
much because the French rejected the substance of the reforms—according to an opinion poll at the time a majority of French, 51 percent to 40
percent, accepted that the government had to put into place drastic social
security reforms (Sofres 1996: 29), as because they objected to the process,
more precisely because the government had failed adequately not only to
communicate to the public how the reforms might legitimately fit with values of 'social solidarity' or its electoral promises but also to inform the
most interested parties of the proposed policies, let alone bring them into
the construction of the policies themselves.

The Socialists in government since June 1997, however, have seemingly
done better in terms of both communication and coordination, as well as
in softening the impact of the neo-liberal policy program. The government's coordinative discourse, to begin with, has been much more accommodating, by opening up policy construction to a less restricted group of
policy elites. Thus, the government has in some cases used expert com-

missions to propose reforms on controversial issues, choosing what to do based on public reaction, while in others it has used corporatist concertation 'in the shadow of the state', which is a long shadow indeed, given the weakness and fragmentation of the social partners that often leaves the state still in a position of having to coerce and control in order to ensure the success of its reform efforts. The 35-hour working week, imposed by government over business objections, is a case in point.

Despite the fact that the government's communicative discourse remains the work of a highly restricted governmental elite—the Prime Minister and select advisers and members of his cabinet—or perhaps because of it, it has been very successful, the proof being the Prime Minister's unprecedented popularity, with a 60 percent approval rating in fall 1999 after two and a half years in office. This is because the government has come up with a coherent discourse which makes appeal to values that the public continues to hold dear. The discourse itself tends to be reasonably moderate and balanced in tone, deliberately using less heroic language to talk about the choices of government. The 'ni-ni' is now being used to suggest that the government will pursue moderate change, with 'neither pause nor acceleration' in the pace of reform, neither slashing benefits to the poor nor doing nothing while the social security system goes into deficit; neither declaring class warfare on the rich nor allowing the privileged not to pay their share; and neither dismantling the welfare state nor failing to address its dysfunctions (Levy, Volume II).

For the first time since the Socialists turned to neo-liberal economic policies in 1983, moreover, they have consistently sought to show how their liberalizing policies actually fit with left-leaning values, by arguing that their reforms are not only economically efficient but also promote social equity, combat social exclusion, and heal the 'social fracture'. This has been evident in the discourse on privatization, where the Socialists have insisted that their privatizations, unlike those of the right, respected rules of efficiency and equity, by seeking to secure investment as well as to guarantee jobs while involving the unions in the negotiations, in contrast to the right's focus on state disinvestment, without regard to its impact on jobs or on industrial strategy, and without worker consultation (Levy, Volume II). The Socialists have made similar arguments with regard to fiscal policy, claiming that instead of the regressive tax policies of the right which targeted wage-earners rather than capital, their policies favored greater redistribution of income toward the poor without increasing spending, in particular by the reduction in payroll taxes in favor of a more universal social security tax on income. And they insisted that by taxing and eliminating benefits for the rich while reducing the burdens on the poor and by raising taxes on business and lowering them on consumers—rather than the other way around, which had been Juppé's solution—they thereby increased public confidence and consumer spending, which in turn has helped the economy. Finally, they have also pointed to the fact that the 'corporatist' negotiation of social security reform has led to the creation of private pensions funds administered by the social partners rather than private companies, as the right had sought to do (Levy, Volume II).

The Jospin Government, in short, seems to have managed to construct an elaborate communicative discourse and the beginnings of a wider coordinative discourse which together have served to facilitate the institution of a wide range of reforms that under earlier governments had been stymied or generated social conflict. The government still confronts great difficulties, however, not only because of the economic pressures that reduce socioeconomic capacity but also because of the institutional context that makes productive coordinative discussions with the social partners difficult, and thus hinders reform efforts. None the less, although the government's reforms are so far reasonably modest, it at least seems to have convinced the public through its discourse that it is possible to reform the welfare state in a way that promotes the values of social solidarity and even egalitarianism and redistribution. In consequence of a more coherent communicative discourse as well as greater concertation, it has made progress where its predecessors had not.

4.6.2.7 Italy In Italy, too, welfare state reforms have been reasonably modest so far. But for Italy, given the state's traditional incapacity, in the 1980s in particular as social expenditures rose astronomically in response to escalating demands (see Ferrera and Gualmini, Volume II), the turnabout is all the more remarkable. How do we explain this turnabout? A good deal of credit must go to the communicative discourse about European integration as the 'rescue of the nation-state', which was the first truly unifying grand objective of the country since the 1950s, and which helped Italy to overcome traditional normative fragmentation (see Ferrera and Gualmini 1999) and problems with its coordinative discourse. In fact, even as France was abandoning European integration as its discursive justification for continued reform efforts in the mid-1990s, Italy was stepping up its use of it to justify much more radical—for it—reforms using a discourse focusing on the '*vincolo esterno*', or external constraint (Radaelli 1998). Becoming part of EMU was not simply an economic necessity to the Italians, however, but also a question of national pride (Sbragia 1998); and, as such, it served to justify any sacrifice. In no other country has the discourse of European integration played such a central and sustained role in promoting acceptance of change, and this even before the 1990s enthusiasms or the pressures of EMU—Eurobarometer surveys have consistently put Italy at the top of the list in terms of support for European integration. This holds even when Italy is compared with countries such as Sweden and Austria, which became members of the EU only in 1995, where the discourse was not nearly as dramatic, nor was it used as legitimization for welfare state reform, although in the case of Austria it also appealed to national pride.

Even for Italy, however, the European discourse alone was a necessary but not a sufficient condition for welfare state reform. Without the political and institutional changes of the early 1990s, the discourse could not have been successful, let alone the welfare policy reform it supported. The changes include the political renewal related to the end of the cold war, which came with the collapse of the old political parties and the system of *'partitocrazia'* that promoted governmental 'immobilism'; the politico-administrative renewal related to the end of the old system of political corruption and deal-making following from the *'tangentopoli'* and *'mani pulite'* investigations; and the electoral reforms that created governments better able to speak in one voice, with the move to a less proportional representation system that produced more of a two party system with a clear majority in power (see Ferrera and Gualmini, Volume II). These changes made it possible for the first time in the postwar period for governmental leaders with clear political responsibility and control to take effective action, and to engage in a communicative discourse which sought to clarify more than to obfuscate, to legitimize rather than to palliate, and, thereby, to gain widespread public support for its actions. Moreover, the changes also made it possible for such governments to coordinate with labor on reform of the welfare state—in those areas where unions have major responsibility—rather than, as in the past, simply to seek to buy them off.

It is as if, once the impasse created by an impossible set of institutional structures was overcome through political and electoral change, everything was possible. In fact, despite the lack of much-discussed further institutional reforms to strengthen the leadership capacity of the executive, the Italian government has managed to engage business and labor in a highly effective coordinative discourse that has produced reforms at critical junctures which the government has then been able to legitimize to the general public through a highly transparent and elaborate communicative discourse. These include not only important changes in the structure of the economy through deregulation and privatization and in the structure of welfare through reforms in 1992, 1993, 1995, and 1997, but also in the structure of work, with the institution in 1992 of an incomes policy that would flexibly adjust to the rate of inflation; the end also in 1992 of the *scala mobile*, the system of wage indexation that had led to spiraling wages; and the reform of collective bargaining by creating two negotiation levels, national and firm or territorial (see Regini and Regalia 1997; Ferrera and Gualmini, Volume II).

Most striking about the new Italy—as opposed not only to the old Italy but also to corporatist polities such as Germany and Austria where coordinative discussions are held behind closed doors, and the subsequent communicative discourse is quite thin—is how extensive the communicative discourse is, and how close it stays to the content of the coordinative discourse, even if the details of the compromises may be left out. It is as if, after all the years of obfuscation that led to public alienation and disgust with politics, governmental leaders have learned to tell the truth, or at least something more closely approximating it, at least some of time.

The welfare reform discourse itself focused on the need to accept sacrifices now, primarily through cuts in benefits and wage restraint, in order to gain in the long run from the '*risanamento*' of the welfare system: not only by the return to financial health and greater efficiency but also by an increase in social equity. The communicative discourse resonated because of the unfairness related to uneven benefit levels and the lack of correlation between benefits and contributions; because of the illegalities of the particularistic-clientelistic system; and because of the runaway spending that threatened to bankrupt the state (see Ferrera and Gualmini, Volume II; Ferrera and Gualmini 1999; Levy 1999b). This is when the government made an impassioned plea for '*Più ai figli, meno ai padri*'—more to the children, less to the fathers—which struck a highly receptive chord (Rossi 1997). By insisting on the importance of balancing economic return to health with social justice, the discourse served to convince both the general public and the social partners of the necessity as well as appropriateness of reform. This was aided, of course, by the acute fiscal crisis of the summer of 1992. But fiscal crisis was not enough to guarantee agreement, as Prime Minister Berlusconi's failure in 1994 attests, when his attempt to impose reform led to major strikes and demonstrations. Another element is discursive style: where governments espoused cooperation, sought 'concertation' with the unions, and entered into a coordinative discourse with them, as did for example the Dini Government in 1995, by contrast with the adversarial stance of Berlusconi, pension reform was particularly successful (Regini and Regalia 1997). The coordinative discourse in the Dini reform, moreover, was an elaborate process that involved not just national union leaders with business and government in tripartite discussions but the entire union rank and file in deliberations which culminated in a referendum, with 65 percent in favor. This process not only served to persuade the majority of union members that the reform was acceptable—even if they were less convinced by the intergenerational justice argument of

political leaders than by the fear of having a harsher reform imposed.
It also ensured that opposing union members accepted the procedural
justice of the vote, and therefore did not stage wildcat strikes (Baccaro
2000).

But none of this would have worked without the overall legitimizing discourse, and reality, of European integration, and the appeal to national
pride related to the question of whether Italy would be able to meet the
Maastricht criteria for European Monetary Union. Although national
interest, both political and economic, of course played a major role in the
decision to go forward with EMU, the necessary steps to prepare the country for EMU could not have been taken without a communicative discourse which has served as a normatively integrating force for a society
torn between north and south, big business and small, management and
labor, right and left, rich and poor, and so forth (see Sbragia 1998). For the
social partners in particular, who have a large say in welfare policies, the
European ideal served as the backdrop for the more consensual, coordinative discourses of the multiple actors involved in reform efforts. More
recently, the only false notes have been in the government coalition itself.
First, the Prodi Government had to scale back some of its proposed
welfare reforms and ultimately fell because of the Communists, who were
less convinced by the European discourse and more concerned to block
welfare reforms that they saw as detrimental to blue-collar workers and
the very poor. And second, the d'Alema Government which took office in
October 1998 and has not departed much from the legitimizing discourse
on Europe as the rescue of the nation-state or on social equity in the
reform of the welfare state, has also had problems negotiating further welfare state reforms. This suggests that the discourse on Europe, once Italy
made it into the EMU, may not continue to exercise the same unifying
power as prior to entry, and that further welfare state reform may therefore encounter increasing difficulties.

4.7 Conclusion

By the late 1990s, most governments in power seemed to have turned
their backs on the starker neo-liberal rhetoric of individual responsibility that had flourished in particular in the 1980s in favor of a more
'humane' discourse which promised to afford the very poor greater protection even as the welfare state was cut, and which pledged to balance
efficiency with equity in the reform of the welfare state. Much of
this discourse comes from recently elected center-left governments,
which have been able to address the 'left' values issues of equity, if not

equality and redistribution, much more directly than the center-right governments previously in power, or even earlier center-left governments. But does this then mean that welfare states are converging in discourse, if not also in policies?

Not really, since the underlying values remain quite different, as do the policies, even when the words used to describe the policies and to appeal to the public are the same. Anglo-Saxon welfare states have reinforced individual responsibility, gender neutrality, and the turn to the market provision of services through both the discourse of the 'third way' and the low level of state provided welfare benefits and services. Scandinavian welfare states continue to enshrine egalitarianism in gender and status in the social-democratic discourse and through the high level of state benefits and provision of services. Continental welfare states, however, have moved away from the emphasis on family values, differentiation in gender and status, and the provision of services by intermediary groups and the state, albeit to differing degrees with differing emphases in the discourse on individualism or egalitarianism in kinds or levels of benefits, on gender-neutral or gender-friendly policies, and on the resort to market provision of services. Intergenerational justice, moreover, has also become a recurrent theme, but only in those Continental countries with pay-as-you-go, earnings-related pensions, where the problems of funding remain significant—for example, in Germany, Austria, Italy, Belgium, and France—and not the Netherlands or Switzerland, where pensions are privatized.

Differences in institutional context also serve to differentiate countries, even when they resemble one another in values, affecting the discourse not just in the way in which reform initiatives are constructed and communicated but even the course taken by reform. Such differences are especially significant with regard to single-actor versus multi-actor systems. In single-actor systems, where power and authority tend to be highly centralized, the coordinative discourse, like the policy it seeks to legitimize, tends to be the construction of a restricted, government-centered policy elite, whether a small governmental-cum-technocratic elite, as in France, or a small governing party elite, as in Britain, or New Zealand until the mid-1990s. Because of such a restricted construction, legitimization of the policy program is at the communicative stage, where this self-same elite focuses primarily on convincing the larger public of the policy's necessity and appropriateness. Here, the debate and deliberation over major policy initiatives tends to go on in the wider public sphere—if at all—as policies formulated unilaterally by a small elite face public scrutiny, and where the discursive process is therefore often adversarial, as it may be opposed by those organized interests most affected: the opposition, the media, and so on.[9] But whether the discourse is persuasive or not, the government has the power to impose.

However, while the government has the power to impose, the public need not accept. Often, the only way to gauge acceptance of reform and, concomitantly, the persuasiveness of the communicative discourse, is in the electoral process. This is where citizens can periodically express their general approval or disapproval of government policies in legislative elections, as in France in 1997 with the defeat of the Juppé Government, or in referenda, as in New Zealand in 1993 with the institutional change in the electoral system. Here, continuity in the policy agenda in the face of party change may constitute the clearest example of public acceptance of previous reform and of the persuasiveness of the discourse, as in Britain with Blair's renewal of Thatcherite neo-liberal policy and discourse. Only in countries with histories of protest may the sanctions be more timely, as in France with the 1995 strikes that led to the withdrawal of the pension reform initiatives, or in Italy—if we consider it as a single actor system 'manqué'—in the periodic protests prior to the 1990s. Occasionally, though, even when the public does not accept a given set of policies, it may nevertheless not sanction the government electorally or through protest if it is distracted by an overriding discourse in another policy area, as in Britain with the Falklands war discourse in the 1983 election or in New Zealand with the nuclear issue in the second half of the 1980s.

In multi-actor systems, by contrast, where power and authority tend to be more dispersed, the coordinative discourse, like the policy its seeks to legitimize, tends to be largely the construction of the multiple participants in the policy formulation process. This may include business, labor, and government with or without coalition partners, as in Sweden and Denmark—along with different religious, regional, ethnic, and linguistic groups, as in the Netherlands, Belgium, Switzerland, and Italy; lower levels of government in federal states, as in Switzerland, Belgium, Austria, Australia, Germany; or even the opposition, as in Germany. Such coordinative discourses, moreover, may be relatively open, as in the Netherlands and Australia, or behind closed doors, with doors that don't leak, as in Austria, or doors that always do, as in Germany. The discussions themselves, in addition, may be highly consensual and cooperative, as in Austria and Switzerland; conflictual before the negotiations behind closed doors which lead to consensus, as in Germany and to a lesser extent Sweden; or simply conflictual, with little consensus ever achieved, as in Belgium and Italy before 1992.

---

[9] This is mainly the case with 'heroic' policy initiatives. More everyday policies may very well look more like multi-actor systems, where the compromises are worked out at the formulation stage (see V. A. Schmidt 1996a).

In all such multi-actor systems, the discourse carries out its major legitimizing function at the coordinative stage, as the negotiating partners deliberate about the policy on which they need to come to agreement. And when they do come to agreement, the different policy actors will ordinarily inform their constituencies of the results, in the terms of their own 'subdiscourse' and values, leaving it to government to communicate the results to the larger public in what is for the most part a much 'thinner' communicative discourse, at least compared with the communicative discourse in single-actor systems.[10] In fact, the more multi-actor the system, the less communicative the public discourse is likely to be, given the number of actors whose preferences must be compromised in order to reach a common agreement and the difficulties of speaking in one voice—for example, compare federal Germany with unitary Sweden or the Netherlands. Moreover, the more multi-actor the system, the greater the dangers of blockage when the multiple actors cannot reach agreement for whatever reason. In unitary states, the government is more likely to be able to go ahead with reform in the face of opposition, as in the Netherlands in the early 1990s—but not in the 1970s—than in federal states, where actors tend to be caught in a joint-decision trap, as in Germany in the late 1990s. Even in federal states, however, forward movement is nevertheless possible where the multiple actors tacitly agree to allow government to decide, as in Belgium beginning in the 1980s.

In election years, however, such multi-actor systems do tend to have a more elaborate communicative discourse. But this may very well work at cross-purposes with the coordinative discourse, since the public pronouncements of the political parties in the election campaign may undermine the attempts to reach compromise in the coordinative discussions between government and opposition and/or coalition partners behind closed doors—for example, Germany in the run-up to the 1998 elections. Only at critical junctures, when the coordinative discourse breaks down, does the communicative discourse have an important role to play, by providing a new frame with which key policy actors can reconstruct their coordinative discourse. Where the government gets it right, providing a new vision or revaluation of long-standing interests and values, major reforms are not only possible but sustainable—for example, the Netherlands in the early 1980s and early 1990s or Italy after 1992. Where it gets it wrong, reform is much less likely to occur—for example, Germany under Schröder 1998–99—unless the key policy actors them-

---

[10] This is not to suggest that actors involved in coordinative discourses do not make public pronouncements, since they often do in an attempt to exert pressure and influence within the context of the coordinative discussions.

selves manage to reconstruct their discourse despite the government's lack of leadership—for example, Austria in the mid-1990s.

In multi-actor systems, however, whatever the problems of achieving consensus among policy elites, once there is such a consensus, public acceptance of the policy, or at least acquiescence, is practically certain. The only exceptions are the few cases where the general public has a say after a policy decision has been taken, as in the case of referenda: for example, in Switzerland. In such cases, there may very well be a second round of fuller communicative discourse, where public debate of a variety similar to what occurs in single-actor systems takes place, as all parties weigh in on the issue prior to the vote. For the most part, however, the public is expected to acquiesce because its interests and values are assumed to be represented by the groups central to the coordinative negotiation process—which is not always true, of course. And it has no recourse, needless to say, if it feels that it is not represented. Even throwing the government out in successive elections doesn't change things where there is agreement among policy elites, as was the case in the Netherlands in the 1990s. But this is also true for single-actor systems where opposing political parties nevertheless espouse, and implement, the same unpopular views, as in New Zealand beginning in the mid-1980s.

The discursive process differs among countries, then, with legitimizing discourses expressed in different voices and different venues in consequence of their differing institutions. In single-actor systems, legitimizing discourses are primarily situated at the communicative stage and found in the pronouncements of governments and in the adversarial public debates, whereas in multi-actor systems they are more likely to be at the coordinative stage, in the consensus-building deliberations of corporate and governmental actors that may or may not take place behind closed doors. The consequences for reform are significant, because even countries that share a similar constellation of values with regard to welfare and work in the postwar period may nevertheless differ greatly in policy outcomes because of differences in the locus of legitimization through discourse, whether at the coordinative or the communicative stage. This came out most clearly in the case of multi-actor Australia, where more gradual, moderate reform was the result of the more coordinative discourse, by contrast with the communicative discourses of single-actor Britain, and New Zealand before the mid-1990s. Such differences help explain the differential development of countries which in the postwar period resembled one another in their constellations of normative values related to welfare and work.

But however important the context and process of discourse, the substantive content of the discourse also matters. Sound cognitive arguments that underline the necessity for reform are clearly essential, for example, when they insist that, in the face of economic crisis, the country must reform the welfare state in order to save it, as in Australia in the mid- to late 1980s, Denmark beginning in the early 1980s, or Sweden in the early 1990s. Reference in the discourse to outside events other than economic crisis also aid reform, as in Italy's use of European monetary integration as a spur to welfare reform beginning in 1992. Generally, however, for the cognitive arguments to succeed they need to be linked to normative ones, as in Italy, where the use of European integration not only made good sense intellectually but also appealed to national pride. Where policymakers have provided the cognitive arguments on the economic necessity for reform without sufficient normative legitimization, they have often encountered great difficulties, as in France in the 1990s prior to the Jospin Government, which failed to link concerns of social solidarity with demands for neo-liberal reform, or Schröder in 1999, when he appealed to Blair's 'third way' or Jospin's French socialist values, which were widely seen as 'inappropriate' in the German context. By contrast, where the discourse has contained not only sound economic reasons but also convincing normative arguments, for example, that neo-liberal reform reinforced values of individualism and entrepreneurialism, as in Britain under Thatcher and Blair or even Australia beginning in the mid-1980s, or that changes in the welfare state that would make for a more competitive economy would also promote a more equitable distribution of public goods, as in Italy since 1992, France under Jospin, or even the Netherlands in the mid- to late 1990s, the discourse has contributed to the success of reform efforts.

Success, however, should be judged not only on whether a discourse provides good legitimizing arguments for policy reform but also whether this has helped the country move toward a solution to its problems. This is of course much more difficult to establish. But if we consider the problems of each of the families of welfare states in turn, we will see that the more successful ones are those which also had coherent coordinative and/or communicative discourses.

If the problems for Continental welfare states are their concentration on protecting the core workforce, their dependence on work-based financing, their lack of security for those with incomplete work histories, and their asymmetric assignment of gender roles, then we could assume that those countries which addressed these problems most effectively in discourse would be most successful. And in fact, if we consider the list of Continental countries, the Netherlands, which returned to a coordinative discourse between the social partners on work-related issues in the early 1980s but moved toward a more communicative discourse on welfare in the early 1990s, appears to have managed adjustment most successfully.

By contrast, Germany seems to have been the least successful so far, having failed to promote reform through either coordinative or communicative discourses in the second half of the 1990s. In between, Switzerland would appear to have done reasonably well with its balance of policies resulting from the combination of coordinative and communicative discourses, as has Italy since 1992. By contrast, Belgium, with the poverty of its coordinative discourse and its seeming lack of communicative discourse, has not done so well. For Austria, the jury is still out, given that the coordinative discourse which has until now facilitated slow, incremental change may implode, given the disruption caused by the communicative discourse—and government participation—of the extreme right. By comparison, France, although also unable to reform in the 1990s, seems to have been doing better since the June 1997 elections of the Jospin Government, given the beginnings both of a more coordinative discourse and of a more complete communicative discourse.

If the problems for Scandinavian welfare states are high taxes and how to accept greater inequalities in some aspects of the welfare state in order not to bankrupt it entirely, even while ensuring basic egalitarian principles with regard to access and services, then Denmark appears the winner. It successfully reformed the welfare state through a coordinative discourse among social partners on the need for wage restraint and a communicative discourse on the need for welfare state cutbacks, while Sweden has not been able to go as far, in part because of insufficient coordinative and communicative discourses.

Finally, if the problems for Anglo-Saxon welfare states are not so much adjustment as adjusting to the problems of adjustment, that is, poverty and the increasing split between the haves and the have-nots in the wake of liberalization, then Britain under Blair seems to have been making some headway through the communicative discourse as well as the policies. New Zealand, by contrast, seems without a coherent communicative discourse or, since the mid-1990s, coordinative discourse to address the problems which resulted from its radical adjustment policies. Only Australia, with its mix of successful coordinative and communicative discourses and its more gradual liberalization, may have successfully avoided the problems of needing to adjust to the fall-out from liberalization.

One question still remains, however. What is the specific explanatory potential of discourse analysis in the context of a project that also seeks to explain differences in national policy responses by reference to differences in economic vulnerabilities, institutional capabilities, and sequences of policy failure and policy learning? The question needs to be discussed with a view to the explanatory strategies used in the previous chapters of this volume. These rely essentially on a combination of quasi-objective problem analyses and bounded-rationality variants of rational-choice institutionalism. Policy responses to given challenges are produced by interactions among policy elites who, within the constraints of a given institutional setting, will advance their own self-interest—organizational or positional—by pursuing solutions that reflect the interests of the constituencies on whose support they depend. In a democracy, there is no question that these interest-based policy interactions will generally be accompanied by continuous flows of communications proposing, exploring, attacking and defending particular policy options. There is also no question that much or most of this communication is a mere epiphenomenon of strategic interaction, reflecting and expressing the interest-based preferences of policymakers anticipating the interest-based responses of their constituents. To the extent that this is true—and it largely is true—discourse analysis would merely restate in a different language and perhaps with different data the explanations that are also, and more directly, obtained by the rational-institutionalist analyses of the preceding chapters.

In this chapter, I have started from the working hypothesis that discourse may be more than 'cheap talk' and more than a mere epiphenomenon without causal influence. I have tried to identify episodes in the policy experience of some countries in which effective discourse was not only able to change taken-for-granted cognitive orientations—which would be compatible with a boundedly-rationalist understanding of 'policy learning'—but was also able to overcome or neutralize interest-based opposition by appealing to commonly accepted or newly activated values and normative criteria of appropriateness. Since we are inevitably dealing with highly contingent multi-factor constellations in policy research, I cannot claim that discourse, so understood, should always have identifiable causal effects. None the less, I was able to demonstrate its influence in certain of the cases discussed above. By comparing matched pairs of countries or the same country at different points in time to control for other variables, it was possible to show that, given similar events, ideas, values, interests, and institutions, the presence or absence of a coherent legitimating discourse made the difference. For example, policymakers in Britain and New Zealand faced similar economic crises, similarly divided constituency interests with welfare-state values shaped by the Beveridge model; they also shared neo-liberal ideas and operated in Westminster single-actor institutions. Nevertheless, the neo-liberal turn-around was stabilized in Britain but failed eventually in New Zealand because the cognitive and normative orientations of the British public were transformed by a highly effective communicative discourse whereas similar policies down under were hardly supported by any public discourse at all.

Similarly, the main difference in Italy between the failed Berlusconi reforms and the successful Dini reforms was that only the latter had extensive and coherent coordinative and communicative discourses, as it was in France between the failed Juppé reforms and the successful Jospin reforms, where only the latter had an extensive and coherent communicative discourse. Similar examples from other countries could be added. But these are sufficient to show that discourse needs to be included among the factors considered by social scientists when they seek to explain welfare state adjustment since the 'golden age'.

Discourse, in short, matters. Countries managed more or less successfully their adjustment to the external economic pressures beginning in the 1970s not only because of their greater or lesser economic vulnerabilities, their greater or lesser institutional capacities, and their better or worse policy responses, but also because of their more or less convincing legitimizing discourses.

5

Conclusions

FRITZ W. SCHARPF AND VIVIEN A. SCHMIDT

This book cannot have a single conclusion that neatly summarizes its three preceding chapters which, in turn, are struggling with the findings of twelve country studies and four special studies. That is the price we pay for undertaking a project which, instead of focusing on a single, well-defined hypothesis—for instance, about the effect of party-political differences on the size of the public sector—attempts to capture the complex causal constellations and sequences of changes in the economic environment and their impact on given employment and welfare-state constellations, policy responses and their effects, and the role of legitimizing discourses over three decades and in a dozen very diverse countries. We chose this procedure, which seems to violate prescriptions of good research design in theory-oriented comparative research (King, Keohane, and Verba 1994), in the hope that the wider net would allow us to capture theoretically interesting and practically significant causal linkages among factors that more narrowly focused designs could not include. The reader must judge whether that hope was fulfilled on the basis of the preceding chapters which have taken three different cuts at the material collected in the project and presented in Volume II. What we will do here is to examine a few crosscutting observations that seem to have great significance for our understanding of the present challenges confronting advanced welfare states and the options which they are facing.

5.1 From Production-Related Employment to Consumption-Oriented Services

The politically most salient criterion of success or failure for advanced welfare states has become the extent to which they are able to provide opportunities for gainful employment for all those who wish or need to find work. Since the countries included in our project differ to such an extreme degree in their employment performance, this has become a dominant theme in our comparative analyses as well. In 1998, in fact,

Switzerland had the highest employment/population rate of all advanced industrial (OECD-18) countries; Italy had the lowest rate, and the difference between the two amounted to almost 30 percentage points (Table A.5). For these differences, we have tried to provide explanations in Chapters 2 and 3. Here we intend to emphasize some commonalties in employment trends.

As was shown in Chapter 2, industrial employment in practically all OECD countries has significantly, and in many countries dramatically, declined over the last three decades. Among the countries included in our project only Denmark and, at a lower level, the Netherlands and New Zealand were able to halt this decline in the 1990s. But although they were declining, the rates of industrial employment were still far above the OECD average in Germany and Switzerland, and they were lowest in Belgium, New Zealand, France, and the Netherlands (Table A.9). In all countries, some of the decline in industrial production was compensated by a shift to production-oriented services: transport, communications, financial and business services (ISIC 7 and 8). Yet if these are considered together with agricultural and industrial production, average OECD-18 rates of production-related employment still declined steeply until the mid-1980s and have not recovered since. Among the countries in our project, the Netherlands is again the only one in which production-related employment, while still below average, did increase somewhat in the 1990s. In the same branches, employment levels are still highest in Switzerland, Austria, Denmark, and Germany—in that order—and they are lowest in Belgium, Italy, and France (Table A.8).

In short, overall employment in production plus production-related services is at best stagnant in advanced industrial economies. The reason seems fairly clear. All of the branches included in this aggregated category are by now exposed to intense international competition, and all are susceptible to the rationalizing effects of new computing, information, and communication technologies on the design, financing, production, marketing, distribution and servicing of tradable products. Thus, while there is no reason to think that the demand for industrial products is already, or will soon be, stagnating, the data suggest that competition and technology-driven productivity increases are at least keeping pace with the expansion of market demand.

By contrast, all OECD-18 countries, and all countries included in our project, had higher employment rates in the 'consumption-oriented services' toward the end of the 1990s than they had in the 1970s and 1980s, but the increases and the current employment rates are higher in the Scandinavian and Anglo-Saxon welfare states plus Switzerland than they are in Continental countries, except for the Netherlands (Table A.10). In this aggregate category, we include employment in ISIC 6—wholesale and retail trade, restaurants and hotels—and in ISIC 9—community and social services. What these 'sheltered branches' have in common is that services are locally provided and locally consumed, so that international competition, except for tourism, plays not much of role. Beyond that, ISIC 6 includes services that are generally provided in the private sector, and that have relatively low skill requirements and low productivity. The composition of ISIC 9 is much more heterogeneous, including the large blocks of education and health care, where skill requirements tend to be high, and where in our set of countries services are either publicly provided and financed or privately provided but publicly financed. The same tends to be true, at somewhat lower skill levels, of the 'social services' which may be provided by regional and local governments as well as by charities and by commercial firms, but which usually are at least subsidized from public funds. In addition, ISIC 9 includes a wide range of high-skilled and well-paid information, entertainment, recreation and therapeutic services that are privately provided and financed, but also less skilled and poorly paid household and personal services.

Unfortunately, it is not possible to separate these diverse categories in the available OECD statistics. What we can say, however, is that the continuing expansion of consumption-oriented services must have occurred in the private sector. In the OECD-18 average, the expansion of publicly provided employment culminated in the mid-1980s and has been declining thereafter. And while public-sector employment rates in Denmark and Sweden are almost twice as high as the OECD-18 average, they also have either stagnated or declined after the mid-1980s (Table A.6). If that is so, it seems safe to conclude that fiscal constraints and attempts at cost containment must also have prevented the further expansion of employment in privately provided but publicly financed health care and social services. Thus the expansion of consumer services since the mid-1980s must be due to an expansion of privately provided and privately financed service employment. Since ISIC 9 does not allow the identification of homogeneous employment areas, we have throughout taken employment in ISIC 6 as a proxy for the larger pattern. Here, present employment levels are highest in Australia, Switzerland, New Zealand, and Austria, and employment increases since the mid-1980s were greatest in the Netherlands, Austria, Australia, and Denmark, whereas Belgium, France, Italy, and Germany had very low and also stagnant levels of employment. In searching for explanations of these differences, supply-side as well as demand-side factors need to be taken into account.

In Chapters 2 and 3, we emphasized the supply side, looking primarily at factors and policies affecting the cost of labor and the flexibility of employment. Given their relatively low productivity, the market for private services could expand only if production costs were low enough to allow prices that consumers would be willing to pay. Our focus was on wage dispersion at the lower end of the wage scale, on the effects of minimum-wage legislation, and on the 'tax wedge' that social-security contributions and consumption taxes could create for jobs whose market wages were close to the reservation wages defined by welfare-state benefits. At the same time, we assumed that the expansion of private-service employment was typically achieved by small firms, often start-ups, exploring and perhaps creating local market niches characterized by uncertain demand. Thus, we also considered the effects of rigid employment conditions and employment-protection legislation that would reduce incentives to hire additional labor under conditions where the permanence of the jobs so created was uncertain. From this perspective, Anglo-Saxon countries and Switzerland with lean welfare states, small tax wedges, low minimum wages, relatively high wage dispersion and low levels of employment protection had conditions that were most favorable to the expansion of private services, whereas conditions in Scandinavian and Continental welfare states were generally unfavorable. The exceptions were Austria with exceptionally high wage dispersion, Denmark with exceptionally low social-security contributions and low employment protection, and the Netherlands with liberal rules regarding temporary employment, attractive conditions for part-time employment and a reduced tax wedge.

The demand-side perspective is less well developed in our project, but it can be reconstructed from analyses in Chapter 4 of this volume and Mary Daly's chapter in Volume II. Its focus is on the socio-cultural and socio-economic preconditions of a sustained expansion of consumption-oriented service employment. At the most abstract level, this expansion seems possible in two very different scenarios, which one might describe as 'the return of the servant society' and 'the rise of service industries', respectively. As a historical review and the comparison with third-world countries shows, the first scenario presupposes socioeconomic conditions in which the distribution of incomes and life chances is so unequal that a sufficiently large class of rich households will be able to buy the services of a much larger class of poor persons, and it also presupposes cultural orientations in which it is considered appropriate to have servants and to work as a servant. In advanced welfare states, neither of these preconditions have been present over recent decades; and the fear that they might be recreated seems to motivate much of the political resistance against proposals that are intended to facilitate the expansion of a 'low-wage labor market'.

The second scenario can be illustrated by present-day Scandinavian rather than third-world and traditional societies. There, the expansion of publicly financed social services, from daycare for young children to home care for the sick and the aged, has transformed into paid formal employment large parts of the 'caring work' that traditionally was performed 'informally' by mothers, wives and daughters in the home. The same is happening when working mothers in the United States rely on the pizza delivery service for preparing dinner and on the cleaning service for keeping the house in order. But, as Chapter 4 makes clear, this scenario is also dependent on socio-cultural norms that encourage, or at least allow, married women and mothers to seek work in the formal labor market, and to rely on public or commercial services to take over some of the caring and home-making functions. Historically, these preconditions were least fulfilled in the Continental, or 'christian-democratic' welfare states; and even though social values are changing here as elsewhere, the supportive infrastructure of day care services and all-day schools and other services facilitating the combination of work and family responsibilities is still less developed. The same is true of the incentive structure of social-insurance and tax systems that still tends to discourage the labor-market participation of married women. As the Dutch and Swiss examples show, where such institutionalized disincentives are absent, the change in social values has led to a rapid increase in the employment rate of married women over the last three decades—which in turn has contributed to a rapid increase of employment in the consumption-oriented services.

Our conclusion is, therefore, that the additional demand that drove the expansion of service employment in those countries where present employment levels are particularly high came mainly from the transformation of 'household work' into formal employment. In the Scandinavian countries, most of this expansion occurred in the public sector which, by providing universal social services, at the same time allowed married women and mothers to enter the labor market and created a wide range of jobs available to women. In Switzerland, in the Anglo-Saxon countries and in the Netherlands, the expansion of private-service employment also went hand-in-hand with a rapid increase of female labor force participation. But even though we have not studied this issue in depth, we think that the process of service expansion was more complex here than in the Scandinavian countries. Since public services did not expand here, it seems likely that the initial impulse came from the rising labor participation of better-educated middle-class women which created a need, and a demand, for affordable services, and that, under the favorable supply-side conditions discussed above, this demand could be met at reasonable prices by commercial or not-for-profit service providers. If that seems plausible then, paradoxically, the disincentives discouraging highly-skilled married women from seeking, or continuing, professional careers in most

Continental welfare states may be the main demand-side obstacle to an expansion of less-skilled service jobs—and they also may explain the very low birth rates and demographic imbalances that are threatening the inter-generational viability of Continental welfare states.

With regard to employment patterns, we may thus conclude that international economic shocks and the increasing intensity of international economic competition have had the overall effect of reducing production-related employment in practically all countries. Those countries that have been doing well in employment terms have achieved their success by an expansion of those services that are not part of the wider process of industrial production, but are provided directly to the ultimate consumer. Since these services are locally produced and consumed, they are not directly affected by changes in the international economic environment. However, their level and their rate of growth are greatly affected by supply-side and demand-side conditions which are shaped by features of national welfare states and industrial relations systems that have indeed come under increasing pressure from international capital and product markets.

5.2 The Growing Vulnerability of National Welfare and Employment Systems

In the early postwar decades, differences in the institutional structures and policies of national welfare states and industrial-relations systems did not seem to matter much for the economic viability of advanced industrial countries. In the international economic environment of 'embedded liberalism' (Ruggie 1982), with capital exchange controls, fixed exchange rates adjusted by political decisions rather than by waves of international currency speculation, and considerable leeway for imposing tariffs and non-tariff barriers to trade, countries were free to choose not only the level of their welfare-state aspirations, but also the institutions and the financing and spending patterns through which they would pursue them.

The importance of boundary control becomes clear if we compare the situation faced by the countries studied here during the postwar decades with that of 'progressive' American states in the three decades preceding the New Deal 'constitutional revolution' of 1937, which finally allowed the US Congress to adopt social security programs and to regulate labor relations at the federal level. Since the progressive movement had gained political strength at the state level at a time when a nationwide market was becoming a reality in the United States while the 'negative-commerce-clause' decisions of the Supreme Court did not allow the states to protect local producers against out-of-state competitors, the ability of progressive majorities to adopt child labor laws, work-safety rules, compulsory health insurance, or minimum wages remained tightly constrained by the pressures of interstate economic competition (Graebner 1977). As a consequence, the welfare-state solutions adopted by the American states were not only very limited in substantive terms, but also structurally very similar, since they were all shaped by the economic pressures of regulatory competition (Skocpol and Amenta 1986; Skocpol 1995).

By contrast, the welfare states covered by our project reached their maturity in a period when the nation state had control over its economic boundaries. Thus, the choice between lean and generous public benefits, between tax-financed and contribution-financed social security, and between restrictive and liberal regulations of production and employment was determined by domestic political preferences, or by the 'power-resources of the labor movement' (Korpi 1983) rather than by the compulsion of international competition. True, all countries had to pay for their imports through exports, but differences in average production costs caused by welfare-state taxes and regulations could be accommodated by the choice of an appropriate exchange rate; and if conditions changed, competitiveness could be restored by the same means.[1] Within wide limits, therefore, national governments and unions were not economically constrained in their choice of the level and type of welfare-state policies or in their choice of who should bear the costs: taxpayers, consumers in the form of higher prices, workers in the form of lower net wages, or capital owners in the form of lower profits.[2] In other words, structural differences between national welfare-state solutions did not matter much for the international viability of advanced industrial economies.

That began to change with the onset of the oil-price crises of the 1970s and early 1980s. As we showed in Chapters 2 and 3, the economic success of countries confronted with the challenges of stagflation was to a large part determined by the capacity of their wage-setting systems to control the increase in the *level* of wages. We will return to this point in the next section. By contrast, the levels and structures of welfare-state spending and financing and of employment regulations were as yet relatively unimportant as factors *influencing* economic success or failure in the international environment of the 1970s. However, the linkages coupling

---

[1] It is true that European 'small open economies' with a high dependence on foreign trade tended to develop 'corporatist' wage-setting institutions in order to maintain the international competitiveness of their exposed sectors without the need for frequent devaluation (Katzenstein 1984, 1985). But countries that did not, like France or Italy, were still viable in economic terms.

[2] While governments could manipulate the rate of return of competing financial investments, expected profits from productive investments still had to be positive and more attractive than the consumption of capital.

economic performance and welfare state structures became much tighter in the late 1980s and in the 1990s, as the gradual processes of international and, above all, European economic integration reached and surpassed the level of integration that the US economy had reached in the early decades of the twentieth century. With the almost complete abolition of capital exchange controls by the early 1990s (Table A.31), capital is no longer restricted to nationally available investment opportunities; and with the increasing abolition of tariff and non-tariff barriers to trade within the WTO, and their complete abolition within the EU, the consumers of traded goods are no longer restricted to nationally produced goods and services. Among the member states of the European Monetary Union, moreover, even the possibility of compensating for changes of international competitiveness through adjustments of the exchange rate is no longer available. In other words, they are fully exposed to the pressures of regulatory competition that had impeded the development of the welfare state at the level of American States.

If all welfare states were structurally alike, the regulatory competition among them might be abated through international agreements on minimum standards; and in the European Union even the more radical post-1937 American option of federalizing welfare-state policies might be considered (Leibfried and Pierson 1995). But although we have not specifically examined these options in the present project, we think that they are not presently available in the European Union, not only because of significant differences among member states in the level of economic development—and hence the ability to pay—but also because of institutional differences between European welfare states that would rule out agreement on common Europe-wide solutions (Scharpf 1999). Beyond the European Union, international agreements are even less likely, since countries with less vulnerable structures will have little interest in seeing their competitive advantages harmonized away. In the following sections, we will explore these differences in vulnerability, first for industrial-relations and then for welfare-state structures.

5.3 The Changing Role of Coordinated Wage Setting

From the perspective of economic viability, the specific importance of industrial relations and wage-setting practices varied significantly over the last three decades. In the stagflation period of the 1970s, what mattered was the impact of *average* wage increases on a macroeconomic constellation characterized by cost-push inflation and demand-gap unemployment. In the period of very high real interest rates in the 1980s, the supply-side effect of *branch-specific* wage settlements on the profitability of investments and production gained in importance. In the environment of the 1990s, characterized by highly contested and volatile markets, finally, the earlier requirements continue to be important, but there is now an added emphasis on wage differentiation and flexible employment conditions.

In the Introduction we used a two-dimensional scheme, reflecting the degree of state involvement and the degree of coordination in collective bargaining, to describe the four constellations that had emerged in postwar industrial relations systems: 'corporatist', 'self-coordinated', 'statist' or 'fragmented' (Fig. 1.1 above). But in view of changes over the last three decades, we now find it necessary to extend the classification to include forms of radical decentralization and the rise of market-determined individual contracting in some countries, and we also find it useful to adopt a form of representation that allows us to describe changes over time in negotiations between employers and workers as well as in the role of the state.

In the first dimension, the basic distinction is between systems where wages and working conditions are negotiated individually and those where they are negotiated collectively. In the first case, the outcome is directly influenced by the state of supply and demand on the labor market, whereas in the second case the outcome will also be affected by the relative bargaining and striking power of organized labor. But there are also significant differences among collective-bargaining systems. Negotiations are conducted in bargaining units defined at different levels and by different criteria, and among these bargaining units agreements may be either 'coordinated' by reference to their overall impact on the national economy, or they may remain 'fragmented' in the sense that outcomes are determined exclusively by reference to the interest and relative power of parties within individual bargaining units. Similarly, countries differ in the degree to which outcomes will in fact be determined by 'free collective bargaining' or by state intervention, and there is also considerable variety in the forms of state intervention, ranging from countries where state legislation merely defines the ground rules and procedures of collective negotiations to constellations where the agencies of the state are actually determining wages and the conditions of employment in great detail.

In the period from the early 1970s to the late 1990s, several countries have changed their positions significantly in the property space defined by these two dimensions. In fact, only Austria and Germany have maintained their original constellations defined by coordinated collective bargaining at the level of branches and regions and minimal or moderate state involvement, whereas coordinated bargaining in Switzerland is even less

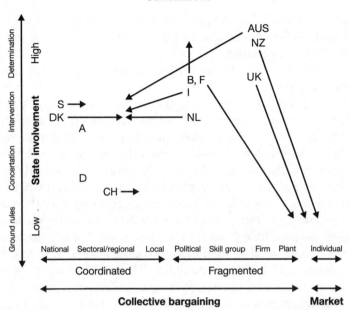

Figure 5.1 Self-coordination and state involvement in wage-setting: early 1970s
to late 1990s

regulated by the state and has recently become more decentralized. Sweden and Denmark had started from centrally coordinated wage setting with a significant 'corporatist' role of the state, and they have moved toward more decentralized, but still coordinated, bargaining patterns. In all other countries, the collective-bargaining patterns in the 1970s could be described as being 'fragmented', but with considerable differences in the type of fragmentation and in the degree and type of state involvement.

In France and Italy, and to a lesser extent in Belgium and the Netherlands, fragmentation in the 1970s was political in the sense that unions associated with different political parties, some of them committed to radical goals, competed against each other in the same industries. In Britain, by contrast, fragmentation and inter-union competition was organizationally rather than politically motivated in a constellation where even the dominant union federation, the TUC, had more than 100 member unions, some of them defined by industry, many by craft, and some with a 'general' jurisdiction that allowed them to recruit members in diverse industries. While the state was legally empowered to intervene in the wage-setting process, it did so at best intermittently and with little effect in all five countries. In Australia and New Zealand, finally, collective bargaining was equally or even more fragmented and decentralized than in Britain, but the role of the state was routinely exercised by arbitration courts issuing differentiated awards for specific branches, skill groups or other local bargaining units.

By the 1990s, the overall pattern had become more or less bimodal. Denmark, the Netherlands, Italy and Australia had converged on models of coordinated collective bargaining that could be described by 'centralized decentralization' where actual wages were determined in local or regional bargaining units, but within guidelines negotiated at national or branch levels. In Sweden, decentralization did not go beyond a shift to branch-level negotiations, and Austria, Germany, and Switzerland more or less maintained their earlier positions. At the other extreme, New Zealand had practically abolished collective bargaining in 1991, and legislation in Britain and France in the early 1980s had radically weakened the bargaining power of unions, with the consequence that negotiations were shifted to the plant level or to individual negotiations, that is, to the market-determined end of the continuum. The one exception from this bimodal convergence on either coordinated collective bargaining or the market is Belgium, where unions were still unwilling to shift to coordinated collective bargaining while governments were neither willing nor able to destroy the bases of union power. Instead, collective bargaining was almost routinely displaced by general wage settlements imposed by the government. It remains to be seen whether the recent willingness of unions to abide by the legislation limiting wage increases to those of Belgium's neighbors and competitors will lead toward another transformation toward the corporatist pattern.

By itself, of course, the classification of industrial-relations regimes would explain nothing. What matters is the goodness of fit between the capabilities of a particular regime and the economic challenges with which it is confronted at a given time. With regard to wage determination, and at the most abstract level, it is theoretically trivial that market-determined regimes will only be able to set wages at the level determined by demand and supply in the labor market.[3] By contrast, all collective-bargaining regimes have the capacity to impose wages *above* the market level. In theory, at any rate, statist and coordinated, but not fragmented, collective-bargaining regimes also should have the power to set wages *below* the level that would have resulted from the operation of demand and supply in the market. While this, clearly, must be a limited power that is continuously eroded by the market pressures of local wage drift, it was exactly the capability that would have been required in those countries that had tried to defend full employment through demand reflation in the stagflation crisis of the 1970s.

---

[3] That is meant to include 'efficiency wages' that may not be market clearing.

As was to be expected on theoretical grounds, fragmented collective-bargaining systems left to their own devices performed poorly under these conditions in all cases. It is more remarkable, however, that none of the governments in these countries—neither in Australia or New Zealand nor in France, Italy, or the United Kingdom—was politically capable of using the formal powers of the state in order to force militant workers and their unions to accept moderate wage settlements when the government was stabilizing the demand for labor. The only countries where wage restraint was achieved under full employment conditions in the 1970s were Austria and Sweden: at the time the two countries with the most effectively coordinated collective-bargaining regimes.

By contrast, the challenge to the capabilities of wage-setting institutions in the 1970s should have been met more easily in hard currency countries where monetary policy gave priority to price stability rather than to full employment. Here economic analysis suggests that unemployment would dampen the rise of market-determined wages, that local wage drift or the militancy of workers would cease to be a problem for statist systems, and that unions in coordinated as well as in fragmented collective-bargaining systems should have preferred to raise the jobs of their members through wage moderation rather than defend real wages. In fact, however, that theoretical expectation was confirmed only in Switzerland and in Germany, but not in Denmark, the Netherlands, and Belgium. Here the explanation for the difference that is suggested in Chapter 2 is not institutional but cognitive: unions that were further removed from the communicative reach of the German Bundesbank were slower to appreciate the true effectiveness of the monetary constraint.

When real interest rates were rising steeply in the 1980s, only Sweden was able to continue its successful defense of full employment, through a massive devaluation of the currency; and, remarkably, its coordinated wage-setting system, although now at the sectoral level, was still able to generate a degree of wage restraint that allowed business profits to rise in parallel with rising real interest rates. All other governments gave up the attempt to defend full employment through macroeconomic reflation and switched to hard currency policies. Confronted with rising mass unemployment, now the unions in all countries with coordinated collective-bargaining regimes were able to practise a sufficient degree of wage restraint to stop the decline of employment by the mid-1980s. This was also true in Australia, which in the early 1980s had been able to achieve an effective coordination of collective-bargaining strategies. By contrast, unions in the fragmented industrial-relations systems of Belgium, Italy, and New Zealand were still unwilling or unable to practise wage restraint in response to job losses. In Belgium, however, the lack of self-coordination was now compensated by statist wage settlements which, under conditions of high unemployment, could be effectively imposed by the government. In Italy and New Zealand, by contrast, governments in the 1980s still did not dare to impose politically unpopular wage freezes.

In Britain and France, finally, fragmented industrial-relations systems were replaced by even more decentralized bargaining patterns that approximate, but will of course not reach, the neo-liberal ideal of a perfect labor market. It is interesting to see, however, that, if judged by the success of wage restraint even under conditions of high unemployment, these countries, while doing better than other fragmented systems, were still less effective than coordinated collective-bargaining systems. One reason seems to be that coordinated wage restraint may anticipate and thus avoid job losses whereas highly decentralized wage negotiations can only respond retrospectively to changes that have taken place. Even more important seems to be the fact that, given the inevitable 'stickiness' of the employment relationship, skilled workers will retain considerable bargaining power to exploit the ability to pay of profitable firms in decentralized negotiations, whereas coordination may define a *general* wage level that ensures the survival of weaker firms in an industry and thus effectively subsidizes more profitable firms.

In short, when confronted with the international economic challenges of the 1970s and early 1980s, countries with industrial-relations regimes that facilitated coordinated wage setting were definitely in a more advantageous situation than countries with fragmented wage setting patterns. By the 1990s, these conditions not only continued but were actually reinforced by more intensive international competition and, above all, by the increasing rigidity of exchange-rate relationships among the future members of the European Monetary Union. Under these conditions, the effect of wage settlements on international competitiveness was no longer buffered by exchange-rate movements, and had increasingly direct repercussions on employment within individual branches or even firms. As a consequence, countries aspiring to EMU membership—most prominently Italy, but also Ireland and Spain—with fragmented industrial-relations systems turned to government-sponsored 'national pacts' in the 1990s in order to persuade unions of the need to orient national wage settlements to those of their nearest European competitors. In Belgium, similar negotiations failed, and the rule had to be imposed by statute—but then was observed in subsequent collective-bargaining rounds (Ebbinghaus and Hassel 2000).

Ironically, it is in Germany, where voluntary self-coordination among sectoral unions was highly effective at the national level, that the move toward the European Monetary Union is creating the greatest irritations.

Under the new conditions, EMU-wide coordination is no realistic prospect. Yet big and powerful unions like the German metal workers find it hard to consider themselves merely as one of many fragmented bargaining units in a much larger European economic space. As a consequence, they resist government efforts to discuss wage guidelines—in the context of an 'Alliance for Employment'—that would be based on a recognition of their own vulnerability to international competition rather than on their former role as strategic interlocutors in bilateral interaction with the Bundesbank (Soskice and Iversen 1998). But these are likely to be the difficulties of an adjustment period, at the end of which unions in all EMU member states will probably have learned the lesson that in a common-currency area wage increases that exceed productivity increases have to be paid for in job losses.

That, however, is not the greatest challenge that industrial-relations systems had to face in the 1990s. From what was said in Chapters 2 and 3, it follows that the pressures of international competition in product and capital markets have created conditions in which employment levels in the exposed and in the sheltered sectors are positively associated with an increase in productivity-oriented wage differentials and flexible employment relations (Eichengreen and Iversen 1999). These requirements are most easily met by extremely decentralized systems in which weakened unions are no longer able to mobilize organized resistance against market forces. In this group, Britain and France were joined by New Zealand, which was moved from 'fragmented' to 'market determined' by the legislation introducing individual contracting in 1991. Switzerland, the most decentralized among the coordinated collective-bargaining systems, is also well placed in this regard.

In theory, coordinated but more centralized industrial-relations systems should have considerable difficulties in allowing the greater differentiation and flexibility required for competitive success in highly contested and volatile product markets. However, Denmark, the Netherlands, and Italy have been able to develop fairly effective forms of 'centralized decentralization', and functionally equivalent solutions are available in Austria and Australia. In all these cases, the basic—minimal or maximal—rate of *general* wage increase is determined at the sectoral or at the national level, presumably—and in the Netherlands explicitly—with a view to average international competitiveness. In the light of these guidelines, effective wage increases are then determined by negotiations at lower levels with a view to the specific conditions faced by individual branches, regions or firms.

The greatest difficulty with the new requirements seem to be encountered in Germany and Belgium, but for different reasons. In Germany, collective bargaining is conducted by highly centralized sectoral unions and employers' associations at the level of regions, and works councils do not have the right to negotiate wages that depart from the regional contract. Coordination is the result of informal wage leadership, typically exercised by the large metal-workers union which tends to choose a region with profitable firms for—often highly conflictual—negotiations over a pilot contract that will then set the pattern for other regions and for other industries. In the 1970s and 1980s, this bargaining pattern often produced very effective *general* wage restraint, which usually went together with above-average increases for the lowest-paid workers. In recent years, however, the commitment to relatively uniform and solidaristic wage setting has contributed to catastrophic de-industrialization in eastern Germany, and even in western Germany smaller firms have increasingly found the general settlements too high and too inflexible for their own survival. Since the unions are unwilling to accept 'opening clauses' in the regional contract, firms have begun to quit their employers' associations in increasing numbers. The emerging pattern is thus more diversified than before, with large and highly productive firms continuing to operate under uniform and relatively rigid rules, while a growing segment of the industry is no longer bound by collective agreements. A similar pattern seems to have existed in Italy all along.

In Belgium, by contrast, free collective bargaining was allowed in only a few years over the last two decades, and when agreement 'in the shadow of the state' was not forthcoming, governments directly imposed wage settlements by statute. While this practice was highly effective in assuring general wage restraint, uniform statutory wage setting could not possibly deal with the need for the continuous adjustment of wage relativities in response to skill-specific, sectoral and regional differences and changes in the supply and demand for labor. Since unions and employers could not be relied upon to perform this function, and since Australian-type procedures for decentralized arbitration are not available, the government was practically compelled to impose and maintain over-standardized settlements. In effect, therefore, Belgium and Germany were the only OECD countries where wage differentiation decreased, rather than increased, from the early 1980s to the mid-1990s (Table A.21).

5.4 How Do Welfare-State Differences Matter?

Industrial relations have a direct influence on wages and employment conditions, and thus on production-related as well as on consumption-related employment, and they are also directly affected by changes in international product and capital markets. For the welfare state, the influences in both directions are less obvious, but they are equally or even more important than is true of industrial relations.

As was pointed out in Chapter 2, Scandinavian, Anglo-Saxon and Continental countries differ significantly in the extent to which the benefits and services that are characteristic of all advanced welfare states are financed from general tax revenues, from wage-based social insurance contributions, or by—often mandatory—private provision. Some functions—social assistance and education, for instance—are tax-financed in all three groups of countries. Health care is tax-financed in the Scandinavian countries and in the United Kingdom, whereas it is financed by wage-based contributions in most Continental countries, and, until recently, by voluntary private insurance in Switzerland. Retirement incomes, finally, are financed by a combination of tax-based basic pensions and mandatory private provision in the Anglo-Saxon countries, Denmark, the Netherlands, and Switzerland, whereas most other Continental countries have systems of compulsory, wage-based contributions which, for the larger part of the population, are supposed to provide a single, earnings-related pension supporting the male breadwinner and his spouse. In general, one could say, therefore, that the Scandinavian welfare state was primarily financed by the progressive income tax, that the Anglo-Saxon countries relied on combinations of tax-financing and private provision, and that Continental welfare states depended primarily on wage-based contributions.

During the postwar 'golden age', all three models performed satisfactorily in terms of their welfare state goals, and all three modes of financing were equally viable economically. In the macroeconomic crises of the 1970s and 1980s, financial burdens on the welfare state increased in all countries that could not prevent major job losses. Anglo-Saxon countries that had only rudimentary systems of unemployment insurance were faced with an increase of social inequality and poverty as private provision could no longer be relied upon to provide income support for those who did not work. As a result, the relative importance of tax-financed social assistance benefits increased considerably. In Scandinavian countries, job losses led to increasing expenditures either on active labor market policy or on generous and long-term unemployment benefits. In Continental countries, where unemployment benefits were not quite as generous, the availability of earnings-related public pensions or disability benefits provided early-exit options from the labor market which came to be preferred over mass layoffs by employers and workers alike, and which added considerably to the long-term financial burdens of the welfare state (Ebbinghaus, Volume II).

Initially, the differences in the sources of financing mattered only in so far as job losses would directly reduce revenue from wage-based contributions, with the consequence that in Continental welfare states contribution rates were pushed up by rising expenditures as well as by fewer contributors. Economically, however, even these differences only became critical as national boundaries lost their effectiveness in sheltering national product and capital markets in the 1980s and 1990s, with the consequence that welfare-state goals could no longer be realized at the expense of captive capital owners and captive consumers. That change had practically no effect on solutions that relied on private insurance or on pension funds for the financing of health care and of earnings-related retirement incomes. It had some effect on tax-financed financed systems, and it had major consequences for systems relying primarily on wage-based contributions.

In the postwar decades, tax-based Scandinavian systems could rely on rising revenues from progressive income taxes in order to finance public services and social benefits and to achieve a considerable redistribution of incomes in the process. Under conditions of high capital mobility, however, taxes on incomes from financial assets were increasingly difficult to collect, whereas taxes on business profits appeared as a disincentive to productive investments and employment. Moreover, both became the object of international tax competition after Ronald Reagan and Margaret Thatcher had cut peak rates of progressive income-tax schedules in the 1980s (Ganghof, Volume II). If nevertheless the GDP share of revenue from personal and corporate income taxes remained stable in the OECD-18 average, and increased considerable in some countries (Table A.24), this seems to be due to a combination of strategies intended to immunize revenues against erosion. The first, generally described as 'tax-cuts-cum-base-broadening', eliminated tax exemptions while reducing peak rates to a level where the relocation of taxable assets to lower-tax jurisdictions became less attractive. The second such strategy found its clearest expression in the 'dual income tax' solutions adopted in Sweden and other Scandinavian countries. It reduces the taxation of all capital incomes to a low, proportional rate while maintaining high peak rates and a progressive schedule for incomes from labor. Denmark, where this scheme had actually originated, decided to move instead to an even more differentiated system where less mobile capital assets are taxed at higher rates than those that are most susceptible to international temptations.

But even if they are able to maintain revenue levels, these solutions weaken the welfare state by counteracting either the redistributive functions of the progressive income tax or the principle that equal incomes, regardless of their source, should be taxed at equal rates. The same can be said of the shift to consumption taxes which played a significant role in New Zealand, and some role in Denmark and the Netherlands (Table A.25). If they are collected in the form of value-added taxes, and according to the 'country of destination' principle, on locally consumed goods and services, their tax base is relatively immobile internationally, and they are thus immune to international competition, but their regressive character also reduces the redistributive potential of the welfare state.

Compared with taxes on capital incomes, social-security contributions also have the advantage that their tax base is immobile and thus immune to the international temptations of tax avoidance and tax evasion. Their major disadvantage is that they directly increase non-wage labor costs. But this disadvantage would not necessarily affect employment under the conditions prevailing in most countries until the 1980s. Regardless of how wage-based contributions were formally allocated between employers and workers, their economic impact could be shifted to consumers as long as effects on international competitiveness could be neutralized through adjustable or flexible exchange rates. It thus appears quite reasonable, from the perspective of national tax authorities, that the GDP-share of social-security contributions increased steeply in the crisis period from the early 1970s to the mid-1980s (Table A.26). By then, however, the situation had begun to change among the countries that had effectively reduced exchange-rate fluctuations by joining the European Monetary System, and by now it has been completely transformed among the members of the European Monetary Union.

With a common currency and in the absence of trade barriers, European consumers can no longer be made to pay more for domestic products than for imports, and with completely integrated capital markets, business profits can no longer be squeezed in order to accommodate higher non-wage labor costs. Thus, any increase of social security contributions, unless it was fully and immediately absorbed by a reduction of net wages, would now reduce the international competitiveness of national products and hence employment. Thus, countries like Austria, Germany, and Italy, that ignored this constraint in the 1990s, paid for it by above-average losses of business employment (Table A.7). As a consequence, and more important for present purposes, wage-based contributions have now become even more vulnerable to international regulatory competition than is true of income taxes. Countries which have come to depend heavily on this source of revenue—that is to say, practically all Continental welfare states—are now greatly tempted to seek competitive advantages by reducing social contributions in general, or at least the part raised from employers, with the consequence that competitor countries will then come under pressure to respond in kind.

But even if beggar-my-neighbor strategies could somehow be ruled out, the situation is complicated by the fact that all countries with high social-security contributions—not only the Continental welfare states, but also Sweden and Switzerland—may also have very good non-competitive reasons to reduce these. As was shown in Chapter 2, at the lower end of the labor market, where net wages are close to the reservation wage defined by social assistance benefits, the tax wedge created by proportional, rather than progressive, social contributions tends to price a wide range of less productive service jobs out of price-sensitive markets. It makes sense, therefore, that, in order to improve the employment opportunities of the most disadvantaged groups, France, Belgium, and the Netherlands have recently adopted very expensive programs reducing employers' social-security contributions—and, in France, the value-added tax also—on low-paid service jobs. While these measures will not affect international competitiveness in the exposed sectors, a major across-the-board reduction of contributions to pension insurance, which is presently being discussed in Germany, would have an impact on competition that could start a round of downward adjustments in other countries. It is here that proposals for internationally coordinated national reforms of the welfare state could have their most beneficial effects (Scharpf 1999).

Coordination would be all the more desirable in light of the fact that wage-based social security systems are in need of reform for other reasons as well: because of their lack of neutrality with regard to demographic changes, to changes of gender roles, and to changes between full-time and part-time dependent employment and various forms of self-employment. By themselves, these changes are not direct consequences of the international challenges that have been the main focus of our project. But the fact that social-security contributions are directly implicated in international economic competition will also increase the difficulties of reforming systems that are in trouble for other reasons. Thus, for example, all countries seem to be struggling with a seemingly inexorable rise of health care costs caused by the progress of medical science and by the graying of the population. But whereas this can be treated as a question of shifting consumption patterns in private-insurance systems, and as a question of budgetary priorities in countries with a tax-financed public health service, it has become an issue that directly implicates the international competitiveness of the economy in countries like France or Germany where health care is financed by wage-based insurance contributions.

Similarly, pension systems in all countries are confronted with the need to adjust to the financial implications of falling birth rates and increasing longevity. But these adjustments have the most significant economic implications and are also politically most difficult in those Continental welfare states which are financing nearly all retirement incomes through wage-based contributions to pay-as-you go public insurance systems. Here, either a shrinking active population must accept having to pay for generous benefits to the present generation of pensioners while knowing that the benefits they can expect after retirement will be much lower, or governments would have to drastically reduce the current benefits of a generation of pensioners whose life plans had been based on expectations defined by the existing system. By contrast, the level of intergenerational conflict is lower in countries where the pay-as-you-go element is limited to a basic pension and where earnings-related elements are supplied by funded systems, whether public, mandated, or entirely private. At the same time, these countries are able to consider reform options with less attention to their implications for international economic competition.

What was said about the lack of intergenerational neutrality of the Continental welfare state applies equally to its implication in changing gender roles and work patterns. If married women are fully insured by the contributions of a working husband, and if a full family pension can be obtained only by a lifetime of full-time dependent employment, married women have less reason to seek employment, and part-time employment and interrupted work biographies will appear less attractive than is true in countries providing a basic pension for all residents or taxpayers. By the same token, contribution-based systems are not well placed for dealing with the widening gray zone between traditional dependent employment and economically secure self-employment that is associated with the outsourcing of specialist functions in industry and the growing importance of freelance work in a wide range of service branches. In their typical form, Continental social insurance systems either have to force these rapidly evolving work forms into the straight-jacket of standard dependent employment, or they would leave workers without any social protection against the risks of their precarious economic circumstances.

In short, the policy legacies that advanced welfare states are carrying forward from the defining choices of the early postwar period—which, in turn, were often path-dependent extrapolations from structural features that had already been in place at the end of the nineteenth century—have come to have much greater importance for their international economic viability than was the case a few decades ago. While it is true, as has been shown in Chapters 2 and 3 above, that the size of the welfare state as such, or the overall tax burden, has no negative impact on economic performance, international competitiveness, or employment levels, it is equally true that the specific shape of national welfare-state institutions and programs, and in particular the different ways in which the welfare state is paid for, have greatly gained in economic importance. At the same time, however, the fact that these characteristics have an effect on international economic competitiveness adds to the difficulties which national reform efforts must overcome.

5.5 The Diverse Politics of Adjustment

Countries are facing different problems that arise from specific character-istics of their welfare states and industrial relations systems, but their abil-ity to cope with these problems is also constrained by institutional settings and, ultimately, by the need for policymakers to respond to political con-stituencies whose interests have been shaped by these very characteristics. That is not meant to say that group interests alone should explain policy outcomes. In Chapters 2 and 3, we pointed to the importance of institu-tional conditions that would facilitate or impede effective policy responses, and in Chapter 4 we discussed value orientations and their influence on the public discourses that might support or impede policy changes. But there is also no question that in a democracy policymakers will generally try to chart courses of action in anticipation of interest-based responses, and that their opponents will similarly choose to con-front them on policy choices that are unpopular among the affected groups. The basic argument is not new (Pierson 1996), but it can be for-mulated more generally and more precisely on the basis of the information collected in our comparative project. Put most simply, we suggest that wel-fare states differ in the functions for which the state has assumed direct responsibility, as distinct from facilitating or ensuring their performance in the private sector. To the extent that these functions are performed effectively, and that people have come to base their life plans on their con-tinuing performance, they will have created political constituencies that can be mobilized to resist their dismantling. By the same token, however, if people have come to rely on private provision for the achievement of these same functions, they can also be mobilized to resist policy changes that would either devalue their existing private investments or reduce their ability to maintain these in the future.

In the lean British welfare state, for instance, most functions beyond education, the national health service, and social assistance for the truly needy are left to private provision, whereas Continental welfare states also provide earnings-related social insurance and retirement incomes, and Scandinavian welfare states provide all of these and also universal and high-quality social services plus the concomitant employment opportun-ities in the public sector. It is not surprising therefore, that taxpayer resist-ance was and is perceived as a critical political issue in low-tax Britain, where New Labour based its successful 1997 campaign on the promise of no tax increases, whereas in high-tax Sweden the social democrats returned to power in 1994 with a consolidation program that involved significantly higher tax rates. With some over-simplification, one could thus say that in Britain a neo-liberal party must have made egregious political mistakes to lose a general election; that in Sweden or Denmark no party could win with a program challenging the full-service welfare state; and that in Continental countries pension and unemployment insurance systems are politically sacrosanct, but that political support is lacking for proposals that would expand consumption-oriented services in the public sector or in the private sector.

5.5.1 Anglo-Saxon Welfare States

In the international economic environment of the last three decades, the characteristic postwar configuration of Anglo-Saxon welfare states—combining very lean public income support for the unemployed and for pensioners with policies ensuring full employment in jobs that allow private savings to provide for retirement incomes—became unbalanced because the state was no longer able to uphold its full-employment promise. Since political support for earnings-related insurance was lacking,[4] the rise of unemployment was associated with an increase in poverty and inequality that challenged the normative foundations of the Beveridgean welfare state: a challenge to which Margaret Thatcher and, less successfully, the post-1991 conservative government in New Zealand responded with a neo-liberal discourse emphasizing individual responsibility (Chapter 4, this volume).

Regardless of the ideological preferences of their governments, however, rising unemployment in Anglo-Saxon welfare states put an increasing burden on social assistance which, at least for low-income families, was and is about as generous as unemployment support is for the same families in Continental or even Scandinavian welfare states (Table A.34). However, since in Britain and later in New Zealand the destruction of union power and the radical decentralization of wage setting had drastically lowered minimum wages, generous social assistance for families with children created a trap in which it wouldn't pay for an unskilled worker to accept one of the available low-paid jobs. Hence even though wage differentiation and employment in the less productive services are increasing, unemployment among low-skilled workers remains disproportionately high, and the large

---

[4] In Britain, a program introduced by the Labour government was immediately scrapped by Margaret Thatcher.

number of families in which no person is working is among the major concerns of present-day British social policy (Jordan 1998). This explains why the transformation of welfare into 'workfare' has become a major preoccupation of social and employment policy in Anglo-Saxon welfare states. Thus unemployment benefits were transformed into a job-seeker allowance by Margaret Thatcher, and in Australia, Britain, and New Zealand social assistance has been complemented by 'in-work benefits' for low-paid workers from poor families that follow the logic of the American Earned Incomes Tax Credit. The intent, in all these cases, is to reduce family poverty in the only way that is politically feasible in societies in which the wide majority of voters have no stake of their own in income-support programs, and in which the willingness to pay for altruistic redistribution to the 'deserving poor' is thus predicated on the reciprocal notion that recipients should be obliged to do all they can to help themselves. By contrast, expenditures to improve universal education and, in Britain, health care appear to be less politically constrained. The same is true, as the Australian and Swiss examples show, for initiatives that transform voluntary into mandatory private pension programs, as long as universal coverage is achieved without devaluing existing investments.

5.5.2 Scandinavian Welfare States

In the Scandinavian countries, the constituency of universal social services includes middle class families that have come to depend on the services as well as on the employment opportunities they provide. By the same token, earnings-related social insurance benefits have wide political support, with the consequence that social assistance plays less of a role in practice and has much lower political salience than is true in Anglo-Saxon countries. Thus, at least in principle, all who must pay are also potential beneficiaries, and the intergenerational conflict is also muted because retirement benefits are divided into a tax-financed basic pension and a compulsory earnings-related occupational pension that is partly funded rather than being financed on a pay-as-you-go basis. Since distributional conflict has low political salience under these circumstances, the comparatively severe cutbacks of welfare-state benefits required by the Swedish unemployment and fiscal crisis of the early 1990s could be discussed pragmatically, and decided by broad political consensus on the basis of perceived need, rather than being fought over in a Manichean battle between freedom and social justice.

There are, however, two unresolved problems of the Scandinavian welfare state. One arises from the fact that international capital mobility and tax competition have required adjustments of income-tax schedules that are normatively incompatible with the exalted aspirations to social equality that have characterized at least the Swedish model. It is as yet unclear whether pragmatic solutions of the 'dual-income-tax' variety can be integrated into a new social-democratic vision of the just society, or whether they will remain reluctant concessions to a capitalist world economy in which the Swedish model must somehow survive. The second challenge is practical as well as normative. From what was said in Chapters 2 and 3, it follows that public-sector employment cannot continue to increase, as it did until the mid-1980s. Hence if the Scandinavian welfare state should stick to its legitimizing commitment to provide employment opportunities for all men and women who seek work, it must create conditions that are favorable to the expansion of consumption-oriented private services. For Denmark, the required adjustment does not seem to be much of a problem, mainly because flexible employment conditions, buffered by very generous unemployment benefits, have long been part of the policy legacy of a country whose economy is dominated by small firms. Moreover, Danish minority governments are free to seek political support for their policy proposals where they can find it. In Sweden, however, greater wage differentiation and less employment protection represent major challenges to the dominant union federation (LO) which, even though it lost its centralized control over collective bargaining, still has an effective veto over the policies that can be adopted by left-of-center governments led by the social-democratic party.

5.5.3 *Continental Welfare States*

From the analyses presented in this volume, it follows that the adjustment of Continental welfare states would benefit from policy changes reducing the dependence on non-wage labor costs and facilitating an increase of consumption-oriented service employment. It also follows that these are changes that are particularly hard to bring about politically. The main difficulty, on both scores, arises from pay-as-you-go, contribution-based, and earnings-related pension systems which, as we have shown, create a large tax wedge, discourage female labor participation, exacerbate intergenerational conflict, and are highly vulnerable to international regulatory competition. But even if everybody agreed on the desirability of a switch to the Scandinavian-Dutch-Swiss combination of a tax-financed basic pension with a funded occupational pension, the transition would be objectively difficult, because entitlements accrued under the present system would have to be honored while the currently active generation would also have to build up the funds for its own retirement. Nevertheless, practicable paths from here to there might be found (Miegel and Wahl 1999). That they have not yet been taken in most Continental welfare states is due to political obstacles.

In Continental countries even marginal adjustments within the existing structure of the pension system can easily turn into a political suicide program as unions and some parts of the opposition will mobilize the fears of present-day and would-be pensioners, while others will play up the burdens that the younger generation must carry, and while business will pillory the government for allowing non-wage labor costs to destroy the competitiveness of the economy. Under these no-win conditions, governments can expect to be punished for whatever they do; thus reforms are likely to fail unless they have the support of a very broad coalition including all major parties and organized interests groups—in which case one should generally expect no more than marginal reductions of benefit levels within the existing structure of entitlements. In fact, none of the countries that find themselves in this trap—Austria, Belgium, France, Germany, and Italy—has so far been able to come up with structural reforms approximating the much more robust solutions which, by lucky historical accident, have evolved in the Netherlands and in Switzerland.

If organized opposition and the anticipation of electoral resistance is blocking pension reform, the lack of progress on service employment is explained by a lack of organized political support. Jobs which do not presently exist have no political constituency demanding their creation, either on the demand side or on the supply side. With the exception of education and health care, where personnel shortages in existing services do create some political pressures for expansion—which generally are running into the fiscal constraints that have prevented the rise of public-sector employment practically everywhere since the mid-1980s (Table A.6)—service employment and the conditions that could facilitate its expansion have no political lobby. In the Netherlands, the rise of part-time employment and of temporary employment had to become a massive reality before unions began to take a serious interest in regularizing and improving the conditions of part-time and temporary workers (Visser 1999a). And even then, the 'flexi' side of the 'flexicurity' strategy—that is, the relaxation of employment protection for workers in regular, full-time jobs—has so far remained very limited, and the Netherlands is still among the countries with the strictest rules protecting workers against dismissal (Table A.34). In Germany, as in Sweden, when the social democrats returned to power, they reversed even the very limited relaxation of dismissal rules that the conservative predecessor governments had dared to enact. In other words, unions tend to represent present job holders, and, wherever they have a *de facto* veto over government policy, the deregulation of employment conditions that would facilitate an expansion of private-service jobs is unlikely to be politically viable.

5.6 Work and Welfare: From Vulnerability to Competitiveness?

This book, and our project as a whole, has focused on the risks rather than on the opportunities associated with economic internationalization and the loss of national boundary control. That is not meant to deny that wider and richer human options are opened up by world-wide communication and exchange, and by the associated acceleration of technical innovations. Nevertheless, for the advanced welfare states included in our project, these new opportunities would come at a high price if they had to be paid for by abandoning the postwar gains in social security and social equality.

Our project demonstrates that all advanced welfare states were confronted with massive challenges over the last three decades, and that, regardless of the political orientations of their governments, none of them could fully defend the achievements of their postwar 'golden age'. At the same time, however, our project shows that the loss of national boundary control is not tantamount to a loss of salient policy choices. While all countries were and are under pressure to adjust, their adjustment paths differ: not only because they started from different initial positions, but also because their policy aspirations continue to differ. We have been able to show that Anglo-Saxon, Scandinavian, and Continental welfare states face very different challenges in an internationalized economic environment, and that coping with these challenges is most difficult in the traditional Continental constellation. But we have also found that in each group of countries there is at least one which was able to maintain or even raise its previous welfare-state aspirations, in modified form to be sure, without endangering the viability of its economy in the international environment. Moreover, some of our 'success stories' had not been successful all along. Australia, Denmark, and the Netherlands had been in deep trouble, exacerbated by manifest policy failures in the 1970s, before they achieved a remarkable comeback in the 1990s. Nor was their success achieved by wholesale welfare retrenchment, let alone by a dismantling of the welfare state. Australia and Switzerland have in fact expanded welfare-state protection during the last decade and a half, and Denmark and the Netherlands continue to be among the most generous social-policy systems in the OECD world.

These countries show, then, that it is indeed possible to achieve and maintain very different levels of welfare-state aspirations in an open economy. But they also show that the achievement of welfare goals at any level presupposes the recognition and acceptance of tight economic constraints on the choice of means. Welfare states remain internationally viable only if their systems of taxation and regulation do not reduce the competitiveness of their economies in open product and capital markets—which implies that, by and large, redistribution must be achieved through public expenditures rather than through the regulation of employment relations, and that the costs of the welfare state have to be collected from the non-capital incomes and the consumption expenditures of the non-mobile population. Within these economic constraints, however, the overall size of the welfare state and the extent of redistribution remain a matter of political choice.

STATISTICAL APPENDIX

Table A.1 *GDP per capita in purchasing power parities (USA = 100)*

Year	A	AUS	B	CAN	CH	D	DK	F	FL	I	IRL	JAP	N	NL	NZ	S	UK	USA
1970	62	70	65	73	104	82	72	72	59	62	38	59	60	70	69	78	66	100
1971	64	72	66	74	106	82	72	74	59	61	38	60	61	71	70	77	66	100
1972	65	71	67	74	104	82	73	74	61	61	39	62	61	70	69	76	66	100
1973	65	71	68	76	103	82	72	74	62	62	38	63	61	70	70	75	67	100
1974	69	72	71	79	105	84	73	77	64	65	40	62	65	74	74	79	68	100
1975	70	74	72	82	100	85	73	78	66	65	42	65	69	74	73	82	69	100
1976	70	74	73	83	96	86	75	78	63	66	41	64	70	75	72	80	68	100
1977	71	71	71	82	96	86	73	78	61	66	42	64	70	73	66	76	67	100
1978	69	70	70	82	93	86	71	77	60	65	43	65	70	72	63	74	67	100
1979	71	71	70	83	93	88	73	78	63	68	43	67	73	72	64	75	68	100
1980	74	73	74	84	99	90	74	80	67	71	45	69	77	74	65	78	68	100
1981	73	74	73	85	98	89	72	79	67	70	45	70	76	72	67	77	66	100
1982	76	74	76	84	100	92	77	83	71	73	47	74	79	73	70	80	69	100
1983	76	72	75	84	98	91	77	81	71	72	45	73	80	72	69	79	70	100
1984	73	72	72	83	94	89	76	77	69	69	44	71	80	70	68	78	67	100
1985	73	73	71	85	95	90	77	76	69	69	45	72	82	70	67	78	68	100
1986	72	72	71	85	95	90	78	76	70	70	44	73	83	71	67	78	69	100
1987	72	73	71	86	94	90	77	76	71	70	45	74	83	70	65	78	71	100
1988	72	72	72	86	94	90	75	77	72	71	45	76	80	69	63	77	72	100
1989	74	73	73	85	96	90	75	78	74	72	48	78	79	70	62	77	72	100
1990	76	73	75	83	97	91	75	79	74	74	52	81	80	73	61	77	72	100
1991	77	72	77	82	97	76	78	81	69	77	55	85	83	73	60	75	70	100
1992	80	72	81	81	99	80	78	82	64	78	59	87	88	76	61	73	72	100
1993	79	73	80	80	96	76	79	77	65	73	59	85	88	73	63	70	70	100
1994	79	73	80	80	94	77	80	75	64	73	62	83	86	73	63	69	70	100
1995	79	73	79	80	94	78	81	75	67	74	65	82	86	75	64	71	67	100
1996	80	73	78	77	89	76	82	73	67	74	65	84	91	75	62	70	69	100
1997	79	72	77	78	88	76	83	72	69	73	69	81	91	75	61	69	69	100

Sources: OECD (1999h): own calculations.

Table A.2 *Growth rates of real GDP (% change from previous period)*

Year	A	AUS	B	CAN	CH	D	DK	F	FL	I	IRL	JAP	N	NL	NZ	S	UK	USA	OECD-18
1970	7.1	6.3	6.4	2.6	6.4	5.0	2.0	5.7	7.5	5.3	2.7	10.3	2.0	5.7	3.3	6.5	2.4	0.1	4.8
1971	5.1	5.2	3.7	5.5	4.3	3.1	2.7	4.8	2.1	1.6	3.5	4.4	4.6	4.2	2.7	0.9	2.0	3.3	3.5
1972	6.2	3.5	5.2	5.4	3.5	4.3	5.3	4.4	7.6	2.9	6.5	8.4	5.2	3.3	1.6	2.3	3.6	5.5	4.7
1973	4.9	5.0	6.1	7.2	3.2	4.8	3.6	5.4	6.6	6.5	4.7	8.0	4.1	4.7	9.0	4.0	7.3	5.8	5.6
1974	3.9	2.2	4.1	4.1	1.2	0.2	-0.9	3.1	3.1	4.7	4.3	-1.2	5.2	4.0	11.3	3.2	-1.7	-0.6	2.8
1975	-0.4	2.9	-1.4	2.2	-6.7	-1.3	-0.7	-0.3	1.1	-2.1	5.7	3.1	4.2	-0.1	-5.1	2.6	-0.7	-0.4	0.1
1976	4.6	3.7	5.6	5.5	-0.8	5.3	6.5	4.2	0.3	6.5	1.4	4.0	6.8	5.1	3.3	1.1	2.8	5.4	4.0
1977	4.7	0.9	0.5	3.5	2.4	2.8	1.6	3.2	0.1	2.9	8.2	4.4	3.6	2.3	-1.3	-1.6	2.4	4.7	2.5
1978	-0.4	3.2	2.8	4.1	0.6	3.0	1.5	3.4	2.2	3.7	7.2	5.3	4.5	2.4	-6.4	1.8	3.4	5.4	2.6
1979	5.5	4.7	2.2	4.2	2.4	4.2	3.5	3.2	7.3	5.7	3.1	5.5	4.3	2.2	1.5	3.8	2.8	2.8	3.8
1980	2.3	2.3	4.4	1.4	9.9	1.0	-0.4	1.6	5.3	3.5	3.1	2.8	5.0	1.2	0.4	1.7	-2.2	-0.3	2.4
1981	-0.1	3.6	-1.3	3.0	1.6	0.1	-0.9	1.2	1.6	0.5	3.3	3.2	1.0	-0.5	4.7	0.0	-1.3	2.3	1.2
1982	1.9	-0.6	1.4	-2.9	-1.4	-0.9	3.0	2.5	3.6	0.5	2.3	3.1	0.2	-1.2	3.3	1.0	1.8	-2.1	0.9
1983	2.8	1.0	0.0	2.8	0.5	1.8	2.5	0.7	3.0	1.2	-0.2	2.3	3.5	1.7	2.5	1.8	3.7	4.0	2.0
1984	0.3	7.0	2.5	5.7	3.0	2.8	4.4	1.3	3.1	2.6	4.4	3.9	5.9	3.3	8.5	4.0	2.4	7.0	4.0
1985	2.2	4.7	1.0	5.4	3.4	2.0	4.3	1.9	3.3	2.8	3.1	4.4	5.2	3.1	1.6	1.9	3.8	3.6	3.2
1986	2.3	2.2	1.5	2.6	1.6	2.3	3.6	2.5	2.4	2.8	-0.4	2.9	3.6	2.8	0.6	2.3	4.2	3.1	2.4
1987	1.7	4.4	2.4	4.1	0.7	1.5	0.3	2.3	4.1	3.1	4.7	4.2	2.0	1.4	0.7	3.1	4.4	2.9	2.7
1988	3.2	3.8	4.7	4.9	3.1	3.7	1.2	4.5	4.9	3.9	5.2	6.2	-0.1	2.6	2.7	2.3	5.2	3.8	3.6
1989	4.2	4.2	3.6	2.5	4.3	3.6	0.3	4.3	5.7	2.9	5.8	4.8	0.9	4.7	-0.8	2.4	2.1	3.4	3.3
1990	4.6	1.2	3.0	0.3	3.7	5.7	1.2	2.5	0.0	2.2	8.5	5.1	2.0	4.1	0.3	1.4	0.6	1.2	2.6
1991	3.4	-1.3	1.6	-1.9	-0.8	5.0	1.4	0.8	-7.1	1.1	2.0	3.8	3.1	2.3	-2.3	-1.1	-1.5	-0.9	0.4
1992	1.3	2.7	1.5	0.9	-0.1	2.2	1.3	1.2	-3.6	0.6	4.2	1.0	3.3	2.0	0.6	-1.4	0.1	2.7	1.1
1993	0.5	4.0	-1.5	2.5	-0.5	-1.2	0.8	-1.3	-1.2	-1.2	3.1	0.3	2.7	0.8	4.8	-2.2	2.3	2.3	0.8
1994	2.5	5.3	2.4	3.9	0.5	2.7	5.8	2.8	4.5	2.2	7.3	0.6	5.5	3.2	6.1	3.3	4.4	3.5	3.7
1995	2.1	4.1	2.6	2.2	0.6	1.2	3.2	2.1	5.1	2.9	11.1	1.5	3.8	2.3	3.3	3.9	2.8	2.3	3.2
1996	1.6	3.7	1.3	1.2	0.0	1.3	3.2	1.6	3.6	0.7	7.4	3.9	5.5	3.1	2.7	1.3	2.6	3.4	2.7
1997	2.5	2.8	3.0	3.7	1.7	2.2	3.3	2.3	6.1	1.5	9.8	0.8	3.4	3.6	3.1	1.8	3.5	3.9	3.3
1998	3.1	3.6	2.9	3.0	1.7	2.7	2.4	3.1	5.0	1.5	9.1	-2.6	2.3	3.8	0.2	2.8	2.7	3.5	2.8

Sources: OECD (1999g); own calculations.

Table A.3 *Consumer prices (% change from previous period)*

Year	A	AUS	B	CAN	CH	D	DK	F	FL	I	IRL	JAP	N	NL	NZ	S	UK	USA	OECD-18
1970	4.4	3.9	3.9	3.4	3.6	3.4	5.8	5.2	2.8	5.0	8.2	7.7	10.6	3.6	6.5	7.0	6.4	5.9	5.4
1971	4.7	6.1	4.3	2.8	6.6	5.3	5.8	5.5	6.5	4.8	8.9	6.1	6.2	7.5	10.4	7.4	9.4	4.3	6.3
1972	6.3	5.8	5.4	4.8	6.7	5.5	6.6	6.2	7.1	5.7	8.7	4.5	7.2	7.8	6.9	6.0	7.1	3.3	6.2
1973	7.6	9.5	7.0	7.6	8.7	6.9	9.3	7.3	10.7	10.8	11.4	11.7	7.5	8.0	8.2	6.7	9.2	6.2	8.6
1974	9.5	15.1	12.7	10.9	9.8	7.0	15.3	13.7	16.9	19.1	17.0	24.5	9.4	9.6	11.1	9.9	16.0	11.0	13.3
1975	8.4	15.1	12.8	10.8	6.7	6.0	9.6	11.8	17.9	17.0	20.9	11.8	11.7	10.2	14.7	9.8	24.2	9.1	12.7
1976	7.3	13.5	9.2	7.5	1.7	4.5	9.0	9.6	14.4	16.8	18.0	9.3	9.1	8.8	16.9	10.3	16.5	5.8	10.5
1977	5.5	12.3	7.1	8.0	1.3	3.7	11.1	9.4	12.6	17.0	13.6	8.1	9.1	6.4	14.3	11.4	15.8	6.5	9.6
1978	3.6	7.9	4.5	8.9	1.1	2.7	10.0	9.1	7.8	12.1	7.6	3.8	8.1	4.1	11.9	10.0	8.3	7.7	7.2
1979	3.7	9.1	4.5	9.2	3.6	4.1	9.6	10.8	7.5	14.8	13.3	3.6	4.8	4.2	13.8	7.2	13.4	11.3	8.3
1980	6.4	10.2	6.6	10.2	4.0	5.5	12.3	13.6	11.6	21.2	18.2	8.0	10.9	6.5	17.1	13.7	18.0	13.5	11.5
1981	6.8	9.6	7.6	12.4	6.5	6.3	11.7	13.4	12.0	17.8	20.4	4.9	13.6	6.7	15.4	12.1	11.9	10.4	11.1
1982	5.4	11.2	8.7	10.8	5.7	5.2	10.1	11.8	9.6	16.4	17.1	2.7	11.3	5.9	16.1	8.6	8.6	6.1	9.5
1983	3.3	10.1	7.7	5.8	3.0	3.3	6.9	9.6	8.3	14.9	10.5	1.9	8.4	2.7	7.4	8.9	4.6	3.2	6.7
1984	5.7	3.9	6.3	4.3	2.9	2.4	6.3	7.4	7.1	10.6	8.6	2.3	6.3	3.3	6.1	8.0	5.0	4.3	5.6
1985	3.2	6.7	4.9	4.0	3.4	2.1	4.7	5.8	5.9	8.6	5.5	2.0	5.7	2.3	15.4	7.4	6.1	3.5	5.4
1986	1.7	9.1	1.3	4.2	0.8	-0.1	3.7	2.7	2.9	6.1	3.8	0.6	7.2	0.1	13.2	4.2	3.4	1.9	3.7
1987	1.4	8.5	1.6	4.4	1.4	0.3	4.0	3.1	4.1	4.6	3.1	0.1	8.7	-0.7	15.7	4.2	4.1	3.7	4.0
1988	1.9	7.3	1.2	4.0	1.9	1.3	4.5	2.7	5.1	5.0	2.1	0.7	6.7	0.7	6.4	6.1	4.9	4.1	3.7
1989	2.6	7.5	3.1	5.0	3.2	2.8	4.8	3.6	6.6	6.6	4.1	2.3	4.6	1.1	5.7	6.6	7.8	4.8	4.6
1990	3.3	7.3	3.4	4.8	5.4	2.7	2.6	3.4	6.1	6.1	3.3	3.1	4.1	2.5	6.1	10.4	9.5	5.4	5.0
1991	3.3	3.2	3.2	5.6	5.9	3.6	2.4	3.2	4.3	6.5	3.2	3.3	3.4	3.2	2.6	9.7	5.9	4.2	4.3
1992	4.0	1.0	2.4	1.5	4.0	5.1	2.1	2.4	2.9	5.3	3.1	1.7	2.3	3.2	1.0	2.6	3.7	3.0	2.9
1993	3.6	1.8	2.8	1.8	3.3	4.4	1.3	2.1	2.2	4.2	1.4	1.2	2.3	2.6	1.3	4.7	1.6	3.0	2.5
1994	3.0	1.9	2.4	0.2	0.9	2.8	2.0	1.7	1.1	3.9	2.3	0.7	1.4	2.8	1.8	2.4	2.5	2.6	2.0
1995	2.2	4.6	1.5	2.2	1.8	1.7	2.1	1.8	0.8	5.4	2.5	-0.1	2.5	1.9	3.8	2.9	3.4	2.8	2.4
1996	1.5	2.6	2.1	1.6	0.8	1.4	2.1	2.0	0.6	3.8	1.7	0.1	1.3	2.0	2.3	0.8	2.4	2.9	1.8
1997	1.3	0.3	1.6	1.6	0.5	1.9	2.2	1.2	1.2	1.8	1.4	1.7	2.6	2.2	1.2	0.9	3.1	2.3	1.6
1998	0.9	0.9	1.0	1.0	0.0	0.9	1.8	0.8	1.4	1.7	2.4	0.6	2.3	2.0	1.3	0.4	2.4	1.6	1.3

Sources: OECD, *Economic Outlook* (various years); own calculations

Year	A	AUS	B	CAN	CH	D	DK	F	FL	I	IRL	JAP	N	NL	NZ	S	UK	USA	OECD-18
1970	1.4	1.6	1.9	5.8	0.0	0.6	1.3	2.5	1.9	4.0	5.6	1.2	1.4	0.9	0.1	1.5	2.4	5.0	2.2
1971	1.2	1.9	1.8	6.2	0.0	0.7	1.6	2.7	2.2	4.0	5.3	1.2	1.4	1.2	0.3	2.5	3.0	6.0	2.4
1972	1.0	2.6	2.3	6.3	0.0	0.9	1.6	2.8	2.5	4.7	5.9	1.4	1.7	2.1	0.5	2.7	3.1	5.6	2.7
1973	1.0	2.3	2.4	5.6	0.0	1.0	1.0	2.7	2.3	4.7	5.4	1.3	1.5	2.2	0.2	2.5	2.1	4.9	2.4
1974	1.1	2.7	2.5	5.4	0.0	2.1	2.3	2.9	1.7	3.9	5.1	1.4	1.4	2.6	0.1	2.0	2.2	5.6	2.5
1975	1.7	4.9	4.5	7.0	0.3	4.0	5.2	4.0	2.2	4.3	7.0	1.9	2.2	3.8	0.3	1.6	3.6	8.5	3.7
1976	1.7	4.7	5.9	7.2	0.6	3.9	5.3	4.4	3.9	4.9	8.7	2.0	1.8	4.1	0.4	1.6	4.8	7.7	4.1
1977	1.5	5.6	6.7	8.1	0.3	3.8	6.3	4.9	5.9	5.3	8.5	2.0	1.5	3.9	0.6	1.8	5.2	7.0	4.4
1978	1.8	6.3	7.3	8.4	0.3	3.7	7.2	5.2	7.3	5.3	7.9	2.2	1.8	3.8	1.7	2.2	5.0	6.1	4.6
1979	1.7	6.1	7.6	7.5	0.3	3.2	6.1	5.8	6.0	5.7	6.9	2.1	1.9	3.6	1.8	2.1	4.5	5.8	4.4
1980	1.6	6.0	8.0	7.5	0.2	3.2	6.9	6.2	4.7	5.6	7.0	2.0	1.7	4.0	2.5	2.0	6.1	7.2	4.6
1981	2.1	5.7	10.3	7.6	0.2	4.5	9.0	7.4	4.9	6.3	9.5	2.2	2.0	5.8	3.3	2.5	9.1	7.6	5.6
1982	3.2	7.1	12.0	11.1	0.4	6.4	9.7	8.0	5.4	6.9	11.0	2.4	2.7	8.5	3.6	3.2	10.4	9.7	6.8
1983	3.8	9.9	13.3	11.9	0.8	7.9	10.3	8.3	5.4	7.7	13.5	2.7	3.4	11.0	5.2	3.5	11.3	9.6	7.7
1984	3.9	8.9	13.4	11.3	1.0	7.9	9.9	9.7	5.2	8.5	15.0	2.7	3.2	10.6	4.5	3.1	11.4	7.5	7.6
1985	4.2	8.1	12.4	10.5	0.8	8.0	8.9	10.2	5.0	8.6	16.8	2.6	2.6	9.2	3.5	2.8	11.6	7.2	7.4
1986	4.5	8.0	11.8	9.6	0.7	7.7	7.7	10.4	5.4	9.9	17.1	2.8	2.0	8.4	4.0	2.5	11.8	7.0	7.3
1987	4.9	8.0	11.5	8.8	0.7	7.6	7.7	10.5	5.1	10.2	16.9	2.8	2.1	8.0	4.1	2.1	10.2	6.2	7.1
1988	4.7	7.1	10.4	7.8	0.6	7.6	8.4	10.0	4.5	10.5	16.3	2.5	3.2	7.8	5.6	1.7	7.8	5.5	6.8
1989	4.3	6.1	9.4	7.5	0.5	6.9	9.2	9.3	3.5	10.2	15.1	2.3	4.9	6.9	7.1	1.5	6.1	5.3	6.4
1990	4.7	7.0	8.8	8.1	0.5	6.2	9.4	8.9	3.2	9.1	12.9	2.1	5.2	6.0	7.8	1.6	5.9	5.6	6.3
1991	5.2	9.5	9.4	10.4	1.1	6.7	10.3	9.4	6.6	8.6	14.7	2.1	5.5	5.5	10.3	3.0	8.2	6.8	7.4
1992	5.3	10.7	10.4	11.3	2.5	7.7	11.0	10.4	11.7	8.8	15.1	2.2	5.9	5.4	10.3	5.3	10.2	7.5	8.4
1993	6.1	10.9	12.1	11.2	4.5	8.8	12.1	11.7	15.1	10.2	15.7	2.5	6.0	6.5	9.5	8.2	10.3	6.9	9.4
1994	5.9	9.7	13.1	10.4	4.7	9.6	12.0	12.2	16.6	11.3	14.8	2.9	5.4	7.6	8.1	7.9	9.4	6.1	9.3
1995	5.9	8.6	13.1	9.5	4.2	9.4	10.1	11.6	15.4	12.0	12.2	3.1	4.9	7.1	6.3	7.7	8.6	5.6	8.6
1996	6.3	8.5	12.8	9.7	4.7	10.3	8.7	12.3	14.6	12.1	11.9	3.3	4.8	6.6	6.1	8.1	8.0	5.4	8.6
1997	6.4	8.6	12.7	9.2	5.2	11.4	7.7	12.4	12.6	12.3	10.3	3.4	4.1	5.5	6.6	8.0	6.9	4.9	8.2
1998	6.1	8.2	11.8	8.4	4.0	11.2	6.5	11.8	10.9	12.2	9.1	4.2	3.4	4.1	8.3	6.5	6.5	4.6	7.6

Sources: OECD (1999g); own calculations.

Table A.5 *Employment rates: total employment* [a]

Year	A	AUS	B	CAN	CH	D	DK	F	FL	I	IRL	JAP	N	NL	NZ	S	UK	USA	OECD-18
1970	66.9	68.2	59.9	63.3	76.6	68.8	74.8	66.0	69.7	56.1	63.2	71.2	67.5	61.6	65.0	73.2	70.8	61.9	66.9
1971	67.5	68.1	60.1	61.6	76.9	68.4	75.1	65.7	69.2	56.0	62.4	70.8	67.7	61.1	64.5	73.0	69.7	61.3	66.6
1972	67.5	67.7	59.6	62.0	77.2	68.3	74.9	65.7	68.2	54.8	61.5	70.4	67.9	59.7	63.9	73.1	70.2	62.3	66.4
1973	68.2	68.4	59.7	63.6	77.4	68.5	75.7	66.0	69.1	55.0	61.2	70.8	67.7	59.0	64.5	73.6	71.5	63.4	66.8
1974	68.5	68.4	60.3	64.7	77.1	67.4	75.4	65.7	70.6	55.9	61.0	69.8	67.6	58.3	65.5	75.3	71.6	63.6	67.0
1975	68.3	67.0	58.9	64.2	74.3	65.7	73.3	65.1	70.0	55.9	59.3	69.0	69.1	57.0	65.0	77.2	71.1	61.8	66.2
1976	68.4	66.9	58.2	64.1	73.0	65.4	74.4	65.1	71.5	55.5	57.8	69.1	71.9	56.2	65.1	77.7	70.3	62.8	66.3
1977	68.6	66.4	57.5	64.1	73.2	65.2	74.8	65.2	69.9	56.1	57.9	69.5	73.0	55.8	65.5	77.7	70.1	63.6	66.3
1978	68.3	65.5	57.2	65.1	73.4	65.4	75.1	65.1	68.6	55.9	58.4	69.9	73.7	55.5	64.6	77.9	70.3	65.7	66.4
1979	68.0	65.4	57.4	66.7	73.5	65.9	75.6	64.7	70.0	56.1	59.2	70.3	74.1	55.5	65.2	78.8	70.8	66.6	66.9
1980	67.5	66.3	57.3	67.5	74.3	66.1	74.8	64.1	72.0	56.8	59.0	70.3	74.0	55.4	64.3	79.5	69.7	65.9	66.9
1981	66.7	66.4	56.2	68.3	74.9	65.1	73.3	62.9	72.3	56.1	57.6	70.5	74.6	54.1	64.3	79.0	66.9	65.8	66.4
1982	65.0	65.1	54.8	65.2	74.3	63.4	73.1	62.3	72.4	55.1	57.0	70.6	74.3	52.4	63.9	78.6	65.3	64.6	65.4
1983	63.6	62.9	53.9	64.8	73.8	61.9	73.0	61.4	72.3	54.4	55.1	71.1	73.9	51.1	61.9	78.5	64.6	64.8	64.6
1984	63.0	63.7	53.4	65.9	73.9	61.6	74.0	60.2	72.6	53.7	53.5	70.7	74.3	50.8	62.5	78.9	65.5	66.9	64.7
1985	62.8	64.9	53.7	67.2	74.8	62.0	75.6	59.6	73.0	53.4	51.8	70.6	75.5	50.9	64.1	78.7	66.0	67.6	65.1
1986	62.9	66.0	53.9	68.5	75.9	62.8	77.3	59.6	72.7	53.5	51.4	70.4	77.7	51.6	63.6	79.3	66.0	68.5	65.6
1987	62.7	66.2	54.1	69.7	77.2	63.2	77.6	59.5	72.4	53.1	51.8	70.4	78.6	52.0	63.4	79.8	67.5	69.7	66.0
1988	63.0	67.3	54.7	71.3	78.5	63.5	76.9	59.8	72.6	53.3	51.8	70.9	77.5	52.8	61.0	80.4	70.0	70.8	66.4
1989	63.8	69.2	55.6	72.0	81.3	63.9	76.1	60.3	73.8	53.0	52.0	71.7	74.8	53.5	59.0	81.3	71.8	71.8	66.9
1990	64.2	69.1	56.4	71.5	83.2	64.8	75.2	60.6	74.7	53.5	53.9	72.6	73.9	54.8	58.8	81.3	72.0	72.2	67.4
1991	64.6	67.0	56.5	69.3	83.7	66.0	74.5	60.4	70.3	53.7	53.0	73.6	72.9	55.8	57.3	79.5	69.7	71.0	66.6
1992	65.2	65.8	56.2	67.8	81.7	65.0	73.6	59.8	65.2	53.2	52.5	74.2	72.3	56.4	57.1	75.8	68.2	70.9	65.6
1993	63.9	65.5	55.5	67.7	80.6	63.8	72.3	58.8	61.0	51.7	52.4	74.2	71.9	56.5	58.0	71.3	67.8	71.3	64.7
1994	63.8	66.8	54.8	68.2	79.8	63.0	71.8	58.7	60.4	50.7	53.3	74.2	72.6	56.2	59.9	70.2	68.3	72.2	64.7
1995	63.3	68.8	55.1	68.5	79.8	62.6	72.5	59.0	61.6	50.4	55.1	74.1	74.0	57.4	62.0	70.8	68.8	72.6	65.3
1996	62.6	68.7	55.3	68.5	79.9	61.7	73.1	58.8	62.2	50.6	56.0	74.3	75.5	58.5	63.3	69.7	69.3	72.8	65.6
1997	62.5	68.2	55.5	69.0	79.3	60.7	74.6	58.8	63.4	50.6	57.5	75.2	77.3	60.3	62.7	68.9	70.2	73.8	66.0
1998	62.8	68.5	56.3	69.9	79.8	60.5	75.8	59.4	64.7	50.8	59.3	74.8	78.5	61.8	60.9	69.6	70.3	73.9	66.5

[a] Total employment as % of pop. 15–64 years.
Sources: OECD (1999g); own calculations.

Table A.6 *Employment rates: government employment* [a]

Year	A	AUS	B	CAN	CH	D	DK	F	FL	I	IRL	JAP	N	NL	NZ	S	UK	USA	OECD-18
1970	8.9	8.2	8.3	12.2	7.6	7.7	13.9	11.8	8.4	6.7	7.4	5.5	12.1	7.4	10.1	15.1	12.8	9.7	9.7
1971	9.1	9.1	8.4	12.4	7.8	8.0	14.7	12.0	8.7	7.0	7.6	5.5	12.6	7.5	10.2	16.1	13.2	9.8	10.0
1972	9.5	9.3	8.6	12.4	8.1	8.3	16.1	12.2	9.0	7.2	7.7	5.7	13.0	7.6	10.2	16.9	13.5	10.0	10.3
1973	9.8	8.3	8.7	12.6	8.3	8.5	16.7	12.3	9.4	7.3	7.9	5.8	13.5	7.6	10.4	17.5	13.9	10.1	10.5
1974	10.2	9.0	8.9	12.8	8.6	8.8	17.6	12.4	9.9	7.5	8.2	5.9	13.5	7.7	10.6	18.7	13.9	10.2	10.8
1975	10.6	10.5	9.3	13.4	8.9	9.0	18.3	12.5	10.4	7.7	8.4	6.0	15.0	7.7	11.1	19.7	14.8	10.5	11.3
1976	11.1	10.7	9.6	13.3	9.2	9.2	18.7	12.7	11.0	7.9	8.6	5.9	15.8	7.8	11.2	20.7	15.1	10.5	11.6
1977	11.2	11.2	9.7	13.5	9.5	9.3	19.5	12.8	11.3	8.1	8.7	6.0	16.4	7.9	11.2	21.5	14.9	10.4	11.8
1978	11.3	11.3	10.1	13.4	9.7	9.4	20.2	13.0	11.8	8.1	9.0	6.1	16.8	8.0	11.5	22.6	14.9	10.6	12.1
1979	11.7	10.8	10.6	13.1	9.8	9.6	21.0	13.0	12.1	8.2	9.3	6.2	18.0	8.0	11.6	23.5	15.0	10.6	12.3
1980	11.6	10.8	10.8	13.2	10.0	9.6	21.7	13.0	12.5	8.2	9.5	6.2	18.6	8.1	11.3	24.4	14.8	10.6	12.5
1981	11.7	10.7	10.9	13.4	10.0	9.6	22.4	13.0	12.9	8.3	9.7	6.2	18.6	8.2	11.3	24.8	14.7	10.3	12.6
1982	11.8	10.9	10.9	13.5	9.9	9.6	22.9	13.2	13.3	8.2	9.8	6.2	18.8	8.2	10.9	25.0	14.4	10.2	12.7
1983	12.0	11.2	10.7	13.7	10.0	9.6	22.9	13.3	13.6	8.1	9.6	6.1	19.2	8.2	10.7	25.1	14.4	10.1	12.7
1984	12.2	11.3	10.8	13.7	10.0	9.5	22.5	13.4	13.7	8.1	9.6	6.1	19.2	8.1	10.4	25.8	14.4	10.1	12.7
1985	12.3	11.4	11.0	13.9	10.0	9.6	22.4	13.6	14.0	8.1	9.5	6.1	19.6	8.0	10.3	25.7	14.4	10.2	12.8
1986	12.6	11.6	11.2	14.0	10.1	9.8	22.4	13.8	14.3	8.1	9.6	6.0	19.8	8.0	10.5	25.6	14.5	10.3	12.9
1987	12.8	11.7	11.1	14.3	10.2	9.9	22.4	13.8	14.7	8.2	9.6	6.0	20.3	8.0	10.2	25.3	14.6	10.4	13.0
1988	13.0	11.6	11.1	14.4	10.4	9.9	22.3	13.8	15.0	8.3	9.3	5.9	20.5	7.9	9.8	25.3	14.6	10.5	13.0
1989	13.2	11.2	11.1	14.5	10.6	9.9	22.4	13.7	15.2	8.3	9.0	5.8	20.6	7.8	9.6	25.7	14.2	10.6	13.0
1990	13.3	11.2	11.2	14.6	10.7	9.8	22.3	13.7	15.3	8.3	8.9	5.9	21.1	7.8	9.7	25.7	14.2	10.9	13.0
1991	13.5	11.2	10.9	14.8	10.9	10.5	22.1	13.8	15.4	8.3	8.9	5.9	21.7	7.8	9.5	25.3	13.8	10.8	13.1
1992	13.7	10.9	10.9	14.9	11.1	10.4	22.0	14.0	15.0	8.4	9.0	6.0	22.2	7.8	9.1	24.3	13.2	11.0	13.0
1993	14.0	10.8	10.8	14.8	11.3	10.2	22.1	14.3	14.2	8.3	9.3	6.1	22.7	7.8	9.1	23.3	11.6	10.9	12.9
1994	14.3	10.4	10.5	14.7	11.2	9.9	21.9	14.4	14.1	8.2	9.4	6.2	22.9	7.8	9.1	22.5	10.3	10.9	12.7
1995	14.3	10.2	10.3	14.2	11.1	9.7	21.7	14.5	14.3	8.1	9.3	6.2	23.1	7.8	8.8	22.2	9.9	10.8	12.6
1996	14.1	10.1	10.4	14.0	11.0	9.5	22.1	14.6	14.5	8.1	9.3	6.1	23.6	7.8	8.7	21.7	9.6	10.7	12.5
1997	14.0	9.9	10.3	13.8	10.9	9.3	22.6	14.6	14.6	8.0	9.4	6.2	24.0	8.1	8.7	21.2	—	10.7	12.7
1998	13.9	9.8	10.3	13.8	11.0	9.1	23.0	14.8	14.8	8.0	9.4	6.2	24.3	—	8.6	—	—	10.6	12.6

[a] Government employment as % of pop. 15–64 years.

Note: For some countries, OECD data on government and business employment represent full-time-equivalents. In the interest of comparability, we have adjusted data for those countries on the assumption that average working times are the same in both sectors.

Sources: OECD (1999g, 1999j); own calculations.

Table A.7 *Employment rates: business employment*[a]

Year	A	AUS	B	CAN	CH	D	DK	F	FL	I	IRL	JAP	N	NL	NZ	S	UK	USA	OECD-18
1970	58.0	60.0	51.6	51.1	69.0	61.1	61.0	54.1	61.3	49.5	55.8	65.7	55.4	54.2	54.9	58.1	58.0	52.2	57.3
1971	58.3	59.0	51.7	49.2	69.1	60.4	60.3	53.7	60.5	49.0	54.8	65.3	55.1	53.5	54.3	56.9	56.6	51.5	56.6
1972	58.1	58.4	51.0	49.6	69.1	59.9	58.8	53.5	59.2	47.6	53.8	64.7	54.9	52.1	53.7	56.3	56.6	52.3	56.1
1973	58.4	60.1	51.0	51.1	69.1	60.0	58.9	53.7	59.6	47.7	53.3	65.0	54.2	51.4	54.1	56.1	57.6	53.3	56.4
1974	58.3	59.3	51.4	51.9	68.5	58.6	57.8	53.3	60.7	48.4	52.8	63.9	54.1	50.6	54.9	56.7	57.7	53.3	56.2
1975	57.6	56.4	49.6	50.8	65.4	56.6	55.0	52.6	59.6	48.2	50.9	63.1	54.2	49.3	53.9	57.5	56.3	51.3	54.9
1976	57.4	56.2	48.6	50.8	63.7	56.2	55.7	52.4	60.5	48.1	49.2	63.2	56.1	48.4	53.9	57.0	55.3	52.3	54.7
1977	57.3	55.2	47.8	50.6	63.7	56.0	55.3	52.4	58.5	48.1	49.1	63.5	56.6	47.8	54.3	56.2	55.2	53.2	54.5
1978	57.0	54.2	47.0	51.7	63.7	56.0	55.0	52.1	56.8	47.8	49.4	63.8	57.0	47.5	53.1	55.3	55.5	55.1	54.3
1979	56.3	54.7	46.8	53.7	63.7	56.4	54.6	51.7	57.9	47.9	49.9	64.1	56.2	47.5	53.6	55.2	55.8	56.0	54.5
1980	55.9	55.5	46.4	54.3	64.3	56.5	53.0	51.2	59.5	48.6	49.5	64.2	55.4	47.3	53.0	55.1	54.9	55.3	54.4
1981	55.0	55.7	45.2	54.9	64.9	55.4	50.9	49.9	59.4	47.8	48.0	64.3	56.0	45.9	53.0	54.2	52.3	55.5	53.8
1982	53.2	54.2	43.9	51.8	64.4	53.9	50.2	49.1	59.1	46.9	47.3	64.4	55.5	44.2	52.9	53.6	50.9	54.4	52.8
1983	51.6	51.7	43.1	51.1	63.8	52.4	50.1	48.1	58.7	46.3	45.5	64.9	54.8	42.9	51.2	53.3	50.2	54.7	51.9
1984	50.8	52.4	42.6	52.2	63.9	52.1	51.5	46.8	58.9	45.6	43.9	64.6	55.1	42.7	52.2	53.1	51.1	56.8	52.0
1985	50.5	53.4	42.7	53.3	64.9	52.3	53.2	46.0	59.0	45.3	42.2	64.4	55.9	42.9	53.8	53.0	51.6	57.4	52.3
1986	50.2	54.3	42.7	54.5	65.8	53.0	54.8	45.8	58.4	45.3	41.8	64.4	57.9	43.6	53.1	53.6	51.5	58.1	52.7
1987	49.9	54.5	43.0	55.4	67.0	53.3	55.2	45.7	57.7	44.9	42.2	64.4	58.3	44.0	53.3	54.5	52.9	59.3	53.1
1988	50.0	55.7	43.6	56.9	68.2	53.6	54.5	46.0	57.6	44.9	42.5	65.0	57.0	44.9	51.1	55.1	55.4	60.3	53.5
1989	50.6	58.0	44.5	57.5	70.6	54.1	53.7	46.6	58.6	44.7	43.0	65.8	54.2	45.6	49.4	55.6	57.6	61.1	54.0
1990	51.0	57.9	45.2	56.9	72.5	55.0	53.0	46.9	59.4	45.2	45.0	66.7	52.8	46.9	49.2	55.7	57.7	61.3	54.3
1991	51.1	55.8	45.5	54.5	72.8	55.5	52.4	46.6	54.9	45.4	44.0	67.7	51.2	48.0	47.8	54.2	55.9	60.2	53.5
1992	51.5	54.9	45.3	53.0	70.6	54.6	51.6	45.8	50.2	44.8	43.4	68.2	50.1	48.6	48.0	51.5	55.0	59.9	52.6
1993	49.9	54.7	44.7	52.9	69.3	53.6	50.2	44.5	46.9	43.4	43.1	68.1	49.2	48.7	48.8	48.0	56.2	60.4	51.8
1994	49.5	56.4	44.4	53.5	68.6	53.0	50.0	44.3	46.3	42.5	43.9	68.0	49.8	48.4	50.7	47.7	58.0	61.3	52.0
1995	49.1	58.4	44.7	54.3	68.8	52.9	50.8	44.5	47.2	42.3	45.8	67.9	50.9	49.6	53.2	48.6	59.0	61.8	52.8
1996	48.5	58.3	44.9	54.5	68.9	52.1	51.0	44.2	47.8	42.5	46.7	68.2	51.9	50.7	54.4	48.0	59.7	62.1	53.0
1997	48.5	58.3	45.2	55.2	68.4	51.4	52.0	44.2	48.8	42.6	48.1	69.0	53.3	52.1	53.8	47.8	—	63.1	53.1
1998	48.9	58.7	46.0	56.1	68.8	51.4	52.8	44.6	49.9	42.8	49.9	68.7	54.2	—	52.3	—	—	63.3	53.8

[a] Business employment as % of pop. 15–64 years.

Note: For some countries, OECD data on government and business employment represent full-time-equivalents. In the interest of comparability, we have adjusted data for these countries on the assumption that average working times are the same in both sectors.

Table A.8 *Employment rates, production and production-related services* [a]

Year	A	AUS	B	CAN	CH	D	DK	F[b]	FL	I	IRL	JAP	N	NL	NZ	S	UK	USA	OECD-18
1970	44.6	40.3	34.8	30.7	50.8	—	—	41.1	—	—	—	44.2	39.4	—	—	42.8	41.6	32.0	41.3
1971	43.7	39.5	34.8	29.6	50.9	—	—	40.6	45.9	—	40.1	43.4	—	—	—	42.0	41.0	30.8	40.9
1972	43.5	38.4	34.1	29.4	50.8	—	41.6	40.2	44.4	—	—	42.4	40.3	—	39.6	41.3	40.3	31.2	40.5
1973	—	38.9	34.0	30.2	50.5	—	41.5	40.2	44.0	—	—	42.5	39.5	—	39.9	41.4	40.8	32.0	40.3
1974	41.8	38.3	34.3	30.5	49.9	—	40.2	40.0	44.8	—	37.2	41.4	39.2	28.8	40.4	42.1	40.7	31.8	40.3
1975	40.8	36.6	32.9	31.2	47.0	—	39.1	38.8	44.0	—	35.6	40.1	39.2	27.8	39.9	42.4	39.4	29.7	38.5
1976	39.9	36.1	31.8	32.4	45.4	—	38.8	38.3	45.4	—	35.5	41.3	39.9	27.5	39.8	42.1	38.3	30.0	38.2
1977	40.1	35.7	30.9	31.9	45.2	—	38.3	37.9	43.8	33.7	35.5	41.0	39.9	27.6	40.2	41.3	38.1	30.7	37.6
1978	39.8	34.2	30.1	32.5	45.0	—	37.5	37.3	42.5	33.3	35.8	40.9	39.8	27.5	39.0	40.5	38.1	31.9	37.1
1979	39.8	34.6	29.6	33.5	44.8	—	38.8	36.8	43.1	32.9	36.1	40.9	39.3	27.5	38.9	40.7	38.2	32.5	37.2
1980	39.3	34.7	29.2	33.7	—	39.5	—	36.2	44.1	33.0	35.7	40.7	38.4	27.4	38.3	40.9	37.4	31.7	37.1
1981	38.9	34.8	28.0	33.8	—	38.5	35.6	35.0	44.2	32.4	34.4	40.5	38.1	26.9	37.1	39.9	34.9	31.5	35.8
1982	39.5	34.1	26.8	31.3	—	37.1	—	34.2	43.5	31.1	33.7	40.2	37.7	25.8	37.7	39.1	33.5	30.2	35.0
1983	38.2	32.1	26.0	30.5	—	36.1	35.2	33.1	42.5	30.3	32.0	40.2	36.4	25.6	36.1	38.8	32.3	30.1	34.1
1984	37.7	32.3	25.5	31.0	—	35.6	35.0	32.0	42.3	28.7	30.6	39.8	36.6	25.3	35.8	38.9	33.7	31.4	33.8
1985	37.5	32.9	25.4	31.3	—	35.8	36.8	31.2	41.9	28.0	29.2	39.7	37.1	25.6	36.9	39.2	34.1	31.7	34.5
1986	37.7	33.1	25.2	31.7	43.2	36.2	38.3	30.7	41.4	27.7	29.0	39.5	38.3	25.2	39.9	38.8	34.0	32.1	34.7
1987	37.9	32.7	25.1	32.4	43.3	36.1	38.6	30.3	40.7	27.5	28.5	39.0	38.3	26.9	38.9	38.8	34.0	32.5	34.7
1988	37.3	33.4	25.1	33.2	43.4	35.9	38.7	30.2	40.4	27.1	28.6	39.3	37.5	27.5	37.0	39.1	35.4	32.9	34.7
1989	37.4	34.9	25.7	33.5	44.3	36.1	38.1	30.3	40.6	27.0	29.0	39.9	35.2	28.1	35.1	39.5	36.8	33.2	34.8
1990	37.8	34.1	26.1	32.7	43.9	36.7	37.8	31.9	40.2	27.6	30.0	40.3	34.0	28.8	34.4	38.6	37.1	33.0	34.8
1991	37.9	31.9	26.1	31.1	45.8	39.3	37.2	31.5	37.1	27.8	29.2	40.9	32.5	29.1	33.5	37.5	35.6	31.8	34.4
1992	37.9	31.2	25.8	29.9	43.9	38.0	36.6	30.8	33.8	27.6	29.1	41.2	31.8	28.1	32.9	34.9	34.0	30.8	33.4
1993	37.1	30.7	—	29.6	43.0	37.1	35.6	29.8	31.2	28.2	28.3	40.7	31.5	28.0	33.0	32.2	33.2	30.7	33.4
1994	39.1	31.8	25.6	30.2	42.5	36.1	35.8	29.3	30.4	27.3	28.7	40.3	32.1	27.6	35.0	32.3	33.5	31.4	32.6
1995	38.2	32.7	25.7	31.0	43.0	35.8	36.2	29.4	31.9	27.1	29.7	40.1	32.6	29.3	36.0	33.2	33.8	31.4	32.8
1996	37.3	32.7	25.7	30.9	42.5	35.9	35.6	29.1	32.0	27.1	29.7	40.0	—	30.4	36.2	32.9	33.7	31.5	33.3
1997	36.4	32.5	—	31.4	41.8	35.3	36.1	28.8	32.9	27.1	30.7	40.3	35.3	31.2	34.9	33.7	34.8	32.2	33.5

[a] ISIC 1–5 + 7 + 8 as % of pop. 15–64 years.
ISIC 1: agriculture, hunting, forestry, and fishing; ISIC 2: mining and quarrying; ISIC 3: manufacturing; ISIC 4: electricity, gas, and water; ISIC 5: construction; ISIC 7: transport, storage, and communication; ISIC 8: financing, insurance, real estate, and business services.
[b] Data from 1990 onwards estimated.
Note: ____ indicates break in time series.
Sources: OECD (1999)); own calculations.

Table A.9 *Employment rates: industry* [a]

Year	A	AUS	B	CAN	CH	D	DK	F	FL	I	IRL	JAP	N	NL	NZ	S	UK	USA	OECD-18
1970	27.5	24.8	25.2	18.6	35.4	33.4	27.6	25.2	24.0	22.0	18.3	25.2	23.0	22.3	22.2	28.1	31.2	21.3	25.3
1971	28.2	24.5	25.2	18.4	35.4	32.6	27.2	25.1	24.2	22.1	18.6	25.3	23.3	21.8	20.2	27.4	30.1	20.2	25.0
1972	28.4	23.8	24.5	18.4	35.1	32.0	25.1	25.1	24.2	21.5	18.4	25.3	22.9	20.6	19.9	26.9	29.4	20.3	24.6
1973	28.9	24.0	24.4	18.6	34.8	32.0	25.0	25.4	24.5	21.3	18.8	26.4	22.6	20.1	20.2	27.1	29.8	21.0	24.7
1974	28.7	23.6	24.5	18.8	34.3	31.0	23.5	25.3	25.3	21.6	19.2	25.9	22.8	19.5	20.6	27.9	29.7	20.6	24.6
1975	25.7	22.1	23.2	17.9	31.5	29.3	22.7	24.4	25.1	21.6	18.2	24.7	23.4	18.5	20.3	28.2	28.4	18.9	23.6
1976	25.1	21.8	22.3	18.7	29.9	28.9	23.8	24.0	24.8	21.1	17.3	24.7	23.5	17.6	20.3	27.5	27.5	19.3	23.2
1977	25.6	21.3	21.5	18.1	29.6	28.6	23.2	23.8	24.3	21.3	17.6	24.6	23.3	17.3	20.5	26.7	27.3	19.6	23.0
1978	25.7	20.2	20.6	18.4	29.5	28.5	22.7	23.2	23.6	21.0	18.0	24.4	23.0	17.3	19.2	25.7	27.1	20.5	22.7
1979	25.7	20.1	20.1	18.9	29.2	28.6	24.1	22.7	24.2	20.8	18.5	24.5	22.0	17.0	19.1	25.6	27.0	20.8	22.7
1980	25.5	20.3	19.6	18.9	28.3	28.4	22.6	22.3	24.8	21.1	18.5	24.8	21.6	16.7	18.9	25.6	26.1	20.1	22.5
1981	25.2	19.9	18.5	19.0	28.4	27.5	20.8	21.4	25.2	20.8	17.9	24.9	21.5	16.0	17.9	24.7	23.7	19.8	21.8
1982	25.5	18.9	17.4	17.0	27.4	26.3	20.0	20.8	24.4	20.2	17.3	24.5	20.9	15.0	18.2	23.8	22.3	18.3	21.0
1983	24.4	17.3	16.7	16.3	26.6	25.2	20.1	20.0	23.9	19.5	15.8	24.6	19.9	14.3	17.3	23.5	21.1	18.2	20.3
1984	24.3	17.6	16.2	16.8	26.4	25.0	19.5	19.1	23.6	18.4	15.1	24.6	20.2	14.3	17.2	23.5	22.7	19.0	20.2
1985	24.2	17.5	16.0	16.8	26.6	25.0	20.9	18.4	23.3	17.9	14.4	24.5	20.2	14.4	17.8	23.8	22.7	19.0	20.2
1986	24.3	17.5	15.8	17.0	26.9	25.2	21.7	18.0	23.2	17.6	14.4	24.2	20.7	13.8	18.3	23.9	22.3	18.9	20.2
1987	24.3	17.2	15.4	17.3	26.7	25.1	21.8	17.6	22.5	17.3	14.0	23.7	20.9	15.3	17.4	23.8	21.8	18.9	20.0
1988	24.1	17.6	15.3	18.0	26.6	24.9	21.0	17.3	22.1	17.3	14.0	24.1	20.1	15.4	15.9	23.9	22.6	19.1	20.0
1989	24.0	18.1	15.7	18.1	27.1	25.1	20.7	17.3	22.8	18.4	14.3	24.5	18.6	15.7	15.0	24.1	23.1	19.1	20.0
1990	24.2	17.2	15.8	17.2	26.6	25.3	21.0	17.5	22.7	17.4	14.9	24.7	18.0	16.0	14.5	23.4	23.0	18.9	19.9
1991	24.4	15.5	15.7	15.8	26.0	27.2	20.8	17.2	20.2	17.5	14.8	25.3	16.9	15.9	13.4	22.2	21.7	17.9	19.4
1992	23.8	15.4	15.5	15.0	24.3	26.1	20.5	16.6	17.8	17.4	14.5	25.6	16.7	15.2	13.0	20.1	20.5	17.4	18.6
1993	23.3	15.3	15.1	14.7	23.2	25.2	19.2	15.8	16.1	16.7	14.1	25.4	16.3	15.0	13.4	18.1	19.8	17.1	18.0
1994	22.9	15.6	14.8	15.1	23.0	24.3	19.2	15.3	15.9	16.2	14.7	25.2	16.7	14.5	14.7	17.6	18.7	17.3	17.9
1995	22.1	15.7	14.6	15.4	23.3	23.6	20.0	15.3	16.7	16.2	15.2	24.8	17.1	14.6	15.0	18.3	18.6	17.4	18.0
1996	21.1	15.4	14.4	15.3	22.4	23.5	19.8	15.0	16.9	16.2	15.3	24.8	17.4	14.8	15.4	18.2	18.7	17.4	17.9
1997	20.4	15.1	14.4	15.7	21.2	23.1	20.0	14.7	17.3	16.1	16.3	24.9	18.2	15.0	14.5	17.9	18.6	17.6	17.8

[a] Employment ISIC 2–5 as % of pop. 15–64 years. ISIC 2: mining and quarrying; ISIC 3: manufacturing; ISIC 4: electricity, gas, and water; ISIC 5: construction.

Sources: OECD (1999j); own calculations.

Table A.10 *Employment rates: consumer-related services*[a]

Year	A	AUS	B	CAN	CH	D	DK	F[b]	FL	I	IRL	JAP	N	NL	NZ	S	UK	USA	OECD-18
1970	19.9	28.0	23.5	29.5	26.0	—	—	23.2	—	—	—	26.9	22.1	—	—	30.4	28.1	29.9	25.9
1971	20.3	27.6	23.7	29.0	26.3	—	—	23.4	22.9	—	20.3	27.3	—	—	23.5	31.0	27.9	30.5	25.8
1972	20.6	28.4	24.0	29.7	26.7	—	31.5	23.6	23.5	—	—	27.8	26.3	—	23.6	31.8	28.6	31.2	26.9
1973	—	28.8	24.2	30.5	27.2	—	32.1	24.0	24.8	—	—	28.2	26.9	—	23.8	32.2	29.6	31.4	28.0
1974	22.1	28.9	24.6	31.1	27.5	—	32.2	24.3	25.5	—	20.1	28.3	27.0	—	24.3	33.3	29.9	31.8	27.9
1975	21.7	29.3	24.7	29.9	27.4	—	32.6	24.5	25.7	—	20.0	28.8	28.5	24.4	24.4	34.9	30.8	32.1	27.5
1976	22.6	29.5	25.0	30.5	27.6	—	32.0	25.0	25.4	—	20.2	27.7	30.7	24.7	24.5	35.5	31.0	32.7	27.8
1977	22.8	29.9	25.3	31.2	28.1	—	32.3	25.4	25.5	20.6	20.4	28.4	31.6	24.9	24.6	36.4	31.0	33.3	27.7
1978	23.3	30.4	25.7	31.6	28.5	—	33.0	25.7	25.6	20.8	20.7	28.9	32.5	24.7	24.8	37.4	31.2	33.8	28.1
1979	23.7	29.9	26.4	32.1	28.9	—	34.5	25.9	26.4	21.3	20.9	29.3	33.3	24.8	25.6	38.1	31.8	34.1	28.6
1980	24.0	30.9	26.7	32.6	—	25.5	—	25.9	27.2	21.7	20.9	29.5	34.3	25.7	25.3	38.5	31.9	34.2	28.5
1981	24.0	30.8	26.8	33.3	—	25.5	34.8	25.9	27.5	22.1	20.9	29.9	35.1	26.5	24.8	39.1	31.3	34.3	29.0
1982	24.5	30.1	26.6	32.8	—	25.3	—	26.0	28.4	22.5	21.1	30.2	35.3	26.4	25.4	39.4	31.1	34.4	28.7
1983	24.6	29.7	26.5	33.2	—	24.8	35.1	26.1	29.4	22.7	21.0	30.7	36.1	25.5	24.9	39.7	31.0	34.7	29.2
1984	25.9	30.7	26.6	33.8	—	25.1	37.1	26.0	30.0	23.6	20.8	30.7	36.4	25.5	24.8	40.1	30.0	35.4	29.6
1985	25.8	31.0	26.9	34.8	—	25.2	37.1	26.3	30.7	24.2	20.5	30.6	37.1	25.5	25.5	40.5	30.7	35.9	30.0
1986	26.2	31.9	27.3	35.6	32.0	25.6	37.9	26.6	31.0	24.6	20.9	30.7	38.1	26.3	32.1	40.2	31.0	36.4	30.8
1987	26.3	32.7	27.7	36.0	32.2	26.1	37.9	26.8	31.3	24.8	21.5	31.2	38.7	29.4	32.9	41.3	31.8	37.2	31.4
1988	26.9	33.2	28.2	36.5	32.4	26.5	37.8	27.1	31.9	25.2	21.5	31.3	38.5	30.5	32.0	41.8	32.8	37.8	31.8
1989	27.4	33.6	28.6	36.5	33.0	26.8	36.6	27.3	32.9	25.5	21.1	31.4	38.1	30.8	31.9	42.2	33.5	38.6	32.0
1990	27.7	34.1	29.0	36.9	33.2	27.0	37.5	28.1	33.0	26.7	21.7	31.9	38.4	31.5	32.4	42.0	33.7	39.2	32.4
1991	27.8	34.2	29.1	36.5	37.8	27.5	37.2	28.3	31.8	26.9	21.7	32.4	38.8	32.5	31.8	41.5	33.6	39.2	32.7
1992	28.6	34.1	29.2	36.4	37.8	28.0	37.8	28.4	30.0	26.6	22.7	32.7	39.0	32.1	32.2	40.6	33.7	40.1	32.8
1993	28.8	34.1	—	36.7	37.6	28.2	36.7	28.6	28.4	24.1	23.8	33.2	39.1	32.8	32.8	39.0	33.6	40.6	32.6
1994	30.0	34.5	27.8	36.8	37.2	28.5	35.5	28.8	28.6	24.1	24.1	33.5	39.3	33.6	32.9	37.8	33.6	40.9	32.6
1995	31.1	35.6	27.9	36.3	36.9	28.4	36.4	29.0	28.3	23.9	24.9	33.7	40.2	33.1	33.9	37.5	33.8	41.2	32.9
1996	31.1	35.6	28.1	36.4	37.4	28.6	37.5	29.3	28.9	24.1	25.9	34.1	—	33.9	34.3	36.8	34.2	41.3	33.2
1997	31.9	35.4	—	36.3	37.8	28.1	38.4	29.5	30.0	24.0	26.6	34.7	41.3	34.9	33.4	37.1	35.2	41.7	33.6

[a] Employment ISIC 6 + 9 as % of pop. 15–64 years. ISIC 6: wholesale and retail trade, restaurants and hotels; ISIC 9: community, social and personal services.

[b] Data from 1990 onwards estimated.

Note: ____ indicates break in time series.

Sources: OECD (1999)i; own calculations.

Table A.11 *Employment rates: wholesale and retail trade, restaurants and hotels*[a]

Year	A	AUS	B	CAN	CH	D	DK	F[b]	FL	I	IRL	JAP	N	NL	NZ	S	UK	USA	OECD-18
1970	9.2	13.8	9.5	—	13.7	—	—	9.9	—	—	—	14.1	—	—	11.3	10.6	11.5	12.6	—
1971	9.5	13.5	9.5	—	13.7	—	—	9.9	10.2	—	10.0	14.3	—	—	11.5	10.6	12.2	13.0	—
1972	9.7	13.9	9.5	—	13.8	—	11.0	9.9	10.3	—	—	14.4	10.7	—	11.5	10.3	12.3	13.3	—
1973	—	13.9	9.4	—	14.1	—	11.2	10.0	10.9	—	—	14.6	10.9	—	11.5	10.3	12.8	13.4	—
1974	10.3	13.4	9.5	—	14.1	—	10.6	10.0	11.1	—	—	14.6	11.0	—	11.6	10.6	12.7	13.5	—
1975	10.0	13.1	9.3	13.4	13.7	—	10.6	9.9	10.9	—	9.5	14.9	10.8	9.2	11.4	11.1	12.8	13.5	11.4
1976	10.3	12.9	9.3	13.6	13.4	—	10.6	9.9	10.5	—	9.5	15.1	11.8	9.1	11.3	11.2	12.7	13.7	11.6
1977	10.4	13.0	9.2	13.9	13.5	—	10.6	10.0	10.0	9.8	9.6	15.5	12.2	9.0	11.4	11.2	12.8	14.0	11.5
1978	10.9	15.5	9.1	14.2	13.7	—	10.8	10.0	9.8	9.8	9.5	15.6	12.5	9.0	11.2	11.2	12.9	14.2	11.7
1979	10.8	15.2	9.1	14.7	13.7	—	10.9	10.0	9.9	10.1	9.5	15.7	12.3	8.9	11.4	10.9	13.2	14.3	11.8
1980	10.8	15.6	9.0	15.0	—	10.0	—	9.9	10.1	10.2	9.3	15.9	12.4	9.2	10.9	10.9	13.4	14.2	11.7
1981	11.1	15.2	9.0	15.1	—	10.0	10.1	9.9	10.0	10.5	9.2	16.1	12.7	9.4	10.6	10.9	13.0	14.2	11.6
1982	11.0	14.6	8.9	14.6	—	9.8	—	9.8	9.9	10.5	9.0	16.2	12.7	9.1	10.7	10.8	12.8	14.3	11.6
1983	10.7	14.0	8.8	14.5	—	9.7	9.6	9.8	10.2	10.7	8.9	16.3	12.8	8.8	10.5	10.8	12.6	14.4	11.4
1984	11.6	14.5	8.8	15.0	—	9.8	10.9	9.6	10.3	11.0	8.9	16.2	12.4	8.8	10.5	10.9	13.0	14.9	11.6
1985	11.4	14.7	8.8	15.5	—	9.9	11.5	9.5	10.6	11.1	9.0	16.0	13.0	8.8	10.8	11.0	13.1	15.0	11.7
1986	11.7	15.3	8.9	16.0	15.6	10.0	11.1	9.5	10.6	11.2	8.8	16.1	13.6	8.7	13.8	11.0	13.1	15.2	12.2
1987	11.4	15.0	9.0	16.2	15.8	10.1	11.1	9.6	10.4	11.3	8.8	16.3	13.9	9.7	14.3	11.2	13.6	15.5	12.4
1988	11.6	15.8	9.2	16.5	15.7	10.2	11.2	9.8	10.6	11.3	9.0	16.4	13.8	10.0	13.7	11.5	14.1	15.6	12.6
1989	11.9	16.8	9.4	16.5	15.9	10.3	10.7	9.9	11.5	11.4	9.0	16.4	13.5	10.1	13.2	11.9	14.5	15.9	12.7
1990	12.2	16.7	9.5	16.7	16.0	10.5	11.3	10.4	11.7	11.5	9.0	16.4	13.0	10.7	14.1	11.7	14.4	16.1	12.9
1991	12.5	16.5	9.5	16.2	16.0	9.6	11.0	10.3	10.6	11.8	9.2	16.6	12.8	11.0	13.5	11.2	14.1	15.8	12.7
1992	12.6	16.4	9.5	15.9	16.0	9.7	10.8	10.2	9.5	11.7	9.9	16.6	12.7	11.0	13.7	10.8	13.8	15.7	12.6
1993	12.5	16.3	—	15.7	15.9	9.6	11.5	10.0	8.9	10.8	10.5	16.7	12.5	11.2	13.9	10.2	13.4	15.8	12.7
1994	13.2	16.9	10.1	15.9	15.7	9.8	11.8	9.9	8.6	10.7	10.3	16.6	12.4	11.6	14.2	10.7	13.6	15.9	12.7
1995	14.4	17.4	10.1	15.8	15.4	11.0	11.8	10.0	8.7	10.6	10.6	16.6	12.7	12.8	14.4	10.8	13.8	16.0	12.9
1996	14.3	17.4	10.1	16.0	15.2	11.0	12.1	10.0	9.2	10.8	10.9	16.8	—	13.4	14.8	10.6	13.7	16.1	13.1
1997	14.5	17.2	—	16.0	—	10.8	12.4	10.1	9.5	10.7	11.4	16.9	14.1	13.6	14.7	10.6	14.1	16.1	13.1

[a] Employment in ISIC 6 as % of pop. 15–64 years. ISIC 6: wholesale and retail trade, restaurants and hotels.
[b] Data from 1990 onwards estimated.
Note: _____ indicates break in time series.
Sources: OFCD (1999i); own calculations.

Year	A	AUS	B	CAN	CH	D	DK	F	FL	I	IRL	JAP	N	NL	NZ	S	UK	USA
1970	—	45.6	—	41.1	—	48.1	—	49.8	63.5	29.1	34.6	55.4	—	—	—	60.6	53.5	50.4
1971	—	46.1	—	42.2	—	48.4	—	49.5	63.9	29.0	—	54.3	—	30.4	—	62.1	55.5	50.6
1972	—	46.8	—	43.1	—	48.9	—	50.5	64.2	28.4	—	53.5	51.6	30.8	—	63.2	56.2	51.6
1973	—	47.8	—	44.9	—	49.6	—	51.2	66.0	29.0	—	54.1	51.8	31.1	—	63.9	57.2	52.7
1974	—	48.7	—	46.1	—	49.8	—	51.9	67.5	29.5	34.8	52.4	51.2	31.5	—	66.3	58.0	53.9
1975	—	49.7	—	50.5	—	49.7	—	52.9	67.7	29.9	—	51.7	53.6	32.0	—	68.9	58.6	54.9
1976	—	49.8	—	51.8	—	51.0	—	53.5	67.5	30.6	34.0	51.9	57.7	32.2	—	70.1	60.2	56.2
1977	—	51.2	—	53.1	—	51.2	—	55.0	68.2	37.1	—	53.1	58.9	32.8	—	71.4	61.2	57.6
1978	—	50.8	—	55.3	—	51.6	—	54.8	67.9	37.1	35.2	54.2	60.7	33.3	—	73.0	61.2	59.5
1979	—	50.2	—	56.8	—	52.2	—	56.0	68.9	38.2	—	54.7	62.2	34.5	—	74.6	61.7	60.7
1980	—	52.5	—	58.4	—	52.8	—	56.0	70.2	39.2	35.8	54.9	64.2	36.3	—	76.0	61.3	61.5
1981	—	52.1	—	60.1	—	53.1	—	55.9	71.1	39.6	—	55.2	65.8	38.4	—	77.2	60.8	62.3
1982	—	51.7	—	60.3	—	52.9	—	55.9	72.2	40.8	37.8	55.9	65.2	39.4	—	78.0	60.2	63.1
1983	—	51.9	44.5	61.3	—	52.5	72.8	55.6	72.9	39.8	36.9	57.2	67.9	40.5	—	78.7	61.2	63.5
1984	—	52.6	45.2	62.5	—	52.3	74.1	55.9	73.1	40.3	36.7	57.2	68.2	40.7	—	79.2	62.5	64.4
1985	—	54.1	45.3	63.9	—	52.9	75.5	56.1	73.9	40.6	37.2	57.2	70.1	41.0	—	79.9	63.1	65.6
1986	—	56.4	46.0	65.0	—	53.8	77.1	56.9	73.4	42.0	42.2	57.4	73.7	41.4	63.7	80.7	64.4	66.6
1987	—	57.4	45.7	66.3	—	54.5	77.5	57.0	72.9	43.1	41.6	57.8	74.8	48.9	64.3	81.7	64.9	67.6
1988	—	58.8	45.5	67.7	—	55.4	77.5	56.9	73.0	43.6	41.6	58.3	74.4	50.6	63.3	82.5	65.8	68.4
1989	—	60.6	45.7	68.5	—	55.9	77.3	57.4	74.2	44.0	43.3	59.3	72.9	51.1	62.5	83.0	67.8	69.5
1990	—	61.9	46.3	69.2	—	57.0	78.6	57.6	74.0	44.5	44.2	60.4	72.6	53.1	63.8	83.3	68.1	69.7
1991	—	61.7	48.3	69.2	74.8	61.1	78.8	57.9	72.7	44.4	44.2	61.5	72.4	54.5	64.2	82.5	68.0	69.6
1992	—	61.9	49.5	68.7	75.2	61.4	79.1	58.5	70.9	44.9	44.5	62.0	71.9	55.0	64.0	80.9	67.9	70.2
1993	59.6	61.6	50.6	68.7	75.1	61.5	78.4	59.3	70.1	42.8	46.0	61.9	71.9	56.3	64.0	78.9	67.9	70.3
1994	59.6	62.4	51.4	68.5	74.2	61.5	74.1	59.6	69.4	42.7	47.2	62.1	72.3	57.3	65.3	77.7	68.0	71.4
1995	—	64.3	52.0	68.4	73.8	61.7	73.6	60.1	69.9	43.3	47.6	62.3	73.5	59.3	66.3	78.0	67.9	71.6
1996	58.8	64.4	52.3	68.7	75.3	62.0	74.0	60.7	70.2	43.8	49.4	62.8	75.3	60.4	68.0	77.9	68.4	72.0
1997	59.0	63.5	53.1	68.7	75.4	61.8	74.7	60.4	69.7	44.1	50.4	63.8	76.8	62.2	67.7	76.7	68.9	72.5

Note: ____ indicates break in time series.
Source: OECD, *Labour Force Statistics* (various years).

Table A.13 *Labor force participation rates (%): men aged 55–64 years*

Year	A	AUS	B	CAN	CH	D	DK	F	FL	I[a]	IRL	JAP	N	NL	NZ	S	UK	USA
1970	—	85.1	—	84.2	—	80.1	—	75.4	73.9	—	—	86.6	—	80.6	—	85.4	91.2	80.7
1971	—	84.4	—	83.3	—	77.8	—	74.6	73.2	—	91.0	87.1	—	78.7	—	84.7	88.1	80.0
1972	—	84.2	—	82.3	—	75.2	—	73.4	69.4	—	—	86.6	83.9	77.2	—	83.5	88.0	79.1
1973	—	82.6	—	81.3	—	73.4	—	72.1	67.6	—	—	86.8	83.9	74.6	—	82.7	87.7	76.9
1974	—	80.4	—	80.3	—	70.5	—	70.8	68.7	—	—	86.3	82.3	72.2	—	82.0	87.6	76.2
1975	—	78.8	—	79.4	—	69.8	—	69.0	65.6	—	83.8	86	81.9	72.2	—	82.0	87.6	75.6
1976	—	76.2	—	76.7	—	68.1	—	68.2	59.0	71.2	—	86.0	82.2	71.8	—	81.3	86.5	74.3
1977	—	75.3	—	76.3	—	67.2	—	69.5	56.9	73.0	81.8	84.8	83.1	70.9	—	79.7	85.5	73.8
1978	—	72.0	—	76.4	—	66.5	—	66.4	55.3	72.7	—	85.0	82.5	69.8	—	79.1	84.3	73.3
1979	—	69.5	—	76.3	—	66.9	—	69.9	56.3	72.7	77.9	85.2	82.0	65.3	—	79.2	83.2	72.8
1980	—	68.8	—	76.1	—	67.3	—	68.6	56.9	73.0	—	85.4	79.5	63.2	—	78.7	81.6	72.1
1981	—	67.9	—	75.2	—	66.8	—	64.6	57.2	73.5	79.1	85.0	79.0	57.3	—	78.1	79.9	70.6
1982	—	64.9	—	73.7	—	65.5	—	59.8	57.7	67.9	—	85.9	80.0	54.8	—	77.7	75.9	70.2
1983	—	62.0	50.6	72.4	—	63.1	67.2	53.6	54.1	68.9	78.0	84.7	80.3	54.2	—	77.0	71.7	69.4
1984	—	61.1	47.3	71.3	—	60.9	66.6	50.3	53.1	67.6	77.7	83.8	80.3	50.3	—	76.2	70.0	68.6
1985	—	60.4	45.1	70.4	—	60.1	65.8	50.1	51.7	67.2	75.4	83.0	79.9	47.0	—	75.9	69.0	67.9
1986	—	61.1	41.2	68.7	—	60.5	68.6	49.5	50.8	66.2	74.6	82.9	78.2	44.3	66.9	75.5	67.8	67.3
1987	—	60.0	37.4	66.6	—	59.9	67.0	47.7	47.3	65.6	70.5	82.6	78.3	47.1	64.8	74.8	67.7	67.6
1988	—	60.6	36.6	66.6	—	58.7	69.1	47.4	45.2	65.4	69.5	82.3	75.6	46.9	60.4	74.6	68.0	67.0
1989	—	62.4	37.8	66.2	—	57.8	69.2	47.0	45.4	64.4	66.3	82.4	74.0	46.0	56.5	74.5	67.7	67.2
1990	—	63.2	35.4	64.9	—	57.7	69.2	45.8	47.1	65.3	65.1	83.3	72.8	45.7	56.8	75.3	68.1	67.8
1991	—	60.7	34.7	62.6	86.4	53.4	66.2	44.5	45.9	64.2	65.7	84.5	71.0	43.4	56.5	75.3	67.7	67.0
1992	—	61.3	35.5	62.1	84.9	53.2	66.3	44.0	44.0	64.2	65.7	84.9	71.8	43.5	56.7	73.4	65.7	67.0
1993	—	58.9	34.1	61.0	84.7	53.1	65.9	43.5	43.0	61.4	64.6	85.4	71.5	41.5	59.9	70.8	64.3	66.5
1994	39.7	60.7	34.5	60.3	82.2	53.3	63.8	42.1	43.9	59.8	64.7	85.0	71.5	41.8	63.0	70.3	64.1	65.5
1995	42.9	60.9	35.9	58.9	82.3	54.1	67.9	41.5	44.6	57.8	63.9	84.8	72.3	42.3	65.4	70.7	62.4	66.0
1996	41.8	60.3	33.8	59.3	81.7	54.7	62.1	42.3	47.2	56.8	63.0	84.9	73.2	43.1	69.0	72.9	62.9	67.0
1997	40.7	59.6	33.9	60.6	81.9	54.6	63.8	42.0	44.5	55.9	61.7	85.1	75.1	44.2	69.3	71.3	63.6	67.6

[a] Men aged 50–64 years.
Note: ____ indicates break in time series.
Source: OECD, *Labour Force Statistics* (various years).

Table A.14 Employment rates: part-time employment (national definitions) [a]

Year	A	AUS	B	CAN	CH	D	DK	F	FL	I	IRL	JAP	N	NL	NZ	S	UK	USA	OECD-18
1970	—	7.2	—	6.1	—	—	—	—	—	—	—	9.8	—	—	6.4	—	—	9.4	—
1971	—	7.1	—	6.1	—	—	—	3.8	—	—	—	9.8	—	—	6.8	—	—	9.6	—
1972	—	7.5	—	6.1	—	—	—	3.8	—	—	—	9.4	—	—	6.8	—	—	9.8	—
1973	4.4	8.2	2.3	6.2	—	6.9	—	3.9	—	3.5	—	9.8	15.1	—	7.2	—	—	9.9	—
1974	4.9	8.5	—	6.5	—	—	—	3.9	—	—	—	10.0	15.5	—	8.1	—	—	10.0	—
1975	4.9	9.1	2.9	6.8	—	7.3	15.5	5.2	4.7	3.3	4.0	10.7	16.2	8.2	8.1	15.7	—	10.3	—
1976	5.1	9.8	—	8.0	—	—	—	5.2	—	—	—	10.0	18.7	—	8.2	16.8	—	10.5	—
1977	4.8	10.0	3.5	8.4	—	7.7	16.5	5.6	4.2	3.3	4.2	10.0	20.0	8.6	8.5	17.7	—	10.7	—
1978	4.9	10.5	—	8.7	—	—	—	5.1	4.3	—	—	10.2	19.4	—	8.7	18.6	—	10.9	—
1979	5.2	10.4	3.5	9.2	—	7.5	17.2	5.3	4.7	3.0	3.0	10.8	20.2	9.2	9.1	19.2	—	10.9	—
1980	5.1	10.9	—	9.7	—	—	—	5.3	4.8	—	—	11.0	20.0	—	9.0	19.5	—	11.1	—
1981	5.4	11.0	3.6	10.2	—	7.8	17.4	5.2	5.3	2.9	—	11.0	21.1	10.1	9.4	19.6	—	11.2	—
1982	5.2	11.2	—	10.4	—	—	—	5.7	5.5	—	—	11.2	21.4	—	9.5	19.5	—	11.8	—
1983	5.3	11.0	4.3	10.9	—	7.8	17.4	5.9	5.6	2.5	3.7	11.5	21.9	10.8	9.5	—	12.3	11.9	—
1984	4.4	11.3	4.3	11.0	—	7.6	15.6	6.1	6.0	2.9	3.2	11.6	21.7	—	9.9	19.4	13.7	11.8	—
1985	4.2	11.8	4.6	11.4	—	7.9	18.4	6.5	6.0	2.8	3.3	11.6	21.3	11.5	10.5	18.9	14.0	11.7	—
1986	4.2	12.5	5.0	11.6	—	8.1	18.3	7.0	5.8	2.7	3.2	11.7	22.0	—	10.7	18.6	14.2	11.9	—
1987	4.5	13.3	5.3	11.4	—	8.0	18.8	7.0	5.8	3.0	3.7	11.7	22.2	15.3	11.2	20.1	14.9	12.1	—
1988	4.7	13.5	5.4	12.2	—	8.4	18.3	7.1	5.3	3.0	4.1	12.0	21.9	16.0	11.3	19.6	15.4	12.2	—
1989	5.6	14.5	5.7	11.9	—	8.6	17.8	7.2	5.5	3.0	3.9	12.6	19.8	17.0	11.1	19.3	15.6	12.2	—
1990	5.7	14.7	6.2	12.2	—	9.8	17.5	7.2	5.4	2.6	4.4	13.9	19.6	17.4	11.8	18.9	15.6	12.2	—
1991	5.7	15.1	6.6	12.6	21.2	9.3	17.2	7.2	5.3	3.0	4.4	14.7	19.4	18.2	12.1	18.6	15.5	12.4	12.1
1992	5.9	16.1	6.9	12.5	21.7	9.3	16.5	7.5	5.1	3.1	4.8	15.2	19.4	19.5	12.3	18.3	15.7	12.5	12.4
1993	6.4	15.6	7.1	12.9	21.8	9.6	16.8	8.1	5.3	2.8	5.7	15.6	19.5	19.8	12.3	17.8	15.8	12.5	12.5
1994	7.7	16.3	7.0	12.8	21.9	9.9	15.2	8.7	5.2	3.1	6.0	15.9	19.3	20.4	12.9	17.5	16.3	13.7	12.8
1995	7.9	17.0	7.5	12.7	21.8	10.2	15.6	9.2	5.1	3.2	6.6	14.9	19.6	20.8	13.3	17.2	16.6	13.5	12.9
1996	7.9	17.2	7.8	13.0	21.9	—	15.7	9.4	4.9	3.3	6.5	16.2	20.1	21.4	14.2	16.4	15.4	13.3	13.0

[a] Part-time employment as % of pop. 15–64 years.

Note: _____ indicates break in time series.

Sources: OECD, *Full-time/Part-time Database* (unpublished document); OECD (1999g); own calculations.

Table A.15 *Net migration as % of total population*

Year	A	AUS	B	CAN	CH	D	DK	F	FL	I	IRL	JAP	N	NL	NZ	S	UK	USA	OECD-18
1970	0.23	0.90	0.04	0.31	−0.10	0.95	0.24	0.35	−0.78	−0.09	−0.10	−0.01	−0.03	0.26	0.39	0.61	−0.05	0.21	0.19
1971	0.76	0.80	0.24	—	0.03	0.70	0.06	0.28	0.02	−0.06	0.20	−0.02	0.18	0.23	0.31	0.04	−0.02	0.19	0.23
1972	0.04	0.42	0.12	—	0.31	0.54	0.10	0.20	0.11	0.05	0.43	−0.02	0.10	0.12	0.82	−0.15	0.00	0.15	0.20
1973	0.30	0.50	0.17	—	0.12	0.62	0.24	0.21	0.13	0.02	0.49	−0.02	0.08	0.13	1.01	−0.14	−0.07	0.16	0.23
1974	−0.09	0.63	0.24	0.64	0.03	−0.01	−0.14	0.06	0.02	−0.01	0.61	−0.02	0.10	0.24	1.12	0.11	−0.15	0.15	0.20
1975	−0.18	0.10	0.25	0.58	−0.91	−0.32	−0.18	0.03	−0.08	−0.02	0.54	0.00	0.12	0.53	0.65	0.21	−0.07	0.21	0.08
1976	0.03	0.24	0.07	0.41	−0.85	−0.12	0.06	0.11	−0.21	−0.01	0.37	−0.01	0.12	0.15	−0.39	0.24	−0.03	0.16	0.02
1977	0.05	0.48	0.05	0.28	−0.36	0.05	0.12	0.08	−0.23	—	0.24	−0.01	0.12	0.17	−0.32	0.28	−0.06	0.18	0.07
1978	0.01	0.33	−0.03	0.13	−0.11	0.19	0.10	0.04	−0.19	0.01	0.45	−0.02	0.10	0.20	−0.83	0.17	0.01	0.23	0.04
1979	−0.01	0.48	0.02	0.32	0.06	0.40	0.10	0.07	−0.15	0.01	−0.03	−0.01	0.07	0.32	−0.83	0.17	0.03	0.24	0.07
1980	0.12	0.69	−0.02	0.50	0.27	0.51	0.02	0.08	−0.02	0.01	−0.03	0.00	0.10	0.37	−0.38	0.12	−0.09	0.37	0.14
1981	0.38	0.82	−0.20	0.47	0.37	0.25	−0.04	0.10	0.10	−0.03	−0.06	0.01	0.12	0.12	−0.22	0.12	−0.03	0.31	0.15
1982	−0.46	0.68	−0.04	0.27	0.32	−0.12	−0.02	0.11	0.15	0.19	−0.32	0.01	0.15	−0.01	0.35	−0.08	−0.09	0.27	0.08
1983	−0.03	0.36	−0.08	0.17	0.08	−0.19	0.04	0.10	0.12	0.25	−0.31	−0.01	0.10	0.03	0.50	0.02	0.01	0.26	0.08
1984	0.07	0.39	−0.01	0.17	0.18	−0.24	0.08	0.08	0.08	0.16	−0.51	−0.01	0.10	0.06	0.09	0.11	0.01	0.26	0.06
1985	0.11	0.56	0.00	0.17	0.21	0.15	0.18	0.07	0.06	0.15	−0.73	0.00	0.14	0.17	−0.43	0.13	0.13	0.27	0.07
1986	0.12	0.69	0.00	0.40	0.33	0.32	0.23	0.07	0.04	0.13	−0.71	−0.02	0.22	0.23	−0.46	0.18	0.11	0.27	0.12
1987	0.20	0.77	−0.01	−0.02	0.41	0.36	0.14	0.08	0.02	0.15	−0.82	−0.02	0.31	0.30	—	0.24	0.03	0.28	0.14
1988	0.14	0.90	0.38	0.90	0.51	0.79	0.00	0.10	0.02	0.12	−1.19	−0.01	0.24	0.24	−0.84	0.36	0.02	0.27	0.16
1989	0.68	0.93	0.07	0.83	0.51	1.57	0.06	0.13	0.12	0.07	−1.02	−0.01	−0.07	0.26	−0.18	0.52	0.09	0.25	0.27
1990	0.31	0.73	0.20	0.62	0.85	1.63	0.16	0.14	0.18	—	−0.26	0.00	0.05	0.40	0.21	0.41	0.22	−0.31	0.33
1991	0.74	0.50	0.14	0.57	1.01	0.00	0.23	0.16	−0.02	−0.03	0.03	0.03	0.19	0.33	0.21	0.28	0.27	0.29	0.27
1992	0.47	0.39	0.25	0.77	0.58	0.96	0.23	0.16	0.48	0.32	−0.20	0.03	0.23	0.28	0.09	0.23	0.08	0.36	0.32
1993	1.16	0.17	0.19	0.64	0.58	0.57	0.21	0.12	0.18	0.32	−0.17	−0.01	0.30	0.34	0.23	0.37	0.16	0.33	0.32
1994	0.17	0.26	0.18	0.46	0.41	0.39	0.19	0.09	0.08	0.27	−0.22	−0.07	0.16	0.12	0.45	0.58	0.15	0.32	0.22
1995	—	0.45	0.03	0.78	0.34	0.49	0.55	0.08	0.08	—	—	−0.04	0.16	0.21	0.98	0.60	0.18	0.33	0.35
1996	—	0.57	0.16	—	0.01	0.33	0.25	0.07	0.06	—	—	−0.01	0.11	0.23	1.21	0.51	0.07	0.33	0.28
1997	—	0.52	—	—	0.07	0.15	0.28	—	0.10	—	—	0.01	0.23	—	0.90	—	—	0.31	—

Sources: OECD (1999j); own calculations.

Table A.16 *Real hourly earnings in manufacturing (% change from previous year)*

Year	A	AUS	B	CAN	CH	D	DK	F	FL	I	IRL	JAP	N	NL	NZ	S	UK	USA	OECD-18
1970	8.5	4.2	4.9	4.6	—	13.3	—	—	7.4	—	7.9	8.9	1.3	—	8.8	—	3.1	-0.7	6.0
1971	10.4	6.1	6.8	6.1	—	8.3	—	7.0	9.3	7.5	7.2	8.2	5.9	4.6	9.8	—	2.6	2.2	6.8
1972	6.8	3.1	7.8	3.0	—	5.3	5.7	4.3	7.1	5.6	6.1	10.8	1.8	5.4	2.3	12.7	6.0	3.7	5.7
1973	5.9	4.1	9.8	1.3	—	5.4	9.9	7.2	6.1	8.0	7.6	8.0	2.9	5.3	3.6	1.5	3.7	0.8	5.4
1974	6.2	9.7	8.4	2.6	3.7	8.1	6.2	5.3	5.5	7.2	3.3	-0.1	7.4	7.3	2.6	1.1	0.3	-2.7	4.6
1975	9.7	5.2	5.5	4.9	0.6	5.1	9.3	7.0	3.2	7.0	7.9	3.4	7.7	3.5	-1.4	5.0	2.8	-0.1	4.8
1976	1.0	1.2	3.4	6.2	-0.1	1.6	3.9	5.6	0.2	7.1	-1.0	3.5	7.3	0.0	-3.5	7.5	0.2	2.3	2.6
1977	3.4	-1.2	2.2	2.9	0.4	5.0	-1.0	2.7	-3.7	1.0	2.5	1.4	1.7	0.7	-0.2	-4.7	-5.7	2.3	0.5
1978	2.1	-1.0	1.2	-1.7	2.3	4.3	0.4	4.4	-0.3	2.8	6.9	2.8	-0.1	1.7	4.2	-1.3	6.0	1.0	2.0
1979	1.7	-1.6	1.8	-0.4	-1.3	2.4	1.7	2.4	4.0	5.3	2.2	2.8	-1.8	0.2	1.9	0.6	2.1	-2.8	1.2
1980	0.8	0.8	2.3	-0.1	1.1	3.0	-0.9	2.1	1.2	-3.5	3.0	-1.6	-0.9	-1.9	1.5	-4.9	0.3	-4.8	-0.1
1981	0.0	1.6	1.1	-0.6	-1.3	0.7	-2.3	1.7	0.8	3.1	-3.9	0.9	-2.9	-3.4	3.8	-1.5	0.9	-0.6	-0.1
1982	1.1	4.4	-1.2	1.2	0.6	0.4	-0.1	3.8	0.9	1.2	-2.6	2.3	-0.1	0.9	-4.0	0.1	2.9	0.2	0.7
1983	1.5	-3.9	-1.7	-2.3	3.7	0.7	-0.3	0.5	1.2	2.1	1.1	1.8	-0.6	-0.1	-7.0	-1.8	4.5	0.7	0.0
1984	-2.1	3.6	-1.1	2.3	-0.8	0.9	-1.6	0.9	3.1	4.1	1.9	1.3	1.9	-2.1	-3.9	1.5	3.4	-0.2	0.7
1985	2.5	-2.7	-2.0	-0.3	-0.1	1.8	0.1	1.4	1.9	2.8	3.2	1.3	2.3	2.6	-5.5	0.1	3.1	0.3	0.7
1986	2.8	-4.0	-0.1	-1.3	2.7	5.1	1.0	2.4	3.3	0.7	3.7	1.3	2.9	1.5	4.2	3.2	4.2	0.2	1.9
1987	3.6	-4.0	-0.6	-1.1	0.9	4.8	5.4	0.3	2.6	3.0	2.7	1.8	6.9	2.1	-7.9	2.3	3.9	-1.9	1.4
1988	1.5	-1.3	1.7	-0.1	1.1	2.9	2.0	1.1	3.2	2.5	3.2	3.3	-1.0	0.6	1.2	1.9	3.8	-1.3	1.5
1989	1.9	-1.1	1.1	0.4	0.5	1.4	-0.1	1.4	2.4	3.1	0.7	2.4	0.5	0.3	-1.7	3.3	0.9	-1.9	0.9
1990	3.9	-1.0	1.6	-0.1	-0.3	2.8	2.2	1.5	3.6	2.5	2.1	1.4	1.8	0.4	-1.8	-1.0	-0.1	-2.1	1.0
1991	2.6	0.6	2.2	-0.9	1.0	3.8	2.1	2.1	1.8	3.2	2.5	0.2	1.8	0.6	0.0	-4.2	2.3	-0.9	1.2
1992	1.8	1.5	2.1	2.0	0.0	4.5	1.2	2.3	-0.8	1.9	1.7	-0.8	0.8	1.1	-0.1	2.0	2.8	-0.6	1.3
1993	1.3	-0.8	0.4	0.3	-0.2	2.3	1.1	1.9	-0.7	0.8	4.3	0.5	0.4	0.7	0.1	-1.4	2.8	-0.5	0.7
1994	0.8	-0.5	0.2	1.4	—	-0.8	0.4	2.0	3.4	-1.7	0.0	2.0	—	-1.0	-0.5	1.8	2.4	0.1	0.6
1995	2.2	-2.9	0.2	-0.8	—	2.4	1.8	-0.2	6.3	0.1	0.3	3.1	—	-0.7	-2.0	2.5	0.9	-0.2	0.8
1996	1.8	-0.8	-0.4	1.6	—	3.0	1.7	0.6	3.2	1.7	1.6	2.2	—	-0.1	-0.3	5.8	2.2	0.3	1.5
1997	0.5	1.2	0.9	-0.7	—	-0.8	1.7	2.0	1.2	3.5	0.4	1.0	0.6	0.6	0.9	3.5	1.2	0.8	1.1
1998	1.3	1.5	1.6	2.1	—	0.2	2.2	1.5	2.2	1.3	2.6	-0.7	—	1.3	1.2	3.9	2.9	0.9	1.6

Sources: OECD (1985, 1997, 1999g); own calculations.

Table A.17 *Real unit labor costs in manufacturing (% change from previous year)*

Year	A	AUS	B	CAN	CH	D	DK	F	FL	I	IRL	JAP	N	NL	NZ	S	UK	USA	OECD-18
1970	-2.2	1.9	1.6	2.2	2.0	9.5	4.5	1.9	2.7	6.0	—	1.6	-1.5	4.7	—	-1.9	3.2	0.9	2.3
1971	5.2	3.3	5.6	1.1	4.6	4.7	4.2	2.1	6.6	8.0	—	7.5	5.7	2.8	—	1.0	-2.0	-0.9	3.7
1972	0.7	0.4	3.5	1.7	2.9	0.7	-0.9	0.7	1.7	2.7	—	2.8	0.0	0.6	—	1.0	2.1	1.1	1.4
1973	4.1	2.0	1.6	-0.1	1.8	1.6	1.7	1.8	4.2	2.3	—	4.3	1.4	2.9	-1.0	-3.2	-1.2	-0.4	1.4
1974	2.6	11.0	3.1	3.6	-0.1	3.3	4.0	2.4	5.8	0.0	—	4.0	1.1	2.3	-2.8	2.2	5.4	-0.5	2.8
1975	4.3	1.0	3.7	3.3	3.1	-0.3	3.7	6.6	5.1	6.4	—	1.2	2.6	3.0	8.4	7.0	7.5	-2.0	3.8
1976	-2.0	-2.5	0.1	2.2	0.4	-2.0	-1.5	2.0	1.1	-1.6	—	-0.8	-0.6	-2.9	-7.6	7.1	-5.7	0.1	-0.8
1977	0.3	-3.0	1.0	-1.0	-1.1	0.7	-1.9	0.8	-4.3	1.9	—	-1.1	0.0	0.5	1.3	2.9	-7.4	0.0	-0.6
1978	6.7	-2.9	-0.1	-4.4	3.2	0.9	-0.7	0.5	-4.6	-0.4	3.8	-1.2	-3.1	1.6	12.0	-0.5	2.1	-0.3	0.7
1979	-2.5	-4.4	0.1	-1.3	-0.9	-0.3	-1.7	-1.0	-0.8	0.1	7.1	-1.2	-4.5	1.0	-0.9	-1.4	0.7	-2.1	-0.8
1980	-0.7	1.8	-1.0	1.3	-6.2	2.2	-1.7	0.1	-0.3	-2.4	2.3	-2.4	-3.8	-1.5	-1.1	-0.1	3.6	-3.1	-0.7
1981	1.3	1.5	-1.7	-0.5	0.4	-1.5	-2.6	-0.9	1.8	3.3	-5.7	0.2	-1.8	-4.2	2.1	-2.7	-1.8	-2.4	-0.8
1982	-2.6	5.8	-5.5	-0.8	3.3	-1.1	-0.4	0.0	-2.7	-0.5	-5.5	-0.1	0.2	-1.7	-6.5	-4.0	-4.4	1.7	-1.4
1983	-2.3	-7.3	-4.8	-3.8	1.1	-3.0	-0.6	-0.5	-0.8	-1.2	-0.9	0.9	-3.7	-3.4	-4.9	-2.5	-1.5	-1.2	-2.2
1984	-0.5	-0.1	-1.8	-2.4	-1.8	-1.6	-2.8	-1.5	0.7	-1.8	-4.6	-0.7	-3.2	-6.1	-5.9	-2.7	-0.7	-1.1	-2.2
1985	0.5	-2.4	0.0	-1.7	-0.9	-0.3	-1.0	-1.4	2.0	0.0	-1.5	-1.7	-0.3	-1.9	-0.7	-0.5	-1.6	0.3	-0.7
1986	2.0	-0.9	0.9	-0.3	3.6	2.9	0.2	-0.3	1.7	-1.1	3.5	0.8	1.8	1.5	5.3	2.8	0.1	1.0	1.4
1987	1.0	-4.7	-0.7	0.0	2.7	2.4	4.9	-1.1	0.4	0.7	-2.6	-0.7	1.6	2.6	-2.4	0.8	-0.3	0.4	0.3
1988	-0.7	-0.7	-2.5	0.6	0.8	-1.1	4.2	-1.7	0.3	0.9	-3.0	-1.2	-0.2	-0.7	0.0	0.7	1.3	-0.2	-0.2
1989	-0.5	0.5	0.2	0.2	-0.7	-2.0	-1.1	-1.6	-1.0	-0.2	-3.2	-0.1	-4.4	-2.8	-3.1	3.6	1.1	-2.3	-1.0
1990	-0.1	0.2	1.0	0.1	-0.5	-0.7	-0.2	0.6	3.4	3.7	-3.6	0.1	-2.5	-0.8	-3.9	0.6	0.1	-0.3	-0.2
1991	1.6	-0.4	3.1	-0.9	2.3	4.5	-0.4	0.8	3.5	1.6	1.2	0.5	-1.9	0.5	-1.8	-3.4	1.6	-0.1	0.7
1992	1.2	-0.3	1.3	-0.1	-0.5	0.6	-0.4	0.2	-2.6	-0.7	-0.1	0.8	-1.7	0.5	-0.5	-2.4	0.2	-0.4	-0.3
1993	0.0	-2.2	2.0	-2.4	-1.9	-1.1	-1.0	1.3	-5.3	-2.0	3.5	0.8	-3.2	-0.5	-2.4	-4.3	-1.2	-0.7	-1.2
1994	-1.7	-1.2	-2.4	-1.5	-0.4	-2.9	-4.2	-2.1	-1.7	-4.6	-3.2	1.1	-1.8	-4.0	-1.8	-2.3	-3.1	-1.0	-2.2
1995	-0.8	-1.2	-0.9	-1.0	0.0	0.3	-0.1	0.2	-0.5	-4.4	-5.6	0.3	-0.5	-0.9	-1.1	-2.7	-2.1	-0.2	-1.2
1996	-2.0	0.4	-1.7	-0.3	-0.4	-1.7	-0.9	-0.2	0.2	1.5	-0.6	-2.0	0.6	-1.4	0.5	3.8	0.0	-1.6	-0.3
1997	-1.8	2.8	-1.5	-1.5	-2.1	-3.8	0.5	-0.8	-2.9	1.4	-1.1	0.4	1.8	-0.9	0.4	0.1	0.2	0.0	-0.5
1998	-0.9	1.5	-0.1	0.0	0.3	-2.0	2.0	-0.2	-0.8	-2.0	-0.7	1.4	3.8	0.4	-0.4	1.5	1.1	1.1	0.3

Sources: OECD (1999g); own calculations.

Table A.18 *Unit labor costs in manufacturing, national currency basis (Index 1991 = 100)*

Year	A	AUS	B	CAN	CH	D	DK	F	FL	I	JAP	N	NL	NZ	S	UK	USA	OECD-17
1970	47	17	43	30	44	43	26	24	20	13	45	21	54	15	20	15	40	30
1971	51	19	46	30	46	46	28	25	23	15	49	23	59	17	22	16	40	33
1972	54	20	48	31	48	48	28	26	24	15	51	25	62	19	23	18	41	34
1973	61	22	50	32	49	51	31	28	28	16	58	26	66	21	24	19	42	37
1974	66	28	58	36	55	56	37	33	33	20	74	30	73	23	28	23	47	42
1975	77	33	67	42	64	59	40	39	43	26	84	36	85	25	33	31	52	49
1976	76	36	69	45	59	60	43	42	49	29	85	41	86	28	38	34	54	51
1977	81	40	74	47	58	63	46	45	53	33	90	45	90	34	43	38	57	55
1978	83	42	75	50	60	66	51	49	53	36	92	49	91	39	46	44	62	58
1979	82	44	77	55	61	68	54	53	56	40	91	49	93	41	46	52	68	61
1980	86	48	88	63	61	75	56	60	60	45	95	50	97	48	50	63	78	66
1981	93	54	90	69	65	78	61	68	67	53	99	56	99	55	56	70	83	72
1982	96	63	88	80	70	82	66	75	71	61	99	59	103	61	58	73	88	76
1983	96	65	84	80	75	82	67	81	74	68	101	62	100	64	59	73	88	78
1984	95	68	86	77	77	83	72	87	77	71	100	64	95	60	62	74	90	79
1985	97	70	90	79	78	85	76	90	80	76	97	68	96	66	67	78	92	81
1986	100	76	92	83	80	88	82	93	82	78	103	75	98	77	71	82	94	85
1987	101	79	93	85	82	93	91	94	82	80	99	82	100	83	74	86	91	88
1988	97	83	91	88	85	93	90	92	84	81	97	87	98	88	79	87	92	89
1989	96	90	91	91	87	95	92	92	88	86	97	91	95	90	84	87	94	91
1990	98	97	97	94	93	97	98	95	95	93	98	93	97	95	92	94	97	95
1991	100	100	100	100	100	100	100	100	100	100	100	100	100	100	100	100	100	100
1992	103	100	104	99	104	107	102	103	92	102	104	98	105	100	99	101	102	101
1993	104	101	104	97	106	112	98	104	85	105	108	100	108	100	91	101	101	102
1994	99	100	102	96	106	109	96	99	84	102	109	101	102	101	87	99	99	100
1995	98	104	102	96	107	111	97	97	88	101	107	104	101	101	91	102	99	100
1996	98	105	102	99	108	110	99	98	88	107	106	106	101	104	96	107	99	102
1997	96	107	102	100	107	109	102	98	87	111	104	108	101	105	96	109	99	102

Source: OECD (1999g); own calculations.

Table A.19 Relative unit labor costs in manufacturing, common currency (Index 1995 = 100)

Year	A	AUS	B	CAN	CH	D	DK	F	FL	I	IRL	JAP	N	NL	NZ	S	UK	USA
1970	106	117	122	115	45	66	92	104	134	172	245	40	81	124	122	163	100	214
1971	107	121	122	116	47	68	91	100	138	181	250	42	83	126	128	161	102	197
1972	108	122	124	117	50	69	88	103	134	176	255	47	83	129	130	164	104	177
1973	117	140	123	111	56	75	94	105	143	158	252	54	85	134	143	157	91	160
1974	117	157	126	115	58	75	97	99	157	154	247	55	87	137	140	151	90	151
1975	125	146	129	115	61	68	92	111	150	169	240	55	93	142	113	165	98	147
1976	122	151	130	125	66	68	93	111	163	147	221	54	99	140	106	181	89	146
1977	126	137	136	115	62	72	92	104	153	146	219	59	104	137	113	178	88	142
1978	124	126	134	104	75	74	94	104	131	139	215	70	98	133	119	164	96	132
1979	118	118	130	101	72	75	94	105	128	138	216	59	89	130	120	154	114	132
1980	116	118	121	103	62	75	81	110	130	134	213	53	91	123	120	152	139	133
1981	116	133	111	107	62	69	76	108	134	133	185	56	95	111	116	155	144	138
1982	115	140	92	117	69	72	75	103	139	135	190	50	97	115	113	134	134	151
1983	115	133	84	120	73	73	75	103	135	144	177	56	98	112	109	121	124	157
1984	111	138	84	111	71	71	76	104	140	140	163	57	97	101	91	124	118	160
1985	111	116	85	107	71	70	79	106	142	138	157	56	97	99	89	130	121	165
1986	116	98	90	101	78	77	86	109	135	140	167	76	97	106	90	130	113	142
1987	116	96	91	107	82	85	94	108	132	138	153	79	97	111	99	129	115	121
1988	109	107	89	118	83	85	91	102	136	137	141	82	103	107	107	136	122	112
1989	105	117	86	122	78	83	88	97	141	143	129	73	100	100	99	142	117	113
1990	106	117	91	122	84	85	95	101	148	149	135	66	99	101	96	145	119	111
1991	103	114	91	126	85	82	91	100	144	152	129	70	96	99	95	151	121	110
1992	103	103	92	114	83	89	92	101	112	145	122	74	95	102	85	148	114	107
1993	102	95	91	104	84	93	89	102	86	119	112	89	92	103	87	107	101	107
1994	99	101	93	98	92	94	93	100	88	112	108	101	95	98	94	102	103	105
1995	100	100	100	100	100	100	100	100	100	100	100	100	100	100	100	100	100	100
1996	97	112	98	106	97	96	99	98	94	112	100	83	101	97	109	112	104	101
1997	92	117	95	107	91	87	99	91	92	117	88	78	106	91	112	109	125	107
1998	91	109	97	103	95	87	106	92	95	114	83	87	107	94	99	103	140	118

Note: The data report the development of unit labor costs relative to the OECD average (1995 = 100).
Source: OECD (1999g).

Table A.20 *Income from dependent employment as % of national income*[a]

Year	A	AUS	B	CAN	CH	D	DK	F	FL	I	IRL	JAP	N	NL	NZ	S	UK	USA	OECD-18
1970	49.4	62.8	54.5	63.5	60.5	59.1	54.9	54.0	57.2	50.5	53.6	50.2	55.9	61.1	55.4	68.5	64.7	67.1	57.9
1971	51.2	62.7	56.6	63.8	62.1	60.5	56.2	54.9	60.6	53.2	54.6	54.5	58.8	62.6	55.4	69.2	63.8	65.9	59.3
1972	50.9	61.4	57.8	63.3	62.5	61.1	52.6	55.2	60.9	54.4	53.1	55.0	60.0	61.9	54.3	69.2	64.6	66.0	59.1
1973	52.5	62.4	58.4	62.0	63.5	62.3	53.3	55.5	61.3	54.4	53.9	56.0	59.4	62.4	54.4	66.9	65.1	65.8	59.4
1974	53.7	67.3	60.2	61.8	64.6	64.7	59.8	58.1	61.8	54.4	58.9	60.3	60.4	64.1	60.7	68.7	69.6	67.2	62.0
1975	57.0	66.1	62.4	64.3	66.2	64.9	64.0	61.4	67.7	58.8	59.6	63.5	63.0	66.8	62.8	70.1	72.9	66.5	64.3
1976	59.7	65.4	63.1	64.6	65.0	63.9	63.0	61.7	69.6	57.0	58.5	63.1	65.6	64.6	58.1	73.5	70.3	66.2	64.0
1977	59.8	66.5	63.9	65.5	64.7	64.6	64.3	62.4	69.1	57.2	57.4	63.5	68.2	64.6	60.2	76.3	67.2	66.0	64.5
1978	62.5	62.8	64.0	64.4	65.6	63.9	64.6	62.2	66.0	55.9	59.4	62.1	67.7	65.2	61.7	76.5	66.4	66.3	64.3
1979	60.9	61.8	64.3	63.6	65.6	64.1	66.6	62.0	64.3	54.9	63.0	61.9	64.1	66.2	61.4	75.0	65.7	66.7	64.0
1980	61.6	63.1	65.3	64.1	65.9	66.1	71.8	63.7	65.1	53.9	66.7	62.3	59.6	66.1	62.8	74.7	67.8	67.9	64.9
1981	62.8	65.1	65.4	64.9	65.9	66.9	75.4	64.5	66.9	55.6	64.9	63.5	59.2	64.9	62.1	75.5	67.2	67.2	65.4
1982	61.4	67.3	63.9	66.3	67.6	67.1	74.9	64.8	65.9	55.4	65.2	63.8	60.2	64.2	60.9	73.7	64.9	68.8	65.4
1983	59.7	62.4	63.2	64.0	68.5	65.0	71.7	64.8	65.6	54.6	65.5	64.6	58.7	62.4	57.0	71.8	63.2	67.3	63.9
1984	60.1	62.3	62.4	63.0	65.9	64.0	69.1	64.1	65.1	53.2	65.1	63.9	56.4	60.0	56.4	70.1	63.2	66.2	62.8
1985	60.4	62.6	61.6	62.9	66.4	63.9	68.2	63.2	66.3	53.1	65.1	62.6	55.8	58.8	58.2	70.3	62.6	66.6	62.7
1986	61.2	62.5	60.9	64.1	68.2	63.5	65.7	61.3	66.6	51.6	65.0	62.5	62.3	59.8	57.1	70.0	62.7	67.3	62.9
1987	61.5	60.5	59.6	63.5	69.7	63.9	69.3	60.7	66.5	51.1	63.9	61.8	64.8	61.6	57.3	69.9	61.8	68.0	63.1
1988	60.7	59.5	58.3	63.0	69.6	63.1	69.2	59.5	65.2	50.6	61.8	61.0	67.2	61.3	55.5	70.5	61.9	68.0	62.6
1989	60.2	61.1	56.3	63.6	70.4	61.7	68.6	58.8	65.5	50.8	59.9	61.5	63.7	59.1	55.1	72.5	62.8	66.9	62.1
1990	59.8	62.4	57.8	65.3	71.6	61.3	68.3	59.7	68.4	52.1	59.5	62.3	61.9	58.7	54.3	74.6	65.6	67.3	62.8
1991	60.7	61.9	58.8	66.8	73.5	63.8	68.1	60.3	73.9	52.4	60.0	63.1	61.3	59.3	54.1	73.7	66.0	67.7	63.6
1992	61.2	60.7	59.0	67.5	74.4	64.3	67.4	60.8	73.0	52.6	60.5	63.8	61.1	60.3	52.7	73.9	64.5	67.6	63.6
1993	62.1	59.9	58.3	66.2	72.8	64.7	66.4	61.3	68.8	51.7	61.4	64.9	59.5	60.3	51.0	73.3	62.7	67.0	62.9
1994	61.2	59.7	57.3	64.7	72.1	63.2	63.4	60.0	65.3	49.6	60.3	66.2	58.6	57.8	51.3	70.8	61.2	66.8	61.6
1995	60.9	59.4	56.7	63.6	71.1	63.4	63.4	59.9	63.4	47.6	58.5	66.7	57.4	57.4	51.6	68.0	60.9	67.0	60.9
1996	59.6	60.6	55.9	63.7	70.9	62.7	63.4	60.2	62.7	47.6	58.4	65.4	55.5	56.4	54.1	70.4	60.6	66.9	60.8
1997	58.5	60.3	55.2	63.3	69.6	61.0	64.2	59.3	60.0	47.7	58.8	66.2	56.2	55.6	53.7	69.7	60.7	67.3	60.4

[a] Compensation of employees/national income.
Sources: OECD (1999h); own calculations.

Table A.21 *Earnings dispersion between median and first decile (D5/D1), both genders*

Year	A	AUS	B	CAN	CH	D	DK	F	FL	I	JAP	N	NL	NZ	S	UK	USA
1979	—	1.64	—	—	—	—	—	1.67	—	1.96	1.71	—	—	—	—	1.69	—
1980	1.94	1.67	—	—	—	—	1.41	1.69	1.49	1.81	1.71	1.41	—	—	1.30	1.67	—
1981	—	1.68	—	2.24	—	—	1.41	1.67	—	1.90	1.72	—	—	—	1.32	1.68	—
1982	—	1.67	—	—	—	—	1.40	1.65	—	1.61	1.72	1.37	—	—	1.31	1.70	—
1983	—	1.69	—	—	—	1.65	1.38	1.62	1.48	1.70	1.72	—	—	1.70	1.30	1.70	—
1984	—	1.71	1.46	—	—	1.68	1.39	1.60	—	1.67	1.72	—	1.55	—	1.33	1.72	—
1985	—	1.64	1.45	2.43	—	1.59	1.41	1.60	1.47	1.75	1.72	—	1.55	1.70	1.30	1.73	—
1986	—	1.68	1.45	—	—	1.58	1.42	1.62	1.48	1.51	1.72	1.45	1.54	—	1.32	1.74	—
1987	1.93	1.67	1.45	2.39	—	1.55	1.41	1.62	1.46	—	1.71	—	1.56	1.74	1.33	1.77	—
1988	1.96	1.68	1.44	—	—	1.55	1.40	1.64	1.50	1.50	1.70	—	1.57	—	1.34	1.78	—
1989	1.94	1.69	1.45	—	—	1.50	1.39	1.65	1.47	—	1.70	—	1.57	1.75	1.35	1.79	—
1990	1.95	1.69	1.44	2.38	—	1.53	1.38	1.64	1.44	1.58	1.69	1.32	1.57	—	1.32	1.79	—
1991	1.98	1.66	1.44	2.23	1.61	1.49	—	1.64	1.44	1.58	1.67	—	1.57	1.77	1.36	1.77	—
1992	1.99	1.64	1.45	2.33	1.60	1.48	—	1.64	1.42	—	1.64	—	1.57	—	1.34	1.79	—
1993	2.00	1.62	1.43	2.21	1.62	1.44	—	1.64	1.39	1.75	1.65	—	1.54	—	1.34	1.79	2.05
1994	2.01	1.64	—	2.28	1.58	—	—	1.65	1.40	—	1.63	—	1.56	1.73	—	1.78	2.10
1995	—	1.65	—	—	1.59	—	—	—	—	—	—	—	—	—	—	1.81	2.09

Note: D1 and D5 refer to earnings at the upper limits of, respectively, the first and the fifth (median) deciles of employees ranked from lowest to highest earnings.
Source: OECD (1996a: 61–62).

Table A.22 *Public-sector deficits[a] as % of GDP*

Year	A	AUS	B	CAN	CH	D	DK	F	FL	I	IRL	JAP	N	NL	NZ	S	UK	USA	OECD-18
1970	1.2	2.8	-2.2	0.1	—	0.2	3.2	0.9	0.8	-3.9	—	0.6	1.3	-1.4	—	4.4	2.9	-1.1	0.7
1971	1.5	2.3	-3.2	-0.1	—	-0.2	3.9	0.6	0.9	-5.7	—	0.5	1.6	-1.1	—	5.2	1.3	-1.7	0.4
1972	2.0	2.1	-4.5	0.0	—	-0.5	3.9	0.6	0.8	-8.3	—	-0.1	1.8	-0.5	—	4.4	-1.3	-0.3	0.0

Year																			
1973	1.2	-0.4	-3.8	0.4	—	1.2	5.2	0.6	1.4	-7.6	—	0.3	2.3	0.8	—	4.1	-2.7	0.5	0.2
1974	1.2	1.0	-2.9	0.7	—	-1.3	3.1	0.3	1.4	-7.5	—	0.2	2.1	0.0	—	2.0	-3.8	-0.3	-0.2
1975	-2.4	-3.0	-5.0	-1.0	—	-5.6	-1.4	-2.4	1.8	-12.4	—	-1.8	1.7	-2.2	—	2.8	-4.5	-4.1	-2.6
1976	-3.6	-3.2	-5.7	-0.8	—	-3.4	-0.3	-0.7	2.9	-9.5	—	-2.5	1.6	-2.0	—	4.5	-4.9	-2.3	-2.0
1977	-2.3	-1.1	-5.9	-1.4	—	-2.4	-0.6	-0.8	2.3	-8.4	-2.6	-2.8	1.1	-0.8	—	1.7	-3.2	-1.0	-1.8
1978	-2.6	-2.7	-6.2	-1.8	—	-2.4	-0.3	-2.1	1.7	-10.2	-3.7	-4.2	0.5	-2.3	—	-0.5	-4.3	-0.1	-2.6
1979	-2.4	-2.3	-7.0	-1.3	—	-2.6	-1.7	-0.8	1.4	-9.8	-4.9	-3.7	1.1	-3.0	—	-2.9	-3.1	0.2	-2.7
1980	-1.7	-1.8	-8.6	-1.8	0.7	-2.9	-3.3	0.0	1.4	-8.3	-6.2	-3.6	3.0	0.0	—	-4.0	-3.3	-1.4	-2.5
1981	-1.8	-0.6	-12.7	-1.1	0.4	-3.7	-6.9	-1.9	2.0	-11.4	-7.7	-3.3	3.0	-5.4	—	-5.3	-3.9	-1.1	-3.7
1982	-3.4	-0.5	-10.8	-4.0	-1.0	-3.3	-9.1	-2.8	1.2	-11.2	-9.2	-3.1	2.7	-6.6	—	-7.0	-2.8	-3.5	-4.4
1983	4.0	-3.9	-11.4	-5.1	-1.2	-2.6	-7.2	-3.2	0.4	-10.5	-8.7	-3.2	4.4	-5.8	—	-5.0	-3.3	-4.1	-4.4
1984	-2.7	-3.3	-9.4	-5.0	-0.6	-1.9	-4.1	-2.8	2.1	-11.5	-7.7	-1.9	5.5	-5.5	—	-2.9	-4.0	-3.0	-3.5
1985	-2.6	-2.8	-8.8	-5.8	-0.4	-1.2	-2.0	-2.9	2.2	-12.3	-9.2	-0.8	8.1	-3.6	—	-3.8	-2.9	-3.2	-3.1
1986	-3.8	-3.0	-9.2	-4.8	0.7	-1.3	3.1	-2.7	2.7	-11.4	-9.7	-0.9	4.8	-5.1	-6.5	-1.2	-2.8	-3.5	-3.0
1987	-4.4	-0.2	-7.6	-3.5	0.5	-1.9	2.1	-1.9	0.9	-11.0	-7.9	0.4	4.0	-5.9	-2.2	4.2	-1.9	-2.6	-2.2
1988	-3.3	0.9	-6.8	-2.7	0.2	-2.2	1.5	-1.7	3.6	-10.7	-4.3	1.4	2.4	-4.6	-4.8	3.5	0.6	-2.1	-1.6
1989	-3.1	1.0	-6.2	-3.1	-0.3	0.1	0.3	-1.2	6.0	-9.8	-1.8	2.4	1.8	-4.7	-3.7	5.4	0.9	-1.7	-1.0
1990	-2.4	0.6	-5.5	-4.4	-1.1	-2.1	-1.0	-1.6	5.4	-11.1	-2.3	2.9	2.6	-5.1	-4.7	4.2	-1.5	-2.7	-1.7
1991	-2.7	-2.7	-6.3	-7.1	-3.0	-3.3	-2.4	-2.1	-1.5	-10.1	-2.4	3.0	0.1	-2.9	-3.8	-1.1	-2.8	-3.3	-3.0
1992	-1.9	-4.1	-6.9	-8.0	-3.5	-2.8	-2.2	-4.1	-5.9	-9.6	-2.6	1.5	-1.8	-3.9	-3.3	-7.8	-6.5	-4.4	-4.3
1993	-4.2	-3.8	-7.1	-7.6	-4.5	-3.5	-2.8	-6.1	-8.4	-9.5	-2.6	-1.7	-1.5	-3.2	-0.6	-12.3	-8.0	-3.6	-5.1
1994	-5.0	-4.0	-4.9	-5.7	-3.2	-2.6	-2.6	-6.0	-6.6	-9.2	-1.8	-2.4	0.5	-3.8	3.0	-10.3	-6.8	-2.3	-4.1
1995	-5.1	-2.0	-3.9	-4.6	-2.0	-3.5	-2.2	-5.4	-5.7	-7.7	-2.3	-3.8	3.7	-3.7	3.3	-7.8	-5.8	-1.9	-3.3
1996	-3.7	-0.9	-3.1	-2.1	-2.2	-3.5	-0.9	-4.6	-4.1	-6.7	-0.3	-4.4	7.2	-2.0	2.7	-2.1	-4.4	-0.9	-2.0
1997	-1.9	0.2	-1.9	0.9	-2.3	-2.8	0.2	-3.5	-1.6	-2.7	1.8	-3.5	8.6	-0.9	2.0	-1.1	-2.0	0.4	-0.6
1998	-2.2	0.5	-1.5	2.2	-3.3	-2.5	1.0	-3.3	1.0	-2.6	3.0	-6.4	5.0	-1.2	0.9	2.1	-0.4	1.6	-0.3

[a] General government financial balances.

Note: _____ indicates break in time series.

Sources: OECD (1999g); own calculations; for AUS 1970–73, DK 1970–87, UK 1970–77: OECD (1988: 178); general government financial balances for CH: Bundesamt für Sozialversicherung (1998).

Table A.23 *Total taxation as % of GDP*

Year	A	AUS	B	CAN	CH	D	DK	F	FL	I	IRL	JAP	N	NL	NZ	S	UK	USA	OECD-18
1970	34.9	24.2	35.7	31.2	22.5	32.9	40.4	35.1	32.5	26.1	29.9	19.7	34.9	37.1	27.4	39.8	37.0	27.4	31.6
1971	35.6	24.7	36.7	31.2	22.2	33.4	43.5	34.5	34.1	26.9	31.0	20.0	37.8	38.9	27.5	40.6	35.0	25.9	32.2
1972	36.0	23.8	37.0	31.9	22.6	34.8	42.9	34.9	34.6	26.9	29.7	20.7	39.9	39.7	27.2	42.0	33.3	26.6	32.5
1973	36.2	25.3	37.9	31.7	24.8	36.3	42.4	35.0	35.5	24.4	29.9	22.5	40.3	41.2	28.5	41.2	31.2	26.6	32.8
1974	37.2	27.1	38.8	33.7	25.8	36.5	44.2	35.5	34.7	25.7	30.3	23.0	39.8	41.7	31.3	42.4	34.5	27.1	33.9
1975	37.7	27.6	41.6	33.1	28.0	36.0	41.4	36.9	37.7	26.2	30.2	21.0	39.9	43.1	31.1	43.4	35.4	26.7	34.3
1976	37.6	28.0	42.0	32.4	29.6	36.8	41.6	38.7	41.7	27.2	33.5	21.8	41.1	42.7	30.8	47.7	35.2	26.0	35.2
1977	37.9	28.0	43.4	31.4	29.9	38.2	41.9	38.7	41.9	27.6	31.9	22.3	42.1	43.4	33.2	49.9	34.6	26.7	35.7
1978	40.2	26.8	44.6	31.2	29.9	37.9	43.4	38.6	38.2	27.7	30.2	24.0	41.2	44.1	31.8	50.3	32.9	26.6	35.5
1979	39.8	27.4	45.0	31.1	29.4	37.8	44.5	40.2	36.7	26.8	29.8	24.4	41.2	44.5	32.7	49.0	32.2	26.5	35.5
1980	40.3	28.4	43.7	32.0	29.1	38.2	45.5	41.7	36.9	30.4	32.6	25.4	42.7	45.2	33.0	48.8	35.2	26.9	36.4
1981	41.5	29.2	44.1	33.9	29.2	37.7	45.3	41.9	38.9	31.6	33.8	26.2	44.4	44.5	33.9	50.1	36.3	27.3	37.2
1982	40.2	29.5	45.6	33.5	29.8	37.7	44.5	42.8	37.8	33.9	35.2	26.6	43.6	44.9	34.6	49.1	38.9	27.1	37.5
1983	39.9	28.5	45.6	33.4	30.6	37.5	46.5	43.6	37.6	35.9	36.7	27.0	42.5	46.0	32.3	49.8	37.3	25.5	37.6
1984	41.7	30.0	46.5	33.3	30.8	37.6	47.6	44.6	39.2	35.0	37.5	27.2	41.7	44.4	32.5	49.5	37.6	25.5	37.9
1985	42.4	30.0	46.9	33.1	30.8	38.1	49.0	44.5	40.8	34.5	36.4	27.6	43.3	44.1	33.6	50.0	37.5	26.0	38.3
1986	42.4	30.8	46.3	33.8	31.9	37.8	50.8	44.0	42.4	36.0	37.2	28.4	45.5	44.9	33.9	52.5	37.8	25.8	39.0
1987	42.0	31.0	46.6	35.2	31.5	38.0	51.5	44.5	40.2	36.1	37.4	29.7	43.7	47.5	37.1	55.4	36.6	27.1	39.5
1988	42.0	30.6	45.2	34.3	31.8	37.7	51.7	43.8	43.3	36.8	38.7	30.3	43.1	47.6	36.5	54.8	36.9	26.9	39.6
1989	40.9	30.5	43.6	35.2	31.1	38.3	50.7	43.7	43.4	37.9	35.2	30.8	41.3	44.9	39.1	55.5	36.3	27.0	39.2
1990	41.0	30.6	44.0	36.0	30.9	36.7	48.7	43.7	45.4	39.2	34.8	31.3	41.8	44.6	38.0	55.6	36.6	26.7	39.2
1991	41.5	28.9	44.1	36.6	30.6	38.2	48.9	43.9	46.9	39.7	35.2	30.8	41.8	47.2	36.6	53.7	35.6	26.8	39.3
1992	43.0	28.4	44.3	36.2	31.2	38.9	49.2	43.7	46.8	42.2	35.4	29.2	41.0	46.8	37.0	51.0	35.1	26.7	39.2
1993	43.4	28.6	44.9	35.6	32.2	39.0	50.4	43.9	45.4	43.8	35.4	29.1	40.1	47.5	36.9	50.1	33.5	27.0	39.3
1994	43.3	29.6	46.0	35.9	33.0	39.2	51.9	44.1	47.6	41.7	36.1	27.8	41.3	44.7	37.3	50.8	34.5	27.5	39.6
1995	42.3	30.4	46.0	36.0	33.5	39.2	51.4	44.6	46.1	41.3	33.8	28.5	41.5	43.8	37.9	49.6	35.6	27.9	39.4
1996	44.0	31.1	46.0	36.8	34.7	38.1	52.2	45.7	48.2	43.2	33.7	28.5	41.1	43.3	35.8	52.0	36.0	28.5	39.9
1997	44.4	30.4	46.5	—	34.6	37.5	—	46.1	47.3	45.0	34.8	—	42.5	43.4	36.4	53.3	35.3	—	40.9

Source: OECD (1999k).

Table A.24 *Personal and corporate income taxes as % of GDP*

Year	A	AUS	B	CAN	CH	D	DK	F	FL	I	IRL	JAP	N	NL	NZ	S	UK	USA	OECD-18
1970	8.8	13.2	11.2	13.9	9.2	10.7	20.7	6.4	14.4	4.6	8.1	9.4	13.4	12.4	16.7	21.6	14.9	13.7	12.4
1971	9.1	13.5	11.8	13.8	9.1	10.9	23.7	5.9	15.0	4.9	9.0	9.4	14.1	13.3	17.2	20.0	14.3	11.9	12.6
1972	9.5	12.8	12.6	14.7	9.3	11.9	23.0	6.1	15.4	5.4	8.3	9.8	15.2	13.8	17.1	21.2	13.0	12.5	12.9
1973	9.5	14.0	13.5	14.5	10.2	13.0	23.9	6.1	16.1	4.7	8.7	11.6	13.4	14.1	18.8	20.2	12.9	12.4	13.2
1974	10.3	15.7	14.5	15.7	11.0	13.4	26.9	7.1	16.5	5.4	8.9	11.8	13.8	14.3	21.7	20.5	15.1	12.7	14.2
1975	9.9	15.4	16.3	15.7	12.3	12.4	24.4	6.5	18.1	5.6	9.1	9.3	13.7	15.0	20.7	21.9	15.8	12.3	14.1
1976	9.5	16.0	16.0	15.0	13.2	12.8	23.9	7.2	20.5	6.6	10.1	9.5	14.6	14.5	20.9	22.3	15.4	11.8	14.4
1977	9.7	16.1	17.1	14.0	12.9	13.9	23.1	7.3	19.6	7.5	10.1	9.5	15.0	14.4	23.3	22.2	14.5	12.7	14.6
1978	10.8	14.7	18.3	13.9	12.6	13.5	23.6	6.9	16.7	8.4	10.1	10.7	15.1	14.4	21.6	22.8	13.4	12.9	14.5
1979	10.6	15.1	18.8	14.3	12.2	13.2	23.9	7.0	15.6	8.3	10.6	10.9	15.6	14.4	22.6	22.3	12.7	13.3	15.0
1980	10.8	15.9	17.9	14.9	12.1	13.4	25.0	7.6	15.8	9.5	11.9	11.7	17.8	14.8	23.1	21.2	13.3	13.4	15.3
1981	11.2	16.7	17.9	15.1	12.2	12.8	25.0	7.8	17.3	10.8	12.2	11.8	18.9	14.1	23.4	21.5	14.1	13.4	15.4
1982	10.7	16.3	19.3	14.9	12.5	12.8	24.8	7.8	16.8	11.9	12.2	12.0	18.3	13.8	23.7	21.7	14.7	12.9	15.4
1983	10.3	15.1	18.6	14.4	12.7	12.5	25.6	8.0	16.9	13.0	12.2	12.2	17.1	12.6	21.4	21.2	14.4	11.6	15.0
1984	10.7	16.3	19.0	14.4	12.8	12.5	26.7	8.0	17.6	12.6	12.8	12.4	17.0	11.8	21.2	21.0	14.4	11.5	15.2
1985	11.2	16.4	19.0	14.6	12.6	13.3	27.9	7.7	18.4	12.7	12.6	12.7	17.2	11.6	23.1	21.1	14.5	11.8	15.5
1986	11.4	17.2	18.6	15.5	13.2	13.0	28.6	7.9	19.5	13.0	13.5	13.0	16.7	12.4	22.4	22.6	14.5	11.6	15.8
1987	10.9	17.1	18.3	16.6	12.8	13.0	29.1	8.0	17.3	13.1	14.2	14.0	14.6	13.0	22.0	23.0	13.7	12.7	15.7
1988	10.8	17.2	17.5	16.1	13.1	12.9	30.2	7.6	18.7	13.1	14.9	14.5	14.6	13.3	21.8	24.3	13.7	12.3	15.9
1989	9.9	17.3	16.2	16.9	12.5	13.4	29.9	7.6	18.3	14.0	12.4	15.1	13.7	12.8	23.1	23.9	14.0	12.6	15.8
1990	10.5	17.5	16.4	17.5	12.8	11.9	28.4	7.5	19.6	14.3	12.8	15.2	14.7	14.4	22.0	23.2	14.3	12.1	15.8
1991	11.0	16.2	16.0	17.2	12.6	12.1	28.9	7.9	19.5	14.3	13.5	14.5	15.0	15.7	20.7	19.9	13.6	11.9	15.6
1992	11.6	15.8	15.9	16.2	13.0	12.4	29.3	7.5	20.1	15.8	13.7	12.5	13.4	14.7	21.1	19.4	12.6	11.7	15.4
1993	11.7	15.4	16.0	15.7	12.6	12.0	30.2	7.6	17.5	16.2	14.2	11.8	13.5	15.4	21.8	20.5	11.7	12.0	15.3
1994	10.7	16.1	17.2	16.2	13.2	11.5	31.4	7.8	19.3	14.5	14.5	10.5	14.4	12.5	22.4	21.6	12.3	12.3	15.5
1995	11.3	16.8	17.7	16.8	12.5	11.8	31.0	7.8	18.5	14.5	13.2	10.4	14.6	11.5	23.0	20.5	13.0	12.8	15.4
1996	12.2	17.5	17.5	17.4	13.1	10.8	31.4	8.2	20.1	14.9	13.8	10.4	15.0	11.7	21.1	21.3	13.2	13.5	15.7
1997	12.9	17.1	18.0	—	12.8	10.5	—	8.9	19.7	16.3	14.3	—	16.2	11.4	21.5	21.6	13.0	11.5	15.8

Source: OECD (1999k).

Table A.25 *Consumption taxes as % of GDP*

Year	A	AUS	B	CAN	CH	D	DK	F	FL	I	IRL	JAP	N	NL	NZ	S	UK	USA	OECD-18
1970	13.0	7.8	12.5	9.9	6.1	10.5	15.7	13.4	12.9	10.1	15.7	4.4	15.0	10.3	7.5	11.2	10.6	5.5	10.7
1971	13.1	7.7	12.5	10.2	5.8	10.4	15.8	13.2	13.5	10.0	15.3	4.3	16.2	10.5	7.2	12.8	10.0	5.6	10.8
1972	13.3	7.4	11.7	10.3	6.0	10.4	15.7	13.3	13.2	9.3	14.6	4.3	16.3	10.9	7.0	12.5	9.5	5.5	10.6
1973	13.3	7.5	11.3	10.8	5.8	10.1	15.0	12.7	12.8	8.5	14.8	4.1	15.6	10.6	6.9	12.1	8.6	5.4	10.3
1974	13.2	7.5	11.2	11.7	5.5	9.7	14.1	12.7	11.7	8.7	14.4	3.7	14.8	10.1	7.0	11.2	9.1	5.3	10.1
1975	13.0	8.1	11.0	10.6	5.6	9.7	13.9	12.3	12.2	7.7	14.1	3.6	15.0	10.4	7.5	10.6	8.9	5.2	10.0
1976	13.1	8.1	11.6	10.3	5.7	9.6	14.8	12.7	12.3	8.3	16.0	4.0	15.7	10.8	7.1	11.4	8.9	5.2	10.3
1977	12.7	7.9	11.7	10.2	5.9	9.6	15.7	11.9	13.2	8.4	14.9	3.9	16.3	11.4	7.3	11.8	8.9	4.9	10.4
1978	12.8	8.4	11.7	10.1	6.1	10.0	16.5	12.2	13.4	7.6	14.1	4.2	15.7	11.5	7.5	11.8	8.6	4.8	10.4
1979	12.8	8.7	11.7	10.1	6.0	10.3	17.2	12.7	13.2	7.6	13.2	4.3	15.1	11.3	7.6	11.6	8.3	4.6	10.4
1980	12.7	8.8	11.5	10.4	5.9	10.4	17.0	12.7	13.2	8.0	14.3	4.2	15.1	11.4	7.4	11.7	10.3	4.7	10.5
1981	13.1	8.8	11.7	11.5	5.8	10.3	17.0	12.5	13.3	8.0	15.2	4.2	15.4	11.1	7.9	12.0	10.0	5.1	10.7
1982	12.6	9.5	11.9	11.1	5.8	10.1	16.4	12.9	13.2	8.4	16.2	4.1	15.1	10.9	8.2	12.0	11.5	5.0	10.8
1983	12.8	9.6	12.0	10.8	6.0	10.3	16.6	12.8	13.2	9.2	16.9	4.1	15.4	11.1	8.3	12.3	11.0	4.9	11.0
1984	13.8	9.9	11.7	11.0	5.8	10.2	16.7	13.0	13.8	9.2	16.9	4.1	15.1	11.3	8.8	12.5	11.6	4.9	11.1
1985	13.8	9.9	12.0	10.5	5.8	9.8	16.8	13.2	13.9	8.8	16.2	3.9	16.3	11.3	7.8	13.3	11.8	4.9	11.1
1986	13.6	9.6	11.6	10.0	6.0	9.5	17.9	12.9	14.2	9.4	16.4	3.8	17.7	11.6	8.7	13.1	11.7	4.8	11.3
1987	13.6	9.3	11.9	10.2	6.1	9.7	17.5	13.0	14.3	9.6	15.9	3.8	17.6	12.3	12.1	13.6	11.3	4.8	11.5
1988	13.5	8.7	11.7	9.8	6.0	9.5	17.5	12.9	14.8	10.3	16.2	3.9	16.2	12.3	11.5	13.4	11.5	4.8	11.4
1989	13.3	8.7	11.5	9.8	5.9	9.8	16.8	12.6	15.0	10.3	15.6	3.9	15.1	11.8	12.8	13.4	11.3	4.6	11.2
1990	12.9	8.5	11.6	9.3	5.7	9.8	16.4	12.4	14.8	11.0	14.7	4.1	14.9	11.8	12.8	13.9	11.6	4.6	11.2
1991	12.7	8.1	11.7	9.4	5.6	10.3	16.3	12.0	14.9	11.2	14.3	4.2	14.7	12.0	12.9	14.2	11.5	4.8	11.2
1992	13.0	8.1	11.7	9.5	5.4	10.5	16.0	11.8	14.8	11.4	14.2	4.1	15.3	12.0	13.2	13.2	12.0	4.8	11.2
1993	12.7	8.5	12.0	9.5	5.4	10.8	15.8	11.7	14.6	11.4	13.6	4.2	15.4	12.0	12.7	13.6	12.0	4.9	11.2
1994	13.4	8.8	12.3	9.3	5.5	11.2	16.6	12.0	14.5	11.8	14.1	4.3	15.9	11.8	12.6	13.1	12.2	5.0	11.4
1995	11.7	8.9	12.0	9.1	6.2	10.9	16.7	12.2	13.7	11.3	13.8	4.3	16.0	12.0	12.6	12.0	12.6	5.0	11.2
1996	12.6	8.7	12.4	9.1	6.2	10.6	17.1	12.5	14.5	11.2	13.4	4.4	15.6	12.4	12.3	11.8	12.7	4.9	11.2
1997	12.5	8.6	12.4	—	6.1	10.4	—	12.6	14.6	11.2	13.8	—	15.8	12.2	12.6	12.0	12.5	4.9	11.3

Source: OECD (1999k).

Table A.26 *Social security contributions and payroll taxes as % of GDP*

Year	A	AUS	B	CAN	CH	D	DK	F	FL	I	IRL	JAP	N	NL	NZ	S	UK	USA	OECD-18
1970	11.6	0.7	10.9	3.0	5.3	10.2	1.6	13.1	4.4	9.9	2.5	4.4	5.6	13.0	0.4	6.3	6.8	4.4	6.3
1971	11.9	1.0	11.3	2.9	5.4	10.5	1.6	13.3	4.9	10.3	2.7	4.7	6.6	13.8	0.6	7.2	6.1	4.4	6.6
1972	11.9	1.1	11.7	2.9	5.3	11.0	1.7	13.6	5.2	10.5	2.7	4.7	7.4	13.9	0.6	7.7	5.9	4.5	6.8
1973	12.1	1.3	12.0	2.9	6.9	11.8	0.8	13.6	5.7	10.1	2.9	4.9	10.1	15.2	0.4	8.3	5.5	4.8	7.2
1974	12.5	1.6	12.1	3.1	7.4	12.0	0.6	14.2	5.7	10.6	3.5	5.7	9.9	16.1	0.0	10.1	6.0	5.3	7.6
1975	13.4	1.6	13.3	3.3	8.2	12.6	0.6	15.7	6.6	12.0	4.2	6.1	9.9	16.5	0.0	10.4	6.2	5.5	8.1
1976	13.5	1.6	13.3	3.6	8.7	12.9	0.6	16.3	7.7	11.4	4.4	6.4	9.6	16.1	0.0	13.4	6.6	5.3	8.4
1977	14.0	1.6	13.4	3.5	8.9	13.2	0.6	17.0	8.1	10.8	4.3	6.8	9.6	16.1	0.0	15.4	7.1	5.5	8.7
1978	15.1	1.5	13.4	3.6	9.1	13.1	0.6	17.0	7.2	10.7	4.1	7.0	9.7	16.4	0.0	15.2	6.9	5.5	8.7
1979	14.9	1.4	13.3	3.4	9.1	13.0	0.7	17.9	7.1	9.9	4.3	7.1	9.7	17.0	0.0	14.6	7.1	5.7	8.7
1980	15.3	1.4	13.3	3.4	9.0	13.2	0.8	18.7	7.3	11.8	4.8	7.4	9.0	17.2	0.0	15.4	7.4	5.9	9.0
1981	15.6	1.6	13.6	3.9	9.0	13.4	1.0	18.7	7.4	11.7	4.7	7.9	9.3	17.7	0.0	16.1	7.4	6.1	9.2
1982	15.4	1.6	13.6	3.9	9.2	13.6	1.3	19.3	6.9	12.6	5.6	8.0	9.5	18.6	0.0	14.8	7.7	6.3	9.3
1983	15.2	1.4	14.2	4.4	9.6	13.4	1.8	19.9	6.6	12.7	6.2	8.1	9.3	20.7	0.0	15.4	7.3	6.2	9.6
1984	15.6	1.4	15.0	4.3	9.8	13.6	2.1	20.2	6.6	12.2	6.5	8.1	8.9	19.7	0.0	15.1	7.0	6.4	9.6
1985	15.9	1.4	15.1	4.5	9.9	13.9	2.3	20.2	7.3	12.2	6.3	8.4	9.0	19.5	0.2	14.4	6.7	6.6	9.7
1986	15.9	1.6	15.2	4.7	10.0	14.0	1.8	19.7	7.4	12.6	5.9	8.5	10.2	19.2	0.3	15.2	6.8	6.6	9.8
1987	16.1	1.7	15.5	4.8	9.9	14.2	2.2	20.0	7.4	12.6	5.7	8.5	10.4	20.2	0.4	15.5	6.7	6.7	9.9
1988	16.1	1.7	15.0	4.8	10.0	14.1	1.4	19.8	8.3	12.4	6.0	8.5	11.1	20.2	0.8	15.2	6.8	6.9	10.0
1989	16.1	1.7	14.7	4.7	10.0	13.9	1.7	20.0	8.6	12.8	5.6	8.6	11.3	18.5	0.7	16.2	6.3	6.9	9.9
1990	16.0	1.9	14.8	5.2	10.0	13.7	1.8	20.1	9.9	13.0	5.7	9.1	11.0	16.7	0.7	16.5	6.2	6.9	10.0
1991	16.1	1.9	15.3	5.7	10.3	14.7	1.8	20.1	11.3	13.2	5.8	9.3	10.9	17.6	0.6	17.5	6.2	6.9	10.0
1992	16.7	1.8	15.5	6.0	10.6	15.0	1.8	20.3	10.9	13.4	5.9	9.4	11.0	18.2	0.5	16.5	6.4	7.0	10.3
1993	17.3	1.7	15.8	5.9	10.6	15.1	2.1	20.6	12.0	13.9	6.1	9.8	10.1	18.2	0.4	14.4	6.0	6.9	10.4
1994	18.0	2.1	15.3	6.0	11.8	15.3	2.0	20.2	12.6	13.1	5.8	9.8	10.0	18.4	0.3	14.5	6.2	7.0	10.5
1995	18.1	2.1	15.2	5.9	12.4	15.5	1.8	20.4	12.7	13.2	5.3	10.4	9.8	18.3	0.4	15.5	6.3	7.0	10.6
1996	18.1	2.1	14.9	6.0	13.0	15.5	1.8	20.8	12.4	14.9	4.9	10.4	9.6	17.1	0.4	16.8	6.2	7.0	10.7
1997	18.0	2.0	14.8	—	13.1	15.6	—	20.2	11.9	15.2	4.9	—	9.6	17.7	0.3	17.7	6.0	6.8	10.7

Source: OECD (1999k).

Table A.27 *Public social expenditures as % of GDP*

Year	A	AUS	B	CAN	CH	D	DK	F	FL	I	IRL	JAP	N	NL	NZ	S	UK	USA	OECD-18
1980	22.6	11.7	24.6	13.2	14.0	23.7	27.5	23.5	18.9	18.4	17.6	9.9	18.5	28.5	16.5	29.8	18.3	13.4	19.5
1981	—	11.9	26.4	13.7	13.7	24.6	27.8	25.1	19.5	19.8	17.7	10.3	—	29.4	17.1	30.7	19.8	13.5	—
1982	—	13.0	27.0	16.2	14.6	25.0	28.0	26.1	20.7	20.3	18.4	10.7	—	31.0	18.2	30.9	20.2	13.8	—
1983	—	13.5	27.3	16.2	15.0	24.4	28.5	26.6	21.4	21.4	18.5	11.0	—	31.1	18.0	31.3	20.9	14.2	—
1984	—	13.8	26.7	16.0	15.3	24.0	27.3	26.9	22.3	20.9	17.9	10.9	—	29.9	17.0	30.0	21.2	13.2	—
1985	24.4	14.0	27.5	16.3	15.2	24.7	26.4	27.0	23.4	21.6	22.9	11.3	19.7	28.9	17.6	31.1	21.1	13.0	21.4
1986	—	13.8	27.5	16.5	15.3	24.5	25.6	26.7	24.0	21.8	23.1	11.6	—	28.6	17.5	31.2	21.3	13.1	—
1987	—	13.8	26.8	16.1	15.5	24.9	26.4	26.6	24.4	22.1	22.2	11.9	—	28.9	18.6	31.4	20.5	13.2	—
1988	—	13.0	26.4	15.9	15.6	24.9	27.7	26.5	23.9	22.2	20.8	11.6	24.9	28.5	19.9	32.0	19.1	13.1	—
1989	—	13.3	25.5	16.2	15.3	23.9	28.2	25.7	23.5	22.4	19.1	11.4	25.9	28.2	21.6	31.4	18.7	13.1	—
1990	24.2	14.5	25.6	17.6	16.3	23.2	28.1	26.7	25.2	23.1	19.2	11.2	26.5	29.7	22.2	32.2	19.5	13.5	22.1
1991	24.4	15.6	26.3	19.4	17.4	25.3	29.0	27.3	30.5	24.7	19.9	11.3	27.7	29.8	22.6	34.3	21.1	14.7	23.4
1992	24.9	16.5	26.6	20.0	19.0	26.7	29.7	28.2	34.8	25.7	20.4	11.9	28.8	30.2	22.5	36.4	22.8	15.4	24.5
1993	26.4	16.5	27.3	20.0	20.6	27.6	30.7	29.7	34.8	25.9	20.4	12.4	28.5	30.5	19.1	36.9	22.7	15.6	24.8
1994	26.7	16.1	26.8	18.9	20.7	27.5	32.6	29.7	33.9	25.2	20.0	13.0	28.2	28.7	18.9	35.9	22.8	15.6	24.5
1995	26.2	15.7	27.1	18.2	21.0	28.0	32.1	30.1	32.0	23.7	19.4	13.8	27.6	27.8	18.8	33.0	22.5	15.8	24.0
1996	—	—	—	—	—	—	31.4	—	—	—	18.4	—	—	26.7	19.2	—	—	—	—

Sources: OECD (1999f); own calculations.

Table A.27a *Social expenditures as % of GDP (including private mandatory benefits*[a]*)*

Year	A	AUS	B	CAN	CH	D	DK	F	FL	I	IRL	JAP	N	NL	NZ	S	UK	USA	OECD-18
1980	23.9	11.7	25.6	13.2	16.1	25.7	27.5	23.5	18.9	18.4	17.6	9.9	18.8	28.5	16.5	29.8	18.3	13.7	19.9
1981	—	11.9	27.4	13.7	15.7	26.5	27.8	25.1	19.5	19.8	17.7	10.4	•	29.4	17.1	30.7	19.8	13.9	—
1982	—	13.0	28.0	16.2	16.7	26.6	28.0	26.1	20.7	20.3	18.4	10.8	—	31.0	18.2	30.9	20.2	14.2	—
1983	—	13.5	28.4	16.2	17.6	25.9	28.5	26.6	21.4	21.4	18.5	11.1	—	31.1	18.0	31.3	20.9	14.6	—
1984	—	13.8	27.4	16.0	17.7	25.5	27.3	26.9	22.3	20.9	17.9	11.0	—	29.9	17.0	30.0	21.2	13.6	—
1985	25.4	14.0	28.2	16.3	17.7	26.3	26.4	27.0	23.4	21.6	22.9	11.4	20.0	28.9	17.6	31.1	21.1	13.4	21.8
1986	—	13.8	28.2	16.5	18.0	26.2	25.6	26.7	24.0	21.8	23.1	11.8	—	28.6	17.5	31.2	21.4	13.6	—
1987	—	13.8	27.6	16.1	18.5	26.5	26.4	26.6	24.4	22.1	22.2	12.0	—	28.9	18.6	31.4	20.5	13.7	—
1988	—	13.0	27.4	15.9	18.7	26.5	27.7	26.5	23.9	22.2	20.8	11.7	25.3	28.5	19.9	32.0	19.2	13.6	—
1989	—	13.3	26.5	16.2	18.6	25.5	28.2	25.7	23.5	22.4	19.1	11.6	26.4	28.2	21.6	31.4	18.8	13.6	—
1990	25.2	14.5	26.6	17.6	19.6	24.8	28.1	26.7	25.2	23.1	19.2	11.3	27.1	29.7	22.2	32.2	19.6	14.1	22.6
1991	25.5	15.6	27.3	19.4	21.0	26.9	29.0	27.3	30.5	24.7	19.9	11.5	28.3	29.8	22.6	34.3	21.3	15.2	23.9
1992	25.9	16.5	27.8	20.0	22.8	28.3	29.7	28.2	34.8	25.7	20.4	12.1	29.5	30.2	22.5	36.4	23.0	16.0	25.0
1993	27.3	16.5	29.0	20.0	24.7	29.2	31.1	29.7	35.0	25.9	20.4	12.6	29.2	30.5	19.1	37.4	22.9	16.1	25.4
1994	27.6	16.1	28.5	18.9	25.0	29.0	33.0	29.7	34.0	25.2	20.0	13.3	29.0	29.0	18.9	36.3	23.1	16.1	25.1
1995	27.1	15.7	28.8	18.2	25.5	29.6	32.6	30.1	32.1	23.7	19.4	14.1	28.5	28.0	18.8	33.4	22.8	16.3	24.7
1996	—	—	—	—	—	—	31.9	—	—	—	18.4	—	—	26.9	19.2	—	—	—	—

[a] Outlays for (quasi-)mandatory occupational pensions in AUS, DK, NL and S are not included in the figures.
Sources: OECD (1999f); own calculations.

Table A.28 *Public expenditures on services for families and for elderly and disabled persons as % of GDP*

Year	A	AUS	B	D	DK	F	FL	I	IRL	JAP	N	NL	NZ	S	UK	USA	OECD-16
1980	0.58	0.18	0.27	0.84	4.58	0.92	1.75	0.30	0.59	0.39	1.72	1.11	0.04	4.07	1.05	0.46	1.18
1981	—	0.18	0.28	0.87	4.82	0.97	1.88	0.31	0.58	0.39	—	1.21	0.05	4.24	1.05	0.42	—
1982	—	0.21	0.27	0.88	4.93	1.00	2.02	0.31	0.61	0.39	—	1.20	0.04	4.08	1.04	0.36	—
1983	—	0.21	0.27	0.86	4.73	1.02	2.04	0.32	0.65	0.38	—	1.20	0.04	4.30	1.03	0.36	—
1984	—	0.22	0.26	0.85	4.51	1.03	1.97	0.31	0.63	0.37	—	1.01	0.04	4.28	0.99	0.34	—
1985	0.61	0.22	0.26	0.85	4.52	1.01	2.15	0.30	0.64	0.37	1.95	0.91	0.04	4.26	0.94	0.31	1.21
1986	—	0.24	0.25	0.86	4.43	1.03	2.20	0.31	0.64	0.40	—	1.02	0.04	4.33	0.95	0.29	—
1987	—	0.66	0.25	0.87	4.51	1.06	2.24	0.33	0.62	0.37	—	1.02	0.05	4.27	0.95	0.30	—
1988	—	0.69	0.24	0.88	4.61	1.05	2.25	0.34	0.58	0.35	4.06	0.99	0.05	4.33	0.90	0.30	—
1989	—	0.73	0.23	0.87	4.56	1.02	2.31	0.32	0.53	0.36	4.15	1.06	0.08	4.21	0.88	0.29	—
1990	0.65	0.79	0.24	0.89	4.50	1.02	2.55	0.32	0.50	0.37	4.25	1.07	0.14	4.53	0.90	0.28	1.44
1991	0.68	0.95	0.24	1.19	4.50	1.00	2.93	0.33	0.54	0.38	4.74	1.02	0.18	4.66	0.95	0.31	1.54
1992	0.74	0.99	0.26	1.32	4.54	1.01	2.92	0.33	0.55	0.41	4.99	0.91	0.20	5.81	0.99	0.35	1.64
1993	0.78	0.97	0.26	1.41	4.37	1.10	3.23	0.32	0.55	0.43	5.01	0.92	0.15	5.26	1.03	0.36	1.63
1994	0.87	1.02	0.24	1.41	5.10	1.11	3.11	0.31	0.58	0.45	5.04	0.88	0.13	5.19	1.17	0.34	1.69
1995	0.85	0.56	0.28	1.36	5.14	1.14	3.10	0.30	0.60	0.49	5.05	1.03	0.15	5.10	1.16	0.36	1.67
1996	—	—	—	—	5.28	—	—	—	0.60	—	—	1.02	0.15	—	—	—	—

Sources: OECD (1999f); own calculations.

Table A.29 *Real long-term interest rates (%)*

Year	A	AUS	B	CAN	CH	D	DK	F	FL	I	IRL	JAP	N	NL	NZ	S	UK	USA	OECD-18
1970	3.4	2.8	3.9	4.6	2.1	4.8	5.8	3.4	5.0	2.7	1.6	-0.7	-4.3	4.4	-1.0	0.6	2.2	1.4	2.4
1971	3.0	0.8	3.0	4.1	-1.3	2.9	5.6	2.9	1.6	2.2	0.3	1.0	0.2	0.1	-4.9	0.1	-1.5	1.9	1.2
1972	1.1	0.3	1.6	2.4	-1.7	2.7	4.9	1.8	0.9	0.9	0.4	2.4	-0.9	-0.4	-1.4	1.5	1.3	2.9	1.1
1973	0.7	-2.4	0.5	-0.1	-3.1	2.5	3.8	1.7	-2.4	-3.9	-0.7	-4.6	-1.3	-0.1	-2.4	0.9	1.4	0.6	-0.5
1974	0.2	-6.0	-3.9	-2.0	-2.7	3.6	1.2	-2.7	-8.1	-9.5	-2.4	-16.3	-2.3	0.2	-5.0	-1.9	-1.8	-3.4	-3.5
1975	1.2	-5.4	-4.3	-1.8	-0.3	2.8	3.7	-1.5	-8.3	-7.0	-6.9	-3.3	-4.4	-1.4	-8.4	-0.8	-11.0	-1.1	-3.2
1976	1.5	-3.3	-0.1	1.7	3.3	3.7	6.6	0.9	-4.2	-4.1	-3.4	-0.7	-1.8	0.2	-8.6	-0.7	-2.9	1.8	-0.6
1977	3.2	-2.0	1.7	0.7	2.7	3.0	5.9	1.6	-1.8	-2.3	-0.7	-0.6	-1.7	1.7	-5.1	-1.4	-3.8	0.9	0.1
1978	4.6	1.2	4.4	0.3	2.2	3.6	8.2	1.5	2.0	1.0	5.2	2.6	0.3	3.6	-1.9	0.3	3.8	0.7	2.4
1979	4.3	0.7	5.2	1.0	-0.1	3.6	8.6	0.0	2.0	-1.8	1.8	4.7	3.8	4.6	-1.8	3.5	-0.5	-1.9	2.1
1980	2.9	1.4	5.3	2.1	0.8	3.1	7.7	0.2	-1.2	-5.9	-2.8	0.9	-0.6	3.7	-3.8	-1.7	-4.1	-2.0	0.3
1981	3.8	4.4	5.8	2.6	-0.9	3.9	8.4	2.9	-1.0	1.6	-3.1	3.5	-1.3	4.8	-2.6	1.6	3.0	3.5	2.3
1982	4.5	4.1	4.7	3.6	-1.1	3.9	11.3	4.2	1.4	3.8	0.0	5.6	1.9	4.0	-3.2	4.7	4.5	6.9	3.6
1983	4.9	4.0	4.2	6.0	1.2	4.9	8.2	4.8	2.5	3.4	3.4	5.9	4.5	5.5	4.8	3.7	6.7	7.9	4.8
1984	2.3	9.7	5.9	8.4	1.7	5.7	8.2	6.0	4.0	5.0	6.0	5.0	5.9	4.8	6.5	4.5	6.3	8.1	5.8
1985	4.6	7.2	6.1	7.1	1.3	5.1	6.9	6.1	4.8	5.1	7.1	4.5	6.9	5.0	2.2	5.8	5.0	7.1	5.4
1986	5.6	4.3	7.3	5.3	3.4	6.4	6.4	6.4	6.0	5.4	7.3	4.5	6.1	6.2	3.5	6.3	6.7	5.8	5.7
1987	5.5	4.7	6.6	5.5	2.6	6.1	7.3	7.1	3.8	6.0	8.2	4.9	4.6	7.1	0.0	7.5	5.5	4.7	5.4
1988	4.8	4.8	6.8	6.2	2.1	5.3	5.1	6.5	5.2	5.9	7.4	4.1	6.2	5.7	6.7	5.3	4.8	4.7	5.4
1989	4.5	5.9	5.5	4.9	2.0	4.3	5.0	5.6	5.5	6.2	4.8	2.8	6.2	6.1	7.1	4.6	2.4	3.7	4.8
1990	5.4	5.9	6.7	6.0	1.0	6.0	8.0	7.0	7.1	7.4	6.8	3.9	6.6	6.4	6.4	2.8	2.3	3.2	5.5
1991	5.2	7.5	6.1	4.2	0.3	4.9	6.9	6.3	7.6	6.8	6.0	3.0	6.6	5.5	7.3	1.0	4.2	3.7	5.2
1992	4.1	8.2	6.3	7.3	2.4	2.8	6.8	6.6	9.2	8.0	6.0	3.6	7.3	4.9	7.4	7.4	5.4	4.0	6.0
1993	3.1	5.5	4.4	6.1	1.3	2.1	5.9	4.9	6.0	7.0	6.3	3.1	4.6	3.8	5.6	3.8	5.9	2.9	4.6
1994	4.0	7.1	5.3	8.4	4.1	4.1	5.9	5.8	7.3	6.6	5.9	3.7	6.0	4.1	5.9	7.1	5.7	4.5	5.6
1995	4.9	4.6	5.9	6.2	2.7	5.2	6.2	5.9	7.1	6.8	5.8	3.5	4.9	5.0	3.9	7.3	4.8	3.8	5.3
1996	4.8	5.6	4.2	5.9	3.2	4.8	5.0	4.5	5.4	5.6	5.8	3.0	5.5	4.2	5.6	7.2	5.4	3.5	5.0
1997	4.4	6.6	4.1	4.9	2.9	3.8	4.0	4.5	3.7	5.1	5.1	0.7	3.3	3.4	5.9	5.7	3.9	4.1	4.2
1998	3.7	4.6	3.8	4.4	2.9	3.7	3.2	3.9	3.0	3.2	2.6	0.9	3.1	2.7	5.0	4.7	3.1	3.6	3.5

Source: OECD, *Economic Outlook* (various years); own calculations.

Table A.30 *Gross fixed capital formation as % of GDP*

Year	A	AUS	B	CAN	CH	D	DK	F	FL	I	IRL	JAP	N	NL	NZ	S	UK	USA	OECD-18
1970	24.0	26.0	22.7	21.5	28.5	25.5	28.3	24.3	26.3	24.6	22.0	35.5	26.0	26.5	22.7	22.3	18.9	17.9	24.6
1971	25.8	25.7	22.0	22.3	30.3	26.2	27.8	24.7	27.5	24.0	22.9	34.2	29.1	26.0	22.5	21.8	18.9	18.4	25.0
1972	28.0	24.5	21.3	22.1	30.8	25.4	28.1	24.7	27.9	23.2	22.9	34.1	27.2	24.2	24.4	22.0	18.5	19.1	24.9
1973	26.5	24.1	21.3	22.7	30.5	23.9	28.4	25.2	28.8	24.9	24.5	36.4	28.7	23.6	24.2	21.7	19.9	19.5	25.3
1974	26.4	23.4	22.6	23.7	28.6	21.6	27.5	25.8	29.8	25.9	23.9	34.8	29.9	22.5	27.4	21.3	20.9	18.9	25.3
1975	24.7	24.1	22.4	24.5	24.9	20.4	24.2	24.1	31.5	24.9	22.0	32.5	33.5	21.6	29.2	20.8	19.9	17.7	24.6
1976	24.2	24.0	21.9	23.7	21.4	20.1	26.3	23.9	28.1	23.9	24.2	31.2	35.6	19.9	26.2	21.0	19.6	18.1	24.1
1977	25.2	23.8	21.5	23.1	21.5	20.3	25.3	22.9	27.2	23.6	24.0	30.2	36.4	21.6	23.7	20.9	18.6	19.4	23.8
1978	23.3	24.0	21.5	22.7	22.2	20.6	24.8	22.4	24.1	23.0	26.8	30.4	31.2	21.8	22.9	19.3	18.5	20.7	23.3
1979	23.3	23.4	20.5	23.1	22.6	21.7	23.9	22.4	23.3	23.0	29.5	31.7	29.9	21.4	20.5	19.7	18.7	21.3	23.3
1980	24.1	25.0	21.0	23.5	24.7	22.6	21.6	23.0	25.4	24.5	27.7	31.6	26.9	21.4	20.7	20.0	18.0	20.2	23.4
1981	23.9	26.1	18.1	24.6	25.0	21.6	17.9	22.1	25.3	24.1	28.7	30.6	27.1	19.6	23.7	18.8	16.2	19.8	23.0
1982	21.8	23.8	17.1	21.9	23.9	20.4	18.4	21.4	25.3	22.5	25.7	29.5	27.3	18.6	24.8	18.6	16.1	18.7	22.0
1983	21.2	22.6	15.8	20.4	24.5	20.4	18.3	20.2	25.6	21.3	22.4	28.0	27.9	18.6	24.7	18.6	16.0	18.4	21.4
1984	20.8	23.5	15.6	19.6	24.3	20.0	19.7	19.3	24.0	21.1	20.8	27.7	26.4	19.1	25.4	18.7	17.0	19.4	21.2
1985	21.5	24.6	15.7	20.1	24.4	19.5	21.5	19.3	23.9	20.7	18.4	27.5	24.8	19.7	26.5	19.3	17.0	19.4	21.3
1986	21.5	24.3	15.7	20.5	24.9	19.4	23.8	19.3	23.4	19.8	17.4	27.3	27.8	20.4	22.6	18.5	17.0	19.2	21.3
1987	21.9	24.1	16.1	21.5	25.3	19.4	22.6	19.8	23.9	19.7	16.5	28.3	28.0	20.8	21.7	19.3	17.8	18.5	21.4
1988	22.6	25.0	17.8	22.2	26.8	19.6	20.7	20.7	25.2	20.1	16.8	29.6	28.4	21.3	19.4	20.2	19.5	18.1	21.9
1989	23.0	24.1	19.1	22.5	27.4	20.2	20.7	21.3	28.0	20.2	17.5	30.6	25.7	21.5	20.2	22.0	20.5	17.6	22.3
1990	23.3	21.4	20.3	21.1	27.1	20.9	20.1	21.4	27.0	20.3	18.8	31.7	21.6	20.9	19.1	21.5	19.6	16.8	21.8
1991	24.0	19.9	18.8	19.4	25.5	23.0	19.3	21.2	22.4	19.8	17.2	31.4	20.6	20.4	16.0	19.4	17.0	15.4	20.6
1992	23.5	20.4	18.6	18.5	23.0	23.0	18.1	20.1	18.4	19.2	16.7	30.5	19.9	20.0	16.5	17.0	15.7	15.6	19.7
1993	22.8	20.6	17.8	17.6	21.6	21.8	17.3	18.5	14.8	16.9	15.3	29.5	20.4	19.2	18.3	14.2	15.0	16.0	18.8
1994	23.8	21.5	17.4	18.4	22.0	21.8	17.4	18.0	14.5	16.6	16.1	28.6	20.7	18.8	20.3	13.7	15.0	16.5	19.0
1995	23.7	20.7	17.7	17.2	21.4	21.4	18.7	17.9	15.5	17.3	16.6	28.5	20.7	19.1	21.0	14.6	15.5	16.7	19.1
1996	23.8	20.9	17.5	17.5	20.2	20.5	19.0	17.4	16.0	17.0	17.8	29.7	21.2	19.5	21.1	14.8	15.5	17.2	19.3
1997	24.1	21.5	17.8	18.8	19.6	19.9	20.1	17.1	16.9	16.7	18.7	28.3	23.0	20.0	19.9	13.7	15.6	17.4	19.4

Sources: OECD (1999h); own calculations.

Table A.31 *Index of capital exchange controls*[a]

Year	A	AUS	B	CAN	CH	D	DK	F	I	IRL	JAP	N	NL	NZ	S	UK	USA	OECD-16
1970	10.0	8.0	9.5	12.5	12.5	14.0	8.5	11.0	10.5	7.5	7.0	7.5	12.0	5.5	10.0	8.0	12.5	9.8
1971	10.0	8.0	9.5	12.5	12.5	14.0	8.0	11.0	10.5	7.5	7.0	7.5	12.0	5.5	10.0	7.5	12.5	9.7
1972	9.5	7.5	10.0	12.5	12.0	14.0	8.0	11.0	10.5	8.5	8.0	7.5	12.0	6.0	10.5	8.5	12.5	9.9
1973	9.5	7.5	10.0	12.0	12.5	13.5	10.0	11.0	10.5	8.5	8.0	7.5	12.0	6.0	10.5	8.5	12.5	10.0
1974	10.0	7.5	10.0	12.0	12.0	14.0	10.0	11.0	10.5	8.5	8.0	7.5	12.0	7.0	10.5	8.5	13.0	10.1
1975	10.5	7.5	10.0	12.0	12.0	14.0	10.0	11.0	10.5	8.5	8.0	7.5	12.0	7.0	10.5	8.5	13.0	10.2
1976	10.5	7.5	10.0	12.0	12.0	14.0	10.0	11.0	9.5	10.0	8.0	7.5	12.0	7.0	10.5	8.5	13.0	10.1
1977	11.5	7.5	10.0	12.0	12.0	14.0	10.0	11.0	10.5	10.5	9.5	7.5	12.0	7.0	10.0	9.0	13.0	10.4
1978	11.5	8.0	10.0	12.0	12.0	13.5	10.0	11.0	10.5	10.5	9.5	7.5	12.0	7.0	10.0	9.5	13.0	10.4
1979	11.5	8.0	10.0	12.0	12.5	13.5	10.0	11.0	10.5	10.5	9.5	8.5	13.0	7.0	10.0	14.0	13.0	10.7
1980	11.5	8.0	10.0	12.0	13.0	13.5	10.0	11.0	10.5	10.5	10.5	8.5	13.0	7.5	11.0	14.0	13.0	10.9
1981	11.5	8.5	10.0	12.0	13.0	14.0	10.0	11.0	10.5	10.5	10.5	8.5	13.0	7.5	11.0	14.0	13.0	10.9
1982	11.5	8.5	10.0	12.0	13.0	14.0	10.0	10.0	10.5	10.5	10.5	9.0	13.0	8.5	11.0	14.0	13.0	11.0
1983	11.5	10.0	10.0	12.0	13.0	14.0	10.0	10.0	10.5	10.5	10.5	9.0	14.0	8.5	11.0	14.0	13.0	11.1
1984	11.5	10.0	10.0	12.0	13.0	14.0	10.0	11.0	10.5	10.5	10.5	9.5	14.0	11.5	11.0	14.0	13.0	11.4
1985	11.5	10.5	10.0	12.5	13.0	14.0	11.0	11.0	10.5	10.5	10.5	9.5	14.0	12.5	11.0	14.0	13.0	11.6
1986	11.5	10.5	10.0	12.5	13.0	14.0	11.0	11.0	10.5	10.5	10.5	9.5	14.0	12.5	11.0	14.0	13.0	11.6
1987	11.5	11.0	10.0	13.0	13.0	14.0	11.0	11.0	10.5	10.5	10.5	9.5	14.0	12.5	11.0	14.0	13.5	11.7
1988	11.5	11.0	10.0	13.5	13.0	14.0	12.0	11.0	11.5	10.5	10.5	10.0	14.0	12.5	11.0	14.0	13.5	11.9
1989	12.5	11.0	10.0	14.0	13.0	14.0	14.0	11.0	11.5	10.5	10.5	10.5	14.0	13.0	12.0	14.0	14.0	12.2
1990	12.5	11.5	14.0	14.0	13.0	14.0	14.0	11.5	13.5	10.5	10.5	12.5	14.0	13.0	12.0	14.0	14.0	12.8
1991	12.5	11.5	14.0	14.0	13.0	14.0	14.0	13.0	13.5	10.5	10.5	13.5	14.0	13.0	12.0	14.0	14.0	13.0
1992	12.5	11.5	14.0	14.0	13.0	14.0	14.0	13.0	13.5	13.5	11.0	13.5	14.0	13.0	12.5	14.0	14.0	13.2
1993	12.5	11.5	14.0	14.0	13.0	14.0	14.0	13.5	14.0	14.0	11.0	13.5	14.0	13.0	12.5	14.0	14.0	13.3

[a] An economy that is completely closed to transborder capital flows would score 0, an economy with no restrictions at all scores 14.
Source: IMF, *International Financial Regulation Data Set;* provided by Dennis Quinn.

Table A.32 *Nominal effective exchange rates (Index 1995 = 100)*

Year	A	AUS	B	CAN	CH	D	DK	F	FL	I	IRL	JAP	N	NL	NZ	S	UK	USA
1970	58.1	166.8	71.9	118.7	30.3	34.0	87.1	101.6	105.8	266.9	133.3	16.0	98.7	51.2	188.3	156.6	170.4	64.6
1971	58.4	167.1	71.6	122.0	31.1	35.1	86.1	99.2	103.4	264.2	133.3	16.3	98.0	51.7	188.7	155.5	170.4	63.1
1972	58.5	166.7	73.6	122.3	31.3	35.8	85.8	101.1	98.0	261.1	131.4	18.0	98.2	52.4	188.5	157.4	164.8	59.5
1973	60.6	187.5	74.2	118.9	34.0	39.3	89.6	103.1	96.7	231.9	124.9	19.3	102.0	53.7	199.5	155.1	146.6	55.5
1974	63.1	194.7	75.1	122.5	36.7	41.5	89.3	95.8	98.9	208.5	122.7	18.0	107.3	56.2	209.6	152.7	140.9	56.4
1975	64.7	178.8	76.1	117.9	41.1	42.0	91.4	104.5	98.0	198.4	118.1	17.9	110.0	57.7	186.3	158.6	129.6	57.1
1976	66.5	176.2	78.1	123.9	45.9	44.7	92.6	101.0	99.9	165.8	110.1	18.7	112.0	59.1	163.6	161.4	111.2	59.2
1977	69.4	155.5	82.1	114.6	47.0	48.1	91.3	95.5	94.6	152.3	107.5	20.7	113.0	61.6	159.6	154.4	105.9	59.5
1978	69.8	145.6	84.4	104.2	57.7	51.0	91.2	94.1	85.5	142.8	108.1	25.4	105.8	63.0	155.9	139.5	106.9	55.2
1979	71.0	139.2	85.3	100.7	58.4	53.6	90.0	94.2	85.5	137.8	107.5	23.8	103.7	64.0	150.9	139.3	113.6	55.1
1980	73.2	142.0	84.7	101.1	57.5	54.3	83.0	94.9	88.6	133.7	103.3	23.5	105.6	64.3	142.0	140.2	125.4	56.1
1981	72.5	153.4	80.5	101.7	58.7	52.2	77.9	88.8	90.8	121.6	93.3	26.5	107.2	61.4	133.0	138.7	127.2	61.2
1982	74.8	148.1	73.1	102.3	63.9	55.5	75.1	82.5	92.8	115.2	92.7	25.3	108.4	64.7	126.4	125.1	122.5	69.6
1983	76.5	137.4	71.4	105.0	67.5	58.6	75.7	77.8	88.8	114.0	89.9	28.7	106.0	66.4	118.6	111.5	115.3	76.7
1984	76.8	141.4	70.5	102.4	67.3	58.9	73.9	75.5	91.1	111.2	86.4	31.1	104.3	65.8	107.1	114.5	111.2	83.7
1985	77.7	117.1	71.6	98.9	67.7	60.1	75.5	77.3	92.4	107.9	87.4	33.3	103.0	66.5	98.1	115.0	112.0	90.3
1986	81.5	96.1	76.0	93.1	74.3	66.7	79.5	80.4	90.8	111.7	94.0	44.9	97.1	72.7	89.7	113.2	104.2	80.1
1987	84.1	92.0	79.2	95.3	78.4	71.6	82.3	81.1	91.9	112.8	93.4	49.8	93.7	76.9	93.0	112.0	103.2	75.2
1988	84.3	99.4	79.0	102.6	78.4	72.2	81.4	80.2	93.7	111.7	91.6	55.8	94.1	77.4	96.8	112.9	110.3	73.8
1989	84.2	106.8	79.3	109.9	75.2	72.6	80.1	80.1	98.0	115.7	91.0	54.3	94.6	77.9	92.0	114.7	108.0	79.1
1990	87.6	106.4	84.7	112.7	81.5	78.7	86.4	85.9	101.5	122.7	98.7	53.0	96.0	83.6	91.8	115.1	108.9	82.8
1991	87.7	106.8	85.3	115.7	81.1	79.2	85.9	85.0	98.5	123.3	97.4	59.2	94.8	83.8	89.0	115.9	110.8	84.6
1992	89.8	100.1	88.1	109.8	80.6	83.1	88.6	88.7	86.5	122.1	101.7	64.2	96.6	87.1	82.8	118.6	108.1	86.1
1993	92.6	95.0	90.1	104.7	84.0	87.6	92.4	92.2	77.0	105.9	96.3	79.4	95.0	90.7	86.5	97.4	100.0	91.5
1994	95.2	103.1	94.3	100.4	92.3	92.5	95.0	95.6	87.4	107.2	98.0	93.3	96.0	94.2	93.8	99.3	103.3	97.7
1995	100.0	100.0	100.0	100.0	100.0	100.0	100.0	100.0	100.0	100.0	100.0	100.0	100.0	100.0	100.0	100.0	100.0	100.0
1996	99.0	109.2	98.3	102.1	98.6	98.6	99.1	100.3	97.6	110.1	102.5	87.2	100.0	98.5	107.0	110.1	102.2	105.4
1997	97.0	110.2	94.3	102.6	92.9	95.1	96.6	97.2	95.3	111.5	102.3	83.2	100.7	93.8	109.6	106.4	118.9	112.9
1998	99.0	101.5	96.3	98.2	96.7	98.6	99.2	99.8	97.5	114.2	99.6	86.0	98.1	96.5	97.2	106.5	126.7	125.1

Note: Index of trade-weighted averages of a country's bilateral exchange rates.
Sources: OECD (1999g); own calculations.

Table A.33 *Exports as % of world exports*

Year	A	AUS	B-LUX	CAN	CH	D	DK	F	FL	I	IRL	JAP	N	NL	NZ	S	UK	USA	OECD-12[a]	OECD-18
1980	0.9	1.1	3.2	3.5	1.5	9.4	0.8	5.5	0.7	3.8	0.4	6.9	0.9	3.8	0.3	1.5	6.1	11.9	37.8	62.1
1981	0.8	1.1	2.8	3.8	1.4	9.0	0.8	5.2	0.7	3.9	0.4	8.0	0.9	3.7	0.3	1.5	5.6	12.8	36.1	62.7
1982	0.9	1.2	2.9	4.0	1.4	9.8	0.8	5.1	0.7	4.0	0.4	7.9	1.0	3.8	0.3	1.5	5.7	12.5	37.2	63.8
1983	0.9	1.1	2.9	4.4	1.5	9.6	0.9	5.1	0.7	4.1	0.5	8.4	1.0	3.9	0.3	1.5	5.5	12.1	37.2	64.2
1984	0.8	1.2	2.7	4.9	1.4	9.2	0.8	5.0	0.7	3.9	0.5	9.1	1.0	3.7	0.3	1.5	5.4	12.3	36.0	64.6
1985	0.9	1.2	2.9	4.8	1.5	9.9	0.9	5.2	0.7	4.2	0.6	9.5	1.0	3.9	0.3	1.6	5.8	11.8	38.3	66.7
1986	1.1	1.1	3.3	4.5	1.8	11.6	1.0	5.6	0.8	4.6	0.6	10.3	0.9	4.2	0.3	1.8	5.4	11.3	41.7	70.1
1987	1.1	1.1	3.4	4.1	1.8	11.8	1.0	5.7	0.8	4.7	0.6	9.5	0.9	4.1	0.3	1.8	5.5	11.0	42.2	69.2
1988	1.0	1.2	3.2	4.2	1.9	11.7	1.0	5.9	0.8	4.6	0.7	9.5	0.8	3.8	0.3	1.8	5.8	11.9	42.2	70.0
1989	1.1	1.2	3.4	4.0	1.8	11.5	1.0	5.8	0.8	4.7	0.7	9.3	1.0	3.6	0.3	1.7	5.2	12.5	41.5	69.8
1990	1.2	1.2	3.4	3.9	1.9	11.6	1.0	6.1	0.8	4.9	0.7	8.6	1.0	3.8	0.3	1.7	5.7	12.0	42.9	69.9
1991	1.2	1.2	3.4	3.8	1.8	11.5	1.0	6.1	0.7	4.9	0.7	9.0	1.0	3.8	0.3	1.6	5.8	12.5	42.6	70.3
1992	1.2	1.2	3.3	3.7	1.8	11.4	1.1	6.2	0.6	4.7	0.8	9.0	1.0	3.7	0.3	1.5	5.5	12.5	41.8	69.4
1993	1.1	1.1	3.2	3.8	1.7	10.2	1.0	5.7	0.6	4.7	0.8	9.4	0.9	3.9	0.3	1.4	5.2	12.4	39.5	67.4
1994	1.0	1.1	3.3	4.0	1.7	10.4	1.0	5.7	0.7	4.6	0.7	9.0	0.9	3.6	0.3	1.5	5.2	12.4	39.5	67.2

[a] Sum (A, AUS, B, CH, D, DK, F, I, NL, NZ, S, UK).
Sources: Statistics Canada (n.d.): own calculations.

Table A.34 *Strictness of employment protection and net replacement rates (late 1990s)*

	A	AUS	B	CH	D	DK	F	I	NL	NZ	S	UK
EPL ranks (among 27)												
Individual dismissals	17	4	6	5	21	7	14	23	25	9	22	2
Temporary employment	14	8	19	8	18	8	23	24	12	5	13	1
Overall strictness	15	6	16	7	20	8	21	23	13	3	18	2
Net replacement rates (%)[a]												
APW level[b]												
Single worker	57	37	65	77	70	65	76	36	75	37	75	52
APW level												
Couple 2 children	71	72	60	88	80	77	79	47	82	64	85	67
2/3 APW level												
Single worker	57	50	84	76	73	90	85	35	86	52	78	75
2/3 APW level												
Couple 2 children	77	82	76	88	76	95	87	46	86	77	85	80

[a] Including unemployment benefits, family and housing benefits. First month of benefit receipt.
[b] APW: average production wages.
Sources: Employment protection (EPL) ranks: OECD (1999a: tables 2.2, 2.3, and 2.5); replacement rates: OECD (1998a: table 3.1).

REFERENCES

AARTS, LEO J. M., and JONG, PHILIP R. DE (1996). 'The Dutch Disability Program and How it Grew', in Leo J. M. Aarts, Richard V. Burkhauser, and Philip R. de Jong (eds.), *Curing the Dutch Disease: An International Perspective on Disability Reform*. Aldershot, UK: Avebury, 21–46.

ADEMA, WILLEM (1998). 'Uncovering Real Social Spending'. *The OECD Observer*, 211/April–May: 20–23.

ALBER, JENS (1998). *Recent Developments in Continental European Welfare States: Do Austria, Germany, and the Netherlands Prove to be Birds of a Feather?* Manuscript. University of Konstanz.

ALT, JAMES E., and LOWRY, ROBERT C. (1994). 'Divided Government, Fiscal Institutions, and Budget Deficits: Evidence from the States'. *American Political Science Review*, 88: 811–28.

ARGYRIS, CHRIS, and SCHON, DONALD A. (1978). *Organizational Learning*. Reading, MA: Addison-Wesley.

AUER, PETER (1999). *Europe's Employment Revival: Four Small European Countries Compared. CEPR Comparative Review*. Paper presented at ILO Symposium 'Social Dialogue and Employment Success'. Geneva, 2–3 March.

——(2000). *Employment Revival in Europe*. Geneva: International Labour Organization.

BACCARO, LUCIO (2000). *Negotiating Pension Reform with the Unions: The Italian Experience in European Perspective*. Paper prepared for presentation at the 12th Conference of Europeanists. Chicago, 30 March–2 April.

BAIROCH, PAUL (1997). 'Globalization Myths and Realities. One Century of External Trade and Foreign Investment', in Robert Boyer and Daniel Drache (eds.), *States against Markets: The Limits of Globalization*. London: Routledge, 173–92.

BASTIAN, JENS (1994). 'Modern Times: Institutional Dynamics in Belgian and French Labour Market Policies'. *West European Politics*, 17: 98–122.

BATES, ROBERT H., GREIF, AVNER, LEVI, MARGARET, ROSENTHAL, JEAN-LAURENT, and WEINGAST, BARRY R. (1998). *Analytical Narratives*. Princeton: Princeton University Press.

BAWN, KATHLEEN (1999). 'Money and Majorities in the Federal Republic of Germany: Evidence for a Veto Players Model of Government Spending'. *American Journal of Political Science*, 43: 707–36.

BECKER, UWE (1999). *The 'Dutch Miracle': Employment Growth in a Retrenched but Still Generous Welfare System*. SPRC Discussion Paper No. 99/May. University of New South Wales, Sydney: Social Policy Research Centre.

BENNET, COLIN, and HOWLETT, MICHAEL (1992). 'The Lessons of Learning: Reconciling Theories of Policy Learning and Policy Change'. *Policy Sciences*, 25/3: 275–94.

BERGER, SUZANNE, and DORE, RONALD (eds.) (1996). *National Diversity and Global Capitalism*. Ithaca, NY: Cornell University Press.

BLAIR, ANTHONY (1996). 'My Vision for Britain', in Giles Radice (ed.), *What Needs to Change: New Visions for Britain*. London: Harper Collins, 3–17.

BLÖNDAL, SVEINBJÖRN and SCARPETTO, STEFANO (1998). *The Retirement Decision in OECD Countries*. OECD Economics Department Working Papers No. 202. Paris: OECD.

BOLTHO, ANDREA (ed.) (1982). *The European Economy: Growth and Crisis*. Oxford: Oxford University Press.

——(1996). 'Has France Converged on Germany? Policies and Institutions since 1958', in Suzanne Berger and Ronald Dore (eds.), *National Diversity and Global Capitalism*. Ithaca, NY: Cornell University Press, 89–104.

BONOLI, GIULIANO (1997). 'Pension Politics in France: Patterns of Co-operation and Conflict in Two Recent Reforms'. *West European Politics*, 20: 111–24.

——and Palier, Bruno (1997). 'Reclaiming Welfare: The Politics of French Social Protection Reform', in Martin Rhodes (ed.), *Southern European Welfare States*. London: Cass, 240–59.

————(1998). 'Changing the Politics of Social Programmes: Innovative Change in British and French Welfare Reforms'. *Journal of European Social Policy*, 8: 317–30.

BOSTON, JONATHAN (1989). 'The Treasury and the Organization of Economic Advice: Some International Comparisons', in Brian Easton (ed.), *The Making of Rogernomics*. Auckland: Auckland University Press, 68–91.

——(1990). 'The Cabinet and Policy Making under the Fourth Labour Government', in Martin Holland and Jonathan Boston (eds.), *The Fourth Labour Government: Politics and Policy in New Zealand* (2nd edn). Auckland: Oxford University Press, 62–83.

BRAUN, DIETMAR, and BUSCH, ANDREAS (eds.) (1999). *Public Policy and Political Ideas*. Cheltenham, UK: Edward Elgar.

BROMBACHER-STEINER, MARIA VERENA (1999). 'Das Schweizer Drei-Säulen-Modell', in Deutsches Institut für Altersvorsorgung (ed.), *Gesetzliche Alters-sicherung. Reformerfahrungen im Ausland. Ein systematischer Vergleich aus sechs Ländern*. Köln: Deutsches Institut für Altersvorsorge, 43–65.

BROOK, LINDSAY *et al.* (1991). *British Social Attitudes: Cumulative Sourcebook*. Aldershot, UK: Gower.

BUDGE, IAN, and LAVER, MICHAEL (1993). 'The Policy Basis of Government Coalitions: A Comparative Investigation'. *British Journal of Political Science*, 23: 499–519.

BUHR, PETRA (1999). 'Vorbild Schweden? Armut und Sozialhilfe in unter-schiedlichen Wohlfahrtsstaaten'. *Leviathan*, 27: 218–37.

Bundesamt für Sozialversicherung (1998). *Schweizerische Sozialversicherungs-statistik 1998*. Bern: Bundesamt für Sozialversicherung.

CALMFORS, LARS, and DRIFFIL, JOHN (1988). 'Centralization of Wage Bargaining'. *Economic Policy*, 6: 14–61.

CAMERON, DAVID R. (2000). 'Unemployment, Job Creation and EMU', forthcoming in Nancy Bermeo (ed.), *Unemployment in the New Europe*. Cambridge, UK: Cambridge University Press.

CANOVA, TIMOTHY A. (1994). 'The Swedish Model Betrayed'. *Challenge*, 37/3: 36–40.

CARLIN, WENDY, and SOSKICE, DAVID (1990). *Macroeconomics and the Wage Bargain: A Modern Approach to Employment, Inflation, and the Exchange Rate.* Oxford: Oxford University Press.

CASTLES, FRANCIS (1988). *Australian Public Policy and Economic Vulnerability.* Sydney: Allen and Unwin.

——, GERRITSEN, ROLF, and VOWLES, JACK (eds.) (1996). *The Great Experiment: Labour Parties and Public Policy Transformation in Australia and New Zealand.* Sydney: Allen and Unwin.

CERNY, PHILIP G. (1994). 'The Dynamics of Financial Globalization: Technology, Market Structure, and Policy Response'. *Policy Sciences*, 27: 319–42.

COHEN, MICHAEL D., and SPROULL, LEE S. (eds.) (1996). *Organizational Learning.* Thousand Oaks, CA: Sage.

COLLIGNON, STEFAN (in collaboration with Bofinger, Peter, Johnson, Christopher, and Maigret, Bertrand de) (1994). *Das Europäische Währungssystem im Übergang: Erfahrungen mit dem EWS und politische Optionen.* Wiesbaden: Gabler.

COMPSTON, HUGH (1995). 'Union Participation in Economic Policy Making in Scandinavia, 1970–1993'. *West European Politics*, 18: 98–115.

——(1999). *The Politics of Concertation in the 1990s: Ten Countries Compared.* Manuscript (July).

CORTELL, ANDREW P., and PETERSON, SUSAN (1999). 'Altered States: Domestic Institutional Change'. *British Journal of Political Science*, 29/1: 177–203.

CREWE, IVOR (1991). 'Values: The Crusade that Failed', in Dennis Kavanagh and Anthony Seldon (eds.), *The Thatcher Effect.* Oxford: Oxford University Press, 239–50.

CROSLAND, CHARLES A. R. (1956). *The Future of Socialism.* London: Jonathan Cape.

CROUCH, COLIN (1993). *Industrial Relations and European State Traditions.* Oxford: Clarendon.

——and PIZZORNO, ALESSANDRO (eds.) (1978). *The Resurgence of Class Conflict in Western Europe since 1968.* London: Macmillan.

——and TRAXLER, FRANZ (eds.) (1995). *Organized Industrial Relations in Europe: What Future?* Aldershot, UK: Avebury.

CUKIERMAN, ALEX (1992). *Central Bank Strategy, Credibility, and Independence.* Cambridge, MA: MIT Press.

CYERT, RICHARD M., and March, James G. (1963). *A Behavioral Theory of the Firm.* Englewood Cliffs, NJ: Prentice-Hall.

DEARBORN, DEWITT C., and SIMON, HERBERT A. (1958): 'Selective Perception: A Note on the Departmental Identification of Executives'. *Sociometry*, 21: 140–44.

DELSEN, LEI (1996). 'Gradual Retirement: Lessons from the Nordic Countries and the Netherlands'. *European Journal of Industrial Relations*, 2/1: 55–68.

DENVER, DAVID (1998). 'The British Electorate in the 1990s'. *West European Politics*, 21/1: 197–217.

DEUTSCH, KARL W. (1963). *The Nerves of Government: Models of Political Communication and Control*. New York: Free Press.

DICKEN, PETER (1992). *Global Shift: The Internationalization of Economic Activity*. New York: Guilford Press.

DINGELDEY, IRENE (1999). *Begünstigungen und Belastungen familialer Erwerbs- und Arbeitszeitmuster in Steuer- und Sozialversicherungssystemen—Ein Vergleich zehn europäischer Länder*. Graue Reihe des Instituts Arbeit und Technik, No. 4/1999.

DUE, JESPER, MADSEN, JØRGEN STEEN, PETERSEN, LARS KJERULF, and JENSEN, CARSTEN STRØBY (1995). 'Adjusting the Danish Model: Towards Centralized Decentralization', in Colin Crouch and Franz Traxler (eds.), *Organized Industrial Relations in Europe: What Future?* Aldershot, UK: Avebury, 121–50.

DYSON, KENNETH, and FEATHERSTONE, KEVIN (1999). *The Road to Maastricht: Negotiating Economic and Monetary Union*. Oxford: Oxford University Press.

EARDLEY, TONY, BRADSHAW, JONATHAN, DITCH, JOHN, GOUGH, IAN, and WHITEFORD, PETER (1996). *Social Assistance in OECD Countries. Volume I: Synthesis Report, Volume II: Country Reports*. Department of Social Security Research Report No. 46. London: HMSO.

EASTON, BRIAN (1996). 'Income distribution', in Brian Silverstone, Alan Bollard, and Ralph Lattimore (eds.). *A Study of Economic Reform: The Case of New Zealand*. Amsterdam *et al.*: Elsevier, 101–38.

——(1997). *The Commercialization of New Zealand*. Auckland: Auckland University Press.

EBBINGHAUS, BERNHARD, and HASSEL, ANKE (2000). 'Striking Deals. Concertation in the Reform of Continental European Welfare States'. *Journal of European Public Policy*, 7: 44–62.

——and MANOW, PHILIP (1998). *Studying Welfare-State Regimes and Varieties of Capitalism: An Introduction*. Paper presented at the Conference 'Varieties of Welfare Capitalism'. Cologne: Max Planck Institute for the Study of Societies, 11–13 June.

EICHENGREEN, BARRY, and IVERSEN, TORBEN (1999). 'Institutions and Economic Performance: Evidence from the Labour Market'. *Oxford Review of Economic Policy*, 15: 121–38.

——FRIEDEN, JEFFRY, and HAGEN, JÜRGEN VON (1995). *Monetary and Fiscal Policy in an Integrated Europe*. Berlin: Springer.

ESPING-ANDERSEN, GØSTA (1985). *Politics Against Markets*. Princeton: Princeton University Press.

——(1990). *The Three Worlds of Welfare Capitalism*. Cambridge, UK: Polity Press.

——(1996). *Welfare States in Transition: National Adaptations in Global Economies*. London: Sage.

——(1999). *Social Foundations of Postindustrial Economies*. Oxford: Oxford University Press.

European Commission (1998). *Employment Rates Report 1998. Employment Performance in the Member States*. Electronic Edition.

——(1999). *Employment in Europe 1999*. Brussels: DGV, Employment and Social Affairs.

Eurostat (1999). *Sozialleistungen ohne Renten verringern die Armutsquote in der EU um ein Drittel*. Memo. 8/99.

EVANS, BRANDON, and TAYLOR, ANDREW (1996). *From Salisbury to Major: Continuity and Change in Conservative Politics*. Manchester: Manchester University Press.

EVANS, LEWIS, GRIMES, ARTHUR, WILKINSON, BRYCE, and TEECE, DAVID (1996). 'Economic Reform in New Zealand 1984–1995: The Pursuit of Efficiency'. *Journal of Economic Literature*, 34/4: 1856–902.

FAWCETT, HELEN (1995). 'The Privatization of Welfare: The Impact of Parties on the Private/Public Mix in Pension Provision'. *West European Politics*, 18/4: 150–69.

FEATHERSTONE, KEVIN (1999). *The British Labour Party from Kinnock to Blair: Europeanism and Europeanization*. Paper prepared for presentation for the 6th biennial conference of the European Community Studies Association. Pittsburgh: University of Pittsburgh/Johnstown, 2–5 June.

FEICK, JÜRGEN (1992). 'Comparing Comparative Policy Studies: A Path Towards Integration?'. *Journal of Public Policy*, 12/3: 257–86.

FERRERA, MAURIZIO (1996). 'Il modello sud-europeo di welfare state'. *Rivista italiana di scienza politica*, 1: 67–101.

——(1997). 'The Uncertain Future of the Italian Welfare State'. *West European Politics*, 20: 231–49.

——and GUALMINI, ELISABETTA (1999). *Salvati dal'Europa?* Rome: Il Mulino.

FLORA, PETER (ed.) (1986). *Growth to Limits: The Western European Welfare States since World War II*. Berlin: de Gruyter.

FRANZMEYER, FRITZ, LINDLAR, LUDGER, and TRABOLD, HARALD (1996). *Employment and Social Policies under International Constraints*. A Study for the Ministerie van Sociale Zaken en Werkgelegenheid of the Netherlands by the Deutsches Institut für Wirtschaftsforschung in Berlin. BK's-Gravenhage, Netherlands: VUGA.

FREEMAN, RICHARD B. (1995). 'The Large Welfare State as a System'. *AEA Papers and Proceedings*, 85/2: 16–21.

GARRETT, GEOFFREY (1998). *Partisan Politics in the Global Economy*. Cambridge, UK: Cambridge University Press.

GERN, KLAUS-JÜRGEN (1998). *Recent Developments in Old-age Pension Systems: An International Overview*. Kiel Working Paper No. 863. Kiel: Institute of World Economics.

GERSHUNY, JONATHAN I. (1978). *After Industrial Society? The Emerging Self-Service Economy*. London: Macmillan.

GOLDEN, MIRIAM A., WALLERSTEIN, MICHAEL, and LANGE, PETER (1999). 'Postwar Trade-Union Organization and Industrial Relations in Twelve Countries', in Herbert Kitschelt, Peter Lange, Gary Marks, and John D. Stephens (eds.), *Continuity and Change in Contemporary Capitalism*. Cambridge, UK: Cambridge University Press, 194–230.

GOLDSTEIN, JUDITH, and KEOHANE, ROBERT O. (eds.) (1993). *Ideas and Foreign Policy: Beliefs, Institutions and Political Change.* Ithaca, NY: Cornell University Press.

GRAEBNER, WILLIAM (1977). 'Federalism in the Progressive Era: A Structural Interpretation of Reform'. *Journal of American History*, 64: 331–57.

GREENLEAF, WILLIAM H. (1983). *The British Tradition. Volume II: The Ideological Heritage.* London: Routledge.

GREEN-PEDERSEN, CHRISTOFFER (1999a). 'The Danish Welfare State under Bourgeois Reign: The Dilemma of Popular Entrenchment and Economic Constraints'. *Scandinavian Political Studies*, 22: 243–60.

——(1999b). *Welfare-State Retrenchment in Denmark and the Netherlands 1982–1998: The Role of Party Competition and Party Consensus.* Manuscript. Department of Political Science. University of Aarhus, Denmark.

GUGER, ALOIS (1998). 'Economic Policy and Social Democracy: The Austrian Experience'. *Oxford Review of Economic Policy*, 14: 40–58.

GUSTAFSON, BARRY (1976). *Social Change and Party Organization: The New Zealand Labour Party since 1945.* London: Sage.

——(1986). *The First 50 Years: A History of the New Zealand National Party.* Auckland: Reed Methuen.

HALL, PETER A. (1986). *Governing the Economy: The Politics of State Intervention in Britain and France.* Cambridge, UK: Polity Press.

——(1992). 'The Movement from Keynesianism to Monetarism: Institutional Analysis and British Economic Policy in the 1970s', in Sven Steinmo, Kathleen Thelen, and Frank Longstreth (eds.), *Structuring Politics: Historical Institutionalism in Comparative Analysis.* Cambridge, UK: Cambridge University Press, 90–113.

——(1993). 'Policy Paradigms, Social Learning, and the State: The Case of Economic Policy Making in Britain'. *Comparative Politics*, 25: 275–96.

——(1999a). 'Introduction', in Peter A. Hall and David Soskice (eds.), *Varieties of Capitalism: The Institutional Foundations of Comparative Advantage.* Manuscript.

——(1999b). 'The Political Economy of Europe in an Era of Interdependence', in Herbert Kitschelt, Peter Lange, Gary Marks, and John D. Stephens (eds.), *Continuity and Change in Contemporary Capitalism.* Cambridge, UK: Cambridge University Press, 135–63.

——and TAYLOR, ROSEMARY C. R. (1996). 'Political Science and the Three New Institutionalisms', in Karol Soltan, Eric M. Uslaner, and Virginia Haufler (eds.), *Institutions and Social Order.* Ann Arbor: University of Michigan Press, 15–44.

HAMPSON, IAN, and MORGAN, DAVID E. (1999). 'Post-Fordism, Union Strategy, and the Rhetoric of Restructuring: The Case of Australia, 1980–1996'. *Theory and Society*, 28: 747–96.

HARRIS, RALPH, and SELDON, ARTHUR (1987). *Welfare without the State.* London: Institute of Economic Affairs.

HAY, COLIN, and WATSON, MATTHEW (1998). *Rendering the Contingent Necessary: New Labour's Neo-Liberal Conversion and the Discourse of*

Globalisation. Paper prepared for presentation to the annual conference of the American Political Science Association. Boston, 3–6 Sept.

HECLO, HUGH (1974). *Modern Social Politics in Britain and Sweden: From Relief to Income Maintenance*. New Haven: Yale University Press.

HEDETOFT, ULF and NISS, HANNE (1991). 'Taking Stock of Thatcherism'. Department of Languages and Intercultural Studies. Aalborg University.

HEINISCH, REINHARD (1999). *Coping with the Single Market: Corporatist Response Strategies in Germany and Austria*. Paper prepared for presentation for the 6th biennial conference of the European Community Studies Association. Pittsburgh: University of Pittsburgh/Johnstown, 2–5 June.

HEMERIJCK, ANTON (1995). 'Corporatist Immobility in the Netherlands', in Colin Crouch and Franz Traxler (eds.), *Organized Industrial Relations in Europe: What Future?* Aldershot, UK: Avebury, 183–226.

——and KERSBERGEN, KEES VAN (1997). 'Explaining the New Politics of the Welfare State in the Netherlands'. *Acta Politica*, 32: 258–280.

————(1999). 'Negotiated Policy Change: Towards a Theory of Institutional Learning in Tightly Coupled Welfare States', in Dietmar Braun and Andreas Busch (eds.), *Public Policy and Political Ideas*. Cheltenham, UK: Edward Elgar, 168–85.

——MANOW, PHILIP, and VAN KERSBERGEN, KEES (2000). 'Welfare Without Work? Divergent Experiences of Reform in Germany and the Netherlands', in Stein Kuhle (ed.), *The Survival of the Welfare State*. London/New York: Routledge, 113–27.

HENNINGS, KLAUS HINRICH (1982). 'Germany', in Andrea Boltho (ed.), *The European Economy: Growth and Crisis*. Oxford: Oxford University Press, 472–501.

HÉRITIER, ADRIENNE (1997). 'Market-Making Policy in Europe: Its Impact on Member State Policies. The Case of Road Haulage in Britain, the Netherlands, Germany and Italy'. *Journal of European Public Policy*, 4: 539–55.

HETZNER, CANDACE (1999). *The Unfinished Business of Thatcherism*. New York: Peter Lang.

HINNFORS, JONAS, and PIERRE, JON (1998). 'The Politics of Currency Crises in Sweden: Policy Choice in a Globalized Economy'. *West European Politics*, 21: 103–19.

HIRST, PAUL A., and THOMPSON, GRAHAME (1995). 'Globalization and the Future of the Nation State'. *Economy and Society*, 24: 408–42.

————(1997). 'Globalization in Question: International Economic Relations and Forms of Public Governance', in Joseph R. Hollingsworth and Robert Boyer (eds.), *Contemporary Capitalism: The Embeddedness of Institutions*. Cambridge, UK: Cambridge University Press: 337–60.

HOLLINGSWORTH, JOSEPH R., and BOYER, ROBERT (eds.) (1997). *Contemporary Capitalism: The Embeddedness of Institutions*. Cambridge, UK: Cambridge University Press.

HOLMBERG, SÖREN, and WEIBULL, LENNART (1997). *Trends in Swedish Public Opinion*. Göteborg: Göteborg University, the SOM Institute.

HOLMWOOD, JOHN (2000). 'Three Pillars of Welfare State Theory: Thomas H.

Marshall, Karl Polanyi and Alva Myrdal in Defense of the National Welfare State'. *European Journal of Social Theory*, 3: 23–50.

HUBER, EVELYNE, and STEPHENS, JOHN D. (2001). *Political Choice in Global Markets: Development and Crisis of Advanced Welfare States*. Forthcoming in University of Chicago Press.

——RAGIN, CHARLES, and STEPHENS, JOHN D. (1998). *Comparative Welfare States Data Set*. Luxembourg Income Study. http://lissy.ceps.lu/compwsp.htm

HUBER, GEORGE P. (1991). 'Organizational Learning: The Contributing Processes and the Literatures'. *Organization Science*, 2/1: 88–115.

IMMERGUT, ELLEN M. (1992). *Health Politics. Interests and Institutions in Western Europe*. Cambridge, UK: Cambridge University Press.

IRWIN, GALEN, and HOLSTEYN, JOOP VAN (1997). 'Where to Go from here? Revamping Electoral Politics in the Netherlands'. *West European Politics*, 20: 93–118.

IVERSEN, TORBEN (1996). 'Power, Flexibility and the Breakdown of Centralized Wage Bargaining: The Cases of Denmark and Sweden in Comparative Perspective'. *Comparative Politics*, 28: 399–436.

——(1998a). 'The Choices for Scandinavian Social Democracy in Comparative Perspective'. *Oxford Review of Economic Policy*, 14: 59–75.

——(1998b). 'Wage Bargaining, Hard Money and Economic Performance: Theory and Evidence for Organized Market Economies'. *British Journal of Political Science*, 28/1: 31–61.

——(1999). *Contested Economic Institutions: The Politics of Macroeconomics and Wage Bargaining in Advanced Democracies*. Cambridge, UK: Cambridge University Press.

——and WREN, ANNE (1998). 'Equality, Employment and Budgetary Restraint: The Trilemma of the Service Economy'. *World Politics*, 50: 507–46.

JACKSON, KEITH (1993). 'The Origins of the Electoral Referendum', in Alan McRobie (ed.), *Taking it to the People? The New Zealand Electoral Referendum Debate*. Christchurch: Hazard Press.

JAMES, COLIN (1986). *The Quiet Revolution: Turbulence and Transition in Contemporary New Zealand*. Wellington: Allen and Unwin.

JANIS, IRVING L. (1972). *Victims of Groupthink*. Boston: Houghton Mifflin.

JOBERT, BRUNO, and THÉRET, BRUNO (1994). 'France: La Consécration Républicaine du Néo-Libéralisme', in Bruno Jobert (ed.), *Le Tournant Néo-Libéral*. Paris: L'Harmattan, 21–86.

JOCHEM, SVEN (1998). *Die skandinavischen Wege in die Arbeitslosigkeit. Kontinuität und Wandel der nordischen Beschäftigungspolitik im internationalen Vergleich*. Opladen: Leske + Budrich.

JOHNSON, PETER A. (1998). *The Government of Money: Monetarism in Germany and the United States*. Ithaca, NY: Cornell University Press.

JORDAN, BILL (1998). *The New Politics of Welfare: Social Justice in a Global Context*. London: Sage.

JOWELL, ROGER, WITHERSPOON, SHARON, and BROOK, LINDSAY (eds.) (1989). *British Social Attitudes: Special International Report (6th Report)*. Aldershot, UK: Gower.

JOWELL, ROGER, BROOK, LINDSAY, PRIOR, GILLIAN, and TAYLOR, BRIDGET (eds.) (1992). *British Social Attitudes: The 9th Report*. Aldershot, UK: Dartmouth.

KALISCH, DAVID W., AMAN, TETSUYA, and BUCHELE, LIBBIE A. (1998). *Social and Health Policies in OECD Countries: A Survey of Current Programmes and Recent Developments. Annex: Tables and Charts*. OECD Labour Market and Social Policy, Occasional Papers No. 33. Paris: OECD.

KATZENSTEIN, PETER (1984). *Corporatism and Change: Austria, Switzerland, and the Politics of Industry*. Ithaca, NY: Cornell University Press.

——(1985). *Small States in World Markets: Industrial Policy in Europe*. Ithaca, NY: Cornell University Press.

KEELER, JOHN T. S. (1993). 'Opening the Window for Reform: Mandates, Crises and Extraordinary Policymaking'. *Comparative Political Studies*, 25/4: 433–86.

KERSBERGEN, KEES VAN (1995). *Social Capitalism: A Study of Christian Democracy and the Welfare State*. London/New York: Routledge.

KING, DESMOND S., and WOOD, STEWART (1999). 'The Political Economy of Neoliberalism: Britain and the United States in the 1980s', in Herbert Kitschelt, Peter Lange, Gary Marks, and John D. Stephens (eds.), *Continuity and Change in Contemporary Capitalism*. Cambridge, UK: Cambridge University Press, 371–97.

KING, GARY, KOEHANE, ROBERT O., and VERBA, SIDNEY (1994). *Designing Social Inquiry: Scientific Inference in Qualitative Research*. Princeton: Princeton University Press.

KLINGEMANN, HANS-DIETER, and FUCHS, DIETER (1995). *Beliefs in Government. Volume I: Citizens and the State*. Oxford: Oxford University Press.

KOHL, JÜRGEN (1994). *Alterssicherung im internationalen Vergleich. Analysen zu Strukturen und Wirkungen der Alterssicherungssysteme in fünf westeuropäischen Ländern*. Unpublished postdoctoral thesis. University of Bielefeld.

KORPI, WALTER (1983). *The Democratic Class Struggle*. London: Routledge & Kegan Paul.

KREHBIEL, KEITH (1996). 'Institutional and Partisan Sources of Gridlock: A Theory of Divided and Unified Government'. *Journal of Theoretical Politics*, 8: 7–40.

KURZER, PAULETTE (1993). *Business and Politics: Political Change in Economic Integration in Western Europe*. Ithaca, NY: Cornell University Press.

LABBÉ, DOMINIQUE (1990). *Le Vocabulaire de François Mitterrand*. Paris: Presses de la Fondation Nationale des Sciences Politiques.

LANGE, PETER, and GARRETT, GEOFFREY (1985). 'The Politics of Growth: Strategic Interaction and Economic Performance in the Advanced Industrial Democracies, 1974–1980'. *Journal of Politics*, 47: 792–827.

LAVER, MICHAEL, and SHEPSLE, KENNETH A. (1991). 'Divided Government: America is Not "Exceptional"'. *Governance: An International Journal of Policy and Administration*, 4: 250–69.

LEHMBRUCH, GERHARD (1967). *Proporzdemokratie: Politisches System und politische Kultur in der Schweiz und in Österreich*. Tübingen: Mohr.

——(1986). 'Interest Groups, Government, and the Politics of Protectionism', in Heinz Hauser (ed.), *Protectionism and Structural Adjustment*. Grüsch: Rüegger, 111–41.

LEHMBRUCH, GERHARD (1989). 'Wirtschaftspolitischer Strategiewechsel und die institutionelle Verknüpfung von Staat und Gesellschaft', in Hans-Herrmann Hartwich (ed.), *Macht und Ohnmacht politischer Institutionen*. Opladen: Westdeutscher Verlag, 222–35.

——(1994). 'République Fédérale d'Allemagne: le cadre institutionnel et les incertitudes des stratégies néo-libérales', in Bruno Jobert (ed.), *Le tournant néo-libéral*. Paris: L'Harmattan, 201–32.

LEIBFRIED, STEPHAN, and PIERSON, PAUL (eds.) (1995). *European Social Policy: Between Fragmentation and Integration*. Washington, DC: Brookings Institution.

LEVY, JONAH D. (1999a). *Tocqueville's Revenge: State, Society, and Economy in Contemporary France*. Cambridge, MA: Harvard University Press.

——(1999b). 'Vice into Virtue? Progressive Politics and Welfare Reform in Continental Europe'. *Politics and Society*, 27: 239–73.

LEYDIER, GILLES (1998). 'Dimensions of Inequality in French and British Political Discourses since the Early 80s', in John Edwards and Jean-Paul Révauger (eds.), *Discourses on Inequality in France and Britain*. Aldershot, UK: Ashgate.

LIJPHART, AREND (1984). *Democracies: Patterns of Majoritarian and Consensus Government in Twenty-One Countries*. New Haven: Yale University Press.

LINDBLOM, CHARLES E. (1965). *The Intelligence of Democracy: Decision Making Through Mutual Adjustment*. New York: Free Press.

LORDON, FRÉDÉRIC (1998). 'The Logic and Limits of *Désinflation Competitive*'. *Oxford Review of Economic Policy*, 14: 96–113.

MACLEAN, MAIRI (1995). 'Privatization in France 1993–94: New Departures or a Case of *plus ça change*?'. *West European Politics*, 18: 272–90.

MAHON, RIANNE (1998). *Death of a Model? Swedish Social Democracy at the Close of the Twentieth Century*. Manuscript. Ottawa: Carleton University, Faculty of Graduate Studies.

MAIR, PETER (1994). 'The Correlates of Consensus Democracy and the Puzzle of Dutch Politics'. *West European Politics*, 17: 97–123.

MAJONE, GIANDOMENICO (1989). *Evidence, Argument and Persuasion in the Policy Process*. New Haven: Yale University Press.

MARCH, JAMES G. (1994). *How Decision Happen: A Primer in Decision-Making*. New York: Free Press.

MARIN, BERND (1982). *Die Paritätische Kommission: Aufgeklärter Techno-korporatismus in Österreich*. Wien: Internationale Publikationen.

——(ed.) (1990). *Generalized Political Exchange: Antagonistic Cooperation and Integrated Policy Circuits*. Frankfurt/M.: Campus.

MARQUAND, DAVID (1988). *The Unprincipled Society*. London: Fontana.

MARSHALL, GORDON, SWIFT, ADAM, ROUTH, DAVID, and BURGOYNE, CAROLE (1999). 'What Is and What Ought To Be'. *European Sociological Review*, 15/4: 349–67.

MARSHALL, THOMAS H. (1950). *Citizenship and Social Class and other Essays*. Cambridge, UK: Cambridge University Press.

——(1963). 'Citizenship and Social Class', in Thomas H. Marshall (eds.), *Sociology at the Crossroads and Other Essays*. London: Heinemann, 67–128.

MAY, PETER, J. (1992). 'Policy Learning and Failure'. *Journal of Public Policy*, 12/4: 331–54.

MAYNTZ, RENATE, and SCHARPF, FRITZ W. (1975). *Policy Making in the German Federal Bureaucracy*. Amsterdam: Elsevier.

————(1995). 'Der Ansatz des akteurzentrierten Institutionalismus', in Renate Mayntz, and Fritz W. Scharpf (eds.), *Gesellschaftliche Selbstregelung und politische Steuerung*. Frankfurt/M.: Campus, 39—72.

McKELVEY, RICHARD (1976). 'Intransitivities in Multidimensional Voting Models and Some Implications for Agenda Control'. *Journal of Economic Theory*, 12: 472–82.

McKENZIE, RICHARD, and LEE, DAVID (1991). *Quicksilver Capital: How the Rapid Movement of Wealth Has Changed the World*. New York: Free Press.

McKEOWN, TIMOTHY J. (1999). 'The Global Economy, Post-Fordism, and Trade Policy in Advanced Capitalist States', in Herbert Kitschelt, Peter Lange, Gary Marks, and John D. Stephens (eds.), *Continuity and Change in Contemporary Capitalism*. Cambridge, UK: Cambridge University Press, 11–35.

McROBIE, ALAN (ed.) (1993). *Taking it to the People? The New Zealand Electoral Referendum Debate*. Christchurch: Hazard Press.

MIEGEL, MEINHARD, and WAHL, STEFANIE (1999). *Solidarische Grundsicherung private Vorsorge: Der Weg aus der Rentenkrise*. Munich: AKTUELL, Olzog Verlag.

Ministerie van Sociale Zaken (n.d.). *Benefit dependency rates*. Unpublished document.

Ministerie van Sociale Zaken en Werkgelegenheid (1995). *Unemployment Benefits and Social Assistance in Seven European Countries: A Comparative Study*. Werkdocumenten No. 10. Den Haag: Ministerie van Sociale Zaken en Werkgelegenheid.

Ministry of Health and Social Affairs (1998). *Pension reform in Sweden*. http://www.pension.gov.se

MITCHELL, AUSTIN (1969). *Politics and People in New Zealand*. Christchurch: Whitcome and Tombs.

MITCHELL, DEBORAH (1991). *Income Transfers in Ten Welfare States*. Avebury, UK: Aldershot.

MOENE, KARL OVE, and WALLERSTEIN, MICHAEL (1996). 'Redistribution of Assets versus Redistribution of Income'. *Politics and Society*, 24/4: 369–82.

————(1999). 'Social Democratic Labor Market Institutions: A Retrospective Analysis', in Herbert Kitschelt, Peter Lange, Gary Marks, and John D. Stephens (eds.), *Continuity and Change in Contemporary Capitalism*. Cambridge, UK: Cambridge University Press, 231–60.

MORAVCSIK, ANDREW (1998). *The Choice for Europe: Social Purpose and State Power from Messina to Maastricht*. Ithaca, NY: Cornell University Press.

MULGAN, RICHARD (1990). 'The Changing Electoral Mandate', in Martin Holland and Jonathan Boston (eds.), *The Fourth Labour Government: Politics and Policy in New Zealand* (2nd edn). Auckland/ New York: Oxford University Press, 11–22.

MUNDELL, ROBERT (1962). 'The Appropriate Use of Monetary and Fiscal Policy under Fixed Exchange Rates'. *IMF Staff Papers*, 9: 70–77.

MYRDAL, ALVA (1945). *Nation and Family: The Swedish Experiment in Democratic Family and Population Policy*. London: Routledge & Kegan Paul.

NAGEL, JACK H. (1998). 'Social Choice in a Pluralitarian Democracy: The Politics of Market Liberalization in New Zealand'. *British Journal of Political Science*, 28: 223–45.

NANNESTAD, PETER (2000). 'Keep the Bumblebee Flying: Economic Policy in the Welfare State of Denmark, 1973–1994', forthcoming in Erik Albäk, Leslie Eliason, Asbjørn Sonne Nørgaard, and Herman Schwartz (eds.), *Managing the Danish Welfare State under Pressure: Towards a Theory of the Dilemmas of the Welfare State*. Aarhus: Aarhus University Press.

NEGRELLI, STEFANO (1997). 'Social Pacts and Flexibility: Towards a New Balance between Macro and Micro Industrial Relations. The Italian Experience', in Giuseppe Fajertag and Philippe Pochet (eds.), *Social Pacts in Europe*. Brussels: European Trade Union Institute, 45–62.

NEI (Netherlands Economic Institute) (1998). *Inactivity/Activity Ratios. A descriptive analysis for six European countries, the USA and Japan. Final Report for the Ministry of Social Affairs and Employment and the Ministry of Economic Affairs*. Rotterdam: Netherlands Economic Institute.

OBINGER, HERBERT (1998). 'Federalism, Direct Democracy, and Welfare State Development in Switzerland'. *Journal of Public Policy*, 18/3: 241–63.

OECD (1980). *Economic Outlook*, 28. Paris: OECD.

——(1985). *Historical Statistics 1960–1983*. Paris: OECD.

——(1988). *Economic Outlook*, 44. Paris: OECD

——(1994). *The OECD Jobs Study. Part II*. Paris: OECD.

——(1996a). *Employment Outlook*, July. Paris: OECD.

——(1996b). *Income Distribution in OECD Countries*. Social Policy Studies No. 18. Paris: OECD.

——(1997). *Historical Statistics*. Paris: OECD.

——(1998a). *Benefit Systems and Work Incentives*. Paris: OECD.

——(1998b). *Labour Force Statistics*. Paris: OECD.

——(1998c). *Income Distribution and Poverty in Selected OECD Countries*. Economics Department Working Paper 98/2. Paris: OECD.

——(1998d). 'Making the Most of the Minimum: Statutory Minimum Wages, Employment and Poverty', in *OECD Employment Outlook*, June. Paris: OECD, 31–80.

——(1998e). *Employment Outlook*. Paris: OECD.

——(1999a). *A Caring World: The New Social Policy Agenda*. Paris: OECD.

——(1999b). *Employment Outlook*, June. Paris: OECD.

——(1999c). 'Employment Protection and Labour Market Performance', in *OECD Employment Outlook*, June. Paris: OECD, 47–132.

——(1999d). *Implementing the OECD Jobs Strategy: Assessing Performance and Policy*. Paris: OECD.

——(1999e). 'Making Work Pay', in *OECD Economic Outlook*, 66/December. Paris: OECD, 151–59.

——(1999f). *Social Expenditure Database 1980–1996*. Paris: OECD.

——(1999g). *Statistical Compendium: Economic Outlook*. Paris: OECD.

——(1999h). *Statistical Compendium: National Accounts I*. Paris: OECD.

——(1999i). *Statistical Compendium: Business Sector Database*. Paris: OECD.

——(1999j). *Statistical Compendium: Labour Force Statistics*. Paris: OECD.

——(1999k). *Statistical Compendium: Revenue Statistics*. Paris: OECD.

——(various years). *Economic Outlook*. Paris: OECD.

——(various years). *Historical Statistics*. Paris: OECD.

——(various years). *Labour Force Statistics*. Paris: OECD.

——(various years). *National Accounts*. Paris: OECD.

——(various years). *Revenue Statistics*. Paris: OECD.

OLSEN, JOHAN P., and PETERS, B. GUY (1996). *Lessons from Experience: Experiential Learning in Administrative Reform in Eight Democracies*. Oslo: Scandinavian University Press.

PENNINGS, FRANS (1999). 'Flexibilität und Sicherheit: neue Entwicklungen im niederländischen Arbeitsrecht'. *Zeitschrift für ausländisches und internationales Arbeits- und Sozialrecht*, 13: 153–64.

PENZ, REINHARD (1999). *Legitimität und Viabilität. Zur Theorie der institutionellen Steuerung der Wirtschaft*. Marburg: Metropolis.

PESTOFF, VICTOR A. (1995). 'Towards a New Swedish Model of Collective Bargaining and Politics', in Colin Crouch and Franz Traxler (eds.), *Organized Industrial Relations in Europe: What Future?* Aldershot, UK: Avebury, 151–82.

PICHELMANN, KARL, and HOFER, HELMUT (1999). *Country Employment Policy Reviews: Austria*. Manuscript. Geneva: International Labour Organization.

PIERSON, PAUL (1994). *Dismantling the Welfare State: Reagan, Thatcher and the Politics of Retrenchment in Britain and the United States*. Cambridge, UK: Cambridge University Press.

——(1996). 'The New Politics of the Welfare State'. *World Politics*, 48/2: 143–79.

——(1997). *Increasing Returns, Path Dependence, and the Study of Politics*. Jean Monnet Chair Papers 44. Florence: Robert Schuman Centre.

——(1998). 'Irresistible Forces, Immovable Objects: Post-Industrial Welfare States Confront Permanent Austerity'. *Journal of European Public Policy*, 5/4: 539–60.

PIZZORNO, ALESSANDRO (1978). 'Political Exchange and Collective Identity in Industrial Conflict', in Colin Crouch and Alessandro Pizzorno (eds.), *The Resurgence of Class Conflict in Western Europe Since 1968. Volume 2: Comparative Analyses*. London: Macmillan, 277–98.

POLANYI, KARL (1957). *The Great Transformation: The Political and Economic Origins of Our Time*. Boston: Beacon Press.

PONTUSSON, JONAS, and SWENSON, PETER (1996). 'Labor Markets, Production Strategies, and Wage Bargaining Institutions: The Swedish Employer Offensive in Comparative Perspective'. *Comparative Political Studies*, 29/2: 223–50.

PURCELL, JOHN (1995). 'Ideology and the End of Institutional Industrial Relations: Evidence from the UK', in Colin Crouch and Franz Traxler (eds.), *Organized Industrial Relations in Europe*. Aldershot, UK: Avebury, 101–19.

QUIGGIN, JOHN (1998). 'Social Democracy and Market Reform in Australia and New Zealand'. *Oxford Review of Economic Policy*, 14/1: 76–95.

QUINN, DENNIS (1997). 'The Correlates of Change in International Financial Regulation'. *The American Political Science*, 91/3: 531–52.

RADAELLI, CLAUDIO (1998). 'Networks of Expertise and Policy Change in Italy'. *South European Society and Politics*, 3/2: 1–22.

REGINI, MARINO (1997). 'Still Engaging in Corporatism? Recent Italian Experience in Comparative Perspective'. *European Journal of Industrial Relations*, 3/3: 259–78.

REGINI, MARINO, and REGALIA, IDA (1997). 'Employers, Unions and the State: The Resurgence of Concertation in Italy?'. *West European Politics*, 20: 210–30.

RUESCHEMEYER, DIETRICH, and SKOCPOL, THEDA (eds.) (1996). *States, Social Knowledge, and the Origins of Modern Social Policies*. Princeton: Princeton University Press.

RHODES, MARTIN (1996). 'Globalisation and West European Welfare States: A Critical Review of Recent Debates'. *Journal of European Social Policy*, 6: 305–27.

——(2000). 'The Political Economy of Social Pacts: "Competitive Corporatism" and European Welfare Reform', forthcoming in Paul Pierson (ed.), *The New Politics of the Welfare State*. Oxford: Oxford University Press.

RICHARDSON, JEREMY (1994). 'Doing Less by Doing More: British Government 1979–1993', in Wolfgang C. Müller (ed.), *The State in Western Europe*. London: Cass, 178–97.

——and JORDAN, A.G. (1979). *Governing Under Pressure: The Policy Process in a Post-Parliamentary Democracy*. Oxford: Martin Robertson.

RIDDELL, PETER (1989). *The Thatcher Decade*. Oxford: Blackwell.

ROCHON, THOMAS (1999). *The Netherlands: Negotiating Sovereignty in an Interdependent World*. Boulder, CO: Westview Press.

RODRIK, DANI (1997). *Has Globalization Gone too Far?* Washington, DC: Institute for International Economics.

ROGERS, JOEL, and STREECK, WOLFGANG (eds.) (1995). *Works Councils: Consultation, Representation, and Cooperation in Industrial Relations*. Chicago: University of Chicago Press.

ROSE, RICHARD (1993). *Lesson-Drawing in Public Policy: A Guide to Learning Across Time and Space*. Chatham, NJ: Chatham House Publishers.

ROSSI, NICOLA (1997). *Più ai figli, meno ai padri*. Rome: Il Mulino.

ROTHSTEIN, BO (1998a). *Breakdown of Trust and the Fall of the Swedish Model*. Manuscript. Department of Political Science, Göteborg University.

——(1998b). *Just Institutions Matter: The Moral and Political Logic of the Universal Welfare State*. Cambridge, UK: Cambridge University Press.

ROTHSTEIN, BO (1998c). *Social Capital in the Social Democratic State: The Swedish Model and Civil Society*. Paper prepared for delivery at the American Political Science Association Annual meeting. Boston, 3–6 Sept.

RUGGIE, JOHN G. (1982). 'International Regimes, Transactions, and Change: Embedded Liberalism in the Postwar Economic Order'. *International Organization*, 36: 379–415.

SABATIER, PAUL, and JENKINS-SMITH, HANK C. (1993). *Policy Change and Learning: An Advocacy Coalition Approach*. Boulder, CO: Westview Press.

SAUNDERS, PETER (1994). *Welfare and Inequality*. Sydney: Cambridge University Press.

SAUTTER, CHRISTIAN (1982). 'France', in Andrea Boltho (ed.), *The European Economy: Growth and Crisis*. Oxford: Oxford University Press, 449–71.

SBRAGIA, ALBERTA (1998). *Italy and EMU*. Paper presented at the workshop on 'Europeanization and Domestic Change'. European University Institute, 19–21 June.

SCHARPF, FRITZ W. (1987). 'A Game-Theoretical Interpretation of Inflation and Unemployment in Western Europe'. *Journal of Public Policy*, 7: 227–57.

——(1988). 'The Joint Decision Trap: Lessons from German Federalism and European Integration'. *Public Administration*, 88: 239–78.

——(1991). *Crisis and Choice in European Social Democracy*. Ithaca, NY: Cornell University Press.

——(1997a). *Employment and the Welfare State: A Continental Dilemma*. MPIfG Working Paper 97/7. Cologne: Max Planck Institute for the Study of Societies.

——(1997b). *Games Real Actors Play. Actor-Centered Institutionalism in Policy Research*. Boulder, CO: Westview Press.

——(1999). *Governing in Europe: Effective and Democratic?* Oxford: Oxford University Press.

——(forthcoming). 'Institutions in Comparative Policy Research'. *Comparative Political Studies*.

——SCHMIDT, VIVIEN A., and VAD, TORBEN B. P. (1998). *The Adjustment of National Employment and Social Policy to Economic Internationalization*. Manuscript. Cologne: Max Planck Institute for the Study of Societies.

SCHELDE, PALLE A., and ÅKERHOLM, JOHNNY (1982). 'Denmark', in Andrea Boltho (ed.), *The European Economy: Growth and Crisis*. Oxford: Oxford University Press, 610–44.

SCHLUDI, MARTIN, SEILS, ERIC, and GANGHOF, STEFFEN (1998). *Adjustment Data Base*. Manuscript. Cologne: Max Planck Institute for the Study of Societies.

SCHMIDT, GÜNTHER. (1996). 'New Public Management of Further Training', in Günther Schmid, Jacqueline O'Reilly, and Klaus Schömann (eds.), *International Handbook of Labour Market Policy and Evaluation*. Cheltenham, UK: Edward Elgar, 747–90.

SCHMIDT, MANFRED G. (1985). *Der schweizerische Weg zur Vollbeschäftigung. Eine Bilanz der Beschäftigung, der Arbeitslosigkeit und der Arbeitsmarktpolitik*. Frankfurt/M.: Campus.

SCHMIDT, VIVIEN A. (1996a). *From State to Market? The Transformation of French Business and Government*. Cambridge, UK: Cambridge University Press.

——(1996b). 'Loosening the Ties that Bind: The Impact of European Integration on French Government and Its Relationship to Business'. *Journal of Common Market Studies*, 34: 223–54.

——(1997a). 'Discourse and (Dis)Integration in Europe'. *Daedalus*, 126/3: 167–98.

——(1997b). 'Economic Policy, Political Discourse, and Democracy in France'. *French Politics and Society*, 15/2: 37–48.

SCHMIDT, VIVIEN A. (1999). 'European "Federalism" in Its Encroachments on National Institutions'. *Publius*, 29/1: 19–44.

——(2000a). 'Still Three Models of Capitalism? The Dynamics of Economic Adjustment in Britain, Germany, and France', forthcoming in Roland Czada and Susanne Lütz (eds.), *Die Politische Konstitution von Märkten*. Opladen: Westdeutscher Verlag.

——(2000b). 'Democracy and Discourse in an Integrating Europe and a Globalizing World'. Forthcoming in *European Law Journal*, 5/2.

SCHMIDT, VIVIEN A. (2000c). 'Privatization in France: The Transformation of French Capitalism'. Forthcoming in *Government and Politics*.

——(2000d). 'Discourse and the Legitimation of Economic and Social Policy Change', forthcoming in Steven Weber (ed.), *Globalization and the European Political Economy*. New York: Columbia University Press.

SCHMITTER, PHILIPPE C., and LEHMBRUCH, GERHARD (eds.) (1979). *Trends Toward Corporatist Intermediation*. London: Sage.

——and GROTE, JÜRGEN R. (1997). *The Corporatist Sysiphus: Past, Present and Future*. EUI Working Papers in Political and Social Science 97/4. Florence: European University Institute.

SCHRÖDER, JÖRG, and SUNTUM, ULRICH VAN (in collaboration with Mester, Frauke, and Rolle, Carsten) (1998). *Internationales Beschäftigungs-Ranking 1998*. Gütersloh: Verlag Bertelsmann Stiftung.

SCHWARTZ, HERMAN (1994). 'Small States in Big Trouble: State Reorganization in Australia, Denmark, New Zealand, and Sweden in the 1980s'. *World Politics*, 46: 527–55.

SCITOVSKY, TIBOR (1998). 'One More "Trouble" with Globalization'. *Challenge* 41/4: 134–35.

SEIDEL, HANS (1982). 'Austro-Keynesianismus'. *Wirtschaftspolitische Blätter*, 29/3: 11–15.

SHAW, ERIC (1994). *The Labour Party since 1979: Crisis and Transformation*. London: Routledge.

SHEPSLE, KENNETH A., and WEINGAST, BARRY R. (1987). 'The Institutional Foundations of Committee Power'. *American Political Science Review*, 81: 85–104.

SIEBERT, HORST (1997). 'Labor Market Rigidities: At the Root of Unemployment in Europe'. *Journal of Economic Perspectives*, 11/3: 37–45.

SIMMONS, BETH A. (1999). 'The Internationalization of Capital', in Herbert Kitschelt, Peter Lange, Gary Marks, and John D. Stephens (eds.), *Continuity and Change in Contemporary Capitalism*. Cambridge, UK: Cambridge University Press, 36–69.

SIMON, HERBERT A. (1976). *Administrative Behavior: A Study of Decision-Making Process in Administrative Organization* (3rd edn). New York: Free Press.

——(1996). 'Bounded Rationality and Organizational Learning', in Michael D. Cohen and Lee S. Sproull (eds.), *Organizational Learning*. Thousand Oaks: Sage: 175–87.

SINN, HANS-WERNER (1989). 'The Tax Policy of Tax-Cut-Cum-Base-Broadening: Implications for International Capital Movements', in Manfred Neuman and

Karl W. Roskamp (eds.), *Public Finance and Enterprises*. Detroit: Wayne State University Press, 153–76.

——(1997). 'Deutschland im Steuerwettbewerb'. *Jahrbücher für National-ökonomie und Statistik*, 216: 672–92.

SINN, STEFAN (1993). 'The Taming of Leviathan. Competition Among Governments'. *Constitutional Political Economy*, 3: 177–221.

SITKIN, SIM B. (1996). 'Learning Through Failure: The Strategy of Small Losses', in Michael D. Cohen and Lee S. Sproull (eds.), *Organizational Learning*. Thousand Oaks: Sage: 541–77.

SKOCPOL, THEDA (1995). *Social Policy in the United States: Future Possibilities in Historical Perspective*. Princeton: Princeton University Press.

——and AMENTA, EDWIN (1986). 'States and Social Policies', in Ralph H. Turner and James F. Short (eds.), *Annual Review of Sociology, 12*: 131–57.

——and WEIR, MARGARET (1985). 'State Structures and the Possibilities for "Keynesian" Responses to the Great Depression in Sweden, Britain, and the United States', in Peter B. Evans, Dietrich Rueschemeyer, and Theda Skocpol (eds.), *Bringing the State Back In*. Cambridge, UK: Cambridge University Press, 107–63.

SOFRES (1996). *L'État de l'Opinion*. Paris: PUF.

SOSKICE, DAVID (1991). 'The Institutional Infrastructure for International Competitiveness: A Comparative Analysis of the UK and Germany', in Anthony B. Atkinson and Renato Brunetta (eds.), *The Economies of the New Europe*. London: Macmillan.

——(1999). 'Divergent Production Regimes: Coordinated and Uncoordinated Market Economies in the 1980s and 1990s', in Herbert Kitschelt, Peter Lange, Gary Marks, and John D. Stephens (eds.), *Continuity and Change in Contemporary Capitalism*. Cambridge, UK: Cambridge University Press, 101–34.

——and IVERSEN, TORBEN (1998). 'Multiple Wage Bargaining Systems in the Single European Currency Area'. *Oxford Review of Economic Policy*, 14: 110–24.

——and IVERSEN, TORBEN (2000). 'The Non-Neutrality of Monetary Policy with Large Price or Wage Setters'. Forthcoming in *Quarterly Journal of Economics*, 15/1.

STATISTICS CANADA (n.d.). *World Trade Database 1980–1994*. Ottawa: Statistics Canada.

STRANGE, SUSAN (1996). *The Retreat of the State: The Diffusion of Power in the World Economy*. Cambridge, UK: Cambridge University Press.

STREECK, WOLFGANG (1978). 'Staatliche Ordnungspolitik und industrielle Beziehungen. Zum Verhältnis von Integration und Institutionalisierung gewerkschaftlicher Interessenverbände am Beispiel des britischen Industrial Relations Act von 1971', in Udo Bermbach (ed.), *Politische Wissenschaft und politische Praxis*. Politische Vierteljahresschrift. Sonderband, 9/1978: 106–39.

——(1994). 'Pay Restraint without Incomes Policy: Institutionalized Monetarism and Industrial Unions in Germany', in Ronald Dore, Robert Boyer, and Zoe Mars (eds.), *The Return to Incomes Policy*. New York: Pinter, 118–40.

STREECK, WOLFGANG (1997). 'German Capitalism: Does It Exist? Can It Survive?'. *New Political Economy*, 2: 237–56.

——(1999). *Competitive Solidarity: Rethinking the "European Social Model"*. Presidential Address, 11th Annual Meeting on Socio-Economics, Society for the Advancement of Socio-Economics, 8–11 June, Madison, WI.

——and SCHMITTER, PHILIPPE C. (1999). *The Organization of Business Interests: Studying the Associative Action of Business in Advanced Industrial Societies*. MPIfG Discussion Paper. Cologne: Max Planck Institute for the Study of Societies.

SURREY, MICHAEL (1982). 'United Kingdom', in Andrea Boltho (ed.), *The European Economy: Growth and Crisis*. Oxford: Oxford University Press, 528–53.

SVALLFORS, STEFAN (1993). *Labourism Versus Social Democracy? Attitudes to Inequality in Australia and Sweden*. University of New South Wales, Sydney. Reports and Proceedings, Social Policy Research Centre, 107 (June).

SWANK, DUANE (1998). 'Funding the Welfare State: Globalization and the Taxation of Business in Advanced Market Economies'. *Political Studies*, 46: 671–92.

SWENSON, PETER (1989). *Fair Shares. Unions, Pay, and Politics in Sweden and West Germany*. London: Adamantine Press.

TANZI, VITO (1995). *Taxation in an Integrating World*. Washington, DC: Brookings.

TELES, STEVE (1998). *The Dialectics of Trust: Ideas, Finance and Pensions Privatization in the US and UK*. Paper prepared for presentation for the Conference 'Varieties of Welfare Capitalism in Europe, North America and Japan'. Cologne: Max Planck Institute for the Study of Societies, 11–13 June.

THATCHER, MARGARET (1993). *The Downing Street Years*. London: Harper Collins.

THELEN, KATHLEEN A. (1991). *Union of Parts: Labor Politics in Postwar Germany*. Ithaca, NY: Cornell University Press.

——(1999). 'Historical Institutionalism in Comparative Politics'. *Annual Review of Political Science*, 2: 369–404.

TRAXLER, FRANZ (1995a). 'Farewell to Labour Market Association? Organized Versus Disorganized Decentralization as a Map for Industrial Relations', in Colin Crouch and Franz Traxler (eds.), *Organized Industrial Relations in Europe: What Future?* Aldershot, UK: Avebury.

——(1995b). 'From Demand-Side to Supply-Side Corporatism? Austria's Labour Relations and Public Policy', in Colin Crouch and Franz Traxler (eds.), *Organized Industrial Relations in Europe: What Future?* Aldershot, UK: Avebury, 271–86.

——(2000). 'National Pacts and Wage Regulation in Europe: A Comparative Analysis', in Guiseppe Fajertag and Phillipe Pochet (eds.), *Social Pacts in Europe*. Brussels: European Trade Union Institute.

——and KITTEL, BERNHARD (2000). 'The Bargaining System and Economic Performance. A Comparison of 18 OECD Countries'. Forthcoming in *Comparative Political Studies*.

——BLASCHKE, SABINE, and KITTEL, BERNHARD (2000). *National Labor Relations in Internationalized Markets*. Forthcoming, Oxford University Press.

TREU, TIZIANO (1994). 'Procedures and Institutions of Incomes Policy in Italy', in Ronald Dore, Robert Boyer, and Zoe Mars (eds.), *The Return to Incomes Policy*. New York: Pinter: 161–74.

TSEBELIS, GEORGE (1995). 'Decision-Making in Political Systems: Veto Players in Presidentialism, Parliamentarism, Multicameralism, and Multipartyism'. *British Journal of Political Science*, 25: 289–326.

VAN DER VEEN, ROMKE, and TROMMEL, WILLEM (1999). 'Managed Liberalization of the Dutch Welfare State: A Review and Analysis of the Reform of the Dutch Social Security System, 1985–1998'. *Governance*, 12: 289–310.

VARTIAINEN, JUHANA (1998): 'Understanding Swedish Social Democracy: Victims of Success?' *Oxford Review of Economic Policy*, 14: 19–39.

VILROKX, JAQUES (1998). 'Tarifpolitik am Wendepunkt: Zum Wandel der Tarifvertragsbeziehungen in Belgien in den 90er Jahren'. *WSI-Mitteilungen*, 51: 478.

VISSER, JELLE (1998). *Social Dialogue and Industrial Relations in Austria, Denmark, Ireland and the Netherlands*. Report prepared for the ILO Country Employment Policy Review in Selected OECD countries. Manuscript. University of Amsterdam: Amsterdam Institute for Advanced Labour Studies.

——(1999a). *Creating Welfare Reform and Creating Part-Time Employment: The Case of the Netherlands*. Manuscript. University of Amsterdam: Institute for Advanced Labour Studies.

——(1999b). 'The Netherlands: The Return of Responsive Corporatism', in Anthony Ferner and Richard Hyman (eds.), *Changing Industrial Relations in Europe* (2nd edn). Oxford: Blackwell, 283–314.

——and HEMERIJCK, ANTON (1997). *'A Dutch Miracle': Job Growth, Welfare Reform and Corporatism in the Netherlands*. Amsterdam: Amsterdam University Press.

VITOLS, SIGURT (1997). 'Financial Systems and Industrial Policy in Germany and Great Britain The Limits of Convergence', in Douglas J. Forsyth and Ton Notermans (eds.), *Regime Changes: Macroeconomic Policy and Financial Regulation in Europe from the 1930s to the 1990s*. Providence: Berghahn Books, 221–55.

VOWLES, JACK (1990). 'Nuclear Free New Zealand and Rogernomics'. *Politics*, 25: 81–91.

——and AIMER, PETER (1993). *Voter's Vengeance: The 1990 Election in New Zealand and the Fate of the Fourth Labour Government*. Auckland: Oxford University Press.

WALWEI, ULRICH (1998). *Beschäftigung: Formenvielfalt als Perspektive?—Teil 2: Bestimmungsfaktoren für den Wandel der Erwerbsformen*. IAB-Kurzbericht, No. 3.

WATSON, MATTHEW (1999). 'Rethinking Capital Mobility, Re-Regulating Financial Markets'. *New Political Economy*, 4: 55–67.

WEICK, KARL E. (1976). 'Educational Organisations as Loosely Coupled Systems'. *Administrative Science Quarterly*, 21: 1–20.

WILDING, PAUL (1994). 'Government and Poverty in the 1980s: An Exercise in the Management of a Political Issue', in Bill Jones (ed.), *Political Issues in Britain Today* (4th edn). Manchester, UK: Manchester University Press: 344–54.

WILSON, GRAHAM (1994). 'The Westminster Model in Comparative Perspective', in Ian Budge and David McKay (eds.), *Developing Democracy: Comparative Research in Honour of J. F. P. Blondel*. London: Sage, 189–201.

Zukunftskommission der Friedrich-Ebert-Stiftung (1998). *Wirtschaftliche Leistungsfähigkeit, sozialer Zusammenhalt, ökologische Nachhaltigkeit. Drei Ziele—ein Weg*. Bonn: Dietz.

INDEX

Page numbers in **bold** refer to figures, and those in *italic* to tables.